AGRICULTURE IN A TURBULENT WORLD ECONOMY

AGRICULTURE IN A TURBULENT WORLD ECONOMY

PROCEEDINGS
OF THE
NINETEENTH
INTERNATIONAL CONFERENCE
OF AGRICULTURAL ECONOMISTS

Held at Málaga, Spain
26 August–4 September 1985

Edited by
Allen Maunder, Institute of Agricultural Economics, University of
Oxford, England
and
Ulf Renborg, Department of Economics and Statistics,
Swedish University of Agricultural Sciences, Uppsala

INTERNATIONAL ASSOCIATION OF
AGRICULTURAL ECONOMISTS

INSTITUTE OF AGRICULTURAL ECONOMICS
UNIVERSITY OF OXFORD

1986

Gower

Published by
Gower Publishing Company Limited
Gower House
Croft Road
Aldershot
Hants GU11 3HR
England

Gower Publishing Company
Old Post Road
Brookfield
Vermont 05036
USA

British Library Cataloguing in Publication Data

International Conference of Agricultural Economists
    (19th : 1985 : Málaga, Spain)
    Agriculture in a turbulent world economy:
    proceedings.
    1. Agriculture——Economic aspects
    I. Title   II. Maunder, Allen
    III. Renborg, Ulf   IV. International Association of
    Agricultural Economists   V. University of Oxford, Institute of Agricul-
    tural Economists
    338.1   HD1415

Library of Congress Cataloging-in-Publication Data

International Conference of Agricultural Economists
    (19th : 1985 : Málaga, Spain)
    Agriculture in a turbulent world economy.
    "International Association of Agricultural Economists.
Institute of Agricultural Economics, University of Oxford."
    Bibliography: p.
    1. Agriculture——Economic aspects——Congresses.
2. Food supply——Congresses.   3. Agriculture and state——Congresses.
I. Maunder, A. H.   II. Renborg, Ulf.   III. Title.
HD1405.I58   1985   338.1   86-14219
ISBN 0-566-05225-3

Typeset by Activity Ltd., Salisbury, Wiltshire
Printed in Great Britain by Blackmore Press, Shaftesbury, Dorset.

CONTENTS

Contents

PALACIO NACIONAL DE CONGRESOS
DE LA COSTA DEL SOL

MÁLAGA – ESPAÑA

PREFACE

This proceedings volume contains the main papers and reports presented at the Nineteenth International Conference of Agricultural Economists. That conference was held from 26 August to 4 September 1985 at Malaga, Spain. An accompanying volume in the occasional paper series of the IAAE will contain the contributed papers presented at the conference after selection by an international panel.

IAAE members greatly appreciated the kind welcome extended to us at this conference and the support provided for it by the Governments of Spain and Andalucia and various agricultural organisations and firms. Welcoming addresses were made by the Mayor of the City of Malaga, Pedro Aparicio; the Vice President of the Junta de Andalucia, Jose Miguel Salinas; and from the Minister of Agriculture, Fisheries and Food, Carlos Romero Herrera. They spoke on behalf of their governmental units and on behalf of the honorary committee presided over by His Majesty King Juan Carlos I.

The professional programme was developed under the intellectual leadership of Ulf Renborg, University of Uppsala, with the assistance of Bruce Greenshields who chaired the contributed paper committee, William Kibler who chaired the discussion groups committee, and Laurent Martens who chaired the 'poster sessions'. The poster sessions were a much appreciated addition to the programme.

The Elmhirst Lecture entitled 'Food, Economics and Entitlements' was delivered by Amartya Sen from the University of Oxford. His paper is a fundamental one which should be read and utilised by all researchers, administrators and teachers concerned with solving problems of hunger around the world. His address both honoured our founding president, Leonard K. Elmhirst, and demonstrated why we, in turn, honoured Amartya Sen with the Elmhirst medal for his own extensive, high-quality accomplishments as an economist.

The Association owes a debt of gratitude to Allen Maunder of the Agricultural Economics Institute, University of Oxford, for his continuing excellent editorial work on the Proceedings of the

Association. Mavis Hunt served us well by making the Cowbell an even more effective means of quick communication at the Conference.

The Association wants especially to recognise the excellent hard work of the Spanish National Organizing Committee under the capable chairmanship of Antonio Herrero Alcon, ably assisted by Jose Luiz Fernandez Cavada. The Spanish National Organizing Committee served all members of the Association attending the conference well, with grace and competence.

GLENN L. JOHNSON
Immediate Past President,
International Association of
Agricultural Economists

INTRODUCTION

There were a number of reasons for choosing 'Agriculture in a Turbulent World Economy' as the theme for the Nineteenth International Conference of Agricultural Economists. The next ten to fifteen years of adjustment needed in food producing systems will probably take place in a very turbulent economy. In the 1970s there were a number of shocks in the economy; but unsolved economic and political problems indicate that surprises may well await us in the future also. They stem from the uncertainty regarding answers to questions of the following type: what choices will national states make between protectionism and free international markets; how will countries choose between economic growth and environmental protection; what political and economic consequences will follow from east-west and north-south tensions in the world?

This volume follows closely the programme of the conference and after an initial section, containing the Elmhirst Memorial Lecture and the Presidential Address, begins with a consideration of the forces shaping the future and the interdependencies and uncertainties in the world's food production and distribution systems. Then follow sections on overproduction and malnutrition, on pressures on natural resources, and on human capital, technology and institutions. Subsequent sections deal with the structure of agriculture and people in rural societies and with markets and trade. A separate section is devoted to theoretical developments and, finally, the implications for policy and research of the preceding sections are considered by separate authors under five headings and in the 'synoptic view' of the incoming President.

The editors wish to express their thanks to the authors, openers and rapporteurs of the various papers, particularly those who turned in their contributions on time and of the correct length, and to the editorial staff without whose unstinting help this volume could not have been prepared.

The contributed papers presented at the conference, together with summaries of discussion, will appear as *IAAE Occasional Papers IV*.

The reports of the meetings of Discussion Groups will appear in an *IAAE Members Bulletin*. The views expressed in this book are not necessarily those of the IAAE nor those of the institutions with which the various authors are connected.

ALLEN MAUNDER
Editor, International Association of
Agricultural Economists

ULF RENBORG
Vice President Programme

OPENING SESSION

ELMHIRST MEMORIAL LECTURE

AMARTYA SEN

*Food, Economics and Entitlements**

I feel very deeply honoured by the invitation to give the fourth Elmhirst Lecture, and I am most grateful to the International Association of Agricultural Economists for this invitation and to Professor Glenn Johnson for his kind – in fact much *too* generous – introductory remarks. The previous three Elmhirst Lecturers – Ted Schultz, Arthur Lewis and Keith Campbell – all spoke on some broad themes with particular relevance to policy, and I shall try to follow this tradition by discussing some general questions in the economics of food and hunger and their policy implications.

Leonard Elmhirst himself devoted much of his life to social action. On policy matters, he was not only a thinker (a very original one), he was also a great activist. I personally was very fortunate in having the opportunity of knowing him since my childhood. Elmhirst was not only a major figure in my school at Santiniketan, in India, he had initiated various pioneering activities of rural reconstruction in the villages around the school, playing an active part in the local battle against poverty and hunger in that depressed part of Bengal. I thought of Elmhirst, then, mainly as an educationist and a rural reconstruction activist, and it is only later I came to realize how extensive his contributions were to the development of economic and social research, including that in agricultural economics. When, as an undergraduate in England, rather exhausted by my first winter in that astonishingly damp country, I visited Elmhirst at Dartington Hall, I was struck by the extraordinary range of his interests and achievements. It gives me great pleasure to be able to join in honouring the memory of Leonard Elmhirst, the Founder-President of this Association.

I ECONOMICS AND THE ACQUIREMENT PROBLEM

In a warm message sent to the São Paulo conference of this Association in 1973, Leonard Elmhirst gave some wise advice to the gathering economists, after wishing them 'lots of down to earth discussions at the grass roots with plenty of vision for the future'. He wanted 'the boots of

*This paper was prepared at the World Institute of Development Economic Research in Helsinki, and I am grateful for discussions with Lal Jayawardena and Nanak Kakwani.

3

economists [to be] firmly rooted in the soil and their heads in the skies'.[1] He was, of course, right to be worried that we professional economists find it easy enough to dangle our boots in the skies and equally easy to bury our heads firmly in the soil. Elmhirst, who warned us against both, did not tell us which of the two feats he feared more. It is, however, fair to say that in the popular vision, it is the dangling boots in the skies that mostly characterise the folly of economists.

Economists are supposed to be singularly lacking in common sense. This is not a charge that has emerged only in recent years. In a letter to Knut Wicksell, dated 26 July 1904, Alfred Marshall complained that a newly arrived student at Cambridge had told him that 'the founders of Economics of all nations were inferior in common sense to most children of ten'.[2] Marshall was not amused by the remark, and promptly challenged the detractor to a serious argument, even though, as he explained to Wicksell, he regarded 'personal controversies as a great waste of time'.[3] Marshall did not record who won the argument (I suppose one does not get great honour from thrashing a student), but he could not really have disposed of the question. The view that economists unnecessarily complicate problems that are perfectly simple and easily solved by a little use of common sense has certainly outlived Marshall rather substantially, and is regularly encountered today.

This is, in fact, quite an occupational hazard in the field of food economics and hunger. 'Practical' people are easily convinced that they know precisely what the problem is, and even though what they 'know' with such certainty varies from person to person, they are impatient with the economists' tendency to use complicated ideas to tackle apparently simple problems. What may be called 'instant economics' has always appealed to the quick-witted layman impatient with the slow-moving economist. In the field of hunger and food policy, the need for speed is of course genuinely important, and this impatience does make considerable sense. But instant economics is also dangerously deceptive, particularly in this field. Millions of lives depend on the adequacy of the policy response to the terrible problems of hunger and starvation in the modern world. Past mistakes of policy have been responsible for the deaths of many millions of people and the suffering of hundreds of millions, and this is not a subject in which short cuts in economic reasoning can be taken to be fairly costless.

One common feature of a good deal of instant economics related to food and hunger is impatience with investigating the precise mechanisms for acquiring food that people have to use. People establish command over food in many altogether different ways. For example, while a peasant owning his land and the product of his labour simply owns the food produced, a wage labourer paid in cash has to convert that wage into a bundle of goods, including food, through exchange. The peasant does, as it were, an exchange with 'nature', putting in labour, etc., and getting back the product, viz. food. The wage labourer does repeated exchanges with others in the society – first his labour power for a wage and then the wage for a collection of commodities including food. We cannot begin to understand the precise influences that make it possible or not possible to acquire enough food, without examining the conditions of these exchanges and the forces that govern them. The same applies to other methods of acquiring food, e.g., through share-cropping and getting a part of the produce, through running a business and making a profit, through selling services and earning an income, and so on. I shall call the problem of establishing command over commodities, in this case food, the 'acquirement problem', and it is easy to establish that the acquirement problem is really central to questions of hunger and starvation in the modern world.

The acquirement problem is often neglected not only by non-economists, but also by many economists, including some great ones. For example, Malthus in his famous *Essay on the Principle of Population as It Affects the Further Improvement of Society* (1798) leaves the acquirement problem largely unaddressed, though in his less well-known pamphlet *An Investigation of the Cause of the Present High Price of Provisions* (1800), which deals with more short-run problems, Malthus is in fact deeply concerned precisely with the nitty-gritty of this problem.[4] The result of this neglect in the former work is not without practical consequence, since the popularity of the Malthusian approach to population and food, and of the particular metric of food output per head extensively used in the *Essay on Population*, has tended to give that metric undue prominence in policy discussions across the world.

Malthusian pessismism, based on the expectation of falling food output per head, has not been vindicated by history. Oddly enough, what can be called 'Malthusian optimism', i.e., *not* being worried about the food problem so long as food output grows as fast as – or faster than – population, has often contributed substantially to delaying policy response to growing hunger (against a background of stationary or rising food output per head). This is a serious enough problem in the case of intensification of regular but non-extreme hunger (without starvation deaths but causing greater proneness to morbidity and mortality), and it can be quite disastrous in the context of a famine that develops without a decline in food output per head, with the misguided focus leading to a hopelessly delayed response of public policy. While Malthus's own writings are by no means unique in focusing attention on the extremely misleading variable of food output per head, 'Malthusian optimism', in general, has been indirectly involved in millions of deaths which have resulted from inaction and misdirection of public policy.[5] While fully acknowledging the great contribution that Malthus has made in highlighting the importance of population policy, this negative feature of his work, related to his own bit of instant economics, must also be recognised.

The neglect of the acquirement issue has far-reaching consequences. For many years rational discussion of the food problems of the modern world was distracted by undue concentration on the comparative trends of population growth and the expansion of food output, with shrill warnings of danger coming from very respectable quarters.[6] The fear of population outrunning food output on a global scale has certainly not been realised, and the world food output per head has steadily risen.[7] This has, however, gone hand in hand with intensification of hunger in some parts of the world. In many – though not all – of the affected countries, food output per head has in fact fallen, and the anxiety about these countries has often been anchored to the statistics of food output per head, with Malthusian worries translated from the global to the regional or country level. But a causal analysis of the persistence and intensification of hunger and of the development of famines does, in fact, call for something more than attention being paid simply to the statistics of food output per head.

I shall have more to say on the policy questions presently, but before that I would like to discuss a bit further the nature and implications of the acquirement problem. I shall also discuss some arguments that relate to studying food and hunger in terms of what in my book, *Poverty and Famines*,[8] was called the 'entitlement approach'.[9] That approach has been extensively discussed, examined, criticised, applied as well as extended, and I have learned a lot from these contributions.[10] But the approach has also been occasionally misinterpreted, and given the importance of the subject of food policy and hunger, I shall permit myself the self-indulgence of commenting *inter alia* on a few of the points that have been made in response to my earlier analysis.

II FAMINES AND ENTITLEMENTS

The entitlement approach provides a particular focus for the analysis of famines. It does not specify one particular causation of famine only the general one that a famine reflects widespread failure of entitlements on the part of substantial sections of the population. Such failure can arise from many different causes.

The entitlement of a person stands for the set of different alternative commodity bundles that the person can acquire through the use of the various legal channels of acquirement open to someone in his position. In a private ownership market economy, the entitlement set of a person is determined by his original bundle of ownership (what is called his 'endowment') and the various alternative bundles he can acquire starting respectively from each initial endowment, through the use of trade and production (what is called his 'exchange entitlement mapping'). This is not the occasion to go into the formal characterisation of endowments, exchange entitlement mappings, entitlement sets, etc.; I have spelt these out in some detail – some would say *painful* detail – elsewhere (in my book *Poverty and Famines*).

A person has to starve if his entitlement set does not include any commodity bundle with enough food. A person is reduced to starvation if some change either in his endowment (e.g., alienation of land, or loss of labour power due to ill health), or in his exchange entitlement mapping (e.g., fall in wages, rise in food prices, loss of employment, drop in the price of the goods he produces and sells), makes it no longer possible for him to acquire any commodity bundle with enough food. I have argued that famines can be usefully analysed in terms of failures of entitlement relations.

The advantages of the entitlement approach over more traditional analysis in terms of food availability per head were illustrated with case studies of a number of famines, e.g., the Bengal famine of 1943, the Ethiopian famines of 1973 and 1974, the Bangladesh famine of 1974, and the Sahel famines in the early seventies.[11] In some of these famines food availability per head had gone down (e.g. in the Sahel famines); in others there was no significant decline – even a little increase (e.g., in the Bengal famine of 1943, the Ethiopian famine of 1973, the Bangladesh famine of 1974). That famines can occur even without any decline in food output or availability per head makes that metric particularly deceptive. Since food availability is indeed the most commonly studied variable, this is a source of some policy confusion. It also makes 'Malthusian optimism' a serious route to disastrous inaction. But the point of entitlement analysis is not only to dispute the focus on food availability, but more positively also to provide a general approach for understanding and investigating famines through focusing on variations on endowments and exchange entitlement mappings. I have tried to illustrate the use of this approach in various case studies.[12]

Famine can be caused by various different types of influences, and the common predicament of mass starvation does not imply any one common fundamental cause. Droughts, floods, general inflationary pressure, sharp recessionary loss of employment, and so on, can all in their own way deprive large sections of the population of entitlement to adequate food. A decline in food output or availability can, of course, be one of the major influences on the development of a famine, but even when that is the case (indeed even when food availability decline is the primary proximate antecedent), a serious study of the causal mechanism leading to the famine and the precise form it takes will require us to go into the behaviour of the determinants of entitlements of the different sections of the population.[13]

In *Poverty and Famines* two broad types of famines were distinguished from each other, viz. boom famines and slump famines. A famine can, of course, occur in a situation of general decline in economic activity (as happened, for example, in the Wollo province of Ethiopia in 1973, due to a severe drought). But it can also occur in over-all boom conditions (as happened, for example, in the Bengal famine of 1943, with a massive expansion of economic activity related to war efforts). If economic expansion is particularly favourable to a large section of the population (in the case of the Bengal famine, roughly the urban population including that of Calcutta), but does not draw into the process another large section (in the Bengal famine, much of the rural labouring classes), then that uneven expansion can actually make the latter group lose out in the battle for commanding food. In the food battle the devil takes the hindmost, and even a boom condition can lead to some groups losing their command over food due to the worsening of their *relative* position *vis-à-vis* the groups favoured by the boom.

It is also important to emphasise that the entitlement approach is consistent with many different detailed *theories* of the actual causation of a famine. While the approach identifies certain crucial variables, different theories of the determination of the values of these variables may all be consistent with the general entitlement approach. For example, the entitlement approach does not specify any particular theory of price determination, but relative prices are quite crucial to the entitlements of various occupation groups. The entitlement approach by itself does not provide – nor is it intended to provide – a detailed explanation of any famine, and such an explanation would require supplementation by more specific theories of movements of prices, wages, employment etc., causing particular shifts in the entitlements of different occupation groups.[14]

What the entitlement approach does is to take up the acquirement problem seriously. Rather than arbitrarily making some implicit assumption about distribution (such as equal division of the available food, or some fixed pattern of inequality in that division), it analyses acquirement in terms of entitlements, which in a private ownership economy is largely a matter of ownership and exchange (including of course production, i.e., exchange with nature). I would claim that this is not in any way a departure from the old traditions of economics. It is, rather, a reassertion of the continuing concern of economics with the mechanism of acquiring commodities. If I had the courage and confidence that Gary Becker shows in his distinguished work in calling his own approach '*the* economic approach',[15] I would have called the entitlement approach by the same bold name. While the price of timidity is to shy away from such assertive naming, I would nevertheless claim that economic traditions stretching back centuries do, in fact, direct our attention to entitlements in analysing problems of wealth, poverty, deprivation and hunger.

This is clear enough in Marx's case,[16] but the point is often made that Adam Smith was a great believer in the simple theory of food availability decline in explaining all famines, and that he would have thus had little patience for discussion of entitlements and their determinants. Indeed, it is true that in his often-quoted 'Digression concerning the Corn Trade and Corn Laws' in Book IV of the *Wealth of Nations*, Adam Smith did remark that 'a dearth never has arisen from any combination among the inland dealers in corn, nor from any other cause but a real scarcity, occasioned sometimes, perhaps, and in some particular places, by the waste of war, but in by far the greatest number of cases, by the fault of the seasons'.[17] However, in understanding the point that Adam Smith is making here, it is important to recognise that he is primarily denying that traders could cause famine through collusion, and he is disputing the view that famines often follow from artificial shortages created by traders, and asserting the importance of what he calls 'a real scarcity'. I shall have the occasion to take up this aspect of Smith's observation presently when I discuss the issue of anti-famine policy.

We have to look elsewhere in the *Wealth of Nations* to see how acutely concerned Adam Smith was with the acquirement problem in analysing what he called 'want, famine and mortality'. I quote Smith from the chapter called 'Of the Wages of Labour' from Book I of the *Wealth of Nations*:

> But it would be otherwise in a country where the funds destined for the maintenance of labour were sensibly decaying. Every year the demand for servants and labourers would, in all the different classes of employments, be less than it had been the year before. Many who had been bred in the superior classes, not being able to find employment in their own business, would be glad to seek it in the lowest. The lowest class being not only overstocked with its own workmen, but with the overflowing of all the other classes, the competition for employment would be so great in it, as to reduce the wages of labour to the most miserable and scanty subsistence of the labourer. Many would not be able to find employment even upon these hard terms, but would either starve, or be driven to seek a subsistence either by begging, or by the perpetration perhaps of the greatest enormities. Want, famine, and mortality would immediately prevail in that class, and from thence extend themselves to all the superior classes ... [18]

Here Adam Smith is focusing on the market-based entitlement of labourers, and its dependence on employment and real wages, and explaining famine from that perspective. This should, of course, come as no surprise. In denying that artificial scarcity engineered by collusive traders can cause famine, Adam Smith was in no way closing the door to the economic analysis of various different real influences on the ability of different groups to command food in the market, in particular the values of wages and employment.

Perhaps it is useful to consider another argument presented by another great classical economist, viz. David Ricardo, attacking the view that a famine cannot occur in a situation of what he calls 'superabundance'. This was in a speech that Ricardo wrote for delivery in Parliament in 1822, using the third person for himself as if the speech is reported in *Hansard*, though in the event Ricardo did not actually deliver the speech. The reference is to the famine conditions then prevailing in Ireland, and Ricardo examines the point made by another member of Parliament that this could not be the case since there was superabundance of food in Ireland at that time.

> But says the honble. gentn. the people are dying for want of food in Ireland, and the farmers are said to be suffering from superabundance.

In these two propositions the honble. gentn. thinks there is a manifest contradiction, but he Mr. R could not agree with him in thinking so. Where was the contradiction in supposing that in a country where wages were regulated mainly by the price of potatoes the people should be suffering the greatest distress if the potato crop failed and their wages were inadequate to purchase the dearer commodity corn? From whence was the money to come to enable them to purchase the grain however abundant it might (be) if its price far exceeds that of potatoes. He Mr. Ricardo should not think it absurd or contradictory to maintain that in such a country as England where the food of the people was corn, there might be an abundance of that grain and such low prices as not to afford a remuneration to the grower, and yet that the people might be in distress and not able for want of employment to buy it, but in Ireland the case was much stronger and in that country there should be no doubt there might be a glut of corn, and a starving people.[19]

There is indeed nothing surprising in the fact that economists should be concerned with the acquirement problem, and dispute the instant economics that overlooks that aspect of the food problem based on confusing supply with command, as the 'honourable gentleman' quoted by David Ricardo clearly did. It is a confusion that has recurred again and again in actual discussions of the food problem, and the need to move away from instant economics to serious analysis of the acquirement problem and the entitlement to food is no less today than it was in Ricardo's time.[20]

It is not my purpose to assert that the entitlement approach is flawless as an economic approach to the problem of hunger and starvation. Several 'limitations' of the entitlement approach were, in fact, noted in *Poverty and Famines*, including ambiguities in the specification of entitlement, the neglect of non-legal transfers (e.g. looting) in the disposition of food, the importance of tastes and values in causing hunger despite adequate entitlement, and the relevance of disease and epidemic in famine mortality which extends far beyond the groups whose entitlement failures may have initiated the famine.[21]

To this one should also add that in order to capture an important part of the acquirement problem, to wit, distribution of food within a family, the entitlement approach would have to be extended. In particular, notions of perceived 'legitimacy' of intrafamily distributional patterns have to be brought into the analysis, and its causal determinants analysed.[22]

Further, if the focus of attention is shifted from famines, as such, to less acute but possibly persistent hunger, then the role of choice from the entitlement set becomes particularly important, especially in determining future entitlement. For example, a peasant may choose to go somewhat hungry now to make a productive investment for the future, enhancing the entitlement of the following years and reducing the danger of starvation then. For entitlement analysis in a multi-period setting the initial formulation of the problem would require serious modification and extension.[23]

These changes and amendments can be systematically made without losing the basic rationale of introducing entitlement analysis to understand the problem of hunger and starvation in the modern world. The crucial motivation is to see the centrality of the acquirement problem and to resist the shortcuts of instant economics, no matter how respectable its source.

III FAMINE AND POLICY

Focusing on entitlements and acquirement rather than simply on food output and availability has some rather far-reaching implications for food policy. I have tried to discuss some of these implications elsewhere, but I would like to pick a few issues here for brief comment. In particular, the problems of famine anticipation and relief are among the most serious ones facing the turbulent and traumatic world in which we live, and I shall comment on them briefly from the perspective that I have been outlining.

So far as famine anticipation is concerned, the metric of food output and availability is obviously defective as a basis, for reasons that follow from the preceding discussion. In fact, the anticipation of famines and their detection at an early stage have often in the past been hampered by undue concentration on this index, and specifically by what we have been calling 'Malthusian optimism'. Early warnings, as they are sometimes called, may not come at all from the output statistics, and it is necessary to monitor other variables as well, which also influence the entitlements of different vulnerable groups. Employment, wages, prices, etc., all have very direct bearing on the entitlements of various groups.

It is also important to recognise that famines can follow from many *different* types of causal processes. For example, while in a boom famine food prices will sharply rise, in a slump famine they may not. If the economic change that leads to mass starvation operates through depressing incomes and purchasing powers of large groups of people, food prices may stay low — or rise only relatively little, during the process of pauperisation of these groups. Even when the slump famine is directly related to a crop failure due to, say, a drought, there may possibly be only a relatively modest rise in food prices, if the supply failure is matched by a corresponding decline in the purchasing power due to the same drought. Indeed, it is easy to see that in a fully peasant economy in which food is eaten precisely by those who grow it, a crop failure will subtract from demand what it deducts from supply. The impoverished peasants would of course be later thrown into the rest of the economy – begging, looking for jobs, etc. – but they will arrive there without purchasing ability, and thus need not cause any rise in food prices even later. Actual economies are not, of course, that pure, but the impact on prices is very contingent on the relative weights of the different types of systems and organisation that make up the affected economy.[24]

Neither food output, nor prices, nor any other variable like that can be taken to be an invariable clue to famine anticipation, and once again there is no substitute to doing a serious economic analysis of the entitlements of all the vulnerable groups. All these variables have possible significance, and it is a question of seeing them as contingently important in terms of what they could do to the ability of different groups to acquire food. The search for some invariable indicator on the basis of which even the economically blind could see an oncoming famine sufficiently early is quite hopeless. Of course a famine will reveal itself sooner or later, if only through early reports of hunger.[25] But if the aim is to anticipate it even before that, that object cannot be satisfied by some mechanical formula on an 'early warning system'. The various information on prices, wages, outputs, etc., has to be examined with an economic understanding of the determinants of entitlements of the different occupation groups and of the rich variety of different ways in which the entitlements of one group or another can be undermined.

The different processes involved not only vary a good deal from each other, they may also be far from straightforward. For example, in various famines some occupation groups have been driven to the wall by a fall in the relative price of the food items they sell, e.g., meat sold by pastoral nomads in Harerghe in the Ethiopian famine of 1974, fish sold by fishermen in the Bengal famine of 1943. These groups may survive by selling these food items and buying cheaper calories through the purchase of grains and other less expensive food. A decline in the relative price of meat or fish will, of course, make it easier for the richer parts of the community to eat better, but it can spell disaster for the pastoralist and the fisherman.[26] The observed variables have to be examined in terms of their specific roles in the determination of entitlements of vulnerable groups to make sense of them as signals of turmoil.

Turning now from the anticipation to the relief of famines, the traditional form of relief has, of course, been that of providing free food in relief camps and distribution centres. There can be no doubt that relief in this form has saved lives on a large scale in various famines around the world. But to understand precisely what free food distribution does, it may be useful to distinguish between two different aspects of the act of providing, which are both involved in the food relief operation. One is to give the destitute the *ability* to command food, and the other is to give him this ability in the actual form of *food itself*. Though they are integrated together in this form of relief, they need not in general be thus combined. For example, cash relief may provide the ability to command food without directly giving the food.

A person's ability to command food has two distinct elements, viz., his 'pull' and the supplier's 'response'. In the price mechanism the two elements are integrally related to each other. But in terms of the logistics of providing the person with food, the two elements may in some contexts, be usefully distinguishable. If a person has to starve because he has lost his employment and has no means of buying food, then that is a failure originating on the 'pull' side. If, on the other hand, his ability to command food collapses because of absence of supply, or as a result of the cornering of the market by some manipulative traders, then this is a failure arising on the 'response' side.

One way of understanding what Adam Smith was really asserting (an issue that was briefly touched on earlier) is to see his primary claim as being one about the nature of 'response failure' in particular, saying nothing at all about 'pull failure'. His claim was that a response failure will only arise from what he called 'a real scarcity', most likely due to natural causes, and not from manipulative actions of traders. He may or may not have been right in this claim, but it is important to note that in this there is no denial of the possibility of 'pull failure'. Indeed, as is shown by his own analysis of 'want, famine and mortality' arising from unemployment and falling wages (I quoted a passage from this earlier), Smith did also outline the possibility of famine originating on the 'pull' side. There is nothing particularly puzzling or internally inconsistent in Smith's various pronouncements on famine, if we distinguish between his treatment of pull and that of response. It is not the case, as is often asserted, that Adam Smith believed that hunger could not arise without a crop failure. Also he was not opposed to public support for the deprived, and in particular he was not opposed to providing relief through the Poor Laws (though he did criticise the harshness of some of the requirements that were imposed on the beneficiaries under these laws).[27]

Smith's point that response failure would not arise from collusive action of traders has a direct bearing on the appropriate form of famine relief. If his point is correct, then relief could just as easily be provided by giving the deprived additional income and leaving it to the traders to respond to the new pull through moving food to the cash recipients. It is arguable that Smith did underestimate the extent to which traders can and do, in fact, manipulate markets, but at the same time the merits of cash relief do need serious examination in the context of assessing policy options.

Cash relief may not, of course, be quick enough in getting food to the starving in a situation of severe famine. Directly moving food to the starving may be the only immediate option in some situations of acute famine. There is also the merit of direct food distribution that it tends to have, it appears, a very immediate impact on nutrition, even in non-famine, normal situations, and it seems to do better in this respect than relief through income supplementation.[28] These are points in favour of direct relief through food distribution. There is the further point that cash relief is arguably more prone to corruption, and that the visibility of direct food distribution does provide a better check. And the point about the possibility of manipulative actions of traders cannot, also, by any means be simply dismissed. These are serious points in favour of direct food distribution. But cash relief does have many merits as well.

First, the government's inefficiency in transporting food could be a considerable barrier to famine relief, as indeed some recent experiences have shown. In addition to problems of bureaucracy and red tape, there is the further problem that the transport resources (i.e. vehicles, etc.) in the possession of the private sector may sometimes be hard to mobilise, whereas they would be drawn into use if the actual trading and moving is left to the profit-seeking private sector itself. There is here a genuine pragmatic issue of the speed of response, and it cannot be brushed aside by a simple political judgement one way or the other.

Second, as was observed in the Wollo famine in 1973 and the Bangladesh famine of 1984, and most spectacularly in the Irish famines of the 1840s, food often does move *out of* the famine-stricken regions to elsewhere. This tends to happen especially in some cases of slump famine, in which the famine area is short of effective demand. Since such 'food countermovement' tends to reflect the balance of pulls of different regions, it may be preventable by distributing cash quickly enough in the famine-affected region.

Third, by providing demand for trade and transport, cash relief may help to regenerate the infrastructure of the famine-stricken economy. This has some merit in contrast with *ad hoc* use of transitory public intervention, which is not meant to continue, and the lasting benefits from expansion of normal trade and transport may be considerable for the local economy.

Fourth, it is arguable that cash relief is more usable for development investment needed for productive improvement, and this cannot be sensibly organised in relief centres. Even 'food for work' programmes, which can help in this direction, may sometimes be too unwieldy, given the need for flexibility for such investment activities.

Fifth, living in relief camps is deeply disruptive for normal family life as well as for pursuing normal economic activities. Providing cash relief precisely where the people involved normally reside and work, without having to move them to relief camps, may have very considerable economic and social advantages. Judging from the experience of an innovative 'cash for food' project sponsored by UNICEF in Ethiopia, these advantages are indeed quite real.[29]

This is not the occasion to try to form an overall judgement of the 'net' advantage of one scheme over another. Such judgements would have to be, in any case, extremely contingent on the exact circumstances of the case. But the general distinction between the 'pull' aspect and the 'response' aspect of entitlement failures is of immediate relevance to the question of the strategy of famine relief. Adam Smith's long shadow fell over many famines in the British Empire over the last 200 years, with Smith being cited in favour of inaction and letting things be. If the analysis presented here is accepted, that inaction reflected quite the wrong reading of the implications of Smith's economic analysis. If his analysis is correct – and the honours here are probably rather divided – the real Smithian issue in a situation of famine is not 'intervention versus non-intervention', but 'cash relief versus direct food relief'. The force of the arguments on Smith's side cannot be readily dismissed, and the experience of mismanagement of famine relief in many countries has done nothing to reduce the aptness of Smith's question.

IV FOOD AND FOOD POLICY

In comparing the merits of cash relief with food distribution, it was not assumed that there would be more import of food with the latter than with the former. That question – that of food imports from abroad – is quite a distinct one from the form that relief might take. It is, however, arguable that in a famine situation direct food distribution is more thoroughly dependent on food import from abroad than a cash relief scheme need be. This is to some extent correct, though direct food distribution may also be based on domestically acquired food. But if we compare food distribution combined *with* food imports, on the one hand, and simple cash relief *without* such imports, on the other, then an arbitrary difference is brought into the contrast which does not belong there. In fact, the issue of food import is a separate one, which should be considered on its own.

This relates to an issue that has often been misunderstood in trying to work out the implications of the entitlement approach to hunger and famines, and in particular the implications of recognising the possibility that famines can occur without any decline in food availability per head. It has sometimes been argued that if a famine is not caused by a decline in food availability, then there cannot be a case for food imports in dealing with the famine.[30] This is, of course, a *non sequitur*, and a particularly dangerous piece of nonsense. Consider a case in which some people have been reduced to starvation not because of a decline in total supply of food, but because they have fallen behind in the competitive demand for food in a boom famine (as happened, for example, to rural labourers in the Bengal famine of 1943). The fact is that the prices are too high for these victim groups to acquire enough food. Adding to the food supply will typically reduce the food prices and help these deprived groups to acquire food. The fact that the original rise in prices did not result from a fall in availability but from an increase in total demand does not make any difference to the argument.[31]

Similarly, in a slump famine in which some group of people has suffered a decline in their incomes due to, say, unemployment, it may be possible to help that group by reducing the price of food through more imports. Furthermore, in each case import of food can be used to break a famine through public relief measures. This can be done either directly in the form of food distribution, or indirectly through giving cash relief to the famine victims combined with releasing more food in the market to balance the additional demand that would be created. There are, of course, other arguments to be considered in judging pros and cons of food imports, including the problem of incentives for domestic food producers. But to try to reject the case for food imports in a famine situation on the simple ground that the famine has occurred without a decline in food availability (if that is the case) is to make a straightforward mistake in reasoning.

A more interesting question arises if in a famine situation we are, for some reason, simply not in a position to get more food from abroad. Would a system of cash relief then be inflationary, and thus counterproductive?

The answer is it would typically be inflationary, but not necessarily counterproductive. Giving the famine victims more purchasing power would add to the total demand for food. But if we want a more equal distribution of food, with some food moving from others to the famine victims, then the only way the market can achieve this (when the total supply is fixed and the money incomes of others cannot be cut) is through this inflationary process. The additional food to be consumed by the famine victims has to come from others, and this may require that prices should go up to induce others to consume less, so that the famine victims – with their new cash incomes – can buy more. Thus, while having a system of cash reliefs is not an argument against food imports in a famine situation, that system can have some desirable consequences even when food imports are, for some reason, not possible. If our focus is on enhancing the entitlements of famine victims, the creation of some inflationary pressure – within limits – to redistribute food to the famine victims from the rest of the society may well be a sensible policy to pursue.

So far in this lecture my concentration on policy matters has been largely on what may be called short-run issues, including the anticipation and relief of famines. At this late hour, it would be inadvisable to take up more long-run questions, just when I have got only a few minutes left. But it should be clear from the preceding analysis, with its focus on acquirement and entitlements, that long-run policies must be geared to enhancing, securing and guaranteeing entitlements, rather than to some simple formula like expanding food output. I have discussed elsewhere the positive achievements of public food distribution policies in Sri Lanka and China, and also in Kerala in India, along with policies of public health and elementary education.[32] These diverse policy instruments belong as much to 'food policy' as do the economic policies for expanding the production of food and of other commodities.

However, the problem of production composition in achieving economic expansion is also, *inter alia*, an important one in long-run food policy. This complex problem is often confounded with that of simply expanding food output as such, treating it as largely a matter of increasing food supply. This is particularly so in the discussions of the so-called African food problem. It is, of course, true that food output per head in sub-Saharan Africa has been falling in recent years, and this is certainly one of the major factors in the intensification of hunger in Africa. But food production is not merely a source of food supply in Africa, but also the main source of means of livelihood for large sections of the African population. It is for this reason that food output decline tends to go hand in hand with a collapse of entitlements of the masses in Africa.

The point can be easily seen by comparing and contrasting the experience of sub-Saharan Africa in terms of food output per head *vis-à-vis* those of some countries elsewhere. Take Ethiopia and the Sahel countries, which have all suffered so much from famines. Between 1969–71 and 1980–2, food output per head has fallen by 5 per cent in Chad and Burkina Fasso, 7 per cent in Senegal, 12 per cent in Niger, 17 per cent in Mali, 18 per cent in Ethiopia, and 27 per cent in Mauritania.[33] These are indeed substantial declines. But in the same period, and according to the same source of statistics, food output per head has fallen by 5 per cent in Venezuela, 15 per cent in Egypt, 24 per cent in Algeria, 27 per cent in Portugal, 29 per cent in Hong Kong, 30 per cent in Jordan, and 38 per cent in Trinidad and Tobago. The contrast between starvation in sub-Saharan Africa and nothing of the sort in these other countries is not, of course, in the least difficult to explain. Unlike the situation in these other countries, in sub-Saharan Africa a decline in food output is associated with a disastrous decline in entitlements, because the incomes of so many there come from growing food, because they are generally poorer and because the decline of food output there has not been outweighed or even balanced by increases in non-food (e.g., industrial) output. It is essential to distinguish between (i) food production as a source of income and entitlement, and (ii) food production as a source of supply of the vital commodity food. If the expansion of food production should receive full priority in Africa, the case for it lies primarily in the role of food production in generating entitlements rather than only supply.

There are, of course, other reasons as well for giving priority to food production, in particular the greater security that the growers of food might then have since they would not be dependent on market exchange for acquiring food. This argument has been emphasised by many in recent years, and it is indeed an important consideration, the relevance of which is brought out by the role of market shifts in contributing to some of the famines that have been studied.[34] But this type of uncertainty has to be balanced against uncertainties arising from other sources, in particular those related to climatic reasons. In the very long run the uncertainty of depending on unreliable weather conditions in parts of sub-Saharan Africa may well be eliminated by irrigation and afforestation. However, for many years to come this is a serious uncertainty, which must be taken into account along with other factors in the choice of investment policy in sub-Saharan Africa. An argument that is often encountered in public discussion in various forms can be crudely put like this: 'Food output in parts of sub-Saharan Africa has suffered a lot because the climate there is so unreliable for food production; therefore let's put all our resources into food production in these countries.' This is, of course, a caricature, but even in somewhat more sophisticated forms, this line of argument as a piece of economic reasoning is deeply defective. One does not put all one's eggs in the same highly unreliable basket. The need is surely for diversification of the production pattern in a situation of such uncertainty.

In this lecture I have tried to comment on a number of difficult policy problems. The entitlement approach on its own does not resolve any of these issues. But by focusing on the acquirement problem, and on the major variables influencing acquirement, the entitlement approach provides a general perspective that can be fruitfully used to analyse the phenomenon of hunger as well as the requirements of food policy. I have tried to illustrate some of the uses of the entitlement approach, and have also discussed what policy insights follow or do not follow from it. I have also claimed that the approach is, with a few exceptions, in line with very old traditions in economics, which have been, in their own way, much preoccupied with the acquirement issue. The challenges of the terrible economic problems of the contemporary world relate closely to those traditional concerns, and call for sustained economic analysis of the determination and use of entitlements of diverse occupation groups.

NOTES

[1]See Dams, T. and Hunt, K. E. (eds), *Decision-Making and Agriculture*, Agricultural Economics Institute, Oxford, 1977, p. 14.

[2]See Gårdlund, Torsten, *The Life of Knut Wicksell*, Almquist and Wiksell, Stockholm, 1958, p. 339.

[3]*Ibid*, p. 339. Marshall's ire was particularly directed at Bohm-Bawerk, whom the student had cited as 'his authority', and with whom Marshall seemed to have been rather displeased anyway at that time for other reasons, such as Bohm-Bawerk's criticisms of Marshall's own writings, which – Marshall confessed to Wicksell – he had 'decided not to answer, probably not even to read' (p. 341).

[4]On the importance of the latter document, which has received much less attention than the former, see my *Poverty and Famines*, Clarendon Press, Oxford and Oxford University Press, New York, 1981, Appendix B.

[5]This issue is discussed in my 'The Food Problem: Theory and Policy', *Third World Quarterly*, vol. 4, 1982.

[6]The Club of Rome, despite its extremely distinguished leadership, had been responsible for some of the more lurid research reports of doom and decline. But see the later study sponsored by the Club undertaken by Linnemann, H., *MOIRA: A Model of International Relations in Agriculture*, North-Holland, Amsterdam, 1981, which shows the picture to be both less gloomy and more influenceable by policy. See also Parikh, K. and Rabar, F. (eds), *Food for All in a Sustainable World*, IIASA Laxenburg, 1981, especially on the role of policy.

[7]See, for example, FAO, *The State of Food and Agriculture 1984* 'FAO' Rome, 1985.

[8]Clarendon Press, Oxford and Oxford University Press, New York, 1981. See also my 'Starvation and Exchange Entitlements: A General Approach and Its Application to the Great Bengal Famine', *Cambridge Journal of Economics*, Vol. 1, 1977, 'Ingredients of Famine Analysis: Availability and Entitlements', *Quarterly Journal of Economics*, 95, 1981.

[9]Note that the use of the expression 'entitlement' here is descriptive rather than prescriptive. A person's entitlements as given by the legal system, personal circumstances etc., need not command any moral endorsement. This applies both to the opulent entitlements of the rich and to the meagre entitlements of the poor. One of the points to emerge was the recognition that 'famine deaths can reflect legality with a vengeance' ('Ingredients of Famine Analysis: Availability and Entitlements', p. 462).

[10]Particularly from Arrow, Kenneth J. 'Why People Go Hungry', *New York Review of Books*, 29, 15 July 1982; Bliss, Christopher, 'The Facts about Famines', *South*, March 1982; Griffin, Keith, 'Poverty Trap', *Guardian*, 7 October 1981; Hayter, Teresa, 'Famine for Free', *New Society*, 15 October 1981; Joshi, Vijay, 'Enough To Eat,' *London Review of Books*, 19 November 1981; Lipton, Michael, 'The Analysis of Want', *Times Literary Supplement*, 1981; Reutlinger, Shlomo, 'Review', *Economic Development and Cultural Change*, 32, July 1984; Solow, Robert M. 'Relative Deprivation?', *Partisan Review*, 51 1984; Desai, Meghnad, 'A General Theory of Poverty', *Indian Economic Review*, 1984, among others.

[11]See *Poverty and Famines*, chs. 6–10.

[12]*Poverty and Famines*, chs. 6–10.

[13]*Poverty and Famines*, ch. 10.

[14]See Svedberg, Peter, 'Food Insecurity in Developing Countries: Causes, Trends and Policy Options', UNCTAD TD/B/C.1/257, 13 October, 1984; Ravallion, Martin, 'The Performance of Rice Markets in Bangladesh during the 1974 Famine', *Economic Journal*, Vol. 92, 1985; Khan, Qaisar M. 'A Model of Endowment Constrained Demand for Foc l in an Agricultural Economy with Empirical Applications to Bangladesh', (mimeographed) forthcoming in *World Development*.

[15]See Becker, Gary S., *The Economic Approach to Human Behaviour*, Chicago University Press, 1976, and *A Treatise on the Family*, Harvard University Press, 1981.

[16]See, for example, the discussion on wages and capital in *Capital*, vol. I, Sonnenschein, London, 1887, parts VI and VII.

[17]Smith, Adam, *An Inquiry into the Nature and Causes of the Wealth of Nations*, Book IV, ch. V, b. 5. In the edition edited by R. H. Campbell and A. S. Skinner, Clarendon Press, Oxford, 1976, vol. 1, p. 526.

[18]Smith, *Wealth of Nations*, Book I, ch. VIII, 26, pp. 90–1.

[19]*The Works and Correspondence of David Ricardo*, ed. P. Straffa, with the collaboration of M. H. Dobb, vol. 5, Cambridge University Press, 1971, pp. 234–5.

[20]See Lance Taylor's illuminating critique, 'The Misconstrued Crisis: Lester Brown and World Food', *World Development*, 3, 1975.

[21]*Poverty and Famines*, pp. 48–50.

[22]The consequences of particular perceptions of 'legitimacy' of intra-family distributions do have something similar to those of legal relationships. Using that perspective, '*extended* exchange entitlement' relations, covering both inter-family and intra-family distributions, have been explored in an integrated structure in my paper, 'Women, Technology and Sexual Divisions', *Trade and Development Review*, no. 6, 1985, UNCTAD, Geneva. The inter-relations may be of real importance in understanding sex bias, e.g., the effect that outside earnings of women have on the divisions within the family. On this see also Ester Bøserup's pioneering study, *Women's Role in Economic Development*, Allen and Unwin, London, 1970.

[23]See *Poverty and Famines*, p. 50, note 11. For some important and original ideas in this direction, see Peter Svedberg's 'The Economics of Food Insecurity in Developing Countries' (mimeographed), Institute for International Economic Studies, Stockholm.

[24]In the Ethiopian famine in Wollo in 1973, food price rises seem to have been relatively moderate. Indeed, in Dessie, the capital of Wollo, the mid-famine food prices seem to have been comparable with prices outside the famine-affected province. There was more of a price rise in the rural areas, but again apparently not a catastrophic rise, and prices seemed to come down relatively quickly. On the importance of prices as a monitoring device for famine anticipation, see however Seaman, J. A. and Holt, J. F. J., 'Markets and Famines in the Third World', *Disasters*, Vol. 4, 1980, and Cutler, P., 'Famine Forecasting: Prices and Peasant Behaviour in Northern Ethiopia', *Disasters*, Vol. 8, 1984.

[25]One of the major influences on the actual prevention of famine is the speed and force with which early hunger is reported and taken up in political debates. The nature and freedom of the news media, and the power and standing of opposition parties, are of considerable importance in effective prevention of famines. They are also relevant to the priority that may be attached to the elimination of non-acute and persistent 'regular' hunger, but the success of the news media and effective opposition in the former respect does not guarantee success in the latter. On this see my 'Development: Which Way Now?', *Economic Journal*, vol. 93, 1983.

[26]See *Poverty and Famine*, chs. 6 and 7.

[27]Smith, *Wealth of Nations*, Book I, ch. 8, part II.

[28]See especially the series of reports published on this subject by the International Food Policy Research Institute.

[29]See Kumar, B. G., 'The Ethiopian Famine and Relief Measures: An Analysis and Evaluation', UNICEF, 1985. See also Bjoerck, Wendy A., 'An Overview of Local Purchase of Food Commodities (LPFC)', UNICEF, 1984; and Padmini, R., 'The Local Purchase of Food Commodities "Cash for Food" Project, Ethiopia', UNICEF, 1985.

[30]For a forceful presentation of this odd belief, see Peter Bowbrick's paper (with a truly flattering title), 'How Professor Sen's Theory Can Cause Famines', presented at the Agricultural Economics Society Conference 1985; and at the Annual Conference of the Development Studies Association, 1985. Bowbrick also presents an alleged rebuttal of my analysis of the Bengal famine of 1943, showing commendable neutrality between misstating my views and misreading the implications of his own statements. [A revised version of Bowbrick's paper and my reply were later published in *Food Policy*, vol. 11, May 1986.]

[31]See *Poverty and Famines*, sections 6.6 and 9.2.

[32]See my 'Public Action and the Quality of Life in Developing Countries', *Oxford Bulletin of Economics and Statistics*, vol. 43, 1981; and 'Development: Which Way Now?' *Economic Journal*, 93, 1983. The reading of Sri Lanka's achievements has been subject to some controversy recently. It is certainly true that though Sri Lanka has the highest longevity (69 years) among all the poor countries, despite being one of the poorest in terms of GNP per head, the *expansion* of that longevity has not been very impressive in the period following 1960 for which many international comparisons are made; see Bhalla, S, 'Is Sri Lanka an Exception? A Comparative Study of Living Standards', mimeographed, World Bank; to be published in Bardhan P. and Srinivasan, T. N. (eds), *Rural Poverty in South Asia*, Columbia University Press. It should be noted that the food distribution policies (including free food) and public measures of health services and education were introduced in Sri Lanka decades earlier, and there is no doubt that the life expectation of the Sri Lankan has grown very substantially over these decades. Also the pattern of female mortality being higher than that of the male, which Sri Lanka shared with the rest of South Asia (in contrast with most of the world), also changed over the period. In 1920-2 the life expectation figures were 32.7 years for males and 30.7 for females (see Langford, D. M., 'Sex Differentials in Mortality in Sri Lanka: Changes since the 1920's', *Journal of Biosocial Sciences*, vol. 16, 1984, whereas the figures are now 67 and 71 respectively. Bhalla looks at the period 1960-78 and notes that Sri Lanka's performance in longevity, etc., did not grow particularly fast in *this* period. But this is also a period over which Sri Lanka's social welfare *efforts* did not expand fast; indeed the percentage of GNP expended on social welfare programmes came down from 11.8 in 1960-61 to 8.7 by 1977. The big and innovative expansions in food distribution and medical health services had taken place earlier – particularly in the forties. Correspondingly, the death rate in Sri Lanka had fallen from 21.6 per thousand in 1945 to 12.6 in 1950 and to 8.6 in 1960. All this happened *before* the oddly chosen period 1960-78 in Bhalla's much publicized 'international comparisons.'

[33]*World Development Review 1984*, Oxford University Press, Oxford, 1984: table 6.

[34]*Poverty and Famines*, chs. 6-10.

PRESIDENTIAL ADDRESS

GLENN L. JOHNSON

Scope of Agricultural Economics

At this, the Nineteenth Conference of the International Association of Agricultural Economists, I want to consider the scope of agricultural economics. During the earlier conferences of our Association, such leaders as Leonard K. Elmhirst, Alan Ladd, John Maxton, George Warren and others defined the scope of the interest of our Association. The scope they defined was broad, multi-disciplinary and particularly concerned with solving the practical problems of farmers, foresters, rural infrastructure workers and governmental decision makers concerned with agriculture, the environment and non-farm rural resources. They placed considerable emphasis on improving the quality of rural societies and communities. They were also concerned about the quality of agricultural economics work. Their implied definition of quality was one of excellence in addressing practical problems. Research to improve economics and its ancillary disciplines was not a primary concern – the tendency was to leave that to the general economists, statisticians, mathematicians and philosophers. At the most, disciplinary improvements and excellence were sought as a means of doing better work on the practical problems of farmers, rural communities, agribusinesses, and agricultural agencies in government.

Our Association is now establishing its own journal which will be entitled *Agricultural Economics: The Journal of the International Association of Agricultural Economists*. For purposes of establishing this journal, it becomes extremely important that we carefully define the scope of agricultural economics. The Executive Committee and I, in particular, want to maintain a balance between disciplinary and applied excellence in publishing the work traditionally expected of agricultural economists. My main purpose today is to examine the scope of agricultural economics as a basis for a policy statement to guide the editor and editorial board in our efforts to establish excellence in our new Journal and, for that matter, in all the work of our Association.

RECENT INDICATIONS OF THE INTERESTS OF OUR ASSOCIATION

The theme of our Fourteenth Conference was *Policies, Planning and Management for Agricultural Development*. For the Fifteenth Confer-

21

ence our theme was *Technology, Policies and Adjustments*; for the
Sixteenth, *Decision Making in Agriculture*; for the Seventeenth, *Rural
Change: The Challenge for Agricultural Economics*; for the Eighteenth,
Growth and Equity; and, for this conference, *Agriculture in a Turbulent
World*. When one examines the papers presented at these conferences, it
is clear that the interests of the members of this Association tend to be on
the practical rather than disciplinary end of the spectrum running from
the disciplinary to practical problem solving. They are concerned with the
research, teaching, advising and consulting work of agricultural economists. At our meetings, we have many more papers dealing with specific
problems or with multi-disciplinary subjects relevant to fairly well
defined groups of decision makers facing relatively well defined problems
than we do disciplinary papers devoted to improving the theories,
techniques and measurements of economics and its ancillary disciplines.
The relatively few papers we have heard in the past decade or two which
can be classified as disciplinary are also designed to increase the capacity
of agricultural economics to contribute to the solution of practical
problems and to the accumulation of multi-disciplinary subject matter
knowledge more or less directly focused on the practical problems of
agricultural decision makers (Johnson 1984). My perusal of our proceedings volumes also indicates that we pay somewhat less attention to the
solution of specific practical problems for specific decision makers than
we do to multi-disciplinary subjects. The above generalizations hold, I
believe, for the excellent programme Professor Ulf Renborg has created
for this conference.

I believe we should continue to emphasize subject matter and problem
solving activities in this Association without neglecting disciplinary work
relevant for our problem solving and subject matter research and that this
should be true for our new Journal. I now want to examine this conclusion
further.

More than half a century has elapsed since this Association held its first
conference at Dartington Hall in England. The work of agricultural
economists and the number of agricultural economists around the world
has expanded enormously since then. In many parts of the world, and
particularly in the United States, Canada and Australia, there has been
an increased emphasis on excellence in economics and in its ancillary
disciplines: mathematics, statistics, econometrics, and philosophy,
including logic, and the philosophy of science and ethics (McCloskey
1983; McClennen 1983). In my own country, our *Journal of Agricultural
Economics* has become so disciplinary, despite substantive editorial
efforts to avert this tendency, that some now regard it as a second-rate
general economics journal rather than the first-rate agricultural economics journal it once was and still may be, depending on how one defines
the scope of agricultural economics. In the affairs of the European
Agricultural Economics Association and of the *European Review of
Agricultural Economics*, there is a tension between practically oriented
agricultural economists and those pursuing disciplinary excellence in
economics and its closely related ancillary disciplines. Graduate educa-

tion in North America, Europe, and Oceania is commonly criticized as being too abstract, modernist (McCloskey 1983) and theoretical to fill the needs to students from less developed countries (Fienup and Riley 1980; Johnson 1983a).

Agricultural economists the world over are interested in the subject of agricultural development. We in IAAE share that interest. Sometimes our emphasis is on the development of farms or firm/household complexes. At other times our emphasis is on the development of the agrarian aspects of communities, industries, sectors, regions or countries. At our conferences, we have been interested in the development of communities, urban farming in Asia and non-farm rural resources. Our interests in development have by no means been confined to the so-called less developed countries. Our members from Japan and the so-called developed countries of Western Europe, North America and Oceania are as interested in the further development of their agricultural sectors (broadly conceived) as are our members from the so-called less developed countries. Whether we work in our own countries or abroad, we are concerned with development. Once we see this clearly, we can ask ourselves about the mainsprings or driving forces for development.

The work of agricultural economists in the decades since the Second World War indicates clearly that technological advance, institutional improvement and human improvement (capital) are the mainsprings of agricultural development. Also important is growth of the biological and physical capital which provides the means for attaining non-monetary as well as monetary values. This capital can be redistributed to assist the needy and disadvantaged when we become concerned about equality as well as growth, as we were three years ago in Indonesia when we considered growth and equity.

While the first three mainsprings – technological advance, institutional improvements and human development – seem individually necessary but individually insufficient, the growth of biological and physical capital is somewhat different (Johnson 1968). Generally speaking, the first three must all be in place before there is much growth in biological and physical capital to support development. We can have improved technology and human skills at hand but if institutions fail to provide incentives for using the technology and skills, there is little growth of the biological and physical capital necessary for development. Similarly, we can have the institutions and skills but without new and advanced technology major development is unlikely. The same is true when we have advanced technology and good institutions but lack human skills. When we have all three, we seem to be able to develop the biological and physical capital necessary to support agricultural development and growth. More equality may or may not be crucial (Johnson 1983b). The conclusion is clear – agricultural development is a multi-disciplinary subject requiring knowledge of agricultural technology, rural institutions and rural people; it is more than merely applied economics.

One of the difficulties with the neoclassical economic theories of market behaviour is that they often tacitly assume technologies, institutions and people to be fixed. While we have made some progress in recent years in developing theories of induced technical change, institutional change and human development or human capital formation (Schultz 1961; Binswanger and Ruttan 1978), these theories provide only incomplete explanations of the origin of such changes. In order to understand such changes more fully, agricultural economists need to draw on knowledge of the physical and biological scientists who do the basic research to support the research and development efforts which generate new technology. Similarly, we need to draw on the basic social scientists whose work undergirds our designs for new agricultural institutions, policies and programmes. Even in the case of human capital, the very important contributions of my much admired and respected professor, former Elmhirst Lecturer and, since then, Nobel Laureate, T. W. Schultz do not adequately explain the origins of the motivation and drive to invest in human beings and to use the resultant human capital to develop agriculture. There seems to be more to it than a simple application of neoclassical market economics. Though market economics is essential for predicting the consequences of technical, institutional and human change in societies where individuals are free to choose, this does not mean that market economics can provide wholly adequate explanations of such changes. Agricultural economics must often go beyond economics to the other disciplines important in creating the driving forces for growth.

We in the IAAE have also had a long-standing interest in the practical management problems of farmers, co-operatives, agribusinesses and agro-industrial complexes and in multi-disciplinary subjects important to farm and agribusiness management. Our interests include practical problems and multi-disciplinary subjects important to consumers as they use and enjoy food, fibres, forest and marine products, and rural recreational resources. We are also clearly interested in the development of forestry, non-farm natural resources and, at the other extreme, urban farming.

Currently, agricultural economists are re-emphasising their stress of the 1920s and 1930s on international instability in agricultural markets and monetary/fiscal affairs (Schultz 1945; Benedict 1953, 1955; Benedict and Stine 1956). Such instabilities have political, social, military and developmental dimensions which make them multi-disciplinary.

From the above, it is clear that the scope of agricultural economics is broader than that of economics. Its scope is multi-disciplinary as the work of agricultural economists includes so many important multi-disciplinary subject matter and problem-solving efforts.

AGRICULTURAL ECONOMICS IS ORIENTED TO PROBLEM SOLVING (PS) AND SUBJECT MATTER (SM) RESEARCH AND CONSEQUENTLY TO QUESTIONS OF VALUE AND PRESCRIPTIONS

It is the problem solving and subject matter orientation of agricultural economics which makes it so difficult to define its scope. Both PS and SM research are multi-disciplinary in nature but, as the mixes of disciplines vary from problem to problem and from one set of problems to another, there is little that is unique about the mixes of disciplines which agricultural economists deal with in doing their problem solving and subject matter work. A second complexity of agricultural economics is the importance of information about values in defining and solving problems and, in many instances, in doing subject matter research (Johnson 1976, 1977, forthcoming-a, forthcoming-b). These two complexities are characteristic of both micro and macro subfields within agricultural economics. They are as true, for instance, for farm management as for the study of agricultural sector development and national policies – also as true for farm management as for resource economics. In the next two subsections, respectively, I will consider multi-disciplinarity and the need to deal with information about values.

Multi-disciplinarity of subject matter (SM) and problem solving (PS) activities as they influence the scope of agricultural economics
Traditionally, agricultural economics has been multi-disciplinary. In the United States, farm management emerged from the biophysical agricultural sciences and through the addition of rural sociology, marketing and policy work, converted rather gradually into agricultural economics. Europe's agricultural economics evolved either as a speciality within economics which gave considerable attention to agricultural institutions, people and technologies (Nou 1967) or followed a farm management route not so different, in some ways, from the farm management route which led to agricultural economics in the US (Taylor and Taylor, 1952). Our founder president, Leonard Elmhirst, was trained in agricultural economics at Cornell University. Both he and our Association were influenced by German thought and by George Warren's farm management thinking. In the US, Warren was a crucial person in the conversion of farm management into agricultural economics. His strength was not in his command over the theories and techniques of economics and its ancillary disciplines; instead, it was in his multi-disciplinary knowledge of agriculture, rural communities and non-farm natural resources and in his knowledge of how production takes place on individual farms, how farms are organised, how products are marketed, how farm communities operate and how agricultural policies are created. He had a substantial interest in rural sociology and in the biological and physical sciences which contribute to the development and understanding of agricultural technology. He, like Leonard Elmhirst, was broad and multi-disciplinary. Neither were classifiable as great disciplinary economists but they were great agricultural economists.

Unfortunately, in the post Second World War period, farm management, originally broad in scope, became specialised in economics in some schools and in some countries even to the extent of being defined as a subpart of production economics, itself only a rather narrow subpart of economics. Early in my own career I saw the damage I was doing in encouraging the trend towards specialisation of farm management as a subpart of economics and resisted it (Johnson 1957).

Originally, marketing was more closely related to neoclassical market economics than farm management. Since the Second World War, there has been some broadening of marketing so that students of agricultural marketing now investigate institutional change using a structure, conduct and performance or industrial organisation approach (French 1977). Others relate technical and human change to the field of agricultural marketing in various ways including the industrial organisation approach. Institutional changes involving markets are now seen to be crucial for agricultural development.

Though much academic work on agricultural policy and trade remains fairly highly specialised on market economics, successful practising decision makers, advisors and consultants on policy and trade are also keenly aware of the necessity of being multi-disciplinary. Among academic economists, increased attention is being redevoted to institutional change, human development and technological change as the primary shifters of supply and demand functions and as determiners of trading relationships among nations and of the relationships of the agricultural sector to the rest of the economy.

Resource economics is increasingly multi-disciplinary as indicated by the works of Kelso (1977), Bromley (forthcoming), Sagoff (1985), McClennen (1983) and Schmid (1978).

Problem solving is even more multi-disciplinary than is subject matter research and the multi-disciplinary mixes are even more unstable. Generally, each problem requires a unique disciplinary mixture of value and value-free knowledge with economics being but one of the many disciplines involved. The maximising calculus of economics is generally useful in converting value-free and value information into prescriptions to solve problems (Johnson 1976). Some problems are 'solved' with prescriptions as to how to 'manage' as contrasted to 'eliminating' problems. Such prescriptions are commonly reached in addressing farm, agribusiness and public administration problems (Drucker 1954).

Agricultural economics is fundamentally different from the discipline of economics and its ancillaries – statistics, mathematics, philosophy, etc. It is broader than any single one or even all of them together as it requires still other disciplines. Agricultural economics has greater, more immediate practical relevance than pure economics (Johnson 1971). Economic theory and quantitative techniques alone provide only part of the conceptual basis and techniques needed by agricultural economists.

The problems and sets of problems of concern to agricultural economists are in constant flux. And as they change, so do the mixes of disciplines which structure our applied work. In addition to modifying the theory of economics to adjust it to new problems, we also have to find new ways of joining that theory with theories and empirical data from a changing mix of other disciplines. Consequently, we in agricultural economics have to be prepared to improvise in establishing our conceptual and theoretical bases and recognise that it is doubtful whether we can ever have a unique theoretical structure for our field of endeavour. For us to seek disciplinary excellence in pure economics at the expense of attention to other relevant disciplines would be for us to run the risk of being second-rate general economists rather than first-rate agricultural economists working on the crucial multi-disciplinary and multi-departmental subject matter areas and practical problems of agriculture.

The value content of agricultural economics
Historically there has been a close connection between classical economics and ethics. Adam Smith, Jeremy Bentham, J. S. Mill and Karl Marx were classical writers in both economics and philosophy. Even in English neoclassical economics, the impact of Pareto on economics via John Hicks's *Value and Capital* was essentially ethical and philosophic as it raised questions concerning the measurability of utility and welfare (Johnson 1985). In general economics, Nobel Laureate Kenneth Arrow was dealing fundamentally with ethics when he raised questions concerning decision rules for converting positivistic knowledge and knowledge about values into prescriptive conclusions as to what ought to be done (Arrow 1963; McClennen 1983).

In both economics and in agricultural economics, we are concerned about values in our theories and in our more practical, subject matter and problem-solving activities (Johnson 1985). Some of the values are monetary and some are non-monetary. In both of these categories, some value propositions describe intrinsic while others describe extrinsic or exchange values. In classical and neoclassical economics, the importance of values was recognised in courses and in research efforts classified under the rubric of 'value and distribution theory'. In early neoclassical economics, the role of values in production was recognised by defining production as 'the creation of time, form or place utility'. When we examine a production process, we classify that part of the output with positive value as product, that part with negative value as a pollutant or contaminant and that part with zero value as waste. These conceptual comments indicate that knowledge about values and prescriptive knowledge play important and crucial fundamental roles in economics. It should be added that we use the prescriptive knowledge resulting from application of the maximising calculus for two purposes (Pihkala 1964): (1) to prescribe advantageous behaviour and (2) to predict with much success the behaviour of producers, resource owners, consumers and, for that matter, governmental officials.

There have been unfortunate attempts to make both general economics and agricultural economics value free or positivistic by eliminating their value content and prescriptive use (Keynes 1963, orig. 1890; Robbins 1949 and Friedman 1953). When prices and utility are viewed as positivistic, they are interpreted as positivistic descriptions of 'who values what by how much' rather than as descriptive of the 'real values' of conditions, situations or things (Johnson, forthcoming-a). The inroads of positivism in both general economics and agricultural economics have taken the form of Myrdal's conditional normativism (see Appendix 2, 1944) and Pareto-optimality. Pareto-optimality (Hicks 1939) goes three steps beyond Myrdal's conditional normativism by (1) constraining information about values to assumptions or statements about who values what, (2) insisting that knowledge about values is not interpersonally valid and (3) that such knowledge is ordinal rather than cardinal. Before Pareto-optimality and since, for that matter, economists acting as advisors and consultants to legislators and executive officials in government have recommended imposition of progressive income taxes and regressive distribution of government benefits (Pigou 1962); in doing so, they often implicitly rejected the constraints of logical positivism whether expressed in terms of conditional normativism or Pareto-optimality. Recently, Cooter and Rappoport (1984) have argued that the ordinalists went too far. They believe we do, in fact, have some cardinal knowledge of values with a usable degree of inter-personal validity. They argue, for instance, that our knowledge of values is sufficient to conclude that another unit of money is worth more to a person who lacks clothing and shelter and is suffering from malnutrition and cold than it is to another person so wealthy that he or she does not worry about food, clothing and shelter but devotes his or her allocative efforts mainly to choosing among such things as alternative high-priced theatre tickets.

The German Historical School, as I understand it, and American institutionalism have not generally accepted the constraints of logical positivism on the attainment of objective knowledge of 'real' values. The American institutionalists have been pragmatic in the sense that they believe philosophically that the truth of a proposition depends on its consequences (Parsons 1958; Runes 1960). As both value-free positivistic and value concepts influence decisions (prescriptions) about 'what ought to be done' in order to solve a problem, the truth of positivistic knowledge and value knowledge are viewed by pragmatists as interdependent. To a pragmatist, logical positivism is an absurdity (Parsons 1958). Pragmatists would regard a form of normativism that asserts knowledge of values to be independent of value-free knowledge as equally absurd.

For reasons I go into in much more detail elsewhere (Johnson 1960, 1977, 1984, forthcoming-b, 1985, forthcoming-a) and which I cannot present here for lack of space and time, I conclude that the scope of agricultural economics necessarily deals with prescriptions and descriptions of values really possessed by conditions, situations and things. In recent years there has been an expanded interest in the theoretical and empirical study of values and prescription growing, perhaps, out of the reduced acceptability of logical positivism (Achinstein and Barker 1969; Caldwell 1982; Kaplan 1968). This interest of economists is shared by philosophers and political scientists. McClennen (1983) has provided us with an excellent review of formal work done in economics and philosophy with ample coverage of the still more abstract sometimes mathematical works of Von Neumann, Morgenstern, Arrow, Rawls and Nozick. Our Elmhirst Lecturer, Amartya Sen (Sen 1984; Sen and Williams 1982), Sagoff (1985), Cairncross (1985), Posner (1980), Dworkin (1980), Harsanyi (1982) and Coleman (1984) have contributed useful discussions of our ability to research values. Philosophically and methodologically, economics and, hence, agricultural economics are undergoing serious intellectual examination and are moving into a state of flux involving more attention to values and philosophy in general.

POLICY STATEMENT: *AGRICULTURAL ECONOMICS: THE JOURNAL OF THE INTERNATIONAL ASSOCIATION OF AGRICULTURAL ECONOMISTS*

The preceding sections indicate that the scope of agricultural economics is multi-disciplinary in view of the large amount of subject matter and problem-solving research, teaching, extension, advising and consulting activities carried out, not to mention the multi-disciplinary activities of agricultural economists serving as governmental, parastatal, international and agribusiness administrators. The theories and ancillary disciplines of economics are of fundamental importance to the work of agricultural economists. Applied economics is a necessary though insufficient part of the scope of agricultural economics. Also, disciplinary progress in economics and its ancillary disciplines is important to us and is, hence, a part of our scope of work. We note, as well, that the domains of the different subjects we investigate and of the different problems we consider vary as to the multidisciplinary mixes involved. Though theories from other disciplines are important, there does not appear to be a stable multi-disciplinary mix of theories which can be regarded as the theory of agricultural economics. Therefore, the scope of agricultural economics involves being able to put together mixes of disciplinary theories appropriate for the subject and problem at hand but does not require the development of a unique multi-disciplinary mix of theories for agricultural economics.

We have also seen that the disciplinary theory of economics, our own problem solving work and, often, our subject matter work deal with values and makes extensive use of maximising calculus to generate prescriptions as to what ought to be done.

From the above it is clear that our new journal should provide publishing opportunities for agricultural economists doing multidisciplinary subject matter and problem solving as well as disciplinary work. It is also clear that the journal should deal with questions of value and prescriptions. In order to convert these conclusions into a policy for the Association's Journal, a statement has been prepared, cleared with the Executive Committee, modified editorially and is presented here. It will appear inside the front cover of our Journal.

This Journal publishes articles covering the range of work done on agricultural economics. Manuscripts are sought on: (1) disciplinary work – improvement of theories, techniques and descriptive knowledge of economics and its contributing disciplines such as statistics, mathematics and philosophy; (2) multi-disciplinary subject matter areas – such as energy, technical change, institutional change, natural resources, farm management, rural communities, marketing, human development and the environment – which are important to fairly well-defined sets of problems; and (3) problem solving – the definition, solution and management of specific practical problems. Work in each of these three categories may deal with teaching, extension and outreach, consulting, advising, entrepreneurship, and administration, as well as research. All of these may require knowledge of values, non-monetary as well as monetary.

The Editor and Editorial Board, under the general direction of IAAE's President, Executive Committee and Council, are charged with implementing Journal policy to serve members of IAAE around the world. The Journal's Editorial Board is distributed among persons skilled in reviewing and evaluating manuscripts from the disciplinary, subject matter and problem solving categories. The Editorial Board also represents the world's different geographic regions to ensure that manuscripts are relevant to the agriculture and membership in each region. Balance by region and the three categories is maintained with invited papers and special issues devoted to specific topics under the editorship of guest editors from time to time. Manuscripts are refereed by peers appropriate to their category and nature. Excellence is sought, maintained and defined so as to recognize the three categories of the work of agricultural economics across the many activities of the profession, including research, teaching, advisory, consultative, entrepreneurial, administrative and other professional endeavours.

It should be pointed out that the proceedings of our triennial conferences will continue to be published separately from the Journal in essentially their present formats.

OUR CURRENT THEME: AGRICULTURE IN A TURBULENT WORLD

Professor Ulf Renborg has worked long and hard putting together the programme for this conference under the central theme: *Agriculture in a Turbulent World Economy*. We are benefiting from his intellectual leadership. Professor Renborg has been ably assisted by Bruce Green-shields who has taken the leadership with respect to the contributed paper competition. He has also been ably assisted by William Kibler who has been responsible for organising the discussion groups. New at this conference are the poster sessions under the competent direction of Laurent Martens. Mavis Hunt will handle the Cowbell. Allen and Pearl Maunder will edit our proceedings in their own highly efficient, helpful and friendly manner. I am grateful to Ulf Renborg and through him to Bruce Greenshields, William Kibler and Laurent Martens for the contributions they have made to oganising this programme. I am proud that our programmes continue to provide a wide range of opportunities for young and established members to participate. This conference's programme is also undergirded by the work of the Spanish National Organizing Committee which started early and has worked diligently and conscientiously on the logistics of our meeting. For the first time in many years, no visa problems have come to the attention of the President and the Executive Committee to mar our conference. I am also deeply appreciative of the efforts of all those mentioned or referred to above. At the end of our ten-day programme there will be a formal opportunity for me to give more adequate thanks to all of them on your behalf.

The programme which Ulf Renborg has designed both conforms to and supports the scope of agricultural economics I have outlined in this address. His programme recognises the importance of changes in human capital, technology, trade agreements, international monetary systems and changing institutions as causes of the growth and turbulence of world agriculture. Both the invited papers and the contributed papers reflect the concern of agricultural economists with the non-market determination of changes in technology, institutions and people – changes which both create problems and, in turn, solve or manage problems perhaps only to generate the next series of multi-disciplinary problems to be addressed by agricultural economists working in concert with biological and physical scientists, other social scientists and humanists. I am delighted with his programme. I am also delighted with the representation he has attained in the programme of a wide range of points of view from different parts of the world and, particularly, from our younger as well as our established agricultural economists. I am told that approximately 1,000 agricultural economists are here and that that number expands to 1,200 when companions and family members are counted.

I know from years of experience attending these conferences that it is extremely important for agricultural economists from different countries really to get to know one another. Our Association has facilitated this process by meeting for ten days under less hurried and pressing circumstances than we typically encounter at our own national meetings. We now have ten days before us in marvellous Malaga. This offers us a wonderful opportunity to get to know each other well and to advance our professional competence. I urge all of you to spend time really getting to know each other over 'cafe, cervesa y vino espanole que son magnificos'. To the younger members of the conference, whose attendance has been facilitated by the opportunities for participation provided by Ulf Renborg's large traditional programme and the addition of the poster sessions, I point out that this is your opportunity to form a wide circle of world colleagues – of people who will be your friends, supporters and valued professional colleagues for the remainder of your professional lives. I attended my first IAAE conference at Helsinki in 1955. I value the acquaintanceships and the friendships which I made with the people who were then the greyer beards of the Association: Edgar Thomas, Leonard Elmhirst, Jock Currie and others. Those I just mentioned and others are now dead but I am proud to have known them and to have listed them and others as my friends. Still others are now our elder statesmen, some active in the Association and others not. Nils Westermarck is here – Richard Manteuffel and John Raeburn are not. I also note that my own contemporaries are now becoming grey beards. I delight, most of all, in the number of young members here from so many different countries. I have no doubt about the future progress of our Association, the replenishment of our leadership and, for that matter, our Association's ability to maintain a full vision of the scope of agricultural economics.

REFERENCES

Achinstein, P. and Barker, S. F., *The Legacy of Logical Positivism*, Johns Hopkins Press, Baltimore, 1969.

Arrow, Kenneth J., *Social Choice and Individual Values* (2nd ed.), John Wiley and Sons, New York, 1963.

Benedict, Murray R., *Can We Solve the Farm Problem?*, The Twentieth Century Fund, New York, 1955.

——, *Farm Policies of the United States, 1870–1950: A Study of Their Origins and Development*, The Twentieth Century Fund, New York, 1953.

—— and Stine, O. C., *The Agricultural Commodity Programs: Two Decades of Experience*, The Twentieth Century Fund, New York, 1956.

Binswanger, Hans P. and Ruttan, Vernon W. (eds.) *Induced Innovation: Technology, Institutions and Development*, Johns Hopkins University Press, Baltimore, 1978.

Bromley, Daniel W., (forthcoming) 'Resource and Environmental Economics: Knowledge, Discipline, and Problems', *American Journal of Agricultural Economics*, Proceedings of 1985 annual meetings.

Cairncross, Sir Alec, 'Economics in Theory and Practice', Richard T. Ely Lecture, *AEA Papers and Proceedings*, vol. 75, no. 2, 1985, pp. 1–14.

Caldwell, Bruce, *Beyond Positivism: Economic Methodology in the Twentieth Century*, George Allen and Unwin, London, 1982.

Coleman, Jules L., 'Economics and the Law: A Critical Review of the Foundations of the Economic Approach to Law', Survey Article, *Ethics*, 1984, pp. 649–79.

Cooter, R. and Rappoport, P., 'Were the Ordinalists Wrong About Welfare Economics?' *Journal of Economic Literature*, vol. XXII, no. 2, 1984, pp. 507–30.

Drucker, Peter F., *The Practice of Management*, Harper & Row, New York, 1954.

Dworkin, Ronald, 'Why Efficiency?', *Hofstra Law Review*, vol. 8, 1980, pp. 563–90.

Fienup, Darrell F. and Riley, Harold M., *Training Agricultural Economists for Work in International Development*, Agricultural Development Council, New York, 1980.

French, Ben C., 'The Analysis of Productive Efficiency in Agricultural Marketing: Models, Methods and Progress', Part II, *A Survey of Agricultural Economics Literature, Volume 1*, Lee R. Martin (ed.), University of Minnesota Press, 1977, pp. 94–206.

Friedman, Milton, *Essays in Positive Economics*, University of Chicago Press, 1953.

Harsanyi, John C., 'Mortality and the Theory of Rational Behaviour,' *Utilitarianism and Beyond*, A. Sen and B. Williams (Eds.), Cambridge University Press, 1982.

Hicks, J. R., *Value and Capital: An Inquiry into Some Fundamental Principles of Economic Theory*, Oxford University Press, 1939.

Johnson, Glenn L., Forthcoming-a., *Research Methodology for Economists*, Macmillan, New York.

——, Forthcoming-b., 'Holistic Modeling Multidisciplinary Subject Matter and Problematic Domains', *Systems Economics*, Don G. Miles (ed.), Iowa State University Press, Ames.

——, 'Economics and Ethics', Twenty-Fourth Annual Centennial Review Lecture, 9 April, 1985: Michigan State University (printed text of lecture forthcoming).

——, 'Ethics and the Economics of Energy and Food Conversion Systems', in *Food and Energy Resources*, D. Pimentel and C. W. Hall (eds.), Academic Press, New York, 1984, pp. 147–80.

——, 1983-a, 'The Relevance of U.S. Graduate Curricula in Agricultural Economics for the Training of Foreign Students', *American Journal of Agricultural Economics*, vol. 65, no. 5, 1983, pp. 1142–48.

——, 1983-b, 'Synoptic View', *Growth and Equity in Agricultural Development*, Allen Maunder and Kazushi Ohkawa (eds.), Proceedings of Eighteenth International Conference of Agricultural Economists, Gower, Aldershot, 1983, pp. 592–608.

——, 'Contributions of Economists to a Rational Decision-Making Process in the Field of Agricultural Policy', *Decision-Making and Agriculture*, T. Dams and K. E. Hunt (eds.), Oxford Agricultural Economics Institute, Papers and Reports of the XVI International Conference of Agricultural Economists, 1977, pp. 25–46.

——, et al., 'Agricultural Change and Economic Method', *European Review of Agricultural Economics*, 1976, The Hague, Netherlands.

——, 'The Quest for Relevance in Agricultural Economics', *American Journal of Agricultural Economics*, vol. 53, no. 5, 1971, pp. 728–39.

——, 'Capital in Agriculture', *International Encyclopedia of Social Sciences*, Macmillan Company, New York, vol. 1, ch. 5, 1968, pp. 229–36.

——, 'Value Problems in Farm Management', *Agricultural Economics Journal*, vol. 14, no. 1, 1960, pp. 13–25.

——, 'Agricultural Economics, Production Economics and the Field of Farm Management', *Journal of Farm Economics*, vol. XXXVIII, no. 2., 1957.

Kaplan, A., 'Positivism', *The International Encyclopedia of the Social Sciences*, vol. 12, D. L. Sills (ed.), Macmillan and Free Press, New York, 1968.

Kelso, Maurice M., 'Natural Resource Economics: The Upsetting Discipline', Fellows Lecture, *American Journal of Agricultural Economics*, vol. 59, no. 5, 1977, pp. 814–23.

Keynes, J. N. *Scope and Method of Political Economy*, Macmillan, London, 1963 (orig. 1890).

McClennen, Edward F., 'Rational Choice and Public Policy: A Critical Survey', *Social Theory and Practice*, vol. 9, nos. 2–3, 1983, pp. 335–79.

McCloskey, Donald N., 'The Rhetoric of Economics', *Journal of Economic Literature*, vol. XXI, no. 2, 1983, pp. 481–517.

Myrdal, G., *The American Dilemma*, Harper Brothers, New York, 1944, Appendix 2.

Nou, J., *Studies in the Development of Agricultural Economics in Europe*, Almquist and Wiksell, Uppsala, 1967.

Parsons, K. H., 'The Value Problem in Agricultural Policy', *Agricultural Adjustment Problems in a Growing Economy*, E. Heady, et al. (eds), Iowa State College Press, Ames, 1958, Ch. 18.

Pigou, A. C., *The Economics of Welfare* (fourth edition), Macmillan, London, 1962 (orig. 1920).

Posner, Richard A., 'The Ethical and Political Basis of the Efficiency Norm in Common Law Adjudication', *Hofstra Law Review*, vol. 8, 1980, pp. 487–507.

Robbins, Lionel, *An Essay on the Nature & Significance of Economic Science*, Macmillan, London, 1949 (orig. 1932).

Runes, D. D. (ed.), *Dictionary of Philosophy* (15th edition), Philosophical Library, New York, 1960.

Sagoff, Mark, 'Values and Preferences', Center for Philosophy and Public Policy, University of Maryland, 10 January 1985.

Schmid, A. Allan, *Property, Power, and Public Choice: An Inquiry into Law and Economics*, Praeger, New York, 1978.

Schultz, T. W., 'Investment in Human Capital', *American Economic Review*, vol. 51, 1961, pp. 1–17.

——, *Agriculture in an Unstable Economy*, McGraw-Hill, New York, 1945.
Sen, Amartya, *Resources, Values and Development*, Harvard University Press, 1984.
—— and Williams, Bernard (eds.), *Utilitarianism and Beyond*, Harvard University Press, 1982.
Taylor, H. C. and Taylor, A. D., *The Story of Agricultural Economics in the United States, 1840–1932: Men-Services-Ideas*, Iowa State University Press, Ames, 1952.

SECTION I

Forces Shaping the Future

YUJIRO HAYAMI

Poverty and Beyond: the Forces Shaping the Future in Asia

In the first session of the last IAAE Meeting held in Jakarta, V. S. Vyas (1983) characterised good agricultural production performances in South and Southeast Asia relative to other developing regions as follows:

> In most countries of this region agricultural production outstripped population growth; in a number of countries the rate of growth in production was higher than that of the growth in domestic demand; the food self-sufficiency ratio for the region and for the majority of countries improved; the growth of agricultural exports outpaced the growth of agricultural imports ...

He went on to say, 'An equally remarkable feature of development during the past decade is that it made very little impact on the extent of poverty in this region.'

Indeed, persistent poverty despite high rates of agricultural and economic growth is and will continue to be the core problem in the rural sector of South and Southeast Asia. In this paper I will focus on the forces influencing this problem. I will then make a prediction on the problem of a very different nature to emerge, if successful economic development is able to reach a stage to solve the poverty problem, drawing on the experience of East Asia.

ECONOMIC GROWTH AND POVERTY

First, we will try to have an overview of the Asian economy. Viewed from macro statistics (Table 1), the economic performance of the Asian Region has been impressive. Emergence of Japan from a developing-country stage to one of the major industrial powers in the world, within only two decades since the 1950s, is a well-known story. A decade later, Asian NICs (Newly Industrializing Countries) such as Korea, Taiwan (China) and Singapore began to take off in industrialisation and economic growth at a rate even faster than in Japan. This was followed by ASEAN countries. During the 1970s, despite the slow-down in the growth rates of advanced industrial economies after the first Oil Crisis, the annual

37

TABLE 1 *Indicators of industrialisation and economic growth in selected countries*

	GNP per caput (1980 US$)	GDP growth rate (%/year)				Share of manufactures in merchandise exports (%)		Debt-service ratio (%)		
		Total		Manufacturing						
		1960–70	1970–80	1960–70	1970–80	1970	1980	1970	1980	1982
India	240	3.4	3.6	4.7	5.0	45	59	21	9	7
Pakistan	300	6.7	4.7	9.4	4.0	27	50	24	11	9
ASEAN:										
Indonesia	430	3.9	7.6	3.3	12.8	1	2	7	8	8
Thailand	670	8.4	7.2	11.4	10.6	2	29	3	5	8
Philippines	690	5.1	6.3	6.7	7.2	4	37	8	7	13
Malaysia	1620	6.5	7.8	na	11.8	6	19	4	2	5
Korea (Republic of)	1520	8.6	9.5	17.6	16.6	14	90	19	12	13
Brazil	2050	5.4	8.4	na	10.3	3	39	13	34	42
Mexico	2090	7.2	5.4	9.0	5.9	12	39	24	32	30
Developed countries (av.)	10320	5.2	3.2	5.9	3.2	66	72			
Japan	9890	10.9	5.0	11.0	6.4	79	96			

Source: World Bank, World Development Report 1982, 1983 and 1984.

average growth rate of national income in the ASEAN region exceeded 7 per cent and that of GDP from the manufacturing sector exceeded 10 per cent. The share of manufactured commodities in total commodity exports in Malaysia, Thailand and the Philippines rose sharply from less than 5 per cent in the early 1960s to more than 20 per cent in the early 1980s. Judging from increases in the domestic saving rate and improvements in the quality of industrial manpower and know-how, ASEAN's development seems to have reached a self-sustaining stage.

Similar rates of industrialisation and economic growth have been experienced by Latin American NICs such as Brazil and Mexico. yet the process by which the Asian NICs and the ASEAN economies grew seems much healthier and more genuinely self-sustaining than Latin American counterparts. Take, for example, the debt-service ratio (debt service/exports) as an indicator. From 1970 to 1980, the debt-service ratio in the Asian NICs and the ASEAN countries remained at about the same level in the order of 5 to 10 per cent. This implies that the imported capital was successfully converted into the productive assets which increased the productivity and international competitive position of industry at a rate sufficient to pay for the accumulating external debt-service. In contrast, the debt-service ratio in Brazil and Mexico rose sharply from a level of 20 per cent in 1970 to above 30 per cent in 1980. Contraction of developing countries' exports due to the world recession, following the second Oil Crisis, coupled with the high interest rate policy in the United States, has raised the debt-service ratio in most developing countries. In some ASEAN countries it has been reported to approach a 'critical threshold' of 20 per cent. Yet, it is still incomparably lower than in Latin American NICs.

A disquieting aspect is that, aside from the NICs, the impressive records of industrialisation and overall economic growth in most developing countries in Asia have not accompanied increases in the real wage rates of labourers except for the urban organised sector. Data collected by the Asian Development Bank (1978, p. 54), for example, show that the real wage rates of agricultural labourers have declined or, at best, stayed stagnant for the past two decades. What do the declining wage rates imply in the economies where the average income per caput has been rising as fast as 5 per cent per year? It means that the property income rose at the expense of the labour income; poor labourers owning no property have been immiserised relative to the property-owning class.

One of the basic forces underlying the declining wage rates is the population pressure on agricultural land. Developing countries throughout the world, Asia not excepted, have experienced explosive population growth since the Second World War. The increase in industrial employment has been grossly insufficient to absorb the increased labour force. Meanwhile, the possibility of opening new land for cultivation has been exhausted. The man-land ratio has been deteriorating rapidly at a rate of doubling the number of agricultural workers per hectare within a half century. As the larger number of workers seek employment in a limited land area, the wage rate will be bid down and many of them become unemployed or underemployed, whereas the land rent will increase – a widening income gap between landlords and landless tenants/labourers.

In order to illustrate the situation, let me report my study conducted on a rice village in West Java (Hayami and Kikuchi 1981, ch. 8). In this village, owing to continued population pressure for the past several decades, the man-land ratio has become extremely unfavourable. The average farm size is only 0.3 hectare and as much as 40 per cent of villagers own less than 0.1 hectare of land. For the past decade the real wage rate declined by more than 10 per cent from 9.5 kg of paddy per day to 8.5 kg. Meanwhile, the land rent increased by about 40 per cent.

The wage decline involved a change in rural community institutions. A traditional rice harvesting system in Java is called *bawon*; in which every villager can participate in harvesting and receive a certain share of the harvest crop. This system represents the traditional community principle of mutual help and income sharing. The system has recently undergone change. First, stronger limitations have been placed on the participation in harvesting (Table 2); the purely open (PO) *bawon* was successively replaced by the system limiting the participation to villagers only (OV), by another system which placed a limit on the maximum number allowed (OM) and, further, by a stronger limitation to those received specific invitations from farmers (LI).

TABLE 2 *Changes in rice harvesting system in a village in West Java (% of farmer adoptees)*

	Bawon[a]				Ceblokan[b]					
					1/6	1/7	1/7	1/7	1/7	
	PO	OV	OM	LI	(T)	(T)	(T + W)	(H + T)	(H + T + W)	Total
1950s	35	29	18	18						100
1960–61	29	31	21	19						100
1962–63	16	34	33	17						100
1964–65	9	16	16	32	27					100
1966–67	3	10	8	27	52					100
1968–69	1	4	6	19	44	24	2			100
1970–71			2	10	33	51	4			100
1972–73				8	17	67	8			100
1974–75				7	15	67	10	1		100
1976–77				4	7	67	18	2	2	100
1978				4		72	19	1	4	100

[a] *Bawon* system: PO-purely open, OV-open for villagers only, OM-open with maximum limit, LI-limited to invitees.
[b] *Ceblokan* system: 1/6, 1/7-harvesters' share; T, W, H-obligatory works to establish the harvesting right (T-transplanting, W-weeding, H-harrowing).
Source: Hayami, Yujiro and Kikuchi, Masao, *Asian Village Economy at the Crossroads*, University of Tokyo Press and Johns Hopkins University Press, Baltimore, 1981, p. 184.

Later, the *bawon* system was replaced by a new system called *ceblokan* in which the participation in harvesting is allowed only to those who performed the additional service of rice planting without pay. More recently, their share of output was reduced to one seventh, and weeding and harrowing were added in the list of obligatory duties required for harvesters. Through those changes the implicit wage rate per hour of labour employed under the output-sharing contract has been reduced to the same level as the market wage rate of labourers employed under the fixed-wage, time-rate contract. Large farmer employers gained from the wage cost reduction under the guise of fulfilling the traditional obligations of village élites who are expected to share work and income with poorer members in the same community. Through such a process the share of labour wage in agricultural income declined and the share of land rent rose.

FORCES AND COUNTERFORCES

Growing poverty and inequality demonstrated in the case of this village is not unique but rather common in South and Southeast Asia under the surface of rapid economic development. This process will likely continue for some time to come. Even though population growth itself began to decelerate in the 1970s, the growth rates of the labour force will remain high for the next couple of decades because a large percentage of the population has not yet reached the working age. Partly because the industrial sector is still a minor sector of the economy and partly because the industrial technology imported from developed countries has a bias towards high capital intensity, the increase in employment in this sector will be insufficient to absorb the increment of the labour population in the dominant agricultural sector. The increment of population unable to find productive employment in agriculture and industry flows into urban slums, as reflected in the 'pathological' growth of the service sector from the early stage of economic development.

How to cope with the situation? The answer seems simple – it is infertile or even counterproductive to deal with the problem of growing poverty and inequality without assaulting the underlying economic forces. If the core of the problem is the population pressure to reduce the return to labour relative to the returns to land and capital, the maximum effort must be allocated for the expansion of demand for labour. Two obvious fronts are agriculture and small (and medium) scale industries.

The historical experience of Japan as well as Taiwan (China) and Korea has proved the development of labour intensive, small scale industries to be the most effective way to achieve the dual goals of growth and equity. Even today, Japan's industrial strength is, to a large extent, based on a large number of small-scale industries. In order to foster the labour-intensive small-scale industries, it is vital to correct the intervention policies designed to protect capital intensive, large-scale industries by such means as tariff and foreign exchange licensing, so that the labour intensive industries can enjoy the comparative advantage in the free market. I wonder whether relatively poor economic growth perform- ances in countries in South Asia compared with those of East and Southeast Asia might be explained, at least in part, by excessive government intervention and regulations on private economic activities. The government must support the small-scale industries by providing education and training services for workers and management as well as information services about new technology and market conditions. As the standard theory of welfare economics tells, the government would be better to specialise in the provision of public goods such as information, while leaving private resource allocation to the market.

Since agriculture is still the dominant sector, the unemployment/un- deremployment problem cannot be solved without increasing its labour absorptive capacity. The development of land saving and labour using technologies such as more intensive cropping systems combined with higher yielding varieties is the key to achieve both growth and equity in agriculture under labour-surplus condition, as the East Asian experience shows. A precondition for the introduction of such technologies is the development of irrigation systems. The need for government provision of public goods such as irrigation infrastructure and agricultural research and extension services is even greater for agriculture than for industry because of the very small scale of peasant production in Asia. Of course, such efforts should not be limited to irrigable lowland areas. Develop- ments of soil conserving agro-forestry management systems in hills and mountains and of drought resisting varieties and water conserving practices in arid and semi-arid areas are vital to the increase in rural employment and income.

The effectiveness of public investment in irrigation and agricultural research to counteract the problem of growing poverty and inequality may be illustrated by a comparison between a village referred to earlier and another village also located in West Java (Hayami and Kikuchi 1981, ch. 9). In the first village agricultural technology was stagnant because no improvement in irrigation systems was made in recent years and no modern high-yielding variety effective in its environment was made available. Gains in rice yields were not significant. The increase in the labour force against limited land resources resulted in the decline in the economic return to labour. The real wage rate declined, inducing the substitution of hand hoeing for animal ploughing, and labour's income share decreased relative to land's share. The dismal process in this village approximates to the world of classical economists like David Ricardo. As the growth of population presses hard on limited land resources under constant technology, cultivation frontiers are expanded to more marginal land and greater amounts of labour are applied per unit of cultivated land; the cost of food production increases and food prices rise; in the end, the real wage rate will be lowered to a subsistence minimum and all economic surpluses will be captured by landlords in the form of increased land rent. This was exactly what happened in this village.

In contrast, in the second village dramatic improvements in irrigation systems resulted because this village was covered by one of the major government irrigation projects and, also, because modern high-yielding varieties were made available through an experiment station located nearby. Both the double-cropping ratio and the average yield per hectare of crop area increased. Labour demand increased and the real wage rate rose, despite the large inflow of migrant labourers and farmers' effort to substitute animal power for human labour. The relative income share of labour did not decline and the income of labourers increased absolutely if not relative to farmers. The comparison of these two village cases suggests that it is critically important for countries in South and Southeast Asia to strengthen the efforts to improve land infrastructure and agricultural technology in the labour using and land saving direction in order to escape from the Ricardian trap of stagnation with poverty and inequality.

It is important to recognise that government regulations and institutional reforms aimed at preventing widening income disparity without assaulting its basic cause often prove to be counterproductive to the equity goal itself. What would have happened, for example, if the *ceblokan* contract quoted ealier had been banned for its apparent 'exploiting' role of reducing the implicit wage rate for hired labourers? Given the fall in market wage rates due to changes in labour demand and supply relations, employer farmers would have abandoned the traditional output-sharing contract with neighbours in the same community and would have begun to employ labourers through the market at a fixed daily wage contract. The shift from a patron-client relation in the rural community to an impersonal market relation would have increased the labour transaction cost, especially the cost of supervising the work of wage labourers; this could have encouraged the adoption of labour-saving practices and discouraged substitution of hired labour for family labour, altogether resulting in a reduction of the employment and wage earnings of landless labourers.

In fact, I have encountered a large number of cases in which government regulations and reform laws resulted in loss to the poor, despite their original intentions; land reform regulations, such as rent control, resulted in the eviction of tenants in order to establish landlords' direct management; minimum wage laws induced the shift from labour-intensive crops, such as rice, to extensive crops, such as coconuts; and the prohibition of usury increased the effective rate of interest for the poor by the amount of increased risk premium for private money lenders, while the rich managed to receive a disproportionate share of subsidised institutional credit through their pull with government agencies. It is easy to point out loopholes in the laws and regulations and to advocate a stronger political will in order to close these loopholes. Yet the real problem is the economic and social conditions in developing countries that allows the loopholes to exist.

It is common to refer to the success of drastic redistributive land reforms in Japan and the Taiwan area of China in the post-Second World War years as a model for developing countries in Asia. However, major differences in socio-economic conditions severely limit the likelihood of reproducing the East Asian experience in South and Southeast Asia today. It should be recalled that Japan's reform was executed under the authority of US occupation forces and Taiwan's executed by the Nationalist Government which was exiled from the continent and, therefore, alienated from the landed interests of the island. Equally important was the huge backlog of data and administrative experience with landownership and tenure systems accumulated in this area since long before the Second World War. In addition, Japanese tenants had learned how to organise themselves through the long history of co-operative and tenant union movements since before the War. More importantly, the critical difference that should be recognised is the economic conditions specific to East Asia that have preserved the results of the land reforms. In both Japan and Taiwan, rapid expansion of non-agricultural employment has resulted in reduced population pressure on land; the agricultural labour force has declined absolutely and real wage rates have risen. If Japan and Taiwan had continued to be subject to population pressure on land similar to that being experienced in South and Southeast Asia today, the results of the land reforms would have been seriously undermined by such developments as illegal tenancy arrangements similar to those we now observe in Philippine villages.

I am not at all saying that equity-oriented policies and reforms are unnecessary or undesirable. I am saying that the direct importation of the equity-oriented policies from the developed countries without due recognition of major differences in underlying economic forces and in social and institutional environments is often counterproductive, not only to the efficiency goal but also to the equity goal itself. It is important to recognise that institutions are viable only when they are consistent with the traditional norms in society. For example, I have observed sharecropping tenancy still widely practised in Philippine villages even though it is illegal under the land reform laws, because the cropsharing contract is consistent with the traditional moral principles of work and income sharing in rural communities in addition to other merits such as risk sharing. Institutional reforms cannot be viable and effective unless they are considered fair and legitimate in terms of traditional norms ingrained in the mind of people in the society. It is therefore necessary to make positive use of indigenous community institutions and organisational principles in designing modern development institutions that can promote both growth and equity.

One might argue that the growing poverty and inequality in South and Southeast Asia is a transitory phenomenon along the rising phase of the Kuznets inverted U-curve in the changes in income distribution in the process of economic development. But, the real concern is whether the cumulative frustration in the rural sector and the urban unorganised sector might result in social unrest and disruption that induce capital flights and jeopardise industrialisation and economic growth before the declining phase of the inverted U-curve will be reached. Thus, South and

Southeast Asian economies are at the crossroads en route either to growing poverty and inequality which may end up with political disruption and the abortion of economic development or to sustaining economic growth up to the point of eradication of mass poverty. Which route to follow depends critically on the efforts to develop appropriate technology and institution in the rural sector.

BEYOND POVERTY

If the present rates of economic growth can be sustained, most countries in South and Southeast Asia will eventually reach a threshold beyond which the real wage rates begin to rise sharply and inequality to decline; this has been the case of Japan since the 1960s and of Korea and Taiwan since the 1970s, and will likely be replicated relatively soon by the ASEAN countries. In that stage of economic development East Asian countries have had to experience an agricultural problem diametrically different from that of South and Southeast Asia today.

Economic growth in East Asia has been accompanied by a rapid decline in comparative advantage in agriculture. During this period of Japan's most rapid industrial growth, 1955 to 1970, labour productivity in agriculture in Japan grew at a similar pace to that in North America and Western Europe, whereas Japan's labour productivity in manufacturing grew at more than twice the average rate of other industrial countries. A similar but even more extreme contrast occurred for Korea and Taiwan during the 1970s. The chief restraint on raising labour productivity at a faster pace has been East Asia's small farm size. In all three countries, the average farm size is still only a little above one hectare and that severely limits the scope of mechanisation to substitute capital for labour. Indeed by 1980 the level of farm mechanisation as measured by tractor horsepower per hectare of cultivated land area had risen to 8 hp in Japan, compared with 4 hp in France and 7 hp in West Germany. But, because the average cultivated land area per worker in Japan was only about one-tenth that of France and one-fourth of Germany, tractor horsepower per worker in Japan remained only about one-fourth that of France and Germany. As a result, Japan's labour productivity was less than one-fourth that of France and Germany, even though Japan's land productivity was about twice and three times higher than France and Germany, respectively.

Thus, how to adjust the agrarian structure to the new labour-saving and scale-biased technology that is consistent with the high-wage economy seems to be the most serious problem in agricultural adjustment in East Asia. A major impediment to this adjustment has been land tenure regulations since the successful postwar land reforms. Tenancy rights have been so strongly protected in the land reform laws that it has been almost impossible for landlords to evict tenants. In addition, land rent has been controlled at a level so low as to give land owners little incentive to lease out their holdings. Thus non-farmers who inherit land tend to hold on to it and farm it on a part-time basis, even very inefficiently, rather than lease it out. Ironically, the relatively egalitarian agrarian structures and institutions in East Asia that facilitated the development and diffusion of the labour using (and land saving) and scale neutral technology consistent with the low-wage economy in the earlier stage of development are now turning into the major constraint against structural adjustment.

Rapid shifts of comparative advantage away from agriculture in Japan, Korea and Taiwan in the process of very fast industrial development have required major adjustment in intersectoral resource allocations. If this adjustment were left to the market mechanism, its cost should have been shouldered mainly by the agricultural population in such forms as rural-urban income disparity and depopulation in rural communities. Increases in the adjustment cost have induced agricultural producers to demand agricultural trade protection and farm price and income support programmes. Concurrently the resistance of the non-agricultural population against the agricultural protection policies has declined. The share of food costs in urban household expenditure declined appreciably owing to rises in wage rates and income per caput, thereby reducing the influences of food prices on the cost of living. The secular decline in the share of agriculture in national income, employment and consumption made it less burdensome for the nonagricultural population to shoulder the cost to support domestic agricultural producers in the form of either high food prices or direct subsidies.

The increasing demand for and the decreasing resistance against agricultural protection policies have resulted in sharp increases in the level of agricultural protection in East Asia as measured by the rates of difference of domestic prices from international prices (nominal rates of protection) in Table 3. The nominal rate of agricultural protection of Japan in 1955 was only 18 per cent which was considerably lower than the average of the countries that later formed the EEC. It rose rapidly, reaching the EEC level in 1960 and the Swiss level in 1965, which is known to be exceptionally high for reasons of national security and environmental conservation for Alpine tourism. Similar but more dramatic changes occurred in Korea and Taiwan (China) from 1965 to 1980. Until 1965, the NRPs of Korea and Taiwan had been negative, reflecting agricultural exploitation policies that are typical of economies in the early stage of economic development. During the subsequent decade and a half their agricultural protection levels rose sharply, surpassing the EEC level and reaching a level comparable with Japan and Switzerland by 1980.

Such high rates of protection do not only result in significant loss in domestic welfare but also create serious international friction. It is well known that Japan has been under very strong pressure for agricultural trade liberalisation not only from major food exporters in North America and Australasia but also from developing countries with respect to sugar, silk, pineapple and other tropical products. The

TABLE 3   *Comparison of the nominal rates of agricultural protection between East Asian countries and twelve other developed countries, 1955 to 1980*

(per cent)[a]

	1955	1960	1965	1970	1975	1980
East Asia:						
Japan	18	41	69	74	76	85
Korea	− 46	− 15	− 4	29	30	117
Taiwan (China)	− 17	− 3	− 1	2	20	52
European Community:						
Denmark	5	3	5	17	19	25
France	33	26	30	47	29	30
Germany, FR	35	48	55	50	39	44
Italy	47	50	66	69	38	57
Netherlands	14	21	35	41	32	27
United Kingdom	40	37	20	27	6	35
Average[b]	*35*	*37*	*45*	*52*	*29*	*38*
Non-aligned Europe:						
Sweden	34	44	50	65	43	59
Switzerland	60	64	73	96	96	126
Food exporters:						
Australia	5	7	5	7	− 5	− 2
Canada	0	4	2	− 5	− 4	2
New Zealand	na	2	0	5	7	− 3
United States	2	1	9	11	4	0

[a] Defined as the percentage by which the producer price exceeds the border price. The estimates shown are the weighted averages for 12 commodities, using production valued at border prices as weights. The 12 commodities include rice, wheat, barley, corn, oats, rye, beef, pork, chicken, eggs, milk and sugar.
[b] Weighted average for all six countries shown for 1975 and 1980, but excluding Denmark and the United Kingdom for earlier years.

Source: Anderson, Kym and Hayami, Yujiro, *The Political Economy of Agricultural Protection: East Asia in International Perspective*, Allen and Unwin, London, 1986.

pressure will increase on Korea and Taiwan as their weights in the world economy continue to rise.

An important point is that the agricultural protection of countries in East Asia has been raised to the highest level in the world not because they have a unique bias for preserving domestic agriculture but because their comparative advantage shifted from agriculture to industry at such a rapid rate that social and political difficulties involved in intersectoral resource adjustments may have become unbearably large in the absence of protection (Anderson and Hayami, 1986). This suggests that East Asia's experience is likely to be duplicated in future in densely populated, resource-poor developing countries in South and Southeast Asia as they follow East Asia in their economic development and overcome the present overriding problem of poverty. At that stage, the diffusion of

48

Yujiro Hayami

agricultural protectionism in Asia might grow to be a major disruptive element in the international economic order.

REFERENCES

Anderson, K. and Hayami, Y., *The Political Economy of Agricultural Protection: East Asia in International Perspective*, George Allen and Unwin, London, 1986.

Asian Development Bank, *Rural Asia: Challenge and Opportunity*, Praeger, New York 1978.

Hayami, Y. and Kikuchi, M., *Asian Village Economy at the Crossroads*, University of Tokyo Press, Tokyo 1981, and Johns Hopkins University Press Baltimore 1982.

Hayami, Y. and Ruttan, V., *Agricultural Development: An International Perspective* (Second edition), Johns Hopkins University Press, Baltimore and London 1985.

Vyas, V. S., 'Growth and Equity in Asian Agriculture: A Synoptic View,' in Maunder, A. and Ohkawa, K. (eds), *Growth and Equity in Agricultural Development*, Gower, Aldershot, for IAAE, 1983.

MANCUR OLSON

The Exploitation and Subsidization of Agriculture in Developing and Developed Countries*

DEVELOPING COUNTRIES

So far as one can tell from the available literature, the developing areas of the world differ profoundly from the developed areas in their treatment of agriculture. In most of the less developed countries there are a vast variety of public policies and institutional arrangements that make many agricultural prices lower than they would otherwise be, and in particular often lower than the prices on the world market. In many of the poorest countries agricultural marketing boards are given a monopoly over the right to trade in the main agricultural export commodities and the growers of these commodities receive only a fraction of the price their products fetch on the world market. In some developing countries multiple exchange rates have been used to give growers of agricultural commodities a less favourable exchange rate than is accorded to exporters or importers of other products. In most developing countries the production of manufactured goods and certain other import substitutes produced in cities is heavily subsidised through tariffs and quotas. This not only raises the prices that farmers must pay for these products, but also tends to reduce the prices that they receive for their exports; restrictions on imports reduce the amount of a country's currency that is supplied to purchase foreign goods, with the result that the value of the country's currency tends to be higher than it would otherwise be and the prices in domestic currency that agricultural exporters receive are correspondingly lower. Many governments in developing countries also provide disproportionate amounts of social overhead capital in major cities and subsidise some types of consumption only in these cities.

The disadvantage of agriculture and rural areas in most developing countries is reflected not only in product prices and in explicit governmental policies, but also in many urban and rural labour markets and in the often extra-governmental and less conspicuous institutions that

*I am grateful to the International Food Policy Research Institute for supporting some of the research on this paper and to the National Science Foundation, Resources for the Future, and the Thyssen Stiftung for supporting the more general research out of which this paper has grown.

influence wages in these markets. Though I do not know of any comparable world-wide data on urban-rural or intersectoral wage differences, there appears to be virtually a consensus among observers that in most developing countries the real wage rates in the 'modern' sectors of the biggest cities are often vastly higher than they are for comparable labour in the agricultural and traditional sectors. There is important evidence for such real wage differentials in the exceptionally high unemployment rates in many of the biggest cities in the developing world. So conspicuous are the real wages differentials and the associated unemployment rates that one of the better-known models in development economics – the 'Todaro model' – is devoted to explaining how the flow of labour from rural areas to major metropolitan centres could continue in spite of the low probability of employment in the modern urban sector. W. Arthur Lewis's very famous model of 'unlimited supplies of labour' to the modern and mainly urban sectors of the developing economies also explicitly assumes a significantly higher return to comparable labour in the modern sector than is available in the traditional and mainly agricultural sector.

Though references to well-known theories cannot substitute for the systematic and comprehensive international measurements that are needed, it is doubtful that the models I have mentioned would have been so widely used and accepted if the observations of a significant urban-rural real wage differential were not shared by many students of the developing countries. Substantial real wage differentials for comparable labour and high unemployment rates in the very locations with the highest wages cannot be sustained in an entirely unconstrained and unorganised market. The unemployed and low-wage labours will, of course, have an incentive to offer to fill the jobs of the high-wage workers for somewhat less and the employers will have an incentive to accept such offers. It follows that in some sectors of many of the major cities of the underdeveloped world there must be institutions, such as collusions or cartels of relatively fortunate workers, that generate supra-competitive wage levels partly at the expense of potential entrants from the agricultural sector.

DEVELOPED COUNTRIES

In the developed countries, by contrast, agricultural interests are normally among the major beneficiaries of tariffs, quotas, price supports, and other subsidies. In those developed economies that lack comparative advantage in agriculture, such as Japan and most of the highly industrialised nations of Western Europe, the subsidisation of agriculture is quite striking, and probably far higher than the levels of subsidies to many of the principal manufacturing industries in those countries. As T. W. Schultz graphically puts it, many of these countries have carried agricultural protection nearly to the point of 'greenhouse agriculture'. Masayoshi Honma and Yujiro Hayami (1984a) have shown convincingly that the level of nominal protection for the major agricultural commodities among the developed nations is greatest in those countries that are the least likely to have a comparative advantage in agriculture. The subsidies to agriculture are usually much less in the developed nations with a comparative advantage in agriculture, such as Australia, Canada, New Zealand and the United States, and the agricultural interests in these countries (especially in Australia and New Zealand) lose substantially from various forms of protection or subsidy to urban interests in those countries. Nonetheless, agricultural interests in these countries also conspicuously share in the society's subsidies and price-distortions. In the United States, for example, the total government subsidies to agriculture are in many years very large even in relation to total farm income. There are in addition subsidies that do not show up in the government budget. The producers of some farm products, such as fluid milk, are systematically given supra-competitive prices at the expense of consumers.

Unfortunately, I do not know of any data source of quantitative study that documents this seemingly systematic difference in the treatment of agriculture in developing and developed countries. But there appears again to be nearly a consensus among the experts. As T. W. Schultz puts it, 'the political market in a considerable number of high income countries overprices agricultural products at the expense of consumers and taxpayers. In many low-income countries the political market underprices agricultural products'. Kym Anderson and Yujiro Hayami (1986) similarly conclude that 'domestic food prices in Western Europe and Japan are often twice international levels. In many developing countries, on the other hand, agricultural prices are well below those in international markets and manufacturing is the sector protected from international competition.'

THE NUMBERS PARADOX

There is a strength in numbers. In democratic countries, the more numerous interests obviously have more votes that the less numerous. Even in non-democratic countries, the potential physical and social force of more numerous groups should, when other things are equal, give them more power than less numerous groups.

Why, then, is agriculture exploited in countries where farmers or peasants constitute the great bulk of the population, and subsidised in countries where farmers constitute only a tiny minority, often less than five per cent, of the population? This is a question that has also puzzled T. W. Schultz. Honma and Hayami (1984b) have underlined the paradox by showing that Korea and Taiwan had negative nominal rates of protection for agriculture before their rapid industrialisation began in the 1960s, but that they have by now imposed very high levels of agricultural protection. I would add that this change of policy has, of course, occurred during a period when the proportions of their populations in agriculture have declined. Indeed, Honma and Hayami show elsewhere (1984a) with a regression analysis that in ten of the major industrialised countries nominal protection for agriculture increases as the percentage of farmers in the population declines.

The paradox that has just been described should for some purposes have been posed in a less aggregative way. The extent of price distortions varies from one urban industry to another and there are also great differences in the extent of price distortions from one agricultural commodity to another. Casual observation suggests that in urban industries and occupations as diverse as the steel industry, the taxi industry, and the learned professions of law and medicine there are unusually large distortions. In the manufacture of scientific instruments and plastics, and in the restaurant industry, I would guess, the incentives are usually less perverse. I would also guess that there is more price distortion in most countries (or at least most developed countries) in dairying than in beef production, and more in rice production than in soya beans.

Sadly, these vitally important questions about inter-industry, inter-occupational, inter-commodity and inter-group differences in the extent of perverse incentives are usually not even asked, so that the data needed to deal with them have not been collected. Eventually I should like to examine these questions of inter-market and inter-group differences in the perversity of incentives in a more detailed and disaggregated way than one can do when one merely contrasts the agricultural and non-agricultural sectors.

Nonetheless, I think there is some interest and utility in a broad comparison of agricultural and non-agricultural activities of the kind I am attempting here. This comparison is some interest to me, partly because of my farm background, and it should be of professional interest to agricultural economists. There is also, as we shall see, one important respect in which nearly all agricultural industries differ from almost all urban industries, and this makes an agricultural/non-agricultural comparison especially valuable.

IS THE EXPLOITATION OF AGRICULTURE REQUIRED FOR DEVELOPMENT?

In many circles, the resolution of the paradox I have posed will seem obvious. The developing nations wish to develop – to become economically similar to the nations that have already become prosperous. The highly developed nations devote relatively small proportions of their populations and resources to agriculture, so many believe that the developing nations should subsidise and promote industries of the types that are most prominent in the economically advanced countries, and discriminate against those industries, such as agriculture, that have become relatively minor parts of the advanced economies. Because they mainly export primary products, the developing areas are perceived to be the hewers of wood and drawers of water for the economically advanced nations, and they naturally strive to escape from this apparently subordinate and unrewarding role.

It is instructive to compare low-income individuals who are striving to become prosperous with low-income countries that are striving to develop. There are many more individuals to observe than there are countries, and the study of individual advancement has gone on far longer than the study of the development of poor countries, which in one sense began only after the Second World War. Thus much more is known about how individuals should get ahead than about how nations should advance. So let us ask what the low-income individual would do if he approached his personal advancement in the way so many people, in rich countries and poor countries alike, advise the less developed nations to do. He would observe, for example, that rich people consume more champagne and caviare than poor people do. By analogy with the precept that developing nations should try to imitate the developed countries by having more industry and less agriculture, he would then conclude that the way to get rich was to consume more champagne and caviare!

Since knowledge about personal affairs is less ideological and based on more experience than popular knowledge of development economics, everyone knows that imitating the behaviour patterns of the rich is not the best way to become rich. Almost everyone realises that it would be better to note what those low-income people who became rich did when they were becoming rich; it is better to take note of the hard work, the investments in education and other assets, and the profitable innovations (often in combination with good luck) that enabled some individuals to earn a lot of money. Similarly, developing nations ought to examine what the now developed nations did when they first began to develop economically.

There is not enough space to go into this here, but I believe that a careful examination of the economic history of the developed nations shows that the discouragement and exploitation of agriculture is by no means the way to bring about economic development. Indeed, our knowledge of economic history and economic theory is already sufficient, in my opinion, to show that the notion that the developing nations can best develop by protecting heavy industry and discriminating against agriculture and primary production is one of the most onerous burdens that the millions of poor people in the developing nations have to bear. But that is another story that I have told elsewhere and must not repeat here (Olson 1982, 1984).

AGRICULTURE IN PRE-INDUSTRIAL EUROPE

Beliefs are realities even when they are illusions. Thus the belief that the exploitation of agriculture and the subsidisation of industry is necessary for economic development, even if it is (as I claim) wrong, may still help to explain agricultural policy in developing countries. So long as the governments of developing countries, and the foreign advisors and intellectual élites that influence them, believe that the underpricing of agricultural products is necessary for economic development, this belief can influence public policy. Though my main explanation of the discrimination against agriculture in the developing countries is quite different, I think that the prevailing belief that the protection of manufactures at the expense of agriculture is good for economic development is part of the explanation. But not the largest part, as we can see when we look at policy toward industry and agriculture in western Europe (and especially in Britain) in pre-industrial times. When these presently developed nations were undeveloped, pre-industrial areas, they did not have any plans or policies to bring about what we would today call economic development. They did not think sustained and substantial increases in income per caput were possible. What some historians call the 'idea of progress' was largely still in the future. It was usually taken for granted that the overwhelming majority of the people in every country would always remain poor. Malthus's apparent demonstration that this must be so, because of population pressure and the finite supply of land, was promptly and widely accepted. The British in the late eighteenth century not only had no plans to promote an industrial revolution, they did not even really understand that one was going on: it was the 1880s before Arnold Toynbee even coined the phrase 'industrial revolution'. Thus any promotion of industry at the expense of agriculture in pre-industrial Britain and in the rest of Western Europe at this time could not possibly be explained as due to any belief that this was necessary for economic development.

The institutions and government policies in Britain and the rest of Europe before the industrial revolution definitely and strongly overpriced many industrial goods and commercial services and underpriced many agricultural products. This is evident not only from modern work in economic history, but also from the testimony of one of the most observant economists of all time: Adam Smith.

> The government of towns corporate was altogether in the hands of traders and artificers; and it was in the manifest interest of every particular class of them, to prevent the market from being overstocked, as they commonly express it, with their own particular species of industry, which is in reality to keep it always understocked ... In their dealings with the country they were all great gainers ... Whatever regulations ... tend to increase those wages and profits beyond what they would otherwise be, tend to enable the town to purchase, with a smaller quantity of its labour, the produce of a greater quantity of the labour of the country. They give the traders and artificers of the town an advantage over the landlords, farmers, and labourers in the country, and break down the natural equality which would otherwise take place in the commerce which is carried on between them ... The industry that is carried on in towns is ... more advantageous than that which is carried on in the country ... In every country of Europe we find, at

least, a hundred people who have acquired great fortunes ... for every one who has done so by ... raising of rude produce by the improvement and cultivation of land (Bk. I, Ch. X, Pt. II).

The whole emphasis of the mercantilistic policies of the national governments, as well as the guild rules of the towns, was to encourage profit from commerce and manufactures at the expense of agriculture and unskilled workers.

There is a striking similarity between the pro-urban policies of the European nations (and, for that matter, Japan) before the industrial revolution in Britain and those of the developing nations that are at a somewhat similar level of economic development today. The pro-urban and anti-rural policies of pre-industrial countries of Europe could not possibly be explained by any desire to imitate the patterns in more developed countries, for there were no such countries, nor by any beliefs that that would promote sustained growth in incomes per caput, for no such sustained growth was thought possible. The underpricing of most agricultural products in most poor countries must accordingly be explained by the inherent characteristics of poor or developing societies. [1]

COLLECTIVE ACTION

How do the inherent characteristics of low-income societies, whether those in the developing areas today or in Europe before the industrial revolution, generate a tendency to underprice agricultural products and overprice certain industrial products? And how does this tendency disappear as a country becomes developed? And does it sometimes even lead to a reverse tendency in developed countries without a comparative advantage in agriculture?

In this paper I have tried, in accordance with normal scientific procedure, to offer mainly new conceptions and information, and not merely repeat what has already been said in my previous publications. Unfortunately, this means that readers of this paper who have no acquaintance with my books on *The Logic of Collective Action* (Harvard U.P., 1965) and the *The Rise and Decline of Nations* (Yale U.P., 1982) will learn about only a small part of my argument. My explanation of the great differences in the treatment of agriculture in the developing and developed nations is, in large part, derived from these two books. Neither of these books deals with the differences in agricultural policies and institutions in societies at different levels of development, but the theories that are presented in them are the main source of my explanation of these differences.

My explanation begins with the difficulty of collective action, especially for large groups. Suppose any group of firms, workers, or farmers should strive to act collectively to lobby for a tariff, price support, tax loophole, or any other legislation that favours them, or act collectively in the marketplace to restrict supply and thus obtain a supra-competitive price or wage. The benefits of the favourable legislation or the monopoly prices or wages would automatically go to everyone in the relevant industry, occupation, or category, whether or not they had borne any of the costs of the lobbying or the output restriction. It follows that in sufficiently large groups, the benefits of collective action offer no inducement to individuals to engage in collective action – they would get the benefits of any such action whether or not they participated in it, and any typical individual's contribution would have no significant impact. Thus some large groups with common interests, such as the consumers, the taxpayers, the unemployed, and the poor are not organised in any society.

By contrast, the large firms in a concentrated manufacturing industry, where the numbers are small enough so that each firm will get a significant share of the benefit of collective action in the interest of the industry, will usually be able to make a bargain to engage in collective action without exceptional difficulty. In rare cases, the landholdings in a country will be so concentrated that the landowners will also be a small group that can organise fairly readily. Large groups will be able to organise for collective action only when they can work out special 'selective incentives' that punish or reward individuals in the group that would benefit from collective action, if they do or do not support the action. The most conspicuous example of a selective incentive in the compulsory membership and coercive picket lines of labour unions, but all large groups that are able to organise for sustained collective action have analogous, if often very subtle, selective incentives that mainly account for their membership.

There are often particularly interesting examples of this is the agricultural sectors of the developed economies. In the United States, for example, most of the membership of the major farm organisations arises because membership dues are 'checked off' from the patronage dividends of farm co-operatives or added to the premiums of mutual insurance companies associated with the farm organisation. Various tax advantages given to co-operatives and various complementarities between farm organisations and certain types of business organisations can make such arrangements viable even in highly competitive environments. Sometimes farm co-operatives themselves will, in effect, function as lobbying organisations as well as firms.

Because collective action by large groups is inherently difficult to organise, it will emerge only slowly and in favourable conditions. It turns out, for reasons that are explained elsewhere, that most organisations for collective action have incentives to strive to obtain more of society's output for their own clients through distributional struggle, rather than to produce useful outputs themselves, and to persevere in distributional struggle even when the costs to society are very large in relation to the amounts that are won in distributional struggle. In this they are fundamentally different from firms, individuals, and democratic governments in environments free of lobbying organisations. This helps to explain why long-stable societies that have had time to accumulate many of these organisations, such as Great Britain, have in recent times been growing less rapidly than expected. It also helps to explain the economic miracles in Germany, Japan, and Italy after the Second World War, for totalitarian governments and occupying armies had eliminated or transformed most organisations for collective action.

COLLECTIVE INACTION IN RURAL AREAS OF POOR SOCIETIES

What are the favourable conditions that are needed before collective action by large groups is likely to emerge? Clearly organising requires that people communicate with and sometimes meet one another. The success of private cartelisation or collusion will depend on the costs of insuring that all members adhere to the collusive agreement. Thus collective action by large groups will be less likely the higher the costs of transportation and communication. These costs depend on such things as distance, the technology of transportation and communication, and the degree of literacy. Private cartelisation will be dependent not only upon the numbers that must combine, but also upon the distances that picket lines or other forms of collusive enforcement must cover. Since organising large groups for collective action takes a lot of time even in favourable circumstances, the likelihood that large groups will be organised also depends on the frequency with which organisations are destroyed by the upheavals and repression that are common in unstable societies.

Because farmers and peasants are obviously spread out over more space than people in urban industries, their capacity to organise will be particularly dependent on the costs of communication and transportation. In rural areas of low-income societies without dense, modern networks of transportation and communication, such as Europe before the industrial revolution or many developing countries now, sustained large-scale collective action is normally impossible.[2] This is especially true if the society is politically unstable, as most developing societies are. The small number of firms in manufacturing or major urban activities will, on the other hand, often be able to organise even in the pre-modern economy, because of the advantages of small numbers and proximity to each other in cities. Thus my argument predicts that some urban industries and occupations in the pre-modern economy will be organised to lobby and collude, and that the goods and services they sell will be overpriced, and that main agricultural industries will by contrast not be organised and their outputs by comparison will be underpriced.

AGRICULTURAL POLICY IN DEVELOPED SOCIETIES

As transportation, communication, and the levels of education improve and the political system becomes stable, the great difficulties of collective action will be overcome even in the rural areas. Thus farmers will be among the groups that are organised for collective action. Farmers in such societies will be among the beneficiaries of tariffs and government subsidies. Private cartelisation, such as that proposed by the National Farmers Organization in the United States, will remain impractical because of the distances that picket lines or other forms of cartel enforcement must cover. But those highly developed societies, like Japan and most of the countries of Western Europe, that have relatively little good land in relation to the size of their populations, will not have comparative advantage in agriculture. It will therefore be possible to support agriculture in a major way in such societies with tariffs and quotas. The social costs of the overpriced agricultural products that result from this protection will be far less conspicuous than the social costs of open subsidies from the public treasury or compulsory measures to keep productive land idle. Thus countries with a pattern of comparative advantage that leads them to export manufactured products and to import farm products may on average greatly overprice agricultural products in comparison with manufactures.

When the present argument is elaborated it can help to explain differences in the degree of subsidisation or exploitation across different farm commodities and across different urban products. That is, it will allow a more disaggregated analysis of the kind I argued was needed, earlier in this paper. Unfortunately, the inevitable limitations on the length of papers for these meetings make it impossible for me to go into this here. I have, however, been invited to give a comparable address to the annual meeting of the American Agricultural Economics Association in the United States. That address will be a sequel to the present paper, and will go into these matters. If the present paper is read along with that paper and the two books from which my argument is derived, it should be clearer and more persuasive. It would, I hope, then also persuade some agricultural economists that this is a line of inquiry that is worthy of their own research attention. If so, my own initial efforts should happily be supplanted in due course by more precise and informed analyses.

NOTES

[1]Some readers may wonder whether the famous English 'Corn Laws' that were repealed in the 1840s call my generalisation into question. This matter is analysed in note 2, below.

[2]When the landowning interest in a country is so concentrated that a relatively small number of families owns a substantial proportion of the land, my argument about the lesser difficulties of organisation in small groups implies that there can be considerable collective action on behalf of agriculture even in pre-industrial countries. Thus 'landed oligarchies' in these countries sometimes succeed in getting policies favourable to agriculture. There is, for example, some evidence of small group action on behalf of agriculture in Prussia and in some Latin American countries in the nineteenth century. To some extent, the landowning aristocracy in Great Britain has in previous centuries also offset the tendency toward mercantilistic policies, and it was a relatively small group with

a disproportionate share of political power. Adam Smith was nonetheless right on balance in giving the name 'mercantilism' to the policies of Britain and most other European governments. It is sometimes supposed that the English 'Corn Laws', – made so famous by the controversy over their repeal, indicated that agricultural interests were especially favoured in Britain until the 1840s. This supposition is not, in my opinion, correct. The main reason is that Britain was not in typical years a grain importer until about the 1770s, so that the import duties on grain had little effect. There were also bounties on grain exports in years of relatively low prices; but exports were prohibited and import duties and bounties suspended in years of relatively high prices. Thus before 1815 the English Corn Laws are generally believed to have had only a small effect on prices, and in years of dearth that effect favoured consumers. After about 1815, the growth of population and income because of the industrial revolution made Britain a substantial importer of grain and this unanticipated change made the corn laws far more favourable to agriculture than they would otherwise have been. Urban interests then gave a high priority to the repeal of these laws and they were in due course abolished. (I am grateful to John Wallis and Adolph Weber for most helpful criticisms on this point, but they are not responsible for my interpretation.)

REFERENCES

Anderson, Kim and Hayami, Yujiro, *The Political Economy of Agricultural Protection: East Asia in International Perspective*, Allen and Unwin, London, 1986.

Honma, Masayoshi and Hayami, Yujiro, *Structure of Agricultural Protection in Industrial Countries*, 1984a.

Honma, Masayoshi and Hayami, Yujiro, *Determinants: East Asia in International Perspective*, 1984b.

Olson, Mancur, *Australian Economic Review*, 1984, pp. 7–17.

PEDRO SISNANDO LEITE

Forces That Will Shape Future Rural Development: The Case Of Northeastern Brazil

In Northeastern Brazil income growth, both total and per caput, has been sustained at a high level, according to international standards, over many years. The industrial sector performance, the foreign currency earnings increase and other macroeconomic indicators have shown an identical trend. However, these fine results did not fit in with the figures concerning the quality of life and social conditions under which live most of the 37 million Northeasterners, mainly the farm people. In this paper I try to put forward that what has been occurring is a misdevelopment, for the main problems of absolute poverty and income inequalities, hallmarks of the most backward Third World economies are still there unchanged. In fact, most farmland is owned by a few, farm yields are low, too many people are crowded into small holdings, general malnutrition prevails everywhere and there is a high illiteracy rate and lack of job opportunities for a great deal of regional manpower. The agrarian crisis in its turn, has created a rural-urban malfunction in favour of an out of control rural-urban migration which goes along with heavy social costs, both for rural areas and the crowded Southern metropolis. Under such conditions, job opportunities are almost impossible to build up, and economic growth impulses are severely curtailed, all of which produce social tensions of great political expression.

On account of this there is a need for the political and social powers to change course in order to promote economic, social and institutional change of structures and establish a clear definition of goals, as well as a new development style, producing more even distribution than at present in Northeast Brazil and elsewhere in the Third World.

NORTHEAST: UNBALANCED GROWTH

The economic performance of Northeast Brazil during the last 20 or 30 years brought about meaningful results, as shown by macroeconomic indexes. A US$970 per caput yearly income was reached, compared with US$300 in 1954. The gross internal product exceeded US$36.8

billion in 1984, much more than the 1960 US$8.9 billion. The economy
of the Northeast by itself ranked 10–15th in the Third World as stated in
World Bank papers. Northeast GIP is 14 per cent of the Brazilian total.
From 1960 to 1980 NE GIP grew at a normal rate of 7.2 per cent per
annum, but in the 1970s it ran at 9.7 per cent. During this decade only Iraq
increased so rapidly in the whole world, faster than the advanced
countries. In the 1960–80 period, the Northeast could be compared to the
7 fastest growing nations, alongside Japan, Republic of Korea, Thailand,
Iraq, Rumania, Ivory Coast and Brazil. Services and industry were the
economic sectors responsible for this record growth, while agriculture
lagged with an annual growth rate of between 3 and 4 per cent.

Exports grew seven times in the 1960–83 period, reaching US$1.9
billion, from an initial US$240 million. In 1983 the electric power
generation capacity of 23,117 GWh was almost 26 times greater than
20 years earlier. There are today 26,000 km of paved roads linking main
cities to the most important producing zones. This is more than a 1,000
per cent increase on what existed initially. Telecommunications now,
taking the country as a whole, compare favourably with the best in the
world, with a myriad of AM and FM radio stations, private and public,
telephone services (long distance, international, direct dialling etc.) and
more than 20 colour TV channels, covering the whole Northeast territory
through land relay stations and foreign and domestic satellites. The
communications network is implemented and operated by a number of
federal and state enterprises that benefit the Northeast enormously. The
Northeast seaports and airports as well as inter-state bus terminals fully
meet the population's needs. There is a network of shopping centres in
the state capitals and main cities, very similar to those in the advanced
countries. There are 12 public Universities and a number of private ones,
besides a network of agricultural and technological research centres,
mostly government operated.

THE SOCIAL DEBT

In the Brazilian Northeast, as in the underdeveloped countries during the
last decades, there was no spontaneous spread within the population mass
of the results of economic growth, in the way one may suppose occurred
historically in the presently developed countries. There is a unanimous
feeling that the Northeast piled up, during the last decades, an enormous
social debt alongside the steady expansion detected by the general
economic indexes.

Of Brazilian workers in an absolute state of poverty, 84 per cent lived in
the Northeast, a region that comprises only 30 per cent of the country's
population. The degree of personal income concentration can be seen, in
a rather shocking way, when one learns that people in the 10 per cent
upper income bracket used to hold 53 per cent of total income, while 50
per cent in the lower stratum work hard for a meagre 13 per cent.

Population explosion is one of various serious menaces against social stability in the Region. Half of the job holders work in agriculture but the output per caput is very low, as shown by the 46 per cent unemployment index. In the urban areas this rate is 17 per cent.

The number of first grade enrolments became three times greater between 1960 and 1980, high school nine times greater and university 14 times; however the educational shortcomings are still very grave. The Northeast[1] is the Region where 51 per cent of the total 22 million illiterate Brazilians aged 10 years or more live. The literacy rate was 53 per cent according to some very limited criteria. The active population profile aged 10 years or more is very similar, since more than half have had no basic instruction.

Health and sanitary conditions are very precarious. The infant mortality index is 105 for 1,000 born alive. There are 6 million children under 6 years old in the low income category. Life expectancy is 50 years, while Brazil's is 62 years. Only one-fifth of the population is classed as having an adequate diet.

The proportion of private urban dwellings with sanitary equipment (sewer or septic tank) is 16 per cent, while in rural areas it is only 2 per cent. However 27 per cent of all residences have a TV set and in the urban sector this goes up to 50 per cent. Similarly, 60 per cent have radio receivers, in both rural and urban areas. There is a refrigerator in 44 per cent of city and 3 per cent of rural dwellings. Electric power reaches 76 per cent of urban and 8 per cent of rural houses. The house deficit is estimated around 2 million units. 66 per cent of children from one to five years of age suffer from the consequences of malnutrition. Bihariasis affects 4 million people. Chagas disease (trypanosomiasis) affects 3 million and 17,000 new TB cases appear yearly. Of all child deaths of 1 year and older, 23 per cent were victims of infectious diseases.

As one may conclude from the above, the endeavours to develop the Northeast did not bring about the expected results as stated in government plans for the Region. The pursuit for higher economic growth rates, such as income and foreign currency earning, and some public works and physical infrastructure succeeded; but the problems of poverty, social imbalances and economic backwardness were not overcome.

NEW BEARINGS FOR DEVELOPMENT

Adam Smith said, at the beginning of the Industrial Revolution: 'No society can be flourishing and happy if the great majority of its inhabitants are poor and miserable'.

The great social and political challenge of our days, in the Northeast, is to implement the necessary changes to countervail the imbalances of its productive system and achieve a bearable level of human dignity and decency. In fact, certain prejudices against poverty dug deep ditches of hostility against the duty of respecting man's rights to decent living conditions. Brown (1983) says: 'as unemployment increases, starving and malnutrition spread around, pressures to change economic growth course get stronger'.

There can be no doubt that we need in the Northeast a new way leading to a greater participation of society in working out and implementing development plans, in order to guarantee a co-operative progress. José A. Mora reminds us that the tensions of all kinds stirring today in Latin-American societies, derive from the downfall of anachronic forms and systems, besides revealing a longing, sometimes in a dramatic and tumultuous way, to speed up the process of changes. On this subject Pope John Paul II explains: 'The cause of tensions are the unjust and out-of-date social and economic structures that allow a small minority to amass most of the existing goods, leaving the greater part of society poor and miserable. This has to be changed through adequate reform, based on social democracy.'

It is an outstanding fact that people no longer accept simple slogans as solutions. People know that a better life is possible for all. The evidence of this is the increasing disappointment over the Government's incapacity or delay in solving basic economic problems. In view of this, we believe that rules and principles that should guide economic development ought to establish as a goal the social and individual improvement of whole population's standards of living, including rural people. Cutting down infant mortality, dealing with illiteracy, improving elementary standards and pushing ahead cheap housing programmes, increasing production and yields in farming and improving ancillary services to farmers – all this is necessary to build up a real desirable development. As Weitz puts it (1981): 'Development is a continuous process of change that permeates all aspects of human life, manifested in social behaviour', For Streeten (1971) development also means modernisation and transformation of human beings, that is: development as goal and development as process both comprise change in basic attitudes towards life, work and social institutions.

The objectives of economic development and social well-being, ought to be based on the rails of economic growth and technological changes, with priority given to the problems of urban and rural unemployment and underemployment, along with the eradication of extreme poverty. Some vital questions are related to the success of such a project in the Northeast:

(a) direct the economy towards a better spread of development over the territory, mainly through the rural areas where there is the greatest focus of backwardness and poverty;

(b) modernisation and increase of farm productivity, specially yields, to avoid worsening of employment due to wrong mechanisation and destruction of shallow tropical soils;

(c) reorientation of the industrialisation process in order to use regional resources and exploring local markets, connected with industrial complex projects funded by national concerns;

(d) effective participation of every social segment in the economic and social development process;

(e) revision of the production structures to give them impulse through adoption of local technology, more manpower intensive;

(f) changing of educational styles as a way of creating a developing society's own values.

The present production policies whose top priority is to export, import replacement or supply the luxury needs of a few high-income individuals, has reached its saturation point. The economy ought now to expand by supplying the internal market of basic, essential goods. This will motivate the good use of internal opportunities and a corresponding positive chain effect of job creation and higher buying power, which stimulates the market.

These measures now suggested aim at creating economic progress in a climate of society's common interests. That is, according to integrated policies and strategies, comprising social, structural and institutional aspects. It is important to bear in mind the clear knowledge of these new bearings in relation to the now existing ones when dealing with economic policies. It is not a question of destroying present achievements but of improving on them, establishing new alliances and motivations without radicalisms that paralyse initiatives for renewal and deepen social conflicts. Even recognising that both in the capitalistic and socialist regime social and political relations do not harmonise automatically, Garaudy (1970) concedes that, for the first time in history, requirements for technical and economic development and democracy's demands have a sole direction.

It must be admitted that the changes of style and objectives of economic policies are difficult and their effective adoption is complex, for the productive process is conditioned on the social structures under which it is run. In this case, the spontaneous development process can be reduced to an economic growth for the appropriation of the social product by the working classes and does not take place properly. In fact, it is very difficult to benefit those who do not have productive goods, that is, the landless farmers, the urban unemployed, the illiterate adults or the fatherless families very common in the Northeast (Lipton and Shekow 1982).

Economic history proves, however, that economic progress is the outcome of mobilising human skill, social awareness and of a democratic and efficient government, capable of reorientating priorities for resource allocation.

STRATEGIES FOR AN INTEGRATED DEVELOPMENT

Empirical observations and academic studies demonstrate that, as has been stated, the Northeastern growth did not bring about an improvement in the quality of life for most of its population. So it is no wonder that the discussion of this problem occupies today the attention of everybody: technicians, government and communications agencies throughout the country. The priority given to social questions and new development styles are, today, a major worry, for it is known there are many ways of overcoming economic backwardness, but few options combining well-being objectives with democracy and preservation of human rights.

I believe that the XIX International Conference of Agricultural Economists offers a timely forum to discuss this question, having in mind its main purpose of debating rural development problems in an economy under turbulence. Brazil's Northeast experience regarding these problems is a set of useful lessons at the disposal of anyone willing to understand and find solutions, in order to help millions of people, doomed to a wretched, miserable and hopeless condition.

It should be pointed out that the suggested remodelling has its foundation laid not on direct income transfer from the rich to the poor or in giving a more acceptable and human appearance to the 'status quo'. The concept maintained in this paper aims at creating economic opportunities for the less favoured in the current growth process, through effective promotion programmes of productive resources to the working class for their self-sustained development. It is a grave oversight of the orthodox doctrine when it is stated that inequality is indispensable to push development, as economic history has demonstrated. Besides that, 'To live', as Albert Tèvoèdjré says, 'does not mean simply to exist, it is also having ways and means to unfold one's own sharing in mankind'. The inequality cost is really unacceptable from the economic social and ethnic points of view. In his studies on Southeast Asia and Latin America, Gunnar Myrdal concluded that 'the growing unevenness stirs up hindrances and drawbacks against development, there being an urgent need to reverse this trend, in order to bring up equality as a condition to hasten development'. David Colman and Frederick Nixon, in their book *Economic Growth. A Modern Perspective* explain that nowadays a greater equality ought to be seen not only as a social goal, but 'as a means to hasten growth with development'. Thus, state these economists: 'Income redistribution should, therefore, be seen in a dynamic context one can not part it from the social political institutional complementary changes.'

The Northeast experience teaches us that economic progress is carried out successfully only in a proper environment. It is possible only if government officials, politicians, teachers, technicians, enterprise heads, businessmen, union leaders, priests etc., wish for progress and are willing to accept the consequences of eliminating social, political, and economic privileges, that today make up the uneven model of our underdeveloped society. On account of this, popular participation has a fundamental role in redirecting development objectives. It is proper to point out that Brazil's Northeast population for decades accepted poverty for most people as unavoidable and the comfort of a high standard of living fairly reserved only for a small élite. This philosophy was steadily rejected and today it is no longer admitted, even by the most humble. What there is now, is an increasingly strong desire of poor Brazilians to improve their living conditions. More than that, among these people grows the conviction that better health, education and dwelling standards could be obtained by the poor if more adequate economic policies and political will were channelled toward this purpose. Unless political leaders start to care about the causes of poverty, confidence in the institutions will go on being eroded.

On this subject Weitz (1981) concludes: 'The rural masses pressure in poor countries are firmly getting stronger and finding political expression. Unless the people are convinced that the government is adopting well-known generally accepted and workable means to solve their basic problems, the government will be overthrown, no matter how strong it may be.'

In Brazil, the regional development strategy for decades was of high priority dedicated to the rapid expansion of agricultural production for export through great commercial enterprises, leaving without proper support the great mass of small landowners and landless farmers. On the other hand, despite social and regional income disparities, problems recognised as deserving attention, the adopted policies to alleviate poverty really consisted of concentrating public resources in fostering and promoting the great industrial enterprises with the purpose of creating urban workplaces. These policies, as they got older, revealed themselves as deeply wrong and sources of the accumulated distortions by the growth with poverty and social tensions model, implemented in the Brazilian Northeast.

The harmonious development of the underdeveloped countries will be tied in future, to social, political and economic forces which must be taken into account in order to avoid these distortions remaining.

GUIDELINES TO REDUCE RURAL POVERTY

A new balanced development style requires reorientation of the existing educational system to adapt it to the various needs of the poor. In the Northeast case the agricultural production and the land distribution problems worsened in such a way that today these are the main barrier to regional economic development. Thus, agrarian reform seems to be the best option to provide the base for the social and economic changes kept down by economic underdevelopment. Full agrarian reform, aimed at an effective institutional ownership change and modification of the unfair ownership and land-use systems, complemented by basic support services, means that land becomes, for the rural worker, the source of economic stability, well-being and assurance of freedom and dignity.

The co-operative association is the proper tool to change a poor and illiterate community into an active participant in the rural development policy. Likewise, rural industrialisation is a vital strategy to solve the critical metropolitan urbanisation problems and counterbalance social and economic instability. Expansion of small towns may also foster balanced development and provide rural areas with the necessary markets and services and education and health-care facilities.

The building of a new equitable economic order to meet the basic needs of rural people, creating new productive jobs, depends on scientific and technological progress in order to let poor traditional farmers increase their yields. This is proved by what has happened in the Northeast. Due to the rapid population increase and the high underemployment and unemployment rates, the sole compatible solution is the creation of intermediate technology for the small agricultural and micro industrial enterprises, which bring about new jobs and make a better use of local natural resources. The family farm is the best way of promoting rural development along with more social justice and productive efficiency. The big capitalistic farm is the base of power for their owners, but does not help reduce rural poverty.

The rural-regional development model basic guideline, as put forward in this document seeks to transform agriculture and solve the social-economic problems of hinterland communities, following social justice standards in the most equitable way. This approach, Weitz (1981) explains is based on three assumptions: (1) agricultural growth is the key to rural development; (2) simultaneous incrementation of agricultural growth and industrial and service sectors; (3) emphasis on social forces as a component of the rural development process. The key to this approach is to create job opportunities within the rural areas, even in the small interior towns, which must act as social services and production support centres. Now, it is proper to remind oneself, agriculture is a part of the more comprehensive development of the total rural space, which, in its turn, is linked to the global economic development process.

This strategy of integral rural development is already being implemented in the Northeast. It seeks to attack the rural underdevelopment problem by following a multi-sectoral procedure in order to reduce rural migration toward the metropolitan cities through improvement and enlargement of services that meet local needs, and still having in mind that it is necessary to:

(a) build up a managerial structure to co-ordinate resources and programmes of all agencies, according to global planning aimed at full development of the selected place;

(b) mobilise human resources and improve utilisation of natural resources and facilities in the selected geographical areas; and

(c) motivate and mobilise small communities to carry out self-help programmes and participation in setting up priorities and implementing these projects.

To conclude this paper, it must be said again that Northeastern agriculture suffers from low productivity and has unequal and anachronic production relations (between land owner and land worker). It lacks both deep changes in the institutional and social framework and in the farm organisation to adopt new technologies that allows for larger and more efficient production for the sake of farmers. Without these, says Todaro

(1982), 'Agricultural development will never start or, what is more likely, the already wide income gap between the few rich, great landlords and the masses of poverty ridden sharecroppers, small landholders and, landless workers will simply get wider'.

The 'Projeto Nordeste' already in implementation aims at changing deeply the existing rural framework in 15 years. For this purpose, it will dispose of 12 billion dollars provided by the World Bank, besides other national funds. It will bring up 6 million stable farm jobs in rural areas, plus 1.2 million in other rural and small urban nuclei activities. This programme is based on integrated rural development strategies, and seeks in its 15 years implementation to: (a) change rural areas and the forms of economic and demographic occupations in priority areas; (b) enhance food production, specially from small scale farming, already responsible for the larger portion today; (c) achieve maximum use of land and manpower; (d) foster non-farm and industrial activities in rural areas.

NOTE

[1]Brazil's Northeast has a 1.6 million km^2 area, where 37.9 million people live (1984). It contains 20 per cent of the total Brazilian territory and 30 per cent of its inhabitants. There are only 24 countries in the world with a larger population, and 15 greater in size. In Latin America only Mexico and Argentina, besides Brazil itself, are larger territorially.

REFERENCES

Banco do Nordeste do Brasil, *Industrialização rural do Nordeste do Brasil*, Fortaleza, CE, 1978.

Brown, Lester, *Por uma Sociedade Viável*, FVG, Rio, 1983.

Castro, Fidel, *A Crise econômica e social no mundo*, Codecri, Rio, 1983.

Furtado, Celso, 'A Nova Dependência', *Paz e Terra*, Rio, 1982.

Iglesias, Enrique V., 'Los problemas de estilo de desarrollo en la America Latina', In: C+C, Bonn, no. 1, 1980.

Garaudy, Roger, 'A Grande Viraca do Socialismo', *Civilização Brasileira*, Rio, 1970.

Johnston, Bruce F., & Mellor, John W., 'The Role of Agriculture in Economic Development', *American Economic Review*, vol. 51, no. 4: 566, 93, September 1961.

Leite, Pedro Sisnando, Desenvolvimento harmônico do espaço rural, Fortaleza, BNB 1983 – 'Novo Enfoque do desenvolvimento econômico', Fortaleza, Universidade Federal do Ceará, 1983.

Leite, Pedro Sisnando et al., *Subdesenvolvimento e desenvolvimento rural do Nordeste*, Fortaleza, BNB, UFC, 1983.

Lipton, Michael and Shakow, Alexander, *O Banco Mundial e a pobreza. Finanças e Desenvolvimento*, Fundo Monetário Internacional, vol. 2, no. 2, June 1982.

Myrdal, Gunnar *The Challenge of World Poverty*, Penguin, N. York, 1968.

Millikan, Max and Hapgood, Dervid, *O problema da agricultura nos paises subdesenvol vidos*, São Paulo, 1970.

Ruttan, V.W. and Wallace, L.T., 'The effectiveness of location incentives on local economic development', *Journal of Farm Economics*, vol. 2, no. 4, November 1962.

Schreiber, Jean-Jacques Servan, 'O desafio mundial', *Nova Fronteira*, Rio, 1980.

Schultz, Theodore W., *The Economic Organization of Agriculture*, McGraw-Hill, N. York, 1953.

Singer, Hans, Technologias para satisfazer as necessidades essenciais. Genebra, 011.

Stevens, Robert D., *Tradition and dynamics in small-farm agriculture*, Economic Studies in Asia, Africa and Latin America, Ames Iowa, 1977.

Streeten, P., *The frontiers of development studies*, Macmillan, New York, 1972.

Todaro, P., *Introdução à economia:uma visão para o terceiro mundo*, São Paulo, 1982.

Weitz, Raanan, *Desenvolvimento rural integrado*, Fortaleza BNB, 1981.

Weitz, Raanan, *From Peasant to Farmer: a revolutionary strategy for development*, Twentieth Century Fund, New York, 1971. *Agricultural Development Planning and Implementation*, Holanda, 1969.

World Bank, *World Development Report*, Oxford University Press, 1983.

PANEL DISCUSSION – JUAN MUÑOZ, FERENC RABAR, RUFUS ADEGBOYE, IRENE TINKER AND PARTICIPANTS FROM THE FLOOR

RAPPORTEUR: ROBERTO PASCA DI MAGLIANO

In the panel discussion on 'Forces Shaping the Future' a wide discussion developed based on the papers presented by Hayami, Olson and Leite and this was augmented by contributions from the floor.

The three papers provided important contributions to bringing into focus the characteristics of forces shaping the future in developing countries. They may be used as starting points for the analysis of government intervention and an attempt to compare these analyses was made by Ferenc Rabar who found common points in the role of government policies, even if the emphasis was different. Government intervention was a key factor in effecting forces to reduce hunger, but it may – if not properly applied – have adverse effects. In fact, as Hayami himself had suggested, state intervention in developing countries, which are affected both by a high rate of population increase and by a decline in real agricultural wages, should have to sustain small-scale industries as well as labour intensive agriculture. Therefore there are important public roles in agriculture regarding education and introduction of appropriate technologies, such as irrigation, research and extension, as well as the general provision of public goods.

Within the discussion as well as in the papers, a strong emphasis on the use of market policies emerged; for example, the overpricing of agricultural products to force agricultural development. Many speakers, however, expressed serious doubts on the efficacy of price policies to promote a better income distribution and to force new investments. Moreover Olson, Hayami and others had shown that in developing countries there were several barriers against the introduction of price policies, such as political ones (the difficulty of organising collective action and pressures to force governments to move) and economic ones (agricultural products have still some comparative advantages etc.).

Ferenc Rabar's comments also stressed that, despite the impressive agricultural growth which has taken place in the last ten years, hunger and poverty are far from being overcome. This apparent paradox depends on the wide-spread financial crisis which is occurring in developing countries.

African difficulties were pointed out by Rufus Adegboye; these related mainly to the efforts needed to increase export earnings in order to compensate for major import costs. Those countries which already had new technologies have coped with the new trade situation, but more depressed countries are producing what can be easily exported and tend to consume what they do not produce, thereby assisting both a growth in production and an increase in hunger. On the question of whether agriculture has to be exploited to stimulate development, Adegboye felt that the exploitation of agriculture has no alternative as it is often the only productive sector which is available for a surplus.

The intervention of Irene Tinker concentrated on the question of equity particularly with reference to the family situation. Some studies of African countries had shown that there was a tendency towards a feminisation of both poverty and agriculture which brought about major gaps in income distribution. These arguments were questioned by Adegboye who added that in any case data to test them were not available in many African countries.

Juan Muños emphasised the risk of making an easy generalisation of both analysis and policies for developing countries, as there are too many economic and institutional differences and he underlined the importance of inflation as a factor in increasing income discrepancies.

To the impressive and deep analysis of forces shaping the future of developing countries of both papers and panel discussion there was a wide reaction from the floor with many questions as well as specifications coming, among others, from Vanegas, Gunther, D. S. Bole and Weber.

The topics and questions included the following: the poverty trap, the difficulty of transferring production from surplus to deficit countries, the reasons for agricultural exploitation, the constraints on arranging collective actions, the hypothesised inverse relationship between the degree of protectionism and the comparative advantage.

After precise answers from the speakers, the chairman, Theodor Dams, stressed the social as well as the economic tensions which are today created by hunger. This leads to the need for more disaggregated analysis to investigate precisely the dimension of inequity and therefore the best ways to solve it case by case.

The fact that three papers were concentrated on the same item followed by a large panel discussion gave a valuable opportunity to investigate deeply the main ways to overcome poverty and hunger in developing countries.

SECTION II

Growing Interdependencies and Uncertainties

ALAIN DE JANVRY

Integration of Agriculture in the National and World Economy: Implications for Agricultural Policies in Developing Countries

Three facts characterise the growing interdependencies and uncertainties of world agriculture today. One is the rise of the marketed surplus as a share of agricultural output, indicating the growing commodification of agriculture and its increasing exposure to terms of trade movements, be they the result of market forces or of institutional interventions. The second is the rapid growth in international trade for agricultural products and the concomitant increase in food and feed dependency for Third World countries, particularly those incurring rapid rates of economic growth. The third is the increasing instability of prices of tradable agricultural commodities measured in domestic currencies where a significant share of this instability originates in international capital movements and exchange rate fluctuations. This growing integration of agriculture in the national and world economy substantially redefines the options and dilemmas which Third World countries face in the design of strategies of food security and in the making of agricultural policy. I explore in this paper some of the policy options available to developing countries, stressing the role that interdependencies and uncertainties play in the choices that can be made to improve their food security. Of course, there exists no unique and immutable policy package so that the purpose of this discussion is not to provide solutions but to help identify the options available and guide the reasoning in making choices.

MULTIPLICITY OF OBJECTIVES AND PRICE INSTRUMENTS: REDUCE THE NUMBER OF OBJECTIVES OR INCREASE THE NUMBER OF INSTRUMENTS?

One of the great difficulties in using prices as a policy instrument is that they fulfil a large number of contradictory functions. Prices affect both economic growth and social welfare and this in a contradictory fashion since prices are a source of revenue for certain classes and of costs for others. Low agricultural prices can stimulate industrial growth but lead to agricultural stagnation; they can raise the real income of consumers but lower that of producers and reduce employment opportunities for

73

landless workers. There also exist conflicts between short- and long-term redistribution objectives obtained through price manipulation since the short-run effects obtained for a given supply of agricultural commodities are often the opposite of the long-term consequences once the impact of prices on output growth has been felt. The contradictory effects of price policy as a joint growth and welfare instrument are evidenced by simulations in computable general equilibrium (CGE) models for India (de Janvry and Subbarao 1984) and Egypt (Dethier 1985; de Janvry and Subramanian 1985). In the short run, price increases induce supply response and increase the real incomes of farmers with holdings large enough to have a positive marketed surplus. Even though output growth in agriculture creates employment for the landless and stimulates industrial growth (India), higher food prices decrease the real incomes of landless rural workers and of urban workers and the urban poor. In the long run, if prices are allowed to fall under the pressure of increased supply, the real incomes of net food-buying classes increase while those of net-selling farmers fall. The greater the elasticity of supply response, the more the price incentives to agriculture induce industrial growth through sectoral linkages, final demand, and savings-investment effects.

A similar dilemma between growth and welfare effects occurs with food subsidies which are financed out of public investable funds. For India, CGE model simulations show that decreasing urban food subsidies to increase public irrigation investment is expansionary on GNP. The urban classes are hurt in the short run by the loss of subsidies; but enhanced productivity benefits the rural classes immediately, and growth benefits the urban classes in the future as well. In Egypt, when a foreign exchange constraint exists, targeting food subsidies on the poor and diverting to investment the value of subsidies formerly received by the rich is expansionary, deflationary, and increases the real income of all classes except the urban rich. These studies indicate that equitable growth can be reached by a combination of investment allocation toward labour-intensive sectors with high potential productivity gains, such as irrigation of small farms producing mass consumption goods, and targeted subsidies to protect the poor until the income effects of increased investment benefit them.

It is because of these contradictory functions of prices that most governments are reluctant to leave the determination of prices to market forces and try instead to control their effects through a whole range of institutional interventions. Some of the objectives of these interventions are to protect consumer welfare, to generate public revenues, to enhance farm incomes, to create foreign exchange earnings, to increase food security, to stabilise prices, to improve nutrition, and to redistribute income among regions and individuals.

A central dilemma of price policy is, thus, that too few instruments are expected to satisfy too many objectives. The resulting mismanagement of price policy leads to stagnation of production and rural poverty, a phenomenon all too widespread in the less developed countries (LDCs).

Two solutions exist. One consists of reducing the number of policy objectives. This is, in essence, the neoliberal solution which abandons concerns with welfare and assigns to prices (left to determination by market forces) and to individual initiatives the role of efficient resource allocation. The other consists of increasing the number of instruments in order to relieve prices from fulfilling many of the functions which state intervention has attempted to achieve through them. Rural welfare can, for example, be enhanced by land reform and by increasing peasants' labour productivity; public revenues can be raised by land taxes; the nutritional status of the poor can be improved by employment creation and income transfers; etc. Thus, increasing the number of policy instruments allows the confining of prices to the role they best perform: to serve as guides for the efficient allocation of resources in an institutional context moulded by structural interventions.

In this case, prices of tradable goods are determined by border prices at an equilibrium exchange rate and price of non-tradables by equilibrium between supply and demand. This allows elimination of price distortions against agriculture that have typically originated in overvalued exchange rates and protectionism to industrial inputs. Eliminating these distortions permits the removal of credit and input subsidies in agriculture which are sources of socially discriminatory institutional rents introduced in compensation for unfavourable product prices. Price policy interventions remain necessary, however, to manage a system of flexible exchange rates, to stabilise prices, and to supervise through protectionism the transition between price regimes – particularly if the farm sector contains large segments of peasants with limited alternative options in the economy. Short of structural policies that redistribute assets and income (e.g. land reforms), food subsidies are also necessary for that segment of the population with insufficient access to land and employment opportunities.

INVESTMENT PRIORITIES: AGRICULTURE OR INDUSTRY?

Most developing countries have passed through a phase of import substitution industrialisation followed, in the most successful cases during the last 15 years, by a phase of export-led growth. The feasibility of these two development strategies is now limited: the first because of inefficiencies, which indiscriminate protectionism has created, and of increasingly inegalitarian income distribution induced by a luxury goods bias in industrial production and the second because the present international market conditions severely limit exports of industrial products on the markets of industrialised countries.

In the present international economic context it thus seems that an investment strategy that favours food production in the context of peasant agriculture or of labour-intensive business farms and that induces industrialisation on the basis of agricultural growth is the most appropriate to ensure both sustained growth and improved welfare for the masses of the population, at least in countries which still have large rural populations. The history of South Korea and China, both mainland and island, as well as that of the industrialised countries in the eighteenth and nineteenth centuries, shows the possibilities of an industrialisation led by accelerated agricultural development. Rural development-led growth recently has been advocated for India by Mellor (1976) and South Korea by Adelman (1984). For the latter country, Adelman shows how the reallocation of investment from the services and industrial consumption goods sectors to rice production leads to GNP growth and to equality in income distribution which are both greater than in the current strategy of export-led industrialization. Key to the success of this development strategy is to stimulate productivity growth in agriculture and to control the forces of the technological treadmill so that the fall in prices lags behind the fall in costs. Also essential to the results of this strategy are an extensive redistributive land reform; human capital formation; labour markets that perform to translate productivity gains into wage gains; and an industrial sector, most likely created in a prior phase of import substitution industrialisation, able to respond to domestic demand inducements.

The CGE results for India of reallocating investment away from industry toward irrigation infrastructure for wheat production show, similarly, that this is expansionary on GNP and progressive on the distribution of income. Only large farmers lose if the fall in prices associated with increased output is not mitigated by some price protection. In Egypt, CGE results also show that increasing the share of agriculture in total investment increases the GNP and raises the real income of all social classes.

AGRICULTURAL DEVELOPMENT: THROUGH PRICE OR NON-PRICE INSTRUMENTS?

The neoliberal school insists on the need to improve the terms of trade for agriculture, to stimulate production, and to reduce the size of the public sector – the latter, in particular, to decrease the surplus that it extracts from agriculture. It is, for example, the philosophy of the Berg report for accelerated development in sub-Saharan Africa (The World Bank 1981). Even though it is certainly necessary to set prices at the equilibrium level determined by market forces, it is also fundamental to realise that (1) this price system is necessary but not sufficient to induce agricultural development and (2) there exist technologies and structural alternatives that allow raising agricultural output faster and with more progressive consequences on income distribution than price incentives.

The reason prices have a limited inducement effect is that aggregate supply elasticity tends to be low in the LDCs. This is, for instance, the case of Africa where estimates of this elasticity range between .05 and .15 (Bond 1983). This is due fundamentally to the lack of new technological options, to constraints on farmers for access to modern inputs and to exhaustion of possibilities of horizontal expansion. Under these conditions increasing agricultural prices result in income transfers from consumers (and, proportionally, the poorest ones) towards producers with the largest marketed surplus. An effective use of price policy thus requires prior structural change to 'elasticise' the aggregate agricultural supply response.

The CGE model for India shows that the poorer classes (landless agricultural workers, small farmers who are net buyers of foods, and urban workers) benefit from a policy of technological change in agriculture with flexible prices while they are negatively affected by a policy of price support which has as a purpose to stimulate output under conditions of inelastic supply (de Janvry and Subbarao 1984). Comparing the two alternatives of increasing wheat production via a system of farm price incentives (with food subsidies to maintain consumer prices at an unchanged level) and groundwater irrigation and high-yielding varieties, shows a present value cost advantage of the latter over the former of 650 per cent at an interest rate of 8 per cent.

The key to agricultural development is, thus, in the implementation of policies of structural change even if these are more difficult to carry out than are simple policies of price incentives. They must include policies to decrease dualism, reabsorb surplus labour and increase labour productivity through technological change and human capital formation.

THE COST OF UNEQUAL SECTORAL DEVELOPMENT: WHY CAN THE SUCCESS OF SOME SECTORS CREATE POVERTY?

During the 1970s, many countries had a very rapid growth in some export sectors while other sectors producing tradable goods stagnated as a result of the success of the first. When populations are trapped in those stagnating sectors the result can be extensive poverty unless compensatory measures financed by export earnings are instituted. The booming export sectors have typically been primary sectors (petroleum and natural gas) or agricultural sectors with strong international comparative advantages (tea, coffee, animal feeds, drugs, etc.). They have created massive inflows of foreign exchange. Similar effects can originate in the rapid build-up of international debt or in international capital inflows, for instance, through foreign aid. In all cases, the success of a sector generator of foreign exchange creates two types of perverse effects on the sectors' producers of tradable goods, such as domestic industry and the food sector. The first is a reallocation of resources toward both the booming export sector and the sector of non-tradable goods (services and construction) for which demand increases as a result of income effects in the export sector. The second is a negative effect on the domestic prices of imported goods which results from the inflationary pressures created by incomes in the booming sector and the resulting tendency for real appreciation of the exchange rate. The availability of foreign exchange allows the avoidance of a devaluation, always unpopular with urban sectors, and thus the maintenance of low domestic prices of food items and industrial goods.

If the peasantry is principally a producer of staple foods and if fluidity in the reallocation of resources is insufficient to allow peasants to shift their resources to the production of the export or nontradable sectors, the peasantry finds itself cornered in a stagnating sector under unbearable price conditions. The result is outmigration toward the employment opportunities created by the expanding sectors. If employment creation is not sufficient, the result is poverty and often hunger.

The wisest approach is to pace the inflow of foreign exchange earnings to avoid inflationary pressures, an approach successfully followed by, for example, Cameroon. Short of this, five options are available to protect the peasantry from the negative consequences of this unequal sectoral development. Since in many situations the earnings of the export sector create public revenues, these revenues can be used to finance the reforms implied by each of these options:

1. Help the peasantry shift its resources to the booming sectors. This was the case, for example, with peasants producing coffee and cacao in the Ivory Coast and with some family farmers who entered fruit production for export in Chile. Since these export products are often capital intensive (tree growing and irrigation for sorghum in Mexico), assistance to peasants requires important credit programmes and technical assistance as well as a stable insertion in international marketing circuits.

2. Increase the total factor productivity of peasants in food production to enable them to compete with low-priced imports. This is the objective of projects of integrated rural development and of research to improve traditional peasant production systems.

3. Protect the food items which compete with peasant production, support farm prices above consumer prices or subsidise farm inputs to compensate for unfavourable product prices. This is the solution that Mexico successfully implemented under the Lopez Portillo administration showing how part of the booming sector revenues can be used to compensate the losers in the tradable sectors. With falling oil prices and the debt crisis, this high-cost programme had to be sacrificed to austerity.

4. Create enough employment opportunities in the expanding sectors to allow the absorption of the peasants ruined by low food prices.

5. Increase the degree of peasant household food self-sufficiency by allowing them to reduce dependency on purchased inputs and satisfy directly a greater share of consumption needs. This implies, in particular, promotion of organic technologies and garden plots as survival strategies.

STRATEGIES OF FOOD SECURITY: FOR WHOM?

The two extreme solutions to food security are generally untenable: food self-sufficiency because it implies excessively high costs; and direct application of the theory of comparative advantage because it is static, implies risks which are too high and has negative effects on some sectors of the population which are not competitive in an open economy and find themselves dispossessed of sources of revenue. Most countries have attempted to defin strategies of food security which make a balanced combination of these two extremes. The problem is, however, not only to define a strategy that gives access to a national consumption vector with high probability but also to insure food security for all segments of the population. As recent experience with the Green Revolution has demonstrated, in India for example, strong agricultural growth is not sufficient to satisfy this latter definition of food security.

Food security has two aspects: the level *and* variability of satisfying nutritional requirements. It is met through the combination of availability and entitlements where, as has been shown by Sen (1981), small changes in availability can create large changes in entitlements. Availability derives from both domestic production and trade so that the choice variables are what to produce for national consumption, what to produce for export and what to import. Sarris (1983), for example, shows that aggregate Egyptian food security can be improved by reallocating resources between food (cereals) and cash (cotton) crops. The food security problem is defined as the maximisation of the risk-discounted expected value of net export receipts of the agricultural sector subject to satisfying both a fixed national consumption vector and technical and resource constraints in production. The greater the degree of national risk aversion, the more food crops should be substituted for cash crops at the cost of a reduced net foreign exchange contribution of agriculture.

Access to food in both level and variability is defined differently for different social groups: for subsistence peasants it depends on access to resources and productivity; for landless farm workers and net-buying marginal farmers on employment, wages, and low food prices; for net-selling farmers on favourable terms of trade and productivity; for urban workers on employment, wages, and low food prices; and for urban marginals on food subsidies and income transfers. Using a CGE model for South Korea, Adelman, Berck, and Gordon (1982) show how the two components of food security (level and variability) affect differentially specific social classes. Although in that country subsistence farmers are the worst off in terms of average consumption level, the social group with the highest risk of food deficiencies is the urban marginals who are heavily affected by price fluctuations resulting from instability in both domestic production and world prices. Improving food security of different social groups thus requires different policy instruments. For subsistence farmers it calls for policies that can raise their mean income, while it requires for the urban poor policies that reduce their vulnerability to instability.

In Egypt, food insecurity originates in both international price movements and fluctuations in domestic yields; but the first source of randomness has a coefficient of variation 3.8 times larger than the second. Among social classes, fluctuations in international prices and yields affect most the real income of the urban rich through the positive economic growth effects that both rising yields and falling world prices have on overall economic growth. High variability in international prices under conditions of extreme food dependency implies that the coefficient of variation in the real income of the poor is larger in the urban sector than in the rural sector. As in Korea, improving the food security of the rural poor requires raising their level of entitlement, while improving that of the urban poor requires reducing the variability in their entitlements. In India, which is basically a closed economy and where food insecurity originates principally in fluctuations in the yields of food grains, it is the rural poor who are most exposed to the fluctuations in entitlements which yield fluctuations create. Among the rural poor it is the landless workers whose access to food varies most since yield fluctuations create, in the short run, proportional fluctuations in employment opportunities. Falling output thus hurts them both through falling employment and through rising food prices which lowers their real wages. In this case, improving the food security of the poorest requires use of policy instruments that both raise the level and reduce the variability of their food entitlements.

With an increasingly integrated agriculture in the national and world economy, it is important to shift the analysis of food security away from that of the stabilisation of food availability and of food prices to that of security of food entitlements for all segments of the population. This focus shows that a complex package of policies needs to be used for this purpose, including yield stabilisation; optimum allocation of resources between domestic food and export crops; price stabilisation though variable tariffs, currency reserves and storage; and food subsidies for critical groups.

FOOD AID: COMPLEMENT OR SUBSTITUTE TO RURAL DEVELOPMENT?

There is no question that international food aid to refugees and the starving is necessary. But long-term food aid is more questionable. It has often been denounced as a means (1) for reducing the pressure to implement the necessary reforms to improve food production; (2) for lowering prices for domestic food producers; (3) for creating price uncertainty since food aid is erratic; and (4) for encouraging consumption habits (e.g. wheat in the tropics) or types of agro-industries (e.g. wheat mills in Peru) which domestic production can no longer supply.

A more careful analysis of the impact of food aid in Latin America reveals, however, that the same instrument – cheap concessional food imports – can be used with markedly different results according to whether it is an explicit component of a strategy of food security or a substitute to the definition of such a strategy. In Colombia, for example, PL-480 wheat imports have depressed domestic prices, eliminated wheat production from commercial farms and increased wheat dependency from 30 per cent of total consumption in the early 1950s to 90 per cent in the late 1970s. In Brazil, by contrast, the state sells the concessional wheat imports at a price higher than what it pays and uses the revenue created by this transaction to offer domestic producers a price above that paid by the mills. In contrast to Colombia, instead of competing with domestic production, food aid provides a source of public revenues to finance the transition toward greater food self-sufficiency (Hall 1980). In other countries, food aid has been used to finance food-for-work programmes.

In analysing the impact of food aid on agriculture, it is also important to distinguish between short-run and long-run effects. In the Egyptian CGE, when food subsidies are financed by foreign aid, increasing food subsidies is strongly expansionary on GNP as it creates a net inflow of foreign exchange. In the short run, falling food prices hurt all net-selling farmers and increase the real incomes of the urban classes. In the long run, however, the strongly expansionary effect that increased foreign aid creates results in positive real income gains for all classes, both urban and rural. The income effects created by foreign aid thus lead to increased demand for food which both benefits domestic agriculture and increases the demand for commercial imports.

It has often been said that the food-surplus, developed countries prefer to give food aid to reduce their surpluses rather than to provide developmental assistance to Third World agricultures which would eventually lead to reduced opportunities for commercial exports. This is a fallacious interpretation of the potential of aid in stimulating food exports from developed countries. Successful agricultural development in the Third World creates strong income effects which result in increased cereal imports of food grains in the poorer less-developed countries and feed grains in the middle-income developing countries (MDCs). Rapid growth in the Third World stimulated by aid, in particular led by rural development on a broad 'unimodal' basis, will be, for the decades to come, the best guarantee of expanding export markets for food and feed grains produced in the more-developed countries.

I thus conclude on an optimistic note of the possibility of harmony between rapid rural development in the LDCs, to reduce malnutrition, *and* increased export demand for the MDCs, to reduce food surpluses and the associated farm income or public budget crises. Foreign aid to accelerated rural development can thus be to the advantage of both LDCs and MDCs.

CONCLUSION

Probably the most important conclusion derived from this analysis of an agriculture increasingly integrated in the national and world economy is the predominant importance of macroeconomic and of inter-sectoral forces on the production performance of agriculture and on the distribution of welfare gains that it creates. The trade-offs implied between growth of different sectors, security of food entitlements for different social groups, and short versus long-run effects, are far from intuitively obvious and were partially captured in the results we presented from multisector, multiclass economic models for India and Egypt. In this new context, Third World countries must, consequently, design their agricultural policies and their strategies of security of food entitlements with a clear understanding and an explicit quantification of these trade-offs.

REFERENCES

Adelman I., 'Beyond Export-Led Growth', University of California, Department of Agricultural and Resource Economics, Working Paper no. 309, Berkeley, April, 1984.

Adelman, I., Berck, P., and Gordon, K., 'Food Security in a Stochastic World', University of California, Department of Agricultural and Resource Economics, Working Paper no. 251, Berkeley, December 1982.

Bond, M., 'Agricultural Responses to Prices in Sub-Saharan African Countries', IMF Staff Paper no. 30, 1983, pp. 703–26.

de Janvry, A. and Subbarao, K., 'Agricultural Price Policy and Income Distribution in India', *Economic and Political Weekly*, vol. XIX, nos. 52 and 53, December, 22–9, 1984.

de Janvry, A. and Subramanian S., 'The Politics and Economics of Food and Nutrition Policies and Programs: An Interpretation', University of California, Department of Agricultural and Resource Economics, Working Paper No. 349, Berkeley, June 1985.

Dethier, J. J., 'The Political Economy of Food Prices in Egypt' (unpublished Ph.D. dissertation), University of California, Berkeley, February 1985.

Hall, L., 'Evaluating the Effects of PL–480 Wheat Imports on Brazil's Grain Sector', *American Journal of Agricultural Economics*, vol. 62, no. 1, February, 1980.

Mellor, J., *The New Economics of Growth: A Strategy for India and the Developing World*, Cornell University Press, Ithaca, 1976.

Sarris, A., 'Food Security and Agricultural Production Strategies Under Risk in Egypt', University of California, Department of Agricultural and Resource Economics, Working Paper no. 249, Berkeley, March 1983.

Sen, A. K., *Poverty and Famines: An Essay on Entitlements and Deprivation*, Clarendon Press, Oxford, 1981.

World Bank, 'Accelerated Development in Sub-Saharan Africa: An Agenda for Action', International Bank for Reconstruction and Development, Washington, DC, October 1981.

G. EDWARD SCHUH*

The International Capital Market as a Source of Instability in International Commodity Markets

Agricultural economics has grown up with a strong sectoral perspective, rooted in strong training in microeconomics. The theory of the firm has been our primary analytical tool. The theory of markets has not taken us much beyond partial equilibrium analyses of agricultural markets. For the most part we have had little training in macroeconomics, and even less in the economics of general equilibrium. This perspective is less and less relevant to the kind of world we now live in. Changes in the international economy and in how individual countries relate to it make it less and less relevant to think of agriculture as a sector of the economy. It is also less and less relevant to think about agriculture in the context of a closed economy. Instead it has to be thought of as part of a well-integrated, open, international economy.

Changes that have occurred in the international economy these last 20 years have completely altered the economics of agriculture. The failure to recognise these changes has led to mistake after mistake in economic policy, and to lack of success in making projections and planning the economic outlook. An important part of this was caused by failing to appreciate the significance of the international capital market and what it means for international commodity markets. My paper is devoted to an explanation of how the international capital market has created instability in international commodity markets, and is divided into three parts. In the first part I will review the changes in the international economy referred to above. In the second part I will discuss some significant developments in international commodity markets that are a consequence of the changed configuration of international economy. In the third part I will review some of the policy implications of the new situation, and end with some final comments.

CHANGES IN THE INTERNATIONAL ECONOMY

These last 20 years have witnessed a number of dramatic changes in the international economy. These developments have changed both the

*The views expressed herein are the author's alone and in no way should be construed as official views of the World Bank.

economics of agriculture and the context in which agricultural policy has
to be conceived and understood.

One important change in the international economy has been the
dramatic increase in dependence on trade world-wide. This is a process
that has been almost continuous throughout the post Second World War
period. But it accelerated significantly in the 1970s. Those familiar with
agriculture thought this increased dependence was limited to that sector.
But in point of fact, it was a general phenomenon. To illustrate the pace
and extent of change, the dependence of the US economy on international trade doubled from 1970 to 1979. Moreover, if we extend the
period back to 1965, the dependence of the US economy on international
trade actually tripled in less than 14 years.

To understand fully the significance of this increased dependence on
trade, one has to think of it in terms of its obverse – the increased
openness of individual economies to the forces of the international
economy. From this perspective one appreciates that a more open
economy is increasingly beyond the reach of domestic economic policies.
That is one of the reasons why today there is around the world so much
frustration with economic policy and policy-making. The US experience
is again an important example. When the full accounting is made for the
1983 commodity programmes, it will be found that total programme costs
were between $30 and $35 billion. And this was for a sector of the
economy that generated a net farm income of only $18–19 billion! It
obviously was not the case that the government was not doing anything.
But despite that considerable expenditure of money, farmers were still
doing very poorly by the end of the year. Forces from the international
economy were literally swamping the effects of domestic policy.

A second major change in the international economy has been the
emergence of a well-integrated international capital market. This change
may be even more dramatic than the increased growth in trade. Recall
that at the end of the Second World War there was no such thing as an
international capital market. There were some transfers of capital among
countries, but they were largely on a government-to-government basis
and we called it 'foreign aid'. In the 1960s, however, we began to hear of
something called a Euro-dollar market as European banks learned that
they could relend their dollar deposits and make a profit. This market
rapidly broadened into a Eurocurrency market as it grew like the
proverbial Topsy. Then we entered the 1970s and experienced the
petroleum crisis, which generated all those petro-dollars. National
governments and international agencies then enjoined the commercial
banks to recycle the petrodollars so as to avoid a collapse of the
international system. This they did with alacrity, of course, and the result
is today's international debt problem.

There is a general failure to appreciate either the size or the
significance of the international capital market. In terms of size, the total
amount of credit outstanding in the Eurocurrency market alone at the
beginning of the 1980s was about $1.7 trillion. This was approximately

commensurate with the total amount of international trade. But even that understates the full significance of the international capital market. Recent data indicate that in 1984 total international trade flows were of the order of $2 trillion. Total flows in international financial markets in that year, however, were of the order of $40 trillion! Clearly, the financial plans are dominating the foreign exchange markets, not international trade.

The third change in the international economy was the shift, in 1973, from the Bretton Woods fixed exchange rate system to a system of flexible or floating exchange rates. This new system might better be described as a system of bloc-floating exchange rates since many countries tie their currency to the value of one of the major currencies such as the US dollar, the British pound sterling or the French franc. Although fixed in this narrow sense, the values of these currencies vary implicitly as the values of the currencies to which they are tied in foreign exchange markets. The shift to a system of flexible exchange rates takes on its significance from the simultaneous emergence of the international capital market and was the issue I examined at a previous meeting of this Association in Banff, Canada (Schuh 1981). The point is that with a system of flexible exchange rates and a well integrated international capital market, the effects of monetary policy are transmitted in large part through the trade sectors of the economy, which may include agriculture. Hence, in many countries agriculture has now become the sector that has to bear the burden of adjustments to changes in monetary and fiscal policy.

This brings us to the final change in the international economy I want to consider – the emergence of a significant amount of international monetary instability in the period since 1968. The reasons for this increased monetary instability are not fully understood. But it is a fact of life, as any plotting of interest rates and/or monetary aggregates will show. And it has emerged at the very time that, because of the other three changes, agriculture as a sector has become more vulnerable to monetary instability.

Before turning to a discussion of some of the developments of the 1970s and 1980s, I would like briefly to discuss one final point that is implicit in the above changes but that is an issue at a somewhat different level. This is the rather obvious, but little recognised point, that most countries now face a dual constraint in their relations with the international economy: a trade constraint and a capital market constraint. These dual constraints open new opportunities to individual countries, but they also impose new constraints on policy. Consider the net-debtor countries in today's world. To service and repay their debt they need to run a trade surplus. But if they are to run a trade surplus and repay their debt, the creditor countries have to run a trade deficit, and this may impose large shocks to their economies. Moreover, to run a trade deficit, those same countries – such as the United States – have to be net importers of capital.

The key issue – and it is very pertinent to the theme of my paper – is the issue of burden-sharing and symmetry in international adjustment (see Schuh, 1985). It is very popular in today's world to lecture the developing countries to get their prices right. And given the size of the policy distortions in many of these countries, it is little wonder this has risen to the top of the policy agenda of international agencies. But less seldom is it recognized that 'getting the prices right' in many of these countries means that they will almost inevitably increase their exports, and that symmetry in burden-sharing means that the industrialised countries will need to be more receptive to the exports of those countries. So far the US economy has played a major role in absorbing these increased exports. But suppose the US dollar falls and/or the US economy enters an economic slump. Then who will absorb these exports? Europe? Japan? And what if they don't?

DEVELOPMENTS IN COMMODITY MARKETS THAT ARE A REFLECTION OF CHANGES IN THE INTERNATIONAL ECONOMY

The changes outlined above have already brought rather significant developments in and shocks to international commodity markets. In this section I want to review just a few of them, preparatory to a discussion of some of the policy implications.

One of the very significant developments is the emerging link between monetary and fiscal policy and international commodity markets. As I noted in my paper at Banff, referred to above, changes in monetary policies are now reflected in changes in the trade sector of national economies. As a country tries to tighten its monetary policy, the upward pressure it puts on interest rates induces an inflow of capital and this causes the value of the nation's currency to rise. This rise will choke off exports by making the country less competitive in foreign markets. It will also cause imports to rise, creating difficulties for import-competing sectors. The monetary authorities accomplish what they want to achieve, but it is the trade sectors that have born the burden of adjustment. In many cases this will be agriculture. The significance of this is that prior to these changes in the international economy, agriculture was largely immune to changes in monetary and fiscal policy. When monetary authorities want to go the other way, they do just the opposite. Lower interest rates lead to a capital outflow, and this to a decline in the value of the nation's currency; this in turn brings a stimulus to export sectors and sectors that compete with imports.

This sensitivity of world agriculture and international commodity markets to monetary policy and monetary conditions is a new phenomenon, at least in terms of the post-Second World War period. It comes at the very time that monetary instability has increased very significantly and an important corollary is the much strengthened linkage between financial markets and commodity markets. The vehicle for this linkage is the foreign exchange markets and the change in value of national currencies as financial resources shift around the world's economy at the beck of phone calls, telexes and cables.

In this kind of a world, of course, national or domestic commodity programmes that attempt to fix prices at rigid levels become a serious problem. The US experience again illustrates this point very well. Starting in October 1979, the US shifted from the very easy and unstable monetary policies that had characterised the late 1970s (large negative real rates of interest) to the persistent pursuit of a tight or restrictive monetary policy. The main element of this policy was the refusal to monetise the large deficit in the Federal budget. The main consequences of the shift in policy was a dramatic rise in US interest rates, and with it a dramatic rise in the value of the US dollar. As the value of the dollar rose, US exports became less and less competitive, with the result that commodity prices declined. A continuation of this trend would eventually have brought about an adjustment in US agriculture. However, at some point US prices settled on the loan level. As the value of the dollar rose beyond that point, US loan prices as denominated in the currencies of other countries continued to rise. This stimulated production of those commodities in other countries. Hence, US commodity programmes not only stimulated excess production at home, they also stimulated excess production abroad. Moreover, the US finds itself in the anomalous position of having bailed the EC out of its costly commodity programmes by causing the dollar price of traded commodities to rise.

In the absence of US commodity programmes there would have been a natural international adjustment in response to the rise in the value of the dollar. US production would have declined in response to the decline in dollar prices, and production would have expanded elsewhere in response to a relative rise in the price of these commodities in terms of other currencies. Moreover, very strong competitive pressures would have been kept on the EC's Common Agricultural Policy. US commodity programmes prevented this international adjustment from taking place. Moreover, they have laid the grounds for excess production not only in the US agricultural sector, but also in world agriculture. These extensive effects internationally are a consequence of the importance of the US economy in both international financial markets and in international grain markets. The same general principles apply for smaller individual countries, although there will in general be fewer international ramifications.

The significance of the US economy in the world economy raises a related issue that is also of considerable significance – the issue of third country effects of exchange rate realignments. These arise because the international monetary system is essentially one of bloc-floating. For example, a fall in the value for the US dollar will carry with it the currencies of all other countries that are tied to the dollar. Hence, trade sectors in those countries can receive considerable stimulus although policy-makers have changed nothing. Similarly, when the value of the dollar rises, it carries with it those currencies that are tied to it. Those countries will find their exports doing very poorly, while at the same time experiencing a flood of imports. It was precisely this phenomenon that created problems for Brazil, Mexico and Argentina, and which explains why the international debt crisis has been concentrated in Latin America (see Schuh, 1984). Most of those countries fix the value of their currency relative to the US dollar. They experienced serious hardship as the value of the dollar rose.

This brings us to the final set of international disturbances to commodity markets through capital markets. This refers to the changes in policy induced by the international debt crisis. Country after country – Brazil, Mexico, Argentina, etc. – have had to alter drastically their 'domestic' policies in response to their international debt crisis. This has involved draconian realignments in the value of national currencies, and complementary policies to make them more competitive in international markets. These measures promise to change the pattern of trade flows in international agricultural markets in very significant ways. Although the ultimate impact will be in commodity markets *per se*, the impetus for change came from the international capital markets.

SOME POLICY IMPLICATIONS FOR AGRICULTURE OF A WELL-INTEGRATED INTERNATIONAL CAPITAL MARKET

There are at least four important policy implications I would like to discuss. All of these are a consequence of the emergence of a well integrated international capital market and the other changes referred to above.

The first policy implication is that domestic commodity programmes that have strong or rigid price provisions probably make no sense in today's world, even for small countries. This applies with equal force to importers and exporters and to whether the objective of the programme is to raise and support prices or to lower and limit them. The point is that exchange rate realignments change the prices of traded goods (exports and imports) relative to the price of non-traded goods. These relative prices can change by implicit means even though the explicit prices have not changed. The result can be very large distortions and/or very large disequilibria. With international monetary instability being what it is, the consequence of any attempt to fix domestic prices can be very serious.

The second policy implication is the logical extension of this principle to international commodity agreements. Such agreements are still on the agenda of the UNCTAD. But it is very difficult to know what such agreements mean in today's kind of world. In fact, it is very difficult to know how any fixed price provision can be designed into an international commodity agreement when realignments in exchange rates can implicitly change relative prices in a national economy with no explicit change in the absolute price of the traded commodity. Because of these changed conditions, pressures for international commodity agreements to break down will be pervasive and irresistible.

The third policy implication has to do with the meaning of comparative advantage in the context of the new international economy we now have. Comparative advantage is a comparative cost doctrine rooted in conditions of relative demand and supply in national economies. But the *competitive* advantages that are reflected to the international economy in today's world may be very different from the underlying comparative advantage. For example, a low national saving rate may keep a nation that otherwise would be competitive from so being (a special form of the Dutch disease). Similarly, the failure to pursue a proper fiscal policy can drastically alter a nation's competitive position. The US Federal deficit is widely recognised as restricting US competitiveness abroad. But what if we were to run a larger budget surplus and use it to retire government debt? Would other countries be willing to accept the strong competitive position that would arise for the US economy? The point is that in today's world, a nation's monetary policy, its fiscal policy and its savings rate are major factors in explaining its international trade performance. Comparative costs are only one of many factors.

Finally, there is the obvious need to reform international monetary institutions. The monetary instability in today's international economy has at least three sources. The first is the lack of mandate and the lack of resources of the International Monetary Fund for it to act as a true international monetary authority – despite its name and despite the original intent that it act in such a way. The second is the failure of the countries with major reserve currencies to co-ordinate their monetary policies to as to obtain some semblance of international monetary stability. The third is the failure of the United States to manage its monetary policy in a way consistent with its actual role as central banker for the world. Given that the world is in effect on a dollar standard, the US Federal Reserve is in effect the central bank for the world. Unfortunately, except when there are periodic international crises, the Federal Reserve manages US monetary policy primarily on domestic considerations. The result is to impose large shocks on the US economy as well as on the international economy.

In today's world, agricultural commodity markets will continue to be unstable as long as international monetary conditions remain unstable. This will lead to continued inefficient use of the world's agricultural resources, to continued government intervention – often in inefficient ways – to offset the shocks that come from abroad, and to continued international political conflicts over trade policy and domestic agricultural policies. Reform of our international monetary institutions should be at the very top of the policy agenda of every country.

CONCLUSION

These last 20 years have been a period in which the economic integration of the international economy has far outpaced its political integration. In fact, we have witnessed a successive breakdown and growing irrelevance

90 G. Edward Schuh

of international institutions at the very time that our respective economies have become increasingly integrated. Domestic economic policies have less and less relevance in today's world and do little more than create suspicion and lack of confidence in national governments since these policies achieve less and less what they say they will.

The LDCs have rightly seen the need for a new international economic order. Unfortunately, their efforts have largely gone for naught, since they have appealed for resource transfers that are not forthcoming, failed to recognise the shortcomings of their own national policies, and appealed for international commodity agreements and commodity policies that are largely not feasible in today's world.

The developed countries, for their part, largely ignore the appeals of the less developed countries and continue to pursue their own self-interest in national policy, oblivious of the fact that national policies make little sense today. At the same time they lecture the LDCs to get their national policies 'right', without seeming to realise that this would result in important burden-sharing implications for the economies of the developed countries.

It is imperative that we get these issues joined and that we design and establish international institutions consistent with the international integration of our respective national economies. Preserving the present Tower of Babel can lead to disaster – as the experience of the 1930s should have taught us. Economists from all countries have a vital interest in seeing to it that we move in the right direction and that we do not slip back into the economic nationalism and beggar-thy-neighbour policies of the past.

REFERENCES

Schuh, G. Edward, 'Floating Exchange Rates, International Interdependence and Agricultural Policy' in *Rural Change: The Challenge for Agricultural Economists*, Proceedings, Seventeenth International Conference of Agricultural Economists, Glenn T. Johnson and Allen Maunder (eds), Gower, Aldershot, 1981, pp. 416–23.
Schuh, G. Edward, 'Strategic Issues in International Agriculture', The World Bank, Washington DC, May 1985 (mimeographed).
Schuh, G. Edward, 'Third Country Monetary Disturbances in a Changed International Economy: The Case of Brazil and Mexico', prepared for the seventy-fifth Anniversary Colloquium of Harvard Business School, 'Colloquium on World Food Policy', Harvard University, Cambridge, Mass., 8–11 April 1984.

DISCUSSION OPENING I – A. E. IKPI

The two related and complementary papers by Alain de Janvry and G. Edward Schuh have been well written and beautifully presented. They are relevant and well thought out and I strongly recommend that each conference participant takes time to read these two papers thoroughly. However, the more I read and try to relate them to developing countries of Africa, the more I thought of a fitting anecdote that adequately

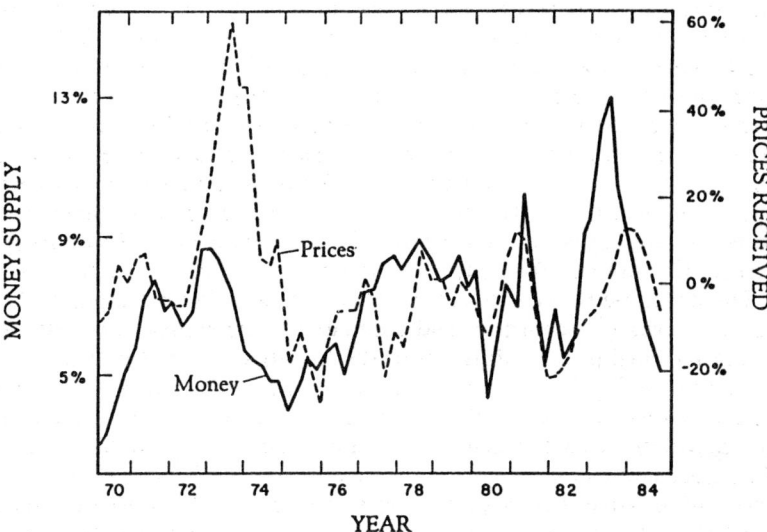

FIGURE 1   Money and Agricultural Prices (Percentage Change)

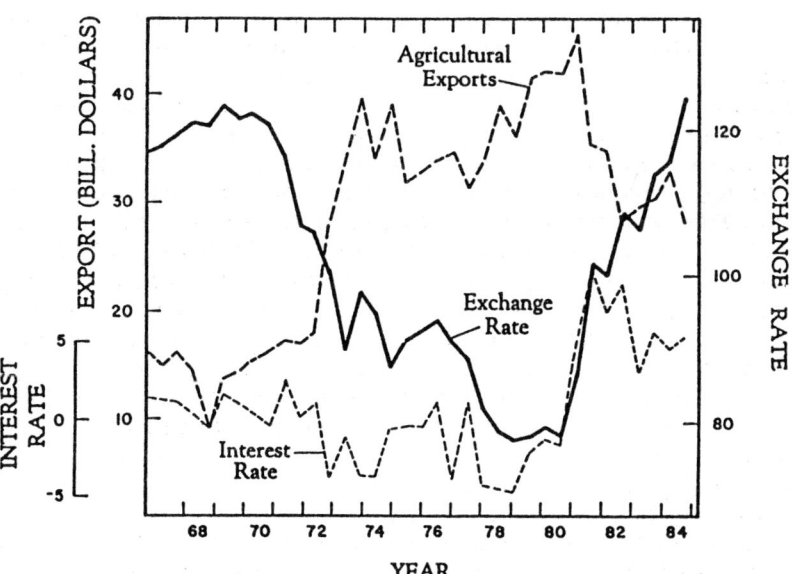

FIGURE 2   Interest Rate; Exchange Rate; Agric. Exports

summarises what is going on between developed countries and developing ones. I shall call it the fable of 'the Giant and the Lilliputian'. It goes
like this:
There once lived a giant (G) who because of his height could see much
further than his poor and hungry neighbour Lilliputian (L).

One day G decided to show L some wonderful land overflowing with
food and other basic necessities of life but with a lot of obstacles that
could only be overcome with his (G's) carefully planned assistance.

One easy way G could have done that would have been to carry L on his
shoulder. But G does not want to stoop down and give L a helping hand;
and L (out of shyness) is reluctant to climb on to G's shoulders. Also, L
believes that getting to the place through his own efforts would be more
advisable, so that he could always go back there on his own.

So G decides to walk with L to the place. But he (G) is in a hurry and
walks too fast for L. Furthermore, each step he (G) takes requires L to
take about 20; and so by the time they get halfway to the place, L is
fatigued and refuses to continue.

Instead of carrying L the rest of the way, G turns back to L and tells
him: 'OK, let us go back. Tomorrow, after you have eaten *in my house*,
we shall go there.' The incident is repeated time and again without
success!

This is exactly what appears to be going on in the various attempts by
developed countries to help their developing counterparts. Developed
countries give everybody the impression that they would like to help or
are, in fact, helping developing countries when in reality their efforts are
aimed at preventing these poor countries from achieving their desired
long-term goals. As Dr Schuh has pointed out in his paper, developed
countries are not exactly anxious to see developing countries (especially
of Africa) implement any 'good plans' that would make them not only
self-sufficient but also export-oriented. Such a success would create
unexportable agricultural and other surpluses in developed countries.
Unfortunately, they appear to ignore Say's simple but true law, namely:
supply creates its own demand.

Both papers have given us a most accurate exposition of some of the
pertinent problems of food and agriculture in Africa and other
developing countries. But in each case I find they come short of giving
logically pragmatic and appropriate economic prescriptions that follow
naturally and could substantially reduce the diagnosed problems, if not
completely remove them.

Since discussion openers in this conference are specifically instructed
not to summarise the papers they discuss, I shall devote the few minutes I
am given to directing our attention to some relevant areas by way of
questions on which I would like participants and authors of the two
papers to focus discussion. For example: (i) Now that developed
donor-countries realise that *ad hoc*, short-term (or stop gap) measures
like massive food aid (mostly with invisible political strings attached) do
not and cannot solve Africa's food problems, what should developed

countries do? Is it, in fact, not apparent by now that a better longer-lasting solution to Africa's food problem lies in the effectuation of a deliberate programme in which graduated increases in food (especially cereal) production can be achieved through selecting and using areas of the continent with known comparative advantages of production? Such planned large-scale food production would have to be made to be inversely related to the volume of food aid from developed countries. A genuine and sincere interest on the part of developed countries to assist African countries should be shown through the provision of either interest-free of low-interest loans to support the planned investment in this increased food production programme.

(ii) In view of what Alain de Janvry has pointed out in his paper concerning the price system being necessary but not sufficient for inducing agricultural development, and there existing some technological and structural alternatives that allow for raising agricultural output faster, it is pertinent to stress here that as long as the international capital market continues to exist in its present form and to operate in its existing mode in relation to agriculture in developing countries, price instruments will continue to have depressing effects on the agricultural output of these developing countries. Therefore, is it not advisable and in fact, feasible, for instance, meaningfully to change the present structure and mode of operation of the international capital market? In fact, should the capital market continue to be used as *the* channel for funnelling development funds to developing countries – especially with cut-throat conditionalities that have been known through experience to do nothing but induce and support 'beggar-thy-neighbour' policies? After all, as Dr Schuh pointed out on the second page of his paper under discussion today, the international capital market, as we know it today, did not exist until 1945, after the Second World War.

(iii) If all of us here really want to help developing countries develop so that all countries can live together happily in God-provided plenty, why can't we (as policy-makers and advisors to our various governments) suggest, for instance, that 'counter-trade' be accepted and adopted by trading partners in both developed and developing countries in order to substitute substantially for international loan financing and all its attendant headaches?

In conclusion, I would like to emphasise that African countries and their market economies differ markedly. Lack of accurate understanding of this basic diversity and difference has led to misconceptions arising on what Africa is or is not; what Africa needs or does not need; and what Africa wishes or does not wish. It is in a forum of this sort that meaningful exchanges of ideas on these issues can be used to plant 'seeds of thought'; these can be germinated to fruition in future publications and policy statements that could change things for the better for developing countries. I appeal to all of us to plant such seeds today and throughout this conference.

DISCUSSION OPENING II – MAURICE SCHIFF

Professor de Janvry's paper is based on the important observation that agriculture has become increasingly integrated in the national and international economy and that these growing interdependencies should be taken into account when analysing agricultural policies in developing countries.

Professor de Janvry uses the results of selected computable general equilibrium (CGE) models to analyse a number of policy options.

I will start with a general comment and then make some more specific ones. In the first part of his paper, the author mentions the contradictory impact of prices on efficiency of resource allocation and on welfare. He suggests that price policy should be supplemented by non-price instruments to compensate for the negative short-term impact of price policy on distribution, nutrition, etc.

Price and non-price instruments are also compared later in terms of their intertemporal allocative efficiency. The author claims that 'there exist technologies and structural alternatives that allow raising agricultural output faster... than price incentives'. He bases his claim on evidence of low aggregate supply elasticity in Africa and India. This claim is widely found in the literature and seems to present price and non-price instruments as alternatives rather than complements.

First, evidence on Africa and India may not be entirely valid for other parts of Asia or for Latin America. Even on India, there is some evidence of more elastic sectoral output. Krishna and Chhibber (May 1983) find that the short-term elasticity of wheat output with respect to agriculture's terms of trade (defined as the price of wheat and of its substitutes relative to a wholesale price index) equals 0.50 and the Nerlovian long-run elasticity equals 1.55.

Second and more important, I believe this claim is based on a rather short-term view of price effects, resulting in a downward bias for the effects of prices on output and an upward bias for the effect of investment expenditures.

Private investment expenditures, which make up the bulk of total investment expenditures in agriculture in LDCs, are carried out by private agents and are therefore expected to respond to incentives. In other words, the impact of prices on output is not limited to movements along a given supply curve, but prices affect the location of the sectoral supply curve through their impact on the intersectoral allocation of labour and capital. In this context, it is interesting to note the contrast between the evidence of the small impact on output of raising agriculture's terms of trade presented here and the evidence of the devastating impact on agriculture of Dutch disease phenomena (e.g. in Nigeria) which lead to a reduction in agriculture's terms of trade through the fall in the relative price of agriculture's tradables and their close non-tradable substitutes. Does that mean that there is a kink in the aggregate supply curve, being elastic downward but inelastic upward?

As the author notes, Dutch disease phenomena result in 'outmigration toward the employment opportunities created by the expanding sectors'. It has been claimed that such outmigration is irreversible. This would result in a kink in the sectoral supply curve. However Dutch disease countries have also tended to use their additional resources on social services for the urban sector. A reduction in the amount of urban services provided and a restoration of agriculture's terms of trade may well lead to a movement back to the rural areas, as some recent evidence on Africa indicates. Furthermore, the productivity of public investment expenditures in agriculture may itself depend on the structure of incentives. There is evidence that farmers may not make full use of irrigation facilities when crop prices are low because it does not pay for them to make the needed private investments (ditches, etc.) at those prices. Public investment facilities thus often operate well below full capacity. Consequently, private investment expenditures, as well as the productivity of public investment expenditures, are not exogenously given but depend on incentives in the agricultural sector.

Nevertheless, a number of these CGE models specify investment as an exogenous variable and therefore do not take into account the interrelationships between prices and investment.

These CGE models do provide an interesting framework for the analysis of agricultural policy options but I believe they should be expanded to endogenise more fully the impact of price policies on intersectoral resource allocation. One model in that direction is that by Cavallo and Mundlak on Argentina (1983), although it is not designed for detailed analysis of the welfare effects of alternative policies. It should be noted that in some cases it may even be necessary to allow for international movements of labour or capital to obtain a realistic picture of the constraints under which policies are made.

I would now like to make some specific comments:

1 The CGE results showing that reallocation of investment from industry to agriculture leads to an increase in growth rates and to an improved distribution of income are extremely interesting and have profound policy implications. Furthermore, these results imply that the impact on growth of reallocation of investment would be much larger still in the absence of a biased price policy against agriculture.

2 On Dutch disease phenomena, I believe it is important to distinguish between effects of a temporary nature and those that are expected to be more permanent. If the phenomenon is a temporary one (say, the coffee boom for Colombia in the 1970s), then it may be a good idea to help the non-booming tradable sector over the transition period. However, if the phenomenon is expected to be more permanent (say, a technological improvement in a tradable sector or discovery of new resources or worker remittances), such a policy will amount to the protection of a sector which has become less competitive in a more permanent sense and will be inefficient.

Even if one would expect technological improvement to be more permanent than a price increase, it is not always possible to know how permanent or transitory such shocks will be and, as the author suggests, the wisest approach is to pace the inflow of foreign exchange earnings to avoid inflationary pressures. This has been recommended by a number of economists (e.g., Harberger).

Even if such a policy were followed and none of the extra revenues were spent, the effect of the boom in a tradable sector would still lead to the contraction of the non-booming tradable sector, although to a lesser degree, as noted by Professor Max Corden (1984). The reasons are twofold. First, the value of the marginal product of labour rises in the booming sector (because of a rise in price or because of technological change or because new resources are discovered). This induces a movement of labour out of the non-booming tradable sector and out of the non-tradable sector. Second, the fall in non-tradable output resulting from the outflow of labour results in a rise in the relative price of non-tradables and thus in an additional movement of labour out of the non-booming tradable sector. That sector will therefore contract even if none of the extra income of the booming sector is spent. The importance of this effect will depend on the absorption of labour by the booming sector.

3   In his section on strategies for the use of food aid revenues to stimulate agricultural development, one might want to consider the fact that in some countries the value of the food aid subsidy may amount to a large share of total import expenditures (30 per cent in Bangladesh) and therefore may indirectly depress output prices through their Dutch disease effect on the real exchange rate.

I turn now to Dr Schuh's paper which was very interesting and added a new dimension to the relationship between capital and commodity market instability, and identified some policy implications.

This is a very important topic which has not received enough attention in the literature and which should be integrated in the analysis of agricultural price policies. The author is, I believe, correct in stating that partial equilibrium analysis is rapidly becoming less relevant because economies have become more open since the end of the Second World War and relative incentives in agriculture are much more affected by domestic and foreign macroeconomic policies. The real exchange rate is one of the crucial variables determining incentives in the agricultural sector and it is therefore important to understand the factors which determine it.

Several policy implications are drawn. First, it is clear that domestic policies which fix nominal prices may lead to large distortions, due to real exchange rate fluctuations caused by an unstable international monetary situation, and that pressures on international commodity agreements to break down may be irresistible in such an unstable world. Dr Schuh is therefore correct, I believe, in suggesting that better co-ordination of the monetary policies of the countries with major reserve currencies would help reduce exchange rate variability and would help to solve the problem of commodity market instability.

Second, it is true that the competitive position of a country may depend as much on fiscal and monetary policies as on underlying resource-based comparative advantage. This point is also made by de Janvry. An interesting question in this context is whether this is only a transitory phenomenon or whether it will also hold in the long run. For instance, the US agricultural sector has become less competitive owing to the increase in the value of the dollar; but one might wonder if the US fiscal and monetary policies which have led to the strong dollar can be maintained.

The main point made in this paper may be applicable in more general conditions than those described. Dr Schuh argues that the flexible exchange rate system is a major determinant of the transmission of capital market instability to commodity markets. I believe that capital market instability will also be transmitted to commodity markets in the case of a fixed exchange rate system. Instability in commodity markets is caused by instability in *real* exchange rates and this may occur even under fixed nominal exchange rates because the price of non-tradables will respond to macroeconomic shocks.

For instance, the rise in interest rates in the US would have led to a much larger inflow of capital under fixed exchange rates than that which took place under flexible exchange rates (because under fixed exchange rates capital would have flowed in until interest rates were equalised). This would have led to an increase in the price of non-tradables in the US and thus to a reduction in the *relative* price of tradables (i.e., to a reduction in the real exchange rates), including that of agricultural commodities. Of course, shocks will be transmitted faster under flexible exchange rates than under fixed exchange rates because the prices of assets adjust faster than those of goods.

Finally, I would like to make some suggestions for future consideration:

1   On the dynamics, what is the minimum duration in real exchange rate shocks required to affect output? If unstable monetary and fiscal policies cause the real exchange rate to fluctuate for short periods of time around a trend, then the effect of output may be small (increased uncertainty). Clearly, in the case of the US dollar in the last few years, the policy has lasted long enough to have dramatic effects on the tradable sector.

2   If the effects of fluctuations of real exchange rates are negatively correlated with other shocks affecting output, then it is not clear that instability in capital markets will increase instability in commodity markets. *A priori* I do not see why this correlation would be negative but knowledge of that correlation is important in determining the exact contribution of capital market instability to commodity market instability.

3   Finally, US policies have led to an increase in interest rates. This should result in lower holdings of stocks and thus in an increase in commodity price variability. In fact, in their 1984 study *International Finance for Food*

Security, Huddleston, *et al.* found a negative correlation between commodity price variability and the ratio of stocks to consumption. However, the opposite will occur in the case of policies which lead to a fall in interest rates.

REFERENCES

Cavallo, D. and Mundlak, Y., 'Agriculture and Economic Growth in an Open Economy – the case of Argentina', IFPRI Research Report 36, Washington, 1982.
Corden, W. M., 'Booming Sector and Dutch Disease Economics: survey and consolidation', *Oxford Economic Papers*, Vol 36, No 3, 1984.
Huddleston, B. *et al.*, *International Finance for World Security*, Johns Hopkins University Press, Baltimore, 1984.
Krishna, R. and Chhibber, A., 'Policy Modeling of a Dual Grain Market – the case of wheat in India', IFPRI Research Report 38, Washington, 1983.

GENERAL DISCUSSION – RAPPORTEUR: A. J. OSKAM

It was questioned whether most governments of LDCs are strong enough to deal with the type of development outlined by Professor de Janvry. A strategy of development requires fine tuning of different types of policy. It is, for example, possible to increase agricultural production, if farmers receive enough incentives. However, what to do if after some period products are stockpiled and there is a strong tendency towards lower prices and agriculture comes into a downward circle? How should such policies be engineered?

Another point concerned the reasoning of Professor de Janvry's paper. At one point one finds statements about the strongly increased prices of grains in Africa, while at another point the very difficult position of the agricultural sector was mentioned because of low priced imports.

In reply, Professor de Janvry stated that he had examined the phenomenon where a strong sector of the economy outperforms other sectors and leads to sectoral unemployment in relation to several African countries. A timely stronger exchange rate can be managed within an economy if one realises this situation and uses specific types of policies for protecting sectors that lag behind.

If the agricultural sector adopts new technology it makes it necessary to lower (real) agricultural prices in such a way that there remain sufficient incentives for continuing technological development, while, at the same time, lower prices increase consumption. However, farmers are very reluctant to give up a favourable position with relatively high prices. More countries, however, face a situation of high imports of grains etc. Here investment in the agricultural sector leads to import substitution.

On the Schuh paper, the point was raised as to whether floating exchange rates and IMF policies are not the main cause behind the relative unstable prices and also low prices for the LDCs. The discussion concentrated on the responsibility for a stable development of trade between LDCs and DCs. If LDCs are asked to maintain a well sustained internal policy, can the developed countries be asked for stability of their economic development, especially with respect to exchange rates? This would not only require more stability in monetary policy, but also a fiscal policy that is effectively used for the internal development of the rich countries.

It was questioned whether there was not an asymmetrical position for LDCs. In a period of expansion they can find financial support; but in a period of contraction they are forced to increase exports and have no opportunities for new loans.

Another question dealt with situations with (regional) commodity surpluses. Are the problems of, for example, US farmers with their relative unfavourable terms of trade not identical to the situation of farmers in many developing countries?

The possibility of counter trade or barter trade (trade arrangements in fixed quantities) was suggested as an alternative for international trade with its dependency on exchange rates.

In reply, Dr Schuh maintained that some means should be established to provide more stable monetary conditions. One must also think about some simple reforms of the IMF and a reduction in the influence of the US dollar – and implicitly US monetary policy – on international trade and capital markets. Countries should stop operating as if they were a closed economy. The fact is that economic integration has far outranged political integration.

Concerning the position of LDCs and DCs and their respective policies he felt that research on the consequences of the particular policies of developed countries and their effects on LDCs should make things clear; but this type of research was limited. Furthermore, many LDCs that have created a large debt load should export more. That is not a point of asymmetry but a result of earlier decisions.

Dr Schuch considered that although there were some common elements in the position of US farmers and farmers in developing countries, the main difference is the existence of many commodity programmes in the US. More flexibility in these programmes could be discussed.

Regarding the final point he felt that counter or barter trade was not or was only a very limited alternative to normal international trade.

Participants in the discussion included Gaymasan, K. S. Parikh, D. R. Colman, G. H. Peters, J. Berthelot, I. Singh, Evestein and A. B. Lewis.

ULRICH KOESTER

Regional Co-operation in the Food Sector Among Developing Countries to Improve Food Security

INTRODUCTION

It is a widely held belief that developing countries should try to make themselves less dependent on trade with industrialised countries. This could be achieved with more import substitution or even autarky. This is rarely recommended, however, especially for the many small developing countries. An alternative could be to increase intra-LDC trade, perhaps through regional co-operation schemes. Actually, this strategy is not at all new. Many regional integration schemes among developing countries were founded in the 1960s and 1970s. But the experience has so far been mostly disappointing. Nevertheless, two new regional schemes have recently been set up in Africa. The Southern African Development Co-ordination Conference, which includes Angola, Botswana, Lesotho, Malawi, Mozambique, Swaziland, Tanzania, Zimbabwe and Zambia, and which came into existence in 1980; and the Preferential Trade Area (PTA), which started with tariff reductions in 1984 and had the following members at that time: Burundi, Comoros, Djibouti, Ethiopia, Kenya, Lesotho, Malawi, Mauritius, Rwanda, Somalia, Swaziland, Uganda, Zambia and Zimbabwe.

The objectives of these new schemes differ somewhat from those of the other schemes. They made food security a special goal. This indicates that regional co-operation might contribute to food security. The potential for improving food security through regional market integration and the institutional and political arrangements that are needed to exploit the potential will be investigated in this paper.

In the following, it is assumed that the objective of integrating the food economy is to improve food security. 'Food security may be defined as the ability of food deficit countries, or regions, or households within these countries, to meet target consumption levels on a year-to-year basis' (Valdes and Siamwalla 1981, p. 2). Consequently, food insecurity may have two facets: real income may be too low to provide target consumption for all groups of the society even in years of normal or above normal domestic production; and real income may fluctuate because of variations in domestic production of food and nonfood products and/or import and export prices. Integrating the food economy of developing countries could affect both aspects of food security.

Regional co-operation to decrease instability in food consumption can be based on a regional insurance approach. Alternative strategies can include regional stockpiling, balancing fluctuations in supply among integrating countries through intra-regional trade, regional market intelligence units, co-ordination in timing exports and imports in cases where port facilities might be a bottleneck, joint ventures to improve marketing infrastructure, a regional food financing facility system and others. Whether countries should co-operate in all or some of these fields depends on the potential benefits for the region as a whole and for individual countries. The benefits to the whole region do not determine whether the scheme might be viable. Experience with existent schemes has proved that the distributional effects among the member countries is crucial for a scheme's viability (Vaitos 1978). Hence, the benefits for individual countries are very important. The distributional effects of the country's net gain from a specific type of co-operation depend largely on the institutional framework chosen. Hence, it can hardly be generalised what fields of integration are the most promising for specific groups of countries. Therefore, the benefits can only be determined on the basis of thorough theoretical and empirical investigation of specific fields of integration by specific regional groupings of countries.

It is not possible in a short paper to evaluate all integration efforts that might stabilise food consumption. Instead, I prefer to concentrate on one selected fields of cooperation which might be adopted by one group of countries, this is market integration of the Southern African Development Conference (SADCC) countries.

THE POTENTIAL TO IMPROVE FOOD SECURITY THROUGH REGIONAL MARKET INTEGRATION

According to the economic theory of integration, regional market integration can only contribute less to food security than world-wide integration. Hence, countries would be well advised to open their economies even if partner countries do not. But, there might be good reasons to prefer regional integration to world-wide integration.

Policy-makers often renounce policies that are best from a purely economic point of view because of political constraints. A country's pattern of protection can only be explained if the political market for protection is taken into consideration (Pelkmans 1980). The argument for world-wide integration is mainly based on economic reasoning, but the arguments for regional integration are founded on political considerations as well. The political will is likely to be stronger for regional integration than for world-wide integration. Moreover, world-wide integration lowers protection without visibly compensating producers. Regional integration, instead, changes the pattern of protection, helping some producers and hurting others. It can be hoped that producers will, therefore, be less opposed to regional integration.

If market integration is supposed to improve food security, regional schemes might be preferred to world-wide integration because they might do more to decrease instability in food consumption. It can be presumed that it is easier to co-ordinate the actions to stabilise food consumption taken by a few selected groups of countries than by all countries. International stabilisation schemes have shown that adherence by member countries to agreed rules of member countries is impossible to enforce if the membership is large and that the possibility of gaining as a free-rider weakens the viability and the functioning of an international scheme.

The traditional approach of the economic theory of integration is likely to lead to false conclusions in valuing the integration efforts of some land-locked countries because transport costs have been disregarded. This assumption is crucial for the conclusion that regional integration can only be less advantageous in economic terms than worldwide integration (Wonnacott and Wonnacott 1981).

Summing up, integration of regional markets may be more beneficial than world-wide integration under some conditions. These conditions will be investigated for the integration scheme of the SADCC countries.

Transport costs as a determinant of regional integration benefits
To highlight the significance of transport costs, import and export parity prices are presented for selected locations in the SADCC region in Table 1. It was assumed that countries trade only with overseas markets without having set up a regional integration scheme. The large difference in prices indicates, first, that a policy of autarky in staple foods is likely to be a reasonable policy if no trade with neighbouring countries is allowed; second, that price ratios of staple prices may differ considerably from country to country; and third, that fluctuations in domestic production are more likely to lead to changes in national carry-over stocks than to changes in trade flows.

The region's and national countries' food balance sheet as a determinant of regional integration benefits
We can presume that the potential for intra-regional trade is greater if the region as a whole is self-sufficient in staple foods, but individual countries are not. Market integration would help to substitute intra-regional trade for inter-regional trade providing higher export prices for exporting countries and/or lower import prices for importing countries.

Table 2 presents the food balance sheet of the region. The region would have been almost self-sufficient in grain equivalents in 1980 if production had equalled the average of 1979–81. Of course, this outcome is not just a mirror of the region's production potential and consumer needs. It is certainly also a consequence of the prices and price ratios set by the governments of individual countries. A different set of producer

Table 1   Import and Export Parity Prices for Maize, Sorghum, and Wheat for Selected Locations in the SADCC Region ($/ton)

	Maize		Sorghum		Wheat	
	Import Parity Price	Export Parity Price	Import Parity Price	Export Parity Price	Import Parity Price	Export Parity Price
			(1977/78)			
Maun, Botswana	203	6	196	− 1	220	23
Maseru, Lesotho	160	49	153	42	177	66
Rumphi, Malawi	222	− 12	215	− 19	239	4
Lichinga, Mozambique	189	20	182	13	206	37
Manzini, Swaziland	132	77	125	70	149	94
Tabora, Tanzania	153	56	146	49	170	73
Lusaka, Zambia	187	22	180	15	204	39
Ndola, Zambia	198	11	191	4	215	28
Harare, Zimbabwe	147	62	140	55	164	79
Bulawayo, Zimbabwe	159	50	152	43	176	67
			(1983/84)			
Maun, Botswana	270	39	255	24	277	46
Maseru, Lesotho	227	82	212	67	234	89
Rumphi, Malawi	289	20	274	5	296	27
Lichinga, Mozambique	256	53	241	38	263	60
Manzini, Swaziland	199	110	184	95	206	117
Tabora, Tanzania	220	89	205	74	227	96
Lusaka, Zambia	254	55	239	40	261	62
Ndola, Zambia	265	44	250	29	272	51
Harare, Zimbabwe	214	95	199	80	221	102
Bulawayo, Zimbabwe	226	83	211	68	233	90

Source: Author's calculations based on data for transport costs from Southern African Development Conference, 'Regional Food Security', *op. cit.* It has been assumed that shipments will be made by train whenever there is a railway connection.

and consumer prices could change the amounts as well as the pattern of production and consumption. However, the figures indicate that the region might be able to produce enough staple food to feed its population. This is quite important for the trade potential created by integrating the markets of these countries, which would promote trade within the region.

In investigating the potential benefits of market integration, it is reasonable to consider the region as nearly a closed economy. Thus, integration would result mostly in trade creation and less in trade diversion, as Viner defines these terms. More trade would be created: (a) the more the food balance of individual countries is unbalanced, either for total staple foods or for individual staples; (b) the more a country's consumption pattern might change due to the creation of intra-regional trade; and (c) the more the region's products differ in quality from the inter-regional traded goods.

Table 2 Food Production/Consumption Balance for the Aggregate of the SADCC Countries[a]

	Wheat	Rice	Maize	Millet and Sorghum	Cassava	Total
	(1000 metric tons of grain equivalent)					
Apparent Consumption	605.1	302.0	4,471.3	908.6	2,314.0	8,601.0
Consumption Pattern (%)	7.0	3.5	52.0	10.6	26.9	100.0
Production	200.6	269.4	4,845.1	870.3	2,400.8	8,586.2
Balance	−404.5	− 32.6	373.8	− 38.3	86.8	− 14.8
Degree of Self-Sufficiency (%)	33.0	89.0	108.0	96.0	104.0	99.8

Note: [a] Production average 1979–81; Consumption 1980.
Source: Author's calculations based on data from Southern Africa Development Coordination Conference. Regional Food Security. Regional Food Reserve. Annex 1 Country Profiles. Prepared by technosynthesis. Harare, May 1983.

Table 3 reveals that there are actually only two of the nine SADCC countries which do not produce a surplus of at least one staple food. The imbalance of an individual country producing a single product would increase if free trade were allowed among the member countries. This presumption is supported by evidence that people in countries that do not produce specific staples, such as rice and cassava, do not include them in the diet.

The potential for growth in intra-regional trade is higher when countries that produce surpluses of some staples are bordered by countries with deficits in the same staples. Table 4 shows that there were five such countries. Thus there is a potential for trade among the SADCC countries with the present production and consumption patterns. If free trade within the region can lead to a change in the prices and availability of specific products, such as cassava, production and consumption in individual countries can adjust and, thus, increase the potential for intra-regional trade in staple foods.

Liberalisation of trade of maize within the region would be of special importance. Consumers in the SADCC countries prefer white maize to yellow maize. Therefore, more of the former is produced. But because international trade is mostly in yellow maize, the markets for white maize in Africa are thin. Thus, prices will fluctuate significantly as production fluctuates or markets will be in disequilibrium if governments set prices. Such situations would be more likely if individual countries chose not to trade in staples or if they only traded outside the region and not with each other. Intra-regional trade would not only help stabilise national maize markets, but it would also allow savings in transport costs. Moreover, exporting countries could capture some of the premium for white maize, which is only paid on African markets and not on international markets. This premium accounts for about 10 per cent of the price for yellow maize (World Bank 1981).

Table 3   Self-Sufficiency Ratio for Staple Food and Consumption Pattern for SADCC Countries

	Wheat		Rice		Maize		Millet and Sorghum		Cassava		Total	
	1	2	1	2	1	2	1	2	1	2	1	2
Angola	6.2	11.0	34.9	3.6	66.6	31.5	56.9	5.9	102.7	48.0	75.6	100
Botswana	3.2	13.0	—	—	7.6	47.5	56.4	39.5	—	—	26.3	100
Lesotho	23.0	34.7	—	—	78.3	47.5	116.7	17.8	—	1.6	65.6	100
Malawi	2.4	1.7	128.4	1.9	104.3	90.8	220.0	4.0	518.8		114.3	100
Mozambique	1.6	6.8	49.8	4.8	50.5	25.9	58.7	13.2	83.1	49.3	64.3	100
Swaziland	180.0	0.8	260.0	1.4	46.1	95.9	107.7	1.9	—	—	51.3	100
Tanzania	48.2	4.6	126.1	6.5	156.6	40.1	137.8	8.7	110.2	40.1	129.4	100
Zambia	6.7	11.3	25.0	1.0	84.7	73.3	96.4	8.1	208.3	6.3	84.0	100
Zimbabwe	167.2	5.0	2.5	0.6	132.5	76.0	80.9	18.4	—	—	124.0	100

Notes: $1 = \dfrac{\text{Average production in grain equivalent from 1979 to 1981}}{\text{Apparent consumption 1980}} \times 100$

2 = Consumption pattern in percentages of the year 1980

Source: Author's calculations based on data from Southern African Development Coordination Conference, op. cit.

Table 4 *Surplus and Deficit in Staple Foods of Bordering Countries in the SADCC Region, 1980[a]*

Country	Surplus Staple Foods	Border Countries	Deficit Staple Foods
Angola	Cassava	Zambia	Wheat, Rice, Maize, Millet, Sorghum
Malawi	Rice, Maize, Sorghum, Millet, Cassava	Mozambique	Wheat, Rice, Maize, Millet, Sorghum, Cassava
		Tanzania	Wheat
		Zambia	Wheat, Rice, Maize, Sorghum, Millet
Swaziland	Wheat, Rice, Millet, Sorghum	Mozambique	Wheat, Rice, Maize, Millet, Sorghum, Cassava
Tanzania	Rice, Maize, Millet, Sorghum, Cassava	Malawi	Wheat
		Zambia	Wheat, Rice, Maize, Sorghum, Millet
		Mozambique	Wheat, Rice, Maize, Millet, Sorghum, Cassava
Zambia	Cassava	Angola	Wheat, Rice, Maize, Millet, Sorghum
		Botswana	Wheat, Rice[b], Maize, Millet, Sorghum, Cassava[b]
		Malawi	Wheat
		Mozambique	Wheat, Rice, Maize, Millet, Sorghum, Cassava
		Tanzania	Wheat
		Zimbabwe	Rice, Millet, Sorghum, Cassava[b]
Zimbabwe	Wheat, Maize	Botswana	Wheat, Rice,[b] Maize, Millet, Sorghum, Cassava[b]
		Mozambique	Wheat, Rice, Maize, Millet, Sorghum, Cassava
		Zambia	Wheat, Rice, Maize, Millet, Sorghum

Notes: [a] Production: Average 1979–81. Consumption: 1980
[b] Negligible consumption so far.
Source: See Table 3.

The following calculation gives an idea of how large the savings in transport costs could be if SADCC countries traded among themselves rather than with overseas countries.

Assume that Zambia's production in staple foods in 1980 was equal to the 1979–81 average. If consumption was normal in 1980, Zambia would have needed to import 96,000 metric tons of maize. Hence, Zambia could have bought all her maize imports and 46,400 metric tons of wheat from Zimbabwe. Assuming that import and export parity prices were the prices in Lusaka and Bulawayo in 1977–8, Zambia would have had to pay US $187 for maize and US $204 for wheat imported from overseas or US $88.56 for maize and US $95.56 for wheat imported from Zimbabwe. Hence, buying from Zimbabwe instead of buying from overseas markets would have saved US $108.44 per ton of Zambia's imports. Total savings which could have been divided between Zambia and Zimbabwe would have amounted to US $15,441,856 (US $5,031,616 for wheat-trading and US $10,410,240 for maize trading without taking into account the premium for white maize). Certainly this is not a neglible amount. Zambia's Agricultural Domestic Product in 1965 prices was equal to US $179.5 million at the 1981 exchange rate.[2] Hence, trading maize and wheat between Zambia and Zimbabwe would have led to savings in transport costs equal to 8.6 per cent of Zambia's Agricultural Domestic Product. Of course, these calculations do not show the potential gain exactly. Some of the gain may have already been captured through trade within the region. Nevertheless, they highlight the comparative advantage that trade within the region has.

Savings in transport cost will not only materialise if one country produces a surplus of a specific commodity and the neighbouring country generates a deficit. They will also materialise if the production and consumption of parts of countries are not in balance and trade is allowed across the border. Thus, it might well be that a country with a deficit in maize in one year becomes an exporter because parts of country produce surpluses of maize that could be exported to parts of a neighbouring country with deficits. This indicates that trade which flows between the countries taking part in an integration scheme would be different without a scheme.

Liberalized intra-regional trade leads to a greater reduction in transport costs in one country if production in regions of the country fluctuates with non-positive covariances of the fluctuations on neighbouring regions of another country. Subregions near the border are normally remote from the central domestic market. Hence, a fluctuation in production will either lead to significant price fluctuations in these regions or will require that additional resources be allocated to transportation. If, however, these border regions are allowed to trade with regions on the other side of the border, the transportation costs incurred would be smaller. They will be smaller the more there are negative or zero covariances between the fluctuations in production of regions on both sides of the border. Correlation coefficients were calculated for projected fluctuations of cereal production between 27 neighbouring zones separated from each other by national borders.[3] Some of these coefficients were negative, indicating that the covariances were negative, and in only one case were not statistically significant, indicating that the fluctuations were statistically independent. Hence, free border trade could help compensate for fluctuations in production between these regions.

Regional market integration and savings in resource costs
The economic theory of market integration deals mainly with the question of whether integration can improve factor allocation and so increase production with a given endowment of resources. It has been concluded that resource costs may be saved through regional market integration if the integrating countries have different comparative advantages, and if integration creates more trade than it diverts. Trade diversion, however, can probably be ruled out for the SADCC countries because import and export parity prices differ greatly, and because the region is nearly self-sufficient in staple foods. That leaves only differences in the comparative advantages of the countries of the region in the production of individual staples to be investigated.

Two indicators of such differences are the differences in the countries' production patterns and in the degree to which they are self-sufficient in individual staples (see Table 3). These are 'revealed comparative advantages'.

Another indicator is the size of the domestic resource costs (DRCs) for individual crops. Unfortunately, DRCs are not available for production of individual staples in all SADCC countries. However, an illustrative calculation will be presented using the DRCs to quantify possible gains from an adjustment of the country's production pattern in accordance with comparative advantage.[4] Assume that incentives to Zambia's farmers were given to expand wheat production, and that if wheat production were increased, the increase in maize production would be reduced. Assume further that the change in the production pattern would be compensated by corresponding changes in imports from Zimbabwe. Yields for maize were 2.14 metric tons per hectare, and for wheat 3.99 metric tons per hectare in 1978–80. Hence, increasing the area sown with wheat by 1 hectare and decreasing the area under maize by 1 hectare would lead to savings in DRC equal to $2.94 \times 2.14 \times Pm + 0.6 \times 3.99 \times Pw$, where Pm and Pw stand for the import parity prices of maize and wheat for imports from Zimbabwe. Taking into account the parity prices for Zimbabwe's exports to overseas markets and adding the transport costs from Zimbabwe (Bulawayo) to Zambia (Lusaka), Zambia's import parity prices for intra-regional trade in 1983–4 were US $111.56 per metric ton for maize, and US $118.56 per metric ton for wheat. Total savings in DRC would be US $985.72 per hectare. This clearly indicates that an adjustment in the domestic production pattern in accordance with comparative advantage can give a high return. Of course, the size of the gain depends on how large the differences between the comparative advantages of the SADCC countries are. One may wonder whether there can be much of a division of labour in agricultural production among these countries. One might argue that these countries are located in the same geographical region and, hence, conditions for agricultural production are the same all over the region. But differences in comparative advantage will arise from variances in climate, variances in soil conditions, and variances in opportunity costs, and these do vary among the SADCC countries.

Specialisation on the basis of comparative advantage will generate even more benefits if the consumption pattern changes significantly over time. An increase in the demand for livestock products and poultry is a case in point. As pork and poultry production is only marginally tied to land endowment, prices for inputs and the final products are most important for choosing where to produce. Experience in developed countries has shown that transportation costs are more important in determining the regional price pattern of feedstuffs than of pork and poultry. Hence, industries tend to be located where feed prices are the lowest. Therefore, integration of the markets of the SADCC countries could reduce the costs of the expanding livestock sector in the region.

Other positive effects on allocation can be expected in food processing. In addition to savings on transportation costs like those for livestock, costs could be reduced through economies of scale. Food processing industries in developing countries rarely use their full production capacity because the domestic markets are so small. Market integration among the SADCC countries might increase the size of the market available to the industries, allowing them to use their resources more efficiently. Significant benefits might arise because the demand for processed food will probably grow. Similar economies of scale effects might be available in the production of agricultural inputs, such as fertilizer and farm machinery.

Savings in administrative costs have been completely neglected by the economic theory of integration. If small landlocked countries have agricultural markets and price policies, and if their domestic prices differ from those of neighbouring countries, incentives for smuggling are built in. This illegal border trade can only be avoided if all border transactions are efficiently controlled. This would absorb a high amount of manpower, which could be used more efficiently to produce goods and services. Moreover, border trade, where legal or illegal, increases welfare in the exporting region because the increase in market prices that results increases the producer surplus more than it decreases the consumer surplus. It also increases welfare in the importing regions, whether changes in consumer surplus surpass changes in producer surplus. Thus, liberalising intra-regional trade can have a twofold, positive effect on welfare.

INSTITUTIONAL ARRANGEMENTS TO CAPTURE MARKET INTEGRATION BENEFITS

Removal of the barriers to intra-regional trade is certainly necessary if all the potential benefits of market integration are to be captured. However, reducing or abolishing these barriers is not enough to guarantee that potential gains will be exploited. An adjustment in the internal and external agricultural trade regime and in exchange rate policies are also necessary. It will be argued that a mere removal of trade barriers might reduce the welfare of some countries if the necessary complementary adjustments in policies are not made. Hence, if countries are not willing or are not able because of political constraints to adjust in the domestic trade regimes and exchange rate policies, they might be well advised to postpone complete market integration. Instead, they might prefer less complete regional trade arrangements to exploit at least some of the benefits of complete market integration.

It should be obvious that integrated markets can only function adequately if trade in agricultural products within the countries is ruled by market forces. Pan-territorial prices and uniform seasonal prices set by the governments of the SADCC countries are obstacles to optimal resource allocation and to international trade.

Pan-territorial prices are political prices enforced by individual governments. They do not reflect a country's comparative advantage. It is hard to find empirical evidence to support the allegation that these prices are set in relation to costs of production (FAO 1984). If free-trading countries were to set different pan-territorial prices, the domestic trade regimes would collapse. Trade would flow from the country with lower prices to the country with higher prices, and this flow might have no basis in the comparative advantages of the two countries. The consequences would be that the country with low prices could not enforce these prices and the country with higher pan-territorial prices would have to build-up government stocks. Neither consequence is acceptable from either a political or an economic point of view.

Harmonising pan-territorial prices among the integrating countries is no solution. Common pan-territorial prices would partly avoid policy-induced trade flows. They would not, however, allow the countries to specialise in accordance with comparative advantage. Resources can be allocated optimally only if prices between countries that trade with each other differ by transportation costs. Transportation costs are important in determining supply prices within the SADCC countries. Hence, prices among the SADCC countries should vary significantly if resources are to be allocated optimally.

Market integration among the SADCC countries not only necessitates liberalisation of domestic price and market policies, it also demands that external trade in agricultural products be harmonised. If integrating countries had different external trade restrictions, trade flows within the region might be distorted. Countries with lower tariffs might import from countries outside the region and sell the imported quantities profitably to other countries in the integration scheme. This would make the higher tariff in the partner countries redundant. But even if the integrating countries agree on common external trade restrictions, the viability of the integration scheme might be weakened. Assume that the difference between import and export parity prices is negligible and that countries agree to set a uniform external tariff. Also assume that production in some countries surpasses domestic consumption, and other countries need to import. The importing country, which could buy its imports at world market prices if it did not join the integration scheme, would have to buy at higher prices from a country also in the integration scheme. Thus, real income would be transferred to the exporting countries from the importing countries. Such invisible transfer flows will always arise if the integrating countries put restrictions on international trade. This problem could be solved easily for the SADCC countries. The borders with neighbouring African countries not in the SADCC would have to be controlled anyway, and since the SADCC region is nearly self-sufficient in staple foods, border trade with African non-member countries might be excluded. Staple foods would only be traded with overseas countries in exceptional cases if the region experienced a bad harvest for which a release of stocks would not compensate. Liberalisation of overseas trade should therefore be considered.

Another obstacle to liberalising trade within the region, exchange rate policies, is much more difficult to overcome. The currency of most developing countries is overvalued, but the extent is hard to quantify. If one could assume that in 1970 the exchange market was in equilibrium for all SADCC countries, the overvaluation of purchasing power for the average 1978–80 period was 1.42 in Tanzania, 1.24 in Zambia, 1.15 in Malawi, and 1.11 in Zimbabwe (FAO 1984). If these countries were to liberalise trade and were to accept the currencies of other SADCC countries in exchange for products, significant amounts of real income would be transferred. For example, Tanzania had to pay 23.5 per cent less for its imports from neighbouring Malawi and received 23.5 per cent more for its exports to Malawi because of the overvaluation from 1970 to 1978–80. Clearly, Malawi would lose and Tanzania would benefit from border trade if each country accepted the other's currency in exchange for products. This problem of weak currencies cannot be solved only by asking for a clearing of the imbalance in trade in hard currencies.[5] Transfer effects are generated, even if trade in national currencies is balanced. In general, countries with stronger currencies are penalised to the benefit of countries with weak currencies. This problem can only be overcome if monetary and exchange rate policies are harmonised. It does not seem likely, however, that countries would be willing to give up an important element of their autonomous national policies. A solution could be to use international prices denominated in US dollars. But, this would not allow for the capture of all the potential benefits from integration as it demands a strict control of all border transactions.

Moreover, partner countries would have to be willing to agree on international prices to be used in intra-regional trade.

To conclude, at least a transitory period is needed, during which the conditions necessary for a complete liberalisation of trade among the SADCC countries would be provided. It might be advisable for the countries to start with a more modest goal. This is actually the strategy which the SADCC countries follow. Even if it is assumed that countries are not willing to liberalise trade within their borders, intra-regional trade can nevertheless be promoted. Countries could at least inform each other about the situation in their domestic markets and they could arrange for trade within the region to be conducted on the basis of international prices.

CONCLUSIONS

Regional market integration would be preferable to world-wide integration as a means of improving food security if specific conditions hold true. However, an exploitation of market integration benefits demands an adequate political and institutional framework. If countries are not willing or able to provide the necessary framework, official trading arrangements should be set up in order to capture some of the market integration benefits. In addition, they could co-operate without significantly impairing their autonomy through the creation of regional insurance schemes such as regional stockpiling, regional food facility systems and others.

NOTES

[1] Actually, the classified stages do not differ only in the degree of discrimination, as has been assumed. They differ as well in their degree of positive policy integration. See Pelkmans, Jacques, op. cit.

[2] This is a five-year moving average. Source: World Bank, Zambia, *Policy Options and Strategies for Agricultural Growth*, Report no. 4764–2A, June 1984, p. 82.

[3] Technosynthesis projected production of cereals in individual zones for the period 1985–94 on the basis of time series for past production.

[4] The size of DRCs depends, of course, on the assumed world market prices. As the World Bank team assumed export and import parity prices for trade with overseas markets, the DRCs are probably underestimated for Zambia's import products, as are maize and wheat.

[5] The Preferential Trade Agreement among the Eastern and Southern African countries asks for a clearing of the imbalances in hard currencies.

REFERENCES

Food and Agriculture Organization, 'Price Policy in Africa', Thirteenth FAO Regional Conference for Africa, Harare, Zimbabwe, 16–25 July 1984.

Pelkmans, J., 'Economic Theories of Integration Revisited', *Journal of Common Market Studies*, XVIII, no. 4, June 1980.

Southern African Development Coordination Conference. 'Regional Food Security. Regional Food Reserve', Pre-Feasibility Study, Main Report, prepared by technosynthesis, Zimbabwe, January 1984.

Vaitos, C. V., 'Crisis in Regional Economic Cooperation (Integration) Among Developing Countries: A Survey', *World Development*, 1978, pp. 719–69.

Valdes, A. and Siamwalla, A. 'Introduction' in Valdes, A. (ed.) *Food Security for Developing Countries*, Westview Press, Boulder, Colorado, 1981.

Wonnacott, P. and Wonnacott, R. 'Is Unilateral Tariff Reduction Preferable to a Customs Union? The Curious Case of the Missing Foreign Tariffs', *The American Economic Review*, September 1981, pp. 704–14.

World Bank, 'Zambia: Policy Options and Strategies for Agricultural Growth', Report no. 4764–7A, The World Bank, Washington, DC, 11 June 1984.

——, 'Malawi: The Development of the Agricultural Sector', Report no. 3459. The World Bank, Washington DC, May 1981.

ALEX F. MCCALLA AND TIMOTHY E. JOSLING

Agriculture in an Interdependent and Uncertain World: Implications for Markets and Prices

I. INTRODUCTION

National agricultural markets in the 1950s and 1960s were relatively stable with the principal linkages among countries occurring through international commodity markets. By contrast, the period since 1972 has been considerably more volatile and uncertain and interdependence is characterised by a much larger number of linkages, including through energy prices, exchange rates and capital markets. This greater interdependence means that national agricultural sectors are potentially vulnerable to a much broader set of external shocks.

To state this now may seem to be emphasising the obvious, but we still need to understand better the nature and causes of the increased interdependence and uncertainty. We begin our analysis with the basic premise that increased interdependence can result from: (1) increased integration of the domestic agricultural sector into the national economy: and (2) increased integration of national economies into world markets. The approach is to develop a framework that allows one to look at both kinds of integration simultaneously. This is developed schematically in Section II. Section III of the paper discusses briefly the variety of situations in which agriculture can find itself. Section IV discusses the implications for world markets of increased interdependence and Section V draws out some policy implications for both individual countries and the international community.

II. THE NATURE OF INCREASING INTERDEPENDENCE

Interdependence for an agricultural sector can come about from two sources: increased integration into the national economy and increased integration of the national economy into the international economy. This is presented schematically in Figure 1. On the horizontal axis is the transformation of the domestic agricultural sector from a traditional subsistence sector to a mature highly integrated part of the economy. The overall process of transformation is well known (Hayami and Ruttan 1985; Mellor and Johnston 1984). Briefly, it involves increased productivity, a greater market orientation, declining relative and then absolute employment of labour, declining contribution to GNP and increased dependence on non-farm sector inputs. The process is, of

114

Increasing Degrees of Domestic Integration

	Traditional Subsistence Agriculture	Transitional Agricultural Sector	Mature Agriculture
Autarkic or Fixed Relations*	1	2	3
Partially Linked**	4	5	6
Completely Integrated Economy	7	8	9

Increasing Degrees of International Integration

*e.g., fixed exchange rates, non-convertible currency and state trading
**may participate in some markets (e.g., commodity) but not all (e.g., capital)

FIGURE 1   Domestic and International Integration

course, a continuum, but for analytical purposes we identify three broad stages: (1) traditional subsistence agriculture; (2) transitional agriculture with partial but not complete integration and (3) a mature integrated agriculture.

On the vertical axis are the degrees of international integration of the national economy. At one extreme, countries may have few if any linkages with the international economy but such an autarkic situation is of limited interest in the present context. Instead, the situation representing the lowest level of international integration is one that would involve limited capital flows, inconvertible currencies and trade managed by the state. A partially linked economy would involve increased participation in commodity markets (with the interface managed or unmanaged), and exchange rate convertibility, but limited or no integration in capital markets. A completely integrated economy would be one where there is heavy involvement in international commodity and product markets and ready capital movements in conjunction with changes in interest rates and exchange rates.

The process of domestic development involves movements from subsistence toward a mature agriculture regardless of the degree of international integration, though its rate and stability may be influenced by such factors. This transformation occurred in the 'developed' countries over the period from about 1850 to the 1960s with the agricultural exporting nations (United States, Canada, Australia and New Zealand) proceeding more rapidly. One could argue that Europe is only now approaching full maturity and that Japan has some way still to go. The rate and character of the agricultural transformation can be influenced by but not halted by policy. Thus, more and more countries will be moving to the right in the figure though at different speeds.

The process of international integration may not have the same degree of inevitability, but the evolution in the post Second World War period has been to move most countries downwards on the chart. Fundamentally the process involves opening the national economy up to the international economy by liberalisation of trade and of capital markets. However, perhaps more so than with the transformation of domestic agriculture, the rate of change and the nature of the openness is more directly dependent on policy choice (McCalla and Josling 1985).

The interaction of both processes has moved more and more countries southeastward towards the combination of a mature agriculture and a fully integrated national economy. With increased interdependence, both in domestic agriculture and because of macroeconomic integration among countries, agricultural commodity markets are subject to a much wider variety of shocks, including weather (the traditional source of instability), from other markets (capital and foreign exchange, for example) and from policy (not only agricultural but monetary, fiscal and exchange rate). The failure to adjust domestic agricultural policy instruments to an interdependent world environment can exacerbate instability as more and more exogenous shocks hit the domestic agricultural sector.

III. THE NATURE OF THE TRANSITIONS

To get the flavour of the various stages of interdependence in this section we characterise the various combinations of the degree of integration, nationally and internationally, in terms of the 'boxes' labelled 1 to 9 in Figure 1. In some cases we risk debate by giving potential examples of countries that seem to fall into a particular category but no formal attempt is made to quantify these criteria.

Case 1
Countries whose agricultural sector is traditional and whose economies are weakly, if at all, linked to international markets would meet the most recurrent description of low-income developing countries: a high proportion of the population in agriculture; heavy emphasis on subsistence food crops with low levels of commercial marketing; the absence of national product and input (particularly credit) markets; near self-sufficiency in food crops at low levels of nutrition; and a relatively small non-agricultural sector in terms of employment and GNP creation. The

international linkages, if they exist, would be highly managed. If export crops are produced they would not be closely linked to the food crop sector and their marketing would most often be managed by state trading agents or parastatal marketing boards. There could be concessional food aid and limited commercial food trade. There would be few if any direct macro and monetary linkages with world markets. Typical would be a fixed exchange rate for inconvertible currencies (or currencies linked to that of a previous colonial power) with most capital movements managed by the public sector. Many countries in sub-Saharan Africa would meet this general description.

Case 2
A country in transition agriculturally but still not linked internationally would exhibit some or all of the following characteristics: the development of national markets for both food and cash crops; a developing but still incomplete distributional sector; improvements in biological technology but still low levels of mechanical technology, resulting in high levels of labour employment; public sector national credit markets; growing inter-sector linkages through product and input markets; a developing national labour market as evidenced by heavy rural to urban migration; more commerical food imports; and declining cash crop exports as rising population and income put pressure on land to produce food. Countries such as Egypt, India and Bangladesh seem to fall in this category with a transitional agriculture but still largely closed macroeconomic markets and policies.

Case 3
Full integration would involve high levels of productivity resulting from biological, mechanical and chemical technology; a well developed distributional sector including sophisticated processing and informational markets including futures trading; declining relative and absolute employment in production agriculture; full integration of agriculture into national capital, labour, product and input markets; high dependence on purchased inputs; most production sold off-farm; declining numbers of commerical farmers and rising numbers of part-time farmers; but with an international interface small and managed to dispose of periodic surpluses or cover occasional shortages. This case seems somewhat rare in practice. Agricultural integration may require the stimulus of international linkages to reach its maturity. Europe in the 1960s during the formation of the European Community seemed to meet most of these conditions: economic integration among Western countries, in particular through the capital market, has moved EC agriculture down at least to case 6.

Case 4
Increasing the degree of international integration for a still traditional agriculture sector would involve greater flows of international goods either as food aid or government purchases for distribution; the development of

the cash crop sector selling on international markets perhaps with some private marketing alongside marketing boards; the deliberate use of trade policy to create conditions to stimulate either cash or food crops; capital inflows both public (e.g., World Bank) and private (multinationals) but incomplete international integration as characterised by fixed and inconvertible currencies and often multiple exchange rates. This case would essentially capture those situations where there are strong international commodity market linkages but these coexist with a large traditional agricultural sector imperfectly integrated in the domestic economy. At the risk of debate, Thailand, several Central American republics and Malaysia seem to fit here.

Case 5
The combination of growing international linkages and internal agricultural linkages is perhaps more typical of middle income developing countries. It can be characterised by strong international linkages through cash crop exports; productivity increases in the food sector but not rapid enough to meet rising demands resulting from income and population growth; consequent rising of concessional and commercial food imports but with prices still generally managed, limiting the impacts of world price changes on agriculture; rising employment in the non-agricultural sector resulting in rising wages and labour migration. Thus in this case both non-agricultural sector and world market linkages are partially developed, but impacts on agriculture come indirectly through policy change often forced by fiscal or foreign exchange constraints. Potential examples here include many of the Centrally Planned Economies of Eastern Europe, the USSR, South Korea, the Taiwan area of China and possibly Brazil. It is in this stage that agriculture may become subsidised rather than taxed.

Case 6
This case is one in which full integration of a commercialised agricultural sector has preceded the development of linkages through capital and trade markets. Therefore, domestic macro but not international shocks hit agriculture. It is plausible to place a number of developed countries in this category particularly members of the EC, where the Common Agricultural Policy has had some success in preventing the opening of the European economies from impinging directly on agriculture.

Case 7
A traditional agriculture with low levels of agricultural productivity but full international integration is another variant. International events have an importance for agriculture, as capital flows influence exchange rates and interest rates. There may be direct foreign investment in the export sector or import competing sectors but few domestic linkages with the non-farm sector. Although examples here are less easy to find,

some of the characteristics appear in the relatively open economies of Argentina, Mexico and Kenya.

Case 8

This case involves full international integration and partial domestic integration. Therefore, exchange rate, world price and interest rate fluctuations impact directly on the commercial export-oriented sector of agriculture. Domestic impacts come through the labour markets. Canada and Australia might fall into this category: world market conditions impact directly on the export grain sector but domestic policies for other commodities partially isolate those producers from domestic macro instability. Japan would also possibly be an example of this situation.

Case 9

This' is the ultimate degree of integration both domestically and internationally. Agriculture competes with a huge non-agricultural sector for capital, industrial inputs and labour. Internal market linkages are well developed. Internationally a relatively open economic policy subjects agriculture to international changes in exchange rates, interest rates, and capital flows. There are well developed linkages between commodity and capital markets. Here the full range of shocks, both domestic and international, impact on agriculture. Clearly the United States is a candidate for this category. The tendency clearly will be for more and more developed countries to move towards it.

IV. IMPLICATIONS FOR STABILITY IN WORLD MARKETS OF INCREASED INTERDEPENDENCE

It is apparent that the general movement of many countries in the 1960s and 1970s was to greater degrees of integration. The implications of this for agricultural commodity markets appears to have been an increase in instability. Increased domestic integration means that domestic macroeconomic policies which influence interest rates and inflation impact on agricultural costs and the demand for food. It seems clear that most nations experienced greater instability in macro prices – interest rates, wage rates, the general price level and exchange rate – in the 1970s and early 1980s than in previous periods. These destabilise agricultural prices more with higher degrees of integration.

Simultaneously, much greater integration and interdependence evolved internationally because of the rising importance of trade relative to GNP, flexible exchange rates and a rapidly growing and highly integrated capital market (Schuh, this volume). Therefore, open economy agricultural sectors could be buffeted both from international sources and domestic sources. Further, in many countries domestic-international macro linkages through money supplies, interest rates, and capital flows reduced the ability of individual countries to attempt to maintain domestic monetary and fiscal stability. In fact, attempts to do so may have exacerbated the international transmission of inflation and recession (McKinnon 1982). These international swings impacted more on agriculture both through domestic and international linkages the more integrated an agriculture was. United States agriculture's roller-coaster ride in the 1970s and early 1980s was much more pronounced because of its highly integrated character.

The implications for international agricultural commodity markets seem clear. Integration leads to a much larger set of sources of external shocks. If domestic policies for agriculture are unable to adjust to external shocks, countries may be less able to prevent the import of international instability than they would be in a world of stable exchange rates, interest rates, and commodity prices. Agricultural policy instruments which fix internal prices and manage trade at the border would be less able to prevent macro impacts from influencing farm prices.

V. DOMESTIC AND INTERNATIONAL POLICY IMPLICATIONS

We sum up this brief discussion by considering the policy implications of the above analysis and posing a conundrum for agricultural policy. The first implication of our approach is that the way in which countries were impacted by the turbulent international events of the last decade depended very much on where they were in the process of two-way integration. Countries in category 1 were the least impacted by events, whereas countries in category 9 were very vulnerable to the full range of international shocks. With greater domestic integration these shocks came from two directions – international commodity markets *and* domestic macro instability. Thus, one conclusion that necessarily follows is that not all countries suffered the same fate from instability.

The related policy question which arises is to ask what could countries have done to reduce the uncertainty and instability. Here the policy options are not symmetrical between domestic and international options. Countries would have a better chance of arresting (or even rolling back) movements towards international integration than they would have of managing domestic integration. This seems obvious. Border instruments – quotas, variable tariffs, licences, multiple exchange rates, state trading etc., – on a limited range of commodities are easier to manage than the full range of agriculture-non-agriculture interactions in an integrated economy. In fact traditional instruments in the latter case may be counterproductive. For example, the United States by fixing target prices and particularly loan rates in domestic currency terms increased agricultural stress when macro events caused a major appreciation of the US dollar.

The second implication of the analysis is that a country's range of options for the support of agriculture change with both kinds of integration. Historically, countries have had two broad options. The first is the attempt to assist the adjustment of a dynamic agriculture to changing conditions. The second is to try to isolate agriculture and prevent integration and, if that is not possible, to prevent the impacts of external policy shocks. But if the isolation is ineffective, agriculture in fact may be worse off. Thus, international turbulence may render the option of domestic isolation less operable and force countries to move towards adjustment policies (Schuh, this volume). Traditional agricultural lobbies and policy officials, used to managing their own affairs in their water-tight compartments, are not generally accustomed to dealing with dynamic adjustments forced by events elsewhere in the national and/or global economy. The events described here alter the set of policy options open to national policy makers. How they respond individually could either move the world towards more isolation or more open markets.

The third implication, for international agricultural policy, is similarly ambiguous. The conventional wisdom has been that trade liberalisation, by the reduction of tariff and non-tariff barriers to agricultural trade, would lead to greater global market stability and international and national food security. But what seems to have happened in the 1970s and 1980s has resulted in both greater integration *and* greater instability. The extent to which a policy of trade liberalisation would reduce instability is now an empirical issue rather than an article of liberal economic faith. Economic theory would suggest that the more integrated markets are (i.e., the greater the number of markets involved in adjustments) the more stable they ought to be. This is one of the standard arguments for flexible exchange rates. Yet exchange rate instability appears to have increased since the demise of the Bretton-Woods agreement. However, it is also true that greater integration *increases* the number of potential exogenous shocks that could impact on a particular sector. This seems to have been the fate of agricultural markets since 1972. The crucial question is which tendency will prevail. Will, in the long run, greater integration and trade liberalisation lead to more stable markets? If the answer is yes, the adjustment policies are appropriate to assist agriculture in moving southeastward towards full integration. If the answer is no, then countries will seek to isolate themselves from both domestic and international shocks. The implication of this, unless complete autarky results, will be further destabilisation of world commodity markets and ever greater uncertainty for both exporters and importers.

REFERENCES

Hayami, Y. and Ruttan, V., *Agricultural Development: An International Perspective* (second edition), Johns Hopkins Press, Baltimore and London, 1985.

McCalla, A. F. and Josling, T. E., *Agricultural Policies and World Markets*, Macmillan, New York, 1985.

McKinnon, R. I., 'Currency Substitution and Instability in the World Dollar Standard', *American Economic Review* vol. 72, May 1982.

Mellor, John W. and Johnston, Bruce F., 'The World Food Equation: Interrelations Among Development, Employment and Food Consumption', *Journal of Economic Literature* vol. 22, June 1984.

Schuh, G. Edward, 'The International Capital Market as a Source of Instability in International Commodity Markets', this volume.

DISCUSSION OPENING I – GERALDO CAMARGO BARROS

The papers presented by McCalla and Josling and Ulrich Koester deal with the basic question of uncertainty or lack of security resulting from world-wide market integration. An interesting complementarity of these papers should be emphasised: the first one approaches the question from a macroeconomic point of view while the second one from a microeconomic standpoint.

Wonnacott and Wonnacott (1981) elaborated the microeconomic setting needed to show that in a world in which tariffs and other obstacles to trade (such as transportation costs) exist, a country can achieve gains from a customs union which are not possible with unilateral tariff reduction. Koester displays some objective conditions under which a specific co-operation scheme (SADCC countries) could be more beneficial than world-wide integration. As pointed out by the author, a major difficulty to be overcome by co-operating countries is of a macroeconomic and political nature: countries should agree on harmonising their monetary and exchange rate policies. This is not an easy task especially among neighbouring countries which tend to be affected more strongly by elements of nationalism.

McCalla and Josling present a bi-dimensional framework where the degree of integration of agriculture into the national economy interacts with the degree of integration of the national economy into the world markets determining the degree of exposure of agriculture to the effects of domestic and international macroeconomic events, including uncertainty. McCalla (1982) and Schuh (1984) discussed the growing interdependence and uncertainty experienced by the international commodity markets and related them to international monetary linkages. The income effects of world-wide growth and recessions, the exchange rate and interest rate effects upon agricultural trade were stressed.

As pointed out by McCalla and Josling, the fundamental question is: 'Will, in the long run, greater integration and trade liberalisation lead to more stable markets?' On one hand, the greater the number of markets integrated the more stable they tend to be under flexible exchange rates. On the other hand, great integration tends to increase the number of potential shocks to agriculture. If the dominant effect turns out to be the second one, a tendency towards isolation, or even autarky, will be observed. Some arguments showing that this late hypothesis is less probable are presented next.

Consider the case dealt with by Koester. Countries characterised by a traditional or transitional agricultural sector and by a low degree of international integration (case 1 in McCalla's and Josling's paper) would be less vulnerable to external shocks and would not have much to gain (in the present context) from isolation.

Other Third World countries, contrary to that observed in the developed countries, have had the integration of their agricultural sector induced and sustained by policy instruments, including monetary and fiscal policies. Plagued by high inflationary levels it is doubtful if these instruments will continue to be used with the same intensity as before. Then, it is to be expected that national agriculture integration will not proceed at the same speed and, therefore, the effects of exogenous shocks upon agriculture would not be aggravated in the future.

Another stronger argument favouring world-wide as opposed to regional integration is associated with the so-called world food equation. Mellor (1983) projects a total deficit of 75 million metric tons of major food crops in the Third World in year 2000, which is nearly three times the deficit of these countries in 1977. Between 1961 and 1978, net imports of food staples by developing countries increased at an annual rate of 13 per cent. The poorest countries in the world, most of them located in sub-Saharan Africa, presented the highest growth rates of imports. Mellor also presents projections of up to a 196 million ton surplus in the developed countries. All these facts clearly favour the expectation of growing world-wide trade.

Mellor (1985) argues that major markets for developed country cereal surpluses are in the developing countries. Schuh (1984) points out that more free trade will be needed in order to create importing capacity by developing countries. This will include fewer trade barriers to increase both agricultural and labour-intensive manufactured products imported from less developed countries.

Finally and perhaps more important, the foreign debt accumulated by Third World countries – around 866 billion dollars in 1985 according to the IMF – will require a sustained trade balance surplus to provide for the needed strong, convertible currencies. This naturally implies more trade among developed and developing countries, since these currencies would not be obtained through regional Third World trade arrangements.

REFERENCES

McCalla, Alex F., 'Impact of Macroeconomic Policies upon Agricultural Trade and International Agricultural Development', *American Journal of Agricultural Economics*, 64, 1982, pp. 861–2.

Mellor, John W., 'Food Prospects for the Developing Countries', *American Economic Review*, 73, 1983, pp. 239–43.

Mellor, John W., 'The Changing World Food Situation', International Food Policy Research Institute, Food Policy Statement, January 1985.

Schuh, G. Edward, 'Future Directions for Food and Agricultural Trade Policy', *American Journal of Agricultural Economics*, 66, 1984, pp. 242–7.

Wonnacott, P. and Wonnacott, R., 'Is Unilateral Tariff Reduction Preferable to a Customs Union? The Curious Case of the Missing Foreign Tariffs', *American Economic Review*, 1981, pp. 704–14.

DISCUSSION OPENING II – GUY DE VISSCHER

Regarding the paper by Ulrich Koester, there is little with which one can disagree. Economic theory is seen to have practical application but there are political inhibitions, which lead to a less than full exploitation of the potential benefits. Africa is not alone in suffering from this. The job now is to encourage the SADCC* countries to pursue the advantages more vigorously.

On page (101) it was pointed out that regional integration was easier to achieve than world-wide integration; but the effect may be less beneficial (to consumers).

Parity prices are referred to in Table 1; but I am not clear what exactly is meant – is it parity with *internal* prices or parity with *world* prices?

Towards the end of the paper the terms 'producer surplus' and 'consumer surplus' are used. Does this mean welfare satisfactions or what? To what does the 'surplus' refer?

I have five points to make on the paper by McCalla and Josling.

1. The simplicity of the presentation of the evaluation of the degree of agricultural integration implies that each country or group of countries can easily regain its place and determine the level of change needed to attain a future objective, fixed or not.

    Viewed in this way, the assertion on page 116 takes on a completely new meaning, as it assigns a secondary role to policy, i.e., agricultural policy. Nevertheless, from the previous paragraph one realises that the degree of change is a function of political choice. Should we see a contradiction in this, or does the author see an increasing role for policy as countries more towards the position illustrated in Case 9 of the diagram?

2. There is no doubt that agriculture is affected by exogenous constraints and that regional and international integration increase the economic risks to agriculture. The authorities are therefore bound to take measures to reduce the harmful effects of disasters, and this is precisely what the developed countries are increasingly doing, since food self-sufficiency is regarded as a vital factor for the rest of the economy. Should not therefore greater significance be attached in future to all development programmes especially when the economically strong countries propose to help the developing ones?

3. Even if the basic criteria for classifying countries can be determined so precisely, the speaker hesitates to classify, with a few exceptions, the states and their respective positions in the diagram. Should one conclude from this that few countries respond to all the constraints, or is the writer avoiding discussion of this subject? In this context the major question arises of whether the USA can be considered as a candidate for Case 9, when in terms of one of the basic elements, i.e., the opening up of its markets, the USA is characterised by the limited

*Southern African Development Coordination Conference

range of its imports (beef, milk, sugar, cereals ... etc.) and inversely, the EL is the largest importer of agricultural products.

4. On page 120, the last phrase of Section IV 'Agricultural policy instruments ... farm prices' contains so many implied elements that there appears to be, without any other definitions, a basic contradiction. Control of trade at frontiers clearly has as its objective to avoid macroeconomic impacts on agricultural prices.

5. Throughout the paper a basic feature has been left out, the cost of market integration. No country once it reaches a certain level of development can forget this item. It is probably the increasing costs of liberalising markets and ensuring a better level of integration which explains (page 121) the growing level of instability during the 1970s and 1980s.

    This is the economic phenomenon which governments need to tackle, particularly to know whether they want to move towards the right hand side of the diagram. But even if the replies were positive, certain factors, such as social factors, cannot be omitted from the integration process.

GENERAL DISCUSSION – RAPPORTEUR: P. ALASSANE SOW

Summary of the discussions following the presentations of Dr Ulrich Koester and of Dr Alex F. McCalla and Dr Timothy E. Josling.

Comments on Koester's paper
Unlike political commitments, three major causes have inhibited the success of agricultural integration among the Andean countries: (a) the products produced by the different countries are very similar; (b) none of the countries involved is self-sufficient; (c) the countries needed hard currencies to import necessary capital goods.

Regional integration may increase the degree of instability in world wide commodity markets. Regional co-operation among LDCs may be unfeasible when EEC countries dispose of large surpluses in agricultural goods.

Dr Koester replied, to comments from the floor, that the degree of protection among LDCs had increased largely due to the CAP of the EEC. This makes the political will of African countries in sub-Sahara very important for the implementation of economic integration. Furthermore, most of those countries are small. Their integration will not damage world-wide market commodities.

To the Opener's remarks he replied that parity prices were hypothetical prices. They were based on export and import prices. The consumer surplus was a concept borrowed from Welfare Economics.

Comments on McCalla and Josling's paper
Available evidence does not support the move from box 1 to box 9. As economic development proceeds, protection of agriculture is almost

inevitable. Also, the diagram does not suggest any identifiable situation beyond box 9.

The authors replied to comments from the floor that they did not argue that countries should move from box 1 to box 9. However, there were welfare gains associated with free trade although countries opened to world trade might incur costs associated with externalities flowing from other countries.

Beyond box 9 we reached a situation of 'world unification'.

To the opener's remarks they replied that although strong political forces (agricultural protection, etc.) might keep a country from moving west to east in the diagram, a country bears important budget costs when it avoids such a move.

One way of measuring the degree of protection of a country was to compare national wages with those prevailing in world markets. Domestic and world price differentials were also another indicator of the degree of protection.

Participants in the discussion included E. L. Casa, G. Schmitt, McColly, Jones, J. Berthelot, S. Tarditi, R. Saint-Louis and J. V. Remenyi.

GEORGE L. BRINKMAN

Farming Under Uncertainty in the 1980s: Some Lessons From Canada

INTRODUCTION

Farmers in Canada, like those throughout most countries of the world, have experienced rapidly changing financial conditions and growing uncertainties in recent years. Canadian farmers have been affected by international changes in interest rates, energy prices, trade relations, and exchange rates, as well as by domestic changes in inflation, credit, taxation, and commodity policies. Of particular importance to Canada is the relationship with the United States, Canada's major trading partner. Canadian prices for beef, pork, grains, oil-seeds, and (to a lesser extent) fruits and vegetables are largely established by the United States, with adjustments in Canada for exchange rate differentials. Dairy, chickens, turkeys, eggs and tobacco, on the other hand, are operated in Canada through supply management systems, restricting supply and establishing prices through cost of production formulae.

Internationally, the most significant impacts in the last ten years have occurred from rising energy prices and interest rates and changes in exchange rates. Canadian energy prices have been adjusting to international price levels in recent years and now are considerably higher than US prices. Interest rates, on the other hand, have followed the US in an attempt to maintain a positive capital account trade flow. Canadian exchange rates have strengthened against most international competitiors except the US, reducing Canada's competitivencss with those countries. Relative to the US, however, the Canadian exchange rate has fallen from about $.97 Can = $1.00 US in 1975 to a low of about $1.40 Can = $1.00 US in March 1985. This drop in exchange rates relative to the US has protected Canadian farmers somewhat from the extreme adjustments occurring in the US, but has not isolated them from these changes.

This paper examines the changes in Canadian agriculture arising from changes in financial conditions and growing uncertainties in the 1980s, and is organised into two parts. The first half of the paper provides an assessment of the changing financial environment in Canada, examining

127

changes in farm incomes, returns from changes in asset values, and the changing capital structure in Canadian agriculture. The second half of the paper examines how these changes affect farm organisation, management and the formulation of related agricultural policies. This final section will address lessons from Canada regarding farm survivability, farm finance, management of asset values, taxation, supply management and quota allocation, minimising long term capital costs, and involvement in the formulation of macroeconomic policies.

THE CHANGING FINANCIAL ENVIRONMENT FOR CANADIAN FARMERS

Farm Incomes
In Canada, the most recent era of high prosperity in agriculture began in 1973, when farm incomes nearly doubled in one year to over $3 billion in total. Since that time, farm incomes have been maintained roughly at the 1973–5 range of $3–4 billion each year, with the notable exception of 1981 when high incomes in the prairies pushed total incomes up to $4.7 billion level. In 1983 total income fell to only $2.7 billion, and is expected to remain around $3.2 billion for 1984 (Statistics Canada 1985).

In assessing incomes throughout this period four important considerations should be noted. First, despite the unusual increases in the prairies in 1981, the steady level of farm incomes across Canada in the last 12 years has meant that in real terms farm incomes actually have been falling. By 1984, the expected Canadian farm income of $3.2 billion in real terms now amounts to only about 83 per cent of the 1970 income and only about 34 per cent of the 1973 income. As a consequence, many farmers feel that agriculture has lost ground in recent years relative to the rest of the economy.

The second consideration involves income instability. Although aggregate incomes have stayed in a narrow range since 1973, individual farm incomes have shown great variations. Statistics Canada (1984) data over the 1967–82 period show that the average year-to-year variability of individual farmers was much greater than the variability of average provincial or Canadian net farm income, and that farmers as a group probably had the greatest variability in their incomes of any group of workers or small businessmen in Canada. Futhermore, farm income instability has actually increased in the latter years. Cash grain farmers are likely to be the group of farmers with the greatest variability because of their dependence on widely fluctuating international markets and exchange rates.

The third consideration that needs to be mentioned is that agriculture is a very heterogeneous industry with really no 'typical farm'. Although incomes worsened somewhat in the 1980s, all farmers have not been affected equally. Established producers, for example, generally have fared much better than new entrants and those making recent expansions. Producers of supply-managed commodities generally have received high returns, while beef producers in particular have experienced a long period of depressed prices and the possibility of significant decreases in demand. Even within similar sized operations, differences in management can make large differences in earnings. As a result, one must be very careful when relating industry aggregates or averages to any particular group or individual.

Finally it must be recognised that farm incomes are only one part of the returns to agriculture. Additional returns may come from changes in the value of assets (such as land and buildings and quotas), and from special taxation treatment provided to farmers. These considerations will be discussed in later sections of this paper.

During the rest of the 1980s, the Canadian farm income situation is likely to remain very weak under normal production conditions (barring a major war, drought, etc.). For grains, there now appear to be abundant supplies of both wheat and feedgrains throughout the world. World prices for these products in turn are heavily influenced by US production levels and grain policies. Grain prices throughout the rest of the 1980s therefore could remain weak if bumper or even good US grain crops were produced and no major catastrophes occurred in other major producing countries. Furthermore, the US has considerable excess capacity in diverted acreage and production capabilities in both coarse grain and wheat production, so that it could probably respond quickly to any single year shortfalls in other countries with increased production, preventing large-scale price recovery. In recent years, for example, the US has had the capacity to produce about 1 billion bushels of corn in excess of its normal domestic commercial and export uses. This excess capacity represents the equivalent of Canada's entire feed grain production and illustrates the kinds of pressures the feed grain sector could face in the rest of the decade.

US grain support programmes also affect Canadian prices. Of particular importance to Canada is the US loan rate for grains, which essentially represents the support price at which the US government will buy US grains from US farmers. Besides supporting US farmers, however, this support price also serves as a price floor for international prices, providing protection for Canadian farmers as well. In 1983 the loan rates for wheat, corn, and barley were dropped from $3.65 to $3.30 US, $2.65 to $2.55 and $2.16 to $2.08, respectively. Present international prices basically are being supported at these levels by the US loan rate. Current discussions (August 1985) are being directed at possibly even lower levels of loan rates for incorporation into the forthcoming 1985 US Farm Bill.

As a result of these conditions I see several years of tight financial conditions for grain farmers, with any improved income positions resulting from unforeseen natural disasters, etc. Substantial improvements may even require two years of crop failures to generate sizeable shortages. Given these conditions, grain incomes are also likely to remain very unstable.

On the livestock side, established producers of the supply-managed dairy and poultry commodities are likely to continue to prosper. Current quota prices, on the other hand, are now so high that they effectively 'eat up' all the operating profit of producing these commodities by new entrants and serve as very effective barriers to entry. In hog production, low grain prices are likely to encourage large buildups with resulting low pork prices over the next few years. Beef breeding herds are now in pretty good shape with herd reductions having occurred over several years in the US, even though slaughter is still up, due to liquidation of heifers. The large herd reductions, however, should improve prices over the next several years. Unfortunately, beef demand appears to have fallen in recent years, and still remains a problem. Some improvements in demand in the US may be occurring with their economic recovery and may help a little. On the other hand, increased pork and poultry production resulting from expansions in response to low grain prices could restrict the recovery for beef. As a result, only a moderate improvement in beef is forecast.

A further important consideration in livestock income is the recent reaction of the US to Canadian stabilisation for pork. The US International Trade Commission preliminarily ruled that Canadian stabilisation for pork production caused injury in the US even though Canadian studies (Martin and Goddard 1985) showed no appreciable supply response from the stabilisation programmes. The US Commerce Department finally imposed countervailing duties for hogs, but not for pork. The move by the US government to impose countervailing duties on hogs and other products is likely to increase uncertainties in trade in the future.

Changes in asset values
The second major influence on farm viability and survivability in the remainder of the 1980s will be changes in the value of farm assets, such as land and buildings and production quotas. Changes in asset values can be extremely important in generating wealth among established farmers, and building up (or reducing) their equity for use as financial reserves in difficult times. Changes in asset values also affect the cost of farm entry, and thereby the credit and potential cash flow requirements of beginning farmers.

In Canada, capital appreciation or depreciation has been largely ignored by farm groups in assessing the returns to agriculture and the viability of the sector. This is unfortunate because capital value changes can increase or decrease a farmer's wealth and total returns from agriculture by greater amounts than his current operating income. For example, real capital appreciation (adjusted for inflation) for Canada as a whole exceeded net farm operating income in four of the last six years of the 1970s (Brinkman 1981). In the 1980s the opposite has happened, with farmers losing more from declining land values than they earned from their operating incomes. In Canada, Statistics Canada (1985) indicates that land values fell between 1982 and 1983 by about 4 per cent. In nominal terms this represents a cumulative loss in farm wealth of about $4.2 billion. Inflationary losses would add another $6.7 billion, resulting in a total decrease of real (adjusted for inflation) farm wealth of about $10.9 billion. In 1983 Canadian farmers only earned about $2.7 billion in operating incomes, or about one-fourth of their losses in wealth. It will take many years of profitable farming to make up these losses, but large capital appreciation could recapture the losses in a single year.

It is unfortunate that farm organisations have not paid more attention to capital value changes in assessing the viability of farming. By ignoring capital value changes, farm organisations underestimate the viability of agriculture when capital appreciation is occurring (as in the 1970s) and greatly underestimate the severity of problems facing farmers when land values are falling. Many farmers cannot ignore falling land values even if they would want to, as banking institutions carefully consider falling equity and collateral values in their decisions to maintain or call in outstanding loans.

Changes in land values are influenced by the profitability of farming, non-farm demand for land, the cost of credit, and the expectations about future land value changes. In recent years, future expectations have played a very major role, as land has been purchased as a hedge against inflation by farmers and non-farmers alike. As such, land investments have taken on many of the characteristics of a growth stock, whereby the overall return to land is determined by both the current return and expected future changes in the value of the asset itself. During the 1970s land values continually increased beyond their capability to generate current returns. Between 1976 and 1979, the percentage rate of real capitalisation even increased while the percentage rate of return to capital was falling rapidly (Clark and Brinkman 1984), indicating a strong growth-stock speculative element. With the decreased profitability in the 1980s, land prices have fallen drastically as the decline in expectations about future returns (over a number of years) has been decapitalised into the present land price. As a result, land values in some areas have fallen much greater than the reduction in profitability because the expectations about future capital gains have also changed.

During the remainder of the 1980s land values are likely to remain relatively weak because of both the expected tight profitability position of grain farmers and the apparent change in future expectations about land values. Further large declines in land values across Canada are not too likely, although nominal land values could be maintained at their present level – causing real decreases each year. Price declines would be good news for new farmers, however, who would be faced with lower capital requirements and greater potential for capital appreciation in the future. Significant land value increases in the next few years, on the other hand, are also not very probable, meaning that farmers probably will not have this added return to supplement their operating incomes. This is a very important consideration, as research examining rates of returns in Ontario (Brinkman 1981) has identified capital appreciation to land as a very important component in generating comparable farm and nonfarm returns. Furthermore, constant or declining land values will not provide farmers with increased equity to help bail them out of difficulties in financing their farms, as occurred in the 1970s.

Capital Structure of Agriculture
The most significant change in the capital structure of Canadian agriculture in the last decade has been the tremendous increase in the value of capital employed on farms (Brinkman and Warley 1983). In nominal terms capital values of farm land and buildings, machinery and livestock increased from 1971 to 1981 by 441 per cent, representing an increase in real terms of 2.3 fold. Of the total capital value, land and buildings account for nearly 79 per cent. Overall this means that agriculture has become an extremely capital intensive industry. In the 1940s, for example, the ratio of capital to value added in agriculture was about 4 to 1. By the first half of the 1970s it had increased to about 8 to 1. In recent years the capital to value added ratio in agriculture has been about four times higher than in mining, about eight times higher than in manufacturing, and over 15 times higher than in construction and forestry (Brinkman 1981). The extremely high capital intensity makes agriculture very sensitive to changes in interest rates, inflation, and policies like credit and taxation affecting capital availability, use and transferability.

IMPLICATIONS FOR FARM ORGANIZATION, MANAGEMENT AND POLICY FORMULATION

Farm survivability
One important implication of the emerging financial environment in Canadian agriculture has been the effect of the changing financial structure of farms on farm survivability. Real incomes in the 1980s are likely to be lower than those in the 1970s, with net income decreasing as a percentage of gross income. Farm debt has been increasing at the same time, so that debt to income ratios may continue to rise from 3.7 in 1971 to 5.4 in 1982. With interest costs also rising from 5.5 per cent of operating expenses in 1960 to 18 per cent in 1981 and likely to remain in the 14 per cent range throughout the 1980s, farmers are now much more vulnerable to changes in prices, interest rates, and input costs, and therefore much more susceptible to financial failure.

In earlier times, farmers hit with low profitability have been able to survive by operating well below their short-run average total cost curves and still being able to meet their immediate cash flow requirements because they have held considerable reserves of earnings to family-provided resources (labour, management and equity) that could be drawn down to cope with short-run crises. In recent years, however, minimum cash-flow requirements have been increased substantially because of greater dependence on purchased inputs, greater debts, and higher debt costs (interest). These conditions have greatly reduced the resilience of farmers, and are particularly acute for new, commercial-sized operators with full-time commitments to farming. As our present generation of established farmers retires from agriculture in the coming decade, these tight survivability conditions will become more and more widespread. As a result, being a good producer will no longer ensure success in the 1980s. Farmers will need to focus more and more beyond the farm gate on both managing their farm finances and on marketing their products. These conditions may also increase the demand for non-farm work and part-time farming to generate non-farm earnings as security against cash-flow shortfalls. Presently we are emphasising the need for farmers to build equity instead of expanding, and consider any farm with less than 50 per cent equity as a potential survival risk.

Farm credit and finance
Credit is a very important part of the financial environment of farmers as it enables them to operate beyond the limitations of their own equity. In 1984 Canadian farmers had $20.7 billion in outstanding credit, with over $10 billion in new credit (short, intermediate, and long-term) taken out in 1984 alone (Statistics Canada 1985). Generally credit in Canada has been adequate, although some specific shortages have occurred. In recent years, many provincial programmes also have emerged to provide additional credit, often at subsidised rates. In comparison with the US, our credit system focuses more on beginning farmers and family-sized operations, with more effective limits than in the US to restrict funds to larger than family units.

In the remaining years of the 1980s, credit availability is not likely to emerge as a major financial limitation to Canadian agriculture. Most lending institutions have switched already from lending on the basis of equity to a more careful analysis of cash flow repayment capabilities, which may make some credit less available. This new emphasis is long overdue, however, and should help prevent new farmers from over extending themselves and getting into financial difficulties because of inadequate cash flows.

Pressures for subsidised credit programmes are also likely to increase in the coming years as financial pressures for farmers in difficulty mount. Subsidised credit programmes available to all farmers may provide short-term relief, but may also eventually become capitalised into higher land values which then serve as additional barriers to new farmers. Selective credit programmes available only to new farmers or to those in serious trouble, on the other hand, may still help these farmers without being capitalised so highly into land values, because the programme would not be available to established producers who want to expand. During the rest of the 1980s, interest rates may fluctuate somewhat, but the very high rates of the 1980–2 period hopefully will not reappear.

Unfortunately, the high capital requirements for Canadian farms are creating some difficulties, as they are making the family farm too expensive for the farm family. Traditionally, Canadians have focused on a system of farming with 100 per cent ownership of land. This system has worked well in the past, but investment costs are now causing a number of highly qualified new farmers to fail or stay out of agriculture simply because they cannot generate the cash flow to service the cost of full ownership. Some of the alternatives to full ownership under conventional credit arrangements that should be explored include better long-term leasing arrangements, variable and indexed farm mortgages, shared appreciation mortgages, equity financing through corporate shares, perpetual mortgages through interest payments only, and agri-development bonds with tax credits or exemptions on depositor interest.

Management of asset values

In the 1980s successful farm operators in Canada are likely to need to devote much more attention to asset value management, rather than emphasising exclusively farm production and even operating financial management. Probably the most useful consideration for asset management is the time of entry, as this determines more than anything else the potential for land value appreciation or depreciation. New farmers must critically evaluate entry or expansion on the basis of maintaining capital values rather than entering simply because they are ready. It makes little sense to work diligently to generate current income only to see asset values fall by similar or greater amounts from falling land prices or declines in other asset values. Other tools of asset management involve more diversification to avoid ending up with low salvage values for specialised assets committed to specific commodity production when the price of the commodity falls and relocation to take advantage of different land values (relative to productive capacity) in different regions.

Taxation

Taxation policies can have a significant impact on the financial environment of agriculture, although they often are not recognised as being as important as they are. Currently there are a number of Canadian taxation provisions available exclusively to agriculture or available to other Canadians but utilised more by farmers because of the particular conditions of farming. These provisions in the approximate order of impact on the financial and organisational structure of agriculture include:

1 Deferment of capital gains taxes on farm property transferred from parent to child;
2 Cash method of accounting;

3 Exclusion of first $500,000 capital gain and half of additional amount*
4 Business inclusion of the farm residence**;
5 Limitations on deductions of up to $5,000 against non-farm income by part-time farmers;
6 Investment tax credits**;
7 Optional inventory livestock valuation method;
8 Depreciation of half of the purchase costs of producer quotas;
9 Clearing and land improvement costs treated as current rather than capital expenses;
10 Income splitting;
11 Hiding the costs of income-in-kind from farm produced food;
12 Forward averaging* and 5-year block averaging provisions.

Overall these taxation provisions typically have

– lowered the incidence of taxes on farm related activities;
– increased the demand and prices for farm assets, especially land;
– promoted larger farms and expansion of existing units over new entrants;
– promoted owning over renting;
– promoted growth within farm families over new entrants from outside agriculture; and
– encouraged production decisions based on taxation benefits rather than market signals.

Although a few features of Canadian tax policy tend to distribute benefits relatively equally to large and small farmers (treatment of the principal residence for business purposes and the hiding of income-in-kind), taxation provisions generally are worth more to those with high incomes than low incomes and particularly to established producers over new entrants.

The impact of taxation policy on farm organisation and management in the remaining years of the 1980s is likely to continue to promote growth from established operations, concentration of land ownership, and entry into agriculture from within established farm families rather than from outside of the sector. Use of the cash method of accounting will continue to encourage livestock producers to expand (even when market signals would indicate contraction) to avoid paying taxes by purchasing more livestock to feed in order to offset their incomes. Tax credits on new machinery also will encourage over-capitalisation of machinery on farms, and provide established producers with a competitive advantage over new producers, who should be starting out with used instead of new machinery. Changes in taxation policy, on the other hand, could alter these impacts significantly.

*Available to all tax payers but utilised more by farmers.
**Available to self-employed businessmen only.

Supply management production systems
In Canada one of the responses to growing financial difficulties in agriculture in the 1970s was the creation of national supply management systems for chickens, eggs and turkeys to complement existing systems for dairy and tobacco. To restrict supply and thereby facilitate the establishment of higher prices these systems grant farmers production quotas, which become the permanent right of the farmer to use or sell. One of the most important lessons to be learned from Canada, particularly for those European countries considering establishing similar systems, is that these systems are not long-term solutions to low income problems. Without a doubt, these systems in Canada have provided very large benefits to the initial producers in both higher incomes and capital appreciation in quota values, thereby generating short and intermediate-run benefits. These benefits, on the other hand, have now become capitalised into the price of the quota which second generation new producers must buy to begin production of the commodity and thereby represent long-run costs. In the province of Ontario in 1984, for example, the quota costs alone for full-sized family units were $180,000 (dairy), $350,000 (turkeys), $400,000 (tobacco), $450,000 (broilers), and $750,000 (eggs) (Warley 1985). In dairy, our calculations show that the quota costs are so high that the return to milk production over variable feed costs, interest and depreciation on the cow and just the interest on the quota generates only about a $100 return per cow, allowing virtually no return to labour and capital invested in land, buildings and machinery. In other words, the only way a dairy farmer can now afford to purchase a quota at current prices is if he has increased his milk production per cow and requires no other additional barn space, milk handling capacity, machinery, land or labour. As a result of the high level of capitalisation in quotas, Canada is rapidly nearing the point in some of the supply management systems when no further adjustments will be profitable, both for new entry and expansion on existing farms.

Policy changes to minimise the long-run cost structure
From a policy standpoint there is an important need to shift the treatment of financial problems in Canada from short run crisis solutions to approaching farm finance, at least in part, from the standpoint of minimising the long-run cost structure and reducing the transfer of benefits out of the sector that were designed to help farmers. As identified in the previous section on supply management, programme benefits designed to help the financial position of farmers typically have simply been capitalised into fixed assets, which have become costs to the new producer and entailed higher future credit requirements. In many cases the selling farmer even ends up taking the capital out of agriculture, requiring that agriculture continually refinance itself out of retained earnings.

   In Canada too little attention has been devoted to the determinants of long-run capital structure and the capitalisation of programme benefits. The discussion on alternative financing methods in the section on Farm

Credit and Finance is an example of the potential for different impacts on long-term costs from different financial instruments. Considerable impact on long-run costs and farm financial viability also could be generated through different rules for quota allocation, transfer and use. For example, the costs of quotas could be greatly reduced, while still providing benefits to operating farmers, by requiring all quotas to be used or returned to the board (to avoid long-term quota leasing), allocating quota rights for fixed periods of production (say 20 years) instead of making them a permanent right, providing graduated entry programmes to new entrants, retaining final rights to the quota in the hands of the board of government and leasing out rather than selling the rights and restricting quota transfer and sale (together with provisions requiring that quotas be used or lost) for new marketing boards to insure that producers holding livestock in anticipation of the new board intended to use the quota for production rather than trying to get rich quick at the expense of other farmers by quickly selling off their new quota rights (Brinkman 1983).

More attention to macroeconomic policies
The final implication of the changing financial environment is that Canadian farmers (and probably all farmers world-wide) need to devote much more attention to macroeconomic policies affecting inflation, interest rates, exchange rates and taxation. Canadian farmers typically have good access to Ministries of Agriculture; but they have been very delinquent in approaching Ministries of Finance, Revenue and External Affairs about macroeconomic policies. This expanded involvement must be a high priority for agricultural producers and organisations in the rest of the 1980s, as changes in macroeconomic policies now can affect farmers more than their traditional commodity policies.

CONCLUSIONS

Without a doubt, the changing financial environment in Canadian agriculture will have a significant impact on farm organisation and management. It must be remembered, however, that despite the weakened financial environment, Canadian farmers as a group still remain in a relatively strong financial position. Overall Canadian farmers own nearly 82 per cent of their assets, and the average net equity of farms producing $2,500 or more gross sales in 1984 was $418,000 (Farm Credit Corporation 1984). Despite falling land values in some areas in recent years, farmers as a group still have, on average, more wealth than any other family-oriented wage or small business operation in Canada. Canadian farmers are some of the best in the entire world, and I am certain that they will be successful in meeting the challenges of the changing financial environment of the 1980s.

REFERENCES

Brinkman, G. L., 'Agricultural Economists and Long-Run Challenges Facing Agriculture', *Canadian Journal of Agricultural Economics*, 3 (1), 1983.

Brinkman, G. L., *Farm Incomes in Canada*, Economic Council of Canada, Supply and Services, Ottawa, 1981.

Brinkman, G. L. and Warley, T. K. *Structural Change in Canadian Agriculture: A Perspective*, Agriculture Canada, Regional Development Branch, Development Policy Directorate, June 1983.

Clark, J. H. and Brinkman, G. L., *Capitalization of Agricultural Land*, Report submitted to Agriculture Canada, August 1984.

Farm Credit Corporation, Canada, *Farm Survey*, Ottawa, 1984.

Martin, L. J. and Goddard, E. W., *The Effects of Canadian Government Payments to Hog Growers on the Canadian Pork Packing Industry*, Report submitted to the US Commerce Dept., February 1985.

Statistics Canada, *Farm Net Income Reference Book*, May 1985.

Statistics Canada, unpublished tax filer data on income instability, 1985.

Warley, T. K., *Canada's Agricultural and Food Trade Policies: A Synoptic View*, S.A.E.E. Working Paper, University of Guelph, 1985.

JÓZEF ST ŽEGAR

Peasant Farms in Economic and Social Crisis: The Case of Poland in the 1980s

INTRODUCTION

Sudden changes of the external conditions which determine the decisions in farm management always exert an impact on the functioning and the behaviour of peasant farms. The economy of the latter is characterised by an important potential to bring into play specific mechanisms and/or processes of adjustment in the respective situations. This has been confirmed by substantial scientific research, performed for many years now, concerning the adjustment of peasant farms to major disturbances of a different nature, such as wars, economic crises and natural disasters. Particular cases of adjustment to such disturbances are of interest to researchers. As one such case one may recognise the adjustment processes of peasant farmers in Poland in the situation of the dramatic and extensive economic and social crisis in Poland in the beginning of the 1980s. The particular nature of this case appears to be determined principally by the fact that it concerns the conditions of a centrally planned economy, which has at its disposal an extensive array of instruments permitting steering of economic processes, including instruments which pertain to the relatively autonomous social and economic system of peasant farming. We are thus interested not only in the evaluation of the adjustment processes taking place in the peasant economy as such but also in an assessment of the effectiveness of actions taken by the Government for the former's possible correction. It is obvious at this point that an assessment of such phenomena must take into consideration the particular economic and social situation in the national economy as a whole.

THE SCALE OF THE CRISIS

The scale and graveness of the economic crisis in Poland is witnessed by the drop in the volume of the national income (in the Material Product System) in the 1981–2 period, compared to the pre-crisis level of 1978, of about one-fourth, an analogical decrease in industrial production of about 10 per cent and a decrease in the volume of the total agricultural production of almost 10 per cent. The turning point of the decreasing tendencies took place in 1983. Nevertheless by the end of 1984 the national income created was still 15 per cent lower than the 1978 figure, while the national income distributed was almost 20 per cent lower. The total agricultural production of peasant farming by the end of 1984 was about 8 per cent lower compared to 1978, while industrial production regained its 1978 level.

The economic crisis in the years 1980–82 was without doubt aggravated by the concurrent social crisis and the phenomena accompanying it, such as strikes, a falling labour productivity, a deterioration of product quality etc. An important factor contributing to the crisis situation and making the recovery difficult, without any doubt, were the restrictions imposed on granting of credit and economic relations with Poland on the part of some countries for political considerations.

As an effect of the phenomena enumerated above, the possibilities of foreign trade, both on the export and the import side, were heavily constrained. The volume of imports which in 1980 dropped by 3.1 per cent compared with 1978, by 1982 dropped by 31.5 per cent. In 1983 it increased by 5.2 per cent and in 1984 by 9.0 per cent but remained nevertheless 20.3 per cent below the 1978 pre-crisis level. The drop in exports was smaller. In 1980 the volume of exports was 4.2 per cent lower compared with 1978, while in 1981 it dropped by 19 per cent compared to the previous year. In the next two years exports grew at the average rate of about 9.0 per cent.

When steering the economy out of the crisis the government chose a strategy of protecting consumption by the population at the expense of economic growth. The real/deflated level of consumption in 1984 was about 6 per cent lower than in 1978 and almost 11 per cent lower when compared with the 1980 level. This took place in line with a decrease in the share of accumulation in the national income distributed from 40 per cent in 1978 to 25.6 per cent in 1980 and approximately 21.5 per cent in the years 1982–4.

THE CRISIS AND PEASANT FARMING

The general crisis experienced by the national economy strengthened the impact of factors of a structural nature causing stagnation of production in peasant farming. This refers first of all to the backward agrarian structure, the average area of a peasant farm being approximately 5.7 hectares but it also exposed the inadequate support which peasant farming is receiving from the non-farming sectors of the national economy, in particular from the industrial branches.

The impact of the general crisis on peasant farming found expression principally in the following areas:

    1. The supply of production inputs for farming, both produced by the domestic industry and imported, dropped sharply. Particularly acute was the decrease in the volume of supply of concentrate

feedstuffs and mineral fertilizers and crop protection chemicals, of spare parts for tractors and agricultural machinery and of numerous farming tools. Thus, for example, the supply/sales of concentrate feedstuffs decreased from 4.4 m tons – this being the average level in the 1976–9 period, to 4.2 m tons in 1980 and 2.2 m tons in 1983, which means a drop of one half. One remarks at this point that these concentrate feedstuffs constituted in the second half of the 1970s approximately one-third of the total amount of concentrate feedstuffs used in peasant farms (Table 1).

2. A deterioration in the supply of both industrial origin durable goods and food products for the agricultural population. The decreasing industrial production constrained heavily the access of

Table 1   Selected statistics on peasant farms in Poland, 1978–1983

Item		1978	1980	1981	1982	1983
Total agricultural production[a]	%	115.0	100.0	106.9	105.0	107.6
Material inputs[a]	%	107.6	100.0	105.2	100.5	100.0
Production added[a]	%	127.7	100.0	109.5	111.6	118.6
Real incomes[a]	%	114.7	100.0	142.0	104.8	98.4
in this earmarked for:						
consumption		103.8	100.0	121.0	101.6	88.5
non-productive investment		100.8	100.0	92.3	85.0	97.5
productive investment		93.2	100.0	116.6	98.4	112.5
Share of crop production in total agricultural production	%	51.0	47.2	53.8	53.2	54.6
Number of cattle per 100 ha of agricultural land		67.0	65.2	62.0	64.3	64.6
in this milk cows		36.6	36.1	35.2	35.4	35.0
Number of swine per 100 ha of agricultural land		108.5	108.2	96.0	102.2	77.6
Yields in tons per hectare:						
Wheat, rye, barley and oats		2.63	2.31	2.50	2.52	2.62
potatoes		19.7	11.3	19.0	14.7	15.7
Sales of concentrate feedstuffs from state resources	m ton	4.9	4.2	3.9	2.0	2.2
Application of fertilizers per hectare of agricultural area	kg of NPK	152	152	156	152	138
Intermediate use of farm products as a percentage of the total production		37.4	40.2	37.7	37.5	36.0
Consumption by the farm family as a percentage of final production		19.5	23.0	20.0	22.3	20.8
Share of sales on the peasant market in the realization of the total production marketed	%	10.5	13.7	18.7	18.6	16.1

[a]Calculated on the basis of 1982 prices.
Source: *Statistical Yearbooks*, published by the Polish Central Statistical Office (Glówny Urzad Statystyczny).

the farm/rural population to these goods. This resulted in a weakening of the economic motivations of producers and also caused a reverse in the secular trend towards limiting the autarky of peasant farms.

3. The disequilibrium on the market in general was further aggravated, this concerning as well the food products market, which resulted in the introduction by the Government of a system of rationing of numerous food products, such as meat, butter, sugar, oil and fats, and cereal products (but not bread). This caused an increased importance of trade on the free private markets. As the peasant population did not receive allotments of meat within the national rationing system, the effect was that the self-supply with meat for consumption increased in importance for the peasant population.

4. The process of inflationary changes taking place in the whole national economy was transferred to the farming sector through the prices of commodities and services purchased by farmers. The index of prices' growth in 1984 compared to 1978 was 375 per cent, while the price index of agricultural products was 340 per cent.

5. The manifestations of crisis both of an economic nature (such as perturbations on the food market) or of a social nature (social emotions in industrial plants) resulted in a more positive evaluation of farming as a mode of work and profession and this was true of the assessment by the farmers themselves. It is without doubt that the farmers felt less endangered by the manifestations of the crisis than the other groups of the society.

The crisis phenomena in agriculture were strongly aggravated by the particularly poor crops of 1980, a drop of production being experienced by all the major crops – grains, root crops, oil crops, hay. Poor crops, but on a smaller scale, were also experienced in 1982, principally root crops.

THE ADJUSTMENT OF PEASANT FARMING TO THE NEW PRODUCTION AND ECONOMIC CONDITIONS

In the assessment of the adjustment processes of peasant farming one should also take into consideration the decisions taken by the Government concerning this group of producers. Of particular importance here is the assumption of the rule of income parity. This began changes of prices in favour of farming, as an effect of which the index of the price scissors in the years 1980–1 was respectively 107.8 and 131.0 per cent but consequently as result of the general reform of prices in 1982 dropped to 70.3 per cent, 95.0 per cent in 1983 and 97.2 per cent in 1984. The income parity, favourable for farming in the years 1981–2, began to deteriorate in 1983.

We are stressing these changes in prices since in effect they were an obstacle to pro-productivity changes and adjustment processes in the peasant economy, such as may be expected in the conditions of maintaining a disparity of incomes unfavourable for the peasant population.

An analysis of the development of peasant farming in the years 1978–84 confirms the thesis that in periods of threat, peasant farms aim at maintaining, or relatively minimising the drop in the consumption level achieved formerly. This is true of farms in all area groups since the indexes of change of consumption are quite identical[1], while the indexes of change of incomes are more favourable for the groups of farms of bigger area. 'In defence' of the consumption level the peasant farms have manifested significant activity and started a number of mechanisms alleviating the impacts of deteriorating external conditions. We will turn our attention to the more important of these.

In the 1970s the production composition of peasant farming was artificially shaped through the considerable imports of grains and feeds. The drastic reduction of these imports disturbed these relations. Farms were forced to develop a new system of relations of production and balances. In order to achieve this, on one hand the livestock numbers were reduced, particularly that of swine and poultry, on the other, the production of grains was increased. One remarks at this point, that small farms reduced their livestock numbers more than the bigger farms, while the latter increased more the production of grains. In this respect the adjustment mechanisms in the scale of agriculture as a whole acted as expected, resulting in flows of grains between groups of farms. In contrast to swine stock numbers, cow numbers were rather stable. The breeding of cows is relatively little dependent on the supply of concentrate feedstuffs and moreover the purchase prices offered for milk were favourable[2]. In the composition of total crop production the share of products earmarked for intermediate use on the farms themselves increased from about 51 per cent in the 1976–9 period to as much as 71 per cent in 1980, to decrease to about 55 per cent in the following years. At the same time sales, particularly of grains, dropped by about one-half, when comparing 1981 with the average for the years 1976–9. It was the group of small farms which reduced the sales of grains the most, since livestock production was of the greatest importance for these considering the accruing incomes. In the years 1983–4 the sales of grains increased significantly, principally as result of relatively good crops but also due to price preferences in the procurements policy.

The disequilibrium on the agricultural and the food products markets resulted in a growth of prices in the peasant market places and a resultant growing volume of turnover there. These peasant market prices in the years 1980–2 were considerably higher than the official procurement prices, e.g. the prices of wheat and rye were 70 to 100 per cent higher, slaughter calves 25 to 30 per cent higher, and the prices of slaughter swine 20 to 50 per cent higher. In 1983 this difference was reduced with a tendency to return to the relationships of the second half of the 1970s. The demand for grains on the private peasant market was created principally by the group of small farms and by the landless breeders of livestock. The supply of grains was increased on the other hand by the farms with a bigger area. The demand for meat on the peasant market was created mainly by the better-off groups of the non-agricultural population for which the allotments of meat products within the rationing system were insufficient.

The agricultural population, in protecting its own consumption increased the natural consumption of products from its own farm. This was true particularly of meat as this population group did not receive allotments of it within the rationing system. Thus the situation was that the non-agricultural population decreased consumption of meat by over 10 kg per caput, while the peasant population increased its consumption by almost 10 kg. The increment of meat consumption was almost identical for farms in all the area groups. At present the consumption of meat on farms with a bigger area, i.e. 10 hectares and over, is about 10 kg higher than the national average.

The peasant farms in defending their level of consumption skilfully manoeuvred the accumulation fund which became a residual position shaped by the changing incomes and the relatively stable consumption. Nevertheless in the group of farms, stronger economically in which the dilemma of consumption versus accumulation (and investment) was not so acute, as well as in the farms with a smaller area and weaker economically, the orientation towards investment, and thus securing further incomes, was strong. An important constraint in this respect without doubt was the insufficient supply of investment goods.

CONCLUSION

1. Polish agriculture has been characterised for many years now by inadequate productivity and income creation. This has its source both in factors of a structural nature, i.e. a backward agrarian structure, poor links between agriculture and the industrial sector, but also in the State's economic policy, which consisted among other things of maintaining relatively low prices for food products and insufficient efforts to reduce the social costs of production. The crisis of the 1980s only strengthened these problems.
2. The impacts of the crisis are transferred to agriculture with some delay. The point is not so much in the supply of agriculture with production inputs but rather in the limited potential for structural transformations within the national economy as a whole, which will not favour structural change, including pro-productivity changes in farming. This is all the more important since we face not a situation of overproduction in Polish farming but quite the contrary. Further development of agriculture is closely dependent on the progress made in the non-agricultural branches of the economy, e.g. material inputs supply, transfer of labour, economic relations.
3. Peasant farming has manifested a considerable capacity for

adjustments to rapid changes in its economic environment. This capacity however concerned only the protection of its economic interests through self-defence mechanisms and the achievement within a short period of a new system of production as well as a skilful employment of the varied production characteristics of farms and the considerable level of self-supply both for production and for consumption purposes. Some symptoms were observed of adjustment of a long-term nature, particularly in farms with a bigger area.

4. The policy of the State, taking into consideration the social and the political aspects, was at times recognised as being too 'nervous', this being expressed for instance in rapid price changes, not linked with material and financial supply. This did not accelerate the processes of adjustment, neither in the short nor in the long term. One may expect change in this respect since this 'protective' policy by the State can no longer be continued. It will not however be possible, on the other hand, to return to a policy which would assume a considerable income disparity between the principal population groups.

5. Income parity will not be possible to maintain in the future without major transformations of peasant farming. Three directions of these transformations, linked to each other, appear justified, these being:
    (a) an acceleration of the transformations of the agrarian structure;
    (b) better equipment of peasant farms with advanced techniques;
    (c) more rapid technological progress in farming, utilising the achievements of biotechnology, organic farming, etc.

NOTES

[1]This observation is confirmed by data from a sample of about 2000 peasant farms performing voluntary agricultural bookkeeping for the Institute of Agricultural and Food economics. These farms were analysed according to 5 area groups, these being (in hectares): 1 to 3; 3 to 7; 7 to 10; 10 to 15 and 15 and over.

[2]An important consideration when introducing the relatively high increases of the procurement prices of milk was the aim to secure for the population a cheap, subsidised source of animal protein in a situation of reduced meat consumption.

DISCUSSION OPENING – DUŠAN TOMIĆ

Our colleagues George Brinkman and Józef Żegar have, in fact, dealt with a similar topic – 'Some Lessons of the 1980s', from Canada and Poland respectively. Although the topic of these two reports is similar, there is a qualitative difference between the agricultures of the two countries.

In Canada there is a great deal of land per inhabitant, and great, modern agricultural commodity production is dominating, as well as firm orientation to the export of food products. But, in Poland, there are small individual properties as well as large socialist holdings, an unsatisfactory supply of agricultural products, a considerable import of food, and a slow process of development of socialistic social-economic relations in the agriculture and in the villages.

Both reports analyse in an interesting way the situation and problems of the two countries in the 1980s. They have in common a short-term approach to some agricultural problems. There is, however, a question whether the critical situations can be solved by short-term actions. What agriculture really needs is a longer-term treatment.

The report of George Brinkman shows that the agriculture of Canada, highly intensified by capital, is not resistant to increasing uncertainty in development and disposal of agricultural production and to the changes in financial economic conditions.

In connection with this report, I would like to present two questions:

The first is concerned with the optimistic conclusion that Canadian farmers have great financial power and that they are among the best in the world. But analysis shows that Canadian agriculture is losing its material base and fails to keep pace with the rest of the economy. This is shown by the great variation of agricultural income, the considerable loss in the farmers' wealth (the capital value of a farm is declining) and by a weakening of the financial power of some more important lines such as wheat production. There is the question of whether the weakness of Canadian agriculture is growing in regard to future instability, if the trend of uncertainty and insecurity persists, connected with some other factors and negative climate conditions, if technological progress fails to make up for a slow increase of productivity and if the profitability of current production is endangered by high costs of expanded production.

The second question is concerned with the lessons. In the report only a short-term approach was used, so there the right lessons were not learned. I agree that credit policy, tax policy, organisation of the production management etc., are important elements of agro-economic policy, but the right solutions cannot be found there. In my opinion the main point should be the function of agriculture in the process of social reproduction. For the right solutions of the critical situations we need complex and long-term agro-economic policy. Accordingly, I believe there is a question about the following strategic lessons: (a) the future of Canadian agriculture and the long-term aims of its development; (b) offensive or restrictive agro-economic policy; (c) the efficiency of the production system and the development of primary agricultural production per unit of all inputs; (d) long-term settlement of social expenses of agricultural production; (e) the excessive industrialisation of agriculture and problems of it being provided with more capital than is really needed; (f) the economic position of agriculture and the economic relations between agriculture, manufacturing, trade and sale of agricultural food products; and (g) world food policy and the export orientation of Canadian agriculture, and its contribution to the world market.

In the second paper, Józef St Žegar discusses the dimensions of the crisis of the 1980s in the individual peasant farms in Poland. The situation is specific there because they deal with a poorly developed small farms agriculture, which is now in the process of socialistic transformation. The general crisis in Poland is reflected very much in the agricultural situation in the country, as shown by the decrease of agricultural production and by farmers' discontent.

The paper deals with the crisis manifestations and agricultural disproportions using certain quantitative indicators. In spite of good climatic conditions in the last few years, a previous level of agricultural production and income has not yet been achieved. Analysis established the facts that bigger peasant farms adapted better to the crisis and that farmers had a better standard of feeding than other citizens.

In connection with the conclusions in this report, I would like to bring out two comments:

First, very slow structural transformation, low productivity and unsatisfactory generation of income are mentioned as the main causes of the agricultural crisis. But, in my opinion, one of the main causes of the crises is a wrong state agro-economic policy, which underestimated agriculture, so that the process of social-economic transformation is treated narrowly and partially. On one side they have carried out the policy of high standards of food consumption, especially of meat, and on the other they have completely neglected farmers and agriculture. It is the state policy which has serious weaknesses, because it has never followed, directed and improved the process of adaptation of agriculture to the new circumstances of development and to the needs of the Polish economy and society as a whole. So there is the question about formation and working out of the complex and long-term agro-economic policy of the social-economic transformation of Polish agriculture.

The second comment is that in the report there are no appropriate lessons to be learned for the present and the future of agriculture. Also, the problems are treated from the peasant farms' point of view, not from the general. In my opinion, important strategic lessons should serve as an example for what is to be done for agriculture to function more efficiently in the process of social reproduction and to be an important support in the building of socialism. The important strategic lessons should be concerned with the following complexes: (a) the strategy of long-term development of Poland and the position of agriculture; (b) the complex model of social-economic transformation of agriculture and the strategy of development of the agricultural state and private sector; (c) social-economic position and the organising of farmers on the basis of self-management (a farmer should be treated as a permanent support and an active subject of agriculture and co-operation with the social sector of the agriculture); (d) a differential approach to the types of peasant farms involving better stimulating of the development of agricultural production in small farms and farmyards; (e) the real aggregate demand for agricultural food products and long-term production orientation of agriculture; (f) establishing balance and inter-dependence between the structure of agricultural production and the structure of consumption of agricultural food products; (g) the increase of plant production is the main problem, because it is the condition of cattle breeding; (h) the formation of an efficient agro-industrial complex on an economic basis between agriculture, industry, manufacturing, trade, sale and consumption of food products; (i) greater contribution of science to the direction of the developing process and social-economic changes in agriculture; and (j) public opinion and the citizens of Poland should have more understanding of agriculture, because it is a biological production which gives results after a long time period. Agriculture should be all society's concern.

GENERAL DISCUSSION – RAPPORTEUR: EIVIND ELSTRAND

It was stated from the floor that overproduction can cause severe problems for farmers and in particular, as in Finland, for young farmers who have high indebtedness and problems of liquidity. At an earlier date these problems might have been solved by an expansion of production, but now this solution is not possible because of the existence of individual production quotas. So far as Poland was concerned, it was felt that the problems of the private farms had been underestimated by the policy markers and that the private farms would be able to increase output if they received the necessary support.

Another speaker stated that in Poland agricultural production in 1984 was 4 per cent higher than before the crisis, while in the non-agricultural sectors it was 14 per cent lower. In a centrally planned economy the answer to the problem of how to avoid a crisis situation in agriculture is clear in principle but in practice one must be more pessimistic.

One speaker felt that more attention should be given to the economic aspects of increased productivity – not simply the technical aspects – and that advisory services should be trained to help here. This was particularly important at a time of surpluses and at both the micro and macro level.

Józef St Žegar restricted his reply to two areas. Firstly, he fully shared the opinion of Professor Tomic that one of the most important reasons for the unsatisfactory performance of Polish agriculture was the neglect of the role of the food sector in the total national economy. It was true that, on the whole, post-war economic policy was not oriented towards agricultural development, in spite of official declarations. In crisis conditions it became quite obvious how important was the role of agriculture. Despite this, however, the process of reorientation of the national economy, particularly the input industry, towards agriculture and food economy is encountering many obstacles both of a technical and a management nature.

Secondly, he could not fully agree with the opinion of Professor Westermarck that the main reason for the agricultural crisis was that the agrarian policy supported too strongly the socialised sector at the cost of the private one. It is true that the needs of the private sector were not always fully appreciated; but one cannot limit the reasons to unsatisfactory aid allocation. The development of agriculture is determined by a whole set of factors: social, natural, technical, political and so on. It is very difficult to select the role.

George L. Brinkman replied to the various points and questions as follows:

What do you mean by equity? – Equity is the difference between the value of assets measured at current market value and liabilities. Equity represents net worth.

What is meant by quota costs? – Since quotas can be bought and sold between farmers in Canada, quota costs represent the amount a farmer must pay to buy the quota from another farmer. Quotas were allocated free to the producers of a commodity when the supply management systems. were first developed, but now farmers wishing to start up or increase their production of quota commodities must buy the quota rights from other producers.

What alternative financing mechanisms, including leasing, are available to help improve farm survivability? – In Canada we have studied a large number of different financing mechanisms both to improve the stability of payment and to increase access to more and/or cheaper credit. Leasing is one alternative that holds promise for better financial solvency. Part-owning and part-leasing is growing faster than either full ownership or full tenancy. Better long-term leasing arrangements will need to be developed, however, for leasing to become the dominant form. It should also be noted that the recent tax provision for exemption of the first $500,000 of capital gain per person from tax could provide some new opportunities for equity financing in agriculture. This tax provision could result in development funds being organised to own farm land for the tax free capital gains returns to the investors and thereby providing either leasing or joint ownership of farm land to farmers.

How can increased productivity at the micro level be reconciled with increasing supplies and decreasing prices at the macro level? – In Canada we face an export demand curve from many of our products that is much more elastic than our domestic demand curve. Furthermore U.S. supply and demand conditions essentially determine prices for beef, hogs, grains, oilseeds and, to some extent, fruits and vegetables. As a result, most of the benefits of research and increased productivity are passed on to the producer rather than the consumer. Agricultural research is therefore one of the most effective assistance measures to Canadian farmers that we can provide.

Have you included in your analysis possible changes to the forthcoming 1985 US farm bill? – US policies are very influential in affecting Canadian farmers because the US loan rate, in particular, serves as an international price floor for crop prices. The 1985 farm bill is not yet completed, but reductions in the loan rate are likely to cause further decreases in international grain prices and worsen conditions further for Canadian producers.

Participants in the discussion included: Estaback, B. F. Stanton, P. A. Power, Rafschneider and N. Westermarck.

Q. B. O. ANTHONIO AND V. O. AKINYOSOYE

The Changing Structure of Nigeria's Agriculture and Prospects for the River Basin Development Reorganisation Programme*

This paper is concerned with the changing structure of Nigeria's agriculture brought about by a reorganisation programme set in motion in the 1970s to improve the deplorable performance of all the participants in the agricultural sector of the nation's economy. This was particularly critical throughout the 1970s in the food subsector where there was a perceptible market disequilibrium which can aptly be described as a situation of permanent excess demand; a market condition in which there was a constant under-production of all major catogories of food items in the country. The food crisis though noticeable before the Nigerian Civil War years (1967–70) as indicated by Anthonio in 1967[1] appeared to have worsened after the Civil War ended in 1970 (Akinyosoye 1984). And some of the unpleasant consequences of the food crisis included large importation of food, (₦1,020.7 million in 1978) soaring food prices which contributed to the high cost of living and stagflation with consequent falls in nutrient intake both in the rural and urban centres.

To solve this crisis, the Nigerian Government initiated the Green Revolution Programme (GRP) late in the 1970s (Idachaba 1980), and adopted the River Basin Development (RBD) approach to achieving its goals. A critical examination and evaluation of the prospects of the reorganisation programme introduced into rural farming communities through the numerous River Basin agricultural projects is the main focus of this paper and some suggestions are made on the future operational strategies needed to make the reorganisation programme contribute more effectively to increased agricultural production in general and food production in particular.

THE GREEN REVOLUTION PROGRAMME (GRP) AND NIGERIA'S RIVER BASIN DEVELOPMENT AUTHORITIES

The GRP was initiated in 1979 as a comprehensive development programme designed to revolutionise not only agricultural production by boosting the production of Nigeria's food and export tree crops, but also

*Paper presented by F. J. Idachaba.

improve life generally in the rural areas of the country. The cardinal goals of the Federal Government of Nigeria in initiating the GRP was the attainment of self-sufficiency in food within the shortest possible time; production of enough livestock products for the domestic and export markets; and the revival of the declining trend in the production of traditional export crops, such as cocoa, oilseeds, rubber, cotton and coffee.

Several policy actions were contemplated and initiated[2] at achieving the goals of the GRP but the most significant, in terms of scope and financial commitment, was the programme that involved harnessing the waters of Nigeria's river basins for food production.

Historically, the river basin development concept had been accepted in Nigeria since 1962 when in the first post-independence National Development Plan (1962–8), a substantial amount of money was allocated to some irrigation projects in the Northern part of the country.[3] At the planning stage of the second National Development Plan (1970–4), planners having grasped a better understanding of the concept of river basin development broadened the scope of the existing river basin schemes to include not only irrigation projects but fishing projects, hydro-electricity generating facilities, flood-control schemes and improved navigational facilities. And in 1976 with the recognition that a more comprehensive regional approach to integrated development within the framework of the existing 19 States was necessary for the economic wellbeing of the Federation, the then Federal Military Government resorted wholly to the river basins development concept and promulgated the River Basins Development Authorities Decree No. 25 of 15 June 1976[4] which led to the establishment of 10 statutory bodies to manage Nigeria's River Basins. The eleventh body was added in 1979.

The 11 RBDs have increased to 18 since the beginning of the 'life' of the present Military administration[5] with one RBDA in each state except for Lagos and Ogun States which jointly have one and are now called River Basins and Rural Development Authorities (RBRDAs).

The River Basins are charged with specific functions as stipulated in the decrees establishing them. This paper is however limited to those aspects of the River Basins' operations connected with structural changes introduced into the Nigerian farm industry.

The main activities planned for change in the farm industry include:

(i)   Building of large dams and provision of water from reservoirs and lakes for irrigation to farmers and farmers' recognised associations, thereby supplementing rain-fed agriculture with irrigation agriculture to minimise uncertainties in crop production and output supply;

(ii) Selection of participating farmers and allocating farm lands in economic sizes (3–4 ha) to each of them, thus increasing the average size of farm holding;

(iii)   Undertaking mechanical clearing and cultivation of land as well as power-assisted harvesting operations thus changing from labour intensive agriculture to a relatively capital intensive agriculture;

(iv)   The timely provision of all forms of non-conventional inputs – fertilizers, pesticides, herbicides and fungicides and improved planting materials, thus changing the industry from a traditional one to a more modern one;

(v)   The provision of an institutional mechanism at each River Basin agricultural project site in form of a continuous physical presence of River Basin operatives including agriculturists, engineers and administrators to provide timely assistance to participating farmers, thus ensuring an improved performance.

(vi)   Equal access to farmland and other productive assets, farm inputs, credit and so on, thus improving the opportunities of those wanting to go into commercial agriculture.

(vii)   Encouragement of farmer co-operatives for joint produce harvesting and processing to ensure that more benefits accrue to rural farmers and to enhance their market power.

(viii)   Encouragement of farmers' representation in some decision-making bodies (e.g. choice of participating farmers) on project sites as a prelude to future active participation of all in the progress of each local community in which RBRDA projects are located, thus giving farmers some degree of 'political' power.

With the foregoing review of the structural changes introduced in the country's farm industry by the River Basins, one is tempted to believe that Nigeria as a whole stands to gain both in the short run and the long run from the huge financial investments on all the established RBRDA projects. From observations during a recent study however, (Akinyosoye 1984), it is doubtful if the country can achieve much from the River Basins if the approach currently adopted is not drastically reviewed and modified. The reasons for associating the future prospects of the River Basins' attempts at changing the structure of the country's farm industry with some degree of uncertainty are now discussed:

Confused objective
The 1979 Act which established the RBDAs was explicit on the statutory functions of the River Basins but failed to assign to them the responsibility of being directly involved in food production. This apparent oversight was indeed deliberate in view of the then existing constitutional arrangement which limited the role of the Federal Government to agricultural research, co-ordination, and external relations, while the state governments had the residual powers including the responsibilities for food production. Some over-zealous River Basins, however, are presently actively involved in food crop and

poultry production. Confused objectives and bureaucratic decision-making contributed significantly to the failure of previous agricultural reorganisation schemes in Nigeria (Oluwansanmi 1966; Olatunbosun, 1971).

Input distribution
At present the River Basins supply all forms of non-conventional inputs to participating farmers; and these are supplied at subsidised prices. The input delivery role of the River Basins has parallels in some state and other federal agencies. The implication of this parallelism in roles is that without a well co-ordinated arrangement, such input delivery system may lead to input trafficking because of varying subsidy rates and inefficiency in input delivery and clearly duplicate efforts and waste resources in an area more effectively handled by the state extension services.

Inappropriate out-growers support
The River Basins are involved directly in almost all farm activities; from land preparation to post-maturity activities such as processing, storage and sales in varying degree. The support in the form of labour, machinery and chemicals is usually priced at rates far below costs to the Basin and well below market prices. From all indications the River Basins' involvements in farm activities seem excessive and may have some unpleasant consequences in the future. Some of these problems are as follows:

(a) There is the danger that farmers may develop a *dependency syndrome* whereby they paradoxically come to regard such River Basin's involvement as a permanent feature of their activities and find it difficult to withdraw from the involvement at a later date;

(b) This level of assistance is obviously a shield against real-life situations in the farm industry and may be protecting marginal and inefficient farmers;

(c) Since the Basins cannot embrace all farmers, their level of activities is biased against non-participating farmers and will lead to greater income inequalities in rural areas; a basic regation of one of the cardinal principles of integrated rural development;

(d) Any level of farmer involvement is expensive, wasteful and clearly not sustainable in the future, with expanding scope of the activities of the River Basins due to larger numbers of participating farmers;

(e) Most of the participating farmers have no legal rights of ownership to the land they are farming. Consequently, the River Basin subsidies will be capitalised into quasi-rent for the next generation and inhibit future investment. The increase in land values will further inhibit farm investment and returns, degenerating into a misappropriation syndrome the Basins cannot afford;

(f) Finally, the level of involvement, and the input price subsidy scheme attached will as a rule 'disturb' private sector participation; consequently, the usual attitude to work that goes with public institutions will ruin a well conceived but badly managed pro-gramme.

'Economies of scale'
The planners of the River Basins irrigation schemes seem to have implicit faith in 'economies of scale', hence the size of all the irrigation schemes at present in full operation (Bakalori in Sokoto, Rima River Basin, Tiga in Hadeja, Jamaiare, and Cyan in Ogun-Oshun River Basin, to mention a few). Such large irrigation schemes require for their effectiveness an abundance of materials, spare parts, high level manpower, reliable communication systems, astute managerial competence and other institutional infrastructures. In addition, a positive gross profit can only be guaranteed for such huge investment provided the crop and livestock enterprises involved are high-priced. Given the level of investment being undertaken by the River Basins, it is extremely unlikely that such enterprises are conceivable in the immediate future.

When some countries (for example, India and Israel) adopted the River Basin Development concept as a means to agricultural develop-ment they started with large irrigation schemes but later realised that 'small is beautiful' and invested more in small schemes with better spatial distribution, more economic to run and less complex to manage.

Poor cost recovery
In the River Basin Development projects of other countries, cost recovery through sales of electricity, potable water and irrigation water is often built into the economic analysis that goes into the planning of such project. In Nigerian River Basins projects this cost recovery aspect is not given much attention. The implication is that when the source of *cheap funds* (through petroleum export) dries up, the establishment of new irrigation schemes as well as the maintenance and effective use of the existing ones will be difficult if not impossible to undertake.

Erratic fund allocation
Contrary to expectations, the method of allocating funds to the RBDAs in Nigeria is vague. This is evident in Table 1 where there is no apparent relationship between funds allocated to each RBDA and estimated land arca of cach Basin area or estimated population of people within the catchment area of each Basin. This contention is given some statistical weight through a simple correlation analysis in which the correlation coefficient (R) between resource allocation and estimated land area was found to be as low as 0.36 and the correlation coefficient between resource allocation and estimated population of each catchment area was as low as 0.31.

Poor intra-state involvement
Finally, these Federal Government projects, with their large investment in irrigation tend to eliminate any urge on the part of the state and local governments to be remotely interested in River Basin Development

Table 1: *Federal Government Allocations, Estimated Land Area and Estimated Population: River Basins Development Authorities, Nigeria.*

RBDA	Allocation 1981–1985 (₦ million)	Estimated Land Area (KM²)	Estimated Population 1979 (millions)
Anambra – Imo	105.00	30,003	10,845
Benin – Owena	132.00	56,791	7,742
Upper Benue	118.00	84,042	3,887
Lower Benue	102.00	105,350	6,643
Chad Basin	170.00	136,361	4,472
Cross River	80.00	28,620	5,188
Hadejia – Jama'are	127.00	64,692	10,439
Niger-Delta	85.00	20,873	2,581
Niger River	146.00	158,540	7,426
Ogun-Oshun	145.00	66,264	12,862
Sokoto – Rima	597.00	166,134	9,829

Source: Akinyosoye (1984) table 10.

Projects. The implication of this is that the Federal Government may be embarking on a programme it cannot eventually handle alone if the other two tiers of government are not involved and assigned specific financial and management responsibilities.

On the strength of foregoing observations and comments there is an urgent need for a drastic reorganisation of the operations of the River Basins if the country hopes to gain from the structural changes they have introduced into the country's farm industry. More important, future projects/schemes have to be organised along the lines suggested later in order fully to tap the resources of Nigeria's river basins for the benefit of its teeming population.

PROPOSALS FOR THE FUTURE

The proposals discussed below, if implemented in a concerted manner, will contribute immensely to a more effective River Basin Development Programme and, also fulfil some of the aims of agricultural revolution in Nigeria.

First, for effectiveness, the RBDAs should enjoy more autonomy and therefore be relieved of the traditional bureaucratic control prevalent in government parastatals.

Second, indigenous financial institutions such as the Nigerian Industrial Development Bank (NIDB), the Agricultural and Cooperative Bank, merchant banks and private entrepreneurs should be involved in the design, funding and operations of projects connected with small, medium and large irrigation agriculture. A broad-based financial commitment will mean a lessening of government *absolute* financial control and thereafter keep political considerations to the minimum in allocating human, material and financial resources needed for effective launching and management of the River Basin projects. In addition, the chief executive (General Manager) of each River Basin will become directly accountable for the success and failure of his projects.

Third, governments have to borrow ideas from the private sector if they want successfully to introduce structural changes in the farm industry through the River Basins farm projects. Using the conventional bureaucratic managerial approach to the management of the operations of the River Basins cannot be very effective. For example, a private company, the Nigerian Tobacco Company (NTC) has shown in the last 50 years that an effective agricultural system based on modern farm technology can evolve in this country with limited government intervention. Prior to 1933, various attempts by the Department of Agriculture in Nigeria to develop commercial tobacco production failed (Akiwowo and Basu 1968). In 1934 the British American Tobacco Company Limited (BAT), the parent company of NTC, on its own started a revolution of tobacco production in Nigeria. With world-wide knowledge about tobacco production, BAT introduced innovations into Nigeria's tobacco farm industry in a way similar to that which the River Basins are now attempting. The salient features of that approach are summarised thus:

(a) a new farming system that guaranteed increased production and allows for a more intensive utilisation of land, labour and other farm resources was evolved.

(b) the use of modern inputs, such as fertilizers, pest and plant disease control chemicals and mechanised farm equipments. As expected of private entrepreneurs, inputs were introduced *after very careful investigation and experimentation* to find the most appropriate ones for the agricultural environment of the tobacco-growing areas. Soil tests, for instance, helped in determining quantity and type of fertilizers and agro-chemicals needed. In addition, *economic prices* were charged for these inputs;

(c) the introduction of a simple and easily acquired method of processing of tobacco leaves (flue-curing) which increased farmers' incomes substantially;

(d) Finally and most important, the introduction of a farm organisation framework unique to tobacco farmers in Nigeria. The tobacco farmers were encouraged to form *organised groups*.

The aftermath of this business approach to farm organisation is that over the years productivity and income in tobacco leaf cultivation have been increasing. With this background, it is proposed that the Federal Ministry of Agriculture, Water Resources and Rural Development should set up a *task force* that will work out a new scheme for the operations of Nigeria's River Basins with a view to introducing business concepts into their management.

Fourth, the River Basins should as a rule limit themselves to the provision of physical and institutional infrastructures and build in a cost recovery mechanism into the financial management of the irrigation projects. The River Basins should not undertake direct food production.

Finally, irrigation schemes should not necessarily be 'large' but small-scale or medium size within the managerial competence of Nigerians.

CONCLUSION

The main theme of this paper has been to suggest new strategies for reorganising the River Basins in Nigeria in order to make them contribute effectively to the goal of restructuring its farm industry. The problem with Nigeria's River Basins does not seem to lie in the concept of River Basin Development *per se* but in the size of investment and the conventional bureaucratic managerial approach to River Basin Management; an approach that is completely devoid of any touch of business efficiency. After all, farming is a business and if the government gives the wrong impression that agricultural development involves the use of heavy machinery, the building of huge dams, and, inadvertently deliberate waste and a level of investment over and above what most investors consider reasonable, agricultural revolution in Nigeria may continue to be a dream. It is therefore suggested within the information available that the private sector should be involved with both the fundamental planning of the programme as well as the technical, economic and socio-political aspects of their (RBDA) activities. A business-like approach should be introduced towards the design, funding and operation of Nigeria's River Basins if the country hopes to benefit from their irrigation projects.

NOTES

[1]See Anthonio (1967) for a detailed exposition on the state of agriculture in Nigeria in the pre-Civil War era.
[2]See Idachaba (1980) for the core of recent policy options for food production in Nigeria.
[3]For details of these early irrigation schemes, see *National Development Plan 1962–68*.
[4]See Federal Ministry of Information, River Basins Development Authorities Decree 25 of June 1976 and Decree 37 of August 1976, for the names of the RBDAs and their statutory functions.
[5]See Federal Ministry of Agriculture, (1984) Agric. News vol. 4 No. 10 July – August.

REFERENCES

Akinyosoye, V. O., *River Basins Development Authorities and Nigerian Food Economy: An Assessment*, Preliminary Report, NISER, Ibadan., 1984.
Akiwowo and Basu, *The Social Organisations of Tobacco Growers in Northern Oyo Division and Adoption of New Farming Ideas and Practices*. NISER, Ibadan, 1968.

Anthonio, Q. B. O., 'Towards An Agrarian Reforms in Nigeria' *Proceedings of the Agricultural Society of Nigeria*. vol. 2, 1984.

F.A.O.   Production Yearbook (various issues)

F.O.S.   Digest of Statistics. (various issues)

Idachaba, F. S. et al., *The Green Revolution: A Food Production Plan For Nigeria*. Vols. 1 and 2, Federal Ministry of Agriculture, Lagos, 1980.

NISH (1983) Federal Office of Statistics, Lagos, Nigeria. Report No RCS/RASS/83/1.

Ogenlaja, S. B. *Nigeria's Food Imports (1960–1980 and some Selected Socio-economic Factors*, Department of Agricultural Economics, University of Ibadan, Nigeria, 1984.

Olatunbosun Dupe, 'Western Nigerian Farm Settlement: An Appraisal', *Journal of Developing Areas*, 1971.

Oluwasanmi, H. A. 'The Israeli Moshav in Nigeria: An Estimate of Returns' *Journal of Farm Economics*, vol. 48, no. 2, 1966.

VLADIMIR IAKIMETS

Adjustment of Regional Agriculture to Expected Climatic Changes

INTRODUCTION

There are many direct observations, indirect facts and theoretical estimates showing that through intensification of industrial production, global climatic changes will occur in future decades. In (Sov-Amer 1982) the following estimates of the observable and probable increase in atmospheric CO_2 concentration up to 2050 are given 280–297 mill^{-1} (pre-industrial period), 336–338 mill^{-1} (1980), 360 ± 6 mill^{-1} (1990), 394 ± 9 mill^{-1} (2000), $700 \pm$ (50 – 100) mill^{-1} (2050). A global warming is expected to be induced by this process. Changes in the mean annual temperature (for example, in several degrees in high latitudes) and precipitation are likely to have a significant impact on agriculture and the environment. Therefore, the assessment of the impact of the adjustment of agriculture in different regions to expected climatic changes is of great importance.

The successful adjustment to such changes will require detailed information on how regional agricultural systems and the environment will react to them. Because experimenting with real agricultural systems is time and cost consuming and is in some sense unrealistic, the development of corresponding models to study possible ways of adjustment and assessment of their economic and ecological consequences is considered as an appropriate approach.

This paper contains the description of such methodology and demonstrates how it operates on the data for the Leningrad region in the USSR.

METHODOLOGY

The proposed methodology included three main interacting tools for:
- (1) generating scenarios of changes in regional weather conditions induced by global climatic changes;
- (2) simulating the behaviour of regional agriculture and environment under different generated scenarios;

160

(3) assessing economic and ecological consequences of adjustment of regional agriculture to changing climate based on results of simulation.

Generating scenarios of changes of regional climatic conditions is implemented with using two alternative approaches: General Circulation Models of the atmosphere, for example GISS model developed by J. Hansen et al. (1983) and modified by W. Bach (forthcoming), simulating anthropogenic effects on climate, particularly CO_2 induced climatic changes; and a second approach which employs empirical climatic data to construct regression models for describing changes in temperature and precipitation for different regions (Vinnikov and Groisman 1979).

For investigating the behaviour of regional agriculture and environment under different scenarios of climatic changes and agrotechnological transformations the VNIISI model is used (Pegov et al. 1983; S. Pegov et al. forthcoming). It is the so-called 'index' simulation model allowing one to study dynamic behaviour of soil, vegetation, water and air indexes based on empirical data and the major trends in regional crop production in response to climatic changes and agrotechnological transformations given exogenously as time series of the scenario's control parameters. This model consists of four parts: a submodel for adjustment to a specific region's conditions (lithology, geographical belt, etc.) a hydrological submodel, an environmental pollution submodel and a submodel of biogeosystem dynamics. For the descriptions of the dynamic processes in these parts of the model, ordinary difference equations are used. As results of simulation, such time-dependent variables as soil productivity, crop yield, soil moisture and salinity, surface, ground and deep ground water pollution with chemicals etc. are generated as outputs. Besides climatic scenarios describing changes in mean annual temperature and precipitation, this model allows one to use scenarios for agrotechnology transformations as the following input time dependent variables: rate of fertilizers and other chemicals application, intensity of irrigation and drainage activity, changes in acreage, changes in acreage for shelter belts, etc.

Based on results of simulation assessing economic consequences for adjustment of regional agriculture to changing climate is implemented on the basis of application of multi-objective decision making methods. For this purpose results of simulation of different variants of adjustment obtained from the VNIISII model are transformed into a number of economic and ecological indicators which are used then for multi-criteria comparison of those alternatives and selection of the most preferable one.

RESULTS OF THE DEMONSTRATIVE APPLICATION OF THE METHODOLOGY

The methodology was applied to conditions of the Leningrad region of the USSR to demonstrate how models are operative. This work was done by IIASA (Laxenburg, Austria) in collaboration with the All Union Research Institute for Systems Studies (Moscow). The complete description of results will be available in a forthcoming publication (Iakimets, Pitovranov 1985). The results of these models fit very well the observed data of the period 1947–80. Some results related to future dynamic changes of winter rye yield (one of the major crops in the region) and several environmental characteristics of the region under 1 reference and 4 selected scenarios of climatic changes and simple agrotechnological transformations are given in Figures 1–3. The scenario of climatic changes used for the region is given in Figure 4 (approximately the same as used in other studies on climatic impacts). The description of 5 considered scenarios is given in Table 1. Table 2 contains comparisons of results of the reference scenario (variant 1) and the scenario of only climatic changes (variant 2). One can see from this table that changes considered for regional weather conditions are unfavourable as a whole for agriculture: the soil index is dropping, surface water pollution with nitrogen and the depth of an already detrimentally high of the first ground water table are increased. These changes lead also, in the second half of the period under consideration, to a decline in winter rye yields. Therefore we tried to find ways of agrotechnological transformations in order to support the level of winter rye yield at the same time as minimising negative ecological consequences. In this paper we do not report about possible changes in cropping patterns. Here only 3 ways for adjustment (variants 3–5) from many other studied are given. Table 3 contains the results of a comparison of those with variant 2 (with climatic changes but without agrotechnological adjustment). A simple analysis of these data shows that variant 5 is the candidate to be the most preferable one because it provides for support of the level of yield more than in 1980 with the least level of surface water pollution with chemicals and an admissible level of first ground water table.

To implement more rigorous integrative assessment of different variants of the adjustment of agriculture to possible climatic changes, three criteria were constructed:

1. Index of the economic efficiency of variants ($E_1(t)$).

$$E_1(t) = \sum_i p_i(t) \cdot y_i(t) - \sum_j c_j(t) \cdot x_j(t),$$

where

$y_i(t)$ is the yield of crop ($i = 1$) and by-products in the year t (for example, the straw ($i = 2$));

$p_i(t)$ is the price of the crop and by-products produced in the year t;

$x_j(t)$ is the value of the j-th agrotechnological input applied in the year t
(for example, nitrogen fertilizer ($j = 1$), phosphorous fertilizer ($j = 2$), etc.);

$c_j(t)$ is the cost of the preparation and application of the j-th input.

YIELD
ton per ha

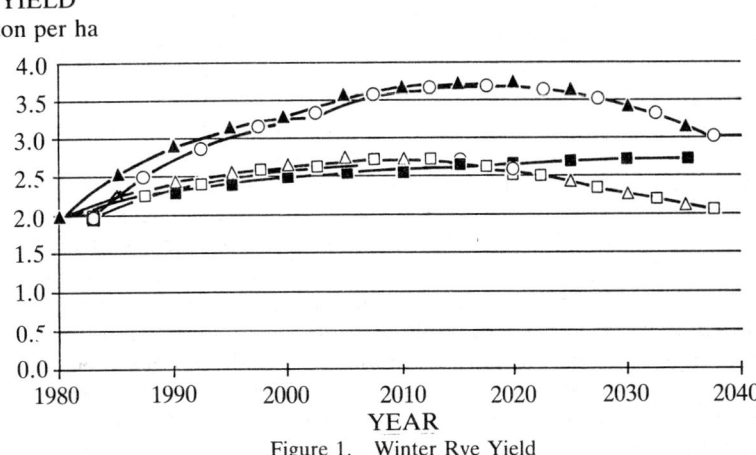

Figure 1.   Winter Rye Yield

ton per ha

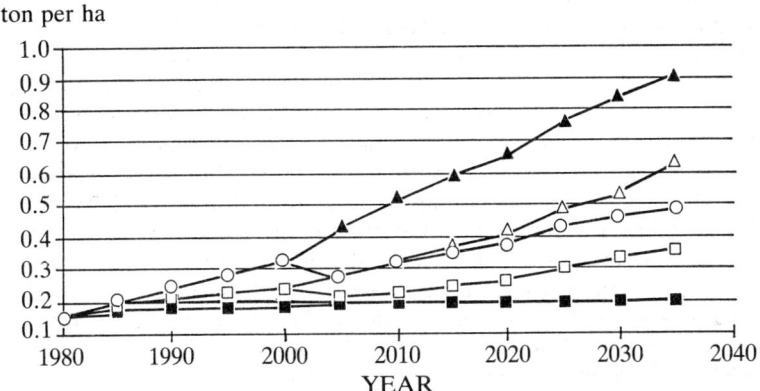

Figure 2.   Surface Water Pollution with Nitrogen

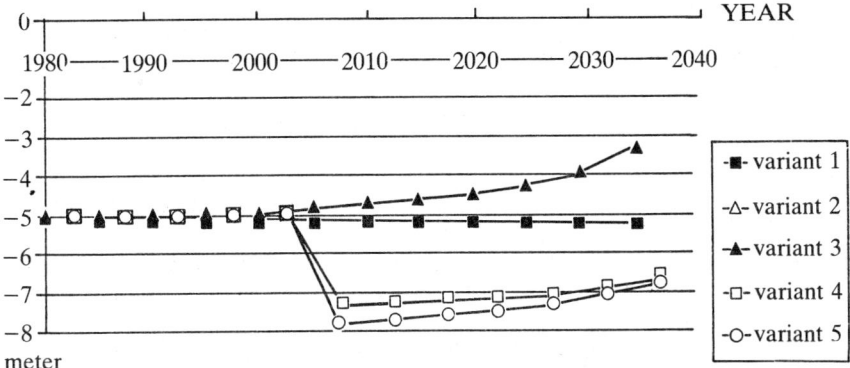

Figure 3.   Depth of the 1 Ground Water Table

degrees

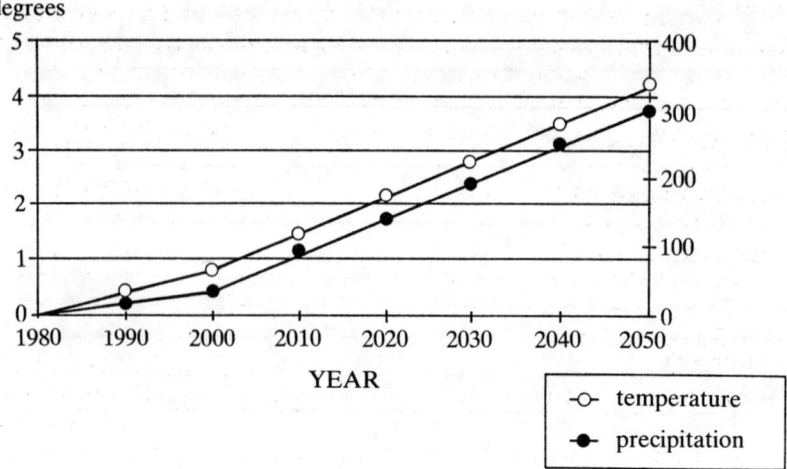

Figure 4. Scenarios of Temperature and Precipitation Increase (relative to 1980)

Table 1. *Selected Scenarios*

	Reference Scenarios of climatic and agrotechnological changes[1] scenario				
	(variant 1)	(variant 2)	(variant 3)	(variant 4)	(variant 5)
Climatic changes (Annual T° and precipitation)	average as for 1980–3 for the whole period		←see Figure 4→		
Annual fertilizer applications (in kg per ha. of nutritional units)	2035	2035	1980– 2000– 2000 2035	2035	as in variant 3
nitrogen	55	55	80 120	55	
phosphorous	45	45	70 100	45	
potassium	45	45	70 100	45	
organic	150	150	250 375	150	
Drainage[2] activity increases				0.5km/km² (2001–2002) 1km/km² (2003)	as in variant 4

[1]Liming effects will be considered in future applications
[2]Expressed as length of surface drains of 5 m depth per km²

Table 2.   *Comparison of results for variant 2 relative to variant 1 (in percentage)*

	1980	1990	2000	2010	2020	2035
winter rye yield	0	+4.3	+5.2	+4.7	−4.1	−23
soil index	0	−1	−4	−11	−22	−42
depth of the 1st ground water table	0	+2	+4	+9	+14	+38
surface water pollution with nitrogen	0	+17.5	+30.2	+75.4	+213.7	+325

Table 3.   *Comparison of variants 3, 4 and 5 relative to variant 2 (in percentage)*

variants	1980	1990	2000	2010	2020	2035
			winter rye yield			
3	0	+19	+25	+35	+45.8	+50.2
4	0	0	0	−2	−3	−3.4
5	0	+19	+25	+34.8	+43.5	+43.4
			soil index			
3	0	+20.5	+24.6	+36.4	+47.2	+49.4
4	0	0	0	−2.5	−1	−4.8
5	0	+20.5	+24.6	+36.4	+44.4	+42.2
		surface water pollution with nitrogen				
3	0	+20.8	+34.6	+56.4	+60.8	+44.7
4	0	0	0	−33	−36	−43
5	0	+20.8	+34.6	−4	−7	−23
		depth of the first ground water table				
3	0	0	0	0	0	0
4	0	0	0	+53.9	+60	+204
5	0	0	0	+64.3	+68	+208

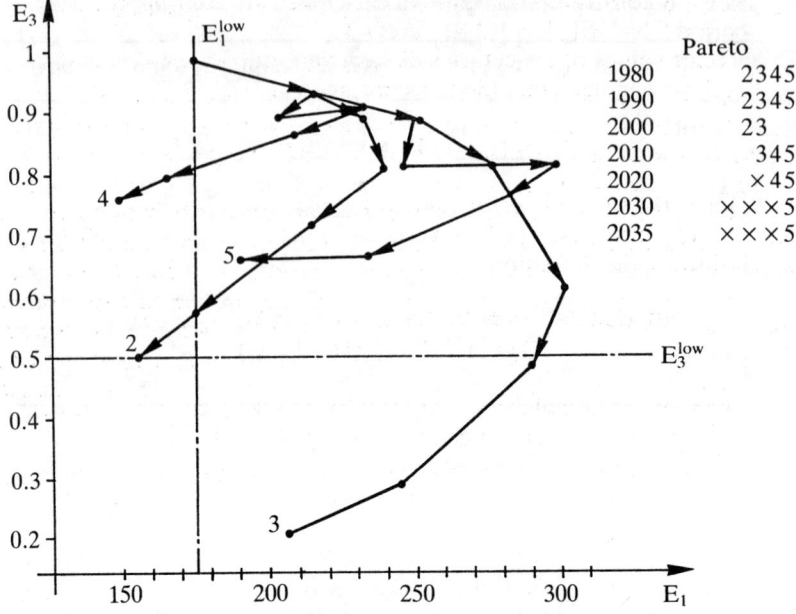

Figure 5.   Projections of trajectories in two-dimensional space

It should be noted that for the sake of simplicity the values of $p_i(t)$ and $c_j(t)$ were taken as constant for the whole period under consideration.
2.   Index of the energy utilization efficiency ($E_2(t)$).

$$E_2(t) = \frac{\sum_i q_i \cdot y_i(t)}{\sum_j q_j \cdot x_j(t)}, \qquad (2)$$

where $y_i(t)$ and $x_j(t)$ have the same meaning as in formula (1) and q_i and q_j are values of energy equivalents of yields and inputs.
3.   Index of the ecological sustainability ($E_3(t)$)

$$E_3(t) = v^\circ - v(t), \qquad (3)$$

where v° is the admissible level of the nitrogen concentration in the surface water (the WHO recommended value of it is 1.13 gN per litre) and $v(t)$ the calculated value of this concentration.
Values of these indices were calculated for all considered variants for each year based on values of simulated variables. Thus the trajectories of variants in three-dimensional space of the above mentioned indices were found. In order to select the most preferable variant of the adjustment the corresponding multi-objective decision making procedure was developed. This procedure has the following main steps:

1. The low constraints on values of each index are fixed for the whole period $E^1 = \{E_k^1, k = 1,2,3\}$, $\forall t \in \overline{O,T}$.
2. Vector values of trajectories of each variant (t) are calculated for each year under simulation, according to (1–3):

$$E_\tau(t) = (E_{1\tau}(t), E_{2\tau}(t), E_{3\tau}(t)), \forall t \in \overline{O,T}.$$

Hence the set V of vector values of variants was determined.

3. Pareto-optimal set (P_t) of variants is determined for each year following the definition

$$\forall t, \tau E_\tau^\cdot(t) \epsilon P_t \iff E_{k\tau}^\cdot(t) \geq E_{k\tau}(t), \forall k \epsilon \{1,2,3\} \text{ and}$$
$$\exists\, k \epsilon \{1,2,3\} : E_{k\tau}^\cdot(t) > E_{k\tau}(t).$$

4. The most preferable trajectory (and hence the preferable variant) is determined as that which for the whole period under consideration was selected more times as the Pareto-optimal one and which did not violate the low constraints or violated these less times than other trajectories.

Based on this procedure the variant 5 was found as the most preferable one. Figure 5 contains projections of all considered trajectories in a space of indexes E_1 and E_2. One can see that only trajectory 5 does not violate both low constraints.

SUMMARY

Illustrative application of the methodology described in this paper shows that possible climatic changes induced by the increase of atmospheric CO_2 concentration can have negative impact on regional agriculture (see Table 2). The analysis of results of different scenarios for adjustment of agriculture to those changes based on simulation runs allows one to select the ecologically and economically appropriate alternative.

REFERENCES

Bach, W., *GCM derived climatic scenarios of increased atmospheric CO_2 as a basis for impact studies*, IIASA, Laxenburg, 1985.

Hansen, J., Russell, E., Rind, D. et al., 'Efficient three-dimensional global models for climate studies: Models I and II', *Monthly Weather Review* vol. 3, 609, 1983.

Iakimets, V. and Pitovranov, S. *The impact of climatic changes on agriculture and environment within the Leningrad region, USSR'*, IIASA, Laxenburg, Austria, 1985.

Pegov, S. A., Khomyakov, P. M., Kroutko, V. N., *Forecasting and estimating environmental changes on a regional basis*, WP-83-83, IIASA, Laxenburg, 1983.

Pegov, S. A., Khomyakov, P. M., Kouzminsky, I. N., Nikitin, E. A., *System of ecological forecasting, second version (SEF.2): User's manual* IIASA, Laxenburg, 1985.

Sov-Amer., 'The impact of atmospheric carbon dioxide increasing on climate', *Proceedings of the Soviet-American Workshop on Atmospheric Carbon Dioxide Increasing Study*, Leningrad, 15–20 June 1981, Leningrad: Gidrometeoizdat, 1982.

Vinnikov, K. Ya and Groisman, P. Ya., *The empirical study of the climatic sensitivity.*, Izvestia Academii Nauk SSSR, ser. Phys. Atmosph. i. Ocean. 6:5–20 (in Russian), 1979.

DISCUSSION OPENING – SHOHSAKU SENDA

The two papers presented were instructive and interesting. However, due to constraints on both my knowledge and time I wish to refer only to the first paper which described river basin development projects in Nigeria.

I have two questions. The first question concerns the motivation and initiatives for the irrigation project. What are the farmers' desires for the irrigation programme in Nigeria? Who established the project originally? Was it government or farmers by themselves?

The second question concerns the organization of the farmers' irrigation association. What is the actual situation of the farmers' activities regarding, for example, allocation and adjustment, maintenance and management of water facilities? To what extent do farmers have to pay for water charges?

GENERAL DISCUSSION – RAPPORTEUR: GLENN T. MAGAGULA

In answer to questions from the discussion opener, the presenter of the first paper, F. J. Idachaba replied that it should be noted that Government involvement began early in the 1970s and the intention was to augment farmers' efforts and to assure an adequate water supply for farmers. Farmers were not involved in policy formulation, articulation of needs and priorities nor in determining the scale of operation. The RBDAs provide and maintain the water systems and the financial contribution by farmers is minimal. The issue of cost recovery had not been adequately addressed in programme formulation.

One questioner noted that river basins are normally characterised by heavy soils and this might lead to high labour costs which might, in turn, reduce the profitability of the programme. He further pointed out that small-scale irrigation projects might be more profitable than the large-scale projects. Finally, he took issue with the concern of the authors regarding non-involvement of State Governments – this might accentuate bureaucratic control.

In reply, while conceding the point that heavy soils might increase labour costs, Idachaba pointed out that the profitability of the schemes could be related to the extent to which high value crops are produced. He agreed that small-scale irrigation schemes e.g. those using small pumps, might be more economical; in fact, there was a high demand for such pumps. He further agreed that bureacratic control should be reduced and this was one of the authors' recommendations.

Another participant asked if these programmes had been examined in relation to other rural development strategies in Nigeria to assess their appropriateness. Idachaba replied that the authors' intention was to evaluate the RBDP's effectiveness in meeting its objectives and to suggest policy changes for improving its performance. He was then asked if the founders of the programme determined the optimal farm size in these programmes and whether the RBD projects were developed simultaneously or sequentially. Idachaba replied that nobody could estimate questions of optimal farm size for Nigeria as a whole. It was true that the farm sizes of the RBDP were small but this was not fundamental, as Japanese, Chinese and Korean experiences indicate. A large number of the river basin schemes were developed almost simultaneously and this was creating a lot of problems.

Another questioner asked what kind of crops were grown in these schemes – cash or subsistence crops? Did men and women jointly participate in producing the crops or was there a division of labour? Idachaba replied that in Nigeria they had abandoned the distinction between cash and subsistence crops. The schemes were created for farm families and it was in this context that the farms were run. He was further asked if the lands on which the RBDPs were established were already occupied or were they Government lands, and were farmers resettled there? Since the construction of large dams was obligatory, according to the Statute, how could the Authorities be expected to construct small-scale dams?

In reply the presenter said that the lands on which the RBDPs were established were originally occupied by farmers. However, the construction of the dams entailed widespread resettlement of farm homesteads and reallocation of fields in such a way that each farm family had about 4 hectares of land. The Act establishing the RBDPs did not specify that dams had to be large. Nevertheless, because the programmes were initiated during the 'oil boom' and money was not wanting, the Authorities took it upon themselves to construct large dams. Now that the 'oil boom' was no longer with us, there was a pressing need for the construction of small dams.

Participants in the discussion included S. Senda, Kiragani, A. C. Nwosu, U. Malik, I. Tinker and S. Bellete.

VICTOR NAZARENKO

Land Resources and Distribution of Agricultural Production in the USSR

The Soviet Union has one of the largest areas of agricultural and arable lands in the world. Out of total area of 2,227.5 million hectares in the country, agricultural lands involve 605.9 mill. ha., including 227.5 mill. ha. of arable lands, 40.6 mill. ha, of grasslands and 332.4 mill. ha. of pastures.

The territory of the country stretches for over 9,500 km. from west to east and for 4,500 km. from north to south. This is associated with a great diversity of natural conditions and methods of land utilisation. The characteristics of land resources in the USSR are defined first of all by the temperature regime from the standpoint of agricultural utilisation. Agriculturally the country is subdivided into a number of natural and agricultural belts, which are first of all characterised by accumulated active temperatures (over 10°C). From this the whole country is subdivided into three main belts:

(1) Cold tundra and taiga natural-and-agricultural belt with accumulated active temperatures below 1600°.

(2) Moderate natural-and-agricultural belt with accumulated active temperatures of 1600°–4000°.

(3) Warm subtropical natural-and-agricultural belt with accumulated active temperatures of over 4000°C.

The belts are subdivided into natural-and-agricultural zones, which are characterised by certain balances of heat and moisture, related to main features of soil formation and plant mineral nutrition. These zones are defined by the nature of the soil and surface. In their turn they are subdivided into natural-and-agricultural provinces, which are characterised by specific features of soil surface, related to macroclimate inside the zone, with annual migration of its elements. The provinces are differentiated by the increase of continentality, severity of winter and its snow cover, changes of thermal and moisture supply during the vegetation period, hydrothermal regime of soil biological productivity. The provinces in their turn are subdivided into natural-and-agricultural regions, which are characterised by well expressed geomorphological and hydrological features, composition of soil-forming rocks, dominating type of soil formation, specific features of climate, soil relief and soil

170

erosion danger. At present 16 zones and 67 types of various contour versions have been identified according to the available taxonomy, which allows the making of very fractional and detailed land taxonomy. The soils are subdivided into seven general categories by their qualitative characteristics. The first involves good arable lands, the second lands primarily suitable for grassland, the third pasture lands, which after reclamation can be suitable for other agricultural purposes, the fourth lands suitable for agricultural purposes after radical reclamation, the fifth lands of low suitability for agricultural purposes, the sixth unsuitable lands for agricultural purposes and the seventh abnormal lands. Most agricultural lands belong in the moderate belt. This includes the majority of arable soils of the USSR, especially in the forest-and-steppe zones and in the steppe zones. The dry-steppe areas are also of great importance.

The main index, characterising the qualitative characteristics of lands in the USSR, is their bioclimatic potential. Bioclimatic potential is the ratio of plant productivity under the given vegetation conditions to productivity under comparative conditions. It is calculated by the

TABLE 1 *Natural-and-agricultural zones of the USSR*

Zone	Total area %	Arable lands %	Ploughed up soils %
Polar-and-tundra	8.9	0.0	—
Forest and tundra-north taiga	10.5	0.0	—
Middle taiga	9.9	0.5	0.5
Total	29.3	0.5	0.2
South taiga-forest	12.6	16.7	12.9
Forest-and-steppe	6.9	30.3	42.8
Steppe	5.6	29.4	50.8
Dry steppe	3.3	12.8	38.3
Semidesert	5.6	2.1	3.7
Desert	2.8	0.1	0.3
Foothills and desert-steppe	0.8	1.3	15.7
Total	37.6	92.7	24.0
Subtropical desert	3.2	0.5	1.7
Subtropical foothills-semi-desert	1.1	2.1	18.3
Shrub-steppe and dry forest	0.1	0.2	22.3
Subtropical moisty forest	0.1	0.1	11.8
Total	4.5	2.9	6.4
The Carpathian and Caucasian	1.0	—	8.6
Middle Asian	1.9	—	5.3
South Siberian	11.3	—	1.7
North Siberian	13.2	—	—
Kamchatka-Kuril	1.2	—	0.1
Total	28.6	3.9	1.3
TOTAL	100.0	100.0	10.1

following formula:

$$BCP = Cp \frac{\Sigma t > 10°}{1000°C} ,$$

where BCP = relative values of bioclimatic potential;
  Cp = coefficient of biological production, which depends on moisture availability in plants;
  $\Sigma t > 10°$ = accumulated temperatures over 10°, reflecting solar energy and heat availability in plants;
  1000°C = accumulated temperatures in the northern border of field crop growing.

In this way, the relative values of BCP represent the product of growth coefficient on moisture availability by growth coefficient on heat availability, i.e. – as the combined coefficient.

The ratio $\Sigma t > 10°$: 1000° reflects the potential soil productivity in a certain area according to the temperature factor in relative values. In this case the minimum bioclimatic productivity is estimated as a unity, and all others in comparative values to it.

It should be mentioned that the bioclimatic potential of agricultural lands in the USSR is on the average not high. It is considerably lower than the average bioclimatic potential in leading farming countries. Soviet climatologists consider that as a whole an average hectare of arable land in the USSR is 2.5 times lower in its bioclimatic productivity compared with a hectare of land in the USA, or 2 – 2.2 times lower in comparison with the countries of Western Europe. Inside the territory of the USSR the diversity of biological productivity and agroclimatic potential of land is extremely high. Under conditions of sufficient moisture, bioclimatic potential is measured from 1.0 in the northern border of farming up to 5.0 and higher in the southern border. Quite considerable amendments in bioclimatic potential can be introduced by the degree of moistening –from 1.0 under irrigation or sufficient precipitation up to the minimum index under desert conditions. The correlation of bioclimatic potential and moistening permits one to estimate the potential zonal productivity of the agricultural zone and province. Such analysis shows that a very limited part of the territory of the USSR has a high bioclimatic potential with sufficient natural or artificial moisture, and the greater part of the territory has a medium or low level of bioclimatic productivity with insufficient natural moisture, and therefore with relatively unsteady agricultural production. These characteristics of land resources are to a great extent a decisive factor in the distribution of agricultural production in the USSR.

The lack of coincidence between favourable accumulated temperatures and moisture availability is quite a serious factor, limiting the efficient utilisation of land resources for agricultural purposes. There is insufficient precipitation in the warm areas of the country in many cases, and, on the contrary, the moist areas, particularly in the central part and in the west of the country, are located in the zone of low heat availability. All these factors demand great work on land reclamation, irrigation, mostly in the south of the country, and drainage, in the central and north-west areas. The irrigation programme of Middle Asia, in the south of the European part of the country, now under way, is of great importance. Sometimes the programme on comprehensive improvement of land resources are accepted for large areas. For instance, the specially accepted programme on the development of the non-chernozem zone of the European part of the USSR involves drainage of 9–10 mill. hectares of marshy lands; irrigated grasslands and pastures are being developed in the area of 8–10 mill. ha. Work on their surface improvement is in the area of 23 mill. ha, including liming. Therefore, the bioclimatic potential is, as a whole, not of a static nature but of a dynamic one, which is changing during the process of intensification through a combination of natural and artificial soil fertility factors.

The efficient distribution of agricultural production in the USSR has been formed historically on the basis of traditional zones of farming. This process of formation however, is subject to considerable modification under the influence of scientific and technical progress and the active planning role of the state. The main idea for the distribution of agricultural production in the USSR is the maximum utilisation of agroclimatic potential of the country with consideration of relative restriction of zones, favourable for production of valuable farm crops. Distribution of farm crops depends first of all on the highest adaptability to biological conditions of growing where these produce the highest yield. At the same time agricultural production is planned first of all for those zones, where the lowest cost price of production is achieved; and not only for plant products but also for animal products. Quite important research for the achievement of this task is under way. Some thousand plots for variety testing of agricultural crops are spread through the whole country, which permits obtaining data on yields of all farm crops, by variety, through the whole territory of the country each year. At the same time the registration of cost price of production for all main types of farm products is being carried out at all agricultural enterprises. Such information allows the planning agencies to introduce certain amendments into the plans for the distribution of agricultural production. Long-term perspectives of scientific and technical progress, of forecasting in yielding ability and cost price of agricultural produce is taken into consideration in long-term plans for changes of agricultural production distribution. This topic is one of the most important in the work of research institutes on agricultural economy both in central institutes and those of the republics.

Intensification of agricultural production, and scientific and technical progress in this field involves, as one of the main elements, a considerable increase in the level of interregional division of labour in agriculture with the formation of specialised zones of agricultural production. These zones are being formed or have already been formed with consideration of specific bioclimatic potential, the level of production cost price, availability of labour resources and centres of consumption and the production infrastructure. These specialised zones involve the Central Asian one, which mainly specialises in cotton production, Transcaucasian republics, specialising primarily in horticultural and vegetable production and production of subtropical crops, sugar beet production zones in the Ukraine and in the south of the RSFSR, zones of market wheat production in Kazakhstan, Western Siberia and the Ukraine and in the south of RSFSR, dairy zones in the Baltic Sea republics and in the centre of RSFSR.

Proceeding from the Food Programme, it is planned to expand in future interregional specialisation with the formation of zones for potato production, greater specialisation in milk production and zones for production of corn, flax and sunflowers. Thus the formation of specialised zones in agricultural production is the main trend in the development of agricultural production distribution. The rates of this zonal specialisation to a great extent define not only the level of intensification in each specialised zone (and possibilities of removal of secondary and non-typical production from it) but also the further development of transport, production and commercial infrastructure. In this case considerable possibilities of changes in interregional divisions of labour are envisaged. For instance, with consideration of a high heat supply and availability of high labour resources, Central Asia can become an important zone for fruit and vegetable production as well as its development of cotton production. A special project, called 'Green Bridge', has been developed for production of vegetables and fruits in Central Asia and their transportation to the Urals and Siberia to supply large industrial centres. The improvement of supplies for Moscow, Leningrad and other central industrial districts with vegetables and fruits from the southern areas of the country is also projected. In view of the construction of the Baikal–Amur Road and the development of areas in Eastern Siberia and in the Far East, it is planned to develop there a large zone of agricultural production, primarily aimed at food supply for the new developed regions.

The development of such an extended interregional system of agricultural production with the large territorial dispersion of different zones leads to increased requirements in transportation. In many cases transport facilities represent the limiting factor in further extension of interregional division of labour. However, it would be wrong to explain all tendencies in specialisation of agricultural production only by the formation of specific zones which produce different types of agricultural products. First, in the majority of cases, agricultural crops are produced within the framework of a crop rotation, which itself provides a number of farm crops. Second, plant production is, as a rule, combined with animal husbandry in all zones. Third, the very important objective of each region is the achievement of a definite degree in self-supply for a number of farm crops, specifically for those which are difficult to transport – such as milk, some types of vegetables and, very important, feeds for the production of some animal products in the areas of their consumption. This leads also to the formation of large suburb zones of intensive agricultural production farming, which is first of all aimed at dairy farming, poultry, swine breeding (to some extent) and the production of potatoes and vegetables. The formation of such suburb zones is particularly specific in central and north-west areas, where large industrial and administrative centres have an historical background. By this means, distribution of agricultural production must not be limited only by increasing the interregional division of labour.

The planning process for distribution of agricultural production, which, as already mentioned, proceeds on the basis of estimation of agroclimatic potential and cost price of agricultural production, is implemented by the planning agencies by means of and due to the establishment of plans for deliveries and sale into the all-union funds of the main specialised types of agricultural production for the particular republic and region. The planning agencies in this case seek to distribute production in zones, which are unique in character, specifically by accumulated temperatures for production of southern agricultural produce, such as cotton, southern types of vegetables and fruits, corn, rice, etc. Distribution of grain production and purchases of grain are also practised first of all in areas of its lowest cost price and highest yielding capacity. However, the requirements of the country for grain and some other agricultural products cannot be satisfied only by low cost price. Therefore some part of production is distributed in areas with the worst climatic conditions and higher cost price. As a result of this, the zonal system of prices has been developed in the country, which stimulates production not only under the best agricultural conditions, but also under the worst.

The adequate process of planning and distribution is practised at the level of a separate republic and district with distribution of the planned tasks for deliveries and sale of the main type of agricultural products to the state. Taking into consideration the cost price of production and zonal agroclimatic conditions, the zones for some types of agricultural production are being developed inside the regional specialisation. But in this case the additional and subsidiary branches as a rule are always developed; their objective is usually to meet local consumption and not to provide the deliveries for centralised funds. In this case the process of planning envisages only the indices of market produce which is sold to the state, but not the sowing areas or livestock population; that creates a certain flexibility in the process of production planning by the farms themselves as well as their high manoeuvrability in the solution of the specialisation process directly at the production level. Planning of market deliveries both at the interregional (all-union level) and at the level inside the regions goes ahead simultaneously with planning means of production of the future produce. These means of production are allotted not only for the procurement volume, but also for the total gross production of a particular region.

The development of agribusiness (agro-industrial complex), in particular the production infrastructure, the system of procurement and trade, the food industry and especially the transformation of agricultural raw material into ready food, introduces certain correctives into traditional schemes of agricultural production distribution. The question is not about the formation of pure agricultural zones of a specialised nature but about the development of agribusiness zones, which would supply the country market with ready types of food and not with agricultural raw material. The accepted measures on the accelerated development of the third sphere of agribusiness (i.e. food industry and supply infrastructure) will permit the formation of such kind of agribusiness zones efficiently. The main part of agricultural produce should be processed on the spot in this case, and should not be transported to large centres of consumption for its subsequent processing. Economic calculations prove that such a type of industrial processing in the zones of raw material production is efficient in practice for all branches of the food industry, except bakery and some others. For instance, as the production of 1 ton of meat requires on average 1.8 tons of raw material and considering, that transportation of livestock is much more expensive than transportation of the finished product, the meat industry is located primarily in the zones of livestock and poultry production. During the 1960s and 1970s 75–80 per cent of new facilities in the meat industries were developed within the zones of raw material production. Annual saving caused by the introduction of meat from raw material areas is 300–400 million roubles, as compared with its production in areas of consumption.

Adequate processing takes place in other branches of the food industry with the objective of comprehensive processing in the areas of agricultural raw materials and of waste utilisation, using them also for feeding purposes. The development of facilities for the food industry in specialised zones has a further effect on the growth of specialisation of agricultural production itself, in particular on the development of the sugar, meat, dairy, butter and fat industry. Specialised agribusiness has been formed in zones of cotton production with ginning and processing of cotton raw material and cotton seeds. It is planned to develop specialised agribusiness zones for potato, fruit and vegetable production with output of final produce ready to use. The development of the refrigerating industry with production of deep frozen products is of particular importance in this case.

From the scientific point of view, the problem of interregional and intraregional division of labour, the combination of branches, striving for utilisation of advantages in bioclimatic potential of different zones, efficient use of differences in cost price of agricultural produce is, as has been already mentioned, one of the main trends in economists' activity regarding USSR agriculture. At present, with the development of systemic studies, modelling and the wide application of electronic computers, these tasks are generally solved by using economic and mathematical methods. The objectives for transportation of agricultural produce (raw materials and finished produce) are solved traditionally, as well as the efficiency of the use of capital investments in zones, considering land reclamation and comparative cost price of agricultural production, the tasks on comparison of production efficiency in different zones, taking into account transportion costs. Such objectives are solved at the level of the whole country (distribution of market produce volumes among republics and regions) as well as at the level inside the region (distribution of production within the region). The further development of these researches, as our experience proves, requires considerable improvement of the information basis, the development of a great number of normative indices, coefficients of flexibility in production functions and corresponding mathematical application. A special programme has been developed at the Academy of Agricultural Sciences. This programme deals with the development of research on the application of economic and mathematical methods, in particular, those for the solution of the problems of agricultural production distribution with the development of imitation models with the possibility of solving multiversion tasks on optimisation of distribution of agricultural production, aimed first of all at the fulfilment of two main objectives: maximisation of production and possible general reduction of the whole complex of expenses in agriculture, the food industry, transport and trade.

I. LUKINOV

The Effect of Scientific-Technological and Social Progress on Development in Agrarian Labour

In a strategic aspect the agrarian policy of the Soviet Union is directed at ensuring economic stability and the acceleration of scientific and technological progress, the changeover of agriculture to intensive industrial technologies.

The socialist system of planned management of economic and social development allows the concentration of resources in decisive directions, to ensure comparatively high rates of technical re-equipment. As early as 1960, despite great damage and a looted economy caused by the fascist invasion (1941–5), the volume of basic production assets increased against the 1940 level 3.2 times, and by 1983 it grew 19.5 times.[1] Power capacities per farmer in 1940 was equal to 1.7 horse power, and 29.7 in 1983. Tractor unit power increased 2.4 times and the fleet of agricultural machinery multiplied, expanded and was radically renewed.

All this provided an opportunity to reduce the share of the population engaged in agriculture (including subsidiary individual plots) from 54 per cent in 1940 to 20 per cent in 1983. The number of workers and employees engaged in the national economy increased from 30.4 to 61.8 per cent, and collective farmers decreased from 44.2 to 10.4 per cent.[2] The total number of workers in agricultural production and its services decreased by 5.2 million. As for the social structure, the number of collective farmers within this period decreased from 29 to 13 million but the number of agricultural workers, on the contrary, sharply increased. Changes also took place in the settlement pattern.

With the total growth of the population from 194.1 million in 1940 to 275 million by 1 July 1984, the urban population accounted for an increase from 32.5 to 64.9 per cent and the rural population for a decrease from 67.5 to 35.1 per cent. Such a ratio is based on the place of residence, whereas with regard to occupation the non-agricultural population at present is 209.8 million or 77 per cent, and the agricultural population is 64 million or 23 per cent.[3]

This is one of the aspects of scientific-technological progress – the shift in the structure of the population and those engaged in social production with a tendency towards the reduction of the share of agrarian labour. But there is another, no less important aspect, characterising final

178

efficiency – the growth of labour productivity, the gross product and national income. The gross social product for the period under analysis increased more than 15 times, including agricultural product by 2.7 times.[4] Gross product in the USSR reached 1,294 billion roubles (in actual current prices of 1983) while the gross product of the agro-industrial complex sphere rose to 451.2 billion roubles, out of which agricultural and forestry produce accounted for 63.1 per cent.[5]

Thus, the two main objectives of scientific-technological progress in socialist agriculture, i.e. labour resources made available for other sectors of economy and raising its productivity, have been reached comparatively successfully. However, the village as a whole possesses even greater labour resources, although there are quite a number of regions where the outflow of rural population to cities is not entirely set off by the introduction of complex mechanisation. There arises a problem of deficits in covering labour demands for agricultural works, especially during the 'peaks' of labour-intensive periods. Agricultural seasonal work often involves workers from cities, which is not always reasonable in terms of the criterion of national economic efficiency.

The level and growth rates of labour productivity in the agrarian sector in the USSR are still much lower than that in the industrial sector. Within the period under analysis the productivity of agricultural labour increased 4.5 times, in industry 8.4 times, and generally in the national economy 11.9 times.[6] The state planned investments, concentrated and distributed in the direction required by society using the criterion of national-economic efficiency, in general also determine the structural shifts in the national economy. More rapid development rates in industry within a long period limited investments to agriculture, resulting in restricted large-scale use of the latest scientific and technological advances and further reduction in the number of the employed. Only from 1965 did the investment rates in this sector start to grow gradually.

In the tenth five-year period (1976–80) investments in the development of the agro-industrial complex (AIC) amounted to 213 billion roubles, including 171 billion roubles for the development of agriculture, and in the eleventh five-year period (1981–5) they were respectively 233 and 190 billion roubles.[7] Grain farming, poultry farming, most of vegetable growing under shelter (large greenhouse farms) and the mixed feed industry have been switched over to machine technologies almost completely in the public sector. The industrialised production of beef, pork and milk is growing. The rates of mechanisation of cultivation of vegetable and fruit crops, potatoes and fodder growing has accelerated. However, there are many problems and difficulties. Many farms lack improved machine complexes and the manual labour involved in looking after and harvesting these crops is great. There are also deficiencies in the mineral fertilizer industry which restricts the intensification process.

The USSR Food Programme, approved at the Plenary Meeting of the Central Committee of the CPSU (May 1982), in order to speed up the transition of agriculture to industrialised methods of production, envisages the increase of agricultural and food industry main production assets by 1.5 times and power capacities of state and collective farms by 1.6 times. The supply of mineral fertilizers (in terms of 100 per cent of nutrients) is to be increased from 23 million tons in 1983 to 30–2 million tons in 1990. A long-term programme of land improvement has been worked out and is at present under way: construction of large new irrigation systems in the arid regions and drainage systems in the high-rainfall regions is designed to secure stable and high guaranteed yields.

As a result, the productivity of agricultural labour throughout the current decade is to be increased 1.5 times, and gross production output from 1 hectare of land is to be raised by at least one-third. The output and structure of agricultural production as envisaged by the Programme will reliably ensure the supply of the country's population with food products within the standards close to those which have been scientifically substantiated. Over 1983–4 the total agricultural output in the USSR increased by 20 billion roubles as compared with 1981–2, including a 7.4 million tons increase in average annual milk production, 1.4 million tons of meat and 4.6 million eggs. Positive changes are also taking place in the structure of consumption – the increase of highly valuable and varied products is accompanied by the reduction in the consumption of bakery products and potatoes. In 1983 the consumption per caput was as follows: meat and meat products, 58.4 kg; milk and dairy products, 309 kg; eggs, 253; fish and fish products, 17.6 kg; sugar, 44.2 kg; vegetable oil, 9.6 kg; vegetables, 101 kg; fruit and berries, 44 kg; potatoes, 110 kg; bakery products, 136 kg. By 1990 the consumption of meat and meat products is to be increased to 70 kg, fish and fish products to 19 kg, milk and dairy products to 330–40 kg, eggs to 260–6, vegetables and gourds to 126–35 kg, fruit and berries to 66–70 kg.[8]

Social aspects are an integral part of the Food Programme, involving further reconstruction of villages on the qualitatively new basis, the conditions of work and life in the village drawing closer to those of the city. The village's social infrastructure at present is being developed at a fast rate with the aim of creating conditions, in particular, for stabilisation and optimisation of the age structure of the workers in collective and state farms, in integrated economic systems, the reinforcement of their strength through the retention of young men capable of quickly mastering modern mechanised and automated technologies. There is a vast network of training and refresher courses for specialists of higher and medium qualifications (agronomists, livestock specialists, veterinary surgeons, engineers, technicians, etc.) as well as workers of mass professions: tractor drivers, machinist tractor-operators, combine operators, automobile drivers, electricians, fitters, turners, builders, repair workers, workmen skilled in the production of various kinds of livestock products and many other professions. The total number employed in the public economy is 1.9 million specialists with higher and secondary education and 4.6 million machine operators and automobile drivers. Their share in the structure of employment is gradually growing. Special significance is attached to the training of master stock-breeders for work on mechanised farms and in livestock breeding centres. Some of the able-bodied workers in the public sector of the economy are still engaged in different farm jobs where manual labour prevails. Mechanisation of these jobs is the main reserve for raising the productivity of labour and using workers made available as a result of it.

State and collective farms functioning on the self-supporting basis of the socialist economy have the appropriate system of management and remuneration of labour. The system is based primarily on the principle of the team contract, although, depending on the current conditions, character and structure of production, there are various forms of teams and sections. Their work, based on the self-supporting principle whereby each team is assigned with their specific sowings, machinery, or cattle and poultry, and other functioning resources, rules out the lack of personal responsibility, shapes an elevated feeling of a collective master as well as an incentive to raise the efficiency of the resources being used to produce more, cheaper and better, and to achieve higher gross and net incomes which are decisive sources for the formation of incentive and accumulation funds.

In the system of the organisational and economic management of the social economy there are many problems that emerge in the course of the progressive movement, the implementation of more cardinal economic updating, the transition of production to the qualitatively new stages of progress. The practical solution of these problems is linked with the overcoming of inevitable difficulties and the achievement of closer unity of national, collective and individual economic interests.

Along with the group of advanced, highly intensive and efficient agricultural enterprises whose labour productivity levels are higher than current world achievements, there are also groups of farms which hold a somewhat intermediate position or are lagging behind, where the structure and technology are still far from perfect, where the share of manual work is still very high and where the average labour productivity is behind that of farms in the USA and Western Europe. The pursuance of the agrarian policy aimed at the acceleration of intensification rates solves the immediate problem of turning sluggish enterprises into highly profitable ones. This is the goal of the Soviet, basically unified, policy of investment, structure, pricing, financing and credit. To ensure social and economic levelling and stabilisation of economic conditions of economic activity there is a system of zonal purchasing pricing for agricultural products, making allowances for farms located on low-fertility lands. As a rule they specialise in those commercial crops and kinds of cattle and poultry which are better adapted to the conditions suitable for their growing. This in itself reduces the cost of labour and material resources per unit of output and raises efficiency. A portion of the rental income is redistributed within the framework of co-operated economic systems and through the state budget. When the resource potential is formed and when the plans of state purchases are determined, consideration is taken of the necessity to level up economic conditions of economic activity with the strict observance of the socialist principle of distribution and remuneration according to the quantity and quality of labour, the final results of meeting the demands of consumers.

The growth rates of the average annual agricultural output and the index of agricultural labour productivity, calculated per man hour, are characterised for five-year periods by the following data.[9]

Years	Agricultural gross output	Labour productivity
1961–1965	100	100
1966–1970	121	136
1971–1975	137	163
1976–1980	150	181
1981–1983	154	184
1984	163	193

The increased gross output with a reduced size of labour force is reflected in the more rapid labour productivity growth rates. In the projected future up to the year 2000, it is planned to accelerate the labour productivity growth rates, first of all, through the technological improvement of land and livestock farming, their further intensification and rise in productivity. Hence, under the condition of farm staff stabilisation, part of the countryside labour resources will pass into the pension age and also will become available due to the movement of a certain number of young people to industry and services. In this case, in the labour structure the share of highly qualified workmen well versed in machine systems will prevail. Here lie tremendous reserves for the saving of public labour.

Nevertheless, manual agricultural labour will still be used for some operations where machinery is difficult to apply, both on public farms and, primarily, on individual subsidiary plots of collective farmers and state farm workers, as well as in orchards and kitchen gardens of urban citizens which are of no small importance for the labour education of children, leisure and physical training of the working people, and in keeping pensioners occupied. The dissociation of man from physical labour and the joys of his links with nature are incompatible with the very essence of human life, prolongation of his life and periods of labour activity.

The socialist system of agriculture is based on ensuring a rational combination of public and personal subsidiary farming. In this connection any attempt at finding artificial contradictions between these two forms, is erroneous. Western literature sometimes suggests that the availability of the subsidiary plots of collective farmers and state farm workers indicates lower efficiency of social production, without taking into account the fact that the very farming on personal plots is run on the basis of the socialist economy which allots not only personal plots but also the machinery for working on them, supplies young stock of cattle and poultry and feeds to maintain them from the public farms. Through existing agreements co-operatives often purchase surplus produce grown on individual subsidiary plots. In other words, counting on the desire of farmers to run their own subsidiary farming, the co-operative encourages it in all ways possible, thereby stimulating their extra activity and interest in collective farming. This is a strictly voluntary business. One who does not have his own subsidiary farming and is satisfied with the earning provided by public farming, may not necessarily have this plot of land. For those who do have it, the co-operative (or the collective farm), as well as the state farm creates the most favourable conditions for running individual subsidiary farming, understandably without damage to social farming.

The public sector at present produces practically all grain, sugar beet, cotton and other technical crops, 97 per cent of sunflowers, 70 per cent of livestock products, 68 per cent of vegetables and only 40 per cent of potatoes.[10] The gross production increase rates in the public sector in 1983 as compared with 1970 were 30 per cent and in the individual subsidiary farming only 6 per cent.[11] In state purchases the public sector accounts for 97–100 per cent for most agricultural products. Individual subsidiary farming sells to the state about one quarter of wool and potatoes and 8 per cent of vegetables of all purchases.[12] It should be underlined that the collective farmers' market in all the trade turnover of food products accounts only for 4.9 per cent.[13] Thus, both far-fetched exaggeration and underestimation of the importance of subsidiary farming in the agrarian sector of the socialist economy are not credible. Its development in the system of public economy at the present stage is of marginal, secondary importance.

Consequently, the most characteristic features and tendencies of the agrarian labour development under the influence of scientific-technological progress in socialist agriculture are as follows:

First, the essential increase in its power and technological capacity, in the level of mechanisation and automation with the introduction of continuous flow process technologies;

Second, more profound division of labour, changes in its sectoral, occupational structure and inner content with the view of transferring many labour functions to machine systems and hence changes in the relationship of manual and mental labour, levels of intellectualisation and qualification and in the rates of transition from simple to complicated labour;

Third, the development of integrated economic systems is accompanied by an increase in the degree of socialisation of production and labour and its gradual conversion from agrarian to agro-industrial;

Fourth, there is a radical change in the socio-class structure of the rural population which has become part and parcel of the new historical community of people – the Soviet people. Agricultural workmen, collective farmers and rural intelligentsia are the indivisible part of it. They, together with other citizens of the USSR possess equal constitutional rights and obligations, free access to common national endowments, social and spiritual benefits, education and science, the gains of culture. In addition to earnings from public farming or individual subsidiary farming, collective farmers get an equal share of social consumption funds, are members of the trade union and are covered by social security services.

However, the solution of the problem of overcoming the essential distinctions between the city and the countryside implies an even greater scope for subsequent changes. The economic upsurge will not only bring agriculture closer to the level of industry in terms of technical facilities and production activity, ensure well-organised co-operation of agriculture and its industrial processing in the agro-industrial systems being formed, but at the same time will help to continue the work in the direction of more rapid development of the production and social infrastructure, development of built-up areas using the principles of the latest scientific accomplishments in the field of architecture, civil engineeering and town planning, achievement of uniformity in the levels of well-being and culture, the service system catering for both urban and rural citizens. These are vital programme targets of the agrarian policy of the CPSU and the Soviet state.

NOTES

[1] *The USSR national economy in 1983*. M., Finansi i statistika, 1984, p. 36 (Rus.).
[2] Ibid., p. 383, 384.
[3] Ibid. p. 5.
[4] Ibid. p. 36.
[5] Ibid. pp. 196–7.
[6] Ibid. p. 36.
[7] Ibid. p. 54.
[8] Ibid, p. 441.
[9] Ibid, pp. 211 and 301.
[10] Ibid. p. 210.
[11] Ibid, p. 211.
[12] Ibid., p. 218.
[13] Ibid, p. 457.

DISCUSSION OPENING – ERIK SWEDBORG

The Soviet Union holds a key position in international food trade. Good or poor grain crops in the Soviet Union influence the world market to a great extent. This can be a good thing from foreign farmers' point of view as well as a bad one. The influence on the farmers is probably most evident in the United States, but it is observable also in Sweden, the country from which I come.

Some 30 years ago with Nikita Krushchev as Head of State and Leonid Breshnev as implementer, the Soviet Union embarked upon a gigantic programme for breaking new land in Kazakstan and adjoining areas east of the Urals. This project, fulfilled in only a few years, was the starting point for a new deal in Soviet agricultural policy. The background to this was the situation at the beginning of the 1950s when the Soviet Union found itself confronted with a grave food supply crisis. There were two alternative solutions: either to intensify agricultural production in the older already existing farming areas, mainly in European Russia, or to break new land east of the Urals. It was decided to adopt the latter alternative, which is understandable since experience from earlier agricultural policy has shown that enormous investments would otherwise be needed to obtain the necessary results quickly.

The guidelines for the new agricultural policy drawn up in 1953 embraced the following:

(1) Extensive land reclamation, mainly east of the Urals (principally in Kazakstan) where the chief crop would be wheat.

(2) The growing of more livestock feed on additional land which would then become available in the older farming districts and in particular maize of different types.

(3) A considerable increase in livestock which would become possible because of the additional acreage of livestock feed.

The first phase in this three-point programme was accomplished with enormous drive, though needless to say not without difficulties, in 1954–6 when the sowed area was increased by almost 40 million hectares (13 times the cultivated area of Sweden), in other words, a 25 per cent expansion. All this produced results. The vital grain crops were greatly enlarged and livestock feed crops also increased and prepared the way for a sharp rise in livestock production.

During the first five years of 'the new deal' up to 1958, total farm production (excluding livestock feed) rose by about 50 per cent, which is about 10 per cent per annum. The increase was somewhat greater in livestock production than in crop production. Thanks to the increase in livestock production the Soviet diet was improved compared with the situation in earlier years. The increase in grain production gave scope for a considerable export of wheat, chiefly to the new Communist states in Eastern Europe which were struggling with difficulties of food supply. During the 1960s however the development of agriculture lost pace and the increases in production were only in the order of 5 per cent per annum. During the 1970s the tempo slowed down even more to between 2 and 3 per cent. Even after the land reclamation, however, the Ukraine retained its traditional status as the granary of Russia; but it also became something of a milk and pork centre. Between 1954 and 1960 the number of cows in the Ukraine rose from 5.5 to 7.7 million – a 40 per cent increase, while the corresponding figures for pigs were 11.3 to 16.5 million – 46 per cent. So far as cultivated area is concerned, Kazakstan took over to a large extent the role as the principal granary of Soviet Russia (though not with regard to the size of harvest). Up until 1959 no less than 18.3 million hectares of new land was broken in Kazakstan, in other words 47 per cent of the total area of newly cultivated land. In a few years the arable land area in Kazakstan increased from 9.7 to 28.0

million hectares and from the crop point of view the emphasis was, and still is, on wheat. Despite the predictions of many pessimists of 30 years ago the special growing problems in Kazakstan and adjoining regions have to a large extent been overcome through a combination of American type 'prairie farming' knowhow and particular techniques of land reclamation.

In other respects agricultural developments in the Soviet Union have been less impressive. This emerges very clearly if we study relative yield levels in crop and livestock farming. For example, during the last period of the 1950s the average wheat yield was about 10 quintals per hectare (this low figure is explainable by the very low yields in the newly cultivated regions). Twenty years later during the 'normal year' of 1976, the corresponding figure was 16 quintals per hectare, in other words, the increase rate was about 3 per cent per annum. By comparison, milk production per cow rose by only something like 1 per cent per annum (1850 kg per cow in 1956/60 to 2200 kg in 1976–80), although the latter figure was influenced to some degree by the unsatisfactory feed conditions resulting from the poor harvests of 1975 and 1979. In the United States, where agriculture is on a larger scale and is therefore better suited to comparison with the Soviet Union than is Western Europe, wheat yields in recent years have been around 21 to 22 quintals per hectare and the yield per cow around 5100 kg per annum. It can thus be safely said that the Soviet Union has been much more successful in increasing crop production than livestock production. This may be a feeding issue and this is a point which is worth a closer examination.

I would now like to ask some specific questions.

(1) Do you agree with my description of what has happened in the Soviet Union during the last few decades and in particular that related to the land reclamation of the 1950s?

(2) Do you agree with my description of the regional pattern of agricultural production made possible by this land reclamation?

(3) What are your views concerning the low productivity in animal production and how can this situation be improved?

(4) It is well known that the 1980s started in a very unfortunate way so far as grain yields were concerned. Crop failures are likely from time to time in the context of a climate like the one in the Soviet Union but it seems that the failure has not happened so frequently before. My question really is whether such a severe drought has occurred for so many years in a relatively short space of time, and are there other reasons than climate which have produced this condition?

(5) Regarding the future, what possibilities are there for the more effective use of water, in particular the idea that some of the Siberian rivers might be used in a more efficient way by making them flow in the opposite direction?

(6) What is the opinion of the agricultural experts in the Soviet Union regarding changes in the near future? What may one realistically

expect regarding the near future development of food supply and production?

GENERAL DISCUSSION – RAPPORTEUR: CSABA FORGÁCS

Replying to the questions of the opener, Victor Nazarenko was of the same opinion with regard to the description of land reclamation as Erik Swedborg in generally emphasising that the main goal was to increase fodder grain production. The low productivity of animal production is a fact. The first aim was to increase the size of the production in general. Productivity is also increasing but it is really slow. The way for the future is to use intensive industrial-type technologies, as has been done in poultry production. But the problem concerning dairy production has to be faced. The number of cows will be stabilised but their productivity should be increased by breeding as well as by larger-scale feed production. The influence of agriculture on the national economy has been analysed on a base of a long-term series. Efficiency has decreased during the last six years where other reasons may also be found besides unfavourable weather conditions. Research on contract farming has shown higher efficiency especially where a labour-intensive production is taking place. He also pointed out that the maintenance of low food prices is a political and social question, being aware of the fact that it has an influence on the budget as well. For the future substantial emphasis should be placed on developing technologies.

Erik Swedborg mentioned the Chinese system of land use which appears to be efficient and he spoke about similar possibilities in the Soviet Union.

In answer to a question focusing on the system of the purchase of grain from abroad, it was made clear that the state has a foreign trade monopoly but a large-scale home trade as well. World market prices, trade situations and other factors are also taken into account by decision-makers with regard to the import of grain.

One questioner asked how it was possible to take into consideration the (around) 400 geographical units in the process of planning. In reply it was stated that resource allocation was investigated unit by unit by institutions thus creating a base for decision-makers. Planning based on administrative units which are not the equivalent of the geographical regions are used mostly in academic works.

It was asked whether net output tendencies are following the pattern of the gross output and also the availability of statistical data on net value product, with reference to the recent problems of organisation and economic management of the Soviet economy mentioned in I. Lukinov's paper. The answer emphasised that there are different ways of calculating net output figures. It was also underlined that there are a lot of publications available on farming but very few in English.

More information was requested on the exact number of people working in agriculture and the share of private production. From the answer it transpired that the number of working people in agriculture and forestry is

20 per cent of the total, but it was previously much higher. The share of private (small-scale) production depends on the basis of comparison. Auxiliary and household plot production is about 27 per cent of the gross output of agriculture. But it is an integrated part of the economy and its role is important, for example, in vegetable, potato and animal production. The output of small gardens is also significant but there are no statistical data available.

Participants in the discussion included F. Fekete and S. Holmstrom.

SECTION III

Balancing Overproduction and Malnutrition

JOHN W. MELLOR

Dealing with the Uncertainty of Growing Food Imbalances: International Structures and National Policies

INTRODUCTION

I start with a Rawlsian (Rawls 1971) view that it is unjust and hence unacceptable that in some countries large numbers of people suffer from food intake inadequate for healthy, active lives, but in others food is stored for uneconomically long periods of time or subsidies are paid to dispose of food or to reduce production.

That the existing distribution of food is unjust is, of course, clearly indicated by the large surpluses that almost all OECD countries have and by their concern with how to dispose of that food. At the same time massive poverty exists in much of the Third World, with as many as 800 million people having an inadequate energy intake. Assuming that such a distribution of food is philosophically unacceptable, we must ask why it exists. I argue that it happens for three reasons.

First, there is a serious inhibition to redistributing income because of the effect of marginal tax rates on incentives. In many countries, perhaps all, the burdens placed on governments, whether well thought out or not, are so large that the marginal tax rates established are now generally thought to destroy incentives and hence growth. This does create a dilemma between growth and equity. One may argue, of course, that a high priority of taxation should be to redistribute food to those who have inadequate food intake. Preferences revealed in actions, which perhaps should not be dismissed as misleading, suggest otherwise.

Second, those who are taxed, generally believe that there is considerable difficulty in identifying the needy and in devising programmes that efficiently transfer resources to them. There is a related ambivalence about the interaction between short-run mitigation of poverty and the creation of conditions that eliminate poverty in the long run. While we all know there is considerable inefficiency in transferring income, it is perhaps also true that the extent of that inefficiency is exaggerated.

Third, there may be a difference between looking at a country from a Rawlsian perspective and looking at the world from that perspective. Since the distribution of income among nations is grossly uneven, it follows that redistributing food from the more well-to-do to the poorer means the redistribution of food from wealthier countries to poorer ones. Do we think only of the probability of being poor in our own country? If so, we may feel that this probability is so low that we can dismiss it. If we take an international view instead, we would favour larger international income transfers, both for development and to increase equity.

GROWING REGIONAL FOOD IMBALANCES

Exports of food from the developed market economies to the developing countries of the Third World have grown rapidly from an annual average of about 11 million metric tons during 1976–80. By projecting production and demand, these exports reach 75 to 80 million metric tons by the year 2000. These figures, by historical standards, are extraordinary. During 1980–2 food aid comprised about 9 per cent of cereal imports into Third World countries. That is a decline from 13 per cent during 1976–8 (Paulino forthcoming; Huddleston 1984). Thus, the market has brought about a tremendous movement of food from the surplus-generating developed countries to the developing countries. Were it not for this commercial flow, food prices in developing countries would have been considerably higher. Since demand for food by the poor is relatively elastic, these commercial transfers clearly increased equity. Given this huge flow of food on commercial account, it is useful to understand the major structural changes in developing and developed countries that explain it. By understanding the structural forces we can understand that this flow is likely not only to continue but perhaps to accelerate. I will distinguish four phases in food-supply demand balance relationships (Mellor 1966; Mellor and Johnston 1984).

Phase one
In the first phase, typical of low income incipient developing countries, the labour force grows modestly and is significantly constrained by high death rates. Income per caput hardly rises at all. Thus demand for food grows at a modest rate, and expansion of the labour force in the dominant rural sector can be expected to cause food production to grow at a comparable rate. Incomes and food intake per caput are low, health is generally poor, and malnutrition is extensive, but food supply and demand are roughly in balance.

While most of sub-Saharan Africa is in an early phase of development, it is importing large quantities of food at a rapidly growing rate. This is because urbanisation has proceeded at a far more rapid rate than domestic agriculture can sustain. That has been made possible by large amounts of foreign assistance and, for a few sub-Saharan African countries, by large increases in oil prices. Combined with a significant marginal product of agricultural labour, this rapid pace of urbanisation has caused agricultural production to increase more slowly and urban demand to grow more rapidly than is typical of this phase of development, particularly when land is in surplus, as it is in sub-Saharan Africa

(Mellor and Ranade forthcoming). The rates of change in this inefficient process are unsustainable without rapidly increasing foreign aid.

Phase two
Economic development begins in the second phase. Food production grows somewhat more rapidly as technological change is introduced. The rate of growth of population may slow in response to lower birth and death rates. Employment and incomes per caput grow only modestly, even though the base for more rapid growth in the future is being prepared. Food supply and demand may shift at a similar pace. Imports may be modest or even decline.

Phase three
In the third phase agricultural production increases quite rapidly, the long slow development of the institutional base having begun to bear fruit. The same process of agricultural growth has very strong linkage and multiplier effects on other parts of the economy and tends to cause rapid growth in the employment and income of the labouring class. Concurrently, other aspects of development, including endogenous capital formation and growth in other parts of the economy also accelerate the growth rate of the economy. The results are rapid growth in the income of people with high marginal propensities to spend on food. Consequently, the demand for food outpaces domestic production, even though domestic production itself may increase rapidly. The result is that imports of food grow rapidly. This importation of food is strongly reinforced by rapid growth of livestock consumption, which quickly uses up the supply of by-product feeds and thus provokes rapid growth of demand for cereals for livestock consumption.

Phase four
In phase four, the phase that high-income countries are in, population grows very slowly and, while income per caput may grow rapidly, the marginal propensity to consume food is low. Thus, demand for food increases slowly. Shifts in the supply of agricultural commodities have been institutionalised and are rapid. Thus, supply grows more rapidly than demand and there is heavy pressure either to have prices fall or to export large amounts of food. The United States entered this phase several decades ago; Europe entered it more recently. The Soviet Union seems yet to enter this phase, primarily because of continued rapid growth in demand.

THE GLOBAL BALANCE

The world has a large population in phase four and another large population moving into phase three. But most phase one countries import large amounts of food. Because the amounts of food involved are immense, particularly relative to the volume of trade in food commodities, it is virtually impossible to predict whether these trends will cause food prices to rise or fall. We should, however, keep clearly in mind that this situation is new and unusual. The future certainly cannot be predicted by the experience of the last four or five years, during which the world has been in a major recession and structural realignment. In the 1950s and 1960s there were too few countries in phase three to have much impact.

How do governments plan food policy in the face of such uncertainty? Two principles stand out. First, since development requires broad participation of a country's population, the food sector, as the generally dominant sector, should be emphasised. Comparative advantage probably supports this emphasis because there is a lack of other short-run opportunities for the massive set of resources invested in agriculture. Second, caution should be used in making long-term investments in agriculture that require agricultural prices considerably higher than at present to justify them.

THE ROLE OF THE MARKET

The powerful and beneficial effect of market forces in the context of structural food imbalances should be noted. Many developing countries, despite widespread popular impression to the contrary, are developing a capacity to expand demand for food more rapidly than even an excellent record in domestic food production can match. Thus, the ability to expand employment and to have the demand for wage goods (primarily food) grow rapidly is great. The potential to expand employment would be constrained by a shortage of wage goods if these were closed economies or if they were open economies but no other countries expanded domestic production of food more rapidly than domestic demand. The rapid generation of surpluses in the developed countries favours employment-oriented growth in developing countries. It should be clear that I am talking about countries that have successfully increased employment. Those are almost inevitably countries in which an agricultural development strategy has been successful (Bachman and Paulino 1979).

These forces reduce poverty because poverty cannot be disassociated from lack of food, the primary component of consumption of the poor. If food is scarce, it becomes expensive, and as it becomes expensive it drives down the real income of the poor. Indeed, a constrained supply of food, or more properly a supply of food that is highly inelastic with respect to price, must necessarily constrain employment, because it drives up the price of wage goods, drives up the real price of labour, and substitutes capital for labour, either through capital intensive production processes in existing industries or by pushing the output mix toward more capital intensive products (Mellor 1974).

Of course, many developing countries have chosen development strategies that are highly capital intensive. India and China based their strategies on the Harrod-Domar and Fel'dman-Mahalanobis concepts, which explicitly push development immediately in a capital-intensive direction. Import substitution strategies may begin by substituting domestic production for labour-intensive imports but they very quickly substitute domestic production for capital-intensive imports, particularly when domestic markets are limited. This process has been most marked in Latin America, where income distribution was initially highly skewed.

WHAT MARKETS CANNOT DO IN DEALING WITH FOOD IMBALANCES

Having made a case that market forces can increase food supplies and equity, we must turn to the limitations of those forces. These limitations are particularly important for equity and have important implications for growth. The problem of market limitations can properly be divided into problems of chronic food deficiencies and problems of fluctuations in food supply.

Chronic food deficiencies
In phases one and two countries can expect to suffer chronic scarcities of food. People are poor and their food supplies are inadequate. In the long run, development must move the country into phase four. Development involves major structural changes, particularly by developing scientific and technological capabilities that require massive quantities of trained people and complex institutional frameworks. Can anything be done to immediately reduce chronic food scarcity? Two measures should be noted in particular: food and employment subsidies and food aid.

Increasing the amount of food those with low food intake consume does much to increase the human capital of a country. There are clear, though not well documented, relationships between adequate diet, physical activity, physical growth, and mental energy. It seems clear that human capital is reduced by poor diets. Thus even for growth – to say nothing of Rawlsian equity – there is much to be said for improving the diets of the poor.

A reasonable way to improve the diets of the poor is to subsidise food, so that the price of food to the consumer is lower than the producer price, or lower than the world price. The problem is that poor countries can have such reductions in food prices only at great cost. They are even less able than rich countries to target food programmes on the poor because they have so few trained people. Thus, they must either have broad programmes and high marginal tax rates, or they must forego important long-term investments. Both reduce future capacity to reduce poverty.

We may distinguish between the efficiency of food subsidies in urban areas and the efficiency of employment subsidies in rural areas. People go to urban areas to find higher-paying jobs. Providing people with low-paid employment that removes them from the search for the kind of employment they came to the urban area for is not likely to work. Food subsidies seem more appropriate.

In rural areas the number of recipients is immense. There is considerable underemployment of labour, that is, labour has low productivity. The marginal propensity of the poor to spend on food is high and the return of rural infrastructure, including roads, is also high. In such circumstances subsidising employment seems an effective way to provide food to the poor.

Global food imbalances can be used to deal with the high cost of food and employment subsidies in low-income countries. Large amounts of food sold on concessionary terms can fuel food and employment subsidies. Such flows, of course, are advantageous to producers of agricultural commodities, because they, in effect, remove food from the commercial market, where demand is inelastic, and move it into markets, such as those for low-income people, where demand is highly elastic. The result is that the average price is higher than it would otherwise be (Mellor 1983). This is a powerful rationalisation for providing much more food aid than is being provided at present.

Food aid is not likely to be used effectively if recipient countries – and donors for that matter – are not interested in development led by agriculture. If agriculture is at the heart of a development strategy, then food aid can be effective in reducing global food imbalances (Mellor 1976).

Food supply fluctuations

The poor have a much more elastic demand for food than the rich – primarily because the income effect of food price change, which is such a high proportion of expenditures, is so powerful. The result is that the distribution of food is much more skewed against the poor during shortages than when supplies are average or above average. The well-to-do maintain their consumption of food when supplies are scarce and prices are high by reducing their consumption of other goods and services. That very act reduces the employment of the poor and thereby reduces their purchasing power, causing the price increases to be considerably smaller than they would be otherwise. Whether one looks at employment or prices, the poor are driven from the market for food when supplies are scarce and they make most of the shifts in consumption.

Thus, using Indian data, if there is a 10 per cent increase in food grain prices, then the bottom 40 per cent in the income distribution reduce their consumption in absolute terms by more than 10 times the reduction of the top 5 per cent (Mellor 1978). In a market economy practically all the adjustment to a food shortage is made by low income people. It is doubtful that that is either good development policy or just.

There are several notable aspects of fluctuations in food supplies. First, weather fluctuations have a tremendous effect on the poor. In India, over two decades, the proportion of the rural population falling below the defined poverty line fluctuated between 40 and 60 per cent, with two complete cycles of such fluctuations (Mellor and Desai 1985). Those huge fluctuations are a result of a large population near the defined poverty line and large fluctuations in weather.

Second, the international price environment fluctuates much more now than it used to (Valdes 1984). This is an indication that food moves across international boundaries less easily now than it did a few decades ago. This is primarily because the United States is no longer a major holder of stocks.

Third, instability in food production has increased substantially during recent decades. This is clearly documented by Peter Hazell for India, the United States, and other countries (Hazell 1984). It seems that, in large countries at least, the covariances among regions are increasing and explain much of the increase in the fluctuations. This may well be because of factors associated with modern technology. For example, practically all a country's production of a crop, as with maize in the United States, might have one parent in common, which makes the crop more vulnerable to pestilence. This is a problem that scientists are now working on, and we can expect a solution. But there is still a problem in the meantime. In a country like India, policies on fertilizer, electricity, or irrigation fluctuate from year to year, having a large effect on production as agriculture becomes more dependent on fertilizer or on electricity for small- or large-scale irrigation.

Thus the poor are tremendously affected by fluctuations in supplies, and supply fluctuations are becoming greater rather than smaller. We need to deal with these problems with a combination of national and international interventions.

The International Monetary Fund's cereal loan facility is a major innovation. It is described by Richard Adams in a recent *World Development* paper (1983). The principle behind the facility is that storage, particularly now, when real interest rates are high, is an expensive way to compensate production fluctuations. Farmers in developing countries typically store heavily after a good year and can take care of one bad year, but not always a second. This is a reflection of the high cost of storage over the long periods necessary for dealing with a sequence of bad years. The best way to solve such problems is through trade: by shipping from areas with good harvests to those with bad. The fluctuations in one country's production are vastly greater than those of the world as a whole. The IMF's cereal facility is designed to finance those flows, particularly for low-income countries that have great difficulty financing the flows themselves.

The facility needs to be improved, separating foods from other sources of fluctuations in foreign exchange availability (Ezekiel 1985). It should not be an integral part of the Compensatory Financing Facility.

Food aid can reduce fluctuations in a similar way. But past uses of food aid are not encouraging. In fact, it may be better to use the IMF cereal facility as a way of dealing with fluctuations in food aid, rather than food aid as a way of reducing use of the IMF cereal facility.

Of course, national programmes must also be relied on to ensure that food flows into rural areas when food is scarce and into urban areas when that is necessary. The national programmes needed are approximately the same as those needed to deal with chronic scarcity.

Uncertainty about global food supplies and financing is a powerful argument against a development strategy that, through emphasis on agriculture and employment, makes poor countries more dependent on uncertain weather. Thus, adding certainty of food supplies through international mechanisms can have a powerful effect on development, as well as on equity.

REFERENCES

Adams, Richard, 'The Role of Research in Policy Development: The Creation of the IMF Cereal Import Facility', *World Development*, vol. 11, no. 7, 1983.

Bachman, Kenneth L. and Paulino, Leonardo, *Rapid Food Production Growth in Selected Developing Countries: A Comparative Analysis of Underlying Trends, 1969–76*, Research Report no. 11, International Food Policy Research Institute, Washington, DC, October 1979.

Ezekiel, Hannan, 'The IMF Cereal Import Financing Scheme', (unpublished paper), International Food Policy Research Institute, Washington, DC, April 1985.

Hazell, Peter B. R., 'Sources of Increased Instability in Indian and U.S. Cereal Production', *American Journal of Agricultural Economics*, vol. 66, no. 3, August 1984.

Huddleston, Barbara, *Closing the Cereals Gap with Trade and Food Aid*, Research Report no. 43, International Food Policy Research Institute, Washington, DC, January 1984.

Mellor, John W., *The Economics of Agricultural Development*, Cornell University Press, Ithaca, NY, 1966.

Mellor, John W., 'Models of Economic Growth and Land-Augmenting Technological Change in Foodgrain Production', in Nurul Islam (ed.), *Agricultural Policy in Developing Countries*, Macmillan, London, 1974.

Mellor, John W., *The New Economics of Growth – A Strategy for India and the Developing World*, Cornell University Press, Ithaca, NY, 1976.

Mellor John W., 'Food Price Policy and Income Distribution in Low-Income Countries', *Economic Development and Cultural Change*, vol. 27, no. 1, October 1978.

Mellor John W., 'The Utilization of Food Aid for Equitable Growth', presented at the World Food Programme – Government of the Netherlands Seminar on Food Aid, The Hague, Netherlands, 3–5 October, 1983.

Mellor, John W. and Johnston, Bruce F., 'The World Food Equation: Interrelations Among Development, Employment, and Food Consumption', *Journal of Economic Literature*, vol. 22, June 1984.

Mellor John W. and Desai, Gunvant M. (eds), *Agricultural Change and Rural Poverty: Variations on a Theme by Dharm Narain*, Johns Hopkins University Press, Baltimore, 1985.

Mellor, John W. and Ranade, C. J., 'Technological Change in a Low-Labour Productivity, Land Surplus Economy: The African Development Problem', (forthcoming).

Paulino, Leonardo, *Food in the Third World: Past Trends and Projections to 2000*, International Food Policy Research Institute, Washington, DC, (forthcoming).

Rawls, John, *A Theory of Justice*, Harvard University Press, Cambridge, Mass., 1971.

Tsujii, Hiroshi, 'Comparison of Rice Policies Between Thailand, Taiwan and Japan: An Evolutionary Model and Current Policies' in Hiroshi Tsujii (ed.), *A Comparative Study of Food Policy in Rice Countries – Taiwan, Thailand, and Japan*, Kyoto University Press, Kyoto, 1982.

Valdes, Alberto, 'A Note on Variability in International Grain Prices', (unpublished paper), prepared for IFPRI Workshop on Food and Agricultural Price Policy, International Food Policy Research Institute, Washington, DC, 1984.

T. N. SRINIVASAN*

Undernutrition: Extent and Distribution of its Incidence

DEFINITION OF UNDERNUTRITION

A widely accepted definition of *malnutrition* is that it is a pathological state, general or specific, resulting from a relative or absolute deficiency or an excess in the diet of one or more essential nutrients (Scrimshaw, *et al*. 1968). Of the various forms of malnutrition such as specific deficiency, imbalance, undernutrition and overnutrition, the primary concern of this paper is with *undernutrition*. This is not because other forms of malnutrition are not prevalent in developing countries but only because either some other deficiencies (e.g. protein) seem to be closely associated with energy undernutrition or their implications are well understood. Undernutrition has been defined as a pathological state arising from an intake of an inadequate amount of food, and hence of energy, over a considerable period, with reduced body weight as its principal manifestation. Implicit in this definition is the notion that energy intake (that is the energy content of food intake measured in kilocalories or megajoules per day) *required* in order to maintain body weight (and to continue performing whatever energy using tasks that are associated with one's occupation) is well defined. This assumption has increasingly come under attack on several grounds. First, it is inconsistent with the observation of several investigators who found a large variation in intakes of otherwise similar individuals engaged in similar activities. An early study by Widowson (1947) showed a coefficient of variation of 20 per cent in intakes of individuals of the same age, sex and similar activity patterns, even after allowances were made for differences in the body weight. There have been several such findings since then. Second, it is now being recognised that an individual can remain in good health and in energy balance with intakes varying over a wide range (Sukhatme and Margen 1982). Third, it has been found (Durnin 1979) that there are individuals, indeed whole population groups, who maintain energy balance at astonishingly low intakes with no apparent consequences in terms of their health or activity. Fourth, the common assumption that dietary induced genesis is a relatively small part of the energy requirement is question-

*presented by J. W. Mellor.

able. Thus a high resting metabolic rate (RMR) instead of signifying a high energy (food intake) *requirement* may instead be a *consequence of* high intake. Sukhatme and Margen (1982) suggest that the thermic effect lasts for several hours and can account for as much as 20 per cent in RMR depending on the quantity and composition of the meal. Finally, in societies in which there are significant seasonal variations in intensity of work and food availability, there appear to be corresponding variations in energy expenditure of individuals. Indeed Sukhatme has argued that a large part of the total energy intake of an individual is dissipated as heat and it is this part (rather than activity) that adjusts to variations in intake. Thus, there is a homeostatic mechanism that adjusts the metabolic efficiency of energy use so that when total energy intake is reduced (increased) the system wastes less (more) energy as heat. Of course there are limits to homeostatic adjustment so that intakes outside these limits lead to deleterious consequences such as wastage or obesity, reduction in activity, etc.

Besides the conceptual problems with the assumption of a constant energy requirement, there are problems with the data base on which the FAO/WHO requirements rest. It consists largely of studies of Caucasian populations of industrialised countries. The applicability of energy requirements derived from these data to populations of differing ethnic and environmental backgrounds is yet to be demonstrated. Yet most of the estimates of the prevalence of undernutrition in the world are based on these requirement estimates.

EXTENT OF INCIDENCE OF UNDERNUTRITION

There are broadly three approaches to the estimation of the extent of prevalence of undernutrition in a population. The first involves the use of clinical and biomedical evidence to determine whether an individual exhibits symptoms associated with dietary inadequacy and/or imbalance and then estimate the proportion of the population exhibiting such symptoms. The second approach uses anthropometric indicators such as body weight, height, skinfold measurements, etc. and judges the nutritional status of an individual in relation to some standards relating height to age, weight for age, height to weight, etc. The third approach involves judging nutritional status by comparing actual intake of a nutrient by an individual with some standards (as for instance, the FAO/WHO energy and protein requirements).

The first two are outcome-based approaches in that they identify an observed outcome such as departure from some standard relationship between anthropometric measures or a clinical symptom with nutritional status. Obviously, in the absence of other supporting evidence, it is often difficult to judge whether the observed outcome is due to dietary inadequacy and imbalance or due to a whole host of other factors of which dietary inadequacy may be one and not necessarily the dominant factor. Even if we ignore the other factors that may have contributed to the observed outcome, there is still a question whether the outcome represents the current or past nutritional stresses.

Just as energy standards have been based on Caucasian populations, so have most widely used anthropometric standards. Further, assessment (of nutritional status) based on anthropometric standards need not, and often do not, correspond to clinical assessments. Ferro-Luzzi, et al. (1975) analysed the dietary intakes of 482 New Guinean children aged 1–18 years. Data on body weight and skinfold thickness were also recorded. They found 'that the high proportion of nutritionally inadequate diets, assessed on an age basis using materially favoured Caucasian population as standards, does not match with physiological or clinical signs and symptoms of malnutrition in these New Guinean children'. If the FAO/WHO standards of energy-protein malnutrition and Western standards of growth were applied to their data,

> growth retardation and the frequent presence of clinical malnutrition would be anticipated. This was only partly substantiated by an assessment of nutritional status. There was a low prevalence of clinical signs of specific nutritional deficiencies. Only occasional cases of Kwashiorkor and Marasmus were observed in the villages and none were encountered in the survey population. Their incidence and severity did not match the degree and frequency of calculated dietary inadequacy. All cases could be traced back to irregular or prolonged untreated infectious diseases.

Nick Eberstadt (1981) quotes several studies that corroborate the conclusion of Ferro Luzzi et al. A study by the then US Agency for International Development showed that 42 per cent of Sri Lankan children were moderately or severely malnourished and less than 10 per cent were normal when American height–weight charts were used to assess growth. Yet life expectancy at birth in Sri Lanka is over 65 years. The Pan American Health Organization apparently found that nearly half the population of Barbados, Costa Rica, Guyana, Jamaica and Panama suffered from some degree of malnutrition by conventional standards. Yet in each of these countries life expectancy at birth was 70 years or more!

In the first section the controversial nature of the theory underlying the FAO/WHO energy requirements was discussed. Given this controversy, the conceptual basis for the third of the above approaches is doubtful, even if it were possible to collect data on intakes of individuals along with information on their age, sex and physical activity so as to be able to compare their intakes with requirements. The widely publicised estimates (see Table 1) of the global extent of undernutrition such as those of Reutlinger and Selowsky (1976) of the World Bank or those in FAO's Fourth World Food Survey are not based on individual specific comparisons of intakes and requirements. It is true that since the objective is not one of determining whether each individual in a

T. N. Srinivasan

TABLE 1 *Percentage of population with energy intakes below requirements*

Source	Region	Period	Percentage undernourished	Definition requirements
Reutlinger and Selowsky (1976)	Asia	1985	65	FAO/WHO requirements, calorie–income elasticity of 0.3
	Latin America		46	
	Africa		61	
	Middle East		51	
	Total		60	
FAO, Fourth World Food Survey (1977)	Far East	1972–74		1.2 BMR
	Latin America		29	
	Africa		15	
	Near East		28	
	Total, developing		16	
	country		25	
Poleman (1982)	Far East (ex. China)	1975	12	50% of infants up to 5 years of age and pregnant and lactating mothers considered malnourished. Number of pregnant and lactating mothers taken as twice the birth rate.
	China		9	
	Africa		14	
	Latin America		12	
	Near East		13	
	Total		11	
Alan Berg (1981)	India	1972–74	47	FAO/WHO requirements
	Bangladesh		77	
	Brazil		43	
	Morocco		50	

population is adequately nourished or not but only of determining the proportion of inadequately nourished individuals in that population, it is not essential to base the estimation procedure on individual specific comparisons. However, the methodology of FAO and the World Bank does not appear to be capable of yielding unbiased estimates of the extent of undernutrition in a population.

There is an important problem with the data on which many of the estimates of the extent of undernutrition are based. Even though undernutrition was defined as a pathological state of an individual arising from an inadequate intake of food over a considerable period of time, the available estimates of global extent of undernutrition are not based on longitudinal data on intakes of food of a suitable chosen sample of individuals from the relevant population groups. Nor are they obtained from anthropometric or clinical and biomedical evidence from such samples of individuals. In other words, the estimates are based neither on individual intake data nor on supposed outcomes of inadequate intakes such as anthropometric or clinical evidence. Very few sample surveys of individual intakes exist and even these few provide data on intakes during a day or at the most a week. Even rarer are surveys that provide data on body weight and activity pattern of surveyed individuals. Needless to say, strong and untested assumptions will be needed to interpret these intakes as habitual or long-term intakes of the individuals surveyed. Most consumption surveys provide data on expenditure on food at the household level over some reference period such as a week, month or even a whole year. Even if one were to set aside the myriad problems associated with obtaining complete and reliable estimates of consumption through questionnaires in developing countries where the components of consumption consisting of home-grown food, food obtained in barter and as wages in kind are significant, a whole host of assumptions of varying degrees of plausibility is needed to go from expenditure on food to estimates of energy intake at the household level. The data situation is even worse since such surveys of consumption expenditures are not available for all developing countries and only for a few countries such as India are data from more than one survey available. Given this situation the brave estimators of the FAO and World Bank literally make bricks without straw. With little more to go on than a not-so-very reliable food balance sheet for a country as a whole and even less reliable data on income per caput, they arrive at estimates of the extent of undernutrition by making heroic and often untested and even untestable assumptions about the distribution of income and food among individuals in the population.

Even if we take the estimates of undernutrition at their face value, there is the further problem of assessing the consequences of undernutrition in terms of human function. While severe malnourishment clearly has adverse consequences, there appears to be a lot of uncertainty surrounding the relationship of less than severe malnutrition to human function. Nor is the relationship between an individual's intake and his work output or productivity firmly established. The available evidence (Srinivasan 1983) suggests that the ill effects of severe malnutrition on human function seem to have been established while mild and moderate undernutrition do not appear to have lasting effects. This does not mean that the ill effects can be ruled out, only that the existing studies may not be sufficiently sensitive to detect them. More sensitive studies are therefore needed.

POLICIES FOR COMBATING UNDERNUTRITION

A variety of nutritional intervention policies have been tried in developing as well as some developed countries, either as part of continuing governmental intervention in matters relating to public health and the food and agriculture sector of the economy or as an experimental effort to determine the appropriate form of intervention. Such policies may either be intended to affect *specific* segments of the population (i.e.

target group oriented policies) or *non discriminatory* in their intent. Examples of target group oriented policies include school lunch programmes, supplementary feeding programmes and in general programmes intended to reach nutritionally vulnerable groups such as young children and pregnant and lactating women. Non-discriminatory policies are exemplified by a food fortification policy and a food subsidy programme that subsidises (or provides free, as used to be the case in Sri Lanka) part of the food consumption of the entire population. In addition to nutrition intervention policies there are other policies which have nutritional side effects – these include a whole host of policies that affect the production, distribution and consumption of food. Berg (1981) provides a summary review of the experience with nutrition intervention policies in developing countries. Taylor et al. (1980) review the evidence on food subsidy and food for work schemes in several countries.

These reviews suggest that while substantial improvements in infant mortality, foetal wastage and morbidity were achieved, the design of very few studies permit an attribution beyond reasonable doubt of the success to the interventions. The cost of intervention is not negligible and replicating successes achieved on a far larger scale without escalating costs remains problematic. Policies towards food and agriculture (a sector in which almost all governments of the world have intervened) can have serious nutritional consequences. Even though a number of studies are available of government intervention in agriculture, it is fair to say that a deeper analysis in a number of socio-economic–political environments is needed of the access to food subsidy programmes, the differences in socio-economic characteristics of participants and non-participants and the extent and significance of leakages to non-target groups. In particular, research is needed in designing subsidy programmes in terms of choice of commodities to be subsidised, of forms of subsidisation, (food stamps, provision free of cost of part of consumption, price subsidy, etc.) and even of the location of distribution outlets.

POVERTY AND UNDERNUTRITION

It is increasingly understood that while the true extent of undernutrition in developing countries may not be known with precision and its causes are many and closely interrelated, the principal cause is *poverty*. This is not to say that all the world's poor, however defined, are necessarily undernourished or that all the world's rich are necessarily well nourished but only to say that most of the world's undernourished may be found among the poor countries (South Asia, Africa) and among the poor in these. Thus policies towards elimination of undernutrition have to address the problem of poverty. Since in many of these countries most of the population is rural and agriculture is the dominant sector in terms of its share in employment, though not necessarily in gross national product, rural poverty accounts for the bulk of the poverty in the world.

It is tempting to conclude particularly from the famine raging in parts of Africa that a major determinant of undernutrition besides poverty is the aggregate availability of food. That this is erroneous should have been obvious: the fact that enough food is available to feed the entire population of a country is no guarantee that no one will starve. Equally, the fact that not enough food is available to prevent starvation of everyone does not mean that everyone will indeed share in the starvation. How the available food is distributed among the population will depend on the institutional arrangements relating to production and exchange (for instance, in a market economy an individual has to have enough purchasing power through his 'income entitlement' to be able to afford a diet above starvation level!), including in particular the nature of transportation, storage and distribution networks. Recent tragic events in Ethiopia show that in the absence of such a network the food shipped by the rest of the world will not reach the starving in time. These elementary and fairly obvious relationships between institutions and access to food and their implications for understanding episodes of famine are elegantly elaborated in Sen (1981).

It will come as no surprise to anyone that the extent of rural poverty is closely related to the ease of access to cultivable land (through ownership or lease arrangements) and to sustained and productive employment. Table 2 provides some interesting data on India from Sundaram and Tendulkar (1982). Nearly 60 per cent of the agricultural labour households are poor and account for over 44 per cent of all poor households in rural India. And these households, not coincidentally, suffer substantial bouts of unemployment. Nearly 40 per cent of other labour households also are poor. It also happens to be the case, though this is not shown in Table 2, that the poor households which are self-employed in agricultural occupations consist largely (though not exclusively) of small and marginal farmers, tenants and share croppers.

The situation in Pakistan and Bangladesh is similar. A World Bank (1982, p. 78) study states that 'the great majority of the absolute poor – over 90 per cent – are rural people who work on farms, or do non-farm work that depends in part on agriculture. More than half are small farmers, who own or lease their land; another 20 per cent are members of farming collectives mainly in China. The remaining one-fifth of one-quarter are landless, and their livelihood is particularly precarious'.

Ensuring access to arable land goes only a part of the way towards reducing poverty. For getting the most out the land in terms of output, access to high-yielding varieties of seed, irrigation, credit for the purchase of inputs, including fertilizers and pesticides, and remunerative prices for output, etc. have to be assured as well. It has been established time and again that given the right incentives the peasants and workers even in poor countries respond by increasing productivity. The tragedy of some of the African countries today is in a significant measure due to misguided

TABLE 2 *Share of different types of Households in (a) All rural households (b) Households below the poverty line (c) Unemployed persondays and (d) Incidence of poverty within each household type*

All India (Rural): 1977–78

Sr. No.	Household type	Percentage share in all rural households	Incidence of poverty within each household type	Percentage share in all rural households below the poverty line	Percentage share of each household type in total number of unemployed persondays		
					Males	*Females*	*Persons*
(1)	(2)	(3)	(4)	(5)	(6)	(7)	(8)
1.	Self-employed in agricultural occupations	46.11	30.37	34.97	20.74	11.44	17.61
2.	Self-employed in non-agricultural occupations	10.60	38.13	10.19	7.82	6.48	7.11
3.	Agricultural labour households	29.88	58.76	44.28	56.24	69.76	60.72
4.	Other labour households	6.88	38.54	6.69	11.10	9.82	0.68
5.	Other rural households	6.65	23.49	3.87	4.10	2.50	3.88
6.	All households	100.00	39.65	100.00	100.00	100.00	100.00

Source: National Sample Survey, Draft Report no. 293.

Notes: 1. Household types are defined by reference to the major source of livelihood for the household in the year preceding the date of survey.

2. All households with the per capita total consumer expenditure of less than Rs. 50 per month constitute the set of poor households. The poverty norm of Rs. 15 per capita month at 1960–61 prices, when adjusted by the consumer price index of rural agricultural labourers, works out to Rs. 48.45. We have approximated it Rs 50 per capita per month.

3. Incidence of poverty within each household type in column (4) is defined by the percentage of households below the poverty line (of Rs. 50 per capita per month) within each household type.

public policy that distorted incentives to produce. Indeed as Mr Williams, the Executive Director of the World Food Council said recently 'it is quite clear that globally the world can produce enough food to feed all its population. And that assumes a yearly increase in population' (*New York Times*, 2 December 1984). He attributed only a small part of Africa's food problems to drought and a large part to the failure of many African governments to provide incentives to small farmers.

CONCLUSION

The current state of knowledge does not permit an accurate estimation of the extent of undernutrition in the world. While there are reasons to believe that the published estimates may be exaggerated there is no doubt that a significant proportion of the population in the developing world suffer from undernutrition. The principal cause of undernutrition is poverty. Most of world's poor live in rural areas and depend on agriculture for their incomes. Geographically South Asia accounts for a large proportion of the world's poor. Whether or not a country produces enough food in the aggregate to be able to feed its population is largely irrelevant to the extent of poverty and undernutrition in the country. The more important determinants are the distribution to productive resources such as arable land, access to gainful employment, to technical knowhow, etc. Above all a policy framework that provides adequate incentives for the poor peasant and worker to increase their outputs and incomes is essential.

REFERENCES

Berg, A., 'Malnourished People: A Policy View', World Bank, Poverty and Basic Needs Series, Washington DC, June 1981.

Durnin, J. V. G. A., 'Energy Balance in Man with Particular Reference to Low Intakes', *Biblthca, Nutr. Dicta* vol. 27, 1979, 1–10.

Eberstadt, N., 'Hunger and Ideology', *Commentary*, July 1981, 40–9.

Ferro-Luzzi, A. et al., 'Food Intake, Its Relationship to Body Weight and Age; and Its Apparent Nutritional Adequacy in New Guinean Children', *Amercian Journal of Clinical Nutrition*, vol. 28, 1975, 1443–53.

Poleman, T., 'World Hunger: Extent, Causes and Cures' in D. Gale Johnson and Edward Schuh: *Role in Markets in the World food Economy*, Westview Press, Boulder, Colorado, 1983.

Reutlinger, S. and Selowsky, M., *Malnutrition and Poverty*, Occasional Paper, no. 23, The World Bank, Washington, DC, 1976.

Scrimshaw, N. S. et al., *Interactions of Nutrition and Infection*, Monograph no. 57, World Health Organization, Geneva, 1968.

Srinivasan, T. N., 'Malnutrition in Developing Countries: The State of Knowledge of the Extent of Its Prevalence, Its Causes and Its Consequences', Economic Growth Center, Yale University (mimeo) 1983.

Sukhatme, P. V. and Margen, S., 'Models for Protein Deficiency', *American Journal of Clinical Nutrition*, vol. 31, 1978, 1237–56.

Sundaram, K. and Tendulkar, S. D., 'Towards an Explanation of Inter-Regional Variations in Poverty and Unemployment in Rural India', Working Paper no. 237, Delhi School of Economics, University of Delhi, 1982.

208 *T. N. Srinivasan*

Taylor, L., et al., 'Food Subsidy Programs: A Survey', Report Prepared for the Food Foundation, December 1980.
Widdowson, E. M., *A Study on Individual Children's Diets, Special Report Series*, Medical Research Council, 257, MNSO, London, 1947.
World Bank, *World Development Report*, The World Bank, Washington, DC, 1982.

DISCUSSION OPENING I – JOSEPH KLATZMANN

I am not really the right person to discuss John Mellor's paper, because I am essentially in agreement with him.

First, I want to underline one point concerning both papers. When food supply objectives are discussed, there is always the question of 'physiological needs'. However, one does not eat merely to survive or to be capable of work. Similarly, one can survive perfectly well without meat. I propose therefore that one fixes as the objective something which should be considered a basic human right, what I call 'satisfying food', something well above the minimal requirement, but still remaining well below the exaggerated rates of the rich countries, which are threatening the health of their inhabitants. This is why I have much appreciated that John Mellor raised this problem in the following phrase: 'there is no question that we would consider the FAO standards too low as a matter of fairness'.

Among the other important points of this paper, some do not need to be discussed, as they are indisputable; for example, the fact that a drop in world food supply essentially affects the poor. We could also have got into too long a discussion of such topics as the growing dilemma of equity.

An extremely important topic is that of food aid, in its various aspects (including 'Food for Work' programmes). Voices are being increasingly raised to denounce the negative effects of this aid, and some go so far as to demand that it be stopped. Many of the criticisms of food aid are undoubtedly justified. But ways need to be found to make the various forms of food aid more effective and to reduce their negative effects, rather than proposing purely and simply that all aid be discontinued.

I was very interested in John Mellor's views on the positive effects of food imports into some Third World countries with rapid economic growth. I appreciated the absence of dogmatism in the way there was recognition of both the positive aspects and the limits of the free market; compared with some who condemn it categorically, while others think it is capable of resolving all problems. According to Mellor, food imports allow a higher level of economic development to be maintained when local agricultural production, in spite of making progress, does not measure up to demand. This point seems one which needs discussion.

Now I shall comment on the question of investments. Mellor writes that those investments should be avoided which are not economically justified as a result of high agricultural prices. I recall that the FAO has estimated that some 100 billion dollars investment per year is needed to ensure a satisfactory rate of growth of agricultural production in developing countries (China excluded). While it is sure that such amounts are not available, the problem is to seek out which types of low level investment can result in increased agricultural production. In other words, if resources are scarce, one must know how to make the best use of those that are available.

Finally, Mellor mentions the variability of harvests. This question poses a problem of statistical interpretation. Thus, I have calculated the variability in the US cereals harvest in the period 1972–82; but I only have to add the figures for one year – 1983 – to give a much greater variability. Care must therefore be taken over choice of years being considered in this kind of calculation.

I have only a few words on Srinivasan's paper. The criticisms he makes of methods of calculating food standards are certainly justified. But the impression which emerges from the paper is that food requirements are actually less than are admitted to. One can also find arguments in favour of the inverse thesis – for example, energy needs being increased by manual labour in a hot climate. I return to my earlier point, that food requirements cannot simply be seen in terms of satisfying minimum physiological needs.

DISCUSSION OPENING II – WOUTER TIMS

Srinivasan's paper on undernutrition makes explicit what many students and observers have, less forcefully no doubt than he, increasingly felt about the numbers of affected persons which have been presented over the past decade, notably by FAO/WHO and by the World Bank. He makes, I think, the point that it is more important to find out why people are poor, and therefore threatened by inadequate nutrition, than to draw lines and estimate numbers below it. And he also attempts to suggest cost-effective means for reducing this threat, both in the short and the long run.

Major issues arising from the paper seem to me to be:

However weak the methods, some estimate of the number of people exposed to inadequate nutrition is nevertheless desirable, because of its mind-setting role and impact; a cautious estimate, no doubt;

Food distribution policies should not be judged by their measured effectiveness alone – even if fully possible – but include an element of risk taking, designing them with errors towards the liberal side;

In the long run there is no way to accommodate poor people, at a more decent level of income, in the agricultural sector even if broadly defined; what is needed is development policies generating employment in all sectors;

Policy failures and institutional weaknesses account for a good part of African food and agricultural problems, but labour scarcity may require quite different incentive policies in Africa than in labour-surplus rural Asia.

The analysis Mellor provides in his paper on dealing with uncertainties in a situation of growing imbalances is a broad one. It is also convincing in its conclusion that, in a general sense, markets have contributed, through international trade in food, to development: countries on the food-receiving end, when pursuing employment-oriented policies, have been enabled to keep prices of wage-goods lower than these would otherwise have been. It is a two-way argument, as the availability of cheap food in international markets has favoured employment oriented growth.

There are, however, a number of questions which still need an answer:

Food importers in the low-income countries were very sluggish compared to middle and higher-income countries; therefore, where the argument of the paper would count most, it does not seem to apply;

A number of middle-income countries do not import food as a complement of employment-oriented strategies, but because of past neglect of agriculture and in substitution of what they should themselves produce, like most low-income countries of Africa;

The main conclusion of the paper should therefore be that major increases of food aid to low-income countries, dovetailed to domestic employment and income generation of the poor, are called for;

Finally, if so many countries are at present importing more food than would be normal for their stage of development, a major issue concerns the adjustment path to a more tenable and in terms of development a more appropriate use of food imports.

DISCUSSION OPENING III – VIJAJ S. VYAS

It is a privilege to comment on the two excellent papers by Professor John Mellor and Professor T. N. Srinivasan. In my view these papers complement each other to a large extent. Professor Srinivasan has concentrated more on the conceptual and the measurement aspects, though he has some pertinent observations on policy too. Professor Mellor has mainly dealt with the policy issues. I have a few comments which apply to both these papers. I am presenting my comments having in the background the two regions of the world where the problems of poverty as well as malnutrition are largely concentrated. These are South Asia and sub-Saharan Africa.

In the first place, I think Professor Mellor should modify the statement where he suggests that developing countries as a group are importing more food grains in recent years and that fastest growing countries are also the larger importers. This statement is only partially true. It was brought out in the Second Asian Agricultural Survey, during the late 1970s, that the net food imports of developing Asian countries had declined after the introduction of High Yield Varieties Programme in South and South-East Asia. Over the period this trend has further strengthened, especially since some of the large countries of the region, like India and Pakistan, have emerged from being net importers to marginal exporters of food grains. This point has importance because in my view more and more developing countries will try to reach that stage.

This is partly because the technologies for augmenting food grains production are already available for some of the principal crops and their coverage is likely to widen. Partly, it is also because of the foreign exchange constraints imposed by the mounting debt servicing obligations as well as the protectionist policies of the developed countries *vis-à-vis* the exports of the developing countries which will goad the developing countries towards import-substitution policies for food grains.

My second comment pertains to the question of market failure. We should first remind ourselves, and Professor Srinivasan has made this point very convincingly, that it is easy to exaggerate the number of chronically malnourished if we are not clear about the concepts or the measures of malnutrition. Even if we equate the malnourished with the poor, the number of those who can have access to adequate food with the removal of the distortions in the government policies is quite substantial. Yet the fact remains that there is a hard core of rural households who would not be able to respond to the market signals in the best of circumstances. Their number may be considerably less but are not inconsequential. These are the people without assets. People who not only do not have physical assets, but who also do not have marketable skills or physical stamina. They are not in a position to respond to market stimuli.

My third and last point is that the nature of intervention suggested by both Professor Mellor and Professor Srinivasan is directed to strengthen agricultural infrastructure or to have access to agricultural land and other factors of production. This strategy has relevance for countries, such as those in the sub-Saharan Africa, where aggregate production falls short of the potential and where enhancing agricultural production will also contribute to raising income levels of a large number of poor agricultural producers. In a strange way, food security problems in Africa are, relatively speaking, more manageable. We have now a clearer understanding about the mainsprings of growth in the agricultural sector.

The problem is a lot harder for the countries where food production at the aggregate level is adequate and yet a large number of people in the rural and urban areas are poor. India is a typical country in this category. Problems of the rural poor, most of whom are landless labourers or marginal producers, cannot be solved simply by augmenting agricultural production. 'More of the same' is not the solution for India. Its capacity gainfully to absorb the labour in agricultural production is seriously limited. The diversification of the rural economy is the major challenge and that would not come automatically. Even after attaining a reasonable degree of sophistication and after providing a reasonable infrastructure, the pace of diversification in the country's economy is still very slow. What sort of trap is arresting the growth of non-farm sectors in such economies? We do not have a complete answer for that. But it is reasonable to assert that without conscious decisions to encourage non-farm activities, the large bulk of rural people cannot be provided with opportunities for gainful employment and income and access to food. Neither paper addressed this question in a satisfactory manner.

GENERAL DISCUSSION – RAPPORTEUR: J. A. AKINWUMI

The importance of the two papers can be judged from the rapt attention paid to John Mellor's presentation by a full house in the Sala Malaga, for a full hour.

In the general discussion regret was expressed at the narrow focus of the Conference theme and the contrasting of the fortunate developed food surplus countries with the unfortunate less developed food deficit countries. The real theme is 'Agriculture in a turbulent *world* economy'. It was suggested that there should be a moratorium on the developed versus less-developed dichotomy for the 1988 meeting. 'Food imbalance' which is the title of this session, is harmful, not only to the countries and people who need food but cannot buy it, but also to exporting countries which are experiencing weak markets owing to inability of food deficit countries to buy food.

Empirical evidence in respect of this turbulence exists in the United States, but first attention was called to another source of turbulence referred to by Dr Schuh. It is the sharp increase in the cost of (borrowed) finance capital that resulted from the second recycling of petrodollars in the late 1970s. It affected not only Third World countries but a sizeable part of the commercial agriculture in developed countries. With regard to the empirical report, an upper fringe of élite farmers in the United States who have no debts is doing well but a third of the full-time farmers in the State of Missouri are being forced off the land and in 1984, 71 farmers in that state committed suicide due to the emotional stress.

It was contended that Mellor was too philosophical in his approach. When the entries are repeated, the outcome would make any illusion of unfair world disappear.

It was argued that it was better to have some data/facts for whatever purpose than not to see facts at all. Some countries do not want to face facts. The task should not stop at feeding the hungry but aim at broadening their choice. One may ask whether the Third World countries are really free. It was suggested that they are in the position of economic dependence. The North–South dialogue of the 1970s has fizzled out. On nutrition, United Nations research concluded that a worker does not need too high an amount of certain sophisticated foods.

It was observed that Ecuador's economy grew by 7 per cent (overall) in real terms in the 1970s, while agriculture grew by 5 per cent and population by 2 per cent; yet importation of agricultural commodities accelerated due to rapid urbanisation at 7 per cent per year. Once in the cities people no longer consumed their traditional food; rather they ate bread and drank Coca Cola, thus creating severe problems of distribution or marketing of their own traditional food products.

It was suggested that markets for the transfer of food from exporting to importing countries are working and benefiting both groups. This, however, failed to emphasise the main issue that there must be self-sufficiency for the developing countries, i.e. they must generate more income and hence purchasing power through production and employment. The first strategy should be to go for rapid increases in food production. Intermediate countries like India and South Asia should attempt to diversify.

It was wondered why Mellor did not disaggregate his data.

The final comment from the floor was a statement that medical evidence showed that limited food plus sufficient essential vitamins made rats live longer. We should there think more about good quality of food and how to prevent contamination.

Professor Mellor replied that food imbalances cannot be discussed without noting the plus and the minus. He suspected that the differences are between the implications not the weights. They are structural. The problems in developing countries put pressure on how to deal with the imbalances from the point of view of developed countries that are ignorant of developing ones. He did not treat the capital problems of developed nations because he felt they should be able at this stage to handle their capital problems.

Professor Mellor was disturbed about the self-sufficiency issue. Benefit of trade refers only to a small margin and something ought to be done to adjust the supply to the poor who happen to be causing the fluctuations in both supply and demand. He submitted that dealing with these through trade results in much greater efficiency compared with storage of surpluses. Other difficulties involve high transport costs and lack of infrastructures. Hence developing countries should raise consumption per caput levels to such a point that they consume their own production at so high a point that they are marginal net importers. This will lead to greater movement of food in international markets. In this way we will deal better with the problem of surplus food production. We should avoid saying that a problem does not exist simply because we do not know about it. We should be talking about larger flows of food in developing countries.

Professor Mellor said it should be emphasised that markets worked well in certain respects but there are deficiencies. We should concentrate on those that work. Finally, food aid is unfashionable. We should see what market forces are doing or not doing. But this may lead to a suggestion of massive food aid. We know what is needed through segmentation of the market so that we can concetrate on aiding the poor in rural and urban areas.

If in Bangladesh with a narrow economic situation, the measure works at 70 to 90 per cent efficiency, we should be prepared to live with much less efficiency in Africa. Intervention should come through market segmentation. Incentive problems may be enormous but they must be handled if food aid is to be managed properly.

Participants in the discussion included Joseph Klatzmann, Wouter Tims, V. S. Vyas, Erhun Kula, K. M. Azam, Bina Cassa and G. S. Bhalla.

CARL K. EICHER AND JOHN M. STAATZ

Food Security Policy in Sub-Saharan Africa

BACKGROUND

At the beginning of the independence period in 1960, the 45 states in sub-Saharan Africa (hereafter referred to as Africa) were basically self-sufficient in food. In fact, a few countries – e.g., Nigeria and Senegal – were significant exporters of groundnuts to Europe. At the same time as African states were winning their independence in the early 1960s, India was caught in a food crisis that led to a large inflow of food aid that lasted for 15 years (1955–70). Today, while much of Africa faces a food crisis, India is feeding 750 million people, has 30 million tons of grain in storage, plans to sell several million tons of wheat in world markets this year and recently donated 100,000 tons of food aid to Africa. Although India has made substantial progress in improving its food security and is now self-sufficient in food, it has neither solved hunger nor poverty. Nevertheless, as Lele (1984) describes in detail, India's experience is instructive for African states and donors; it shows the time that it took (25 years) to achieve self-sufficiency and that food self-sufficiency does not automatically solve other food security goals – i.e. access of all members of society to a nutritionally adequate diet.

DEFINING FOOD SECURITY

The term 'food security' was highlighted during the 1974 World Food Conference in Rome, where discussions of food security were influenced by events of the early 1970s. Rising international grain prices and lagging food production in many low-income Asian and African countries raised the spectre of mass starvation. During the 1974 conference, proposals to increase food security focused on (a) increasing food production in food-deficit countries, thereby reducing their dependence on unstable international markets; and (b) creating a co-ordinated system of national and international grain reserves. However, food security proposals paid little attention to demand issues, such as ensuring that nutritionally vulnerable groups had the resources necessary to gain access to an adequate diet.

While famine has faded from much of Asia since the mid-1970s, both famine and chronic hunger have become more prominent in Africa, leading not only to massive short-term relief efforts but also to crash programmes to increase food production. In dealing with Africa's present crisis and the chronic problems that underlie it, it is important to recognise that many of the hungry in Africa, particularly the chronically hungry, are malnourished not because the aggregate supply of food (domestic production plus potential imports) is inadequate but because the poor lack the resources to gain access to the food that is available. Improving the food security of the poor requires measures to help the poor increase their purchasing power (Reutlinger and Selowsky 1976) or what A. K. Sen (1981) has called their food entitlement. Siamwalla and Valdes have defined food security as ensuring that 'food-deficit countries, or regions or households within these countries ... meet target ievels of consumption' (1984, p. 190), a view that incorporates the effects of both supply and demand.

Our definition of food security is similar to that of Siamwalla and Valdes. We define food security as the ability of a country or region to assure, on a long-term basis, that its food system provides the total population access to a timely, reliable and nutritionally adequate supply of food.[1]

Our definition of food security implies that:

(1)   The food security situation of a country needs to be assessed by looking at the access of *individuals or households* to an adequate diet. It is not sufficient to look at average food availability per caput on a national or regional basis; some notion of how consumption is distributed among the population is also needed. Therefore, a key step in food security analysis is the identification of the malnourished.

(2)   Assuring an individual's access to a nutritionally adequate diet requires that an adequate supply of food be available and the individual has some claim on it, either because he produced it or because he has other sources of real income that can be exchanged for it. Consequently, increasing domestic food self-sufficiency and building domestic grain stocks do not guarantee a country's food security and may actually weaken it if done in a costly manner that reduces the income of the poor. Promoting cotton production or non-farm employment in the Sahel, for example, may do more to increase smallholders' food security than insisting that they increase their production of millet.

The issue of how the cultivation of cash crops affects farmers' food security may also depend on the time horizon one is considering. In many countries (e.g., Mali and Rwanda) state monopoly marketing of cash crops generates a sizeable proportion of total government revenues. Even if cash crop production reduces farmers' food security in the short run, it may be one of the few available means of financing the rural infrastructure needed to improve food security in the long run.

(3) In most food-deficit African countries, however, there is justification for putting substantial emphasis on improving the productivity of the staple food system. The majority of the poor in Africa are engaged in subsistence food production. In the short run, one of the most direct ways of increasing their real incomes is to increase the productivity of their main enterprise, staple food production, which may increase the availability per caput of home-produced foods, raise cash incomes by generating a marketable surplus of grains, or allow subsistence food needs to be produced with fewer resources, thus freeing resources for other income-earning activities. Improving the productivity of the food system involves not only generating improved on-farm technologies but also investing in marketing, processing and transport of staple crops. Farmers are often understandably reluctant to try to increase their income through specialisation if there is not a reliable market for food. In addition, the off-farm components of the food system can generate substantial employment for rural people who have limited access to land and hence would derive few direct benefits from improved farm-level technology. In the long run, efficient input and output markets are a key in developing the intersectoral linkages that characterise economic development, which by generating increased incomes reduces food insecurity.

(4) Food insecurity has both transitory and chronic dimensions.[2] Transitory food insecurity occurs when an individual's food consumption level falls below adequate levels because of short-run (intra or inter-seasonal) fluctuations in supply or effective demand (real income). Chronic food insecurity describes a situation where an individual persistently lacks the real income to assure an adequate diet.

(5) Improving a country's food security typically requires both short-run and long-run measures. Short-run measures involve interventions to assure that the poor have access to food through various forms of real-income transfers, such as rations and subsidised distribution of food. Such short-term solutions are needed to address both transitory food insecurity (e.g. famine relief) and chronic food insecurity (e.g. targeted food subsidies). Long-run solutions involve creating food production and distribution systems that assure adequate access of the poor to food through income generation and an efficient supply system for food, either domestically produced or imported. The long-run solution therefore essentially lies in economic development, with particular emphasis on income generation for the poor. One of the key tasks of food security analysis is to devise short-run solutions that do not have

deleterious long-run effects. For example, how can food aid be used for short-term relief without undermining the long-term development of the domestic food system?

CAUSES OF FOOD INSECURITY IN AFRICA: AN HISTORICAL PERSPECTIVE

What explains widespread hunger in Africa, a continent in which certain areas have substantial agricultural potential (FAO/UNFPA/IIASA 1982), at a time when world food prices are near historic lows? The answer lies not only in recent droughts but also in the failure of African states to develop economic systems that generate sufficient real income for the poor to assure access to adequate food produced at home or purchased in the market. Developing such systems is not easy, but one fact is apparent: since most of the poor live in rural areas, the neglect of agriculture and related rural industries throughout much of the post-independence period has been a major contributor to food insecurity in Africa. This neglect of the rural economy has stemmed from a misunderstanding of the relationships between agriculture and other sectors in the developing economy and a failure of both donors and African governments to make the medium- to long-term investments necessary to stimulate rural development: investments in physical infrastructure, rural institutions, agricultural research and human capital. Many African countries have also been unwilling to face the long-term threat to their food security posed by rapid population growth.

Although statements from the latest OAU summit indicate an increased awareness that underinvestment in agriculture lies at the root of Africa's current economic and food security problems, historically African governments and donors have seriously misunderstood (a) the role of agriculture in national development at this stage of Africa's economic history and (b) the strategic importance of a reliable agricultural surplus as a foundation for the expansion of the industrial sector. As a result, the past two decades have been characterised by scores of poor decisions regarding ranches, state farms, settlement programmes, and government tractor-hire schemes. Gaining political consensus between national leaders and donor agencies on the place of agriculture in the economic development strategy of African states is the starting point in dealing with food security issues over the coming 10 to 15 years. This consensus, in turn, needs to be translated into a commitment to fostering rural institutions (farmer co-operatives, local governments, etc.) that have enough autonomy to respond to local conditions and opportunities and to begin to build a domestic constituency that will support policy reforms that favour rural areas. Obviously, the politics involved are complex and potentially disruptive, which may explain why such changes are often slow in coming (Bates 1981; Johnston and Clark 1982).

A political consensus in favour of paying increased attention to agriculture needs to be reflected in new investment priorities. Chief among these are investments in improved marketing systems, agricultural research and human capital.

Since 1970, food production has been growing at half the rate of growth of population in Africa. With the exception of maize in southern Africa, the recent introduction of hybrid sorghum in the Sudan and a few other local examples, there is no backlog of farmer-tested food crop technology (Spencer 1985; Eicher 1985). After 25 years of independence, most African states and donors do not have well-devised empirically tested strategies to increase production of rainfed crops (especially sorghum and millet), irrigated crops, and livestock.

The evidence of the past 25 years shows that the direct international transfer of technology – especially plant material – from Asia, Europe and North America to Africa – is not working as anticipated (Eicher 1984). In short, there is a gap between technology transfer in theory and practice. The absence of a strong indigenous scientific community in national research services makes it difficult for African states to screen and borrow technology from neighbouring states and regional and international centres and adapt it to local conditions. Finally, there is growing evidence that there is a gap between the expectations and the actual achievements of the International Agricultural Research Centres (IARCs) in Africa (Eicher 1985).

Developing new technologies and rural institutions requires large numbers of trained people. By any yardstick – literacy rates, percentage of school age population in secondary schools and universities, and percentage of expatriates in scientific, managerial and academic staff positions – Africa has fewer trained personnel than any other area in the Third World. What is the response of donors to this situation? The World Bank approved two education projects in Africa in fiscal year 1984, representing 3.6 per cent of its education portfolio, or \$25 million out of \$694 million of IBRD and IDA funds (World Bank 1984). USAID currently spends \$20 million per year to support African institutions of higher education in agriculture and to finance 250 scholarships for overseas training of Africans in agriculture at the undergraduate and graduate levels (USAID 1985, p. 7). What explains the modest response by two major donors to Africa's crushing human resource problems? Investment in human capital should receive greatly increased priority in the coming decades.

Even if increased investments result in rapid growth in the total food supply, availability per caput may grow very little or even decline due to rapid population growth. Africa is the only region of the world where the rate of growth of population is increasing. Population growth rates among African countries of 2.5 to 4.4 per cent are crucial variables in the population, hunger and poverty equation. The total fertility rate (number of living children per woman) is around six in urban areas and eight in rural areas in Africa. But, there is little serious debate in Africa – even among academics – on population and family planning. The distinguished Kenyan economist, Philip Ndegwa, is one of the few African social scientists to advocate family planning. But even he approaches this issue with caution:

> In my view, and here I know I am treading on dangerous and controversial ground, there is little sense in a family having so many children that it cannot look after them properly in terms of food, health, education and employment (Ndegwa 1985, pp. 141–2).

Most demographers agree that family planning programmes have been ineffective in Africa in the 25 years of independence and that no African nation displays any significant sign of fertility decline (Caldwell and Caldwell 1984). Africa's population 'treadmill' is a major challenge to the agricultural sector, implying that the supply of food needs to grow three to five per cent per year through domestic food production and/or imports.

In summary, no single factor can explain the success or failure of agricultural policies in a particular country. Africa's food insecurity problems, the result of a complex interaction of factors, have been building up for two decades. The solution to these problems lies in the development of short-, medium- and long-term policies and programmes to increase agricultural production (food, cash crops and livestock), expand rural and urban incomes and increase the access of the poor to the available food supply. Developing policies to achieve these goals is difficult and involves hard tradeoffs, as the following examples illustrate.

COUNTRY ILLUSTRATIONS

Many African nations have adopted explicit food security strategies and have prepared food security plans. In this section, we briefly examine the strategies of two countries: Senegal, a food-deficit state, and Zimbabwe, a food exporter.

Senegal
Senegal is currently importing about 1,000 tons of rice a day, mostly broken rice from Asia. The Senegalese government is faced with several tough questions: Should food production be increased on rainfed or irrigated land? Are different policies needed to protect the food security of different target groups (for example, urban or rural people)? What role should international trade play in these policies? What are the interactions between short-run and long-run policies to achieve food security? What is the appropriate role of the state in helping assure food security?

Since the nineteenth century, Senegal has followed a policy of agricultural specialisation, exporting groundnuts and importing broken rice, not only to supply urban areas but also for rural areas. The state has historically played an important direct role in agricultural trade, holding the legal monopoly on the groundnut trade, rice imports and, until 1980, coarse grains marketing. Hence, price and marketing policies have had major effects on the government budget as well as on food security.

Over the past 15 years drought has reduced domestic foodgrain and groundnut production; this has combined with a depressed world market for groundnuts and other stresses on the government budget due to oil shocks, world-wide recession and the growth of the 'rural development bureaucracy' to draw into question Senegal's agricultural strategy. In recent years, Senegal has imported on average roughly half its annual cereal consumption and if present production and population trends continue, the country will produce only a third of its foodgrain needs by the year 2000 (Abt Associates 1985, p. iii).

In order to deal with the worsening situation, in 1984 the government announced its 'New Agricultural Policy', part of a general economic reform package (*plan de redressement*) launched in 1979. The plan called for increased foodgrain self-sufficiency, primarily through irrigated rice production in the Senegal River Valley and millet and sorghum production in the Groundnut Basin; a greatly expanded role for the private trade and farmers' co-operatives in input and output marketing; and a reduction in the activities of regional development administrations and parastatals. The goal is to produce 75 per cent of the nation's foodgrain consumption by the year 2000 and to reach self-sufficiency as soon thereafter as possible.

In implementing the new policies the government has had to face competing objectives (e.g., its desires to assure consumers' food security in the short run and to stimulate long-run agricultural growth through higher prices to farmers) and the difficulty of developing an institutional environment favourable to the private trade after years of heavy state involvement in the cereals market. For example, in early 1985 the government raised the price of imported rice by over 20 per cent in order to reduce the government's budget deficit and to stimulate production of millet, sorghum and locally produced rice. Yet, when the price of millet and sorghum rose in response to this change, there were calls by some government officials for strict price controls of these cereals to help protect consumers. Furthermore, the effects on the food security of the poor of the policy of promoting self sufficiency primarily through price policy has probably been mixed. The cost of rice production in the large irrigated perimeters of the Senegal River Valley is extremely high by world standards (Ndiame 1985) and investing in these perimeters has reduced the funds available for development of rainfed crops in higher rainfall areas, such as the Casamance. Because the traditional millet and sorghum varieties respond only modestly to modern inputs, increases in the domestic supply of these foodgrains in response to higher relative prices is likely to be forthcoming only at a high marginal cost (in terms of greater input use and/or diverted groundnut exports). In addition, the lack of clearly defined rules governing the private trade has hindered its ability to play the role envisaged for it in the new agricultural policy. (For details see Sow and Newman 1985).

These high costs of production draw into question the strategy of trying to assure food security through foodgrain self-sufficiency. Dakar is a major seaport and the preferred staple of many Senegalese, broken rice, is usually available on the world market at a relatively low price. It may make more sense to try to assure Dakar's food security through imports, while promoting rural food security through the increased production of local foodgrains and export crops. Alternatives to rice production in the irrigated perimeters of the north (e.g. vegetables and tomatoes for canning factories) need to be considered as Senegal seeks more cost-effective ways of assuring the food security of its people.

Zimbabwe
When Zimbabwe became independent in 1980, it inherited a dual agrarian structure composed of about 5,000 large commercial farms and 700,000 smallholders. At independence, the fundamental problems in agriculture were the low productivity of smallholders, widespread poverty among rural workers on large commercial farms, a large landless population and a rural infrastructure that had been battered during the warfare of the 1970s (Blackie 1981). In 1981, the government identified the 'achievement and maintenance of food self-sufficiency and regional food security (in Southern Africa) as an important national objective' (Zimbabwe 1981). In attempting to improve the food security of its population, the post-independence government has tried to balance redistribution of income to the urban and rural poor, who are at the most risk nutritionally, with the need to maintain the productive capacity of the agriculturally based economy.

Despite the substantial incidence of poverty and malnutrition among families of rural smallholders and workers on commercial farms (World Bank 1983), Zimbabwe has decided to maintain its dual production structure in the short run because its 4,200 commercial farms are producing about 50 per cent of the cotton, 50 per cent of the marketed surplus of maize, and 99 per cent of the tobacco crop, a major earner of foreign exchange. The government has, however, tried to improve the food security of the rural poor by raising the minimum wage of farm workers (to Z$600 per year)[3] and by purchasing commercial farms on a 'willing buyer–willing seller' basis to transfer to the landless. At the same time, aggressive steps are being taken to help smallholders expand their rainfed production, especially of cotton and maize, and to promote smallholder irrigation (Rukuni).

The government has generally followed a price policy favourable to agriculture, even when this may have increased the food insecurity of the urban poor in the short run. In 1983–4, the government eliminated Z$100 million of consumer subsidies on wheat bread, meat, dairy products, and refined maize flour. In an attempt to lessen the impact of these changes on the urban poor, subsidies were retained on coarsely milled maize meal and the minimum wage was increased. Following a three-year drought, the government raised maize producer prices by

28.5 per cent in June 1984, four months before planting time for the 1984–5 crop. With very favourable weather, farmers responded with a record maize crop of approximately three million tons, with a large increase coming from smallholders. Zimbabwe is now developing trade agreements to sell 500,000 to 750,000 tons of maize in southern Africa.

Although the experience of Zimbabwe is frequently cited as an example of the successful use of price policy to stimulate production, not all the increase in production should be attributed to higher prices and good weather. Farmers were able to respond to these because they had access to well-functioning input and output markets, an extension system that has given increasing attention to smallholders in recent years and one of the strongest agricultural research services in Africa. For example, in 1980, Zimbabwe had 201 agricultural scientists and spent 2.52 per cent of its agricultural GDP on research, compared with an average of 1.16 per cent for other countries with a comparable level of income per caput (Evenson 1984). Zimbabwe became the first country after the US to develop hybrid maize varieties, in 1949, after 17 years of research. Yet, although hybrid varieties were available to smallholders ten years ago, it was only with improvements in the marketing, credit and extension systems, an end to the disruption caused by war and a more favourable price policy that smallholders widely adopted the new varieties. The experience of Zimbabwe underlines the important interactions among technologies, institutions and agricultural policies in affecting food security.

In spite of its success in increasing total food production and becoming a maize exporter, the long-term food security of Zimbabwe also depends on its ability to deal with its rapid rate of population growth, nearly three per cent per year, which may undermine availability of food per caput. As the experience of India demonstrates, achieving food self-sufficiency (in the sense of becoming a food exporter) is not necessarily synomymous with achieving food security.

THE RESEARCH CHALLENGE FOR AGRICULTURAL ECONOMISTS

Applied research by agricultural economists has played an important role in more clearly defining the nature of food security problems in Africa; additional work is needed in several areas to contribute to improved food security policy. Yet research on food security in Africa is hindered by two major constraints: the lack of reliable data and the small numbers of African economists engaged in policy research.

The data base for food security analysis in Africa is extremely weak relative to that for Asia and Latin America. For example, the authors of *Food Policy Analysis*, drawing on their Asian experience, argued that the starting point for food policy analysis in the Third World is 'usually a food balance sheet, which most countries now publish on an annual basis' (Timmer, Falcon and Pearson 1983, p. 22). But we are unaware of any

African country that publishes a food balance sheet on an annual basis. Moreover, Lele and Candler (1984) report that the basic data sets on agricultural production (FAO and USDA) vary widely from one another, often showing opposite trends in production for the same crops. In Nigeria, current estimates of the area under given crops vary by up to a factor of five depending on the source of data. The lack of reliable data can lead to highly questionable 'empirical' analyses or the formulation of food security policies almost solely on the basis of economic theory without knowledge of crucial parameters, such as the magnitude of demand and supply response and of institutional constraints, that determine how theory works out in practice.

Experience has shown that economic policy research is just as location-specific as technology development, such as maize breeding. A *relatively* large number of African economists are engaged in preparing feasibility studies for donors, but few are engaged in long-term research on local policy problems. This reflects the small *total* number of African economists, the pressing demands they face in appraising and managing externally funded projects, and the low priority that donors and African states have given to developing indigenous capacity to develop data bases and to carry out economic policy analysis. Developing such capacity is, however, an essential component of the institutional development needed to deal with food security issues and to carry out effective policy discussions with donors. Without a greater commitment of resources to developing indigenous policy analysis capacity, much of food security research in Africa may continue to be characterised by the discontinuities and lack of knowledge of local conditions that often characterise the work of short-term external consultants.

The food security situations in the 45 countries of sub-Saharan Africa are extremely heterogeneous; hence, research needs to be tailored to the needs of each country. Nonetheless, we see four areas where additional research could contribute to improved food security policy in many of these countries.

(1)   Grain reserves, imports and food aid
If food security involves not only increasing the available supply of food but also ensuring that the poor have access to that supply, then there is a need to replace the goal of 'food self-sufficiency' (autarky) with the broader goal of 'self reliance', i.e., developing an appropriate mix of domestic production, trade, price, technology, marketing and other policies to supply food in a cost-effective manner while increasing the real income of the poor. Developing such a policy mix requires a much more detailed understanding of how internal trade and aid can be used to achieve food security goals. Research on the use of trade and stocks to stabilise domestic grain supplies has been a major focus of work by the US Department of Agriculture, IFPRI, and other international organisations. Much of this has focused on the appropriate design of storage facilities; the management of stocks; the relative efficacy of using food reserves

versus insurance approaches, such as the IMF's compensatory financing facility, to ensure stable food supplies; and the possible roles of commercial imports and food aid in achieving food security (see, for example, Goreaux 1981; Huddleston 1984). This research has been very useful in demonstrating the high cost of stabilising grain supplies solely through a system of grain reserves, but it has often implicitly assumed that most agricultural production passes through well-functioning markets and that governments hold a significant share of total stocks, assumptions that are particularly inappropriate in Africa (Lele and Candler 1984). Similarly, researchers have paid relatively little attention to the role of private storage in national food systems.

Given the budgetary constraints facing many African countries in the coming decade, the resources generated by food aid may be one of the few means available to finance improvements in domestic food systems to enhance food security. Yet there is a paucity of research on the efficiency of food aid (Reutlinger 1984) and the management and creative use of the resources generated by food aid (both the funds derived from food aid sales and the physical capital created through food-for-work projects).

But without clear provisions for using food aid and the funds it generates to improve the marketing systems ... food aid may meet short-run needs at the expense of long-term development ... More research is needed on the policy processes and institutional constraints within countries before policy makers can know how much food aid they can use effectively (Huddleston, 1984).

(2)   The interactions among technologies, institutions and policy
Agricultural economists have long been involved in research to describe agricultural production and marketing systems in Africa, diagnose their problems, and prescribe ways of improving performance. Such research produces knowledge that is essential in designing effective food security policies. There is a need, however, to avoid looking at production, marketing and policy issues in isolation; the design of effective food security policies requires an understanding of the *interaction* of changes in institutions, technologies and policy on a country's food security. In addition, those engaged in micro-level studies, such as farming systems teams, need to keep in mind the key policy issues that are important for food security when designing their studies. For example, recent emphasis by donors on policy reform has focused mainly on market liberalization and price policy. How a change in price policy affects farmers' production decisions depends on how the private and public marketing systems work, the nature of the available technology (e.g., what is the yield response of traditional varieties to fertilizer?), access to additional production resources and alternative income-earning possibilities. Planning effective policies to increase food supplies and rural incomes requires knowledge of these factors and of the interactions among them. Yet many of the discussions of policy reform remain at a macro, largely

abstract, and often ideological level. The results of dozens of supply response studies suggest that without complementary agricultural research, extension, and institutional reforms, price policy is unlikely to have a marked impact on increasing aggregate food production (Helleiner 1975; Eicher and Baker 1982). Agricultural economists can make an important contribution to improved food security in Africa by undertaking micro-level research on the combination of price policies, institutional reforms, and technological packages needed to increase agricultural production and improve the access of the poor to food.

(3) Food consumption studies
In order to design effective food security programmes, one must first know who the malnourished are, what they eat and why they are hungry. In much of Africa basic information is sparse on the incidence and causes of chronic malnutrition and on the socio-economic characteristics of the malnourished. Methodological advances are needed to design more cost-effective means of gathering such information; traditional nutrition studies usually fail to elicit information on the relationship between income and consumption and conventional income-expenditure studies, especially when conducted in rural areas, are extremely costly. Yet without such information it is impossible to determine the most cost-effective way of increasing caloric intake in a given rural area; is it through improving home food production, reducing post-harvest losses, or expanding non-farm employment, coupled with improvements in the food marketing system? In urban areas, knowledge of the consumption patterns of the poor is needed to design programmes that protect the poor from bearing an undue burden of the painful structural adjustments that many African countries, Ghana and the Sudan, for example, are undergoing, often at the behest of international agencies such as the IMF.

(4) National food security planning and the design of food strategies
A number of African nations have developed national food strategies, often with external technical assistance from the EC. These documents typically outline broad goals for the food system and discuss general approaches to achieving these goals. More work is needed in examining whether the various goals are realistic and mutually consistent and in developing well-conceived strategies and effective implementation plans, including identification of the essential information needed to formulate food security policies. In some countries, food security planning has tended to be an exercise that is rapidly performed by short-term expatriate consultants and rapidly forgotten by government ministries. If this is to change, it is essential that African researchers and government officials be intimately involved in the generation and analysis of data on the food system and in the policy formation and programme design activities. This reinforces the need for donors and African governments to give high priority to developing local institutions to carry out economic policy analysis.

IMPLICATIONS FOR DONORS

Beyond underlining the need to maintain food aid flows in the short run to deal with the present crisis, what guidance can be offered to donors? Simply increasing the volume of project-related aid is unlikely to solve African food security problems, because aid flows in many countries are constrained by the lack of absorptive capacity. For example, aid flows per caput in some African states are running at $50 to $75 per year compared with an average of $1.50 per year in India over the 1951–70 period (Mellor 1979, p. 89). With a population only 16 per cent the size of Asia's, Africa received $8 billion of Official Development Assistance in 1982–3 from the OECD, OPEC, and the multilateral aid agencies, a larger amount of aid than Asia (excluding the Middle East) received. Kenya, for example, is finding it difficult to manage and impossible to evaluate the 600 projects that are currently being funded by 30 major donors.

Rather, there is a need for donors to reconsider the nature of the food insecurity in Africa and the types of programmes and policies required to deal with it. First, in planning longer-run policies, it is important to recognise that food security involves more than just expanded food production and grain reserves; ensuring access of the poor to food means attention has to be given to improving the efficiency of the food system and increasing the real income of the poor through a combination of employment generation, income transfers and redistribution of assets (e.g. access to education). Second, the current emphasis on 'policy dialogue' between donors and African governments, though useful, needs to be based on a better understanding of how the food system in a particular country works. How farmers, merchants and consumers respond to a higher relative price for a given crop is an empirical not an ideological issue; without a better knowledge base, much of food security planning in Africa will continue to be an exercise in 'planning without facts'. Hence, in the longer run, donors can make a major contribution to food security in Africa through helping expand indigenous scientific capacity in both the biological and social sciences, improve the quality of data on the food system and facilitate the development of the African scientific community to deal with both the biological and economic issues underlying food security. Donors should also recognise that policy reforms require time, both to build the domestic political support required to maintain them and to change the expectations of participants in the food system and hence their behaviour. It would be extremely unfortunate if policy reforms needed to improve food security were undermined because donors were impatient about the lack of immediate results.

NOTES

In preparing this paper, the authors have benefited from discussions with numerous colleagues at Michigan State University, the Institut Senegalais de Recherche Agricole, USAID (especially Don Anderson and Curt Reintsma), the University of Zimbabwe and the World Bank (especially Shlomo Reutlinger and J. Price Gittinger). All responsibility for

228   *Carl K. Eicher and John M. Staatz*

errors remains with the authors. The research supporting this paper was financed by the US Agency for International Development, Bureau for Science and Technology, and Bureau for Africa under a 'Food Security in Africa' Cooperative Agreement (DAN-1190-A-00-4092-00) with the Department of Agricultural Economics, Michigan State University.
[1]Because of space limitations we do not enter into the debate concerning the standards for a 'nutritionally adequate diet' (see Poleman 1977).
[2]We are indebted to Shlomo Reutlinger for this distinction.
[3]Z$1 = US$0.65.

REFERENCES

Abt Associates, *Senegal Agricultural Policy Analysis*, Report to USAID/Senegal, Cambridge, Massachusetts, 1985.
Bates, Robert H. *Markets and States in Tropical Africa: The Political Basis of Agricultural Policies*, University of California Press, Berkeley, 1981.
Blackie, Malcolm, 'A Time to Listen: A Perspective on Agricultural Policy in Zimbabwe', Department of Land Management, University of Zimbabwe, Working Paper 5/81, 1981.
Caldwell, John C. and Caldwell, Pat. 'Cultural Forces Tending to Sustain High Fertility in Tropical Africa', Australian National University, 1984. (draft).
Eicher, Carl K., 'Facing Up To Africa's Food Crisis', *Foreign Affairs*, Fall, 1982.
Eicher, Carl K., 'International Technology Transfer and the African Farmer: Theory and Practice', Department of Land Management, University of Zimbabwe, Working Paper 3/84, 1984.
Eicher, Carl K., 'Agricultural Research for African Development: Problems and Priorities for 1985–2000', paper presented at a World Bank Conference at Bellagio, Italy, 25 February–1 March 1985.
Eicher, Carl K., and Baker, Doyle C., *Research on Agricultural Development in Sub-Saharan Africa: A Critical Survey*, MSU International Development Papers, no. 1, Michigan State University, Department of Agricultural Economics, East Lansing, 1982.
Eicher, Carl K., and Staatz, John M., (eds.), *Agricultural Development in the Third World*, Johns Hopkins University Press, Baltimore, 1984.
Evenson, Robert E., 'Benefits and Obstacles in Developing Appropriate Agricultural Technology', in Eicher and Staatz, op. cit. pp. 348–61.
FAO/UNFPA/IIASA, *Potential Population Supporting Capacity of Lands in the Developing World*, Report of Project FPA/INT/5/3, Land Resources of the Future, FAO, Rome, 1982.
Goreaux, Louis M., 'Compensatory Financing for Fluctuations in the Cost of Cereal Imports', in Valdes, Alberto (ed.), *Food Security for Developing Countries*, Westview Press, Boulder, Colorado, pp. 307–33, 1981.
Helleiner, G.K., 'Smallholder Decision Making: Tropical African Evidence', in Reynolds, Lloyd G. (ed.) *Agriculture in Development Theory*, Yale University Press, Harvard, 1975.
Huddleston, Barbara, *Closing the Cereals Gap with Trade and Food Aid*, International Food Policy Research Institute, Washington, DC, 1984.
Johnston, Bruce F. and Clark, William C., *Redesigning Rural Development: A Strategic Perspective*, Johns Hopkins University Press, Baltimore, 1982.
Lele, Uma, 'Rural Africa: Modernization, Equity, and Long-Term Development' in Eicher and Staatz, op. cit. pp. 436–52.
Lele, Uma and Wildred Candler, 'Food Security in Developing Countries: National Issues' in Eicher and Staatz, op. cit. pp. 207–21, 1984.
Mellor, John W., 'The Indian Economy: Objectives, Performance and Prospects' in John W. Mellor (ed.) *India: A Rising Middle Power*, Westview Press, Boulder, Colorado, 1979, pp. 85–110.

Ndegwa, Philip, *Africa's Development Crisis and Related International Issues*, Heinemann, Nairobi, 1985.

Ndiame, Fadel, 'A Comparative Analysis of Alternative Irrigation Schemes and the Objective of Food Security: The Case of the Fleuve Region in Senegal', (Unpublished M.S. thesis) Department of Agricultural Economics, Michigan State University, East Lansing, 1985.

Poleman, Thomas T., 'World Food: Myth and Reality', *World Development*, 5, 1977, pp. 383–94.

République du Sénégal, Ministère du Dévéloppement Rural, *Nouvelle Politique Agricole*, Dakar, 1984.

Reutlinger, Shlomo, 'Project Food Aid and Equitable Growth: Income-Transfer Efficiency First', *World Development*, vol. 12, no. 9, 1984, 901–11.

Reutlinger, Shlomo and Selowsky, Marcelo, *Malnutrition and Poverty: Magnitude and Policy Options* (World Bank Staff Working Paper no. 21), Johns Hopkins University Press, Baltimore, 1976.

Rukuni, Mandivamba, 'An Analysis of the Economic and Institutional Factors Affecting Irrigation Development in Communal Lands of Zimbabwe', (Unpublished D. Phil. dissertation) University of Zimbabwe, 1984.

Sen, Amartya K., *Poverty and Famines: An Essay on Entitlement and Deprivation*, Clarendon Press, Oxford, 1981.

Sow, P. Allasane and Newman, Mark D., 'La Réglémentation et l'Organisation des Marches Céréaliers au Sénégal: Situation des Campagnes de Commercialisation 1983:84 et 1984:85', ISRA/BAME Document de Travail 85–2, Dakar, 1985.

Spencer, Dunstan, 'Agricultural Research in Sub-Saharan Africa: Using the Lessons From the Past to Develop a Strategy for the Future', Background paper for the Committee on African Development Strategies, New York, 17 January, 1985.

Timmer, C. Peter, Falcon, Walter P. and Pearson, Scott R., *Food Policy Analysis*, Johns Hopkins University Press, Baltimore, 1983.

USAID, *Plan for Supporting Agricultural Research and Faculties of Agriculture in Africa*, Washington, DC, May 1985.

World Bank, Population, Health and Nutrition Department, *Zimbabwe Population Health and Nutrition Sector Review*, Washington, DC, 1983.

World Bank, *Annual Report, 1984*, Washington, DC, 1984.

Zimbabwe, Government of, *Growth with Equity*, Harare 1981.

COLIN KIRKPATRICK AND DIMITRIS DIAKOSAVVAS

Food Insecurity and the Foreign Exchange Constraint in Sub-Saharan Africa

I. INTRODUCTION

The problem of food insecurity in less developed countries (LDCs) continues to demand the attention of the international community. Despite the progress that has been made in increasing world production of cereals and other major foodstuffs, many LDCs continue to face immense difficulties in ensuring an adequate level of food supplies on a regular year-to-year basis. The current African food crisis has once again demonstrated the vulnerability of low income economies to a sudden shortfall in food supplies and has highlighted the need for additional measures to strengthen food security in the Third World. Despite a significant increase in food imports, the growth in consumption in sub-Saharan Africa was less than that of population, with consumption per caput declining over the last two decades (Mellor and Johnston 1984).

The problem of food insecurity has a long-term and a short-term dimension. The longer-term aspect relates to the chronic and persistent malnutrition of significant sections of the population in many LDCs, while the shorter-term insecurity is caused by year-to-year fluctuations in food consumption levels.

The focus of the present paper is upon the second dimension of food insecurity. The paper seeks to identify the extent to which short-run changes in the level of food imports have offset shortfalls in domestic production, thereby protecting consumption levels. The paper is structured as follows. Section II presents some evidence of the foreign exchange burden of food imports in sub-Saharan Africa. Section III develops the paper's main argument, that fluctuations in food consumption levels per caput are related to the difficulties that low-income countries face in financing the shortfalls in domestic production and/or increases in the price of imports. Empirical evidence relating to a sample of 30 African economies for the 1965–83 period is presented in Section IV. Section V contains a brief summary and concluding comments.

II. RECENT TRENDS IN FOOD IMPORTS[1]

International trade is an increasingly important element in the food supply

230

equation of many low-income countries, with commercial imports and food aid accounting for a significant share of total consumption. This growing dependence on food imports, and the short-term insecurity problems with which it is associated, are particularly acute in sub-Saharan Africa. Empirical evidence indicates that cereal imports by this region have increased more rapidly than for the LDCs as a whole (Huddleston 1984). Commercial imports rose by 63 per cent between 1976–8 and 1981, while the share of food aid in total imports increased from 18 to 23 per cent over the same period. The foreign exchange burden of food imports varies both across countries and over time. Table 1 shows that for a sample of 30 sub-Saharan countries covering the period 1965–83, expenditure on cereal imports accounted for more than 10 per cent of export earnings in half the sample economies. In particular years, the share of cereal costs in export revenues exceeded 25 per cent in 13 countries. Thus, for many African economies,

TABLE 1 *Cereal imports as share of total merchandise exports in African economies, 1965–83 (%)*

Country	Mean	Maximum
Benin	22.0	77.2 (1982)
Botswana	19.1	66.2 (1968)
Burkina Faso	26.3	66.9 (1978)
Cameroon	4.6	6.1 (1983)
Central African Republic	5.2	9.2 (1975)
Chad	6.0	16.2 (1974)
Ethiopia	6.4	16.1 (1980)
Gambia	15.3	37.3 (1981)
Ghana	5.1	9.5 (1983)
Guinea	10.2	18.0 (1973)
Ivory Coast	4.2	7.3 (1981)
Kenya	2.3	6.2 (1982)
Lesotho	67.3	127.3 (1977)
Madagascar	11.6	34.4 (1982)
Malawi	4.2	15.6 (1970)
Mali	19.2	96.8 (1974)
Mauritania	11.2	22.9 (1978)
Mauritius	15.2	22.3 (1969)
Mozambique	10.5	27.3 (1977)
Niger	8.0	47.2 (1974)
Rwanda	10.1	18.0 (1982)
Senegal	20.6	35.4 (1973)
Sierra Leone	12.4	32.3 (1982)
Somalia	29.5	77.1 (1981)
Sudan	6.5	11.9 (1980)
Tanzania	9.3	30.4 (1975)
Togo	5.1	10.2 (1981)
Uganda	2.2	4.5 (1982)
Zaire	7.6	23.8 (1981)
Zambia	2.9	10.1 (1980)

expenditure on food imports, is a serious strain on the balance of payments.

III. FOOD CONSUMPTION INSTABILITY AND THE FOREIGN EXCHANGE CONSTRAINT

Short-term food insecurity arises from two interrelated sources – domestic production and foreign exchange availability. Fluctuations in production are an obvious potential source of insecurity, but on their own they are neither necessary nor sufficient to generate food insecurity. In a world of perfect capital markets a country which experienced a production shortfall could simply borrow in international markets to finance additional imports and repay these loans when production returned to normal levels. In practice, there are a variety of economic and institutional factors which make such a simple solution impossible.[2] These can be summarised as representing a foreign exchange constraint. A constraint on the availability of foreign exchange causes food insecurity by limiting a country's ability to buy on the international market in order to stabilise consumption in years of production shortfalls. In the same way, a tightening of the foreign exchange constraint through a rise in the world price of food imports, or a decline in export earnings, will impact directly on food security.[3] The effect of fluctuations in production and import prices on food insecurity can be manifested in a variety of ways. Consider a country which is faced with a shortfall in food production and a severe foreign exchange constraint. Such a country may attempt to sustain domestic food consumption levels, or at least moderate the decline in consumption, by various means. These could most obviously include: drawing on existing food reserves, reducing food exports, obtaining increased food aid, or increasing food imports.

In practice, the choice among such measures is likely to be severely limited. In the majority of low-income food-importing countries domestic food stocks are either non-existent or much below target (IWC 1983). Empirical analysis has shown the lack of correspondence between food aid inflows and the import needs of individual LDCs (Huddleston 1981). Reducing food exports is obviously not an option available to a majority of LDCs. An increase in commercial food imports will have a high opportunity cost, since it can only be financed by a cutback in non-food imports, many of which are essential for sustaining the development effort.

The *a priori* expectation is therefore that the majority of low-income food deficit countries will be unable to increase significantly their year-to-year food imports in response to a sudden decline in domestic production or increase in the price of food imports. The result is likely to be downward adjustments in consumption standards.

Many sub-Saharan economies have indeed experienced considerable short-run variability in consumption levels. Table 2 displays the estimated coefficients of variation in cereals consumption per caput for 30

TABLE 2   *Instability in food consumption per caput in sub-Saharan Africa, 1965–83*

Country	Coefficient of Variation[1] %	Probability of a given percentage shortfall 5%	2.5%
Benin	10.6	31.9	40.7
Botswana	9.6	29.7	39.7
Burkina Faso	10.2	30.9	40.2
Cameroon	30.5	43.7	46.7
Central African Republic	10.6	31.5	40.5
Chad	7.8	25.8	37.2
Ethiopia	10.3	30.9	40.2
Gambia	15.5	37.2	43.5
Ghana	21.5	40.6	45.3
Guinea	10.3	30.9	40.2
Ivory Coast	5.9	19.1	33.4
Kenya	10.0	30.6	40.0
Lesotho	20.2	40.1	44.9
Madagascar	4.2	10.6	26.6
Malawi	10.1	30.6	40.0
Mali	12.1	33.6	41.6
Mauritania	11.6	33.2	41.4
Mauritius	32.5	43.5	46.8
Mozambique	9.7	30.1	39.8
Niger	15.1	36.6	43.2
Rwanda	9.8	29.9	39.6
Senegal	20.4	40.2	45.0
Sierra Leone	8.1	26.2	37.5
Somalia	20.2	39.9	44.9
Sudan	17.7	38.5	44.2
Tanzania	14.6	36.0	42.9
Togo	12.5	34.2	41.9
Uganda	14.9	36.8	43.3
Zaire	9.3	28.9	39.0
Zambia	22.1	40.8	45.4

[1]The data are trend adjusted cereal consumption per caput.

countries during the period 1965–83. The results indicate sizeable cross-country variation, ranging from 4.2 per cent in Madagascar to 32.5 per cent in Mauritius. An alternative way of representing this variability in consumption is to compute the probability of consumption falling below trend by more than a given percentage. Columns 2 and 3 of Table 2 show the probabilities that actual consumption per caput falls below 95 per cent and 97.5 per cent of trend. For 28 countries a shortfall in consumption per head of more than 5 per cent occurs with a 25 per cent probability, that is, once every four years. When we consider shortfalls in consumption per head of at least 2.5 per cent, however, only Madagascar did not experience such a shortfall one year in three, and all the countries in the sample experienced a shortfall one year in four. Where the shortfall is unevenly distributed, the impact upon the already uneven consumption pattern can be severe for the poorest sections of the population, and under plausible assumptions, an average shortfall of 2.5 per cent could translate into a shortfall of 10 per cent for as much as 30 per cent of the adult population (Green and Kirkpatrick 1982).

To summarise, the relationship between food production, imports and consumption cannot be analysed in isolation from the balance of payments position. If a country faces a foreign exchange constraint, the *ex post* data on the volume of food imports will provide a poor indicator of the country's food import requirements, and it would be a misleading simplification to interpret a low level of short-run variation in food imports as evidence of the absence of a food insecurity problem.

IV. EMPIRICAL EVIDENCE ON THE USE OF IMPORTS TO ATTAIN FOOD SECURITY

The analysis of the way in which imports respond to changes in domestic production and world prices is undertaken in two stages. First, an estimate is made of how food imports have responded to variations in domestic production and international prices; second, the relationship between consumption instability and foreign exchange availability is examined. The data used consisted of FAO statistics on production, consumption and trade in cereals. Price data were taken from World Bank (1984) and refer to the real international price of cereals.[4]

To evaluate how food imports have responded to changes in domestic production and world prices the following equation was estimated:

$$(M_t - \hat{M}_t) = a_1(Q_t - \hat{Q}_t) + a_2(P_t - \hat{P}_t) \tag{1}$$

where M_t = volume of cereal imports in year t
Q_t = domestic production of cereals in year t
$\hat{M}_t$, $\hat{Q}_t$ and $\hat{P}_t$ denote the linear trend estimated values of the variables in year t.[5]

The coefficients a_1 and a_2 reflect the extent to which variability in domestic food production and world market price are reflected in adjustments in food imports. If fluctuations in domestic production are totally offset by trade, then the coefficient of the production variable, a_1, will be equal to minus unity. If a_1 is different than minus one then domestic production shortfalls are not completely offset by trade and some adjustments have to be made in domestic consumption. The price coefficient, a_2, captures the extent to which short-run fluctuations in international food prices create adjustments in food imports. Again, we would expect to find an inverse relationship, implying that as prices rise imports are reduced.

The results obtained when equation (1) was estimated are shown in Table 3. As can be seen, the coefficient of production is correctly signed in the majority of cases, and in all cases is (statistically) significantly different from minus one. It can be argued, therefore, that trade has not made a significant contribution to food security and a significant proportion of production variability is likely to have been transmitted directly to consumption instability. The price coefficient estimates are less satisfactory. The coefficient is correctly signed in 14 cases, and is statistically significant in only two cases. There are six instances of statistically significant positive coefficients, a result consistent with consumption stabilising behaviour. One possible explanation for the apparent unresponsiveness of imports to cereal price changes might be that, contrary to our *a priori* expectations, countries managed to stabilise import volumes despite price volatility, and adjusted the level of non-food imports accordingly. A more plausible explanation is that the price variable is a poor proxy for the change in the foreign exchange constraint. If, for example, the increase in world food prices is part of a general increase in commodity prices, increased export earnings may offset the adverse effect of food prices on foreign exchange purchasing capacity.

The finding that cereal imports by sub-Saharan countries have been unresponsive to variations in domestic production is consistent with the results reported in several recent studies for LDCs as a whole. Morrison's (1984) study of the pattern of LDCs' cereal imports concluded that short-term factors were relatively unimportant determinants, as compared to long-term structural factors such as the level of income per caput and the degree of urbanisation. Of particular interest for the present study is Morrison's failure to find a statistically significant relationship between fluctuations in domestic cereals production and cereals imports per caput. Blandford's (1983) study reports estimated values of the production coefficient, a_1, for different country groupings. For the low-income LDCs group the coefficients for wheat and coarse grains imports over the period 1960–81 were -0.41 and -0.12 respectively. In other words, significantly less than half of the variation in domestic production was transmitted to imports.

The second stage in the empirical exercise was to examine directly the impact of foreign exchange availability on food security. To do this, deviations in food consumption from 'target' levels were regressed on the ratio of 'food security' costs to export earnings. Food security imports (M_t^*) are defined as the volume of imports needed to close the gap between target consumption ($\hat{C}_t$) and domestic food production (Q_t). The cost of food security imports can be written as:

$$M_t^* = (\hat{C}_t = Q_t) P_t$$

where $\hat{C}_t$ = the target level of consumption, defined as the estimated trend value[6]

Q_t = domestic food production

P_t = real international food price.

To allow for movements in overall foreign exchange availability, the cost of food security imports is expressed as a ratio of real total export

TABLE 3 *Results of regression analysis*

| Country | Import Equation | | Consumption Equation |
	a_1	a_2	b_1
Benin	−.025	72.162	−2.456
	(28.327)**	(0.890)	(7.081)**
Botswana	−0.014	−180.367	−3.025
	(10.935)**	(1.685)	(3.710)**
Burkina Faso	−0.002	437.218	−3.004
	(29.748)**	(3.410)**	(10.329)**
Cameroon	−0.322	−179.199	−12.464
	(17.900)**	(2.033)*	(2.475)**
Central African	−0.56	1.409	−3.841
Republic	(36.117)**	(0.015)	(13.032)**
Chad	0.277	−29.500	−4.265
	(6.582)**	(1.257)	(3.778)**
Ethiopia	0.014	−358.072	−18.102
	(37.083)**	(0.733)	(9.171)**
Gambia	−0.015	−28.983	−2.589
	(14.998)**	(0.872)	(7.898)**
Ghana	−0.032	177.470	−45.113
	(19.246)**	(0.626)	(8.534)**
Guinea	0.002	100.640	−10.738
	(53.946)**	(3.079)**	(6.362)**
Ivory Coast	−0.281	−14.478	−59.839
	(9.559)**	(0.059)	(3.771)**
Kenya	−0.163	72.182	−35.712
	(20.767)**	(0.116)	(3.200)**
Lesotho	−0.078	−107.771	−1.026
	(13.095)**	(0.794)	(7.563)**
Madagascar	−0.027	−15.053	−18.504
	(51.370)**	(0.273)	(15.458)**
Malawi	−0.095	−8.949	−6.836
	(30.501)**	(0.050)	(5.503)**
Mali	−0.025	121.488	−8.119
	(23.291)**	(6.312)**	(8.436)**
Mauritania	−0.799	379.417	0.119
	(13.244)**	(4.019)**	(0.060)
Mauritius	−0.743	2.762	1.437
	(6.764)**	(0.135)	(0.440)
Mozambique	−0.237	−97.020	−6.966
	(8.415)**	(0.250)	(2.680)**
Niger	0.023	101.025	−4.985
	(34.911)**	(4.752)**	(6.168)**
Rwanda	−0.005	−5.637	−2.841
	(70.774)**	(0.410)	(8.682)**
Senegal	0.006	177.041	−16.727
	(16.007)**	(0.497)	(4.906)**
Sierra Leone	0.038	100.417	−10.883

TABLE 3   *Results of regression analysis (cont.)*

	(15.262)**	(1.096)	(12.040)**
Somalia	0.956	610.722	−5.396
	(8.596)**	(1.706)	(3.096)**
Sudan	−0.030	−381.688	−32.832
	(40.262)**	(0.981)	(22.050)**
Tanzania	0.033	171.081	−35.519
	(12.727)**	(2.077)*	(5.904)**
Togo	−0.116	−188.541	−6.982
	(18.846)**	(2.603)**	(8.105)**
Uganda	−0.007	9.755	−20.949
	(48.433)**	(0.061)	(9.033)**
Zaire	−0.534	111.703	−4.006
	(3.307)**	(1.781)	(0.468)
Zambia	−0.129	−101.049	−50.667
	(17.118)**	(1.466)	(4.101)**

[1]The numbers in parenthesis under the coefficients are the t-ratios. Stars stand for confidence (risk) levels of the two-tail test: * 5% ** 1%.

earnings (X_t).[7]

The equation was estimated in the following form:

$$(C_t - \hat{C}_t) = b_0 + b_1 \frac{M_t{}^*}{X_t} \qquad (2)$$

The coefficient b_1 is expected to have a negative sign. If the cost of 'food security imports' increases (due either to a domestic production shortfall or an increase in the world price), or export earnings fall, then a country will find it more difficult to stabilise consumption.

The results displayed in the right-hand signed column of Table 3 show that the coefficient of 'food security imports' is correctly signed and statistically significant at the one per cent level in all but three cases (Mauritania, Mauritius, Zaire). On average a ten per cent change in the cost of 'food security imports' has led to 2.12 per cent change in food consumption. Of the 30 countries included in the sample, only two fail to show the predicted inverse relationship (Mauritania, Mauritius).

Given the unsophisticated nature of the testing procedures employed, and the poor quality of the data, the results in Table 3 are encouraging. They provide strong support for the argument that limited foreign exchange availability has been a constraint upon the ability of sub-Saharan countries to obtain the level of food imports needed to ensure short run food security, and has therefore contributed directly to the significant year to year fluctuations in consumption experienced by these economies.

CONCLUSION

In this paper it has been argued that the short term insecurity problem in sub-Saharan Africa, as evidenced by high levels of consumption variability, is the direct result of a foreign exchange constraint which limits the ability of low-income countries to adjust their level of food imports in response to shortfalls in domestic production and/or variations in international food prices. Section IV provided strong empirical evidence consistent with this hypothesis.

An important qualificiation to this paper relates to the aggregate nature of the analysis. There is considerable diversity in the experience of individual economies, and the importance of any particular factor in explaining food consumption instability will vary across countries. Furthermore, the impact of a given variation in consumption or imports will depend, *inter alia*, on the existing level of consumption per caput, the share of food imports in total consumption and the share of 'essential' imports in total non-food imports. It is recognised that these complexities are not captured by cross-section analysis, and the sources of food insecurity in individual countries require further detailed study.

Nevertheless, we believe that the analysis presented in the paper provides a new perspective to the serious food insecurity problems of sub-Saharan Africa and has important implications for international food security policy. The international community can play a significant role in the alleviation of food insecurity through the provision of concessionary finance for the funding of exceptional food import requirements. The IMF's 'Food Facility', which is specifically designed to help members with balance of payments difficulties to finance an increase in cereal imports, is one channel through which assistance can be provided. The use of the IMF's Buffer Stock Financing Facility to finance the setting up of food security reserves would be a further means of alleviating the short-term foreign exchange constraint on food security (Kirkpatrick 1985). Improving the LDCs' capacity to finance short-term fluctuations in food requirements will not eliminate the food security problem. Domestic policies towards income maintenance, pricing and distribution of food supplies will also play an important role in determining the degree of consumption instability and deprivation experienced by vulnerable sections of the population. But taken in conjunction with appropriate internal policies, increased financial assistance by the international community could make a significant contribution to the reduction of food insecurity in sub-Saharan Africa.

NOTES

[1]In the rest of the paper we refer to 'food' and 'cereals' interchangeably. In the majority of developing countries both the share of human consumption in total cereal consumption and the share of cereals in total foodstuffs consumption (measured in calorie intake), is high (FAO 1977, Tables I.1.3 and I.4.1). In addition, world trade in foodstuffs consists mainly of cereals.

[2]The consideration that food insecurity is in part related to inperfections in world capital markets suggests the relevance of intervention by international lending agencies in alleviating international food insecurity. See Green (1983) on this point.

[3]There is evidence to suggest that the variability of both cereals production and prices has increased in recent years. See Hazell (1984) and Blandford (1983).

[4]Real cereal prices were obtained by deflating nominal prices by the World Bank manufacturing unit value index.

[5]Equation (1) has been derived from a simple free trade model.

[6]The trend value of consumption was defined in terms of a permanent income consumption function. A detailed description of the procedure used is given in Diakosavvas (1983).

[7]Nominal exports were deflated by import unit values from IMF's *Financial Statistics*, to derive real export earnings series.

REFERENCES

Blandford, D., 'Instability in World Grain Markets', *Journal of Agricultural Economics*, vol. XXXIV, no. 3, 1983, pp. 379–95.

Diakosavvas, D., 'The Measurement of Commodity Market Instability with Particular Reference to Food Consumption Instability', *Manchester University Discussion Papers in Development Studies*, no. 8302, Manchester, 1983.

Food and Agriculture Organization (FAO), *The Fourth World Food Survey*, Rome, 1977.

Green, C., 'Insulating Countries Against Fluctuations in Domestic production and Exports: An Analysis of Compensatory Financing Schemes', *Journal of Development Economics*, vol. 12, 1983, pp. 302–25.

Green, C. and Kirkpatrick, C., 'A Cross-Section Analysis of Food Insecurity in Developing Countries: Its Magnitude and Sources', *Journal of Development Studies*, vol. 18, no. 2, 1982, pp. 181–200.

Hazell, P., 'Sources of Increased Variability in World Cereal Production since 1960s'. *International Food Policy Research Institute*, Washington DC, 1984.

Huddleston, B., 'Responsiveness of Food Aid to Variable Import Requirements' in Valdes A., (ed.), *Food Security for Developing Countries*, 1981, Westview Press, Boulder, Colorado.

Huddleston, B., 'Closing the Cereals Gap with Trade and Food Aid', *International Food Research Institute*, Research Report 43, Washington DC, 1984.

Huddleston, B. and Kirkpatrick, C., 'World Food Security: The Need for Balance of Payments Support to Meet Exceptional Variations in Food Import Bills' in *Approaches to World Food Security*, FAO Economic and Social Development Paper 32, Rome, 1983.

International Monetary Fund (IMF), *International Financial Statistics*, various issues.

International Wheat Council, (IWC), *National Stockholding Policies*, Secretariat Paper no. 13, London, 1983.

Kirkpatrick, C., 'Improving Food Security in Developing Countries: A Role of the IMF', *Banca Nazionale Del Lavoro Quarterly Review* (1985).

Knudsen, O. K. and Scandizzo, P. L., 'Nutrition and Food Needs in Developing Countries', *World Bank Staff Working Paper no. 328*, Washington DC, 1979.

Mellor, J. W. and Johnston, B. F., 'The World Food Equation: Interrelations Among Development, Employment and Food Consumption', *Journal of Economic Literature*, vol. XXII, June, 1984, pp. 531–74.

Morrison, T. K., 'Cereal Imports by Developing Countries', *Food Policy* vol. 9, no. 1, 1984, pp. 13–26.

World Bank, *Commodity Trade and Price Trends*, Johns Hopkins University Press, Baltimore, 1984.

DISCUSSION OPENING – L. A. MSAMBICHAKA

Both papers bring enormous work and concern to the problem of food in Africa. These two good papers have attempted to present the following:

(i) The food security and insecurity situation which by facts and figures is said to be disastrous.

(ii) The causes of the situation.

(iii) Remedial measures as well as a suggested research agenda (first paper).

Notwithstanding the above observations, however, I would like to raise the following issues for discussion as well as an emphasis to the information provided in the two papers.

On the Eicher and Staatz paper:

1. Sub-Saharan Africa's ability to feed itself
It is true that many sub-Saharan African countries were before independence net exporters of food or at least they could meet their own domestic demands. This ability has over the years been eroded and many of these countries are now almost permanently net importers. Despite the fact that reasons behind this anomaly do substantially vary from country to country, is there a common denominator to the problem? In other words has the inability to feed oneself got anything to do with the following?

  (a) the national agricultural policies:
    —wrong policies were prepared
    —wrong emphasis in wrong areas was made or
    —wrong priorities were made
  (b) the mismanagement of the agricultural sector (food and cash)
  (c) external factors: for example, Aid Donors have over the years provided assistance in wrong areas of the national economy and at the wrong time. This has compounded the problems inherent in the food sector.
  (d) Inability to predict and plan for the future.

2. Nutrition and vulnerable groups
No one would dispute the fact that the issue of nutrition is important. However as the situation is now in Africa and given the level of development we have, what could we consider as the major point of departure for our discussion? Is it the food production, availability or accessibility problem which African countries and agricultural economists should attempt to discuss and look for alternative solutions? I pose this question for the following reasons:

  (a) Sub-Saharan Africa is basically made up of a poor rural population.
  (b) With the exception of a few countries, most of the food is produced by the majority of the population who are the rural poor.
  (c) Sub-Saharan Africa's potential natural resources are enormous.

In such a situation when the majority poor are the majority of producers, land resource is not a threatening problem and yet food is in severe shortage. What should be the issue for discussion? The truth is that many households are not capable of producing enough for themselves, let alone for the market. I would imagine that for sub-Saharan Africa and given the state of our development, the problem is at the production level and the ability to use reasonably what has been produced.

On the Diakosavvas and Kirkpatrick paper:

1. Food consumption
Financing capability of food imports. In years of foreign exchange constraint one would expect less of commercial food imports. Nevertheless there are countries which import enormous amounts of food even when their foreign exchange situation is in a precarious situation. How can this be explained? Is it because of political and humanistic reasons?

2. Food insecurity
Discussions on food security/insecurity are being conducted in various countries in Africa and the respective sub-regions. In a span of 12 months I have attended about four meetings which were discussing food crisis at a national, sub-regional and the entire African level. In each meeting food crisis has always been equated with 'cereals or grain crisis'. The role of traditional crops such as bananas, cassava, yams, sweet potatoes, etc. in ensuring food security has never been treated exhaustively. How correct are we as agricultural economists to neglect these foods which could substantially reduce the magnitude of human disaster? Agricultural economists would do a greater service to human development in Africa if they sorted out ways and means of propagating the traditional foods by way of improving productivity, transport and storage logistics as well as their preparations.

3. Imports per caput v. consumption per caput
Most of the countries in the sub-Saharan region import food. Many of these countries have rural transport problems which have a direct negative impact on the distribution system. Quantitative food import per caput figures show a rising trend and so are the figures for consumption per caput.

Despite these rather impressive figures, we note an increasing number of malnourished children and expectant mothers who suffer from nutritional anaemia and face maternal death. How can these be explained?

4. Food aid imports v. commercial food imports
Food aid imports in developing countries declined during 1961–3, 1976–8 and 1981. Regionwise, food imports in sub-Saharan Africa have been on an upward trend. However the region received less aid than each of the areas discussed, except for 1976–8 when it received more than Latin America. However total food aid received by sub-Saharan Africa during

the period under discussion was about 10 per cent of the total. A combined volume of food aid to Latin America and sub-Saharan Africa accounted for around ⅕ of the total food to developing countries.

Except for sub-Saharan Africa, where a parallel increase in both commercial and food aid imports took place, in other regions the trend was in opposite directions. The questions which can be derived out of this trend are twofold:

(a) Food prices have been volatile over the years and yet commercial imports have been rising and food aid declining. Are developing countries putting more and more of their foreign exchange resources into food imports rather than other non-food imports?

(b) Does the declining trend of food aid to developing countries indicate that donors are increasingly becoming more reluctant to extend food aid to the developing countries?

Many questions could be derived from Table 3, but I hope participants will be able to raise them.

In conclusion I wish to make the following observations:

(1) Since independence African governments have not seriously addressed their policies towards the problem of food and human nutrition. Many countries have no 'food and nutrition policy'. This is a big drawback in human development.

(2) Food aid has not made a significant contribution to the promotion and stabilisation of domestic food production in sub-Saharan Africa.

(3) Food aid has not made a significant contribution towards stabilisation of food security in sub-Saharan Africa. The percentage of the malnourished is still on the increase.

(4) Certainly we do need external assistance to improve our agriculture and food production. However, the international community can play a bigger role in alleviating food insecurity by channelling their assistance towards direct production.

(5) Domestic policies should aim at increasing production first. This would need an improvement in four basic areas:
  (a) rural infrastructural supportive services;
  (b) agricultural marketing incentives;
  (c) agricultural technical services;
  (d) resource deployment, especially investment allocation for direct food production and an increase of productivity (yields per person and per hectare).

(6) Stepping-up the overall socio-economic development is the only sure way of resolving the problem of food insecurity in Africa.

DISCUSSION OPENING – S.D. SAWANT

On the Eicher and Staatz paper

This paper covers a wide canvas of short-run and long-run measures to be adopted to deal with food insecurity arising from lack of effective purchasing power on the part of the poor. Two case studies, namely of Senegal and Zimbabwe, are briefly discussed to bring out the contrasts in policies followed and their consequent impact. In this context the authors have very rightly emphasised the vital importance of development of an indigenous science community and a decentralised research system for evolving locally adaptive technology for agriculture. Preference for a strategy of self-reliance, rather than an insistence on self-sufficiency in food by totally disregarding the relative costs of production of foodgrains *vis-à-vis* non-foodgrains, is also well placed. But there are some serious discrepancies in the authors' remarks about Zimbabwe. It was initially stated that, 'the fundamental problems in agriculture were the low productivity of smallholders, widespread poverty among rural workers on large commercial farms, a large landless population and a rural infrastructure that had been battered during the warfare of the 1970s'. On the other hand we were further told that a substantial increase of 28.5 per cent in the price of maize, a major food staple, elimination of the food subsidy offered on wheat bread and substantially reduced consumer subsidies on meat, dairy products etc. induced favourable growth in agricultural exports. The disastrous consequences of this latter package of increased prices of major food staples and reduced subsidies on other foods to numerous small farmers and particularly to the large landless population, hardly need to be stressed. While not denying the fact that the backlog of indigenously evolved, proven, on-shelf maize technology for both commercial and small farmers is a very laudable achievement of Zimbabwe, it is difficult to accept the authors' judgement that Zimbabwe represents a successful policy model for African countries, when we have not been informed about the consequences of increased food prices for poverty stricken rural workers and the large landless population in the rural areas. Notwithstanding the above discrepancies, however, the general agenda of research to be undertaken for African countries, stated by the authors towards the end of the paper, is very extensive and instructive.

On the Diakosavvas and Kirkpatrick paper

The concept of food security as defined by the authors with reference to aggregate availability has limited relevance to the major problem of 'entitlement failure', either temporary or chronic, faced by a large majority of the undernourished population in the LDCs. This is not to indicate that the authors are not aware of this limitation but to bring out the limited usefulness of the study for a more vital problem of food security to the poor, especially the rural poor, in developing economies. Secondly, an approximation of food availability by availability of cereals is not a very satisfactory approximation, particularly for quite a few African countries in which non-cereals, such as root crops, pulses, nuts, oilseeds, plantains etc., play an important role in food consumption.

I shall now make a few remarks about the crucial issues suggested below for discussion. So long as the concept of food security is restricted to the supply side, and that too with a short-run time horizon in sight, the solutions are not very complicated, though they may be expensive, owing to difficulties arising from the balance of payments situation. However, partial reliance on national food stocks, supported by the programmes of international co-operation may provide substantial relief in this case. If an objective is to attain target levels of food consumption per caput and thereby increasingly improve the status of nutrition for all in the community in the long run, we need to concentrate on growth of agricultural production or more specifically food production, if food self-sufficiency is not a relatively high cost strategy compared to a broader goal of self-reliance. However, availability of food does not necessarily guarantee physical and economic access of the poor to food. But extension of the food security concept to cover the demand aspect takes us to a much wider canvas of strategies which aim at (i) building up an efficient food distribution system supported by adequate infrastructural development particularly in the rural areas and (ii) generation of 'food entitlement' to the rural poor in LDCs. Obviously, we assume in this context that adequate food availability and increased real incomes (to ensure food entitlement) of the poor would push up their level of food consumption and consequently their nutritional status and thereby increasingly reduce their vulnerability, both to food supply variations and real income variations. An important question that crops up in this context is: do the consumption behaviours of the poor justify such a strategy without any reservations? The evidence emerging from Indian data does indicate (i) a preference for 'taste' rather than 'nutrition' of the undernourished at various income levels[1] and (ii) that diversion of income for non-food commodities and services begins at an income level much below the poverty line income.[2] In other words, there is a reason to believe that a mere increase in real incomes may not lead to improved food security to the poor in LDCs unless conscious efforts are made to modify their preference systems and life styles associated with chronic poverty so as to motivate them to increase their food consumption and also acquire adequate levels of nutrition with increased incomes.

NOTES

[1]C.H. Shah, *Demand for Higher Status Food and Nutrition in Rural India: Experience of Matar Taluka*, Bellagio Workshop (Italy), March 1985.

[2]Rao, V.M. and Vivekananda, M., 'Food Problems and Policy Priorities' in Shah, C.H. and Vakil, C.N. (eds.), *Agricultural Development of India: Problems and Policies*, Orient Longman, New Delhi, 1979.

GENERAL DISCUSSION – RAPPORTEUR: CARLISLE A. PEMBERTON

The discussion on the first paper centred on two major issues. First, whether increased export or cash crop production (for example, cotton production in the Sahel) could be valid policy for the alleviation of the food security crisis in sub-Saharan Africa and second, an appropriate definition of the concept of food security.

Dr Staatz noted that the paper considered two time perspectives: while increased cash crop production may not increase food availability in the short run, in the longer term it provides a source of revenue for improving rural infrastructure and it also allows, through income generation, great access of the poor to food via the market mechanism. He conceded however that most countries must produce the majority of their own food with only residual amounts being met by food imports, financed perhaps by the sale of cash commodities. In this context he accepted the criticism of a neglect in the paper of the contribution of livestock to food production in sub-Saharan Africa.

On the definition of food security, discussants expressed some concern with the one provided in the paper, especially since 140 countries had accepted a clear definition of food security at a recent FAO meeting.

Another issue discussed was the informal food sector, where it was noted that so-called 'street foods' may represent some 20–25 per cent of the food budgets of poor households, but that such food consumption may be neglected in more macro-oriented studies or studies concentrating solely on foods eaten within the home.

In reply to the discussion opener, Dr Staatz stated that there was no simple or single cause of the loss of ability of sub-Saharan African countries to feed themselves. To the list of causes noted in the paper and expanded upon by the opener, another cause could be added 'unfavourable weather'. He agreed that Zimbabwe might not be quite the success story that was presented in the paper distributed to the Conference and stated that a revised paper would deal with some of the difficulties of the Zimbabwean experience.

The discussion of the second paper centred on the points raised by the discussion openers: the use of cereals to represent food (in the paper) and the increase in food imports with increase in foreign exchange in developing countries.

Dr Diakosavvas stated that cereals were used as a proxy for food since, as noted in the paper, for most developing countries the share of cereals in total food consumption as well as the share of human consumption in total cereal consumption were both high. Also, he noted that there was general unavailability of data on non-cereal food consumption in developing countries.

On the second issue, Dr Diakosavvas argued that food imports increase as foreign exchange reserves increase in developing countries because food imports 'crowd out' non-food imports in the use of foreign exchange. The need for food imports arises from shortfalls in domestic food production perhaps caused by changes in consumer tastes as a consequence of rising incomes. Fluctuations in foreign exchange reserves could then result in a short-term food insecurity problem.

The need for an adequate definition of food security was raised in the discussions and Dr. Diakosavvas noted that he was aware of and accepted the definition agreed to at a recent FAO meeting. He therefore had not offered any alternative definition in his paper.

Participants in the discussion included J. Berthelot, R.C. Agrawal, F.S. Idachaba, M. Vanegas, E. Iveri and I. Tinker.

JAN DE VEER

National Agricultural Policies, Surplus Problems and International Instability

SURPLUSES AND SHORTAGES

There is a painful contrast between the agricultural surplus production problems of the developed market economies and the protein–calorie malnutrition problems of large groups of the population in many developing countries. It is tempting to link these two problems. A transfer of about 2 per cent of the world's grain production from surplus areas to the malnourished in the developing countries could eliminate malnutrition in the developing countries (World Bank 1980).

However the hunger problem in the developing countries is not a matter of counting calories and proteins that can be solved by logistic measures. It is also not a matter of an insufficient food production potential. Available estimates of the global population supporting capacity indicate a potential to feed a multiple of the present world population.[1]

Food shortage in developing countries is not primarily rooted in the insufficient production of food or in physical constraints for the expansion of food production, but is a feature of the general poverty problem and, therefore, more a problem of distribution than of production. Chronic and temporal lacks in the entitlements to food on the level of countries, regions, social groups or individual families due to a chronic low level of income or a temporary fall in income are the main cause of food problems (Sen 1981). An analysis of the connection between the agricultural policies of the developed countries and the food problems of developing countries should, therefore, focus on the impacts of these policies on the economic development and the income distribution in the developing world. However, a characteristic of developing countries is also that agriculture is an important source of income and still more of employment. The majority of the poor people in the developing countries live in the rural areas and, directly or indirectly, depend strongly on agriculture for their living. Particularly in the developing countries, agricultural policy is not only an instrument for the

247

national agriculture and food policy but also for regulation of the personal and regional income distribution with opposite effects on the low-income groups in the rural and in the urban areas.

The agricultural policies of the developed countries with their extensions of export, food aid and surplus disposal policies are important determinants of the agricultural and food policies of the developing countries. They affect the terms of trade for (potential) exporters of competing products and the political conditions for the national market and price policies of food-importing countries. The agricultural sector is also an integral part of the total economy and agricultural products are an important factor in international trade. The national agricultural policy is, therefore, also strongly connected with economic and monetary developments.

After a discussion of the agricultural policy and particularly the surplus problems of the developed countries and their direct impacts on international trade and agricultural development we shall, therefore, discuss the position of the agricultural sector in the context of the total economy and the impact of international economic and monetary developments on the development of agriculture.

AGRICULTURAL POLICY AND SURPLUS PRODUCTION

Agricultural production in the industrialised countries is expanding steadily whereas domestic demand is stagnating, due to reduced growth rates of population and consumer expenditures and decreasing income elasticities of demand. This has resulted in increasing self-sufficiency and the development of mounting production surpluses. The disposal of these surpluses through subsidised exports or domestic market outlets, the accumulation of stocks and the financing of deficiency payments, premiums on output restriction, etc. cause an increasing financial burden for the national treasuries which increasingly conflicts with the necessity to reduce budget deficits.

Countries with important shares in the world exports of a specific commodity and a correspondingly lower price elasticity of export demand also face a deterioration of their terms of trade resulting in low or even negative marginal export revenues (Meester and Oskam 1983.) Such countries also suffer from the growing self-sufficiency rates of importing countries and particularly by the penetration of their traditional export markets by countries which have turned into exporters to dispose of their surpluses. This adds considerably to existing tensions in international trade relations arising from economic recession, the restructuring of the world economy and monetary imbalances.

The increasing budgetary expenditures and, to a much less extent, international trade considerations force governments and politicians to consider revisions of the current policies. They are generally much less worried about the national social costs which arise from allocation losses in production and consumption and negative terms of trade effects for agricultural exports. These social costs are much less conspicuous and their exposure requires a rather complicated theoretical and quantitative economic analysis. Generally the social costs are, moreover, small in comparison with the total transfer of income from consumers and taxpayers to the farming sector and in relation to total national income.[2]

The quantification of the national social costs of the price support policies is generally based on a comparative static and partial analysis of the price effects on supply and demand and results in a recommendation of more market-oriented policies with a preference for direct income payments above price supports as an instrument for income redistribution in favour of the farming sector (see a.o. the Siena Memorandum, 1984). Politicians and governments, however, have to deal with interregional (within the EC also interstatal) and intersectoral conflicts of interests and with with the 'social actions' of strong pressure groups. A system of direct income payments generally faces a strong opposition from these pressure groups and, certainly in the short run, also does not solve the budgetary problems.

The political solutions, therefore, generally aim at the continuation of price policy as the main instrument for the allocation of income to farmers with supplementary measures to reduce surplus production and to diminish the budgetary expenditures for surplus disposals on external and domestic markets. Such measures include individual quota systems and production thresholds, in combination with levies on the total farm deliveries or excess deliveries, home consumption price schemes, etc. and measures to divert production from surplus products to products with an import surplus. The ultimate effect of these measures is generally a rather modest reduction of the surplus production and a shift of the financial burden from taxpayers to domestic consumers. From the viewpoint of international trade this is an unfavourable development. It must be feared that with the alleviation of the budgetary problems also the preparedness to strive for more discipline in international trade will diminish and that to a greater extent the costs of the policy will be rolled off to less protected producers in the rest of the world.

SOME REMARKS ABOUT PRICE POLICY

The analysis and recommendations of economists with respect to price supports are generally based on a strong 'price fundamentalism' (Krishna 1982 and Evenson 1983). Overproduction and underconsumption are attributed to price distortions; downward price and adjustments are recommended to eliminate or at least reduce these imbalances. Particularly with respect to supply the attention is focused on the comparative static effects with a neglect of possible long-run dynamic effects of prices and of the effects of other policies like research, development and extension policies, irrigation and rural development programmes, investment subsidies, etc.

In actual practice agricultural price policy consists of a range of policies for the direct and indirect support of the prices of the various farm products. There is a great variation in policies depending on the specific characteristics of products and markets (a.o. price flexibility, rate of self-sufficiency, international trade considerations, perishability and seasonality). Because of the interdependencies between the products a lowering of administered prices will work out in a general lowering of all farm prices including the products which are indirectly protected and supported by the price supports of 'base products'.

We have many estimates of single crop responsiveness to price changes but very few on cross-supply-responsiveness and aggregate price elasticities of supply; generally the long run aggregate price elasticities of supply are in the 0.2–0.4 range (Krishna 1982 and Evenson 1983). Compared with the supply shifters (trend variables) and the growth rates of global productivity, crop and milk yields and the total agricultural production, which are generally in the range of 1.5–2 per cent, the aggregate price elasticity is low. The once-over effect of a price reduction of say 20 per cent will be overtaken in only a few years. Price policy, therefore, is rather to be considered as a conditioning factor co-operating with other factors at the inducement of innovations and the creation of conditions which raise land productivity.

The major share of agricultural production (70–80 per cent) in the developed countries is presently produced by a relatively small part of the farms (20–30 per cent). These farms are in many countries sufficiently large to capture most of the economies of scale attainable at the present stage of technological development (e.g. Penn 1981). It is, therefore, true that the price policy above all benefits the bigger and more efficient farms. However, owing to non-farm income, lower indebtedness, less employment of hired labour, etc. the differences in total disposable family income between the larger and smaller farms are surprisingly small (USA: Penn, 1981; Canada: Brinkman, 1981; Japan, Ministry of Agriculture and Forestry 1984; Fed. Rep. of Germany: Krüll 1984 and Netherlands: de Veer 1985). Taking into account the necessary financial reservations for the future of the farm and the family and differences in the number of dependent family members, the differences in the level of family expenditures are even smaller (de Veer 1985). The standard of living of farm families is moreover generally not above that of wage earning families.

The mechanisation and use of labour-saving farming systems furthermore does not depend directly on farm product prices but on the price ratios between labour and labour-saving equipment. The contribution of farm prices is indirect via the opposite impacts of an increased availability of capital from savings and borrowing and a reduced supply of land from liquidating farms due to the retarding effect on structural adjustment.

As a consequence high farm product prices tend to creep into the value of assets, particularly of agricultural land. However, most of the farm land and other assets is financed by own capital or rented at a low rent, and the imputed interest does not affect disposable farm income. For the farming sector as a whole high land prices affect mainly the refinancing of the outflow of capital in relation to taking over the assets from outgoing farmers and intergenerational farm transfers. The debt-to-asset-ratios are generally low for the Netherlands – 20 per cent on the average (L.E.I. 1985) – and for the USA on cash grain farms (1974) even less (Penn 1982). Taking into account the income situation of farmers it is difficult to maintain that a vicious circle exists of high product prices–high lands prices–high product prices.

The popular statement that high farm product prices and high land prices stimulate land saving and yield increasing technological develop- ment also should be qualified. At the economic optimum farms will extend the use of yield increasing inputs and cultivation practices up to the point where marginal revenues equal marginal costs. That optimum is not directly affected by the level of land prices but depends on the price ratios of outputs and yield increasing inputs.

In modern science-based farming the levels of yields are moreover not very sensitive any more to price; for many of the yield increasing inputs – e.g. fertilizers – further yield increases do not require higher inputs and vice versa (de Wit et al. 1985). The 'green revolution' which in the developed countries started in the 1950s may have been supported by favourable product prices, but is not reversible by lowering these prices (see Figure 1).

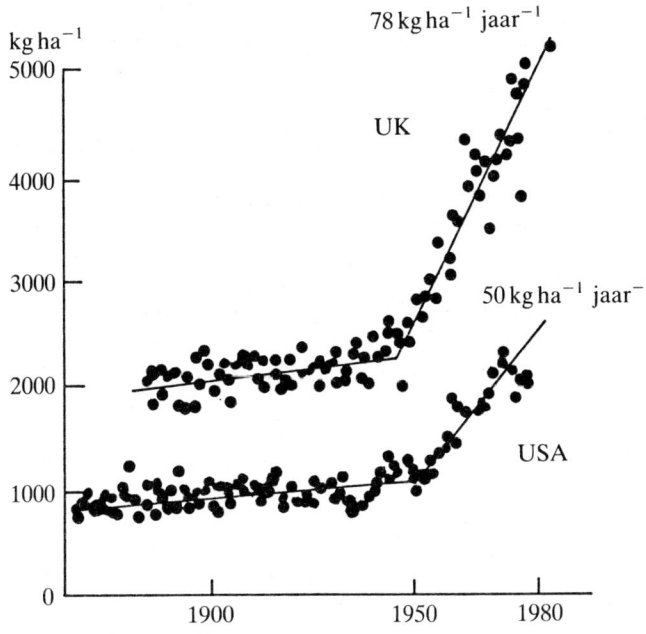

Source: FAO-handbooks, de Wit 1985.

FIGURE 1   The course of the yield of wheat in kg/ha in the United States and the United Kingdom during the last 100 years

Favourable product prices may have contributed to induce not only the yield increasing technological innovations but also the government policies in the field of rural reconstruction, soil improvement, irrigation, water management, farm development, land reclamation, etc. This, however, is also an irreversible process. As in modern farming bigger farms tend to have a comparative advantage in the acquisition of technical know-how and the application of science; an accelerated structural development may even result in a more rapid diffusion of yield increasing technology, as has been the experience with the expansion of modern dairy farming in Western Europe.

There is little research on the type of adjustments which will take place after a radical lowering of farm product prices. As it must be expected that the impact on the productivity of land and livestock will be small, the adjustment of supply will mainly have to take place by putting out of use marginal land. If this is solely to be performed by the price mechanism, it will be a lengthy process, require a long period of depressed prices and farm incomes and have far-reaching consequences for the regional distribution of agricultural production and the fate of peripheral, agriculturally less favoured and economically less developed regions. Taking also into account the ecological inpact, it is unthinkable that such consequences will be socially and politically acceptable.

The introduction of more market-oriented policies will require flanking measures to mitigate the income consequences and to regulate the adjustments of the regional distribution of agricultural production and of agricultural land use which are appended to such a policy.

IMPACTS ON INTERNATIONAL TRADE AND AGRICULTURAL DEVELOPMENT

Part of the social costs of agricultural policies in the industrialised countries are rolled off to other countries through the depressing and destabilising effects on world markets. The agricultural protection resulting in a reduction of the domestic demand and an increase of supply diminishes the export demand for exporters and potential exporters of competing products. These are not only limited in their access to the domestic market of the industrialised countries but also face the competition with subsidised exports of surplus products on other export markets. In particular, less developed countries with a comparative advantage for the development and expansion of the agricultural sector are impeded in the full exploitation of their natural resources and the creation of employment in rural areas, and are deprived of a source of foreign currency.[3] These countries are, moreover, generally not in a position to compensate their farmers by interventions on their domestic market at the cost of domestic consumers or taxpayers.

Valdès and Zietz (1980) calculated the total increase of developing country exports if industrial countries reduced their exports by 50 per cent for 99 agricultural products to be $3.4 billion at 1977 prices or 12.4

per cent of their total agricultural exports in 1975–77. A third of this increase was attributed to a lower level of protection for sugar. Also beef and fruit exports are relatively strongly affected. By their isolation from world markets the industrialised countries also roll off the instability of their domestic supply and demand to the residual world market and do not take their part in the absorption of world market instability. However, actually – and particularly for cereals – the major part of the domestic instability and even part of the external instability in the 1970s have been absorbed by storage, price and quota adjustments or offset by incidental variations (Blom 1982; Josling and Barichello 1984). The USA especially is found to act to stabilise world cereal markets.

Cereal importing countries, therefore, in the second half of the decade could benefit from low and stable world market prices and rely on world markets to cover their fluctuating import needs. Some countries, moreover, acquired food aid or could purchase at concessionary terms. This enabled many countries, particularly in Africa, to conduct cheap food policies in favour of urban consumers. This had a very depressing impact on the development of their domestic food production and contributed to increasing balance of payment deficits and debts. The accumulation of debts and the strong rise of interest rates now require socially painful and politically difficult adjustments (see a.o. Pinstrup Andersen 1984). It can be questioned if the price support, export and food aid policies of the industrialised countries can be held responsible for this situation. However, they certainly created the conditions for a policy which discouraged domestic food producers and frustrated agricultural development.

The agricultural price support policies of the industrialised countries, therefore, presumably have had a negative effect on the development of agriculture and food production in developing countries – not only for food exporters but also for many food importers (see also Linneman et al. 1979).

INTERNATIONAL ECONOMIC INSTABILITIES AND NATIONAL ADJUSTMENT POLICIES

In the 1980s the instability of agricultural world markets and of the international terms of trade for agricultural imports and exports has become increasingly dependent on the overall international economic and monetary instability. These disturbances arise primarily from developments in other markets – including the monetary and capital markets – and the national macroeconomic and monetary adjustment policies to these disturbances.

Under the prevailing system of floating exchange rates there is no mechanism by which national adjustments to world inflation and to changing international terms of trade evolve directly from the impacts on the national internal macroeconomic and monetary equilibrium, domestic prices and sectoral terms of trade. Individual countries can isolate themselves, and avoid, or at least postpone, the necessary adjustments by letting their exchange rates float.

Because of the development of the international capital market exchange rates are also increasingly dependent on international capital flows and expected returns on capital (Schuh 1983). These expected rates of return in turn depend strongly on the macroeconomic and monetary policies of the economically powerful industrialised countries, particularly the USA. The relationships between international purchasing power parities and exchange rates of national currencies have become weaker. There are also, moreover, important impulses from fluctuations on financial markets (real interest rates, exchange rates, etc.) on commodity prices (Frankel 1984). In particular, the rapid appreciation of the US dollar and the strongly fluctuating dollar exchange rates in combination with the rigidity of the USA's agricultural export prices and the dollar-prices of other basic commodities in the past years have increased the instability of the international (commodity and income) terms of trade, particularly for agricultural importers and exporters. The rather erratic fluctuations in agricultural terms of trade reinforce the tendency to isolate the national agricultural and food sector from world market prices.

There are also, particularly for depreciating countries, short run macroeconomic and monetary policy considerations for such an isolation. Exchange rate adjustments have immediate effects on the terms of trade for the tradable sectors of the economy. These sectors which are exposed to international competition either on export markets or on the domestic market benefit from higher export and import prices after a depreciation and vice versa. A contraction rather than expansion of these exposed sectors is needed to restore the external equilibrium. However, if not followed by appropriate measures to adjust the internal macroeconomic and monetary equilibrium the price changes in the tradable sectors will soon work their way through the entire national economy and offset the primary effect of the exchange rate adjustment. To be effective a depreciation of the national currency should be followed by a deflationary policy or price regulations to achieve a contraction of the non-exposed sectors such as servicing industries and the public sector and an appreciation by an expansion of the non-exposed sector (Corden 1980).

In this macroeconomic and monetary policy framework the agriculture and food sector takes a special position. On the one hand, agricultural goods are tradables and the agriculture and food sector is an exposed sector; on the other hand agricultural prices in most countries are administered prices. A rise in food prices, moreover, has a strong impact on the cost of living – especially of the low-income groups – and on wages. Agricultural goods are both tradables and wage goods. Because of the low short-run price elasticities of supply and demand, price adjustments in the agriculture and food sector also in the short run contribute little to restoring the external equilibrium.

For depreciating countries it is, therefore, attractive in order to suppress inflationary tendencies and to facilitate the internal adjustment process not to raise farm product prices. Such a policy in the first instance also does not face much opposition from the farming sector, which reacts much more strongly on abrupt nominal price changes than on a gradual decline of real prices. In appreciating countries, on the contrary, a nominal price reduction of farm prices, although it would contribute to the internal adjustment, will face a strong opposition of farmers. Also the institutional rules will often not allow a nominal lowering of administered prices in response to an appreciation of the national currency.[4]

In the longer run the isolation of the national agriculture and food sector from both the national general price development and the development of the international terms of trade will raise difficulties. This is especially the case for countries with a tendency to inflate more strongly than their trade partners which regularly have to depreciate in order to restore the external equilibrium. This upward rigidity of agricultural prices has a depressing effect on the agricultural development and results in a deterioration of the agricultural trade balance. Particularly in many developing countries this results in increasing food deficits and a structural deterioration of their balance of payments position. The international debt problems now force such countries to painful adjustments of these policies.[5]

THE AGRICULTURAL SECTOR AS AN INTEGRAL PART OF THE TOTAL NATIONAL AND INTERNATIONAL ECONOMY

It is, of course, a platitude to say that agriculture is an integral part of the total economy. However, both nationally and internationally, the linkages with general economic developments have become more intense. This raises the need to widen the scope of the analysis of agriculture and food policy problems. On the national level the linkages with macroeconomic and monetary development and policies have to be included in the analysis of agriculture and food policy problems. On the international level, not only the linkages between agricultural supply and demand and the national agricultural policies of the various countries but also the interdependencies with respect to the general development of the world economy, world trade, and international capital markets and monetary developments need to be integrated in the analysis.

National agricultural policies affect not only the internal regional, sectoral and personal income distribution and the agricultural balance of trade and the international repercussions are not limited to agricultural world markets. The impacts expand over the whole world trade system and through the balance of payments also have repercussions on the international competitiveness of non-agricultural sectors of the national economies. The further development of global models which integrate these various factors and take proper account of the interdependencies in the world economy can therefore contribute to a better insight

(Linneman et al. 1979; Parikh and Rabár 1984; Gunning, Carrin and Waelbroeck 1984; Burniaux 1984). Agricultural protection and the isolation of domestic markets from world markets therefore also constitute obstacles for the overall world economic development and international trade.

In my opinion, it is, however, an illusion to think that national governments – particularly in the industrialised countries – will be prepared to fully expose their national farming sector to the hazards of the world market and let farm prices and farm incomes go beyond their control. It will not be politically and socially feasible to leave the radical adjustments in farming structures, regional distribution of agricultural production and adjustments in land use completely to the operation of market forces and to accept the consequence of a lengthy period of depressed prices and farm incomes needed to achieve in the end a better balance of agricultural supply and demand in line with the international terms of trade. Such a policy will also conflict with objectives regarding a balanced regional development, protection of rural landscapes, natural resources and ecological macro-systems and the long run development of agriculture. Flanking policies to regulate the adjustments, which are needed anyhow, will be required even if they conflict with the rate at which adjustments take place.

However, the repercussions on international trade relations and the conflicts with national interests of trade partners will also enforce more disciplined behaviour and more regard for the international impacts. The lack of international co-ordination of national policies increasingly threatens the development of international trade and adds to the danger of a wave of protectionism and cut-throat competition with subsidised agricultural exports.

A revision or a sharper application of the GATT rules on agricultural trade imposing more severe restrictions on national price and income support policies with respect to a further decline of agricultural imports and, particularly, the subsidising of agricultural exports and, allowing more penetration of world market price fluctuations on domestic markets seems the highest attainable in the coming international trade negotiations. The recommendations of the GATT's Committee on Trade in Agriculture go in this direction. The disturbances of international terms of trade arising from macroeconomic and monetary instabilities could, however, hamper progress in achieving more co-ordination of agricultural policies and might require additional rules allowing countries to take temporary stabilising measures to protect their farmers.

NOTES

[1] For a survey of recent estimates of the global population supporting capacity see Parikh and Rabár, 1981, p. 40.
[2] For the European Community the gain of a transition to world market prices has been estimated to be approximately 0.40% of total GNP.
[3] For a discussion of these effects see Lutz and Bale (1980); Mackel et al. (1984) and

Tangermann (1982). Quantative estimates have been made a.o. by Valdès and Ziets (1980), Koester and Schmitz (1982), Tangermann and Krostitz (1982). For a recent survey see Matthews (1985).

[4]These specific characteristics of the agriculture and food sector can explain the system of border taxes and subsidies – monetary compensation amounts – set up within the European Community during the 1970s to compensate for the impact of exchange rate adjustment on national farm prices.

[5]Also within the European Community the long-run effects on agricultural supply and demand and on the development of intra-community trade have led to the abolition of monetary compensation amounts.

REFERENCES

Blom, J.C., *Stabilization of the International Grain Market*, Royal Dutch Grain and Feed Trade Association, Rotterdam, 1982.

Brinkman, G.L., *Farm incomes in Canada*, Supply and Services, Ottawa, 1981.

Burniaux, J.M., *A Rural-Urban North-South Equilibrium Model: theoretical overview of the R.U.N.S.-model*, CEME-Discussion Paper No. 8404, Free University of Brussels 1984.

Corden, W.M., *Inflation, Exchange Rates and the World Economy: lectures on international monetary economics*, Oxford University Press (2nd ed.), 1983.

Evenson, R. discussion in Johnson, D.G. and Schuh, G.E., *The Role of Market in the World Economy*, Westview Press, Boulder, Colorado, 1980.

Krüll, H., 'Wieviel Bauer unterschreiten die amtliche Armutsgrenze?' *Agrawirtschaft*, vol. 9, 1984.

Krishna, R. *Some aspects of agricultural growth, price policy and equity*, Food Research Institute Studies in Agricultural Economics, Trade and Development 18. no. 3, Stanford University, 1982.

Frankel, J.A., 'Commodity prices and money: Lessons from International Finance', *American Journal of Agricultural Economics*, vol. 66, no. 5, 1984.

Gunning, J., Carrin, G., Waelbroeck, J. et al., *Growth and Trade in Developing Countries: A general equilibrium analysis*, CEME-Discussion Paper no. 8216, Free University of Brussels, 1984.

Josling, T. and Barichello, R., 'International trade and world food security since the World Food Conference', *Food Policy*, vol. 9, no. 4, 1984.

Koester, U. and Schmitz, P.M., 'The EEC-sugar market policy and developing countries', *European Review of Agricultural Economics*, vol. 9, 1982.

Linneman, H., De Hoogh, J. and Keyzer, M.A., *Moira: Model of International Relations in Agriculture*, North-Holland, Amsterdam, 1979.

Lutz, E. and Bale, M., 'Agricultural protectionism in industrialised countries and its global effects: a survey of issues', *Aussenwirtschaft*, Vol. 35, no. 4, 1980.

Mackel, C., Marsh J. and Revell, B., 'The Common Agricultural Policy (Western Europe and the South)', *Third World Quarterly*, Vol. 6, no. 1, 1984.

Matthews, A., 'La politique agricole commune et les pays sous-développés: un examen des faits', *Economic Rurale*, vol. 165, January–February, 1985.

Meester, G. and Oskam, A.J., *Analyse van de Vereldvraag naar Zuivelprodukten uit de EG*, L.E.I., The Hague, 1983.

Ministry of Agriculture and Forestry, Japan, *The State of Japan's Agriculture, 1983. A summary report*, April 1984.

Parikh, K. and Rabár, *Food for all in a sustainable world*, IIASA Food and Agriculture Program, Laxenburg (Austria) 1984.

Penn, J.B., 'Economic developments in USA-agriculture during the 1970s' in Johnson, D.G. (ed.), *Food and Agricultural Policies for the 1980s*, American Enterprise Institute, Washington, 1981.

Pinstrup Andersen, P., *Food Prices and the Poor in Developing Countries*, Fourth European Congress of Agricultural Economists, Kiel, 1984.

Schuh, G.E., 'The role of markets and governments in the world food economy', in Johnson, D.G. and Schuh, G.E. (eds). *The Role of Markets in the World Food Economy*, Westview Press, Boulder, Colarado, 1983.

Sen, A.K., *Poverty and Famines*, Oxford University Press, 1981.

Tangermann, S., 'Policies of the European Community and agricultural trade with developing countries' in Johnson, G. and Maunder, A. (eds) *Rural Change: The Challenge for Agricultural Economists: Proceedings of the Seventeenth International Conference of Agricultural Economists*, Gower, Farnborough, 1981.

Tangermann, S. and Krostitz, W., *Protectionism in the Livestock Sector with Particular Reference to the International Beef Trade*, Institut für Agrar Oekonomie, Göttingen, 1982.

Valdès, A. and Zietz, J., *Agricultural Protectionism in OECD Countries: its cost to less developed countries*, International Food Policy Research Institute, Washington, DC. 1980.

de Veer, J. et al., *National impacts of different agricultural policy reform proposals for the Common Agricultural policy developed within the Socialist Group of the European Parliament*, European Parliament, Brussels, 1985.

L.E.I., *Overzicht van de financiele positie van landbouwbedrijven 1983/84*, Landbouw-Economisch Instituut, The Hague, 1985.

de Wit, C.T., Huisman, H. and Rabbinge, R., *Agriculture and its Environment: are there other ways?* Netherlands Scientific Council for Government Policy, The Hague, (unpublished draft paper), 1985.

World Bank, *World Development Report*, Oxford University Press, 1980.

GÜNTHER FISCHER, KLAUS FROHBERG, KIKIT S. PARIKH AND
FERENC RABÁR

The World Economy:
Resilient for the Rich, Stubborn for the Starving

The concept of a world food system is defined by D. Gale Johnson (1984) as 'a system in which food and other agricultural products that can be transported at reasonable costs produced anywhere in the world, is actually or potentially available to any person in the world *if that person has the means to purchase it*' (emphasis added).

In this sense one could not but conclude that the growing interdependence of the world (as measured by the percentage of agricultural production that is traded internationally) has led to a resilient well functioning world food system. It has been able to withstand shocks of severe bad weather as well as of sudden policy shifts by major actors on the world market. Supplies have resiliently responded to price signals and to incentives and the long-term trend of world food prices has been, if anything, downward in spite of large increases in demand due to increasing population of the world with a rising income.

Yet the system has functioned well only for those who have the means to purchase food. Most estimates show that a large number of people in the world remain hungry and do not get enough to eat. Though the proportion of world population getting inadequate food is estimated to go down, the improvements are too slow and still leave many or even more people suffering from hunger. A system that leaves people hungry is not functioning satisfactorily. As economic analysts it behoves us to ask why is the system malfunctioning? What are its characteristics and what can we do about it?

For the poor who do not have means to purchase food, the world economic (and political) system is malfunctioning and stubbornly so. No matter what happens, left to itself, the system seems to transfer the major burden of adjustment to the people too poor to buy or produce all the food they need. For these people the biological requirements are higher than their effective demand. In a system where effective demand has no lower bound, *hunger is just a part of the normal adjustment process* as it was in the former natural economies where population had to adjust to natural resources either by emigration or by dying.

In a world where everyone agrees that there should be no hunger (all nations who subscribe to the UN Charter agree to it) the persistence of hunger must be considered a sign of the malfunctioning system. The world economic system produces shortages and surpluses at the same time. While farmers are protesting against low prices in some countries (although leading to substantial surpluses), people starve in others.

In the world economy those which have more resources have also more power. And the domination by the powerful perpetuates itself. The dominating powers do not give up their positions and the dominated ones are by definition too weak to change them. Thus the burden is always shifted to the weak. (If it were not, then accepting more burden by the strong, equity could be achieved). So far as hunger is concerned, this leads to something like an *institutionalised disaster area*. If there is a drought in India, more people die in India. If there is a drought in the USA, the same number of people die in India. The system shifts the burden to the same areas and to the same income groups. (Just to clarify the idea the example is simplistic. In fact a drought in the USA will not change anything, except the buffer stocks and acreage set asides, thus keeping up the same artificial level of prices).

The effectiveness of the means to transfer the burden and the means to protect oneself against it is *disproportional*. A small change in a big country might still result in a big change in the small ones.

This description of the nature of the world economic system is to be demonstrated through simulation using our system of linked national models for food and agricultural policy analysis which cover the whole world economy. In particular we show that hunger is stubborn. It will not go away by merely increasing production; it will not go away by removing barriers to agricultural trade; it does not go away if the rich countries restrict their consumption or if they increase their production or even if they reduce their agricultural production, thus giving economic incentives to agricultural producers in developing countries.

The modelling system, which we call the Basic Linked System (BLS) consists of 20 national models and 15 regional models linked through trade, aid and capital flows. The national models are of general equilibrium type and their parameters are *empirically estimated*. The models are constructed such that not only physical flows but also financial flows balance both at national and international levels. The commodity flows balance at the level of each nation and at the international level. The financial flows balance at the level of each actor, the consumer, the government and the nation. The models distinguish nine agricultural commodities and one non-agricultural sector covers the rest of the economy. Thus the whole economy is included and there is no unaccounted supply (sources) or demand (sinks) in the system. It is run in a year-by-year simulation mode. The modelling system was developed at the International Institute for Applied Systems Analysis (IIASA) by its Food and Agriculture Program (FAP), with the help of a network of collaborating institutions. The objectives, approach and scope of FAP are described in Parikh and Rabár (1981). The methodology and algorithms are given in Keyzer (1981). Fischer and Frohberg (1982) provide the technical description of many of the models of the system.

WOULD LOWER WORLD PRICES OR REDUCED CONSUMPTION BY THE RICH HELP THE HUNGRY?

There is some evidence to show that world foodgrain prices are kept high by the government policies of some big exporters and that this prevents poor countries from importing more. Thus, not just prices but also hunger are kept at a given level. What would happen if we kept prices low and allowed the poor countries to import more than they do now?

As a first step we assumed that a hypothetical country enters the market with the firm intention of selling 35 million tons of wheat each year, at any price, to help poor importers.

A new additional input channel that does not follow the rules of the market is thus opened in the system. It continues supplying just the missing amount of grain that is needed to eradicate hunger.

A series of adjustments starts as soon as the first 35 million tons appear on the market. The international market response is instantaneous. The major wheat exporters reduce their exports by increasing their stocks and the importers increase their imports. Yet the quantity is too high to be completely absorbed at prevailing prices. The wheat price drops and it stays depressed.

The second-level adjustment on the part of the exporting countries, after reducing their exports, is reducing their production as well. This happens with different time lags, different speeds and different intensities. This is, though, the general response of all the exporters.

The second-level adjustment on the part of the importers, after increasing their imports and their home demand, is the reduction of their home supply. In other words, they substitute their home production with cheaper imports. Of course, they reallocate their production capacities to other products. Because of these substitutions the consumption of wheat increases only marginally and hungry people do not eat much more.

The real advantage seems to be in the beef market. In almost all countries there is an upward shift in feed consumption: either wheat is directly used as feed or producers substitute wheat with coarse grain production. Bovine production and export figures in the exporting countries and imports in the importing countries go up and for some years after the shock an upswing in the beef market is created, until prices and production begin to adjust.

After all these adjustments we may ask the question: where are the additional 35 million tons of wheat, put on the market by an imaginary country? The answer is that it was absorbed in the system. Very little of it reaches the hungry people of the countries represented. They increased their buffer stocks, they changed their export structures and they substituted their wheat production with feedgrain, bovine, dairy and non-food production. Consequently, hunger was not eradicated; instead a new export and production structure was created that seemed more profitable from the point of view of the new relative prices. The present market mechanism did not solve the problem. A solution by the market could not have been rationally expected anyway, since we already knew that effective demand does not always reflect biological needs and that the market is distorted in many ways by conflicting agricultural policies.

This scenario can be interpreted in other ways too. If people in developed countries were to eat less wheat, it would also put more wheat on the world market and the effects would be similar; changes in the structure of production, trade and prices but a marginal impact on the hungry in the world.

WOULD NOT THE FREE MARKET TAKE CARE OF HUNGER?

In this heyday of 'supply side economics' one sometimes hears that if only governments would not intervene in the markets, price signals and profit motives would solve the problem of hunger. Though no simulation with any model (after all, models abstract from reality and can on that excuse be rejected) can shake religious beliefs, we test this through simulation that introduces free trade in agricultural commodities in the world. In our simulations which run from 1980 to 2000, we introduce free trade gradually over 1982 through 1986, and the relative prices in the world market and national markets are equalised from 1986 onwards. Important production or demand restraining measures are also removed in the market economies.

TABLE 1 *Economic and welfare effects of agricultural trade liberalisation at country group level, percentage change compared to reference scenario in year 2000.*

	World	Developed market economies	Developing countries
GDP (at 1970 world prices)	0.25	0.58	−0.30
GDP (at 1970 domestic prices)	−0.05	0.15	−0.32
Agricultural GDP	0.02	−1.45	1.22
(at 1970 domestic prices)			
Per caput consumption of			
calories	—	—	−0.03
proteins	—	—	0.33
Persons hungry*	—	—	0.22

*Calculated from cross-country regressions, see Hrabovszky, Parikh, Zeold (1985).

Some economic and welfare effects of free trade are shown in Table 1. The figures given are for the year 2000 and indicate percentage changes of the free trade run compared with the reference run. As can be seen from this table, there are only minor changes in GDP, agricultural GDP and consumption per caput at world level. Though GDP calculated at 1970 world prices shows a modest improvement, GDP calculated at domestic 1970 prices shows a slight fall. When one investigates the developed market economies and the developing countries separately, a different picture emerges. While the former group of countries increase their GDP the latter shows a decline. Under the hunger aspect the nutritional status of the population in developing countries even worsens under agricultural trade liberalization and the number of persons in hunger goes up.

TABLE 2   *Changes (in per cent) in food index, GDP per caput, calories and equivalent income for developing countries identified in the BLS: free trade run compared to reference scenario, year 2000.*

	Food Price Index		GDP per caput		Calorie intake		Equivalent income*	
	1990	2000	1990	2000	1990	2000	1990	2000
Argentina	31	22	0.3	−0.2	−2.2	−1.5	1.0	3.8
Brazil	14	16	−0.4	−0.7	−1.8	−2.0	−1.3	−1.9
Egypt	−3	−4	−0.6	−2.5	0.4	−0.4	0.8	−1.2
India	11[1]	7[1]	0.2	−0.0	−0.1	−0.4	−0.3	0.6
Indonesia	11	8	0.4	1.1	−1.0	1.8	−5.1	−3.6
Kenya	19	14	1.7	3.2	2.6	2.9	—	—
Mexico	−1	−4	−1.6	−4.2	0.0	0.2	−2.0	−4.7
Nigeria	−5	−9	−0.4	−0.6	1.1	1.2	0.5	0.2
Pakistan	−2	−3	1.2	2.2	−0.2	1.1	1.9	2.1
Thailand	11	8	0.1	0.1	−0.2	−0.3	—	—
Turkey	−6	−3	0.6	1.2	0.0	0.2	2.5	2.1

*Income required to get the same utility at base year prices as provided by current consumption.
[1]Agricultural price index is used as a proxy for the food price index.

Table 2 gives more detailed information on consumption for those developing countries which are identified in the BLS. Food prices rise in Argentina, Brazil, India, Indonesia, Kenya and Thailand as a result of the removal of trade barriers. This happens because these countries have negative protection on the major food commodities and world market prices do not fall in the free trade run so that the price rise due to these negative protections cannot be offset. The income gain (measured as GDP per caput) is too modest – if there is one at all – to counterbalance the loss in purchasing power due to the price increase. Hence in 1990 except for Kenya, these countries consume less calories. By 2000 Indonesia shows a small increase in calorie intake.

The other countries shown in Table 2 – Egypt, Mexico, Nigeria, Pakistan and Turkey – have lower food prices in the free trade run compared to the reference run, and increases in calorie intake when they take place are modest (highest is 1.2% in Nigeria). In terms of changes in equivalent income, the picture is in general similar to calorie intake changes. Brazil, Indonesia and Mexico suffer a fall in equivalent income whereas Argentina, Pakistan and Turkey show clear gains. Others show modest or changing gains. But the main point in this run is that the number of hungry in the world shows little change and if anything, increases.

WOULD A 'GREENS' REVOLUTION IN THE OECD COUNTRIES PROMOTE A GREEN REVOLUTION IN THE LESS DEVELOPED WORLD?

To test the hypothesis that less developed countries (LDCs) would benefit and that hunger would be reduced if the OECD countries were to reduce their agricultural production, one could envisage that the environmental concern represented by the 'Green' parties in Europe could culminate in attempts to reduce use of chemical fertilizers and restrict the extent of land cultivation. A tax on fertilizer prices may be introduced to provide for the cost of cleaning up the resulting environmental pollution. To simulate such a scenario we stipulated the following. A tax of 50 per cent was levied on fertilizer prices in the OECD countries. Moreover, total cultivable area was reduced by 25 per cent in these countries.

TABLE 3   *Impact on LDCs of lower agricultural production in OECD countries. Percentage change over reference run. Selected indicators for year 2000.*

Country	GDP Domestic world (1970) prices		GDP Agriculture (1970) prices	Calorie intake kcal/person/day	Utility indicators
Argentina	0.2	1.4	11.2	−0.6	3.7
Brazil	−0.3	−0.6	2.6	−1.7	−1.8
Egypt	−4.6	−4.7	10.5	−0.9	−9.4
India	0.1	0.1	0.1	−1.4	—
Indonesia	0.7	1.3	0.6	−0.4	6.9
Mexico	−3.9	−3.6	7.9	−1.4	−6.7
Nigeria	2.3	4.0	13.5	2.7	−16.4
Pakistan	0.2	2.2	9.2	−2.6	3.2
Turkey	1.0	0.7	11.8	−0.4	0.3

These changes were introduced over a five-year period from 1981 to 1985. Our expectations were that this measure would reduce production in these countries and result in higher world market prices. This in turn would lead to higher prices in LDCs which would stimulate increased production in these countries and after some time, and not too long a time, these countries would be better off.

The scenario results showed that (compared to the reference run) the world prices do go up and so do agricultural prices and production in the LDCs for which we have elaborate national models in the system. Their agricultural GDPs also increase and so do the total GDPs in most of them. Yet the higher domestic prices that promoted increased agricultural production also led to lower intake of calories in most LDCs. Moreover, in terms of utility all LDCs but Argentina showed a decline. The utility measure is based on the underlying utility functions behind the expenditure systems which characterize consumer behaviour. These results, summarised in Table 3, indicate that even when agricultural production increases substantially as it does in Mexico, Nigeria, Pakistan and Turkey, the average calorie intake and utility indicators fall.

Thus the passive bystanders, the poor LDC consumers (especially in urban areas) are hurt by the actions of people in faraway countries and adjust in the only way they can by reducing their food consumption.

SUMMARY

What these scenarios have shown is emphasised by many others that we have generated. That hunger persists stubbornly and does not respond to easy solutions. The world economic system adjusts and adapts in favour of those who have. Similarly, national economic systems also adjust and adapt in favour of the rich groups within the nation.

Active redistribution policies that alter the structure of the system in favour of the poor within nations and between nations are needed if hunger is to be reduced effectively, substantially and in reasonable time. The reconciliation between overproduction on the one hand and hunger on the other would otherwise take a long time to come.

REFERENCES

Fischer, G. and Frohberg, K., 'The Basic Linked System of the Food and Agriculture Program at IIASA: An Overview of the Structure of the National Models', *Mathematical Modelling*, vol. 3: 453–66, 1982.

Hrabovszky, J., Parikh, K. S. and Zeold, L., 'Income and Nutrition: Welfare Indicators and Proxies', contributed paper presented at XIX International Conference of Agricultural Economists, Malaga, Spain, 26 August–4 September 1985.

Johnson, D. Gale, *A World Food System: Actuality or Promise*, a paper presented at the 75th Anniversary Colloquium on World Food Policy, Harvard Business School, 8–11 April 1984.

Keyzer, Michiel, 'The International Linkage of Open Exchange "Economies"', PhD dissertation, Free University, Amsterdam, Holland, 1981.

Parikh, K. S. and Rabár, Ferenc, *Food For All in a Sustainable World: the IIASA Food and Agriculture Program*, SR-81-2, The International Institute for Applied Systems Analysis (IIASA), Laxenburg, Austria, 1981.

DISCUSSION OPENING – MICHELE DE BENEDICTIS

Jan de Veer and Fisher, Frohberg, Parikh and Rabár (whom, for brevity, I will call the IIASA group) should be complimented for delivering two stimulating papers.

The first point I would like to stress is the complementarity existing between the two papers: one could read them as the first two acts of a play. In the first act de Veer tells us quite convincingly that it is unlikely to expect, in the immediate and also in the intermediate future, any substantial change in the agricultural policies of the developed countries. In the second act the IIASA group produces some surprising and we could say shocking research results: even if dramatic changes – and, as we have been told in the first act today, unthinkable changes – were introduced in the policies of the developed countries the perspective of persistence of chronic and substantial malnutrition for many in Third World will remain unaffected. Among other things, the myth of free trade – at least, so far as the elimination of hunger is concerned – comes out shattered.

A third act remains to be written, which should answer this fundamental question: *is there then any way out of the deadly over-production/nutrition trap?* We cannot blame the authors for not attempting to give the answer to this question which, perhaps, more appropriately should collectively come out of the entire conference.

I will say more about this question in a moment; but first I would like to call your attention to a few selected points listed or hinted at in de Veer's paper which, in my opinion, deserve consideration for discussion.

The *first* group of points concerns the *supply behaviour in developed agricultures*. De Veer underlines, and I tend to share his views:

(a)   The low aggregate price elasticity in comparison with the powerful impact of other supply shifters;
(b)   That the level of yields are not very sensitive any more to price;
(c)   That an accelerated structural development may result in a more rapid diffusion of yield increasing technology;
(d)   That we are quite ignorant about the type and the size of adjustment that will take place after a radical lowering of farm product prices.

The *second* group of points concerns the *policy behaviour in developed agricultures*.

First of all, I feel that de Veer is quite right in stating that there is going to be *no major revision of* the agricultural policies, and of the price policies in particular, on the part of the developed countries, only collateral adjustments to alleviate the budgetary constraint. He points out several reasons that support his belief (the presence of other objectives assigned to agriculture – regional development, environmental control, the power of the traditional pressure groups, among others).

There is, however, another factor which pushes toward the continuation of the present situation, which, in my view, has not received sufficient attention in de Veer's analysis. Or, more appropriately, my position is more pessimistic than that which can be read between the lines in de Veer's paper. I refer to the role that is going to be assigned in the future to agricultural exports by the developed countries. It is my impression that the maintenance of a substantial flow of agricultural exports will continue to receive the highest priority in the policies of this group of countries. In no minor part this is also due to the appearance on the policy making scene of a new group of characters with no direct interest in farming – the agribusiness export firms.

The impacts of aggressive export policies will be substantial both in the First and the Third World. Looking only at the developed nations, one should point out that the internationalisation of agriculture pursued through these means has increased instability, thus generating greater needs of government intervention and deepening the vicious circle of overprotection and overproduction in which developed agricultures seem to be trapped.

The *third* group of points concerns some tendencies in the international division of labour which will influence agricultural development both in the First and the Third World. In addition to the points mentioned by de Veer I would like to stress the following significant trends, largely imputable to the behaviour of developed economies:

(1)   The growing *internationalisation of capital*, taking the form of (a) foreign investments in plantations or the contracting of agribusiness with foreign products; (b) investment by food processors and distributors in retail and marketing in the Third World, (c) the opening of new markets for agricultural exports.

(2)   Increasing *capacity for agribusiness to gain control over farming*: specifically in the:
  generation of technology;
  control of the production process;
  dramatic expansion of specific crops.

In the Third World these tendencies, together with other structural forces, tend to generate situations characterised by:
  diversion of agricultural production away from basic needs towards what it profitable on either the domestic or international markets;
  surplus labour in agriculture with lack of absorptive capacity in the rest of the economy.

All this raises a permanent conflict between agricultural and rural development and tends to create situations – to use the expression of Prof de Janvry – of a 'cornered peasantry' that experiences the worst form of poverty.

Finally, a few conclusive comments around the central question that should dominate the third act of the play mentioned before: is there any way to curb and dominate the stubbornness of hunger?

The final suggestion of the IIASA group is to point out the need for active redistributive policies that alter the structure of the system in favour of the poor. I would expect that they have in mind 'feasible' policies, i.e. applied through some form of reformism, not calling for revolutionary changes in the economic and social structure of the system.

At this point a methodological question seems to be in order. Do we possess the appropriate conceptual and empirical knowledge to identify the kind of policies that, though compatible with the structure and the functioning of the system, would allow, at least in perspective, a way out of the 'poverty and deprivation' trap? I don't want to sound too pessimistic but I have the impression that we still have some way to go before we succeed in putting together an articulated conceptual framework capable of identifying regular patterns in the relations between the economic and social structure of specific societies, the forms, functions and limits of public action, the adoption of specific food and agricultural policies, the economic and social impacts of these policies both within agriculture and the entire economy. I wonder whether what I would call 'our excessive faithfulness' to the neoclassical equilibrium analysis of markets is not partly responsible for hindering the search for alternative or complementary theoretical frameworks. But I do not want to conclude these comments on a pessimistic note: I am convinced that significant progress has been accomplished in recent years toward the specification of more satisfactory theoretical frameworks and the possibility of incorporating them in quantitative models. The papers given so far to the conference confirm this general impression. However, more courageous doses of 'methodological reformism' and phantasy are needed if we want to write the third act of the play as well as the first two.

GENERAL DISCUSSION – RAPPORTEUR: CATHY L. JABARA

To start off the discussion of Dr de Veer's paper, his statement that countries isolated themselves and postponed necessary adjustments by letting their exchange rates float was questioned. In the view of the questioner, the opposite is true, that is, countries fix their exchange rates to avoid this adjustment.

Another speaker agreed with Dr de Veer that agricultural policies were effective in increasing agricultural production, but wanted to make two additional points. First, if price incentives are biased towards a specific crop, they may cause a surplus of that crop, but may not cause a surplus of agricultural production as a whole. At the same time, there could be a shortage of other crops. This point was made from the experience of Japanese agricultural price policy. Second, when agricultural surpluses emerge, it may not be possible to solve this problem by exporting because of the financial constraint of the government to subsidise the product on the world market or because of poor product quality.

In reply to the first comment, Dr de Veer stated that a devaluation or revaluation of the exchange rates, while a means to adjust the prices of import and export commodities, was not a direct mechanism which forced countries to adjust their policies so as to solve internal disequilibria. In his argument, agricultural commodities were special, regulated products due to their importance in the cost of living and influence on real wages. Countries used the effects of devaluation as time to take care of their internal problems. Dr de Veer cited the case of the Federal Republic of Germany which had difficulty in lowering agricultural prices after a revaluation of its currency.

With regard to the second paper a number of questions revolved around what was in the 'black box' of the IIASA model and how the scenarios in the paper were carried out. Specifically, it was asked whether the IIASA model results given in the paper were sensitive to the supply and demand elasticities, whether transport costs from exporting to importing countries were taken into account when the increase in wheat supply appeared in the market, and if the model examined changes in demand for intermediate products (inputs). Another question asked whether the model included the impact of changes in relative prices on the total economy or on the agricultural sector.

With regard to the overall results of the paper, the need to examine the economic and social mechanisms which produce the result that the poor do not benefit from increased food supplies was stressed. It was also pointed out that the poor might have the means to absorb production variability through the extended family. However, the extended family system is in the process of breaking up in many developing countries, a process which makes the poor even more vulnerable.

A final comment was that the scenarios in the paper involved regional or global changes while many of the problems in agriculture were national ones. In this regard, it was asked whether or not the IIASA model had been used as a policy tool in co-operation with a national group to examine national food problems.

In reply, Dr Parikh, who presented the paper, first stated that the paper did not include specific redistributive policies, and that national governments were left free to redistribute food through existing systems. He stated that specific redistributive policies could be designed through fair price shops, or food for work programmes, but knowledge of existing systems for redistributing food were currently limited.

With regard to the model results, Dr Parikh stated that the overall thrust of the results presented in the paper were robust with respect to the model's parameters and that transport costs from exporting to importing countries were taken into account. He also stated that the IIASA model was a general equilibrium model with consistent physical and monetary flows. Thus data presented in Tables 1 and 2 were consistent.

With regard to the more general comments on the paper, Dr Parikh stated that the model had been used for analysis of national agricultural problems for several countries, including Bangladesh where the model was used in developing that country's five-year development plan. National policy changes were also included in the global scenarios. For instance, a decrease in OECD countries' production was achieved through a decrease in land and fertilizer use in those countries.

Finally, Dr Parikh observed that the inability of the developing countries to benefit from the types of scenarios examined in his paper was due largely to a lack of financial resources and of specific policies designed to redistribute purchasing power or food to the poor in these countries. Thus there was a need for additional financial aid to these countries combined with specific redistributive policies in order for the poor to benefit from global actions that increase food supplies. Dr Parikh also observed that the free trade run did not eliminate hunger, but it did eliminate surpluses. Therefore, the costs in terms of foregone income were much less than expected.

Participants in the discussion included Takeo Misawa, Günther Schmitt, Leroy Quance, Carlos Arnande, Ewa Rabinowicz, Lyndon Moore and Gordon Macaulay.

SECTION IV

Pressure on Natural Resources

KENNETH R. FARRELL AND SUSAN M. CAPALBO

Natural Resource and Environmental Dimensions of Agricultural Development

INTRODUCTION

The productive capacity of world agriculture has grown impressively during the last half century. Although erratic over time and uneven among countries and regions, that growth, coupled with increased international trade, has afforded a modest improvement in food availability per caput in most parts of the world. Yet the global capacity to feed a population projected to increase to about 6.0 billion in 2000 and perhaps 10–11 billion before levelling off in the second half of the twenty-first century remains the subject of widespread discussion and debate. In part, the concern continues to be defined by the notion of 'limits to growth' – the mathematical imperatives of compound population growth rates pressing upon a finite supply of natural resources. This theme, so central to the projections and conclusions of the Club of Rome school prominent in the 1970s, dates back to Malthus nearly 200 years ago.

The environmental movement has added new dimensions to the Malthusian thesis. The very goals of economic efficiency and present patterns of productivity growth in agriculture are coming under increasingly intense scrutiny. Agriculture is viewed as an inseparable part of the larger ecosystem and as an increasingly important source of environmental pollution. A plethora of 'command-and-control' regulations to limit the use of environmentally-damaging technologies and production practices in agriculture is evolving in the United States and other industrial countries, with possible consequences for future agricultural productivity growth. This, the future productive capacity of agriculture may be constrained not only by the quantity of natural resources available but also by the quality of those resources and by market and non-market measures to assign to agriculture the environmental costs of externalities created by the sector.

It is not our purpose to develop still another assessment of potential future states of agriculture, natural resources and the environment. Most such assessments are subject to very large 'errors of estimate' because so many of the critical relationships between agricultural development and

273

environmental quality indicators are themselves unknown or poorly measured. Nevertheless, we are convinced that the growing public concern in many parts of the world concerning agriculture and its relationship to natural resources and quality of the natural environment is neither ephemeral nor transitory. We suggest that these increasingly complex issues will pose formidable challenges to agricultural institutions for decades to come.

Our remarks are in three principal parts. We begin with a review of agricultural development in the United States and the nature of relevant current and emerging resource and environmental issues. Although institutions, resource endowments and public policies shaping US agricultural development are to some degree unique and the results therefore cannot be generalised, the US experience may nonetheless be instructive in considering agricultural development issues in other countries, particularly industrialised market economies. We turn then to a brief exposition of analytical approaches to assessing development and environmental tradeoffs in agriculture. Finally, we develop implications of the issues for agricultural economists and agricultural economic research.

DEVELOPMENT, NATURAL RESOURCES, AND THE ENVIRONMENT: THE U.S. EXPERIENCE

By conventional measures, productivity and output of US agriculture have increased dramatically since the Second World War. Based on our recent research, total factor productivity grew at an average annual rate of 2.2 per cent in the 15 years immediately after the Second World War, 1.0 per cent in the 1960s, and 1.7 per cent in the 1970s (Capalbo, Vo and Wade 1985).

A large part of the growth stemmed from development and application of land and labour saving technologies – new and improved mechanical power, improved seeds and animal genetic stock, hydro-electric and fossil fuel based energy, fossil fuel based fertilizers, pesticides, herbicides and fungicides, and other chemicals to aid livestock and crop production. Pesticide and fertilizer use, for example, increased annually at more than 6 per cent between 1948 and 1978. Several major publicly-financed water development projects became operational in the 1950s and 1960s. Irrigation, in response to low water and energy prices and new water application technologies, expanded rapidly from both surface and underground sources to 50 million acres in 1980 – almost double that of 1950.

Productivity of land, as measured by yield per acre, grew nearly 50 per cent between 1948 and 1978. Although the harvested cropland area was variable, acreage in 1982 was virtually identical to that in 1950; but crop production nearly doubled in that period. Labour inputs declined by nearly 70 per cent; labour productivity grew at an annual average rate of 4.8 per cent during 1948–78.

The regional effects of these patterns of agricultural development on the natural resource base have been uneven, as they depend on the physical properties of land, climate (and weather related variables), water and agricultural production systems and management. Evidence of effects on environmental quality is partial and incomplete, sometimes circumstantial and anecdotal. Yet the presumptive evidence continues to mount that 'high-tech' agriculture is a major source of environmental pollution and a source of significant risk for human and animal health and wildlife habitats.

A comprehensive recent assessment of the resource and environmental effects of agriculture in the United States suggests that the major environmental threat emanating from agriculture is that of soil erosion and associated effects on water quality (Crosson and Brubaker 1982). Sheet and rill erosion now exceeds the level that permits crop yields to be maintained economically and indefinitely on some 27 per cent of US cropland. Sediment delivered to the nation's waterways is projected to nearly double by 2010 under economic and technological assumptions of the study. These estimates derive in large part from a 60–70 million-acre increase in cropland to meet projected domestic and foreign demand for US agricultural products. Crosson and Brubaker conclude that such an expansion in cropland would further induce agricultural production on erosion-prone land and thus cause a significant decline in marginal agricultural productivity growth rates. A more recent RFF assessment of global food prospects suggests a lesser but still substantial increase in cropland by 2010 given no major breakthroughs in technology (Farrell, Sanderson and Vo 1984). In either case the pressure could be high on natural resources and environmental quality.

For most of the last half-century, US agriculture had access to low-cost energy and publicly subsidised low-cost water for irrigation. As a result, farmers have made profligate use of both. Current irrigation levels with average precipitation result in the 'mining' of over 22 million acre-feet of water from aquifers in the western United States. Nationally, nearly a quarter of the groundwater used by agriculture is not replenished. Falling groundwater levels coupled with higher energy costs are forcing major adjustments in agricultural production in a multimillion acre area in the central and southern Plains states.

Beyond these physical and economic dimensions of water resources are major problems of water quality. Groundwater contamination from agricultural as well as non-agricultural sources has become serious in many parts of the country. Western irrigation practices have raised groundwater salinity. 'Perhaps one-quarter of the lands currently under irrigation in the West are heavily dependent on non-renewable water supplies, and the productivity of several million additional acres is threatened by rising salt levels' (Frederick 1982).

Other water quality problems – dissolved oxygen; suspended solids carrying bacteria, nutrients, and pesticides; excessive phosphoric and nitrogenic nutrients – derive in part, occasionally in major part, from agricultural production practices and runoff into streams and lakes. Growing public pressure to control non-point pollution could significantly increase agriculture's future production costs.

About 1,000 new chemicals are introduced each year in the United States. Some 55,000 to 60,000 chemicals are marketed annually. Comparatively little is known about the potential toxicity of many of these chemicals, about precisely how they are used, whether and how they enter the food chain and other ecosystems, and their ultimate effects on human health and other species. Controls on use of pesticides in agriculture and forestry have become more stringent, and progress has been made in developing less toxic but effective pesticides and integrated pest management systems that reduce application rates. Nonetheless, pesticide use remains pervasive in the production of major field crops.

The presumptive evidence seems compelling that high agricultural productivity growth rates are linked with some types of undesirable consequences for natural resources and the natural environment. But presumptive evidence must be carefully interpreted: cause and effect are not easily specified among complex relationships of the type under discussion. Many technologies now in use appear quite compatible with public goals of long-term resource conservation and retention of environmental quality hospitable to complex ecosystems, e.g. plant genetic improvements, control of endemic diseases, production technologies to control erosion. Further, the effects of technology depend not only on the inherent technical properties of the technology but also on the economic and managerial environments that govern its use. Improper management of the technology may create or exacerbate environmental externalities; economic incentives, sometimes reinforced by public policies, may induce private, short-term profit-seeking entrepreneurs to use technology in ways that generate longer-run resource and environmental costs. Thus, attribution of the resource and environmental costs of technology cannot be disassociated clearly from the institutional and economic environment that conditions its use.

Population and economic growth also generate pressures on the natural resource base and environmental quality. The demand for land for urbanisation, industrialisation and transportation resulted in an average annual conversion of about one million acres of agricultural land from 1967 to 1982. Competition for water, particularly in the centres of population growth in the West, may yet bring about major changes in water pricing and allocation schemes to the economic disadvantage of agriculture. Demand continues to grow for resources for recreation. Although rising competition for natural resources is unlikely to seriously impair the US agricultural productive capacity as a whole, dislocations may be substantial in some regions.

Some of the most flagrant damages to environmental quality are the direct products of population growth and industrialisation – disposal of human and industrial wastes that contaminate water supplies, for example. Air pollution from industrial activity and high consumption of fossil-fuel energy pose potentially serious threats to atmospheric quality and as yet largely undetermined effects on agricultural productivity in the form of acid rain and the 'greenhouse effect'.

The long-term implications of these changes in agriculture's relationships to larger environmental and ecological systems may not be fully understood but it is clear that agriculture must be viewed in the context of interdependence in those systems as well as economic systems. The production of food and fibre affects and is in turn affected by the quality of the natural environment. The goals of enhancing agricultural productivity and output *per se* without due regard for the costs of externalities on natural resources and quality of the environment are becoming less acceptable to society as a whole.

Ultimately, trade-offs between high rates of productivity growth as currently derived in favour of greater protection of the resource base and reduced levels of environmental pollution could mean higher real costs of food and fibre. However, as Barnett and Morse remind us, the nature of future trade-offs among goals related to agricultural development, natural resources and environmental quality can best be viewed as a dynamic process:

> as one of continual adjustment to an ever-changing economic resource quality spectrum. The physical properties of the natural resource base (and quality of the natural environment) impose a series of initial constraints on the growth and progress of mankind; but the resource (and environmental) spectrum undergoes kaleidoscopic change through time. Continual enlargement of the scope of substitutability – the result of man's technological ingenuity and organisational wisdom – offers those who are nimble a multitude of opportunities for escape (Barnett and Morse 1963).

Therein lies a major challenge to science, agricultural research and economists.

TOWARD ASSESSING DEVELOPMENT AND ENVIRONMENTAL TRADE-OFFS IN AGRICULTURE

In this section we sketch possible approaches to modify current economic analysis better to reflect the environmental and resource trade-offs in agricultural development. We examine selective models and measures to reflect these economic trade-offs as well as the economic health or performance of the agricultural sector.

The methods we examine fall within the realms of resource and agricultural economics. This area is important because some of the natural resources of concern are not exchanged through markets as are other agricultural resources, have common property aspects, and/or cause externalities to other users and non-users. Yet by the same token, these resources are extremely important to the continued efficiency and productivity of the agricultural sector. Furthermore, while the non-market and common-property characteristics of these resources provide a solid rationale for government intervention, this rationale is often quite removed from the current objectives and effects of agricultural policies. These policies may have little to do with the economic efficiency criteria for using natural resources.

Zilberman notes that the depletion patterns for water from a non-replenishable aquifer depend highly on technical change and agricultural price policies. Technical improvements in irrigation practices and some types of agricultural price support policies may operate in opposite directions on the output price. The former tends to depress the output price because of a shift in the producer's marginal cost curves; the effect of the latter may be to increase output price in the early periods. With respect to the depletion of the resource, technological improvements operate to reduce water use , while the price support policy tends to indirectly increase water use by increasing the quantities of output producers are willing to provide.[1] Over the long run the more rapid depletion of the aquifer will increase water prices and reduce output levels. While the extent that Zilberman's results can be generalised to other resources and policy scenarios is an open research area, the evidence illustrates the importance of addressing both agricultural policies and technological change in systematic analysis of agricultural development and environmental trade-offs.

The pesticide controversy offers a second illustration of the need to incorporate both technological change and agricultural policy options in a dynamic manner. The public policy solution to this externality problem in the past has been to restrict or prohibit the use of many chemicals. Restricting or eliminating the use of a particular pesticide of course reduces or eliminates its beneficial as well as its detrimental effects. Understanding the economic incentives that induce farmers to use chemical-intensive technologies is important in addressing the policy implications of pesticide bans. To assess properly the environmental trade-offs, one needs to know how using a pesticide in period t may affect the future ability to control target pests. For example, pesticides are likely to be temporarily beneficial but have declining marginal products. Thus, it is important to understand and incorporate the marginal benefit relation into a dynamic model.

The results of pesticide productivity studies are consistent with the high adoption rates of chemical-intensive technologies in post-Second World War agriculture. Headley found a high marginal productivity for pesticides and chemicals based on aggregate (state-level) production function analysis for the mid-1960s. Evidence at the micro level confirms the highly productive nature of chemical pesticides through the 1970s (Archibald 1982). This expansion in the use of chemical inputs has been encouraged by price and income policies for agriculture that restricted land inputs, increased crop land prices and provided output price supports. Since the market price of pesticides to farmers has not reflected both the private and social costs due to externalities, the current combination of land, pesticides and other inputs may not be the socially least-cost option for producing a given output.

The above concerns underscore the types of dynamic and inter-disciplinary analyses needed to explore the economic growth and environmental trade-off problems in agriculture. The short-run static nature of many models, combined with the limited information concerning the effects of continued use patterns for environmentally damaging inputs or the assimilative capacity of the environment, severely restrict the empirical analysis to provide anything more than an estimate of the current benefits and costs. These limitations have been well documented and attempts are being made to relax the static assumption and replace the analysis with a dynamic framework.[2]

One distinguishing feature of this new generation of models is that they should be based explicitly on dynamic economic optimisation incorporating costs of adjustments for the adoption of new technologies as well as biological relations that link intertemporal uses of environmental resources. That is, the speed with which firms adjust to new technologies should be endogenous and time varying, rather than exogenous and fixed. Also, the quality and quantity of the resource stock in period t should be explicitly related to the utilisation and conditions of the stocks in period $t-1$. This last component of the dynamic framework takes on a variety of forms and complexities. For a water resource problem, a single equation of motion describing the stock of water as a function of previous use levels may suffice. If the production involves agricultural runoff, the dynamic component is likely to involve complex interactions among many subsystems.

While integrating research on agricultural policy and resource management is paramount in evaluating the private and social cost of the growth/environmental trade-offs, the models developed for this purpose tend to be both commodity and policy specific. This is partly dictated by data requirements and limitations on model specifications, but there is a parallel need to provide some means of comparing the trade-offs at a more aggregate level. In our introductory comments we employed the familiar yardstick of the economic health of a sector – total factor productivity (TFP). The evidence suggests that the largest gains in TFP in US agriculture occurred during the decade and a half immediately following the Second World War, with slower growth rates observed during the 1960s and 1970s. In the most narrow sense one might suggest that there has been a relative decline in the economic performance of the sector. This conclusion needs to be qualified by examining the components of the productivity index.

The broad productivity criteria concentrate on *measurable* outputs of goods and services and neglect environmental quality. Some attempts are being made to adjust the conventional inputs to reflect quality change, but explicit recognition of the role of non-market inputs is lacking. A sector is productively efficient if it is producing as much as possible of every good and service given the amount of resources used. The neglect of the environmental quality components from these measures is a serious misstatement of the economic performance of the sector and, thus, TFP is inadequate for assessing economic efficiency and the trade-offs between environmental quality and economic growth.

To incorporate these trade-offs, one might utilize a more inclusive concept – augmented TFP[3] – which includes measurable agricultural output as well as the value of improvements to the resource base and environmental quality. This measure would reflect the social output as well as the private output from using a given bundle of inputs. Inputs devoted to restoring the quality of the environment or slowing resource depletion would have a beneficial value on the output side. Likewise, if the production of marketable output involved a decrease in the environmental quality, then this would show up as a diminution to the augmented output index, relative to the traditionally measured output index.

To illustrate the implications of this modification to TFP, one might correlate the growth rates of the potentially damaging inputs such as fertilizer and pesticides with the growth rates of the conventionally measured output. The 1948–60 period in US agriculture saw a large displacement of labour by agricultural chemicals; TFP also grew at a phenomenal rate of over 2 per cent per year. By contrast, the 1970s showed a slowdown in the rate of growth of chemicals and a slowdown in the exodus of labour from the agricultural sector. Given the changes in the input composition that occurred, one might hypothesise that an augmented TFP measure would be less than the observed TFP in the 1948–60 period and possibly greater in the 1970–8 period. In the absence of any statistical analyses our point regarding the TFP measure can only be suggestive: using the conventionally measured TFP index is likely to be misleading if one is concerned with environmental trade-offs. A decline in this TFP index may be a Pareto improvement and the high growth rates of the 1948–60 period for US agriculture may be less attractive using the augmented TFP measure.

Alternatively, the process can be viewed as an adjustment on the input side. Define the production function of a sector as:

$$Y = F(v, x, \dot{x}, t)$$

which represents efficient combinations of the conventional inputs v, and the environmental inputs x that can be used to produce output Y at time t. If the level of quality of the environmental inputs declines ($\dot{x} \neq 0$), output produced with any given amount of the conventional inputs would decline because of the necessity to utilise inputs to increase the stock of x rather than produce output. This diminution in output constitutes an internal cost of adjustment to the agricultural sector.

The apparent inverse relationship between environmental quality and increasing productivity leads to several implications concerning public policies to raise agricultural productivity. Obviously, it is not enough that such policies should simply encourage individual farmers to become more efficient. Equally important is ensuring a high rate of gross investment in both the capital stock and the environmental stock. The relation described above in principle is the basis for an intertemporal model in which the accumulation of capital and environmental resources link the production processes through time.

CONCLUSIONS AND IMPLICATIONS

We view trade-offs between agricultural development and natural resource and environmental quality as a dynamic, ever-changing process in responding to changing technological, institutional and economic criteria and the goals of society. There is need to define and measure the trade-offs more fully and accurately so that more informed choices can be made. And new or improved institutional designs are needed to facilitate effective expression of those choices. Nevertheless, the environmental risks associated with agricultural production cannot be reduced to zero.

Clearly, science and technology must play a major role in enlarging the future scope of substitutability between environmental resources and other resources in meeting future world needs for food and fibre. For some, the *sine qua non* of future agricultural technologies is that of biotechnology and the promises of dramatic productivity-enhancing breakthroughs in both plant and animal science. But before 'the genie is unleashed from the bottle' we should inquire rigorously of the potential effects of such technology on variables other than agricultural productivity as conventionally defined. In the thesis of this paper those variables include natural resources and quality of the natural environment.

If our perceptions and conclusions are valid, major implications ensue for agriculture and related institutions and for public policies. In concluding we single out four such implications of particular significance to agricultural economists and offer recommendations for addressing each.

(1) Agricultural research and extension programmes need to be re-examined – possibly reoriented – to more fully reflect that 'natural resources are an integral part of the ecosystem, and they have values transcending that of production for today's harvest' (Batie). Agricultural research and extension programmes in the United States and, we suspect, in other countries, have been heavily influenced by 'technological determinism' – a tendency to develop and extend agricultural productivity and output-enhancing technology sometimes without due reference to potential natural resource and environmental effects of the technology. If joint objectives of maintaining agricultural productivity, protecting natural resources and quality of the environment are to be achieved, more purposeful research and extension programmes reflective of those objectives are called for.

(2) Much of the research required to better identify the terms of trade-off between agricultural productivity and natural resource and environmental quality will be perforce interdisciplinary. Research

administrators should seek ways to provide incentives to induce more extensive and effective participation of scientists in cross-disciplinary research. We suggest that agricultural economists should play a larger role in such research. Current micro and macro analyses need to be modified to reflect dynamic forces in the use of natural resources.

(3) Data and information systems concerning the physical and economic attributes of natural resources should be strengthened and made more consistent within and across countries. Measures for monitoring environmental quality should be improved; monitoring should occur more frequently and rigorously; data should be systematised and made readily available for research and policy purposes.

(4) Agricultural, natural resource and environmental policies and programmes should be brought into closer harmony. The public goals underlying many current agricultural policies should be re-examined in the light of evidence of conflict with other public goals concerning natural resources and the environment. The rationale for such policies has often been tied closely to enhancement of agricultural production. We may now be seeing, all too clearly, the true social costs of these policies.

Perhaps the most basic implication of our perceptions and conclusions is the need for agricultural economists to perceive themselves and to define their agenda in a context that recognises and reflects the interdependence of agriculture in larger and more complex environmental and ecological systems as well as economic systems. If that is done, agricultural economists have much to offer in identifying the trade-offs between agricultural productivity, natural resource use and protection and environmental quality, and in the design of institutions to facilitate implementation of those trade-offs.

NOTES

[1]This latter result assumes that the demand for water is fairly responsive to output price.
[2]The studies by Zilberman and Archibald are two such examples.
[3]Augmented GNP was originally proposed by Dorfman and Dorfman.

REFERENCES

Archibald, S., 'A Dynamic Approach to Measuring Productivity and Technical Change in the Presence of Externalities in Production', (unpublished research), University of California, Davis, 1982.
Barnett, Harold J. and Morse, Chandler, *Scarcity and Growth*, Johns Hopkins University Press, Baltimore, 1983.
Batie, S. A., Shabman, L. A. and Kramer, R., 'U.S. Agriculture and Natural Resource Policy' (unpublished paper), National Center for Food and Agricultural Policy, Resources for the Future.
Capalbo, S., Vo, T. T. and Wade, J. C., *An Econometric Data Base for the U.S. Agricultural Sector*, Discussion Paper Series no. RR85–01, Resources for the Future, Washington DC, 1985.
Crosson, P. R. and Brubaker, S., *Resource and Environmental Effects of U.S. Agriculture*, Resources for the Future, Washington, DC, 1982.

Dorfman, R. and Dorfman, N., *Economics of the Environment* (second edition), W. W. Norton and Company, Inc., New York, 1977.

Farrell, K. R., Sanderson, F. and Vo, T. T., 'Meeting Future Needs for United States Food, Fiber, and Forest Products' in *Reference Document: Needs Assessment for the Food and Agricultural Sciences*, Joint Council on Food Agricultural Sciences, Washington, DC, January 1984.

Frederick, K. D., *Water for Western Agriculture*, Research Paper, Resources for the Future, 1982.

Headley, J. C., 'Estimating the Productivity of Agricultural Pesticides', *American Journal of Agricultural Economics*, vol. 50, no. 1, 1968.

Zilberman, D., 'Technical Change, Government Policies, and Exhaustible Resources in Agriculture', *American Journal of Agricultural Economics*, vol. 66, no. 5, 1984.

ACHMAD T. BIROWO AND DIBYO PRABOWO

The Pressure on Natural Resources in Indonesian Agricultural Development

INTRODUCTION

Resources are basic for the economic development of any country, particularly those in the early stages of economic development. For that matter, a country like Indonesia, has to be fortunate with the luxury of abundant natural resources. In the old days people used to call the country 'An Emerald of Natural Resources in the Equator'.

However, up to the present, there are still many poor people in certain parts of the country. Growth in economic development in some parts of the country has been very slow and in others very rapid. Certain sectors of the economy enjoy a high rate of economic growth whereas others remain stationary. Compared with countries like Japan and Singapore, the wealth of natural resources in Indonesia is exorbitant, whereas economic development of Japan and Singapore is high compared with Indonesia. Does it mean that a wealth of natural resources are not that important in economic development? Or maybe, resources are overexploited so that their productive services soon become zero? Or maybe, the resources are managed inappropriately?

The objective of this paper is to unveil policy issues in the management of natural resources for the agricultural development of Indonesia under serious population pressures. The discussion will be centred around two categories of agricultural development activity, namely, crop husbandry and forestry.

GENERAL TOPOGRAPHIC RESOURCES BASE

Indonesia is an archipelago with a land surface of about 190 million hectares, situated between 94° 15'E and 141° 05'E meridian and 6° 08'N and 11° 15'S parallel, running right through the equator. The archipelago consist of 13,677 islands of which 931 or 6.8 per cent are inhabited by around 147 million people. Most of the land surface is covered by forest (60 per cent). The remaining surface are: 8 per cent agriculture, 7 per cent bare lands and 25 per cent other. 41 per cent of the land area is mountainous, 31 per cent hilly and 28 per cent lowland. Some 80 per

284

cent of the country's 147 million people live in rural areas and agriculture employs about two thirds of the total labour force. In 1980, the agricultural sector provided 31.4 per cent of the total GDP, of which food crops (19.1 per cent) provided the largest share, followed by cash crops, estate crops, forestry, livestock and fishery. In the decade 1970–81, agriculture grew at a rate of 3.8 per cent per annum against a 7.9 per cent growth in total GDP. Hence a decreasing role of agriculture.

According to the 1980 Population Census there were in 1980 around 17.5 million farm households, of which 11.0 million (63 per cent) operated on land of less than 0.5 ha. The corresponding figures in 1973 were 14.4 million farm households, of which 6.6 million (44 per cent) operated on land of less than 0.5 ha. During the period 1973–80, then, the number of farms increased by 2.8 per cent annually, of which, the 'mini-farmers' with less than 0.5 ha increased annually by 7.7 per cent. In 1980 the number of landless farmers were 8.1 millions, which, during the period 1977–80, increased annually by 2.2 per cent. Land fragmentation also became a serious problem.

Java is the most fertile and densely populated island. There, 60 per cent of Indonesia's people live in an area of about 7 per cent of the total land surface. In Java the number of agricultural population per ha was 7.5 in 1973, as compared to 4.9 for the whole of Indonesia. The area of arable land per person actively engaged in smallholder agriculture, except in Kalimantan, is about the same in all parts of the country, i.e., 0.109 ha for Java-Madura, 0.107 ha for Sumatra, 0.090 ha for Sulawesi and 0.113 ha for the total of Indonesia. These figures indicate the limited level of farming technology in the small-holder sector, where, despite an abundance of land resources, the level of technology puts a limit on the amount of land a farmer can operate.

Out of a total of farm households in 1980 of 17.5 million, 73.6 per cent were owner operated, 14.9 per cent tenanted and 11.5 per cent farming a combination of the two. The corresponding figures in 1973 were 74.8 per cent, 3.2 per cent and 22.0 per cent, respectively. Hence, during the period 1973 to 1980 the number of tenants increased annually by 28.2 per cent, owner operator by 2.6 per cent and mixed −6.3 per cent. Although the number of owner operators are still more than two-thirds of the total, the number of tenants is increasing very rapidly.

The above figures indicate that although the resource base for agriculture is abundant, its distribution is uneven. The technology of resource utilisation for agriculture was still limited. With this background, an analysis is made of policy issues on resource management under population pressure in crop husbandry and in forestry.

CROP HUSBANDRY

Management of natural resources in crop husbandry has been pushed mainly towards reaching food self sufficiency, particularly in rice[1]. In the massive efforts to reach food self-sufficiency, intensification programmes called *Bimas* and *Inmas* have been launched since the late 1960s. *Bimas*, an acronym for *Bi*mbingan *Mas*sal which literally translated means *mass guidance*, is basically a package programme consisting of: (1) intensive extension activities, (2) provision of fertilizers, pesticides and high yielding rice varieties at subsidised prices, (3) provision of credit at subsidised low interest rates and liberal terms to purchase modern inputs as well as to meet the increasing production costs due to the application of improved technology, and (4) a floor-price guarantee at farm gate level. The intensive extension is directed towards stimulating *Panca Usaha*, or *Five Proper Crop Husbandry Practices*, i.e. (1) proper soil preparation, (2) appropriate irrigation management, (3) application of sufficient fertilizer, (4) proper pest and disease control through the use of modern inputs, and (5) appropriate crop husbandry. *Inmas*, the twin programme of *Bimas*, is practically *Bimas* without credit provision, assuming that the farmers are in a financial position to join the intensification programme. In 1981 around three quarters of the total farm land was either under *Bimas* or *Inmas* programme, as compared to a corresponding figure of 25 per cent in the late 1960s. The results of *Bimas* and *Inmas* programmes have indeed been very impressive. National average yield of milled rice per hectare increased from 1.2 tons in the period 1960–7 to 1.65 in 1968–75 and 1.9 tons in 1980–81. After Japan, Taiwan and Korea, today Indonesia has the highest land productivity for rice growing in Asia. Rice production increased from 12.2 million tons in 1969 to 22.9 million tons in 1982. Rice imports were 1.862 million tons in 1973, 1.842 million tons in 1978 and down to 0.458 million tons in 1982. In fact with an annual stock of rice reserves of over 1.5 million tons by 1981, with a 22.3 million ton milled rice production, Indonesia has already reached a situation, in which national consumption needs could be met by domestic production even at a consumption standard of 150 kg per caput per year. Imports were still needed then to provide the annual reserve stock for controlling floor and ceiling prices, as well as for emergency in cases of natural catastrophes. A prerequisite for joining the intensification programme is good irrigation in land management. In 1977 around 5 million ha were under irrigation. Of those, around 3.9 millions ha were under the Department of Public Works and the rest under village administration.

Effective irrigation depends on efficient water management as well as water supplies. The first and second Five Year Plans, 1969–74 and 1974–79, emphasised the large-scale development of irrigation. Quite recently, however, emphasis was put on small-scale irrigation and simple irrigation.

Dibyo Prabowo and Affendi Anwar (1982; pp. 52–3) quoted a study indicating that there was evidence that irrigation water management and utlisation is inefficient at the farm level. They mentioned (ibid, p. 52) that farmers in fully irrigated areas in Klaten, Central Java, typically receive and apply 50 per cent more irrigation water than is necessary for optimum production. Thus, half of the irrigation water currently applied is wasted.

By water reallocation, a significantly larger area could be served in a normal year. Poor management and low irrigation efficiency in Indonesia is partly due to physical facilities that are worn out because of age and lack of maintenance. There has been a lot of discussion about who should pay the costs of operation and maintenance as well as the repayment of the construction costs of the irrigation system. Presidential Instruction No. 1/1969, specified that the costs of water distribution and maintenance of the irrigation system should be borne by those obtaining the direct benefits from irrigation water. The provincial governors were then authorised to charge land owners certain fees. But by long established tradition, irrigation water is free and no water charges are levied. Thus the payment for O & M (Operation and Maintenance) is regarded as a contribution of the land owner to irrigation development, abbreviated as IPEDA, (*Iuran Pembangunan Daerah*). The financing of the main system O & M is assisted by a Central Government subsidy of around 50–80 per cent of the total costs. A recent study from East Java (Dibyo Prabowo et al. 1982, p. 55), indicated that O & M expenditure for the primary through the tertiary canals should at least be $21.10/ha. If the large investments allocated in irrigation construction should be followed by efficient water management, the issue of water charge to cover O & M expenses should be solved immediately and appropriately.

FORESTRY

Through Indonesia, forest land covers around 122 million hectares, roughly 60 per cent of the total land surface. In 1979, almost 75 per cent was rain forest. The second largest forest types – secondary or idle forest and swamp forest – occupied less than 15 per cent of the total forest area. The remaining four types – coastal, peat, deciduous and mangrove – each covered about 2–3 per cent of the total forest land. The predominance of rain forest is not surprising because the country is an archipelago within the monsoon rain belt (Birowo 1981, p. 117).

As shown in Table 1, between 1972 and 1979 forest exploitation jumped by around six times to reach 63.1 million hectares. Similarly,

TABLE 1   *Forest area by function in 1972 and 1979 (million ha)*

Forest function	1972	1979	Change in %
Protection	11.5	14.2	23
Production	11.1	63.1	568
Nature conservation	3.5	7.9	126
Reserved	96.1	37.0	−62
Total	122.2	122.2	

Source: Directorate General of Forestry, 1980.

protection forest increased by 23 per cent and nature conservation forest more than doubled. These increases were possible because the area of reserved forest was reduced by more than 60 per cent. The changing structure of the export market, with decreasing supply from the Philippines, produced a tremendous demand, resulting in the rapid growth of forest exploitation. In terms of geographic distribution, more than 90 per cent of the total forest lands are in Sumatra, Kalimantan and Irian Jaya. However, the forest uses differ in the various provinces.

Because of excessive over-exploitation it was reported that around 30 million hectares were critical (Birowo 1975). The critical lands are those, which, (a) regarding the hydro-orological functions are very bad, (b) from the national economic viewpoint have no productive value and (c) from the physical and technical properties have no more value for agricultural development.

On Java, intense population pressure causes people to be land hungry. People are cultivating more crops on steep lands. They go to the forest to gather firewood for own consumption or to sell for cash. The land is often put under cultivation after the trees have been cut. Outside Java, land is not so scarce but the soil is generally much less fertile, more fragile and more subject to erosion if denuded or cultivated. Shifting cultivation, extensive logging and development or transmigration settlements were creating soil depletion problems. Erosion rate and sediment concentration are two indicators of the extent of critical lands. Erosion rates on river basins on Java range from 0.1 to 23 mm per year, whereas in areas outside Java they range from 0.03 to 0.87 mm per year (Dibyo Prabowo et al., 1982, pp. 39, 40). Sediment concentration on river basins on Java ranges from 1,500 to 20,000 mg/l, whereas outside Java it ranges from 150 to 10,000 mg/l.

The erosion rate is continuously rising, as indicated by a study in the Cimanuk river basin (Dibyo Prabowo et al., 1982, p. 43) in which the erosion rate in 1952 was 0.6 mm/year while in 1967 it had increased to 5.3 mm/year. Sedimentation has a serious effect on the dams of reservoirs, decreasing capacity to store water and hence, shortening service life. Due to sedimentation, Karangkates reservoir in East Java is losing its capacity by 1.2 per cent annually.

To solve the problem of the critical lands, reforestation and afforestation are two important efforts. Massive development budgets have been allocated to finance these two programmes. To give an example, in the fiscal year 1975–6, US $140 million were allocated for these two programmes, corresponding to about 20 per cent of the total agricultural development budget, five times the budget for livestock development, three times the budget for commercial crop development and twice the total development budget for fisheries (Birowo 1975). However, up to the fiscal year 1982–3 only around 1.5 million hectares were the result of afforestation and 2.0 million hectares for forestation, just over 50 per cent of the prescribed plan. Skilled personnel are the major bottleneck. Because a huge amount of funds are managed by a very limited number of project personnel, a number of mass media have lately reported project financial mismanagements. Hopefully with the establishment of a Ministry of Forestry in the new cabinet starting in 1983, the implementation of reforestation and afforestation should be handled more efficiently.

ECONOMIC VIABILITY OF THE RESOURCE CONSERVATION PROJECTS

This section attempts to evaluate the economic viability – the costs and benefits of the technology that has been extended through the resource conservation projects. When the estimate of benefits is not available, at least the estimate of costs will be presented.

Check Dams

These check dams are budgeted not to exceed $150.00/ha of upstream watershed. Once constructed, maintenance costs are minimal. Direct costs are primarily for local labour (60 per cent). which is paid the prevailing wage rate, and material (40 per cent) obtained at the site (except cement). The construction costs vary from $20,000 to $30,000 and required 12,000–15,000 mandays of labour. Compensation is paid to owners of the land flooded by the dam at a rate of $7.50/ha. After the check dam silts up, the land is returned to the original owner.

Terracing on 50 per cent slope or less

The cost of bench terracing and associated structures is largely a function of the slope of the hillside to be terraced. Estimates of labour requirements per hectare suggest a significant manpower input is needed, ranging from 500 to 1,800/md/ha depending on the slope. Some projects paid the farmer to construct the terrace and others did not. Yet, even if the farmer is not paid, he must forgo opportunities to earn a daily wage. At full ($0.70/md) and 50 per cent opportunity costs of labour these manpower requirements imply construction costs of $263 to $1,283/ha. Costs of planning material, tools, and fertilizer required to build and establish a crop on the terrace in year one average $70/ha. Total labour and material costs would range from $1,293 to $1,319 depending on slope and assumed labour costs. While maintenance requirements are reported to be minimal and may be considered as a normal part of land preparation, waterways and drop structures will require yearly maintenance. Consequently, building bench terraces requires a significant investment of time and money.

Improved cropping patterns

Upper Solo River Basin Projects. Results suggest that the improved practices more than double labour demand/ha on severely eroded slopes and increase labour requirements by 27 per cent on the moderately eroded land. The implicit daily wage the farmer earns for himself by adopting the technology is about three times the pre-adoption level. Net farm income – the consequence of both more days worked per year and a higher wage/day – ranged from 3.5 to 8.3 times that without project, on severe and moderately eroded slopes respectively.

Citanduy River Basin Project. The improved pattern makes possible triple cropping. For the farmers who grew only one crop before development, the improved pattern tripled the labour requirements, tripled the daily wage and increased net income ninefold. For the farmer who grew two crops before the development, the improved pattern increased labour demand by 35 per cent, doubled the wage rate earned, and increased net income by two and a half times.

Livestock component. The cost of establishing a grass cover on the terrace is approximately $45.00 for material and 2–5 md/ha of labour, if 20 per cent of the area is in terrace rises and lips. A mature female sheep/goat costs about $40–45 per head.

The major variable input in small ruminant production is labour. Owning these animals provides an opportunity for the household to self-employ family labour, often child labour with a low opportunity cost. Typically, livestock forage needs are provided by men or boys who cut grass along the roadways and on other public land and carry it back to the pens in which the animals are confined. To feed small ruminants, the household must spend 1 hour/animal/day in the wet season and 2 hours/animal/day in the dry season. Consequently, flock size seldom exceeds 4–8 animals per household. Establishing grass intensively on the terraces greatly reduces the time required to harvest daily food requirements. This enables the household to either raise a greater number of animals with the same labour input or raise the same number of animals with perhaps only 20 per cent of the labour input required under the traditional extensive cut and carry system. Hence, the grass/livestock enterprise can be expected to increase labour productivity and the implicit wage earned from ruminant production by 2–3 times. Furthermore, livestock provide farmers with an additional income stream, reducing vulnerability to crop failure. At the same time, livestock provide a mechanism by which farmers can accumulate capital. Whenever the occasion arises, this asset can be sold to meet family consumption and investment needs.

Development on slopes greater than 50 per cent. The cost of establishing tree crops/grass is dependent on the type of tree planted and the spacing. The long run returns to tree crops such as cloves and citrus are significantly greater than food crops, once they reach maturity. For example, a clove plantation with trees planted at a rate of 250 seedlings per ha gives an annual gross return of over $1,500 per ha.

PRODUCTION AND EXPORTS

In 1981 Indonesia produced 24.6 million m³ of timber of which 21.2 million m³ were logs and 3.4 million m³ were sawn timber. Both the composition and total production have changed since 1970. Log production has increased twofold, whereas sawn timber production has expanded more than 10 times. In general, increasing amounts of processed forest products were produced.

In 1980 forestry exports amounted to US $1.8 billion and were more than ten times that of 1970. In terms of volume, exports had doubled. The general upward trend of export prices indicated the increasing gap of demand over supply. However, major constraints to the development of exports of forest products have been inadequate harbour facilities, high shipping costs, poor quality control and lack of trade skill and management. Between 1969 and 1980 timber exports varied between about 60 per cent and 85 per cent of total production. The period when a high percentage of total production was exported (1975–77) was followed by a decline. Apparently, with increasing incomes, domestic markets are able to use more of the output, particularly of processed wood products.

The market rise in the value of wood as a commodity in the Pacific area has occurred because of the supply and demand in the 1980s, the interest in wood as a renewable energy resource, and the emergence of South Korea and China as significant purchasers. This may stimulate government and investors to channel their resources of capital, land and personnel into a belated but still necessary effective afforestation effort. Today in Indonesia there are 525 firms holding forestry concessions with a total invested capital of about US $1.5 billion. Of these, 430 firms are operating under domestic investment facilities and 95 under foreign investment facilities. The government has encouraged the firms to produce more processed wood and fewer logs. In 1980, a new regulation was issued under which firms would export no more than 50 per cent of their logs and were required to process 50 per cent locally. A few months later, the requirement was increased so that an export permit would be issued for one unit of logs if the firm could produce evidence that it had sold two units for local manufacturing.

From an international perspective it seems likely that Indonesia will become a producer of plywood and other manufactured goods. The major constraint would seem to be the availability of managerial skill. Special plans are being considered to encourage the establishment of timber manufacturing. Under these plans no new forest concessions will be granted to applicants who do not submit plans for establishing a wood-processing plant.

CONCLUSION

Management of natural resources for agricultural development under population pressure cover development activities in crop husbandry and forestry. The abundant vast resources of Indonesia are unevenly distributed among regions. Limited levels of technology, however, put a limit on the application of resources per unit of agricultural population. Due to rapid population increase the number of mini farmers is increasing vastly, the number of landless farmers likewise growing rapidly and the number of tenant farms are increasing alarmingly.

In crop husbandry, land management in general has been satisfactory. To maintain and operate water management efficiently, however, the problems of how to finance the operation and maintenance of the irrigation system need to be solved appropriately. Improvement of water at the farm level may increase the efficiency of irrigation services.

In forestry, erosion and sedimentation due to excessive forest eploitation are growing at an alarming rate. Programmes for reforestation and afforestation need to be given more serious attention. Reforestation and afforestation projects need more skilled personnel urgently in order to manage the development activities efficiently. The government has encouraged forestry firms to produce more processed woods and fewer logs.

If all bottlenecks could be tackled successfully, proper management of natural resources in agricultural development even with the serious population pressure in Indonesia may definitely increase farm incomes and maintain and improve a healthy and sound environment.

NOTE

[1] Others include expansion of cash crops to increase exports; these issues will not be discussed in this paper, since they have little bearing on population pressure.

REFERENCES

Birowo, A. T. 1975, 'Agro-economic aspects of rehabilitation of critical lands', a paper presented at a symposium on *Control and Rehabilitation of Critical Lands in the Framework of Regional Development*, Jakarta, Ministry of Agriculture, 27–29 October 1975 (in Indonesian language).

Birowo, A. T. 1981, 'Development prospects for forestry in Indonesia' in English, H. E. and Scott, Anthony (eds) *Renewable Resources in the Pacific*, Proceedings of the 12th Pacific Trade and Development Conference, Vancouver, Canada, 7–11 September 1981.

Birowo, A. T. 1983, 'The growth and equity issues in Indonesia', lecture delivered at Department of Economics and Statistics, Swedish University of Agricultural Sciences, Uppsala, Sweden, 25 April 1983 (mimeograph).

Birowo, A. T. 1983, 'Coconut Production in Indonesia', paper prepared for Symposium on Food Problems held for the Anniversary of World Food Day, Bangkok, FAO Regional Office for Asia and the Pacific, 17 October 1983.

Birowo, A. T. 1983, 'Two-way Process in agricultural and rural development planning in Indonesia', paper written for the Expert Consultation on Two-Way Process in Agricultural and Rural Development Planning, Bangkok, FAO Regional Office for Asia and the Pacific, 1–4 February 1983.

Birowo, A. T. 1983, 'Renewable resource problems and policies in Indonesia', paper presented at the VI Biennial Conference of the Agricultural Economic Society of South-East Asia (AESSEA), Bangkok, Thailand, 16–20 November 1983.

Prabowo, Dibyo and Anwar, Affendi, 'Natural Resources, Agriculture and the Environment' in *Mubyarto* (ed.), *Growth and Equity in Indonesian Agricultural Development*, Jakarta, Yayasan Agro Ekonomika, 1982.

Notodihardjo, Mardjono and Mahbub, Badruddin, 'Erosion and sedimentation in Indonesia: An Overview', *Proceedings of the South-East Asian Regional Symposium on Problems of Soil Erosion and Sedimentation*, Bangkok, A.I.T., January 1981.

'Report of the watershed assessment team, 1983', Government of Indonesia/US-AID, Jakarta, 1983.

Wiersum, K. F., 'Plattelandsontwikkeling, erosie an bos op Java', *Landbouwkunde*, no. 9., 1980. (Rural development, erosion and forestry on Java).

DISCUSSION OPENING I – JOSEPH VON AH

Experts all over the world agree that pressure on natural resources is an important issue at the present time, and, even more so in the future. The Vice President Programme was, therefore, well advised to invite two prominent members of our association to introduce the topic. We are grateful for two comprehensive, informative and competent papers: Farrell and Capalbo covering the situation of the United States as a case of an industrialised country; Birowo and Prabowo presenting prospects of populous Indonesia, situated in the Asian tropics. As discussion opener, I want to highlight four points – needless to say they reflect (in part at least) my background, present interests, personal biases and preferences.

(1) What are really the *facts* on the environmental issues: locally, nationally and world-wide? Both papers have an optimistic undertone: there are problems, certainly, alarming signals due to rapid deforestation (e.g. in Indonesia); dangers and risks of a modern, hard line, chemically based agricultural technology (e.g. in USA). Neither of the two speakers indicated, however, that the situation would deteriorate into chaos and global catastrophe. Similarly Kramer writes in his 'International Overview of Soil Conservation Policy'[1]: 'Soil erosion is not the imminent threat to mankind that some doomsday prognosticators would claim …'.

This position I set in contrast to widely read, quoted and discussed publications (especially in the Swiss media and by students) like *Global 2000 – Report to the President*, or Fritjof Capra *The Turning Point*[2] – to name just two. At this Conference, Bromley in his highly stimulating paper 'Natural Resources and Agricultural Development in the Tropics: Is Conflict Inevitable?'[3], puts the production of tropical cash crops for export under the heading of 'International Resource Degradation'. Do university professionals or journalists know better? Are administrators in responsible positions always ignorant or biased? How about experts in all camps who hold contrary views to each other?

(2)   What is the place of glamorous *biotechnology* for the problem at hand? Birowo does not mention the term; for Farrell it is 'a genie in the bottle' whose release should be carefully evaluated beforehand.

Ricardo has described the scenario of a world with a decreasing man-land ratio and agricultural technology remaining constant; Malthus formulated his dismal solution to the problem as vice, misery and death – also, it seems to me that past trends of agricultural technology must not be simply carried into the future. In fact, today we are 'eating oil' with our highly developed agricultural technology. On the other hand, oil resources are going to be depleted in the foreseeable future. Health hazards for man and beast as well as environmental hazards of an oil-based civilisation and of food production techniques cannot be overlooked (Farrell gave a list of examples.) For these reasons, it is puzzling to me why biotechnology has found such a small place in the two papers. Moreover, the Conference paper by Fishel and Kenny[4] and the Poster Paper no. 63 by L. D. Hill and W. Florkowski[5], both on biotechnology, make no reference at all to possible relief of pressures on natural resources by the new technology.

(3)   Do *people* and *villages* matter? Implied in both papers, and explicitly stated in numerous contributions at the Conference sessions, as well as in the 'poster' presentations, we find the *leitmotiv* of how important the main actors, the people in the countryside, are. Agriculture has the unique quality of being a highly location-specific human activity. This concerns the natural conditions (soils, topography, climate, altitude) as well as the man-made organisations and institutions in their history, religion and social structure. An overall consensus seems to prevail that narrowly defined economic analysis is fading into the history of our profession.

(4)   Some *more questions* listed:
    Poverty and environmental degradation;
    Role of organic farming;
    Olson's theory on collective action;
    Relative impacts of on-farm and off-farm pollution, e.g. of soil and water;
    Tourism as a factor of preservation and degradation;
    The UNESCO-approach 'Man and Biosphere' (MAB).

I wish to conclude my brief contribution with reference to the Presidential Address by Glenn Johnson. Our profession can make an important contribution to the solution of the problems of natural resources as they relate to the feeding of mankind. A necessary condition for achievement is to widen the 'Scope of Agricultural Economics'[6] and to apply the appropriate mix to theory:
    in a multidisciplinary approach
    with proper problem solving activities, and
    sufficient information about our quantifiable and unquantifiable
    values', (i.e. the normative and ethical base).

REFERENCES

1. Randall Kramer, 'An International Overview of Soil Conservation Policy', this volume, p. 307.
2. Fritjof Capra, *The Turning Point*, Simon and Schuster, New York, 1982, Chapter on agriculture, p. 226 ff.
3. Daniel W. Bromley, 'Natural Resources and Agricultural Development in the Tropics: Is Conflict Inevitable?', this volume, p. 319.
4. Walter, L. Fischel and Martin Kenny, 'Challenge to Studies of Biotechnology Impacts in the Social Sciences', this volume, p. 353.
5. Lowell D. Hill and Wojciech Florkowski, 'Economic Consequences of Biotechnology on International Corn Production and Marketing', (Poster Session Paper no. 64).
6. Glenn L. Johnson, 'Scope of Agricultural Economics', Presidential Address, this volume, p. 21.

DISCUSSION OPENING II – JEAN-PIERRE BERTRAND

The two papers which have been presented focus on the same topic: Does the intensive model of agricultural development exert tremendous pressure on the natural resources?

In the case of the US Susan Capalbo and Kenneth Farrell argue that the increase in the productivity in agriculture has occurred without taking into account the natural resources and environmental quality, as the process of erosion and degradation of water quality created by the use of huge amounts of pesticides and fertilizers show. The main hypothesis of the authors is that there does exist an inverse relation between an increase in productivity and the maintenance of environmental quality. They think, however, that this relation could be reversed and they propose to take into account the costs of protecting the environment. They then suggest a new approach to measure the productivity.

Agricultural productivity growth at the expense of environment would be made more costly. How, we may ask, could we measure this economically? How to take into account the loss of diversity of systems which are more and more specialised and concentrated? One example of this loss could be found in the case of the soybean system in the United States and of the soybean-wheat system in Brazil. They are very simple, and, without doubt, agronomically balanced, but are they able to resist a biological, climatic or economic shock?

Susan Capalbo and Kenneth Farrell argue that trade-offs between high rates of productivity growth in favour of greater protection of the natural resources and reduced levels of pollution could mean higher real costs of food. They suggest that the magnitude of this cost increase will depend on the difference between the rhythm of development of technologies to maintain production and attempts to reduce the degradation of the quality of natural resources.

In this evolution the price policy will be very important. We could also ask if in the international situation, there should exist a new relation between the movement of prices and the mobilisation of natural resources? Do we have a succession of agricultural booms which put more pressure on national resources and agricultural busts which, paradoxically, favour conservation practices and policies? Can the acceleration of erosion in the United States during the 1970s be attributed to cultivation of marginal land? On the contrary, what will be the consequences of the present overproduction crisis upon the protection of the environment?

The paper of Achmad Birowo and Dibyo Prabowo raises also the question of the pressure on the natural resources as a consequence of the choice of an intensive model of agricultural production. The authors have shown very well how Indonesia has combined rice self-sufficiency strategy and a vigorous agro-export wood and products policy. The import substitution of rice was obtained thanks to small producers who have adopted new packages of inputs. The rice yield has doubled in the last 20 years which is quite remarkable. What I would like to know is what has happened to the income distribution and if there was not a disruption, or at least deep changes, in the social structure.

In the lumber industry the results have been remarkable too but the effects on environment were more dramatic. On the international demand side, after the 1975–7 boom with high lumber prices, prices have dropped. Indonesia has tried to develop a more complex strategy and has begun to export more processed products, but the country has faced the interests of the developed countries and has suffered from its own lack of managerial skill.

I think it would be very interesting to discuss a little more the specific difficulties of excessive dependence of a strategic sector in very unstable and turbulent international markets.

GENERAL DISCUSSION – RAPPORTEUR: MAURIZIO MERLO

Comments and questions mainly concerned the general analysis of pressure on natural resources as presented by the two papers and the problems of evaluating externalities which have 'non-monetary, intangible' values. Contributions to the discussion also concerned agricultural-environmental policies and special attention was devoted to the environmental impact of foreseeable development in biotechnology.

With regard to the general analysis the opinion was expressed that more attention should have been given to welfare economics, especially Pigou analysis, quite neglected by the Farrell and Capalbo paper. Also multi-objective analysis in its dynamic version was advocated as a more appropriate tool for optimising the trade-offs between farmers' profits (first objective) and 'ecological sustainability' (second objective). Other discussants supported the importance of ecosystems analysis which should be able to give a more comprehensive view of agriculture in the context of the environment and its role in natural resource development and depletion. It was also pointed out that agriculture, besides being a polluter, was very much affected by the pollution created by other activities. Farmers were usually very sensitive to ecological problems and to natural resource conservation but they were under such economic pressure they were obliged to use the more sophisticated techniques even if polluting.

Several discussants posed the more practical (as well as theoretical) question of how to evaluate costs and benefits of various agricultural techniques. It was observed that various items can often be evaluated in an incorrect way or even ignored. The case of soil overexploitation was raised, underlining its consequences, not only in terms of erosion (as shown by Birowo and Prabowo's paper) but also in terms of more general environmental and social degradation.

Several discussants felt that even when the best theoretical solution of the trade-off between productivity and conservation was found, the crucial problem would remain of evaluating the shadow prices of non-monetary externalities.

It was observed that the modified aggregate production functions proposed by Farrell-Capalbo seemed to be only a first step which needs further sound and consistent evaluations. In this context the problem of intertemporal relationships was also raised; that is, consideration of future generations' welfare. It was pointed out that in various cases solutions to apparent problems are generating more serious problems for the future. Others observed that we are passing the bill to the next generation because we are too selfish on environmental issues. In other words, what really matters is the willingness to pay which seems to be lacking in our societies. It was then felt that this crucial issue was missing in the papers as well in the discussion.

Coming to more political considerations, the free market, and its distortions, was blamed as the main reason for environmental degradation. A 'stick and carrot' policy was then called for to cope with externalities. A supra-national authority at regional level should supervise the policy in order to achieve a better quality of the environment and a more balanced economic growth.

Political issues concerning biotechnology development were also raised with reference to the papers and to the openers' remarks. The modified aggregate agricultural production functions proposed in the Farrell-Capalbo paper were considered a step forward in order to broaden the traditional analysis by taking account of environmental quality as a separate outcome of the production process. However it was observed that what really counted was the attitude of the administration of research stations and the behaviour of farmers. It was pointed out that there should be some implications for environmental policy of a situation of market surplus and a highly intensive use of land in agriculture.

In their replies the authors of the two papers largely agreed with most comments. Birowo and Prabowo particularly stressed the fact that unfortunately many questions up to now had no answers. To a very large extent the demographic pressure, the growing food needs, the development of new technologies were a vicious circle. However, environmental and social problems were constantly in the focus of political intervention.

Farrell and Capalbo first underlined the fact that linkages between productivity analysis and applied welfare economics were unclear. This was an area for further research. Second, with reference to several objections regarding shadow values they agreed about the difficulty of measurement. However, this should not prevent further enquiry into possible adjustments to the familiar production functions. They observed that agricultural economists were famous or maybe 'notorious', depending on one's point of view, for pushing ahead in relatively unexplored frontiers of research and applied empirical work. They also agreed that the suggested modifications were only one of the possible means of incorporating and evaluating the environmental/productivity trade-off; of course other methodologies could be employed.

With reference to questions concerning biotechnologies and the impact of agricultural policies on natural resources, Farrell and Capalbo pointed out the possibility that new biotechnologies might simultaneously increase agricultural productivity and enhance environmental quality. However this possible outcome was dependent on many variables about which we now know very little. These variables included technical characteristics of the technologies themselves, substitution possibilities with more conventional production inputs, and economic variables which affected the rate of adoption and the returns to agricultural producers. This implied a unique opportunity and need for agricultural economists to collaborate with other scientists from other disciplines to assess the potential effects and the environmental impact of the new biotechnologies. This assessment was needed for shaping the future course of development and defining the more appropriate public policies able to encourage the most desirable outcomes.

With respect to agricultural policies, Farrell and Capalbo expressed the opinion that price, income and other policies exerted strong effects on producers' choices and thereby on environmental quality. Consequently there was an obvious need to explicitly incorporate agricultural policy variables in models designed to explore the trade-offs between productivity and environmental quality.

Participants in the discussion included J. Berthelot, F. de Casa Bianca, T. Dams, V. Iakimets, E. K. Ireri, A. Kahan, E. Rabinowicz, P. Söderbaum and G. Weinschenk.

CSABA CSÁKI

Land Utilisation and Agricultural Development:
The Case of Hungary

INTRODUCTION

Agriculture has traditionally played an important role in the Hungarian national economy. Hungary's primary national resource is her arable land. The relatively high growth of agricultural production and the introduction of new intensive technologies have combined in recent years with increasing signs of environmental damage. Not surprisingly, study of land use options and analysis of future potentials in agriculture have become crucial tasks of national planning.

Two recently completed research projects analysed ecological and biological potentials of production growth in agriculture up to the year of 2000.[1] These two nationwide projects offered an excellent framework for further investigations in which the economic, technical, ecological and environmental elements of land utilisation were considered equally. The first results of these investigations are presented in this paper. The study was sponsored by the Hungarian Ministry of Industry and by the Hungarian Academy of Sciences and has been carried on in co-operation with the Food and Agriculture Program of the International Institute for Applied Systems Analysis[2] (IIASA, Laxenburg, Austria). The centres of actual work are the K. Marx University of Economics, the Bureau for Systems Analysis and the Institute of Soil Sciences in Budapest. The work has been conducted by an interdisciplinary team of researchers including Z. Harnos, K. Rajkai, I. Válvi and the author of this paper as major contributors, as well as C. Forgács, A. Pusztai, G. Módos, M. Sebestyén and F. Tóth.

LAND RESOURCES IN HUNGARY AND OBJECTIVES OF THE STUDY

The area of Hungary is 9,303.6 thousand hectares, with the following land use structure in 1980 (in thousand hectares):

ploughland	4734.7
meadows and pastures	1294.2
vineyards, orchards	306.2

299

gardens	291.4
forests	1610.3
other (settlements, infrastructure	
etc.)	1066.8

On the whole, 72.3 per cent of the territory of Hungary is utilised by agricultural production. The fertility of the soils in Hungary can be characterised as follows:

- 27.2 per cent of the arable area is high fertility tchernozem-type soil with rich humus content and good water- and nutrient-holding capacity;
- 30 per cent is represented by brown forest soils, which are often subject to acidification with unfavourable nutrient budget and physical characteristics. These soils are generally of good or fair fertility;
- 23 per cent is represented by meadow and alluvial soils with medium nutrient and humus content and good or fair productivity;
- The rest is in general of low fertility.

These soils provide relatively favourable conditions for high level crop production in Hungary. These endowments may, however, change in time, since soil is a conditionally renewable natural resource. Agricultural use has already impacted upon soil fertility unfavourably. High rates of fertilizer application have been accompanied by increasing rates of soil acidification. About one-third of Hungary's arable area, namely the hilly areas with strong relief, are endangered by erosion. On 25 per cent of the arable area characterised by sandy and silty soils of light mechanical composition, deflation (or wind-borne erosion) appears with its damage. Salinisation occurs on a significant part of the Great Hungarian Plain.

As the above discussion indicates, the future of soil conditions is controversial. On one hand, we can establish that soils with high fertility have a favourable share so far while on the other hand it appears that more than half the arable area has already been endangered by detrimental processes which decrease fertility. We also have to reckon with the ambitious plans envisaging substantial increases in agricultural production. This, in general, means the intensification of technologies, eventually contributing to the aggravation of undesirable processes. There is no question that in this situation realistic long-term planning requires investigating the long-term environmental consequences of attaining the targeted agricultural growth levels and this cannot be done without studying the environmental limits of agricultural production potentials.

The question can be raised of whether we should continue to introduce technologies which cause an increasing environmental damage and whether the overall objectives and the technological technical tendencies of production development should be decided merely according to short-run consideration of economic efficiency. The detailed objectives of our study were set along the line of these problems. The following questions were investigated as the major objectives of the study:

– What are the production potentials of the existing soil resources, and how can these be increased and utilised?
– What are the long-term impacts of continuing present practice in plant cultivation upon soil quality?
– Can productivity and efficiency be increased with rational combinations of existing technological alternatives?
– What are the economic consequences of an environmental protection-oriented agricultural development?
– Will increasing the level of environmental protection limit the growth of agricultural production?
– How efficiently are existing biological resources being used?
– How efficient is energy transformation in Hungarian agriculture?

The study is focused on plant production which is the area of primary utilisation of land potential. Producing regions (soil types) were treated as the basic units of investigation. The region is the framework within which the major technical, technological and physical processes were studied. The coverage of the study can be characterised as follows:

– The territory of Hungary has been divided into 35 agro-ecological regions whose climatic characteristics make them homogeneous units.
– From the point of view of soil fertility, 31 soil types were identified.
– Their distribution within the regions led to a division of 205 habitat types.
– The study was related only to plant production. 12 major field crops have been considered (wheat, barley, rye, rice, corn, sugar beet, potatoes, sunflowers, soybeans, peas, alfalfa, red clover).
– Agricultural technology has been represented by the types of major machines, the level of fertilisation and manure application as well as by the level of irrigation.

METHODOLOGY OF THE STUDY

The study analyses the processes of production, land use and technological change which will be required for a long-term period, i.e. about 20–25 years. Therefore a feasible model system was elaborated on two levels in order to describe the major physical, biological, agrotechnical and economic processes of Hungarian agriculture.

Using the experience gained from agricultural and ecological modelling work previously conducted in socialist countries, and the results of IIASA's methodological research on the centrally planned food and agriculture systems, as well as on the assessment of the long-range consequences of technological development in agriculture, we adopted a relatively new methodology for our study. The main goal of the model is not merely optimisation, but to provide a tool for a detailed, many-sided, dynamic investigation of the consequences and limits of technological development in agriculture. On the whole, the structure has a descriptive character. Use of the model might also allow for the calculation of optimal states of some of the subsystems. The overall methodology used by the model system is a simulation technique. The time horizon of the analysis is 20–30 years. The model system consists of two submodels:

The Plant Soil Model is used to describe the major plant-soil-agrotechnology relationships.
The Plant Production Model is designed to integrate soil and crop specific subsystems into a national plant production system and to draw conclusions on the national level upon optimal resource allocation in land use and development.

Plant-Soil Model
In describing the relationships between the plant and its environment, we sought an answer to the following questions:

– How does plant production develop under given soil conditions and agricultural technologies?
– How does the habitat change as a consequence of the applied agricultural technology?

The separation of the questions is justified by the fact that agricultural technology and land quality affect the level of the output in the given

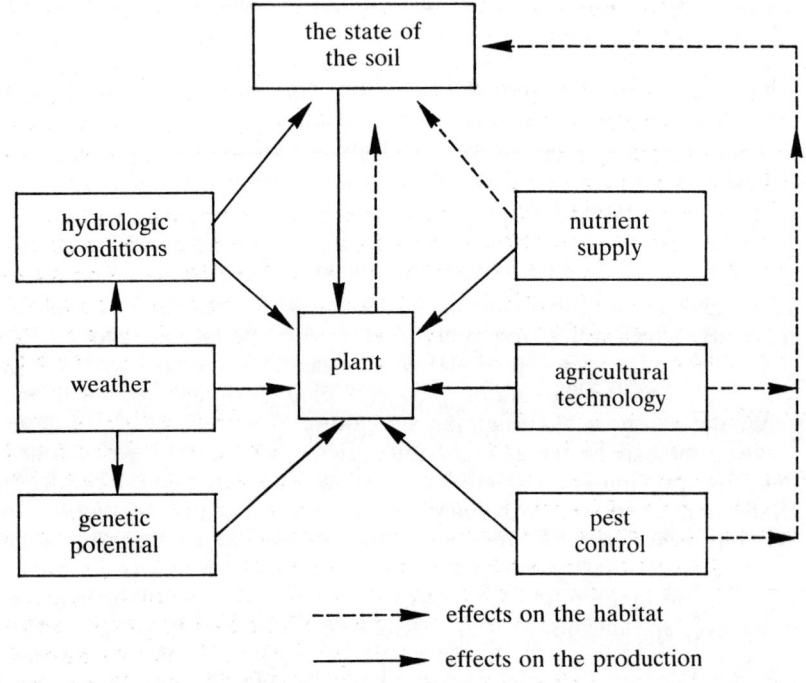

effects on the habitat

effects on the production

FIGURE. 1.   *Major inter-relationships of the Plant-Soil Model*

year, already, while the changes in the state of the habitat usually involve longer delays and extend to longer periods.

The Plant-Soil Model simulates the major inter-relationships among plant growth, soil conditions and agricultural technologies. Each run of the model is related to a given crop on a given soil type assuming the use of a given agrotechnology. The main relationship considered in the Plant-Soil Model are shown in Figure 1 in a schematic way. It includes two major modules:
- generation of yield
- modelling of impacts upon habitat conditions.

The formation of the yield is given in our Plant-Soil Model as a function of:
- genetic potential,
- habitat conditions
- applied agricultural technology.

The second major block in the Plant-Soil Model is devoted to the description of the effects of plant cultivation upon soil characteristics. Among the rather complex soil-agrotechnology inter-relationships in our model, six major environmental effects of agricultural production are considered, which we represented by six indicators. Table 1 gives an overview of the environmental effects treated in the study. The data base for developing this model block included experimental data and the results of a field survey.

TABLE 1 *The environmental processes, their causes and indicators as represented in the model*

Environmental effects	Causes	Indicators
1. Erosion	relief	soil lars
2. Decrease of pH	non-calcareous sands	pH ranges
3. Secondary salinization	potentially salinisable territory	critical ground water level
4. Degradation of soil structure	application of heavy machinery under unfavourable climatic conditions	bulk density
5. Decrease or overload of soil nutrient level (NPK)	deviation from the nutrient balance in the application of chemical fertilizers	soil nutrient balance
	insufficient or no application of manure	organic matter content

National Plant Production Model
The second submodel of the model-system describes the national plant production system. The results of the Plant-Soil Model are used as inputs for setting the variables in the Plant Production Model. This model is focused on the dynamic inter-relations between the state and transition of production and habitat on the national level.

The National Plant Production Model is actually a large-scale linear optimization model formulated in the form of a linear control problem. The output of the model is the product mix of plant production in a given period of time computed on the basis of sowing structure and yields.

POTENTIALS AND LIMITS IN THE USE OF HUNGARIAN LAND RESOURCES

The study was focused on the questions listed in the first section. A large number of calculations have been completed both by using the whole model system and its two major components and the calculations have not yet been completed. The detailed discussion of the results already available exceeds the scope of this study.[3] Here we present only the main conclusions according to overall production potentials, the impacts of a rational crop allocation plan and of amelioration and environmental limits upon further growth.

Our calculations resulted in a finding that Hungarian ecological potentials permit a 40 to 50 per cent higher output in plant production than was attained in the late 1970s. The actual utilisation of these potentials, however, depends on a number of different economic conditions as follows:

- the choice of an ecologically based sowing structure;
- the conservation of soil productivity by applying ameliorative agricultural technologies and additional ameliorative investments;
- the expansion of the share of the irrigated areas;
- the ensuring of a sufficient nutrient supply;
- the spreading of new agricultural technologies.

According to currently accepted conceptions a 50 per cent overall increase in plant production is envisaged. The growth potential is, however, not the same for each crop. In some areas no growth in planned because the aim is only to meet domestic demand, which has already been reached. There are other commodities, such as protein feeds, where output may multiply relative to the present level. The greatest increase in volume is expected in grain production. A yearly 19 to 20 million tons of total production seems to be a realistic target around the turn of the millenary.

The impacts of sowing structure optimally suited to ecological conditions upon production potentials have also been investigated. According to the computations through a more rational allocation of crops the productivity of plant production can be boosted by 10 to 15 per cent and the risk of production due to random weather fluctuations can be substantially decreased. The extent of the risk due to the variability of weather in the case of the optimal sowing structure is according to the calculations (in percentages): cereals 5–7, maize 10–15, sugar beet 13–18, sunflower 10–20, alfalfa 21–23. These figures are substantially lower than those experienced up to the present.

The effects of amelioration have been investigated according to three criteria:

1 the relationship between amelioration and sowing structure,
2 the relationships between the extent of amelioration and total production,
3 the time order of amelioration interventions at different locations.

As amelioration does not bring fundamental changes in the natural conditions of the habitat, the volume of ameliorative investments have no significant impacts on the optimal sowing structure. However, they have a major influence on the upper level of production potentials. In the case of maximal ameliorative efforts a production surplus of 10 per cent can be achieved relative to the analogous variant without amelioration. This increase in terms of grain production in Hungary corresponds to more than 3 million tons yearly. The total amount of resources that can be devoted to ameliorative investments was set to different levels, and on this basis the individual investments were selected by the model according to their efficiency.

The impacts of postponing ameliorative investments upon production potentials have also been projected. Without any further amelioration the reduction of realistic potentials will be equivalent to at least 1 million m.t. of grain by the year 2000. It is worth pointing out that, according to the calculations, it seems to be more expedient to carry out ameliorative interventions in areas of higher base productivity than in those of lower productivity.

Concerning the nutrient supply two questions have been investigated so far:

– What is the role of the of different nutrient sources in the total nutrient supply?
– How are the sowing structure and product mix related to nutrient input quantities and what is the impact of reducing nutrient supply upon production potentials?

In the study, nutrients for the crops have been considered from the following sources: chemical fertilizers, manure, plant residues, N-fixation by phaseolus crops, precipitation supply of phosphorus and potassium. According to our calculations, the desired share of the individual sources is as follows:

	fertilizers	manure	residues	N-fixation	air
Nitrogen	66%	9%	13%	5%	7%
Phosphorus	74%	11%	15%	–	–
Potassium	69%	12%	27%	–	–

Based on these figures one is led to three main conclusions:
(1) Sources other than chemical fertilizers should play a significant and

increasing role, with their share ranging between 26 and 34 per cent depending on the type of nutrient.

(2) The application of manure not only conserves chemical fertilizers, but also increases the organic matter content of the soil, thus affecting the soil's structure, water-holding capacity etc., moderating acidification processes and contributing in a large extent to the supply of the soil with micro elements.

(3) In planning the nutrient balance, consideration of other materials besides chemical fertilizers, constitutes a part of environmentally beneficial agrotechnologies, by reducing such processes as nutrient leaching and nitrification of subsurface and surface waters (eutrophication).

Several model runs have been made in order to investigate the effects of reducing fertilizer supply. The reduction of N-fertilization by 15 per cent reduces the demand for phosphorus and potassium fertilizers by 10 to 15 per cent. Among the conditions of today's technologies the decrease of fertilizer application (not surprisingly) leads to a very substantial drop of production potentials. The decrease of production potentials in the extreme case amounts to about 3 million m.t. of grain equivalent. The increase of the share of phaseolus crops in the overall sowing structure can be observed in this case, with the wheat to corn ratio significantly modified in favour of wheat. In the runs without limitation on N-fertilizer inputs this ratio was 40:60, while it was 52:48 in a fertilizer constrained variant. The impacts of soil conditions upon the utilisation of genetic potentials have been investigated on a soil-plant-technology basis by using the Plant-Soil Model component of our system. These investigations have not yet been finished.

NOTES

[1]For details see Csáki, Harnos and Láng (1984); Csete, Harnos and Láng (1981); Láng, Harnos, Nagy and Valyi (1985).
[2]The study has been considered at IIASA as one of the country case studies upon long-range environmental impacts of agricultural development, see: Caśki et al., (1985).
[3]Some of the results are presented in details in Csáki et al. (1985).

REFERENCES

Csáki, C., Harnós, Z. and Láng, I., *Agricultural Development and Ecological Potential: The Case of Hungary*, Kieler Wissenschaftsverlag Vauk, 1984.
Csáki, C., Harnós, Z., Rajkai, K. and Vályi, I., *Development Potentials and Environment in Hungarian Agriculture*, (unpublished manuscript) Budapest, 1985.
Cseté, L., Harnós, Z. and Láng, I., 'Measuring the Agroecological Potential of Hungary and its Expected Trends up to 2000', Third Congress of the European Association of Agricultural Economists, Belgrade, 1981.
Láng, I., Harnós, Z., Nagy, A. and Vályi, I., 'The Biopotential of Hungary', *International Agrophysics*, 1985.

RANDALL A. KRAMER

An International Overview of Soil Conservation Policy

There is a growing recognition that soil erosion is a serious problem in many parts of the world. Although erosion has always been a byproduct of human cultivation of the earth, many observers argue that erosion has increased considerably this century because of changes in production practices and the large increase in ploughed acreage in some parts of the world (Brown and Wolf 1984; Dregne 1982). As shown in Table 1, there were substantial increases in cropland from 1960–80 in South America, sub-Saharan Africa, and Southeast Asia. Converting forests to cropland can increase erosion rates by 5 to 100 times the natural uncultivated rates (Wolman 1983).

TABLE 1   *Cropland in selected regions of the world*

	North America	South America	Western Europe	USSR	sub-Sah. Africa	South Asia	SE Asia	China	World
			Million hectares						
1960	256	87	94	221	124	192	53	103	1,320
1980	280	126	87	232	156	211	72	99	1,452
% change	9.4	44.8	−7.4	5.0	25.8	9.9	35.8.	−3.8	1.0

Source: Urban and Vollrath 1984.

The extent of the world erosion problem is difficult to assess because few nations have systematically surveyed the condition of their soil resources. In the US, where millions of dollars have been spent in recent years to inventory soil resources, 40 per cent of the cropland is estimated to be eroding at an excessive rate (greater than 5 tons per acre annually). The erosion is concentrated on a small proportion of cropland; nearly 70 per cent of the erosion in excess of 5 tons per acre annually occurs on 8.6 per cent of the cropland (Batie 1983). In India, about 60 per cent of the cropland is eroding excessively. The Worldwatch Institute, working with rather limited data, concludes that the world-wide annual loss of soil in excess of new soil formation is approximately 25 billion tons with half of that occurring in India, the US, China and the Soviet Union (Brown and Wolf 1984). The highest erosion rates over large areas are found in Asia (Wolman 1983).

307

Soil erosion over time can lead to lower and more variable food production. It is estimated that erosion and other factors associated with continuous cultivation have resulted in fertility losses as high as 40 per cent in some parts of the Soviet Union and 25 per cent in portions of the US. A simulation study comparing eroded and uneroded soils used for corn production in Haiti found that yields were 30 per cent lower on the eroded soils and the *variance* of yield was 4 times greater (Wolman 1983).

If left unchecked, soil erosion can lead to desertification, which is referred to as soil degradation. The east coast of the Mediterranean is a historical example (Hudson 1985). Several thousands of years ago, large quantities of timber were exported from what is now Syria and Lebanon. Erosion has changed much of the area to barren slopes where only goats can survive. Degradation has occurred in many other parts of the world (Dregne 1982). In Africa, severe degradation of rangeland, due in part to extended droughts, has occurred north of the equator and has contributed to falling food production. Historically, agricultural output has been hindered by degradation in Southwest Asia and more recently in Southeast Asia. Overgrazing and erosion have contributed to desertification of a large portion of the Australian rangeland. In Europe, there has been a reversal of desertification in some countries due to reforestation, but severe erosion persists in parts of Greece, Italy and Spain. The worst degradation problems in South America are found in the Andes Mountains (Dregne 1982).

Considering the extent of erosion problems, there has been surprisingly little governmental effort to encourage soil conservation. Although there are some notable exceptions, many countries have assigned a low priority to soil conservation. The purposes of this paper are to discuss economic reasons for excessive erosion, to describe alternative policy tools for encouraging conservation, and to provide an overview of existing policies in various countries. Finally, factors which may limit the expansion of soil conservation programmes will be delineated.

THE ECONOMICS OF SOIL CONSERVATION

Why do farmers allow their soil to erode? Conservation measures require the use of scarce funds. Unless farmers perceive a direct benefit from conservation expenditure, they will generally not choose to invest in conservation practices. The primary benefit to farmers from soil conservation is the maintenance of future productivity. A farmer may not realise that his soil's productivity is diminishing because the decline is slow and is masked by other inputs such as fertilizers. Education can be an effective remedy in such cases. On the other hand, a farmer may realise he is losing productivity, but because of scarce funds, cannot afford to practise soil conservation. Government subsidies can help in this case.

The most difficult problem to attack from a policy point of view is when conservation does not earn sufficient economic returns to justify the cost. In such a case, society may decide to intervene in order to maintain a safe minimum of soil resources for future food production needs. Additional justification for intervention may arise from off-farm damages including water pollution and sedimentation of navigation channels and hydro-electric reservoirs.

Some argue that the concern about soil erosion is exaggerated because future technological advances will reduce the importance of the soil resource in producing food. However, given the expected increases in demand from expanding populations and the uncertainty of the timing, extent and cost of technological advancements, such a cavalier approach to soil erosion is risky.

Although farmers in a market economy may find conservation to be unprofitable, it is not clear that soil conservation will be any more attractive to decision-makers in non-market economies. The manager of a collective farm who is faced with production quotas will be unlikely to voluntarily use conservation practices which reduce output (Brown and Wolf 1984).

Soil conservation practices include changes in production practices, as well as structural measures. Changes in production practices include minimum tillage, crop rotation and fallowing. A major portion of the cost of these practices is the opportunity cost of giving up the more erosive and presumably more profitable (in the short run) existing production practices. For example, the shifting cultivation techniques of the native population in Central and South Amercia are giving way to large-scale clearing for the more profitable and more erosive production of crops such as maize, coffee and tobacco. A return to shifting cultivation might reduce erosion but would also result in an income loss.

Structural measures such as terraces may not alter production practices very much but do require large amounts of labour and capital to construct. They are, however, very effective soil conservation measures. Probably the most extensive construction of terraces is in China. Terraces have been constructed for hundreds of years, particularly along the heavily silted Yellow River. Terrace construction has increased significantly in China in recent years (Hudson 1985).

In some cases, land is so erosive that the only realistic erosion control measure is to take it out of agricultural production and plant it in trees. Because timber production is often less profitable than agricultural production, landowners are unlikely to take this step without governmental involvement. Cropland in Europe has declined (see Table 1) because of reforestation efforts. Between 1950 and 1980 2.3 million hectares in Italy and 1.5 million hectares in France were taken out of agriculture due to reforestation policy (Urban and Vollrath 1984).

ALTERNATIVE SOIL CONSERVATION POLICIES

Government policies to encourage soil conservation can take many forms. Three major types are: (1) research and education, (2) economic incentives, and (3) regulation. Examples of each of these are discussed below.

Government-supported research and education can develop less erosive production practices and encourage their adoption through demonstrations and technical assistance. For example, minimum tillage has been widely adopted in the US, in part because of efforts of publicly supported universities and the extension service. Education is also important for developing a cadre of soil conservation workers with the technical training necessary to implement conservation programmes. In several African countries, a major constraint to achieving soil conservation goals appears to be an extreme shortage of trained conservation manpower. For example, Botswana attempted in the 1960s to reduce rangeland erosion but gave up because of lack of staff (Stocking 1985).

Because in many cases soil conservation does not provide sufficient return to justify private investments (at least in the short run), farmers may not voluntarily make conservation investments unless provided economic incentives by the government. These incentives may take the form of cost-share subsidies, low interest loans or reduced taxes.

Cost-sharing has seen its widest application in the US. Most cost-sharing has occurred under the Agricultural Conservation Program which has paid out more than $8 billion since 1936. A drawback to this approach is that politics can result in a widespread distribution of programme benefits with little regard to geographical differences in erosion rates. For example, over half of the US cost-shared practices have been applied to land without serious erosion problems (Easter and Cotner 1982). To correct this, there is a move in the US toward targeting the funds to areas with the worst problems.

Cost-share programmes can take a variety of forms. A Nigerian programme shared the cost of constructing hand-built terraces between farmers and the government. Participating farmers contributed one day of work per week as their share and were paid wages by the government for the rest of the week. It is reported that farmer acceptance of this project was better than for other projects carried out entirely by the government without farmer involvement (Jones 1977).

In those countries with an income tax for farmers, tax reductions can be used to provide incentives for the use of conservation practices. In Canada, which does not now provide conservation incentives, a recent legislative study recommended the use of tax credits (Senate of Canada 1984). However, a distributive aspect of this approach, which may make it politically unpopular, is that it will provide greater assistance to higher income farmers.

Regulation is another alternative for public intervention. Erosive practices or the cultivation of highly erosive land can be banned. In the Caribbean, a common management practice in sugarcane production is to burn the crop prior to harvest. This leaves the soil susceptible to erosion for several months. This practice was declared illegal in Barbados after erosion was observed to reduce sugarcane yields by about 4 tons per hectare (Ahmad 1977). A more politically acceptable form of regulation, commonly referred to as cross-compliance, is to require the use of conservation practices as a precondition for obtaining various government benefits. Although not yet implemented, public support for this approach is growing in the US.

FACTORS WHICH MAY LIMIT EXPANSION OF SOIL CONSERVATION POLICY

In 1981 the FAO adopted a World Soil Charter which called for conservation of the world's land resources for future generations. Governments were asked to implement research and education programmes in soil and water conservation and to create favourable economic and institutional conditions including 'providing security of land tenure and adequate financial incentives (e.g., subsidies, taxation relief, credit) to the land user' (Kelley 1983).

There are a number of forces which may discourage an effective implementation of the World Soil Charter. Because erosion is a long run problem, soil conservation programmes have difficulty competing for limited public resources. Governments tend to be most responsive to short-run problems and are reluctant (like farmers) to make investments whose pay-off may be far into the future. Furthermore, land pressure from growing populations may override any measures which could decrease food production in the short run.

Institutional constraints can also hinder government conservation policy. Although some components of soil and water conservation services exist in many developing countries, they are sometimes located in different departments of a ministry or even in more than one ministry. Co-ordination and co-operation between agencies is frequently non-existent. Thus, reorganisation of agencies or creation of a new agency may be required for effective conservation programmes.

Another factor hindering soil conservation efforts in some countries is the stigma of it having been promoted by colonial governments. In some previously colonised countries, soil conservation policy has been de-emphasised since independence. Under colonial governments, African farmers were frequently forced by law to engage in conservation practices (Stocking 1985). Technical assistance and needed machinery was paid for out of an unpopular 'Native Maize Pool' which was funded by paying a price below market price to African maize farmers. In contrast, it was common for farmers of European origin to receive conservation subsidies and free technical assistance. Although considerable progress was made in soil conservation in many African countries, it is not surprising that there has been a backlash against conservation because of its association with colonial regimes. After independence, peasants expected to be left alone to do what they wished with the land. For example, the ruling party in Tanzania denounced soil conservation as a part of colonial repression; conservation institutions in Kenya and Zambia were dismantled after independence.

Land tenure arrangements can affect the success of soil conservation efforts. Farmers who share-crop or who farm land to which they do not hold a clear title will be reluctant to invest in soil conservation. Furthermore, if the flatter and more fertile land is concentrated among a few owners, this may cause overuse of the more marginal land by the majority of farmers. This implies that in some cases land reform may be a necessary component of a successful soil conservation programme. To the extent that current landowners hold political power, they can be expected to strongly oppose conservation policies linked to land reform (Blaikie 1983).

CONCLUSION

Soil erosion is not the imminent threat to mankind that some doomsday prognosticators would claim, but in many parts of the world it is causing irreparable losses in productivity as well as substantial off-site damages. Although there is a growing recognition of erosion problems, there has been relatively little policy response. As Wolman concludes: 'Unfortunately, roughly 50 years of conservation science and demonstration have not alone convinced farmers throughout the world of the wisdom of adopting conservation practices, even where appropriate practices are known ... much more attention needs to be given to the economic and social incentives and disincentives which influence farmers' decisions to use or, more often, not to use known techniques of conservation management' (1983, p. 16).

REFERENCES

Ahmad, N., 'Erosion Hazard and Farming Systems in the Caribbean Countries', in Greenland, D. J. and Lal, R. (eds), *Soil Conservation and Management in the Humid Tropics*, John Wiley, New York, 1977.

Batie, Sandra, S., *Soil Erosion: Crisis in America's Croplands*, The Conservation Foundation, Washington DC, 1983.

Blaikie, Piers, 'The Political Economy of Soil Erosion' in O'Riordan, Timothy and Turner, R. Kerry, (eds), *Progress in Resource Management and Environmental Planning*, vol. 4, John Wiley, New York, 1983.

Brown, Lester, R. and Wolf, Edward C., *Soil Erosion: Quiet Crisis in the World Economy*, Worldwatch Institute Paper no 60, September 1984.

Dregne, Harold E., *Impact of Land Degradation on Future World Food Production*, US Department of Agriculture, ERS-677, March 1982.

Easter, K. William and Cotner, Melvin L., 'Evaluation of Current Soil Conservation Strategies' in Halcrow, H. G., Heady, E. O. and Cotner, M. L., (eds), *Soil Conservation Policies, Institutions, and Incentives*, Soil Conservation Society of America, 1982.

Hudson, N. W., 'A World Review of the Development of Soil Conservation', *Agricultural History*, vol. 59, no. 2, 1985, pp. 326–39.

Jones, O., 'Training, Extension, and Implementation of Soil Conservation Programmers in Developing Countries', in *Soil Conservation and Management in Developing Countries*,

Food and Agriculture Organization of the United Nations, Rome, Soils Bulletin No. 33, 1977.

Kelley, Hubert, W., *Keeping the Land Alive: Soil Erosion – Its Causes and Cures*, Food and Agriculture Organization of the United Nations, Rome, Soils Bulletin no. 50, 1983.

Senate of Canada, Standing Committee on Agriculture, *Soils at Risk, Canada's Eroding Future*, June 1984.

Stocking, Michael, 'Soil Conservation Policy in Colonial Africa', *Agricultural History*, vol. 59, no. 2, 1985, pp. 326–339.

Urban, Francis and Vollrath, Thomas, *Patterns and Trends in World Agricultural Land Use*, US Department of Agriculture, Economic Research Service, Foreign Agric. Econ. Rep. 198, April 1984.

Wolman, M. Gordan, 'Soil Erosion and Crop Productivity: A World-Wide Perspective', paper presented at the Soil Erosion and Crop Productivity Symposium, Denver, Colorado, 1–3 March 1983.

DISCUSSION OPENING I – CARLOS ROMERO

My comments on the two papers presented in this session are organised in the following way. First, I will try to discuss some common aspects of both papers, trying to raise some general points. Second, I will pose some more specific points on each.

Until recently the profession has considered land as a non-destructible natural resource which produces a renewable services flow (i.e. land can produce utilities indefinitely). Within this conceptual framework the optimum management of this resource is based only on economic criteria of efficiency. We know nowadays that this kind of analysis is rather obsolete. Land is not completely a non-destructible resource and may produce utilities indefinitely only if it is managed correctly (the overview by Kramer shows this point). Furthermore the optimum management of land cannot be based only on economic criteria of efficiency but also ecological and environmental elements should be considered; and as Csáki shows in his paper, there is usually a conflict between economic criteria (e.g. short-term profits) and environmental objectives (e.g. soil erosion).

According to this framework the optimum management of land represents a problem where it is necessary to find a compromise among economical, ecological and environmental criteria. This conclusion leads me to some queries.

First, how can the market system, which considers land as a private property resource and maximisation of profits as the objective of the decision-maker, cope with problems such as the one analysed by Kramer?

Second, how can traditional planning techniques devised to optimise a single objective be adapted to the actual problem of land management under a multidimensional utility function with economical and environmental arguments, as is implicit in the model by Csáki?

Third, can the new multiple criteria decision-making techniques play an essential role in the management of land within the framework presented by Csáki and Kramer?

Csáki's paper

(1)   There is a lack of explanation of the methodology used in the paper. I understand the situation because of constraints of length and time, but some clarification on this matter would be welcome. According to the paper we only know that a simulation technique with a time horizon of 20–30 years has been used and that the national plant production model is a large-scale linear optimisation model formulated in the form of a linear control problem. Perhaps questions from the floor related to these matters could contribute to improve our understanding of the methodology used.

(2)   Professor Csáki is in clear favour of using manure as an important source of fertilisation. He gives good technical reasons in support. This claim perhaps deserves discussion, taking into account some possible negative effects of manure as: price, bulk, possibility of weed infestation, etc. Also in some kind of soils nitrate pollution problems have been shown in ground waters due to heavy manuring of soils.

(3)   Questions related to possible extensions of the model should be useful. For instance, I wonder if the structure of the model would allow us to obtain the trade-offs or opportunity costs among some negative environmental effects (e.g. erosion, salinisation, etc.) and some economic effects (e.g. yields, agricultural growth, etc.).

Kramer's paper

(1)   According to Kramer, farmers in market and non-market economies usually find soil conservation practices of little interest because they represent sacrifices in important objectives, such as profits or the achievement of production quotas. In this situation the role of political institutions is essential. But I wonder if politicians are nowadays aware of the importance of this matter and if there are significant differences in terms of practical support to the application of soil conservation policies between market and non-market systems.

(2)   Among the economic incentives for implementing soil conservation programmes, Kramer cites the use of low interest loans. In my view this measure could be difficult to implement in many cases because of the very low internal rate of return (IRR) of soil conservation investments. In fact, it would be necessary to fix the interest rates lower than the IRR, and this rate is extremely low, being even negative in some cases if private criteria of profitability are applied to assess an investment in soil conservation.

(3)   Kramer, in one of his final remarks, states that in some cases land reform measures may be a necessary component of successive soil conservation programmes. This claim allows me to connect with the beginning of my comments. Land is nowadays a strategic natural resource with a renewable services flow only under certain management conditions. A resource with these characteristics cannot be managed only

according to short-run interests of sometimes non-rational private ownership. Because of that, although in many countries land is a private-property resource, a certain kind of legal framework is necessary (perhaps, in some countries, within a land reform programme) to regulate its use according to certain social objectives (to provide adequate levels of employment, to restrict the degradation of soil fertility, etc.).

DISCUSSION OPENING II – CARSTEN THOROE

'We have not inherited the Earth from our fathers, we are borrowing it from our children.' This ethical statement, on which much of the discussion on future development and ecological questions is based, is a demand for a sustainable future. But what does sustainability mean? Some people equate sustainability with food sufficiency, others regard it primarily as an ecological question or focus their attention primarily on rural life conditions (Douglas 1984). Whatever belongs to agricultural sustainability it is certainly endangered by environmental damage. This has already been discussed in the plenary session this morning. Some kinds of this damage are presented in Csaba Csáki's paper. Others can be added, as mentioned in the paper of Farrell and Capalbo. But we should not only concentrate on environmental effects of agriculture production. Negative influences on agricultural sustainability also result from negative influences due to industrial production or private consumption.

In spite of intensified research efforts in recent years the connection between environmental damage, its causation and its consequences is, to a large extent, unknown. Therefore, efforts to model the manifold connections between environment and agricultural production, as in Csáki's paper, are very commendable although they cannot accomplish all the claims Farrell and Capalbo set up for a new generation of models. For me it is a hopeful example for multidisciplinary research. I do not want to go into the model in detail, but a few general problems of such modelling and of its use for policy decisions and planning should be discussed thoroughly:

(a) Formulating the aims. The most common aim in agricultural research in land use is maximising plant production, considering in a dynamic context the inter-relationship between agricultural production and soil fertility. This is an inadequate narrowing of the focus because it ignores the inter-relationship between agricultural production and other uses of land. Surplus production is a problem in many developed countries, not shortage (Baden 1984). With respect to environmental questions, for instance, not only those environmental effects which influence agricultural production potential are relevant but also agricultural effects on ecological targets. How misleading the results of models which neglect ecological targets may be for political policy purposes may become clear

in the field of ameliorative investment. Much effort has been put into adjusting farm layouts and geographical conditions to the requirements of modern agriculture with the effect of increasing homogeneity of landscape, declining diversity of species and so on. To put it bluntly, optimal agricultural conditions require uniformity, optimal ecological conditions require variety of natural resource conditions.

(b) Regarding maximum plant production in a dynamic context needs the definition of potential agricultural production over time. For this Csáki combines a plant-soil model with a plant production model. This follows a very old tradition in agricultural science, as can be seen in the work of famous agricultural scientists of the eighteenth century, Arthur Young (1741–1820), Albrecht Thaer (1752–1828), or, empirically based by Carl von Wulffen (1785–1853) in his static law. We can·treat the problem of soil conservation and depletion utilising neoclassical capital theory (Clark and Furtan 1983); but how reliably can we define actual and future agricultural production potential? The lessons of history show that prediction, for example, on the basis of Wulffen's static law, is meaningless because of unforeseen progress in knowledge about optimal nutritional provision of plants. If we agree the hypothesis of turbulence in the world agricultural economy, how much confidence can we then have in empirical models, which inevitably have to be based on past developments? Long-term analysis has to take care of the openers of the system. Agreement can easily be reached that the use of natural resources and especially land use is not optimal, although we shall probably disagree about what we would regard as the optimum.

Current environmental problems are not primarily caused by irresponsible individual behaviour by property owners. To me they are caused by a problem of insufficient knowledge, information and institutional arrangements. And they reflect changing social values. A good example of this is ameliorative investments and their negative effects on ecological systems. These investments are a result of planning in centrally planned economies, and in market economies they have been organised and assisted to a more or less extent by public policy.

In market economies individual self-interest is the main mechanism directing the development and use of productive resources. Lessons of history show that this mechanism has been quite efficient for preventing problems of depleting renewable natural resources, if the constitutional framework allows for private appropriation of the earnings of private resource conservation. But this mechanism can only work in a socially satisfying manner, if externalities are as low as possible. As in other fields of environmental policy, externalities in land use, positive as well as negative, should be internalised where possible, either by means of efficient institutions, including changing liability and property rights, or by means of subsidising and taxation (Runge 1984).

No plausibility can be given to the argument that it would be in the interest of individuals to destroy renewable natural resources instead of caring for them. There is only little empirical evidence for the argument that private time preference is less than social, if politicians are regarded as representing social preferences. The process of political decision-making shows much short-term crisis management rather than meeting long-run problems.

REFERENCES

Baden, J., (ed.), *The Vanishing Farmland Crisis. Critical Views of the Movement to Preserve Agricultural Land*, University Press of Kansas, 1984.
Clark, J. S. and Furtan, W. H., 'An Economic Model of Soil Conservation/Depletion', *Journal of Environmental Economics and Management*, vol. 10, 1983, pp. 356–70.
Douglas, G. K., (ed.), *Agricultural Sustainability in a Changing World Order*, (Westview Special Studies in Agriculture Science and Policy) Westview Press, Boulder, Colorado, 1984.
Runge, C. F., 'Strategic Interdependence in Models of Property Rights', *American Journal of Agricultural Economics*, vol. 66, 1984, pp. 807–13.

GENERAL DISCUSSION – RAPPORTEUR: GERT GÖRANSSON

One contributor from the floor said that many industrial countries had a fringe on the Mediterranean where the problem was not intensifying but abandoning land because it was no longer competitive. This land had therefore been covered by natural vegetation, very sensitive to fire, with subsequent consequences of erosion. The result was huge costs for fighting fire. Two errors were often made in coping with this situation. First, the role of animal breeding was in general considered as negative; but goats were useful in preventing fire. Second, forest was generally taken as an alternative and conifers were planted; but this was not a good solution because it did not prevent fire at all.

Another speaker said that in France they were just trying to cure the symptoms not the disease, because the problems were the social situation which was causing a bad relationship between man and nature.

Another participant stated that an analysis of the interval rate of return must be superior to the interest rate of the loans. This was a purely financial approach to the problem while a wider, long-term cost-benefit analysis would be more appropriate. He considered that the social benefits for humanity deriving from soil conservation policies would be very difficult to compute in quantitative terms.

In reply, Carlos Romero said that he thought that the colleague raising the question relating to the relationship between interest rates and interval rates of return had misunderstood him. He was, in fact, not speaking in a normative way. He had just wanted to say that if only the private criterion on profitability were used then the policy would fail because interval rate of return was lower than the interest rate. He agreed that cost–benefit analysis should be used in a global soil conservation policy evaluation.

Csaba Csábi said that he had two general comments to make in reply to the questions:

(1) Environmental problems were a new challenge to agricultural economists, both for our theory and our methods.

(2) About the methods, there were a number of difficulties when using models. Land use was a difficult problem not only for economists but also for soil scientists. But the politicians needed help, so he hoped there would be more approaches.

He went on to say that he could not describe the details of the model here because of the short time for the presentation. With regard to manure, he was not a soil scientist but in Hungary it was believed that manure was as good as described in the model.

Randall Kramer replied that multi-attribute utility functions were mentioned as applicable to analysis of soil conservation decisions. Such an approach might be helpful in understanding soil conservation decisions made by farmers because in some cases conservation investments were made which were unprofitable even in the long run. Such investments might result from a land stewardship ethic, concerns about the environment, or a desire to pass farms on to heirs in as good a shape as possible.

Several comments had been made about interval rates of return (IRR) to conservation investments, and he agreed that if the IRR were very low or negative, low interest loans, or any other economic incentive provided by the government, might not be sufficient to encourage conservation. The IRR calculations made by a farmer would ignore environmental costs. If IRR analysis were conducted for policy purposes then such costs should be included.

In response to the question about any significant differences between soil conservation efforts in market compared with centrally planned economies, he felt that this was difficult to assess. There was more information in the literature about efforts in market economies, but there were reports of some successful conservation programmes in centrally planned countries as well. With the limited and mostly anecdotal information available, it would be unwise to attempt to determine which political and economic structure had fostered the greatest encouragement of soil conservation.

It was suggested that minimum tillage might hold considerable promise for promoting conservation because in some settings it was less costly than conventional tillage. In fact minimum tillage had been widely adopted in the U.S. However, it might not be the panacea that some had hoped because there was some evidence of environmental problems associated with it, including greater pesticide use and increased nitrogen infiltration of groundwater.

Participants in the discussion included F. de Casabianca, J-P. Berlan and G. P. Caponera.

DANIEL W. BROMLEY*

Natural Resources and Agricultural Development in the Tropics: Is Conflict Inevitable?

ON RESOURCE DEGRADATION

I suggest that there are three general classes of resource degradation in the tropics: the first arising from explicit policies to exploit natural resources (or resource-based agricultural commodities) for economic gain, and the latter two arising from more subtle policy choices. While the first category of degradation receives much of the attention of environmentalists, I will suggest that it is the latter two categories that may, in the long run, pose more serious threats to the natural resource base in the tropics.

INTENTIONAL DEGRADATION

The explicit policies that generate conflict between economic development and the natural resource base are those where intentional resource degradation is carried on by governments to promote the sale of tropical timber, minerals, fish, or other natural resources for purposes of export. Equally serious is the cultivation of certain agricultural crops that are important in export markets and the disregard for the environmental implications of those practices because of the critical need for the export income. The foreign exchange earnings are then used to import manufactures or heavy machinery with which to satisfy an industrial need, or fancy consumer goods to satisfy the wants of an urban élite that requires solicitude on the part of governments. The problem is one of an important macroeconomic demand for foreign exchange, the use of the natural resource and agricultural sectors to generate that foreign exchange and the unwillingness of the government to confront the interests of those engaged in resource destruction. This reticence on the part of government is often reinforced by a need to ensure that the foreign exchange requirements are met. After all, there are not only things to

*I am indebted to Bruce Larson and Abdel Moneim El Nageeb for assistance in preparing this paper.

import, but much foreign assistance consists of loans that must be repaid in hard currencies.

The colonial history of most tropical countries can be understood as a major contributing factor in this particular pattern of resource use. Their early economic development was one of an imposed structure with the explicit intent being to provide the colonising power with desired raw materials or agricultural products. With export-driven resource policies being the accepted norm, we cannot expect a rapid reorientation.

The most recent (1980) data for 24 tropical countries considered by the World Bank to be 'low income' reveal that, on average, the two most important export commodities in each of the countries accounted for 64 per cent of foreign exchange earnings. Of these 24 countries – 17 of which are in sub-Saharan Africa – coffee and cotton were the primary exports of 12, with 12 other commodities being first in the remaining 12 countries (rice, gas, textile fabrics, alcohol, copper, clothing, animals, tea, pearls, ores, fertilizers, and cocoa) (World Bank 1984b; United Nations 1983). Eleven of the 24 countries derived more than 50 per cent of their foreign exchange from only one commodity – five of them from the export of coffee, then one each from rice, cotton, animals, pearls, ores, and cocoa. These 24 low-income countries used, on average, 66 per cent of their foreign exchange earnings to import just two general classes of imports – manufactures, and machinery and transport equipment; only in three cases did the top two imports show up as something else – in one case it was food and in two cases it was fuels.

Turning to the 31 middle-income countries, a similar picture emerges. Here, these 31 countries derived almost 60 per cent of their total foreign exchange earnings from two primary commodities: nine of them had petroleum as the first export, while six had coffee as the first export. That is, 15 countries had only two commodities (petroleum and coffee) as the primary earner of foreign exchange. Only nine other commodities were the major export of these 31 countries (iron ore, copper, fruit, rice, fertilizers, sugar, chemicals, clothing, and cotton). Ten of these 31 countries had more than 50 per cent of their foreign exchange from only one commodity, of which petroleum was the dominant export in five countries, followed by ore, copper, sugar, chemicals, and coffee in the remaining five countries.

As with the 24 low-income countries, these 31 middle-income countries used, on average, 66 per cent of their foreign exchange earnings for the importation of machinery and transport equipment and for manufactures. In contrast to the low-income countries, the middle-income countries are more serious importers of fuels, with approximately 39 per cent showing fuels as either the first or second most important claimant on foreign exchange.

We have the familiar situation of these 55 low- and middle-income tropical countries relying on one or two commodities for the vast majority of their foreign income, and using the greater part of that foreign exchange to import manufactures or fuel.

The direct relationship between explicit government policy and natural resources can be illustrated with reference to gum arabic (*acacia senegal*) in the Sudan. The Sudan has historically accounted for approximately 80 per cent of the world's total production of gum; gum exports from the Sudan account for approximately 10 per cent of total foreign exchange earnings. These conditions render the Sudan vulnerable to swings in the demand for gum and in recent years the development of synthetics has posed a serious threat. But an equally serious threat arises from internal management of gum pricing by the state buying organisation, the Gum Arabic Company.

When prices are set too high there is an incentive to over-harvest gum by excessive tapping; this is compounded in times of drought when the trees are less hardy. Many of the gum trees are found on state lands with uncertain tenures and so these are particularly vulnerable to herders moving through. Conversely when prices are set too low, farmers will move into other crops and often cut down the gum trees for fuel or charcoal, and to make room for other crops.

The government can ill afford to lose even 10 per cent of its foreign exchange earnings; over the recent past the average annual rate of change in exports has been a minus 5 per cent, while imports have been growing at about 4 per cent per annum (World Bank 1984a). Recently, energy imports have required about 40 per cent of total export receipts. Hence gum arabic exports are essential and yet the gum sector is in disarray. A failure to manage this particular resource – rather insignificant on a global scale, yet of paramount importance to the Sudan – would bring added hardship to a country already suffering severe financial and environmental stresses.

This same story could be told about a number of other developing countries. For the non-oil exporting developing countries in Asia (excluding China), current-account deficits in 1984 averaged 4.1 per cent of the export of goods and services. Yet for similar countries in Latin America the percentage was 15.5, and in Africa it was 28.7 per cent (IMF 1984). A sample of 90 developing countries shows that between 1970 and 1983 the ratio of debt to GNP doubled (from 13.3 to 26.7 per cent), the ratio of debt to exports increased by 20 per cent (from 99.4 to 121.4), the debt service ratio (interest plus amortisation divided by the value of exports) increased from 13.5 to 20.7 per cent, and total debt outstanding increased almost tenfold (from $68.4 billion to $595.8 billion) (IMF 1984). For the period between 1965 and 1981, all developing countries taken together increased the value of their exports by a factor of 11 (in constant dollars). Over that same period the low-income Asian countries increased their exports by a factor of 7, while the low-income African group managed to increase the value of their exports by a factor of only 3.5 (World Bank 1984b).

The export structure of the developing countries is absolutely dominated by the natural resource sector either directly through minerals, timber, petroleum, or fish, or indirectly through the export of

agricultural crops whose future production depends upon the wise use of
land and water resources. We will return to this below.

UNINTENDED DEGRADATION

The second class of resource degradation arises from government
policies that may actually be formulated with resource protection in
mind. As new nation states emerged following the demise of colonial-
ism, governmental organisations were created reflecting those observed
in more industrialised societies. Ministries of agriculture were created,
often with a division of forestry or forest management. A few countries
elevated forestry or mining or fisheries to the full status of a ministry.
With these organisations in place it was not long until the myth of
management was given effect by the passage of laws and the development of administrative rules that redefined an individual's rights and
duties with respect to the forest, to minerals or to the fishery. A
number of countries passed laws that prohibited the cutting of firewood
or that outlawed certain fishing practices. This evolution of resource
management by proclamation created perverse incentives at the local
level where it suddenly became an act of honour to defy absurd
institutional arrangements – as well as a necessity for survival.

In Nepal the government in 1957 nationalised all forest lands that had
previously been under the management and control of the local village
(*panchayat*). The villagers were thus moved to get what they could from
these lands before the transition took place. Villagers who had
previously operated under a well defined set of rights and duties
vis-à-vis the forest suddenly found themselves with no rights and only
duties (Bromley and Chapagain 1984). The government of Nepal is now
attempting to restore those local-level management systems – really
institutional arrangements – in the hope of arresting continued resource
destruction.

Some would argue that contemporary resource degradation in the
Sahel is quite often the fault of government policies that divorce local
users from responsibility for conservation, while at the same time
creating negative incentives that discourage villagers from innovating
local-level institutional arrangements that might result in improved
resource-use practices (Thomson 1977). Forestry codes that outlaw
cutting of necessary fuel wood without accompanying programmes of
supply augmentation simply invite open defiance of the law and are,
over the long run, quite counterproductive. This long-run problem is
caused by an attitude of contempt for the national government, the
knowledge that certain individuals have bribed their way out of
difficulties, and the realisation that the national government has no plan
to deal with the very real resource shortages at the village level.

It is this myth of management at the national level and indifference or
contempt at the local level that poses a very serious threat to natural
resource integrity in the newly independent states in the tropics.

Turning from government-mandated institutional change, there are instances of government-promoted technological change in fisheries that resulted in the destruction of fish stocks and which set in motion social processes that destroyed long-standing institutional arrangements defining the fishing population with respect to the natural resource, as well as with respect to others also fishing (Cordell 1978). We find this problem particularly acute where governments have thought they were 'helping' a fishery by subsidising more powerful fishing boats and gear.

COMMERCIAL AGRICULTURE AND NATURAL RESOURCES

The final class of resource degradation arising from economic policies are directly related to agricultural development strategies. Specifically, I have in mind national policies directed toward self-sufficiency in certain food crops and the export of certain cash crops that may be grown under plantation conditions. While not openly directed toward resource extraction, this policy-level determination of land use imperatives often holds important implications for the structure of agriculture and hence its technological aspects. As part of this determination, we must be aware of the human implications of modern agriculture and its labour-absorptive capacity.

When agriculture cannot absorb increased population growth because of policy-induced mechanisation or because it is inherently capital intensive, then individuals become marginalised. Forced from the lowlands, they end up in the swelling urban slums of Manila, Calcutta, Bombay, Lagos, Abidjan, Nairobi, Jakarta or Bangkok, or, more critically for natural resources, in the uplands, on lands of decided inferior quality, or on fragile habitats that can ill afford more human pressure.

Recently published data from the Philippines indicate that (in 1970) approximately 30 per cent of the total population of the country resided in the uplands. This represented over 50 per cent of the total migrant population in the Philippines – the remainder having gone (apparently) to urban areas in the lowlands [Cruz 1984].

This marginalisation of people occurs in precisely those areas where institutional arrangements are the least developed regarding their ability to deal with this new resource pressure. That is, in the uplands resource use has traditionally been guided by custom and local-level institutional structures that were based upon an individual's membership in the group. When migrants invade the uplands, not only are indigenous institutions unable to adjust rapidly enough but, more importantly, they are not even appropriate for the new mix of resource users. Here we are talking about the derived resource destruction in the tropics that emanates from commercial agricultural policy that may seem quite removed from natural resource integrity. Of course part of this can be found in the heavy use of chemicals in agriculture; that too causes unintended problems for resource integrity. But an equally serious problem – and one that has not received much attention – is that associated with the marginalisation of people. In Indonesia we see it in the form of government-organised migration to the outer islands; in Latin America it takes the form of colonisation efforts in remote regions. While in other countries these practices may be less obvious, they are still present.

The serious threat for natural resources, as indicated above, is that the migrants bring with them an alien institutional structure for guiding resource use and these patterns of use may fit in quite badly in the new location. If they have the ability to impose their will on the original residents then serious problems can arise in terms of resource use. Even if they fit in with prevailing resource-use patterns, their numbers will be enough to pose a serious threat to the resource base.

THE ECONOMIC ISSUES

Agricultural development and resource degradation are serious problems over the long run because the poor tropical countries now lack the critical management skills in the biological and social sciences relevant to natural resource policy. More important, the major development-assistance agencies seem unwilling to help these countries obtain such skills. There seems to be a sustained drift away from investments in human resources; what investments do seem probable on the horizon are likely to be concentrated in the glamorous fields of biotechnology. The hard work of devising resource management schemes that are supportive of needy rural populations, yet protective of the long-term resource base, will be ignored. Science will proceed in search of the 'miracle technical fix' in agriculture and it will relegate to a secondary role the very real needs for innovative resource management.

The food problem in much of the developing world, coupled with conscious government policies to extract foreign exchange from the resource sector, will surely continue to cause severe pressure on the natural resources of the tropics. At the extensive margin the most serious problems are found in overgrazing, deforestation, the killing of wild animals, and the compression of slash-and-burn systems into shorter fallow cycles. As crop agriculture moves into new areas, habitat is destroyed and soil erosion can become serious. At the intensive margin the conflicts are likely to come from the increased use of chemicals in agriculture and from the homogenisation of the ecosystem to conform to the economic imperatives of modern commercial agriculture (Norgaard 1981). Continued reliance on chemical pest control will simply result in increasingly resistant pests; cotton pests in the Sudan are now much less controllable by chemical means and this situation is surely duplicated elsewhere. The plant geneticists are but a 'few steps ahead' of ever more creative enemies.

In the intermediate zones of agriculture – much of South Asia, and parts of Africa and Latin America – increased food production is coming not from increased yields but from an expansion of the cultivated area.

When this expansion moves agriculture into ever more fragile areas (and particularly steep slopes) the potential for resource degradation increases dramatically.

In regions where slash-and-burn agriculture is still practised, the encroachment of sedentary agriculture, coupled with local population growth, has brought a compression of the fallow period and a resulting serious loss of productivity.

Finally, at the extensive margin (parts of South Asia and North Africa) resource destruction is bound to continue into the foreseeable future and there seems to be little that can be done. In contrast to an 'urban' agriculture such as rice or even wheat, the nomadism of this part of the world makes public policy most difficult to implement. The very discipline of intensive agriculture lends itself to policy adjustments. By way of contrast, nomadism is much less amenable to policy implementation.

Economists concerned about agricultural development and natural resource problems in the tropics must bring to the enquiry a very clear understanding of colonial history; there are but four or five countries in all of Africa and Southeast Asia that were not colonised at one time. Agriculture and natural resource management are profoundly influenced by this history. At the local level, economic and social behaviour will have at least three guiding norms: (1) traditional; (2) colonial; and (3) newly independent nation state.

Under traditional norms, certain agricultural practices and also natural resource practices were proscribed by a variety of sanctions and taboos. Colonial administrations imposed markets and cash on many local areas and rendered local resources subject to exogenous prices and demand conditions. Now, newly independent nation states are attempting to impose yet a third layer of institutional arrangements on resource users. This 'institutional layering' is a situation where traditional and colonial institutions that favoured one particular use of resources in a particular manner are now confronted by new and exogenously imposed institutions that are the product of an emerging state. Independent agents are then faced with three overlapping but not coincident opportunity sets from which they will choose how to behave. In any society where enforcement of the rules is haphazard, it should not surprise us that problems arise when enforcement must deal with several institutional structures (Bromley 1985).

Economic policy will require much more attention to matters of compliance and enforcement; economists cannot assume compliance with the mandated rules precisely because there are several incongruent institutional structures (rules) that bear on the individual's relationship to natural resources, and to others who have traditionally used those resources. This matter of *institutional dissonance* presents a rich opportunity to economists concerned with natural resources in the developing world.

Economists will need also to reconsider their preoccupation with rather conventional benefit-cost analysis when addressing resource questions in the developing countries (Hufschmidt and Hyman 1982). I suggest that most economists, feeling good about the very notion of 'development', regard economic change in rather standard Paretian terms. That is, once we have conducted a benefit-cost analysis and found that the net present value of benefits from doing something is positive, then it seems safe to conclude, at least on 'efficiency' grounds, that it is good to proceed. This sanguine view of change overlooks a critical aspect of life 'out on the ground'.

Often overlooked by the optimistic notion of potential Pareto improvements is that there is some disagreement about whether agricultural producers are 'attracted to' change, or are rather 'forced into' change (Boserup 1966). This is relevant in the context of an individual producer attempting to decide about particular agricultural practices. If a farmer is less than confident that all the promises of some new approach will be realised – and many farmers in the developing world have ample empirical grounds for such caution – then change may not be undertaken until the costs of not changing become quite high. This is a subtle, yet important, distinction. That is, the benefits of change are here suggested to be often different than the costs of not changing.

As every good welfare economist knows, the promise of a Pareto improvement tends to confuse the *potential* for compensating those made less well off by the proposed change with *actual* compensation. Since actual compensation rarely, if ever, occurs, the losers from change may be excused their lack of enthusiasm. To be told not to worry, that net national income will go up even though you will be harmed, is scant solace to the losers.

But the real issues in natural resource policy in the developing world pertain to the rate of use of renewable resources and the nature of capital formation that attends the exhaustion of non-renewable resources. Much resource degradation is the result of harvesting rates that exceed the sustainable yield rate of renewable resources. If renewable resources are driven to exhaustion and if non-renewable resources are depleted without making constructive use of that capital for sustained development purposes into the future, then the tropical countries are clearly mortgaging their future. Natural resources are not only the literal frontier of most tropical countries but they are the institutional frontier as well. It is with respect to natural resources that the public policy process is most hampered by conceptual, biological, and political problems. In parts of the world the concept of time – so important in the concept of conservation – is not linear, as it is in the West, but is instead cyclical; try discounting the future in that view of time.

As economists, our contribution to these resource degradation problems will require a sense of purpose and commitment. We will often deal with politicians whose rate of time preference is exceedingly high. We will deal with biologists whose notion of 'wise use' may mean 'no use'. And we will deal with some economists who favour doing whatever is judged on Pareto grounds to be efficient. Our most lasting contributions, however, will be found in the way that we help policy-makers to understand: (1) the nature of the existing problem; (2) the feasible alternatives to solve that problem; and (3) some general sense of the winners and losers that will result from the possible solutions. The ability of many tropical countries to avoid ecological disaster may well depend on the nature of our involvement in that process.

REFERENCES

Boserup, E., *The Conditions of Agricultural Growth*, Aldine Press, Chicago, 1966.

Bromley, D. W., 'Resources and Economic Development: An Institutionalist Perspective', *Journal of Economic Issues*, vol. 19, no. 3, September 1985.

Bromley, D. W. and Chapagain, D. P., 'The Village Against the Center: Resource Depletion in South Asia', *American Journal of Agricultural Economics*, vol. 66, December 1984.

Cordell, J., 'Swamp Dwellers of Bahia', *Natural History*, June/July 1978.

Cruz, M. C., 'Population Pressure, Migration and Markets: Implications For Upland Development', University of the Philippines, Institute for Development Studies, Working Paper 84–05, 1984.

Hufschmidt, M. M. and Hyman, E. L. (eds), *Economic Approaches to Natural Resource and Environmental Quality Analysis*, Tycooly International, Dublin, 1982.

International Monetary Fund, *World Economic Outlook*, Washington, DC, September 1984.

Norgaard, R. B., 'Sociosystem and Ecosystem Coevolution in the Amazon', *Journal of Environmental Economics and Management*, vol. 8, September 1981.

Thomson, J. T., 'Ecological Deterioration: Local-Level Rule Making and Enforcement Problems in Niger' in Glantz, M. (ed.), *Desertification: Environmental Degradation in and Around Arid Lands*, Westview Press, Boulder, Colorado, 1977.

United Nations, *Statistical Yearbook*, New York, 1983.

World Bank, *World Development Indicators*, Washington, DC, 1984(a).

World Bank, *World Development Report*, Washington, DC. 1984(b).

NIK HASHIM MUSTAPHA*

Pressure on the Malaysian Fisheries Arising from Current Modernisation Programmes and Management Conditions

Fisheries resource constitutes a sizeable portion of food and nutritional needs of the Malaysian population. The resource also provides income and employment to fishermen and others involved in the industry. Because of its importance and common property nature fish supply is anticipated to be adversely affected. A number of factors contribute to this effect: (i) current and future trends in the domestic supply of and the demand for fish, (ii) the ecological condition affecting the living environment of the fisheries, and (iii) the effectiveness of maritime enforcement of its exclusive economic zone (EEZ) to prevent loss of fisheries. For instance, increased fish prices coupled with the improvement of technology can lead to increased production through intensification of fishing effort. The problem arises only if increased production acts to depress stocks as this is related to the future food supply, fishermen's income and employment. This paper attempts to investigate the supply side of the Malaysian fisheries, that is, to project levels of effort, catch and fish stocks as the result of allowing the fisheries to be managed under open-access and limited-entry policies.

General problems facing the Malaysian fisheries will be discussed and a specific problem related to the future management of the resource will be chosen for the analysis.

DEVELOPMENT AND MODERNISATION PROGRAMMES.

The development of the fishing industry has always been emphasised as the ultimate goal of the national fishery programme. This programme has two parts; (i) to upgrade the productivity of the small-scale capture; and (ii) to create mechanised large-scale offshore fishing operations.

Development programmes implemented by the government in recent years include mechanisation of small-scale fishermen, extension and training, and institutional improvement in pricing and marketing facilities. Attention and effort are given to developing the poverty-stricken fishing

*The author wishes to acknowledge the invaluable assistance and suggestions given by Prof. Walter R. Buctcher of the Department of Agricultural Economics, Washington State University.

328

areas. For instance, a subsidy scheme was launched for the construction of new fishing vessels, purchase of vessels' engines, improvement of existing vessels, replacement of gear, conversion of old to new fishing vessels and for the purchase of modern fishing equipment (Fisheries Division 1976). In addition, the Fisheries Division of the Ministry of Agriculture is responsible for providing training for fishermen (Third Malaysia Plan 1976–80, 1976). Modern and intensive fishing techniques, like trawlers, are encouraged.

Development efforts in the fishing industry have generally ignored overfishing and stock depletion problems that accompany the management of most fisheries.

Indications of overexploitation of the demersal and semi-pelagic species of the West Coast have been reported by several authors (Lawson 1974; Pathansali 1976; Yap 1977 and 1978). A recent study reported that the fishery situation in the East Coast area of Kelantan showed indication of overexploitation based on a low level of the Maximum Sustainable Yield (Azmi et al., 1981). This finding is contrary to the commonly held belief that an abundant supply of fish resource exists in this region because of a broader fishing jurisdication. Careful consideration of overfishing is therefore, relevant for a number of reasons: (1) Malaysian fisheries are open-access resources and hence will tend to be overfished if not subjected to stringent regulations; (2) government development programmes geared towards fishermen's economic wellbeing may inflict pressure on the resource use; and (3) development and modernisation efforts disregard the biological and optical economic management of the fisheries.

ENVIRONMENTAL CONDITIONS AFFECTING FISHERIES RESOURCE

Deteriorating environmental conditions affecting fisheries have been reported in several studies. For instance, in 1976 Jothy (in Ruddle 1982) reported the effect on industrial waste of fisheries which included the destruction of oyster beds from sawmills, boat yards and iron foundries. Rapid increase in oil palm production in past years added a significant number of oil palm refineries in the major producing areas. The discharge of their wastes into rivers and eventually the sea, polluted some of the Malaysian water resource systems.

The South China Sea has received increased attention in the oil industry's search based on its proximity to existing off-shore oil production. Oil production in Peninsular Malaysia began in 1974 with an initial production of 80,900 barrels per day. By 1979 the daily oil production had reached 282,000 barrels (Economic Report 1980). Since then increasing exploration activities were undertaken to discover new off-shore hydrocarbon fields along the East Coast of West Malaysia. The latest information reported that PETRONAS had discovered 52 gas and oil wells in its exploration activities between 1977 to 1982 (*Daily News*

15 January 1984). It is expected that extensive off-shore extraction and the construction of processing, storage and transportation facilities are likely to threaten vulnerable ecosystems which support the marine fisheries.

ENFORCEMENT OF THE MALAYSIAN EXLUSIVE ECONOMIC ZONE

Malaysia claimed her exclusive economic zone (EEZ) on 25 April 1980 which resulted in 200 nautical miles territorial gains of the South China Sea adjacent to the East Coast (Ibrahim 1982). Thus, the right of ownership to EEZ is defined for economic, administrative and political purposes. From the economic viewpoint this territorial gain has somehow affected the national fishery policy especially pertaining to policy and development of some 138,700 square miles within the EEZ. The immediate problem faced by Malaysia is to identify the EEZ's resource potential.

The Ministry of Agriculture reported that throughout 1982–3 a total of 73 foreign fishing vessels were caught violating Malaysian fishing grounds (*Daily News*, 17 June 1984). Such occurrences not only inflict losses on the Malaysian fisheries but also threaten the security of small fishermen. For security purposes enforcement is desirable.

ECONOMIC ANALYSIS OF THE MANAGEMENT PROBLEM

A comparative analysis of the Malaysian fisheries using 1969–81 data was undertaken to investigate resource use under the open-access, steady-state and the dynamic conditions. The analysis used several equations to simulate levels of fishing effort, catch, stock and economic rent. This section attempts to investigate what will happen to resource supply if fisheries are left to be managed under open access in comparison to the alternative limited-entry optimal management. Thus under these policy alternatives, food supply, income and employment of fishermen in general are discussed.

Analytical procedures
The following equations are used in the analysis of the Malaysian fisheries.

π_t	$= PQ_t - cE_t$	(economic rent equation)	(1)
$E_t^{\#}$	$= [(pk\,X_t^b)/c]^{1/1-a}$	(open-access equilibrium effort equation)	(2.1)
$E_t^{\bullet}$	$= [(pak\,X_t^b)/c]^{1/1-a}$	(steady-state optimal effort equation)	(2.2)
$E(t)$	$= [p-u(t+1)\,ak\,X(t)^b/c]^{1/1-a}$	(dynamic optimal effort equation)	(2.3)
Q_t	$= kE_t^a X_t^b$	(production/harvest function)	(3.0)
X_{t+1}	$= \Theta X_t - Q_t$	(stock-growth equation)	(4.0)

Where π_t is the economic rent in dollars in time t, Q_t is the total harvest in tons in time t, E_t is the total effort in vessels horsepower in time t, X_t is total stock of fish in tons in time t (the symbols #, ● and (t) are used to differentiate variables attributed to open-access equilibrium, steady-state and dynamic optimisations respectively), p is unit price of catch in $ per ton, c is unit cost of effort in $ per vessels' horsepower, u(t+1) is the scarcity rent value in $ of the *in situ* fisheries resource. a, b, and Θ are parameters of the estimated equations and k is a constant term of the production function.

Specifications of condition that must hold under open-access equilibrium, steady-state and dynamic optical limited entry are identified. Under the open-access fishing, effort will be expanded until the marginal cost of production equals average revenue of catch because an individual fisherman will compare his marginal cost with the average return of other fishermen in the industry. As long as fishermen expect average returns greater than cost of effort they will continue to increase fishing effort. If they do not fish, their shares will be captured by other fishermen. As effort expands to the open-access equilibrium, economic rent diminishes. The open-access condition becomes p = c/APPe, where c/APPe is the average cost of effort.

Management under the steady-state limited-entry optimization is assumed to maximise the economic rent. The government or its agency can be regarded as the controlling manager that aims at maximum profit from fishing undertakings. This analytical procedure yields the temporal limited entry condition as $p = c/(\partial Q_t/\partial E_t)$ where $c/(\partial Q_t/\partial E_t)$ is the marginal cost of effort. Unlike the static optimisation the dynamic limited-entry considers optimisation over time. The management objective is to maximise the present value of the economic rent subject to the stock-growth equation. Transforming into the Hamiltonian expression and using the discrete optimal control maximum principles, the intertemporal optimal condition for effort is $p = \mu(t+1) + (\partial Q(t)/\partial E(t))$, where $\mu(t+1)$ is the scarcity rent for the *in situ* fisheries resource and $c/\partial Q(t)/\partial E(t))$ is the marginal cost of production.

If the initial stock level is known, open-access equilibrium and limited-entry optimal efforts at time t = 1 can be estimated from (2.1), (2.2) and (2.3) respectively. Simulations proceed by substituting fishing effort and stock at time t=1 into (3.0) to obtain the initial level of catch and finally into (4.0) to obtain the next year t+1 stock. Projections of stock, effort, catch and the leftover stock can then be performed for t=1,2 ..., n number of years by the interactive process.

Results and discussion
Four Malaysian Fisheries Stocks were identified for the analysis. But only one of the four identified stocks was statistically accepted after data were fitted to OLS technique to obtain estimates of harvest and stock-growth equations. Thus fisheries stock adjacent to the coastal areas of Perlis,

Kedah, Penang, Perak and Selangor was chosen for simulation and projection.

Simulation results using open-access condition at varying cost-price ratios are shown in Table 1. For a decreasing return to scale production function the open-access fishing effort, catch and left-over stock eventually decline over time. A smaller effort would result in lesser catch and a larger leftover stock. Hence, a less extensive effort application can preserve fisheries resource for a relatively longer period of time than the extensive effort.

Effort-catch price ratios undoubtedly influence the open-access levels of fishing efforts, catch and leftover stock. The stock fails less rapidly for relatively higher effort-catch price ratios and vice versa. It therefore follows that taxation imposed on the fishermen operating in the industry would have the same effect of increasing effort-catch price ratio. As noted a 20 per cent tax on catch produces equivalent effect on price ratio as a 25 per cent tax on fishing effort. On the other hand, any subsidy programme that acts to reduce cost of effort relative to the price of catch will have an adverse effect on resource utilisation. Such a policy programme would have increased pressure on fisheries and hasten depletion of the potential fishing stocks. Usually, benefits derived from subsidy programmes are taxed back as a source of additional revenues to the government. In this instance the effect on effort-catch price ratio arising from subsidies and taxes might be somewhat balanced if properly planned.

Alternative management simulations of the limited-entry steady-state and the intertemporal optimisation are shown in Tables 2 and 3 respectively.

On comparison one can easily observe that the limited-entry optimisations allow for the maximisation of economic rent as contrast to zero rent under the open-access condition. Moreover, if the fisheries authority were in a position to exercise control over the resource, it is likely that effort could be limited to the optimal level. Limited-entry situation would exert less pressure on resource use compared to the open-access fishing operation. Food supply from fisheries resource can be preserved for a longer period of time although at the beginning of the planning horizon lower catches are observed. Additional gains may be realised by the fishermen in terms of higher prices because of the reduction in supply.

Results of the intertemporal optimisation are presented in Table 3. The intertemporal simulations recognise the year-to-year linkages between effort, stock and catch. Changes in stock level as the results of changes in effort and catch affect the scarcity rent value of the *in situ* resource. Thus, depressed stock resulting from increased effort application and fisheries extraction would directly increase the value of the *in situ* stock and therefore raise the future scarcity rent value. Given this situation the management usually revalues decisions in favour of future economic benefits. The fisheries resource will be captured less now and will be kept for future use. Intertemporal results showed that effort, catch and stock

TABLE 1 *Open-access levels of effort, catch, stock, total revenue, total cost and economic rent at varying catch/effort price ratios predicted for the periods 1979, 1983 and 1988, West Coast Peninsular Malaysia.*

	Open-Access ('000)					
	Effort (hp)	Catch (ton)	Stock (ton)	Total revenue($)	Total cost($)	Economic rent($)
1. *Price = $3,500/ton; cost = $1,500/hp*						
t = 1 (1979)	767	329	1,565	1,150,450	1,150,450	0
t = 5 (1983)	552	236	739	827,580	827,580	0
t = 10 (1988)[a]	145	62	40	217,400	217,400	0
2. *Price = $3,000/ton; cost = $1,500/hp*						
t = 1 (1979)	559	280	1,565	839,010	839,010	0
t = 5 (1983)	441	221	929	661,870	661,870	0
t = 10 (1988)	243	122	251	364,580	364,580	0
3. *Price = $3,000/ton; cost = $1,800/hp*[b]						
t = 1 (1979)	385	231	1,565	693,100	693,100	0
t = 5 (1983)	329	198	1,108	592,550	592,550	0
t = 10 (1988)	240	144	555	432,320	432,320	0
4. *Price = $2,400/ton; cost = $1,500/hp*[c]						
t = 1 (1979)	354	221	1,565	531,260	531,260	0
t = 5 (1983)	307	192	1,146	461,020	461,020	0
t = 10 (1988)	233	146	625	349,910	349,910	0

[a]Infeasible since catch is greater than stock.
[b]20% tax on effort.
[c]20% tax on catch.

TABLE 2 *Temporal limited-entry levels of effort, catch, stock, total cost and economic rent at varying catch/effort price ratios for the periods 1979, 1983 and 1988, West Coast Peninsular Malaysia.*

Simulation	Temporal Limited Entry ('000)					
	Effort (hp)	Catch (ton)	Stock (ton)	Total revenue($)	Total cost	Economic rent($)
1. *Price = $3,500/ton; cost = $1,000/hp*						
t = 1 (1979)	446	249	1,565	871,890	446,140	425,750
t = 5 (1983)	371	207	1,041	724,260	370,560	353,700
t = 10 (1988)	248	139	432	485,180	248,260	236,920
2. *Price = $3,500/ton; cost = $1,300/hp*						
t = 1 (1979)	261	189	1,565	662,310	338,900	323,410
t = 5 (1983)	237	172	1,271	602,570	308,330	294,240
t = 10 (1988)	201	146	881	510,030	260,980	249,050
3. *Price = $3,500/ton; cost = $1,500/hp*						
t = 1 (1979)	195	163	1,565	570,080	291,710	278,370
t = 5 (1983)	183	154	1,377	537,920	275,250	262,670
t = 10 (1988)	167	140	1,116	488,780	250,100	238,680
4. *Price = $2,400/ton; cost = $1,500/hp*						
t = 1 (1979)	90	109	1,565	263,257	134,706	128,551
t = 5 (1983)	91	111	1,599	265,917	136,067	129,850
t = 10 (1988)	92	113	1,653	269,891	138,101	131,790

TABLE 3 *Intertemporal levels of effort, catch, stock and economic rent under changing scarcity rent and quantity demanded for the period 1979, 1983 and 1988, West Coast Peninsular Malaysia.*

Simulation	Price[a] ($/ton)	Scarcity Rent ($/ton)	Intertemporal Limited Entry ('000)					
			Effort (hp)	Catch (ton)	Stock (ton)	Total revenue ($)	Total cost ($)	Economic rent ($)
1. *Cost = $1,500/hp*								
t = 1 (1979)	3,500	676	124	126	1,565	452,893	186,048	266,845
t = 5 (1983)	3,500	741	116	124	1,521	435,112	174,180	260,932
t = 10 (1988)	3,500	870	103	116	1,480	406,221	154,073	252,148
2. *Cost = $1,500/hp*								
t = 1 (1979)	3,927	676	166	150	1,565	589,343	248,567	340,776
t = 5 (1983)	4,006	741	160	144	1,429	578,264	239,620	338,644
t = 10 (1988)	4,140	870	149	135	1,235	557,518	222,869	334,649
3. *Cost = $1,500/hp*								
t = 1 (1979)	3,927	700	162	149	1,565	583,468	243,748	339,720
t = 5 (1983)	4,006	799	153	142	1,438	566,928	229,921	337,007
t = 10 (1988)	4,140	1,006	136	129	1,269	535,101	203,296	331,805

[a]Changes in the price level are caused by the change in quantity demanded which is estimated from the demand function $P_{(t)} = 1,629,598.23$ $Q_{(t)} - 0.5119$

would be quite stable throughout the period studied. Depletion of the fisheries resource is marginally felt with considerable benefits in terms of economic rents. In such a case food supply is assured and employment to the fishermen will persist for a longer period of time.

CONCLUSIONS

Proper management of the Malaysian fisheries is essential to ensure sufficient domestic supply of fish to its growing population. Projections based on the existing open-access management policy do not guarantee a lasting supply of fish as this tends to deplete current stocks faster than the alternative steady-state and dynamic optimisations. Not only the fisheries resource would deplete but additional problems in the forms of income and employment would follow the depression of stocks: The study also illustrates the possibility that fisheries would be more extensively captured by following a subsidy instead of a taxation programme.

To ensure a longer period of domestic fish supply alternative management policies of temporal and intertemporal optimisations were found appropriate. The temporal analysis directly limits the fishing effort that can enter the fishing industry to the optimal level. The intertemporal analysis considers the value of the *in situ* resource and weighs benefits between the present time and the future. Results show that economic optimisation policies are preferred to open-access in terms of preserving the fisheries resource.

REFERENCES

Azmi, A., Azni, H. and Mohsin, A. D., 'Assessment of The Demersal Stock off Kelantan, East Coast of Peninsular Malaysia', *Pertanika*, vol. 4, no. 2, pp. 156–9, Universiti Pertanian Malaysia, Serdang, Malaysia, 1981.

Government of Malaysia, *Third Malaysia Plan 1976–80*, Government Printer, Kuala Lumpur, 1976.

Ibrahim, M., 'Impact of the Exclusive Zone on the Malaysian Fisheries', Working paper of the Faculty of Fisheries and Marine Science, Universiti Pertanian Malaysia, Serdang, 1982.

Jahar, Y., 'Some Implications of the Fisheries Subsidy Scheme, Peninsular Malaysia', *Seminar on Development of Fisheries Sector in Malaysia*, Kuala Lumpur 1976.

Lawson, R. M., 'Fisheries Development and Planning in the Indo-Pacific Region – its Objections and Constraints', *Symposium on the Economic and Social Aspects of National Fisheries Planning and Development*. Bangkok, 1974.

Ministry of Finance Malaysia, *Economic Report 1980–81*, National Planning Department, Kuala Lumpur, 1980.

Pathansali, D., 'Assessment of Potential Yields From Coastal Marine Fisheries Resources of Malaysia', *Fisheries Bulletin, No. 15. Ministry of Agriculture*, Malaysia, Kuala Lumpur, 1976.

Ruddle, K., 'Environmental Pollution and Fishery Resource in Southeast Asia Coastal Water', *Man, Land and Sea: Coastal Resource Use and Management in Asia and Pacific*. (ed.) Chandra, H. S. et al., ADC, Bangkok, 1982.

Yap, C. L., 'Trawling: Its impact on Employment and Resource Use on the West Coast of Peninsular Malaysia', *Small-Scale Fisheries Development: Social Science Contribution*. (ed.) B. Lockwood and K. Ruddle, East-West Center, Hawaii, 1977.

Yap, C. L., 'The Diseconomics of Technological Progress: A Note on Fishery Regulations', *Regional Conference on Technology for Rural Development*, Kuala Lumpur, 1978.

DISCUSSION OPENING – U. K. SRIVASTAVA

The paper by Daniel Bromley discussed three main causes of resource degradation in developing countries – resource-based exports; inept policies regarding resource use at the local level; and side effects of commercial agricultural policies.

The first cause raises the issue of diversification of export structure, i.e., exporting more value added products rather than primary products from developing countries. This solution, of course, needs to be discussed in a somewhat long-term perspective. The discussion should recognise the constraints faced by developing countries relating to appropriate technology and markets of developed countries.

The second cause raises the issue of how to obtain the much needed local participation in implementing policies relating to the natural resource sector. Therefore, the question of appropriate organisational/ institutional design is extremely important in formulating and managing agricultural projects.

The third cause raises the issue of the choice of appropriate technology. The policy of commercialisation of agriculture pursued without regard to available human resources is bound to cause side effects. Since it is well known that net transfer of rural population to urban areas which can be sustained by the rate of growth of the industrial sector is very slow, the crucial issue is how to find gainful employment for rural labour in villages without natural resource degradation.

The paper also raised the issue of the rate of use of renewable resources and the nature of capital formation that accompanies the exhaustion of non-renewable resources. But the point is whether we have adequate data to arrive at harvesting rates that do not exceed the sustainable yield rate of renewable resources. The paper rightly emphasises the gap between the biologists' and economists' notion of 'wise use'. While the former are conservative, the latter are liberal. In this context a crucial issue to be discussed is how to develop the critical skills in biological and social sciences relevant to natural resource policy in developing countries.

The second paper by Nik Mustapha emphasises that the development efforts in the fishing industry have generally ignored accompanying overfishing and stock depletion problems. It also points out that the open access policy does not guarantee a lasting sufficient domestic supply of fish over time in Malaysia, because the current stocks deplete faster than the steady-state and dynamic optimisation. The subsidy on boats and gear further accentuates the resource depletion effect. This overall depletion of stocks creates problems of income and employment in the fishing community, which is relatively poor. To avoid fishery and stock depletion problems, the temporal and inter-temporal optimisations, which directly limit the fishing industry to optimal levels, could be an answer.

The findings of the paper are theoretically sound. I would, however, like to add that management policy of temporal and intertemporal optimisations in the fishing industry assume that we have extremely good estimates of resource availability and its growth pattern over time. Without this reliable information it is not possible to limit the fishing effort at optimal level. Unfortunately, this data is not available in many developing countries. For example, this is one of the constraints in limiting the fishing effort in India. If fishing effort is to be limited in the absence of such data, there is a danger of missing the opportunity of increasing the catch and the possibility of augmenting the domestic supply and exports.

Another aspect relates to the fact that the use of aggregate models for a country as a whole could be misleading. For example, although marine catch in India has become stagnant around 1.6 million tonnes and there is pressure to limit the entry of fishing effort in in-shore waters, there are coastal areas where there is a possibility and need for additional fishing effort to exploit both prawn and fishery resources without the fear of resource depletion.[1]

Therefore, keeping the findings of this paper in mind, the issue to be debated is whether fishery scientists and biologists are in a position to generate accurate data on resource potential and sustainable yield without resource depletion. We have also to examine whether the developing countries have the resources and trained manpower to undertake this task.

In the context of resource depletion due to demand pressure in the fishery sector, we have also to examine whether the existing catch in developing countries is processed into edible products to the maximum possible extent. In many developing countries, the lack of infrastructure facilities and fishing practices cause a great deal of spoilage which enhances the demand-supply gap and puts pressure on increasing the supply to meet the needs of a growing population and supplies for export.

NOTE

[1]Srivastava, U. K., Reddy, Dharma, M. and Gupta, V. K., *Management of Marine Fishing Industry*, New Delhi, Oxford and IBH Publishing Co., 1982; Srivastava, U. K. and Reddy, M. Dharma (eds), *Fisheries Development in India – Some Aspects of Policy Management*, New Delhi, Concept Publishing Co., 1983; Kulkarni, G. R. and Srivastava, U. K., *A Systems Framework of Marine Foods Industry in India*, New Delhi, Concept Publishing Co., 1985; Gupta, V. K. *et. al.*, *Marine Fish Marketing in India*, vol. I to VI, Indian Institute of Management, Ahmedabad, 1984.

GENERAL DISCUSSION – RAPPORTEUR: ELISABETTA CROCI-ANGELINI

While showing a general agreement with the authors of the two papers, the discussion was mainly aimed to elaborate on the more interesting points as follows:

The difficulties faced in project implementation were pointed out. Development assistance is too often provided through big projects substituting new products for traditional crops and employing new technologies totally alien with respect to local experience. The lack of human capital and its inability to cope with this situation increases the risk of crop failures. The likelihood of wide discrepancies between the calculated and the actual cost/benefit ratios (i.e. the probability of success of the project) should be taken into account as well as the possible environmental burdens.

While the causes for 'market failure' should be studied more in-depth, a new direction of enquiry was acknowledged in the study of 'institutional failure' as an additional source of externalities. In this respect the ability to avoid ecological disaster in the tropics may well depend upon the attention paid to how peasant farming is organised. For instance, the dependence upon firewood for energy uses (mainly for cooking) is almost complete because the farmers do not have access to other fuels while *de facto* the access to firewood is open, although frequently illegal.

Whether fisheries should have open or somehow regulated access, was related to the Exclusive Economic Zone. Self-limiting rules may not be the solution for small countries unless an agreement is reached with neighbouring countries to limit their exploitation of natural resources as well.

All the above issues stress the role of government. Governments usually know the consequences of their intervention on land and other natural resources. The behaviour therefore can be explained along the following lines: (a) they cannot do otherwise, either because of the constraints they face on the foreign exchange side or because of the impossibility of effectively counteracting private behaviour (e.g. private tree cutting); (b) their own instability leads them to favour short-run policies in order to please the people; (c) they cannot avoid favouring large profit-making agencies controlled by foreign capital, whose philosophy is explicitly oriented towards exploiting existing resources and later move to other countries. A solution to this problem could be found in compelling governments to submit to land and natural resource conservation rules in order to obtain international agencies' intervention and aid (e.g. loans accorded by the IMF).

In reply, Daniel Bromley stated that in his opinion social scientists were observing two crises at present: one was conceptual and stemmed from the simplistic application of welfare economics also in cases of market failure or when independent optimisation may lead to overall damage. The assumption of benevolent government assistance might become a perverse factor and bring about very severe failures. The second one referred to the presumption of development assistance. Much of it had resulted in a quite hard impact on the resource base, so the problem should be reconsidered. A distinction should also be made between government (bureaucracy, explicit state) and institutions (set of uses, habits, legal foundations of society, implicit state) the latter being often missing after the government had broken the social contract. Cost/benefit analysis should be framed into a certain environment including cultural elements; while they should be improved, such analyses are however an unavoidable check in order to avoid more serious mistakes.

As to the problem of fisheries, Nik Mustapha replied that the lack of a reliable database is very serious, however what is really needed is to find out the trends. Fishermen would profit from fleet modernisation rather than subsidy allowances. More disaggregation would certainly improve the model and technical assistance is of the greatest importance for the problem of the Exclusive Economic Zone.

Participants in the discussion included Michel Petit, Kamil I. Hassan, Carlisle Ford Runge, Morag Simpson, Ewa Rabinowicz, John Antle, Patrice Dofonsou and J. Viaene.

SECTION V

Human Capital, Technology and Institutions

JEAN-PIERRE BERLAN

From the United States to a World System: Technological Change, International Trade, Agricultural Policy in the Twentieth Century

This paper attempts to build a comprehensive framework of the transformations of agriculture in the twentieth century, focusing mainly on the case of the United States where they first took place. The moving force behind these transformations is an enduring overproduction crisis which began at the end of the First World War, exploded during the 1930s, was more or less under control after the Second World War and is again becoming particularly threatening. Overproduction has triggered the search for a new system of agricultural production and food consumption based on the transformation of grain into meat. This could be done economically thanks to high protein concentrates (soybean meal). Soybeans appear in Agricultural Statistics for the first time in 1924 and now are grown on as many acres as maize. The corn belt has become a corn soybean belt. A general process of capital accumulation and commoditisation of the farm economy has led to a powerful agribusiness system which has little to do with previous forms of organisation of agriculture.

This new model has spread in most parts of the world, making it possible to rebuild the US share of world trade in basic agricultural products. New forms of agricultural policies corresponding to the new situation have been implemented to foster capital accumulation. Family farms, considered the most efficient method of organising agricultural production, have undergone such structural changes that they now appear obsolete and a drastic change of agricultural policy appears possible.

Statistics of international agricultural trade show that the present dominant situation of the US on world markets for staple food or feedstuff is not nature's gift but the result of an historical process. The US was a very large exporter at the end of the nineteenth century but her position started to erode under the competition of Argentina, Australia and Canada. At the end of the 1930s the US was a marginal supplier of world markets and only 2 per cent of US cropland was cultivated for export in 1940. Now it is one-third.

The situation of the 1930s is in sharp contrast with the present situation where the US makes up 50 per cent of world maize production, 80 per cent of world exports of maize or soybeans, and 40 to 50 per cent of world wheat exports. World grain exports have tremendously increased since the Second World War.

The index of total agricultural production shows a progressive slowing down of the rate of growth from the Civil War to the Second World War.[1] The yearly rate of growth of agricultural production declines from 2.8 per cent during the period 1870–97, to 0.9 per cent during the period 1897 to 1939. These periods can be themselves subdivided: 4.7 per cent between 1870 and 1880; 2.1 per cent between 1880 and 1897. From 1897 to 1920, the rate of growth is 1.2 per cent and declines to 0.7 per cent from 1920 to 1939. Whether including the drought years of 1934 and 1936 artificially lowers the rate of growth of the period is uncertain: they did also restore the balance between supply and demand, and laid the ground for the recovery of the late 1930s. Moreover, statisticians compute the volume of *final* agricultural production, and not the volume of *total* agricultural production. The difference between the two is the production being used as an input, that is seeds and feed for horses and mules. The amount of seeds does not change significantly during the period but the amount of feed declines drastically because tractors and trucks replace horses. This concept overestimates the actual growth.

USDA computes for research purposes an index of total agricultural production.[2] This index shows that the volume of agricultural production remained stable during the period 1920–39.

Last, the moving average of the index of agricultural production per caput shows a regular decline from 1897 to 1939; the keystone of the present food system has seen for 40 years a *steady decline* of the volume of food production per caput! In the 1920s, it was doubted whether the United States could feed her population!

This overall picture is in sharp contrast with the Second World War and its aftermath which sees a steady and vigorous growth: 1.8 per cent during a period of more than 40 years, with a noteworthy acceleration in the 1970s and the early 1980s. This growth has been largely fuelled by exports.

Many factors have contributed to such a recovery: economic recovery in Europe and Japan, 'finely tuned' agricultural policies, trade liberalisation, rise in real incomes, the political and economic might of the United States to shape favourably to her interests the course of economic policies in Europe and elsewhere etc. However important, these factors are of the second order of magnitude. What has to be dealt with is the structural transformation which has laid the ground for the post war growth of agriculture and the shaping of the present world food system.

AGRICULTURAL DEVELOPMENT IN THE US

The technological frontier and the roots of overproduction
Beginning in the 1920s, the dominant problem of US agriculture

becomes overproduction (Johnson and Quance 1972). It still is. Quickly stated, draft animals on farms were using 28 per cent of the harvested cropland in the late 1910s, while 72 per cent was used for final consumption (which includes draft animals used in cities or in industries). In two decades, the replacement of draft animals by gasoline motors increased by 39 per cent (28/72) the potential final production, while motorisation in cities suppressed another important outlet of agriculture (Barger and Lansberg, 1942, p. 29). Hence the development of a rampant overproduction crisis in the 1920s and its explosion in the 1930s.

The oat crop, 20 per cent of the corn crop, and part of the hay crop was grown for horse feed. With the advent of automobiles, tractors and trucks, the number of horses began to decline regularly while the remaining ones were doing lighter work and needed less feed.

If the geographical 'frontier' was closed by 1910, a new frontier, a technological one, opened. It was invisible since it ran through each farm and could not justify any 'manifest destiny'. Huge amounts of cropland became free for final production and consumption. From the point of view of available food resources, the development of this new frontier is the equivalent of the discovery and of the development of a new continent, of a new North America right into the 20th century! The same process took place in Western Europe, after the Second World War.

The distribution of a stable volume of production between final uses and agricultural input began to shift. The agricultural recovery of Europe decreased its imports needs, while Canada, Australia and Argentina took a larger share of world exports the percentage of US cropland harvested for exports declined. Domestic markets were increasingly unable to absorb this excess capacity: food consumption per caput did not show any drastic changes. Cereal consumption declined notably and meat slightly. Fruit and vegetable consumption went up as well as milk but these products are marginal in the heart of US agriculture, the Midwest.

In 1929, the underlying tendencies broke out: agricultural markets collapsed, entailing a severe and lasting overproduction crisis alleviated by the droughts of 1934 and 1936.

Power farming and its problems
Power farming is touted as a gigantic progress. From the point of view of capital accumulation, it certainly is. However, it also opened the farmers' Pandora box; difficult problems had to be solved and fewer farmers were able to solve them! Farmers who had mechanised were confronted with a threefold problem: finding a crop that would fit into crop rotations, be easily mechanised, and more importantly provide cash.

Crop rotations. A crop had both to provide fertilizer since the volume of horse manure decreased and to fit into a balanced rotation system. The decline of corn yields during the 1920s and early 1930s is evidence of the disruption brought about by power farming to the old order. Oats (not a profitable crop by itself) as well as some of the pasture or hay had become useless. the ideal crop had to be a legume since legumes fix the nitrogen from the air into root nodules.

The mechanisation problem. The new crop had to be handled with the machinery and implements already available on farms.

The cash problem. Since cash was going out to pay for the machinery, parts and replacement (while draught mares could be left idle to breed), energy and car transportation, cash had to come in. Up to then, the farm economy of the Corn-Belt was working to a large extent under the simple exchange, commodity-money-commodity. In sociological terms: 'For a large number of farmers the production of agricultural commodities is not carried on as a means of making money, but rather as a mode of existence' (Barger and Lansbury 1942, p. 6).

Farm records of Iowa or Illinois show that farmers were working largely alongside a market economy: a typical farmer on his quarter section would grow 50 acres of corn, 20 acres of oats, maybe some wheat with the rest of his land with hay, clover, timothy and alfalfa. His rotations were based on corn-oat-pasture with a number of variants depending upon fertility of his land, location, markets etc. Corn was fed to hogs and horses. Farmers got their main source of cash from hogs, sometimes dubbed 'land whales' because they provided the fat for candles, cooking and other uses, and from butter or cattle. His wife was raising chicken or eggs and covered her current outlays with this 'chicken money'.

A typical farmer and his team of horses could plant and cultivate about 50 acres of corn in the spring. Ploughing and preparing the seed bed was a very arduous operation and when the soil was particularly wet or dry, horses could not work. Cultivating corn was the most time-consuming farm operation (Wallace and Bressman 1937) at a time when the work load was important. Horses had to rest; increasing the acreage of corn or the size of operation entailed the use of a second team of horses, the hiring of another driver and the purchase of other implements. A farmer had to incur a large increase of his fixed costs for a dubious benefit. There were hardly any economies of scale under corn belt conditions (Barger and Lansberg 1942, p. 4).

Production itself did not involve much expense: implements were relatively simple and lasted for a number of years, little commercial fertilizer was used on corn until the late 1930s, draft animals were bred on farms, repairs could be handled by farmers or by the local craftsman. Land prices were still reasonable and debts low. These years prior to the power age are remembered as a golden age.

Automobiles were the first sign that times were changing. The 6 million plus farms had 50,000 automobiles in 1910, 2.1 million in 1920 and 4.1 million in 1930. Farmers converted part of their large windfall war income – the net income of farm operators of 4 billion dollars in 1915 reached 9 and 9.6 billions in 1918 and 1919 – into cars, tractors and trucks. Few realised that the operating costs of these glittering wonders would drain their cash year after year and subvert the very sense of farming.

Power farming began to make money the driving force. It replaced the simple exchange by the more complex and contradictory capitalist circuit of money-commodity-money which makes sense only if the amount of money at the end of the circuit is larger than the one at the beginning, i.e. accumulation is the aim of production.

Tractors created important economies of scale. They worked faster than horses and they worked longer under difficult conditions. They removed directly and indirectly the bottleneck of preparing the seed bed and cultivating corn. In Illinois one-third of the farms that had acquired a tractor in 1916 and 1917 were cropping a larger acreage in 1918 (Yerkes and Church 1918), and this at the very beginning of the tractor age, when the machines left much to be desired.

Thus, the tractor – and more generally power farming – simultaneously made capital accumulation necessary and possible. Necessary by subverting the simple exchange into a capitalist one; possible by creating economies of scale. Growth and elimination of individual farms through the competitive system has ever since been a permanent feature of the farm economy.

But all this hinged upon the development of a new crop.

Soybeans were the obvious solution – with hindsight! This mere botanical curiosity in the Corn Belt until the 1930s now occupies as much land as corn. It is a legume plant, it is easily mechanised and when processed into oil and meal, it brings in cash. The ultimate triumph of soybeans is not the result of some masterminded design but of a necessary historical process and struggle which span the two decades of the 1920s and the 1930s.

Towards a solution

Space does not permit a description of the development of the soybean oil market (Berlan et al. 1976), except to mention four breakthroughs.

In 1928, a few industrialists, co-ops and processors (some large companies) offered to contract farmers their bean production at a fixed price. Thi event symbolises the very close links between farming and industry. It marks the birth of the soybean complex as the core of the modern agribusiness complex.

In 1930, soybean production was protected through the Hawley-Smoot tariff. The US imported only one staple: vegetable oils. Replacing foreign oils with domestic oils was an obvious demand from farmers and processors at a time of shrinking markets. However, this tariff could not keep out coconut oil from the Philippines and soybean oil only found limited markets in industrial uses, particularly paints and varnishes.

In 1934, hydrogenation of soybean oil became feasible on a large scale. Soybean oil could be stabilised and used in margarine manufacturing or other food uses. Research had a key role in shaping the American soybean.

In 1935, the margarine manufacturers agreed 'to use only domestically produced oils and fats' at a *Domestic Oils and Fats Conference*.[3] The industry had no choice: it had shifted progressively away from domestic fats to tropical oils, particularly copra oil fron the Philippines and had lost all support from farmers – western cattle ranchers had lost interest, dairy states took more and more retaliatory measures and corn-belt states were becoming hostile. Rather than taking the risk of having margarine banned by law, as several bills in Congress had attempted the industry decided by this move to placate the opposition of dairy interests. In addition, a first processing tax had made Philippines oils less attractive. Within a few years, soybean oil became the largest component of margarine and shortening and the acreage of soybeans for beans – as opposed to hay or green manure – increased dramatically (Table 1).

TABLE 1   *Soybean production and use (1,000 metric tons)*

	soybean for grain	processing	oil	% used in margarine	shortening	other	meal
1931–33	420	111	15	1	1	2	82
1939	2,453	1,543	208				1,224

Source: Soybean Blue Book, various years.

These first victories would have been short-lived if economical uses had not been found for the meal. Meal (some 80 per cent of the weight of the bean) had to be a full commodity and not only a byproduct. In the 1930s, the work of experiment stations and USDA showed that this source of concentrated protein had magic properties after heat treatment: (i) it made it possible greatly to improve the ratio of feed consumed per unit of gain in meat animals (ii) the growth rate was considerably increased, (iii) the meat was leaner. Electricity was reaching farming communities and land was becoming useless.

Most pigs were raised on a corn ration sometimes with minerals added. More advanced farmers were adding tankage, a byproduct of the meatpacking industry, high in protein content. Being a byproduct, the quantities of tankage available were set by slaughtering. By contrast, soybean meal could be a full commodity by itself. By the end of the 1930s, meal was worth as much as oil and in the post-war period, the ever-increasing market for meal was the driving force behind the expansion of soybeans. A large part of the oil had to be disposed of through the various aid programmes. To put it in a nutshell, a much more 'efficient' system of animal production becomes feasible.

The control of this source of raw material was immediately an important stake. The first instances of *vertical integration* took place in the Delmarva Peninsula in the late 1930s and the supply of feed enriched with soybean meal, that is of a more 'efficient' ration, was the reason and the means of this new organisation of agricultural production. Within ten to twenty years, poultry production, scattered all over the United States in 1935, moved to the south-eastern states where impoverished small farmers were numerous. These farmers had no choice but to sell cheaply their labour power under the disguise of contracts and without the fringe benefits of a wage worker (National Commission 1966). At times strikes and violence have erupted in the south.

At the eve of the war, the core of the new system of agricultural production and consumption based on a more efficient transformation of grain into meat and other animal products was well established. During the following decades, it was technologically, economically and socially perfected and expanded first in the United States and later abroad.

The consequence has been a profound decline over the long term of the cost of meat and a corresponding increase in consumption per caput. Poultry meat consumption has increased more than threefold and beef has doubled between the 1930s and 1970 (*Historical Statistics* 1975). The use of soybeans, the development of a new source of energy (carbohydrate) in the Great Plains (sorghum) has led to an entirely different pattern of production: fattening previously done on scattered lots on a number of farms is now concentrated in few huge feedlots in the west. Some cattle funds have been introduced on the NY stock exchange!

NEW AGRICULTURAL POLICIES

This period of emergence of the modern agribusiness complex saw, of course, the birth of new ideas on agricultural policies. Historians (Rasmussen 1960; Schlesinger 1957) but not economists (Benedict 1953) have remarked that G. Peek and H. Johnson, advisers to Henry Wallace and agricultural policy-makers of the 1930s (the principle of which was that the price system was unable to shape a smooth path of capital accumulation through the agribusiness complex, and that this situation has to be corrected by the State), were, in 1921, directors of the Moline Plow Company (later to become John Deere) which was thrown into insolvency by the price collapse in the fall of 1919. As a result, they published in early 1922 a small book *Equality for Agriculture* (Peek and Johnson 1922), which elaborated, albeit in a confused manner, what should be the new principles of an agricultural policy serving the needs of the emerging agribusiness complex. The book fed the heated discussions around the McNary-Haugen Bill. New ideas, to be implemented later, took shape (Fite 1953).

The shaping of modern agricultural policies was triggered by the crisis of the 1920s which occurred at a time when agriculture became a market for the mechanical industries that are characteristic of the first part of the twentieth century. It is an *agribusiness policy*.

Agricultural policies in the modern sense, that is a sophisticated system of state interventions to foster capital accumulation in an agribusiness complex dominated by large corporations has little to do with what was done earlier – basically a tariff policy as noted somewhere by Hathaway. These policies create the illusion of working independently of the structural transformation which they accompany and foster and which in its turn define their characteristics. In fact, their success is accounted for by the emergence of a new technological and social base of capital accumulation which reduced the overproduction crisis to a manageable proportion. It remains to be seen if they can work at a time of sagging markets.

The same movement took place in Western Europe which has adopted a specific version of the corn-soybean model: giving up the protection given to its traditional colonial sources of vegetable oils and meals in favour of American soybeans, while at the same time protecting its cereal and particularly its wheat production. This trade-off founded the Common Market agricultural policy but in this period of increasing overproduction becomes the source of conflicts.

Food production is now a high technology activity (people often are surprised to see the US exporting foodstuff *and* electronics or weaponry as if there was a contradiction between the two). These technological advances are capitalised under high land prices, that is under the form of a Ricardian rent. Hence, agricultural production has tended to move back from Third World countries to industrial countries. Third World countries, turned into sources of agricultural commodities during the colonial era, are becoming now the dumping ground of agricultural surpluses which are a powerful means of political control and jeopardise their own agriculture.

CONCLUSION

Food production and consumption has now little to do with traditional agriculture. A farmer of the 1910s is closer to farmers of the Roman Empire (slavery not taken into consideration) than to his grandson. In France, 50 years ago, feeding wheat to poultry or hogs would have been considered as a capital sin. Now it is a way of life and three-quarters of wheat production goes to animal feed. The 'wasteful' (as often stated) transformation of cereal and high protein feed into meat is the historical response to the challenge of overproduction. When American agribusinessmen call soybean 'the miracle bean', they are right to the point, for in the absence of this technological revolution, it is doubtful if US agriculture would have pulled out from the doldrums of stagnation into a period of rapid capital accumulation.

The seventeenth and eighteenth centuries saw, first in Flanders and later in other parts of Europe, the abandonment of fallowing. Historians have stressed how important this agricultural revolution has been and how it laid the ground for the Industrial Revolution. What has happened in the twentieth century deserves also to be called a revolution leading in few decades to an entirely new technical, economic, cultural and social world system of food production and consumption. However, this system remains still beset by overproduction in spite of the opening of the markets of the communist world. This framework may be useful, we hope, to examine the present crisis.

NOTES

[1]Among early studies of aggregate output, one may cite: Strauss, Frederick and Bean, Louis H., *Gross Farm Income and Indices of Farm Production and Prices in the United States, 1869–1937*, USDA, Technical Bulletin 703, 1940. Bressler, R. G. and Hopkins, J. A., *Trends in Size and Production of the Aggregate Farm Enterprise, 1909–1936*, National Research Project, Philadelphia, 1938.

[2]I would like to thank Dr. D. Durost for making available to me this index in manuscript form.

[3]This *Domestic Fats and Oils Conference* is mentioned once in the *Proceedings of the American Soybean Association* and is alluded to in some issues of *Soybean Digest* (August 1946, editorial and p. 19). A bibliographic search (including the National Archives) with the help of Wayne Rasmussen, head of the history branch of USDA has been unsuccessful in uncovering any further material illuminating this important point. It is likely that this conference was unofficial and was held discreetly to prepare the defeat of the bills introduced in Congress to ban margarines.

REFERENCES

Annuaire du Commerce International, Organisation pour l'Alimentation et l'Agriculture, Rome, diverses années.

Barger Harold and Landsberg Hans H., *American Agriculture, 1899–1939, a Study of Output, Employment and Productivity*, National Bureau of Economic Research, 1942. 'In the cultivation of the soil there is discernible scarcely any tendency toward that growth in the size of the entrepreneurial unit which has characterized other types of industry' p. 4. 'At the turn of the century, hay represents 2.1% of agricultural output and almost nothing at the eve of W.W.II' p. 29.

Benedict, Murray R., *Farm Policies of the United States*, 1953.

Berlan, Jean-Pierre, Bertrand, Jean-Pierre and Lebas, Laurence, *Le Complexe soja des Etats-Unis*, I.N.R.A. 1976.

Fite, Gilbert C. in Peek, George N., *Fight for Farm Parity*, University of Oklahoma Press, 1953, covers at length what we have to summarise in a few sentences.

Johnson, Glenn L. and Quance, Leroy, 'Since 1917 (and possibly some time before), United States agriculture has been characterized by a capacity to expand production every twenty to twenty-five years by as much as it produced in 1875.' *The Overproduction Trap in U.S. Agriculture*, Resources for the Future, 1972, p. 3.

amer, Mirko, *The World Fertilizer Economy*, Stanford University Press, 1957; 'The average application of fertilizers materials (in the Corn Belt states of Illinois and Iowa) quadrupled in the decade 1938–1948', pp. 495–6.

Historical Statistics of the United States, *Colonial Times to 1970*, USGPO, 1975, p. 484.

National Commission on Food Marketing writes: 'A question remains why the system of coordination that developed was not ownership integration at all stages, including growing the broilers? At this stage, coordination was achieved by contract instead. The answer is to be found in the fact that many underemployed farmers with facilities had few or no alternatives. Also, contracts were attractive to integrators because they involved no social security, no workman's compensation and other employee costs. Capital of feed companies and poultry processors could earn higher returns in other uses' (1966:2).

Peek, George N. and Johnson, Hugh S. *Equality for Agriculture*, 1st and 2nd edition, H. W. Harrington, Moline, Illinois 1922.

Rasmussen, Wayne, D. *Readings in the History of American Agriculture* University of Illinois Press, 1960, is to my knowledge one of the few to have realised that the ideas which underly the New Deal are rooted in the material transformation of the 1920s.

'Thus the Moline Plow Company, managed by George N Peek and Hugh S. Johnson, was thrown into insolvency (by the post war decline in farm purchasing power). Peek and Johnson, who had served on the War Industries Board and believed that government action could promote economic stability, decided that farm prosperity must be restored before the farm machinery could prosper' (p. 228). Rasmussen ends his presentation of 'Equality for agriculture' with the following words: 'Pressure for farm relief continued until by 1929 the federal government was committed to the idea of accepting some responsibilities for farm prices' (p. 228).

Schlesinger, Arthur M. Jr, *The Age of Roosevelt: Crisis of the Old Order 1919–1933*, 1957.

Stern, Robert M., World Food Exports and United States Agricultural Policies', Ph.D Thesis, Columbia, 1958.

USDA, Economic Research Service, *World Trade in Selected Agricultural Commodities 1951–1965*, vol II, Foreign Agricultural Economic Report 47, 1968.

Wallace, Henry A. and Bressman, Earl N.: 'The average Corn Belt farmer with 50 acres of corn spends 300 hours of man labor and 600 hours of horse labor cultivating corn. This takes more time than any other farm operation except corn husking. Moreover, corn cultivation conflicts to some extent with haying and oat harvest.' *Corn and Corn Growing*, John Wiley and Sons 1937, p. 102.

Yerkes, Arnold P. and Church, L. M., Tractor Experience in Illinois', *Farmer's Bulletin* vol. 963, June 1918: 'Approximately one-third of all Illinois farmers reporting increased the acreage they were farming after purchasing a machine.'

WALTER L. FISHEL AND MARTIN KENNEY

Challenge to Studies of Biotechnology Impacts in the Social Sciences

Much has been written in recent months about the impending technological revolution in agriculture that will result from biotechnological innovations (NRC 1982; NAS 1984). Even the more conservative among these writers foresee changes in agriculture and related economic and social institutions that overshadow even that of the often discussed Green Revolution in developing countries. Unlike the Green Revolution, this set of technological changes will have even greater, if not different, impacts on the economic and social structures of the developed countries (Kenney forthcoming). In addition, there will be few economic and social components of agriculture and related institutions and infrastructures unaltered to some degree because of the source, nature and rate of change in biotechnology introductions (Kenney 1984).

This paper contends that social scientists interested in the consequences of technical change on agriculture and related economic and social infrastructures, whether in developed or developing countries, must begin now to analyse the implications of the new product introductions and processes resulting from biotechnology. This includes the biotechnologies already on stream and at least those that may be readily anticipated from the research now under way in the biological sciences. Several factors differ from the circumstances that have been involved in past studies of technological change that suggests no small degree of urgency in this endeavour. Further, this paper will indicate a number of characteristics of biotechnology that have significant implications to the study of impacts and suggests the need for added attention being given to the study perspective and methodology.

A CHANGING ENVIRONMENT FOR TECHNOLOGY ASSESSMENT IN AGRICULTURE

Economists and sociologists have a rich history in the study of technological change and its impact on agriculture and related institutions and structures (Hayami and Ruttan 1971). Consequently, there already exists a solid foundation of studies and methodologies applicable to most technological change situations encountered. Yet, in reviewing the relatively sparse literature relating to biotechnology applicable to agriculture, some concern with the adequacy of this foundation arises. There are a number of characteristics and factors associated with the advent of biotechnology and its adoption that strongly suggests the need for careful reappraisal of both our perspective and our methodology for assessing the impacts of biotechnology on agriculture.[1] In the following discussion, it is important to note that for the most part these characteristics and factors are not conjectural, nor are the direction of effects; the extent and rate of change necessarily must be conjectural, based on the limited amount of study done to data.

The principal source of change in the study environment originates from the extent to which biotechnologies are being developed and disseminated outside the traditional sources of agricultural technologies. While many technologies have come from other than public sector research institutions, especially in recent years, nothing approaching such a stream of private sector technologies has ever been encountered before in agriculture. Certainly, such a change extends well beyond that experienced in the Green Revolution. The significant effect of this will be reflected in a radical change in the source of control of technology related information, in its relative dependence on the information source and consequently its relative objectivity, and in its price and relative availability. Both developed and developing countries face many dilemmas from this shift in the transport of new knowledge (Kenney 1984).

In addition, the nature of the technical changes will be much different than most of the past technological changes that have been studied. Biotechnology innovations and introductions are being driven by large infusions of capital from outside the traditional sources of new technologies, namely from the private sector. These efforts are being applied only to areas of high technology in which the high risk of development is associated with high expectations of profits, and all that goes along with it. Technologies to be developed are being selected on this basis. The resulting biotechnologies will have incremental and disjointed impacts on agricultural productivity. Only the hybridisation of corn and possibly the current adoption of computers and microprocessor control systems can be expected to have a comparable impact to what may become commonplace for many biotechnologies.

Nearly all past technical changes in agriculture have been gradual enough for adjustments to be partially governed by tolerable rates of capital consumption. The decline of marginal operations has been at a rate that acceptable, of not preferable, adjustments could be made, short of impending disaster. The nature of the high tech, capital and knowledge intensive biotechnology based systems will greatly aggravate the adjustment problems by accentuating the differences in levels of productivity between capital and knowledge intensive versus more labour-intensive systems and units. Rates of capital consumption will be less important as a decision factor in adoption and, consequently, adoption rates will be greater to an as yet unknown degree than for most new technologies. The significant implication of this is that issues related both to management decisions and to governmental adjustment programmes will need to be anticipatory rather than reactive.

Because relatively few biotechnologies have yet to come on stream, possibly the most deceptive and least recognised cause of concern in this changing technological environment is the sheer magnitude of the number of new biotechnologies that are or will be developed. Changes will be coming from many directions simultaneously. As a later section of this paper indicates, virtually every biological aspect of agriculture is the subject of biotechnology innovations. And these are occurring concurrently. At no time in the history of agriculture has such a proliferation of new technologies been introduced in such a short period of time with each one having potential for substantial impact on productivity. Such an occurrence presents few possibilities for segmenting out relatively narrow areas of agricultural technology for individual study.

SOURCES OF CHANGES IN THE BIOSCIENCES

All changes start with altered technical relationships in agriculture and related industries, whether these are productivity changes or commodity or product substitutes. Sources of change from biotechnologies can be grouped in four major categories: (1) plant genetic manipulation and improvements, (2) advances in animal husbandry, (3) industrial tissue culture and (4) genetically engineered micro-organisms. Each category includes a number of heterogeneous techniques and each will have particular impacts based on the component of the farming system that it will affect. Certain of these techniques will be economically and socially more important than others, some in the short term, others in the longer term. The following overview provides only a brief summary of the power biotechnology has to transform both the production and distribution of agricultural products.

Plant breeding was the key to the Green Revolution and still remains the single most important discipline in agricultural research. However, in the last ten years, the increased capabilities of molecular and cellular biologists have provided new techniques to manipulate plant genetic material. Potentially, the most impressive of these techniques is the ability to move selected genes from one species to another. Researchers are attempting to move the gene complex for nitrogen fixation from legumes to cereal grains. However, this research may be most successful initially in moving single gene traits from one species to another. These genetic engineering techniques are still at the research stage and useful products probably will not be available before 1990.

Other less sophisticated techniques for plant improvement using tissue culture are already in use in both developed and developing countries (Sondahle 1984). The techniques using tissue culture range from the growth of potato microcuttings in a liquid medium to protoplast fusion involving the fusing of two cells to secure a more complete genetic mixing than is achievable by traditional sexual means. A 'pomato' having the roots of a tomato but the stem and leaves of a potato has been grown using protoplast fusion. Potatoes, cassavas, orchids and a number of other plants have been grown commercially using tissue culture. The International Rice Institute is currently field testing a cold-tolerant high-yielding rice variety in Korea that was developed using another culture. There is no doubt that tissue culture will hasten the spread of high-yielding varieties into areas formerly outside their growth range because of environmental constraints. These new plant propagation techniques, as with those that undergirded the Green Revolution, provide the stimulus for new social, political and economic arrangements.

The application of biotechnology to animal husbandry is already making an important contribution to increasing livestock productivity. Genetic engineering has provided researchers with new tools for developing vaccines against animal diseases, many of which are endemic in developing countries. Researchers in two companies in the United States are near to developing a microbially-produced foot and mouth disease vaccine. Other researchers have developed microbially-produced animal growth hormones and bovine interferon with the expectation that these will increase the efficiency of animal production. Farmers can now hormonally induce élite cows to superovulate and then manually extract and transfer these embryos to surrogate mothers. Commercial operations can sex and freeze the extracted embryos, transfer them anywhere in the world, thaw and then implant them into surrogate mothers. The possibilities for drastically upgrading the quality of cattle herds in developing countries are considerable.

Industrial tissue culture, keeping single plant or animal cells alive in a nutrient medium, makes it possible for scientists to select a single plant cell producing a desirable chemical, grow the cell *in vitro* and harvest the cells. This is an expensive process, but any plant chemical costing greater than $600 per kilogram is a candidate for displacement by industrial tissue culture. The first tissue culture plant chemical was shikonin, an Asian medicinal herb developed by one Japanese firm and already being used as a colouring agent in cosmetics by another. Tissue culture produced berberine will also shortly enter the market in Germany. The displacement of agriculturally produced plant chemicals by bio-industrially produced identical substitutes can have a substantial impact on regional economies (Kenney forthcoming).

The final area in which biotechnology will affect agriculture is in the use of micro-organisms to develop products that will displace agricultural commodities. The successful commercialisation of fructose corn sweetener to replace sugar through the use of immobilised enzymes is in many respects the seminal example of the potential for a significant impact on existing agricultural production systems from industrial biotechnology. The USSR is attempting to genetically engineer micro-organisms to convert methanol into single cell protein more efficiently. If the research is successful, the USSR will become self-sufficient in protein for animal feed (OTA 1981). This would have a severe impact on plant protein exporters such as Senegal, Brazil, Argentina and the United States. At the same time, if more efficient ethanol-producing micro-organisms were engineered, developing countries likewise would have the capacity to 'grow their own' feedstocks.

The complexity of bioscience research and development provides many difficulties for social scientists attempting to anticipate the future of biotechnology. So much of the main thrusts in biotechnology remain in the basic research stage. An increasing share of new developments are in industrial laboratories hidden behind the cloak of proprietary information (Kenney forthcoming). The varied nature of the biotechnologies makes it inevitable that many of these technologies will compete against each other. While a number of companies are preparing to microbially produce bovine growth hormones for dairy herds, other scientists are attempting to genetically engineer cattle to produce more growth hormone internally. Such a lack of any semblance of stability in the state-of-the-art for anticipated biotechnologies provides innumerable hurdles to realistic technology assessment studies.

CHALLENGES TO THE STUDY OF BIOTECHNOLOGY IMPACTS

The presumption in the following is that technological assessments of biotechnology impacts are performed to provide decision and policy makers with information that will be beneficial in their respective activities. This presumption specifies that the information required, and not the theoretical constructs of economics and sociology, is the predominant driving force in the design and conduct of biotechnology impact studies. As such, the parameters of the information required are specified first and only then are the dimensions of the study model, data acquisition and analytical methodologies determined. The latter will be varied both in design and degree of measurement precision as necessary to provide the required information. This is contrary to the usual approach in agricultural economics and rural sociology studies. Typically, information to be produced by a study is seldom determined with any degree of finality until after data availability is determined and analytical precision requirements are met. Rigorously reversing these roles may be the hardest of the challenges, especially for academic researchers. However, proper and rapid response to anticipated impacts of biotechnology introductions will be much too important not to provide less than the best possible information that is clearly oriented to the decision- and policy-maker's needs.

There are three additional factors related to perspectives about technology assessment studies that need to be carefully considered. All three have a significant effect on how one approaches the development of models, data acquisition and selection of analytical methods. The first of these is the need to orient one's perspective to the fact that both decision-makers and policy-makers will have to pre-act rather than react or respond to anticipated impacts of biotechnology. Both the rate and pervasiveness at which impacts will occur as well as the scale of effect of the impact will not permit waiting for the occurrence before studies are conducted and counter action is taken. A greater stress on anticipation (not projection!) rather than measurement will need to characterise our studies.

A second challenge to perspectives about biotechnology impact studies will be to attitudes about change itself. Anticipated impacts arising from the introduction of new biotechnologies should not be viewed as positive or negative. The object of concern should be how the economic and social systems will change as a result of the adoption of a particular biotechnology. Then, how do the units or components of that system change or adapt to the system changes? Up front neutrality of perspective will be necessary in order to preserve study objectivity in confronting the complexity of issues and effects that are presented in studies of biotechnology impacts. Changes resulting from biotechnology will be so pervasive that the *status quo* cannot be considered a relevant base for comparison.

The third factor related to perspective is the need to realise that the topic being studied is inherently multidisciplinary. Consequently, studies of biotechnology impacts must reflect this characteristic in their design and conduct. Multidisciplinary involvement must start with the conceptualisation of the problem, be reflected in the design of the study model and be present in the data acquisition procedures and analysis. There will be few biotechnologies that will permit a single discipline approach to assessments with any degree of usefulness in the information produced.

The foregoing is not intended to suggest that existing technology assessment methods should be abandoned. Existing methods will still be as useful and necessary in future studies as they have been in past. The contention here is that there must be some analytical extensions to these methodologies in order to generate the kind of information that is going to be required by decision- and policy-makers.

For most studies of biotechnology impacts, the model design will need to become a more explicit activity of the total study. It is common in economics and sociology to take a single category of economic or sociology theory as the given logical construct and then build the data and analysis methods based on its assumptions. Even for studies on biotechnologies having a relatively specific application, the model will need to be more explicit, larger and more involved. The design of the model will need to reflect the disciplinary inputs of bioscientists, institutional or organisational theorists and possibly the business component, as well as that of economists and sociologists. This suggests more of a discipline-free systems or systems analysis approach to the design of the overall model structure as a bridge to multidisciplinary participation. Although properly designed studies will still permit individual problem analysis within a single discipline, the critical element in the analysis is a notable reduction in the number of assumed conditions by the overall study structure. The latter point is a critical error to be avoided in studying biotechnology impacts.

Accepting the anticipatory goal in biotechnology impact studies and the pre-eminence of information requirements, a significant problem encountered is that data bases are either totally lacking or at best inadequate. Basically we are faced with a situation in which not only the impacts exist in the future but so do the data needed to determine the probable impacts. Further, with so much of the biotechnology research being conducted under a proprietary mantle, data that does exist simply will not be available to other researchers. Both of these conditions require some significant rethinking, especially on the part of social scientists, about their techniques for acquiring data. Absolute reliance on secondary data is not possible. Even budgeting techniques are limited in their application. The concept of precision in data measurement, as well as its currently pre-eminent role in study design, must be reconsidered. It is suggested that a greater reliance may need to be placed on subjective data sources.

In conclusion, it is our contention that the challenges to social scientists involved in biotechnology impact assessment studies are substantial ones. The nature of the environment within which biotechnologies are being developed is different than is commonly realised and certainly different from that of agricultural technologies experienced in the past. The nature of the resulting impacts will be more pervasive, more complex and occur at a more rapid rate than anything previously experienced. The practice of making management and policy adjustments *after* an impact has occurred and its effects become clearly visible in the market place or to the general public will result in very great economic and social losses. The role of and challenge to the social scientists, as it has been in the past, is in providing the information that will help anticipate these changes and impacts and their economic and social costs. The circumstance that is different now is that the task of providing truly useful information will require a significant re-examination on the part of social scientists of how they go about conducting their studies.

Undoubtedly, the greatest challenge will come in modifying the way in which we conceptualise the overall problem and formulate our analytical structures. The information required by decision- and policy-makers must become the pre-eminent force in study design. Expected disjointed-ness in impacts suggests the need to re-examine traditional techniques of data acquisition and analysis. More than ever, we will need to consider including the methodologies used in other disciplines. At the same time, we must develop theories that better anticipate the general trajectories of technological, economic and social change that evolve out of the peculiar circumstances created by biotechnologies. Finally, there is a great deal of

Walter L. Fishel and Martin Kenney

urgency in getting social scientists started on examining these issues. There are a number of methodological problems in particular to be resolved before social scientists can expect to provide a steady flow of useful information to managers and policy-makers.

NOTE

[1] Only the principal factors are indicated here. A more complete discussion of these factors is contained in Kenney (1984), Swaminathan (1982), Kenney and Buttel (1985) and Buttel et al. (forthcoming).

REFERENCES

Buttel, Frederick, Kenney, Martin and Kloppenburg, Jack, Jr., 'From Green Revolution to Biorevolution: Some Observations on the Changing Technological Bases of Economic Transformation in the Third World', *Economic Development and Cultural Change*, (forthcoming).

Hayami, Yujiro and Ruttan, Vernon W., *Agricultural Development: An International Perspective*, Johns Hopkins Press, Baltimore, 1971.

Kenney, Martin, 'Biotechnology and Third World Farming Systems', Symposium on Science and Technology as Factors of Change, UNESCO, Paris, 1984.

Kenney, Martin and Buttel, Frederick H., 'Biotechnology: Prospects and Dilemmas for Third World Development', *Development and Change*, January 1985.

Kenney, Martin, *High Tech Biology: Corporate Influence on American Universities*, Yale University Press, New Haven, (forthcoming).

National Research Council, *Priorities in Biotechnology Research for International Development*, National Academy Press, Washington, DC, 1982.

National Academy of Sciences, *Genetic Engineering of Plants*, National Academy Press, Washington, DC, 1984.

Office of Technology Assessment, *Impacts of Applied Genetics*, U.S. Congress, U.S. Government Printing Office, Washington, DC, 1981.

Sondahl, Maro R., Sharp, W. R. and Evans, David., 'Biotechnology for Agriculture of Third World Countries', *ATAS Bulletin*, 1984.

Swaminathan, M. S., 'Biotechnology Research and Third World Agriculture', *Science*, vol. 218, 3 December, 1982.

DISCUSSION OPENING I – CLAUDIO GONZÁLEZ-VEGA

The unifying theme of these two papers is the impact of technological change on economic structures and on social institutions. One of the papers, by Jean-Pierre Berlan, looks at the past. It attempts to explain the historical evolution of the share of the United States in the international trade of grain by looking at the consequences of farm mechanisation and of the introduction of soybean cultivation. The other paper, by W. L. Fishel and M. Kenney, looks at the future. It urges the profession to look closely at the potential consequences of biotechnological innovations, because these may be equivalent to or even more dramatic than those examined by Berlan. Both papers are very general and highly speculative. They do not provide empirical evidence of the kind that would be required to validate their arguments, but the issues raised are very important and are treated in imaginative and provocative ways.

Berlan offers an interesting historical treatment of the evolution of grain production in the United States and of the accompanying structural transformations. It contains multiple details that it will not be possible to examine in detail here. I have no problems with the accuracy of most of the individual facts and events reported in the paper, many of them examined in an insightful way. The same events, however, can lead to a different interpretation of the dynamics of the story, particularly when one brings into the picture other facts, not sufficiently acknowledged by the author.

Increased grain production after the Second World War, for example, owes much to the hybridisation of corn and the extensive use of fertilizer. Since the late 1930s there has been at least a four-fold increase in corn productivity in the United States. These innovations made possible not only rapid growth of corn production but the release of land for soybean production. Similarly important in increasing productivity has been the increasing specialisation of American farmers.

Although Berlan recognises the cost-reducing factors that made possible the expansion of soybean production and exports, from the perspective of supply, he does not consider the equally important demand influences. As a result, he ignores the role of tastes and incomes, elasticities, and relative prices. An alternative interpretation of the events would identify demand as a driving force, as a market for meat products was created by rapidly rising incomes. Without these changes in consumption patterns, the transformations described by the author would not have been possible.

Before the War, the proportion of the world population with incomes sufficiently high to demand livestock products was minimal. Even today, 50 per cent of this population enjoys incomes per caput of less than US $400 a year. It was not until the American and European population became sufficiently affluent, that the demand for meat products increased. It has been shown that the income elasticity of demand for meat is quite high. Moreover, in the earlier days this limited demand for meat was satisfied with production from grass-fed livestock. It is only when incomes grow and consumption patterns shift, that grain is demanded for feed purposes. Similarly, the surge in poultry production can be explained by changes in relative prices and tastes.

Berlan claims that the United States has taken away the role of food producer from the Third World. The fact is that in the past the low-income countries sent little food to the industrialised nations. The periphery was never an important exporter of grain to the centre; at best, it was a supplier of desserts: sugar, coffee, bananas, cacao. Actually, during the period of decline of the American share in international grain trade, it was countries with a very similar natural resource endowment, – Canada, Australia, Argentina – that took her place. In any case, it can hardly be claimed that these were low-income countries. Moreover, policies adopted by these other countries, like the very protectionist import-substitution industrialisation strategy adopted by Argentina after the War, may explain her declining share in grain exports. I do agree, however, with his interpretation of the negative impact of PL-480 on low-income country agriculture.

Given low incomes, in the past the periphery did not demand much feed grain. As incomes increased and with them the demand for meat, imports of feed grain grew. A clear example is Taiwan which faces a severe land constraint. Over the past two decades, the ratio of consumption to output of grain increased from 1 to 1.6. That is, while in the 1960s domestic production was sufficient to meet her needs, Taiwan today imports 40 per cent of her consumption of grain. Does this reflect a poor performance? No, it does not, as Mellor suggested earlier. During these two decades, productivity in grain doubled, output was growing at 5 per cent per year, but consumption increased well in excess of this, given high income elasticities of demand.

The alternative interpretation, that a driving force in the growth of American exports of grain has reflected a demand expansion, has important implications. As one looks at the evolution of world patterns of production and consumption, it becomes clear that the market for grain may be potentially greater than is usually recognised. As incomes per caput increase in other parts of the world, the newly industrialising countries will generate an accelerating demand for meat. At present this demand is met with livestock fed on grasslands and on waste products, the supply of which is extremely limited and will not expand sufficiently. Livestock and poultry producers will turn to feed grain, but these countries do not possess comparative advantages in grain production. Their demand may become an important factor in alleviating the overproduction syndrome highlighted in Berlan's paper.

My main concern with the paper is a methodological one. One cannot justify an argument on the basis of isolated facts and events, while ignoring others, and on cleverly selected citations. I would have preferred to see some reference to tastes and preferences, incomes, relative prices, elasticities, and comparative advantages. From this perspective one cannot claim, as Berlan does, that the economic recovery of Europe and Japan, trade liberalisation, and the rise of real incomes have been 'factors of the second-order of magnitude'.

The difficulties associated with the analysis of the impact of technological change on economic structures and social institutions are also examined in the informative paper by Fishel and Kenney. If the interpretation of past history and a determination of the relative contribution of the multiple determinants of structural adjustments is a difficult task, anticipation of future impacts and adjustments is even more complex and risky. The researcher not only does not know the precise nature of the innovation itself, but must also project the constellation of relative prices and public-sector interventions that will influence the pace of adoption and counterbalancing reactions.

Fishel and Kenney claim that the biotechnological innovations in the pipeline are numerous, will be introduced simultaneously, will have a major impact on productivity, and will require rapid and substantial adjustments. They insist that their potential impact requires not only urgent study, but also anticipatory management and policy action. Their paper, unfortunately, does not even suggest what some of these actions may look like. It would be important to discuss what some of the predictable consequences of this revolution may be, if the dislocations announced by the authors are going to be properly dealt with.

For example, the authors insist that these developments raise important questions about property rights. They claim that the new technologies are being developed mainly by the private sector, protected by secrecy, patents and other proprietary restrictions. At the same time, they require enormous infusions of capital and have a high risk of development. The usual dilemmas resulting from the imperfections of the market for knowledge are evident. It is in the social interest to protect the profitability of these endeavours, to promote investment in this kind of research and innovations, while at the same time guaranteeing the widest adoption. Divergences between private and social costs and benefits must be compensated for in ways that do not slow down the pace of progress. Fishel and Kenney implicitly suggest that existing mechanisms for the generation and diffusion of innovations are no longer adequate, but their paper does not even outline the measures that must be taken to improve them.

Although the authors challenge the adequacy of existing methodologies for the study of technological change and of its impact, again they do not spell out explicitly and precisely what the deficiencies are and what is the nature of the corrections and extension required. They claim that larger and more complex models will be needed, with exceptionally high information requirements, but this is a change of magnitude, not of approach. Their recommendations of up-front neutrality, a multidisciplinary approach, and relevancy of the data one can hardly disagree with. At times it seems that the authors are unhappy about existing theoretical paradigms, but they do not state it explicitly.

There is a clear link between the two papers. If indeed biotechnological innovations will be as significant as Fishel and Kenney claim, largely increasing the productivity of firms and activities relatively intensive in knowledge, capital and management, they will have a substantial impact on the comparative advantages of the United States in world agricultural markets. Developments like these will further increase American dominance and will have significant consequences on the direction and pattern of international trade.

DISCUSSION OPENING II – W. J. MARTIN

Unless we learn the lessons of history, we are doomed to repeat the mistakes of the past. For this reason, it is fortunate that the two papers presented this morning are extremely complementary. As Claudio González-Vega noted in his comments, the first analyses the historical impacts of a major technological change while the second considers the likely effects of future technological advances.

The two papers each cover three main topics:

(1) Technological change
(2) Its economic effects
(3) Social and policy effects.

Turning first to M. Berlan's paper, the technological advance considered was power farming – the mechanisation of US agriculture. Interestingly, this technological advance was largely the result of research and development undertaken in the private sector. The patent system defined property rights over most technical advances and made investment in research worthwhile for the private sector.

The economic effects of power farming were both direct and indirect, with the indirect effects being considerably more important in the long term. The indirect effects required that considerable endogenous technical change take place to exploit newly profitable opportunities in soybean and livestock production. These advances included development of new varieties, development of soybean meal and hydrogenation of soybean oil, and involved both public and private research investments.

M. Berlan has pointed out that power farming brought farmers further into the market economy – 'subverting the simple exchange into a capitalist one'. He goes much further than this, suggesting that the capitalist system is inherently prone to a crisis of overproduction because of capital accumulation on farms and in agribusiness. This claim *completely* ignores the role of relative prices in balancing supply and demand – a role which they perform adequately if not distorted by policy. I am afraid I do not understand how this important balancing item can be ignored in developing a framework for analysing technical change, particularly when the role of lower prices in increasing the demand for meat is acknowledged. Any analysis of future technological change must surely consider the role of price in balancing supply and demand.

In the second paper, Fishel and Kenney argue that biotechnology is likely to have a greater impact on agriculture than the Green Revolution. They would probably argue that it is likely to be comparable in impact to the power farming revolution discussed earlier. The authors describe a range of technological advances such as tissue culture and genetic engineering, and point out that most research is taking place in the private sector. This raises an important question of whether today's institutions are adequate to allow efficient allocation of research resources. Patent systems generally do not provide property rights so that private investments in agricultural research can be recouped. Other systems such as Plant Variety Rights are only in their infancy.

As we have seen in the case of power farming, the economic effects of technological advance are likely to extend well beyond the direct effects. Even the direct effects of advances which transfer production of agricultural commodities from the farm to the factory will, of course, be substantial.

Fishel and Kenney argue that a great deal of research into biotechnology impacts is needed and that this research should be problem-oriented, should use a systems approach and should be subjective, if necessary, to overcome data limitations. I endorse most of their suggestions about methodology, particularly their argument that research should be addressed to the important policy problems, rather than merely those that are readily solved given current data availability. However, I have some concerns about their orientation to forecasting, or even anticipating, the effects of technological change. While providing some general information on technological developments is likely to be useful to decision-makers, I simply do not believe that the impacts of new technology can be forecast with any degree of accuracy. This is particularly the case with the indirect effects which can be very complex, as we have seen in the first paper. A far more important issue, I believe, is ensuring that the policy environment allows needed adjustments to take place. Any welfare problems resulting from rapid technological change can be dealt with directly by compensation policies which do not distort prices. Agricultural policies which do not allow prices to move in line with market trends can severely inhibit adjustments needed to respond to emerging market opportunities. The problems of over-production currently evident in Europe are indicative of how costly such interventions can be.

The actual conduct of research also requires an appropriate institutional framework. If research is to be undertaken efficiently in the private sector, careful attention needs to be given to the design of property rights for research achievements. For the public sector, research is needed to ensure that scarce research resources can be efficiently allocated.

In summary, it is clear from the two papers that technological change has caused, and will continue to cause, massive change in agriculture. As history has shown, these effects are extremely complex, involving long chains of indirect effects. Because of this complexity, and the difficulty of forecasting future technical change, I do not believe that we can accurately predict where we will end up. However, as long as we have the right institutional environment, I am confident that our journey will be a welfare-maximising one.

GENERAL DISCUSSION – RAPPORTEUR: GERT VAN DIJK

The reactions to Berlan's paper were concerned with the theoretical approach and the interpretation of data and also with specific facts. Quite a few questions took the implications of Fishel and Kenney's paper into account and applied these to Berlan's analysis.

Regarding the surplus problem in US agriculture, it was stressed that conversion of foodstuffs into livestock products was an important feature. However, although international trade in these products was important, the meat trade was in fact rather restricted. Possible favourable effects were thus impeded.

The more general observation was made that international trade was strongly influenced by differences in rates of change in technology. The effects of these differences might be more important than the differences in resource endowment or comparative advantages. Countries lacking competitive power needed political power in order to compensate. The question was raised whether this necessitated other production models.

Related to the previous point it was pointed out that the well known Public Law 480 led to the shipment of large quantities of grain to countries like India. The discussant stressed that this had many negative effects in the sense of depressed prices and disincentives to agriculture in importing countries. Smaller acreages were more under wheat than necessary, development policies were based on food aid, most cheap grains were consumed by the urban population.

Some discussants applied Fishel and Kenney's paper to Berlan's subject. The main line of reasoning was that the role of biotechnology was thought to be important for future world food supplies. For example, fractioning of biomass might in due course improve the conversion ratios of animal production, also more fibres might become suitable. The origins of raw materials for human food would similarly broaden because of applying biotechnological methods to biomass. New technology might, in total, increase the competitiveness of agricultural raw materials versus non-renewable natural resources in the field of agrochemistry and agro-energy. The examples of latex, alfalfa, forestry products and alcohol were mentioned. Such new opportunities could help to overcome the surplus problem. Other more specific points on Berlan's paper were the following:

Thanks to new varieties of soya and their adaptation to climatic conditions in Western Europe this crop has expanded rapidly in the recent past. A continuation of this explosive increase may occur, as happened with maize.

The idea of capital accumulation in agriculture was questioned; currently capital volume is stagnant or decreasing both in the US and Belgium.

In the early 1950s US agriculture not only lost the feedstuff market for draft animals but also textiles were substituted for by plastics.

It was considered difficult to judge in retrospect the assertion that Third World countries had now become the dumping ground of agricultural surpluses.

Doubts were cast on the applicability of Fishel's paper. Was this not too speculative? Could the future be sufficiently quantified?

Berlan's reply could not deal with all points raised because of time limitations. He unfolded his analytical framework and added that instead of gathering all relevant demand elasticity estimates, discussions with farmers – who had to make use of the opportunities for change – might be more relevant. He stressed once more that a static approach was not fruitful. Instead one was dealing with long-term historical processes. In our time social forces might need new economic policies. A new model by which new markets were developed by, among others, agronomic research had to be judged in the light of historical processes. As a way of getting rid of surpluses it should be remembered that currently 85 per cent of US oil exports is shipped as food aid. Consequently oil production in LDCs is under severe pressure. Berlan agreed that the international meat trade was restricted. The multiplying effect of meat exports with regard to surplus disposal was moreover reduced because of improved conversion ratios. Solutions of the problem now were therefore bound to be different from those in the 1980s.

In response to the discussion openers and the audience, Fishel recognised the lack of examples in the paper about the problems of methodology, data sources and acquisitions. This was due to space limitations. Against the scepticism as regards the relevance of analysis as stressed in the paper, the author maintained that we indeed could quantify the future. There was a difference, however, in the view of the past-oriented world of economists and sociologists and the future which existed in the minds of our bio-scientists who could rather easily perceive what was possible. Our methodologies had therefore to be adapted from a concern about precision and an approach was required which permitted the concept of anticipation – not always correct, but more often correct than not. Was it justified to consider future problems that might not even happen? Things could be worse and could be better, but would, anyhow be different. If we as agricultural economists did not provide policy-makers with more information about what it might mean, who would?

Participants in the discussion included J. M. Boussard, G. Bublot, D. Farris, M. S. Kenal and E. Tollens.

FRANCIS S. IDACHABA

The Evolution of National Agricultural Research Systems in Sub-Saharan Africa

I. INTRODUCTION

The poor performance of sub-Saharan agriculture is now well documented.[1] The decade of independence in the 1960s has been followed by about 15 years of stagnation and decline in production, yields and cropped land area in the key staple food and export crops. Recent estimates from IFPRI[2] disaggregate this dismal performance by subregions and commodity groups. Using 1976–80 averages, West Africa accounted for almost half of the output of sub-Saharan Africa, with Nigeria accounting for more than half of West Africa's food output or about 25 per cent of all sub-Saharan Africa. West Africa witnessed the highest rate of growth of population but the slowest rate of growth of food production: output of major food crops grew at only 1 per cent during 1961/5–1976/80. These trends have resulted, especially in Nigeria, in soaring domestic food prices and mounting imports of palm oil, rice, wheat, sugar and cotton, among others.

There are at least five sources of incremental food and fibre production: extensive agriculture involving cultivation of virgin lands and increases in productivity per man; improvements in allocative efficiency[3] and increases in cropping intensity through irrigation which makes possible two, sometimes three, crops a year. Others are massive infusions of new chemical, biological and management inputs and the introduction of drastic reforms in policy to remove such policy disincentives as implicit and explicit taxes on crops, overvalued exchange rates, which make food imports cheaper than they should otherwise be, and urban bias in food policies, to mention a few.

National agricultural research systems in sub-Saharan Africa face enormous challenges in efforts to realise the production potential from these five sources. The objective of the paper is to review national agricultural research systems in sub-Saharan Africa and to identify the critical issues that need to be addressed if these systems are to meet the historical challenge. The rest of the paper is structured as follows. Section II briefly reviews the evaluation of agricultural research in sub-Saharan Africa. We are constrained by our heavy dependence on experiences from Anglophone West Africa, especially Nigeria. It is hoped that the issues addressed are of a sufficiently general nature to have wider continental relevance. Section III identifies the key issues for consideration in evolving effective national research systems and redirecting research priorities while section IV concludes the paper.

II. BRIEF REVIEW

Most agricultural research institutes were established to cater for the needs of the oil seeds industry of Western Europe during the first half of this century. Some of the institutes owe their origin to the disruptions in supplies of raw materials during the Second World War. In Nigeria, agricultural research dates back to 1893 when the first botanical garden was established. The critical focus of the institutes was on export crops not only to provide the raw material needs of Western Europe but also to provide the needed foreign exchange for imports of consumer goods and capital items needed especially for the transportation networks in the colonies. Pan-territorial research institutes were established along broad ecological zones, (e.g. the West African Cocoa Research Institute, Tafo, Ghana (1944), The West African Institute for Oil Palm research, Benin, Nigeria (1951) and the West African Institute for Trypanosomiasis Research, Kaduna, Nigeria (1947)).

The advent of independence witnessed the dissolution of the West African Research Organization in 1962 and the creation of corresponding national research institutes in individual countries, for example, the Cocoa Research Institute of Nigeria (1964), the Nigerian Institute for Oil Palm Research and the Nigerian Institute for Trypanosomiasis Research. This has resulted in a duplication of research facilities. It also marked the beginning of the progressive abdication of national responsibilities for research of a less applied nature.

An important feature of the colonial system was the active involvement of the private sector in research. For example, the British Cotton Corporation provided a stable core of cotton breeders, soil scientists, entomologists, etc. at the Institute for Agricultural Research Samaru, Nigeria, during 1926–67. A striking feature was the network of close informal links between the private sector researchers and policy-makers and bureaucrats who took the major decisions affecting agricultural research. This ensured good funding and a much faster appreciation of the problems of the research establishment.

There is a variety of institutional arrangements for managing agricultural research. In some countries agricultural research institutes are under the Ministry of Agriculture while in others they are under the Ministry of Science and Technology. Some countries have created parastatals to manage agricultural research institutes while in countries such as Nigeria, all institutional modalities have been tried in an almost endless search for the most effective institutional arrangement.

On research impact, there are only isolated pieces of evidence on quantum production gains which can be directly and unambiguously attributed to dramatic breakthroughs in agricultural research. This has led some observers to suggest that African agriculture is backward largely because decades of agricultural research have produced few usable technologies.[4] Agricultural extension systems have proved largely ineffective because of poor and erratic funding, low staff morale and vague specifications of programmes for extension staff. Training programmes have been largely *ad hoc* and usually geared towards the needs of the extension system and totally unrelated to the training needs of the agricultural research system. Finally, research extension and training have not been completely integrated, with the result that there is no effective two-way communication channel between researchers and farmers.

Against the background of these characteristics, what have been the main constraints?

Constraints of national agricultural research systems
National agricultural research systems in sub-Saharan Africa face a set of constraints. These include lack of coherent agricultural research policies, lack of operational agricultural research resource allocation criteria, inadequate and unstable research staff (see Tables 1–2) and poor management of national agricultural research systems.

TABLE 1   *Instability in funding of agricultural research institutes, Nigeria, 1975/76–1980*

Institute	Total allocation 1975/76–1980 (₦million)	Index of funding instability (%)
AERLS	6.276	32.40
CRIN	18.175	40.67
FRIN	22.400	36.20
IAR	28.614	105.80
IAR & T	14.023	162.10
KLRI	10.352	92.65
LCRI	7.876	20.10
LERIN	8.468	199.85
NAPRI	7.713	55.85
NCRI	24.600	53.80
NIHORT	11.852	37.53
NRCRI	21.451	35.95
NVRI	29.862	23.00
NIOMR	10.674	35.80
NIFOR	25.291	89.65
NITR	11.519	47.36
NSPRI	4.976	156.73
RRIN	12.500	106.31

Source: Underlying data from *Report of Research Institute Review Panel for the National Committee on Green Revolution*, vol. 2, Green Revolution National Committee, Ibadan Office, Moor Plantation, Ibadan, 1980–1.

TABLE 2 *Research staff turnover rates for selected agricultural research institutes*

Discipline	IAR		FDAR/NCRI	NIFOR
	1962/63 to 1967/68	1967/68 to 1977/78	1967/68 to 1973/74	1963/64 to 1973/74
	(per cent)			
Agronomy	66.67	66.67	12.50	100.00
Botany	57.14	80.00		
Cotton breeding	40.00	100.00		
Pathology	50.00	60.00	25.00	
Crop physiology	100.00			
Entomology	71.43	80.00	20.00	
Soil science chemistry	60.00	100.00	60.00	100.00
Soil survey	71.43	60.00		
Animal husbandry and grassland	100.00			
Agricultural engineering	100.00			
Plant breeding			20.00	66.67
Statistics/information			100.00	
Agricultural economics		100.00		

Notes The rate of research staff turrnover (I_j) is defined as:

$$\sum_{i=1}^{k} N_{ji,t-n} - \sum_{i=1}^{k} N_{ji,t} \Big/ \sum_{i=1}^{k} N_{ji,t-n} \times 100,$$

where N_i stands for the ith individual researcher whose value is set equal to 1 if he is on the job or 0 if he has left the research institute; j stands for the discipline, commodity programme, or department; k stands for the number of researchers; t stands for the time period; and n is some chosen time interval.

The full names of the institutes listed in the table are as follows: Institute for Agricultural Research (IAR), Federal Department of Agricultural Research/National Cereals Research Institute (FDAR/NCRI), and Nigerian Institute for Oil Palm Research (NIFOR).

III. KEY ISSUES IN MAKING NATIONAL AGRICULTURAL RESEARCH SYSTEMS MORE EFFECTIVE

After almost a century of agricultural research in many African countries and the continuing stagnation of African agriculture, the time is ripe for redirection.

National objectives and agricultural research priorities
How should African countries reduce the time lag involved in transforming national objectives into agricultural research priorities, programmes and projects? Several lags are involved: the lag between the existence of a national problem (e.g. production shortfalls and increasing dependence on food imports) and the articulation of a national objective (e.g. food self-reliance/self-sufficiency); between the formulation of a national objective and the translation into an agricultural sector objective

and the specification of agricultural research priorities (e.g. varietal selection and trials to stimulate domestic production and processing of wheat, long grain rice, sugar etc.; between agricultural research priority specification and the formulation of research programmes and projects; between programme formulation and execution; between agricultural research formulation execution and agricultural research results (which may take several years); and finally the time lag between research results from the experimentation phase and agricultural research impact (the mass adoption phase). The convolution of these lags in most African countries compounds the resource allocation problem further. The discipline that this imposes on research managers is the need for continuous demonstration of how research, extension and training priorities are directly derived from national objectives.

Criteria for determining priorities in redirecting research, training and extension
The redirection of research, extension and training involves a reallocation of resources. Criteria for such reallocation include: foreign exchange contribution of commodities, self-reliance and import substitution considerations, nutritional significance and the relative significance of food items for the diet of poor people. Others include employment potential, value of production and value added, and contribution to national food security with special focus on irrigation research and drought research.[5]

Micro management of research
Micro research managers, institute directors, division chiefs and departmental heads must achieve technical efficiency in the transformation of research resources (funds, researchers, equipment, materials) into research output of practical value in agricultural production, distribution and consumption. Constraints on this transformation process include low calibre of research staff which results in poorly formulated and executed research projects, poor allocative abilities of institute directors and division chiefs on grounds other than competence and demonstration ability for research leadership, the proliferation of divisions, departments and units within research institutions sometimes to satisfy the personal ambitions of particular individuals or from the utility that directors get from presiding over 'big' institutes. How do we get institute directors to become good managers? How do we ensure that institute directors continue to provide professional leadership for their institutes rather than become mere administrators?

Macro research management
Proper macro management of research institutes is probably a more serious problem than paucity of funds or skilled manpower in many national systems of sub-Saharan Africa. The institutional arrangements for administering research institutes are in a continuous state of flux: the

TABLE 3   *Frequent changes in institutional arrangements for managing Nigeria's national agricultural research system, 1970–1979*

Date	Decree/Act	Remarks
1970	National Council for Science and Technology (NCST) Decree	Pulled together under one agency research units of various Ministries.
1971	Decree establishing Agricultural Research Council of Nigeria (ARCN)	One of four Councils provided for under NCST Decree to co-ordinate all agricultural research.
1973	Agricultural Research Institutes Order (Decree No. 33)	Formally established present federal agricultural research monolith in place of past joint federal-state system.
1975	Research Institutes (Establishment) Order	
1977	Research Institutes (Establishment) Order	
1977	National Science and Technology Development Agency Decree	Repealed 1973 Decree. Took over all functions of the NCST.
1979	Science and Technology Act, 1980	Abolished National Science and Technology Development Agency established only 2 years earlier. Created a Ministry of Science and Technology.
1984	Ministry of Science and Technology scrapped and merged with education to form Ministry of Education, Science and Technology	Ministry too large to pay attention to the needs of agricultural research.

supervising ministry for research institutes gets changed almost as frequently as there are changes in regime; parastatals with statutory responsibility for research institutes are created and abolished with alarming frequency and ease, again almost as frequently as regimes change (see Table 3). Frequent institutional changes of this nature impart a basic instability to a national research system, resulting in frequent policy revisions, changes and reversals. Components of this instability include: instability in programme formulation as new ministerial or parastatal leadership imposes its own programme priorities; unstable relationships between macro managers and micro research managers and consequently an unstable system for transforming national objectives into agricultural research priorities and finally, instability from researchers who migrate from the system in protest against the uncertainty created by the frequent institutional changes at the macro level.

On the best macro institutional arrangement for managing the research institute system, can we say one is better than the other, as a general rule as between a ministry at the national level and a parastatal? Nigeria has gone full circle with these forms and the verdict is still open. Results from other African countries and Latin America are mixed. In the final analysis, we are forced to conclude that it all depends on the individuals operating the ministry or the parastatal.

Granted that a minsterial mode is chosen, should agricultural research institutes be under a Ministry of Science and Technology, a Ministry of Education or a Ministry of Agriculture? This is relevant for purposes of funding, co-ordination, linkages with mainstream agricultural programmes, the reduction in the time lag between specification of national objectives and the translation into agricultural research priorities etc. There is also the central issue of the need for an explicit national science and technology policy of which a national agricultural research policy is only a part. Some African countries have such a policy statement but for most, it is only implied. When an explicit statement exists, what role does the agricultural establishment play in its formulation?

A central issue of macro management of a national system is the absence in most African countries of any effective mechanisms for monitoring and evaluating national agricultural research systems – the absence of a 'monitoring and evaluation culture' that must be distinguished from the periodic investigative panels which are more of the nature of episodes. To effectively monitor, headquarters (macro) managers of national agricultural research systems need to develop technical capabilities in the relevant disciplines in order to be able to guide research activities at the institute level, i.e., monitoring without superior technical support capability is virtually useless.

Locations of some research institutes, subcentres and stations have been more the product of history and circumstances than of logic and relocation efforts have been hampered by lack of political will, funds for capital projects, etc. (see Table 4).

Macro managers should direct institute directors to concentrate less on grandiose headquarters complexes and more on a network of adaptive research centres with the requisite infrastructures (water, electricity, schools, hospitals, etc.) that would attract sufficiently senior and experienced researchers. Otherwise, national adaptive and operational research capabilities will remain weak.

Finally, macro managers must appoint research institute directors on the basis of their professional expertise rather than political patronage. Their performance must be closely monitored by Governing Councils and Boards made up of relevant professionals rather than politicians.

Funding, research, extension and training

Though Nigeria and a few countries have recorded substantial increases in funding for agricultural research, the general picture for most countries is one of gross underfunding. Any recorded recent gains are only illusory as they reflect the high wages and salaries which are generally higher in Africa (especially West Africa) than in Southeast Asia. The gross inadequacy in funding can be attributed to a lack of political will or commitment or inability to link research with technology and production. Inadequate funding is further compounded by funding instability

TABLE 4 *Suitability of agricultural research institutes headquarters location by crop, Nigeria, 1968/69 to 1974/75*

Institute	Nearest three states to headquarters	Crop	Index of location suitability
			(per cent)
IAR	Kaduna	Groundnuts	65.60
	Kano	Sorghum	55.14
	Sokoto	Millet	50.29
		Melons	7.35
		Benniseed	15.65
NCRI	Oyo	Maize	40.75
	Ondo	Rice	35.10
	Ogun	Beans	3.95
		Soybeans	0.00
		Sugarcane	.....
NRCRI	Imo	Yams	22.80
	Anambra	Cassava	29.49
	Cross River	Cocoyams	65.98
NIFOR	Bendel, Ondo, Imo	Palm Kernels (1969–71)	56.40
RRIN	Bendel, Ondo, Imo	Rubber	.....
NIHORT	Oyo, Ogun, Ondo	n.a.	.....
CRIN	Oyo, Ogun, Ondo	Cocoa (1968/69–1970/71)	90.05
NAPRI[a]	Kaduna, Kano, Sokoto	Cattle	n.a.
NVRI[a]	Plateau, Kaduna, Bauchi	Cattle	n.a.
NITR[a]	Niger, Plateau	Cattle	n.a.

Note The full names of the institutes listed in the table are as follows: Institute for Agricultural Research (IAR), National Cereals Research Institute (NCRI), National Root Crops Research Institute (NRCRI), Nigerian Institute for Oil Palm Research (NIFOR), Rubber Research Institute of Nigeria (RRIN), National Institute for Horticultural Research (NIHORT), Cocoa Research Institute of Nigeria (CRIN), National Animal Production Research Institute (NAPRI), National Veterinary Research Institute (NVRI), and National Institute for Trypanosomiasis Research (NITR).
[a]Though indexes of suitability are not available, indications are that the locations of livestock research institutes in Kaduna State are suitable.
Source Idachaba, F. S. *Agricultural Research Policy in Nigeria*, International Food Policy Research Institute, Report 17, August 1980.

comprising unpredictable and uncontrollable fluctuations in year-to-year funding and untimely release of funds.

The funding situation in extension is equally alarming. Many extension departments have ground to a complete halt because salaries are delayed, also transport claims, where they have not been scrapped altogether, motor cycle loans have been abolished, among other debilitating austerity measures.

Private sector involvement in research, extension and training
The earlier strong presence of the organised private sector in agricultural

research has given way to the monolithic dominance of government in research support. The real issue here in trying to redirect research is: how do African systems dominated by the small-scale farmer provide private sector support for research? Of fundamental importance here is the limited relevance of traditional supply side approach to discussion of national agricultural research systems to the total neglect of the demand side. How are demands of small-scale peasant farmers for research results/output to be articulated? The experience from Latin America reveals that private sector farmers do indeed support research though they tend to be large-scale farmers. Do African countries have to wait for the new generation of large-scale farmers before private sector farmers support research? What is required is a forging of the links between farmers, farmers' groups and research institutes.

There are now frantic efforts in Nigeria and other African countries to involve the organised private sector in farming. Government should provide incentives for the organised private sector to participate in agricultural research.

Manpower utilisation, migration of researchers and research staff instability
Efforts to redirect research, extension and training must focus on the efficient utilisation of available indigenous manpower within the system.[6] How should research staff productivity be raised? How can internal migration of research staff be minimised to reduce staff instability and turnover? The issue centres around the identity crisis of the civil servant-scientist. He is not a full civil servant and he is not a university researcher. His is a dubious status promoted by successive governments and tolerated by institute researchers whose career has thus been linearly tied up with length of service. Any effort to redirect research must therefore start with a redefinition of the status of the hybrid called the civil servant-scientist.

Integration of research, extension and training
The historical origins of research institutes in most African countries have almost guaranteed the non-integration of research, extension and training. African systems have ended up with the worst of both worlds: they have neither the unique features of a Rothamsted Experimental Station nor the integrated system of the United States Land Grant system. Elsewhere, India broke out of this colonial legacy and implanted an integrated system through a network of agricultural universities. Is the agricultural universities route the best option and do African countries have the funds to establish them? And what are workable institutional modalities for joint collaborative research between research institutes and university faculties of agriculture, especially when they lack the advantage of close physical proximity?

National research institutions and international agricultural research centres
CGIAR Centres see their roles primarily in applied research of regional

and world-wide relevance. As many African countries dismantled the colonial pan-territorial research institutes, the CGIAR Centres have come to fill in some of the vacuum. What are the best modalities for integrating work at the CGIAR Centres with work in the national institutions? There is no reason why African countries cannot emulate the Colombian example where CIAT and the national institutions collaborated to breed new rice varieties. Another issue is: what is the optimal division of responsibility between national institutions and CGIAR Centres? And should African national research systems continue to abdicate their responsibility for basic research to the faculties of agriculture and specialised laboratories and research institutes of developed countries?

Research on the macro environment
Agricultural research in most research institutes and in the faculties of agriculture has neglected the larger macro environment. Thus, there is an urgent need to conduct more research on the impact of trade policies (exchange rate policy included) on domestic food and fibre production; the effect of fiscal and monetary policies on the agricultural sector; agricultural sector modelling to simulate effects of policies such as devaluation and removal of petroleum subsidies on the agricultural sector; agricultural planning within the framework of national economic planning; the allocative and distributional consequences of pricing policies and the impact of world prices on domestic agricultural production, to mention a few.

Interface of research and development programming
In most countries, there is still the issue of how to integrate agricultural research, extension and training into practical development programming. This is due to the fact that there is often no effective linkage between research work in the research institutes and the universities and the executive ministries and the organised private sector that is supposed to translate these results into commercially useful commodities and services. The research establishment, the executive ministries of government and the organised private sector all seem to be running in parallel with a very urgent need for convergence.

Returns to investment in research
There are very few studies on the returns to investment in various types of agricultural research in sub-Saharan Africa. This lacuna in empirical knowledge cannot entirely be blamed on lack of reliable crop output time series data. Yet *ex post* rate of return analysis remains vital for allocation of resources to different types of research.

Responsibility for agricultural research, extension and training by different tiers of government
Still an unresolved issue in many countries is the delineation of

responsibilities among local, state and national governments for different kinds of research, extension and training. What should be the allocative criteria here? Suggested criteria include, among others, the category of research as between basic and applied, geographical or ecological spread of the crop and the strategic (national) importance of the crop. Nigeria has gone full circle: from a national research system initially dominated by the federal government to one jointly supported by federal and state governments and, since the oil boom era, to a situation wherein the federal government alone finances all agricultural research.[7] Extension on the other hand has been the traditional responsibility of state governments while training at the level of Colleges of Agriculture and the Universities has been the joint responsibility of the state and federal governments.

Perennial mistakes in agricultural research, extension and training policy
After almost one century of organised research in much of sub-Saharan Africa, are we not entitled to ask why mistakes in priorities, resource allocation, research management, etc., continue year after year, decade after decade, from one regime to the next and also from one country to another? To say that the stagnation of the agricultural research establishment can be explained by 'perennial mistakes' which persist from year to year is to confess the inadequacy of our analytical framework. The problem of persistent mistakes in public policy to which I have alluded elsewhere[8] has been succinctly put in another context by Professor George Stigler, the Nobel Laureate:

> ... To believe year after year, decade after decade that the protective tariffs or usury laws to be found in most lands are due to confusions rather than purposeful action is singularly obfuscatory. Mistakes are indeed made by the best of men and the best of nations, but after a century are we not entitled to question whether the so-called 'mistakes' produce only unintended results? ... Alternatively stated, a theory that says that a large set of persistent policies are mistaken is profoundly anti-intellectual unless it is joined to a theory of mistakes.[9]

What is increasingly required is more research on the demand side to balance the present undue concentration on the supply side.

IV. SUMMARY AND CONCLUSIONS

This paper has been concerned with issues in redirecting agricultural research, extension and training to achieve accelerated agricultural development in sub-Saharan Africa. We have been more concerned with raising the issues than with providing answers that are universally applicable in this area.

These issues are identified and discussed against the background of a brief review of salient features and constraints of African national research systems. The issues centre around those factors that determine the internal technical efficiency of research institutes in transforming research resources into research output; those that relate to macro research management at the headquarters level and finally those determinants of research, extension and training productivity and performance that are external to the national agricultural research system. Unless these issues can be clarified and workable solutions found that are relevant within the environmental context of different sub-Saharan African countries, there will still be no viable packages of new technology to extend to the millions of African farmers.

NOTES

[1] See The World Bank (1981).

[2] See Paulino (1983).

[3] Significant output gains can however be realised through changes in policy incentives that favourably affect relative prices and induce efficiency movements along a given production function using traditional inputs. For the earlier statement of the allocative efficiency hypothesis, see Schultz (1964).

[4] For some discussion of broad strategies regarding new technologies, see Johnson (1969).

[5] Allocative criteria are essentially country specific, reflecting a country's peculiar constraints and opportunities and are therefore not necessarily applicable to other countries. Also, allocative criteria are essentially dynamic, reflecting changes over time in a society's goals, opportunities and constraints.

The literature on allocative criteria for agricultural research is extensive. For a small sample, see Fishel (1971); Arndt, Dalrymple and Ruttan (1977); Daniels and Nestel (1981); and Ruttan (1982).

For specific Nigerian case studies, see Idachaba (1980); and Idachaba (1981).

One issue which can only receive brief mention here is conflict in allocative criteria. One way out is to streamline the process by which national goals are translated into specific agricultural research priorities to eliminate some inherent conflicts. Another solution is to identify a set of policy instruments which will shift the trade-off curves outwards and to the right. See Idachaba (1985).

[6] Eicher (1985) has provided some evidence on continued domination of some national research systems by expatriates in Senegal where 'the French dominated research until 1975' and French dominance of tree crop was terminated only recently.

[7] Unlike the development of the decentralised co-operative system in the United States, the research institutions in sub-Saharan Africa did not develop in response to local, state and national movements and pressure groups. African national systems developed largely to cater for the regional export economies prompted by the needs of imperial transnationals and nurtured by the colonial civil service. The achievements of research institutions have hardly ever become hot political issues in sub-Saharan Africa in the same way that they became campaign issues in State elections in the United States in the 1880s and 1890s. See Peterson and Fitzharris (1977).

[8] See Idachaba, (1984).

[9] See Stigler (1982).

REFERENCES

Arndt, T. M., Dalrymple, D. G. and Ruttan, V. W. (eds.), *Resource Allocation and Productivity in National and International Agricultural Research*, University of Minnesota Press, Minneapolis, 1977.
Daniels, D. and Nestel, B. (eds), *Resource Allocation for Agricultural Research*, International Development Research Centre, IDRC 182e, Ottawa, 1981.

Eicher, Carl R., *Agricultural Research for African Development: Problems and Priorities for 1985–2000*, 1985.

Fishel, W. L. (ed.) *Resource Allocation in Agricultural Research*, University of Minnesota Press, Minneapolis, 1971.

Idachaba, F. S., *Agricultural Research Policy in Nigeria*, International Food Policy Research Institute, Report 17, Washington DC, 1980.

Idachaba, F. S., 'Agricultural Research Resource Allocation Priorities: The Nigerian Experience' in *Resource Allocation to Agricultural Research*, Daniels, D. and Netsel, B. (eds.), op. cit.

Idachaba, F. S., 'Agricultural Research Policy in Nigeria', in *Proceedings of Agricultural Research Policy Seminar*, Department of Agricultural and Applied Economics, University of Minnesota, Minneapolis, 1985.

Idachaba, F. S., 'Self-Reliance Strategies for Nigerian Agriculture: Cornucopia or Pandora's Box?' in *Proceedings of Annual Conference of Nigerian Economic Society*, 1984.

Johnson, G. L., et al. (eds), *Strategies and Recommendations for Nigerian Rural Development, 1969–85*, CSNRD 33, Michigan State University, East Lansing, 1969.

Paulino, L. A. 'The Evolving Feed Situation in Sub-Saharan Africa', Paper presented at International Food Policy Research Institute Conference on Accelerating Agricultural Growth in Sub-Saharan Africa, Victoria Falls, Zimbabwe, 29 August–1 September 1983.

Peterson, W. L. and Fitzharris, J. C., 'Organization and Productivity of the Federal-State Research System in the United States' in *Resource Allocation and Productivity in National and International Agricultural Research*, Arndt, T. M., Dalrymple, D. G. and Ruttan, V. W. (eds), University of Minnesota Press, Minneapolis, 1977.

Ruttan, V. W., *Agricultural Research Policy*, University of Minnesota Press, Minneapolis, 1982.

Stigler, G. J., *The Economist As Preacher and Other Essays*, University of Chicago Press, 1982.

World Bank *Accelerated Development in Sub-Saharan Africa: An Agenda for Action*, International Bank for Reconstructions and Development, Washington, DC, 1981.

HANS P. BINSWANGER AND PRABHU PINGALI

Agricultural Intensification and Technical Change in Sub-Saharan Africa

This paper provides the main conclusions of a research project on the evolution of farming systems and agricultural technology in sub-Saharan Africa. These conclusions are based on a detailed literature review complemented by field visits to 50 villages in 10 countries of sub-Saharan Africa. We explore the impact of population growth and/or improvements in market access on the overall nature of the farming system, on land use patterns and yields, on the use of mechanical technology and the production of organic fertilizers, and on the institutional restrictions to the acquisition of land.

African farmer-generated solutions to increasing food production from a given area of land have been identical or strikingly similar to the solutions found in other parts of the developed or developing world. Farmers respond to increasing population densities and/or increased demand for agricultural output with an expansion in the area cultivated, an increase in land investments and innovations in mechanical technology and manuring systems. These changes are capable of sustaining slow and steadily growing agricultural populations with modest increases in agricultural output.

This research supports the view that more rapid growth in output can be achieved where agricultural policy promotes: (a) an expansion in transport infrastructure; (b) the installation of core agricultural support services; (c) trade policies that do not restrict the availability of new technology; and (d) a rational agricultural price policy that does not suppress farmer initiative for expansion in output. Appropriate agricultural policies could lead to rapid expansion in food output resulting in higher levels of food consumption and increase in income per caput[1].

Population growth and market access are the main determinants of agricultural intensification
Agricultural intensification is defined here as the movement from forest and bush fallow systems of cultivation to annual and multicrop cultivation systems where plots of land are continuously cultivated. The existence of

a positive relationship between population density and agricultural intensification has been hypothesised by Boserup. An increase in population density causes a reduction in fallow periods due to increasing land scarcity, hence the movement to more permanent cultivation of land. Our research in addition to verifying the Boserup hypothesis also finds improvements in market access (through better roads and transport facilities) to have a similar positive effect on the intensity of land-use. Intensification in the latter case occurs because: (a) higher prices and elastic demand for exportables implies that the marginal utility of effort increases, hence farmers in the region will begin cultivating larger areas; and (b) higher returns to labour encourage immigration into the area from neighbouring regions with higher transport costs. We have not come across any cases of sparsely populated areas under forest or bush fallow systems. Presumably, the former could occur if market access is excellent, while the latter could not occur even under poor market conditions.

Heavier soils are used only under high population densities or where market access is good
Heavier soils are the ones which are deeper and have a higher clay content; these soils therefore have higher water and nutrient holding capacity. Although these soils provide a higher and more certain yield they are often impossible to cultivate in the absence of investments in water control and drainage. Therefore, under low population densities and in the absence of animal or motor power more easy to work soils with a low clay content are preferred over the deep clayey soils. As population densities increase the heavier soils are intensively cultivated due to the relatively higher returns offered to labour, fertilizer and land investments, especially for rice cultivation. Also, as population densities increase labour supply increases, making it possible to undertake the labour investments in irrigation, drainage etc. Therefore, population pressure leads to a reversal in preference (price) of different types of land with the deeper heavier soils being preferred over the lighter more easy to work soils.

Agricultural intensification leads to an increase in yields per hectare
The higher yields are obtained due to two reasons: (a) the movement to heavier soils which are more responsive to intensification; and (b) more careful husbandry of existing fields. However, intensification of farming in the absence of a new power source (animal or motor power) could lead to a decline in yield per man-hour. This is because the heavier soils require high levels of power for land investments and land preparation and because sustaining yields on existing soils requires extremely labour intensive manuring and interculture.

Agricultural intensification, in the absence of labour-saving technical change, leads to an increase in agricultural employment
The total labour input per hectare is positively correlated with the intensity

of farming, holding technology constant. The movement from forest fallow to annual cultivation in West Africa using the hand hoe results in an increase in total labour input per hectare from 770 hours in Liberia to 3,300 hours in Cameroon (Ruthenberg 1980). Increased labour is required for investments in irrigation, drainage, levelling or terracing and for the development of more evolved manuring techniques. In addition to these overhead labour requirements permanent cultivation also warrants extremely labour intensive land preparation and interculture.

Organic fertilizer use is positively associated with land scarcity
In land abundant areas long-term soil fertility is maintained by periodic fallowing of land. As the fallow periods become shorter due to an expansion in the area under cultivation the use of organic fertilizer begins to emerge. At first these fertilization techniques are fairly rudimentary, often involving no more than a periodic transport of household refuse to the fields. As farming intensifies more evolved composting and manuring techniques are used. Under extreme land scarcity one observes the incorporation of legumes in a crop rotation cycle as green manure. At this stage also one tends to observe increased use of chemical fertilizers as a substitute for labour intensive manuring techniques. Such general use of chemical fertilisers is still very rare in sub-Saharan Africa although the use of fertilizers for select crops such as cotton and groundnuts which are produced for the market is becoming increasingly common.

The transition from hand hoes to animal-drawn ploughs is only profitable at higher intensities of farming
The transition from digging sticks and hand hoes to animal-drawn ploughs is closely correlated with the evolution of the farming system and cannot be understood by using a simple choice of techniques analysis familiar to economists. This transition would not be cost-effective in forest and bush fallow systems due to the very high labour requirements for destumping and levelling the fields. As the length of fallow decreases the costs of destumping decline because of reduced tree and root density. Destumping requirements are minimal by the grass fallow stage and it is here that animal power becomes the economically dominant technology. Also, by the grass fallow stage trypanasomiasis becomes less of a constraint on animal ownership and use and grazing land becomes prevalent. The transition to animal-drawn ploughs would occur first on soils which are hard to work by hand (clays) because the returns to ploughing are highest on these soils. It is only later that animal-drawn ploughs are used on all other soils. The use of animal-drawn ploughs leads to substantial labour savings and a timely completion of the land preparation operation.

Lack of animal husbandry/mechanical skills are at most a short-run constraint to the use of animal/tractor power
Our study finds that, where conditions were appropriate, African farmers acquired the skills required for operating animal draught/tractor

equipment readily. Moreover, we found that many of the skills required for the efficient use of animal draught/tractor equipment had been acquired by these societies prior to the acquisition of this equipment. For instance, a majority of the tribes in sub-Saharan Africa (outside the humid forest zone) are crop cultivators who keep cattle for milk, meat and as a store of wealth. These farmers already possess animal husbandry skills, although they may lack the ability to train their animals for draught purposes. As farming intensifies, however, they acquire this additional skill and begin using animal-drawn ploughs. Even in the humid forest zone where trypanosomiasis caused a historic absence of livestock we found that farmers could and did acquire livestock husbandry skills, when it was possible and profitable to do so. Similarly, the use of bicycles, motorcycles and mechanical mills has become very common all over sub-Saharan Africa, even in areas where animal traction and tractors are not used. The mechanical skill required for the use of this equipment is as complex as that required for animal-drawn implements and perhaps even tractors. We also found that where animal draught or tractor equipment was in use, workshops capable of servicing this equipment emerged fairly rapidly and were located within accessible distance of the users.

In general, it is economically infeasible to bypass the animal traction stage and move directly to tractors
This is because the quality and hence the cost of destumping is much higher for tractor operations than for animal-drawn ploughs. Tractor operations also require more elaborate systems for repair and mainten- ance. Moreover, the societies concerned are usually characterised by extreme capital scarcity and cannot usually afford the substantially higher capital costs associated with tractors. Once animal draught power has been successfully incorporated in the farming system, however, tractors and animals become close substitutes for ploughing. The choice of techniques analysis finally becomes relevant. The factors involved are the relative costs of land, labour and capital, the seasonality of agricultural production and the cost of tractors. There are two exceptions where the direct transition to tractors may be cost-effective: (a) valley bottom lands where irrigated or flooded rice is cultivated; and (b) the grassy savannas in the semi-arid zone. In both cases the land is open and grassy and hence destumping is not a major problem. The profitability of using tractors, however, continues to depend on domestic and external market demand.

The profitability of animal/tractor-drawn equipment is constrained by the length of the growing season.
The length of the land preparation period is an important determinant of the capacity utilisation of animal and tractor-drawn ploughs. Utilisation rates are lower the shorter the period of land preparation, accordingly, costs per unit of equipment are higher the shorter the season. The period

during which mechanical tillage equipment can be used in the arid and semi-arid tropics is extremely limited. Timeliness of ploughing is crucial to assure adequate time for crop growth before soil moisture stress becomes a problem. Due to the acute timeliness problem in the dry tropics, rental markets for equipment are not well established and therefore equipment costs cannot be spread over a larger area. Longer ploughing periods exist in the sub-humid and humid tropics, in areas with a bi-modal rainfall regime and in high altitude areas. Well developed rental markets exist in these areas and the cost of equipment is spread over several users. In the case of tractors, capacity utilisation can be increased by providing contract hire operations across several rainfall zones.

It is not unusual for some intensively cultivated regions to persist in the use of hand hoes
The tropical highlands are a primary example of intensively cultivated areas that persist in the use of hand hoes. There are two reasons for the continued use of the hoe in the highlands: (a) the steep terrain is often a constraint on the use of animal/tractor power; (b) the tropical highlands have a comparative advantage in the production of tree crops rather than field crops and therefore the opportunities for the use of mechanical tillage equipment is limited. Although small quantities of field crops are grown for subsistence purposes the plot sizes are small and the season length is long, therefore hoes continue to be the dominant technology.

The simultaneous transfer of all agricultural operations to a new power source (animal or motor) is not economically attractive
Agricultural operations can be grouped in terms of the relative intensity with which they require power (or energy) relative to the control functions of the human mind (or judgement). Operations such as land preparation, transport, milling, grinding and threshing are power-intensive, while weeding, sifting, winnowing and fruit harvesting are examples of control intensive operations. New power sources are always used first for power intensive operations even when wages are low. It is for these select operations that the use of the new power source has the highest comparative advantage. The transfer of control intensive operations to the new power source becomes profitable only when wages are high or rising. In land-scarce economies where non-agricultural demand for labour is low, operations such as weeding, interculture and harvesting continue to be done by human or animal power. Therefore, agricultural projects which promote a package of equipment designed to mechanise all agricultural operations usually fail.

Specific rights to land become well defined only in the face of land scarcity
The institutional arrangements for the acquisition of land by individuals within a society and by 'outsiders' are not rigid but change as increasing population densities or improved market access make land scarce. In land

abundant economies cultivation rights are easy to obtain, often for no more than a nominal gift to the head of the lineage. Land acquisition becomes more and more difficult as intensification leads to more narrowly defined groups or lineages and therefore results in the exclusion of large numbers of people from acquiring the rights to cultivate. The ultimate institutional change, and one which commonly occurs under high population densities, is one of clearly defined rights to cultivate specific plots of land often with the ability to buy and sell land. The above institutional changes in land acquisition induced by population growth were already outlined by Boserup in 1964. During our field visits we asked a series of questions that allowed us to determine the process of land acquisition in a particular society. Our findings support Boserup's theory on population growth and rights to land. The transition to specific land rights improves incentives to undertake investments which are required for the intensification of production and preservation of fertility.

NOTE

[1]For a detailed account of the methodology and findings of this study, see Pingali and Binswanger (1984) and Pingali, Bigot and Binswanger (1985).

REFERENCES

Boserup, Ester, *Conditions of Agricultural Growth*, Aldine Publishing Company, Chicago, 1965.
Boserup, Ester., *Population Growth and Technological Change – A Study of Long-Term Trends*, University of Chicago Press, 1981.
Pingali, Prabhu L. and Binswanger, Hans P., *Population Density and Agricultural Intensification: A Study of the Evolution of Technologies in Tropical Agriculture*, Agriculture and Rural Development Department Discussion Paper, no. ARU 22, World Bank, Washington, DC, 1984.
Pingali, Prabhu L., Bigot, Yves and Binswanger, Hans P., 'Agricultural Mechanization and the Evolution of Farming Systems in Sub-Saharan Africa', Draft Manuscript, Agriculture and Rural Development Department, World Bank, Washington DC, 1985.
Ruthenberg, Hans, *Farming Systems in the Tropics* (3rd edn.), Clarendon Press, Oxford, 1980.

DISCUSSION OPENING – A. T. BIROWO

In general I should like to admit that I know very little about agriculture in Africa. If I may put some comments at all, it is because I have some experience in development administration and research on similar issues in Indonesia and in other Asian countries.

Professor Idachaba has put forth a comprehensive paper on issues in redirecting agricultural research, extension and training to achieve accelerated agricultural development in sub-Saharan Africa. The paper has indeed unveiled important issues in research management to meet the challenges in efforts to realise the production potential for food and agricultural development. It is interesting to learn the recognised facts that as a colonial heritage research was initially directed to meet the needs of the colonial powers in Europe, instead of directly formulated to meet the needs of national agricultural development. It also explains why data on the socio-economic environments of the research systems in the independent nations of present sub-Saharan Africa are not clearly unveiled. At the present level of economic development of the regions, social and institutional environments are very important determinants of the agricultural research system. Whether the research system is under the jurisdiction of the Ministry of Agriculture or Ministry of Science and Technology, depends on the socio-economic environment. One thing is certain, one needs to have an explicit national science and technology policy of which national agricultural research policy is a part, as the author has rightly mentioned. The need to monitor and periodically evaluate the programme is beyond question. In the face of obvious scarcity of research managers and research skill the fragmentation of previous institutes into scattered 'national' institutes is to be discouraged. Indeed I support the author in proposing relocation of the centre to make efficient use of scarce skilled resources.

I do not agree with the so-called 'perennial' mistakes as being too much concentration on 'supply research' which actually should address demand aspects as well. Within the current socio-economic context it is only natural that supply issues come forth more apparently than demand problems. The market aspects are organised by few elements and may be relatively imperfect, whereas supply problems are technically more apparent.

The authors of the second paper have richly disclosed important facts and analyses from empirical research on sub-Saharan agriculture. The issues are very close to my heart as we have many similar problems with rice intensification in Indonesia. I am particularly interested in the propositions relating to the process of technology transfer, especially the social and institutional aspects. In my opinion it is rather dangerous to move directly to tractors and to bypass the animal tradition. The penultimate finding indirectly supports this. I would, however, question the last statement. In our experience, in the social setting of Indonesia, specific rights to land became well defined in areas where land was not scarce. It seems to depend on the social institutions and levels of economic development. Since information on this is incomplete, perhaps the authors may give a further explanation.

GENERAL DISCUSSION – RAPPORTEUR: J. L. STANNING

The discussion of the first paper was opened by a speaker from the floor who commented that whilst the paper had outlined five possible sources of incremental agricultural production he wanted to know which of these measures was of immediate relevance to the present food crisis situation in sub-Saharan Africa. Other speakers questioned whether the poor production performance was related to poor research performance. Concern was expressed about the apparent past failure of international and national agricultural research programmes to provide appropriate technological packages to realise the production potential in Africa. How could national agricultural research programmes be made to function more effectively and how should critical areas for research be identified?

The second paper provoked controversial discussion and a number of questions were raised. In view of the observations regarding institutional arrangements with respect to land, the authors were asked to comment on the effects of increasing population density and market access on land use beyond the intensification issue emphasised in the paper. Another speaker asked whether the observed topographic effect illustrated by rice was also the case for traditional African crops like sorghum, millet and root crops. There was disagreement with the statement that it was economically infeasible to bypass the animal traction stage. The authors were asked if they were aware of the tsetse fly problem and it was suggested that although tractors might be more costly than animal traction they were a more feasible alternative in tsetse-infested areas. More details were also asked for concerning the survey techniques used in the research reported in the paper.

In reply to the questions raised, Professor Idachaba emphasised the need for national research programmes to pay greater attention to the research demands of small farmers. He suggested that in this regard farm systems research might have an important role to play in articulating the research demands of small-scale producers. Turning to immediate priorities, he said that each country had to identify its own commodity priorities for research and that factor endowments also had to be taken into account. Since in many African countries labour was a production constraint, greater emphasis in national research programmes should, in his view, be placed on researching appropriate labour-saving technologies. Finally, he stressed that effective linkages between research workers, executive ministries and private research organisations was a key factor in making national agricultural research systems more effective.

Dr Pingali responded by explaining that cross-sectional surveys were the basis of their study although some time series surveys had been possible at particular locations (for example in Tanzania). He felt that where data sources for time series surveys were available this could be an interesting avenue of further study. More research was also required concerning the effect of agricultural intensification on land tenure patterns, on land rental and ownership exchange markets, and on land consolidation and fragmentation. It was confirmed that the topographic effect was observable for traditional African crops such as millets and sorghum. He maintained the view that it was economically infeasible to bypass the animal traction stage and argued that the widespread failure of tractor projects in tsetse areas supported this thesis.

Participants in the discussion included L. A. Msambichaka, S. Bellete, J. C. Martinez, S. Simons, Sara J. Scherr and J. A. Akinwumi.

GÜNTHER SCHMITT

The Role of Institutions in Formulation of Agricultural Policy: Their Repercussions on the Challenges of an Agriculture in a Turbulent World Economy

INTRODUCTION

In dealing with agricultural policy, agricultural economists traditionally either analyse the economic effects of various policy measures on allocation of resources and distribution of income or they model optimal policies by given policy objectives based on welfare economics. The design of such optimal policies has often been criticised as a 'Nirvana approach' (Demsetz 1969) due to its remoteness from real policy decisions of prevailing governments. Welfare economics as an instrument for evaluating and designing economic policies is strictly based on methodological individualism assuming that each economic agent (*homo oeconomicus*) is striving for a maximum of individual utility in terms of economic rents (Sohmen 1976). Consequently, the society as the aggregate of those individuals prefers those policies maximising welfare. Policy decisions contrary to those principles do not therefore reflect the true preferences of individuals and have to be changed towards optimal decisions according to economists' reasoning. In other words, they are in fact (at least implicitly) in favour of an 'omnipotent, wise, benevolent and wholly informed dictator' (Buchanan 1959). Fortunately in many countries policy decisions are not up to dictators. In other countries being governed by dictators, those dictators are mostly neither wise nor benevolent. In countries mentioned first policies of governments are made legitimate by a majority of citizens due to regular votes within the institutional framework of a democratic constitution. With respect to the role of economists as designers of an optimal policy, the basic question arises whether those government decisions based on the consensus of the citizens reflect the true and unfalsified preferences of those citizens. Economists deny this. However, given that this is actually the case, 'welfare losses' of society due to factual policies have to be interpreted as 'welfare gains' of the society contrary to traditional welfare analysis.[1]

However, those implications of real (farm) policies are not the problem we have to deal with here, at least at the moment. Instead, we have to deal with the role of institutions in formulation of agricultural policies.

390

But we have already demonstrated that, first, institutions do play a rather important role in policy decisions, second that institutional arrangements are unavoidable in organisation and formulation of public policies and, third, that the outcomes of the decision-making process depend to a large degree on the design and structure of the relevant institutional settings.[2] It has to be added, fourth, that in reverse the design and the structure of institutional arrangements do of course direct and determine individual behaviour and decisions.

Institutions, and this has to be kept in mind, are man-made. Therefore they are subject to changes which are often interpreted as 'institutional innovations' in terms of changes favouring welfare increasing realloca- tion of resources.[3] However, sometimes it is very doubtful whether institutional changes are directed towards such an objective in any case. With respect to this, it is rather surprising that economists have failed until recently to analyse the process of the design and change of institutions, although economic reasoning may be able to explain those processes. It is therefore even more astonishing that agricultural economists have neglected the economic aspects of the creation and change of institutions in the field of agriculture and agricultural policies. Farmers (as well as other members of society) make use of three different strategies in order to increase their economic status: first they may organise the economic performance of their farm businesses as efficiently as possible; second, they may increase their profits by restricting competition. Both strategies and the economic implications thereof are traditional subjects of agricultural economists' analysis. Farmers, however, may additionally try to influence the outcome of the political decision-making process *qua* pressure groups. But this strategy of political rent-seeking[4] by farmers within the existing institutional pattern or by changing it, has been almost neglected by agricultural economists.[5] This in spite of the fact that the basic question of which of the three strategies (or combinations thereof) is to be preferred as a matter of economic efficiency involves, besides their different benefits, costs of co-ordinating individual decisions. The adjustment of individual actions to prevailing and expected market conditions (reflected in relative prices) is bound to such costs of co-ordination as well as the mutual adjustment of individual decisions towards collective actions in order to restrict competition or to influence the processes of political decisions by interest group activities.

Mentioning such costs of co-ordination leads back to the 'transaction costs' – the term which was introduced by Richard Coase in his famous article on 'The Nature of Firm' first published in 1937. Transaction costs determining whether production of goods and services is co-ordinated by markets directly or by other types of institutional arrangements (such as firms, co-operatives etc.) has stimulated economic research in analysing the role of institutions. Furthermore, it has also stimulated a bundle of new branches of economic sciences such as Modern Economic History,[6] the Theory of Property Rights[7] and the New Political Economy

(Economic Theory of Politics),[8] which are now summarised as the New Institutionalism. New Political Economy has enabled economists to analyse and to explain political decisions as collective actions subject to relative economic costs and benefits to individuals (public choice).

In this line of the economic theory of politics we have to describe and analyse the decision-making process with respect to agricultural policy. We have to restrict this analysis to parliamentary democracies as the institutional framework (constitution) of those decisions. The principle of those democracies is that political decisions are the result of elections in which (as a rule) the majority legitimates a government to use its power based on a corresponding majority in the parliament.[9] With respect to farm policy, the basic question to be answered is the following one: in developed countries farmers and farm populations constitute only a minority of total population as well as of constituency. According to our definition of democracy as the dominion of the majority it has to be expected that farmers do not have any chance to exploit the majority (of consumers and taxpayers). However, the contrary can be observed, as stated above. Consequently we have to explain this obvious paradox that political decisions in a democratic society are in favour of a minority of farm population by protectionistic measures, subsidies, tax reliefs etc. We will next try to explain why agricultural policy in those societies is as it is, and is not as it should be according to agricultural economists arguing in terms of economic welfare. Next, we will discuss the implications of the result of our analysis on the (new) economic theory of politics and, in relation to this, the role of (agricultural) economists as analysts and advisors of public policy. Third, we will consider the implications of those political decisions on the challenges of an agriculture in a turbulent world.

FARM POLICY DECISIONS IN A DEMOCRATIC SOCIETY

Formulation and application of (farm) policies in a democratic society is a complicated and interrelated process determined by numerous factors and forces. These factors are among others the specific structure of institutions, their mutual connections, rights and competences, the quite different influences of voters, political parties, pressure groups, bureaucracies, parliaments, committees and experts, partly regulated by constitutions and laws, restricted by national and international regulations (such as GATT or the Rome treaty) etc. Therefore, it is not astonishing that there are quite a number of hypotheses concerning the explanation of the privileged position of agriculture in most developed countries subject to a parliamentary democracy. These hypotheses have in common that agriculture is competing with other (organised) groups on the political market in order to enforce favourable decisions, by policy-makers. However, the answer to the crucial question why the farm population as a minority as compared to other groups seems to be more successful in its political rent-seeking differs rather widely among those theories: Most prefer the relative strength of interest groups,[10] others consider farmers as marginal voters attracting all political parties in order to gain majorities of constituency,[11] still others emphasize the role of bureaucracies,[12] whereas only few have some ideological (agrarian) 'fundamentalism' in mind common to all voters, politicians and political parties.

We are convinced that all these hypotheses offer some insight; but are only of a partial nature. We therefore think that a more integrated and holistic 'theory' is needed which includes all those partial elements. Such a holistic model of the process of public legitimation of farm interests has to be based, first on the theory of the role of agriculture within economic growth, rather familiar to agricultural economists.[13] This theory, explaining factors affecting 'income disparity' of agriculture such as a secular attribute of the farm sector, seems to be the basic source of political preferences of society in favour of agriculture. Next, the economic theory of democracy originally founded by Schumpeter (1942) and Downs and further refined by Herder-Dorneich and Knappe has to be used in order to analyse the steering capacity of general elections with respect to farm populations respecting farm policy decisions of the government and Parliament. Third, the economic theory of political competition among various interest groups set forth especially by Posner, Stigler, Peltzman (1976) and more recently by von Weizsäcker has to be used in order to evaluate the impact of the organised interests of farmers on farm policy decisions. Finally, the economic theory of bureaucracy put forward by Tullock, Downs, Niskanen and Roppel may demonstrate the reactions of bureaucracy to the claims of agriculture.

Such an integrated theory may take into account the mutual interdependences and influences of all participants, actors and institutions being relevant on the economic as well as on the political market. We have analysed the elements of such a theory explaining the politically privileged position of agriculture mentioned above elsewhere in more detail (Hagedorn and Schmitt 1985; Schmitt 1984, 1985). Space available only allows one to summarise the findings such as:

1. The distribution of economic costs and benefits of structural adjustment of agriculture within economic growth is asymmetrical in so far as the benefits are transferred to consumers whereas the costs have to be borne by farmers (sunk costs of disinvestments).
2. The coincidence of rather low opportunity costs of resources used in agriculture and the institutional regulation of resource allocation in agriculture result in the well-known intersectoral income disparity.
3. Agriculture as a social group of many 'small' farmers is confronted by the free-rider problem in organising effective interest group activities. However solidarity seems to be rather strong among farmers due to agriculture's situation as described above.
4. Farmers in most Western countries are characterised by more or less strong identification with (conservative) political parties. Therefore

the 'political mobility' of farmers as voters seems to be rather weak. Consequently they do not behave as median voters and their impact on election results is rather negligible.

5. At best agriculture is able only to steer farm policy decisions rather roughly by political election. Agriculture therefore is incapable of a fine tuning of farm policy in the sense of a choice between competing policy measures.

6. The optimal strategy of income distribution according to the model of a pure democracy does not in reality provide politicians with a stable majority of voters and, consequently, there are no stable farm policies.

7. Theoretically the majority of consumers and taxpayers and their greater political mobility (between competing political parties) should result in policy decisions discriminating against farm populations because the political opportunity costs of privileging agriculture are basically most expensive to those voters.

So far, agriculture seems to be in a rather weak position in enforcing its interests on the political market. However, those disadvantages are obviously compensated by specific *advantages* of agriculture as an interest group:

1. The coincidence of irreversible investments and the economic pressure on farm income and structural adjustment leads to intensive as well as homogenous political preferences by farmers. Selective incentives (offered by organised interest groups) and an ideology result in solid group behaviour as a base of the institutional organisation of group interests.

2. Organised agriculture is able to formulate, represent and articulate fundamentalistic ideologies which are not restricted to the farm population. These ideologies are used in order to justify and to back up the consensus of society and the approval of the majority to policy decisions favouring agriculture. The arguments put forward by agricultural interest groups according to which farmers are supplying cheap and healthy food, that they are responsible for a secure food supply, that farmers are conserving the landscape, that they are rather poor and underprivileged, that they only ask for 'parity income', that they are politically stable etc. are forceful 'weapons' in order to manipulate public opinion. By neglecting or discriminating against agriculture, society may lose those 'public goods' supplied by agriculture. The exercise of solidarity, justice and stability of the majority of voters as well as political parties as against farmers offer some sort of satisfaction to the general public.

3. Ideological commitments of the majority with the minority of farmers are the basic motives for policy decisions favouring agriculture in advanced economies subject to a democratic decision making process. Farm pressure groups play a major role in so far as they have to strengthen and to revive those ideological commitments by demonstrating the specific position of agriculture within and with

respect to the more or less consistent sets of normative statements as to the best or preferred state of the world – usually defined as ideologies. But very often an additional 'power' is acting in the same direction as agricultural interest groups: the farm bureaucracy. The farm sector is usually administered by a bureaucracy specific on agricultural matters. On the top of this agriculture-oriented bureaucracy you will find in most of those countries a specific ministry of agriculture contrary to most other sectors or branches of the economy which are not administered by their own political departments. The officials of these administrative bodies (especially of the ministry) including the ministers (Secretaries of State) themselves are *ex officio* responsible for agriculture's well-being. In order to reach the consent of their clientele as well as the financial resources and competences by governmental and parliamentary decisions (which of course are status symbols) farm bureaucracy uses similar arguments although on a more sophisticated level.[14]

4. It seems that the mechanism described above enables agriculture to protect its own political preferences and to neutralise opposing preferences of voters in the course of political decisions. In reverse, the mechanics of control of constituency and of competition between various political parties are open to agriculture as an effective instrument to influence those policy decisions: agriculture is consequently more efficient as compared to other groups or branches with respect to the 'production' of political power.

It has to be added, of course, that the specific type and structure of the existing institutional settings of the decision-making bodies differing between various countries may accentuate or mitigate the efficiency of agriculture in influencing the output of those bodies. For instance, it might make a difference whether we find a two-party system or numerous parties in a country, whether the country is subject to a centralised system of government or federally organised, whether we have a presidential type of government or a system more similar in Western Europe, whether some countervailing power outside parliamentary control, such as independent central banks, is established or not, etc. However, as far as we can see, there is a lack of theoretical as well as of empirical studies in terms of international comparative analyses, especially with respect to the formulation and execution of agricultural policies.

However, the present agricultural policy of the European Community offers an impressive example of the influence of institutional arrangements of decision-making bodies in policy output, quite diverging from that found in Western parliamentary democracies. We have analysed this elsewhere (Schmitt 1984; Hagedorn and Schmitt 1985) in detail. In summarising our findings, the following may be said: Farm policy decisions are made exclusively by the Council of Ministers of Agriculture, not being subject to either parliamentary control (by the European Parliament) or by Ministers of Finance or by a medium-range budget planning process (as in the case in fiscal policy decisions in most member countries). Furthermore, financial resources of the CAP are so far unrestricted and only partially related to farm policy decisions as financial contributions to FEOGA (the farm budget of EEC) are to a large extent dependent on the size and growth of the national income of member states. Finally, decisions of the Council of Ministers are subject to unanimity, exposing each country to a position of blackmail. It has to be added also that member states are free to execute national farm policy measures outside the common price policy, especially in the field of social and, to a limited extent, structural policy. For most member countries such complementary policies are advantageous because the output effects can be externalised by FEOGA due to the budget regulation of the CAP. As a consequence of this 'unusual' type of institutional setting (which has to be analysed in relation to the fact that within the Community there is no common or harmonised economic and monetary policy), the CAP is hypertrophic compared to farm policies within the institutional framework of 'normal' parliamentary democracies. The specific outcomes of EC decisions on farm policies are well known and have been analysed by agricultural economists often and extensively.[15] We will come back to some implications in the last part of this paper.

THE IDEOLOGICAL FOUNDATIONS OF FARM POLICY DECISIONS: WHAT AGRICULTURAL ECONOMISTS CAN DO ABOUT IT

The central finding of our analysis of the factors affecting decisions on farm policies within the institutional arrangements of a parliamentary democracy privileging farm populations to an exceptional extent, has been the ideological commitment of the participants of the decision-making process. With respect to those ideological commitments two basic questions arise to (agricultural) economists. The first is related to the role of agricultural economists as analysts and advisers of policy authorities, given that farm policy decisions of 'society' in fact reproduce the undistorted preferences of society's members: are economists still authorised to apply traditional welfare economics in analysing farm policy outcome, given that welfare economics refers to maximisation of individual and pecuniary utility? The next question to be answered refers to the problem of analysing ideological commitment in terms of cost-benefit relations determining the (political) decision of all participants of the decision-making process. Since both questions are highly inter-related, we will start with the question mentioned last.

The second question is related to the problem whether the ideological commitment of public policy decisions has to be interpreted as of a purely altruistic nature. In this case, economists have nothing to add to what political scientists and sociologists have to say about ideologies as something which does play an important role in policy decisions but being quite of an irrational nature which cannot therefore be analysed by sciences based on the rationality of human behaviour and decisions.[16] However, until recently the economic theory of politics was merely restricted to the view that political decisions (especially in the field of economic policy) are exclusively determined by pecuniary (materialistic) costs and benefits to the participants of decision-making. Since every (economic) policy produces transfers of wealth in one way or the other, it is always possible to relate with certainty political outcomes to these distributional impacts. This approach, in fact, leaves open the question whether the behaviour and results we observe in the political arena are the product of something else than the paradoxical pecuniary interests of affected parties. Probably the most basic proposition of economic (capture) models of state regulations is the assertion that the altruistic, publicly interested goals of individuals are such insignificant factors in processes that they are empirically uninteresting and dispensable.

However, such a proposition is obviously inconsistent with respect to farm policy decisions as we have demonstrated above. Altruistic motives play a decided role at least in farm policy decisions. They might be in the form of a sense of civic duty, that is, a duty to serve the interests of the public. Pursuit of such a duty therefore is a consumption activity that yields utility in the form of a warm glow of moral rectitude. A number of recent studies have suggested that policy-makers' self-defined notions of 'public interest' are dominant explanatory factors in their voting behaviour.[17] It has therefore to be asked whether the same should not be relevant for all political decisions of the participants involved.

Political ideologies are more or less consistent sets of normative statements as to the best or preferred states of the world. Such statements are moralistic and altruistic in the sense that they are held as applicable to everyone. Accordingly, political ideologies are to be taken in our context, as statements about how governments can best serve their proponents' conception of the public interest. Behaviour in accordance with such statements has the appearance of altruism in the actors' preference function. The returns from the furtherance of an ideology appear either in the form of satisfaction to individuals of knowing that they have concretely improved the lot of others or in the form of deriving satisfaction from having done the 'right thing'. Political behaviour based on ideology may arise from either the public by interested objectives of constituents or the publicly interested objectives of their representatives. In any case, the pursuit of ideologically based objectives gives satisfaction similar to the pursuit of materialistic objectives. No difference can be seen between the rationality of 'economic' decisions of individuals as compared to 'political' decisions of those individuals directed by 'altruistic' motives exclusively or in connection with economic incentives.

We are consequently, as economists, not authorised to blame ideologically motivated decisions by the participants of the (political) decision-making process as 'irrational'. The question is, however, whether the output of the decision-making process reflects the real preferences of the constituency, including preferences towards altruism.

And these preferences, given that they are not distorted by the decision-making process,[18] include not only the objectives of public policy – most economists are willing to accept that these objectives reflect the true preferences of society; but they reflect also the policy instruments used by the government to reach the objectives. Such a view of public policy is, of course, contrary to the traditional application of welfare economics as a method of formulating and defining optimal policy instruments as well as evaluating prevailing policies. This seems to be the real source of the mutual misunderstanding and misinterpretation of real farm policies (and farm policy-makers) on the one hand and agricultural economists on the other.

ON THE ROLE OF AGRICULTURAL ECONOMISTS AS POLICY ANALYSTS AND POLICY ADVISORS

Some final remarks have to be added to the last statement according to which farm policy decisions on parliamentary democracy are the result of the 'real' preferences of the society, being not only restricted to individualistic and pecuniary cost-benefit calculations. These remarks are directed to the role of agricultural economists within this policy-making process. In general, agricultural economists have analysed relevant farm policy by the application of welfare economics. These analyses have in most cases resulted in the findings that the prevailing farm policies are third-best solutions and society would be, of course, better off by changing policies towards first-best or, at least, second-best solutions. Based on this perception, agricultural economists implicitly asked for the 'dictator' mentioned above, ignoring the fact that society is willing explicitly to pursue ideological oriented objectives and policies and even renounce economic advantages. With respect to our reasoning from above, it might possibly be true that these third-best solutions are in fact first-best solutions in relation to the political preferences of the constituents.

Does this mean that agricultural economists are misconceived in arguing within the boundaries of traditional economic reasoning?[19] We do not think so. We are convinced that agricultural economists have to return to the old tradition of social science, that is the old tradition of enlightenment by demonstrating the real costs to society of the pursuit of ideological objectives. Arguing in the tradition of social sciences, agricultural economists can and will contribute to a more rational world, to more rationality of the political decision-making process, which of course leads to benefits for all members of society.

THE REPERCUSSIONS ON THE CHALLENGES ON AGRICULTURE IN A TURBULENT WORLD ECONOMY

Agricultural economists have analysed the consequences of regulation on income distribution, resource allocation and stability of agricultural markets by governmental and parliamentary decision very extensively. The implications of non-market interventions such as social and structural policy measures have been less intensively studied. However, we are also informed on those implications although in a more qualitative sense. We need not therefore repeat here the relevant findings. Instead, we will concentrate on the implications of institutional arrangements steering and directing farm policy decisions on the specific causes and consequences of the present situation of agriculture in a turbulent world. With reference to the geographical dimension, i.e. the world, we have of course to include institutional arrangements which relate to international trade relations, such as:

1. National policy decisions in the field of agriculture very often have world-wide consequences in so far as farm policy measures by various countries stimulate other countries to protect their own farm sector. The history of protectionism demonstrates the fact that the introduction of protectionistic measures by some importing countries has led other importing as well as exporting countries to counteract those policies by import restricting and/or export stimulating policy instruments (Luard 1984). As a consequence of this, international division of labour in agricultural resource allocation is highly distorted and world markets are characterised by great instability. This instability of world markets seems to be still further accelerated by the fact that some countries are transferring their internal instabilities in food supply to world markets to a rising extent. This is to be observed so far as socialist countries are concerned. Within the context of a liberal world market, the impact of this 'structural' change would be rather limited. However, in the context of the present world market conditions subject to import restricting and export subsidising policies of many countries, instability of world markets are enhanced to a great extent (Runge 1984).

2. As a consequence of what is called 'the turbulent world', reflected in economic instability with respect to economic growth, employment and inflation, governments are under pressure to enlarge protectionism of national agriculture. This pressure is the consequence of expected instability of world food supply, the implication of inflation on agriculture's income situation, the deficits in external trade balances as well as the restricted outflow of farm labour due to general unemployment. These tendencies towards extended protectionism by tariff and non-tariff restrictions of international trade, by increased subsidies, tax reliefs but also by voluntary export restraints etc. of course accelerate the instability of world markets of agricultural products, again stimulating state intervention by importing as well as exporting countries (Johnson 1973).

3. Of course, there are some international institutional arrangements, which aim to control or to prevent these implications of national policy measures directly or indirectly. In this respect we have to mention first

GATT, but also international agreements concerning stability of exchange rates such as the Bretton Woods agreement. However, the latter has disappeared and the former has become increasingly irrelevant to international trade of agricultural products. So far these international institutions have shown themselves to be increasingly inefficient in countervailing national policy measures, special bilateral or multilateral trade agreements, etc. As a consequence of an increasing 'demoralisation' of international trade behaviour and performance, stability of world markets has to a large extent been reduced. This in reverse has stimulated protective measures by governments still further. A reform of these international agreements is urgently needed (Schuh 1984). However, the chances of realisation of such reforms are very poor, because the direction of such reforms is subject to very large controversies.

4. Necessary reforms of international agreements relevant for trade in agricultural products directly (such as GATT) or indirectly (such as a system of international monetary policies) are furthermore bound to a high degree to reforms of national farm policies. However, as stated above, present political and economic turbulence in the world economy as well as world agriculture is the pretext for the conservation and the expansion of national protectionism. The best example to illustrate this automatism is given by the European Community where the increasing economic problems confronting national authorities have resulted in a further retreat into protectionistic policy by national governments especially in the field of agriculture ('renationalisation' of farm policies). Additional distortions in factor allocation, international trade and income distribution are the direct outcomes; the stagnation of the process of integration of the EC is an indirect one.

5. Compared to markets and relative prices steering the adjustment of resource allocations, institutions are extremely inflexible towards necessary changes. The rigidity of institutions is reflected in an inflexibility of decisions to be made within the existing institutional arrangements. Therefore the repercussions of institutions on the rapidly changing conditions of the turbulent world economy (partly a consequence of rigidities of institutions and the decision-making process therein) are to be seen not only as the consequences of those institutions exclusively, but also as a consequence of the incapability of flexible reactions of the decision-makers. Changes in demand and supply in the short run as well in the long run do most often find an inadequate and insufficient reaction of institutions which are theoretically free to respond adequately. The most striking example may be found with respect to the reaction of the policy-making process to the rapid increases in agricultural production in Western countries due to technological innovations. Instead of practising a restrictive price policy, passing productivity gains of technical progress to consumers, political decision favoured a more income-oriented price policy (especially in the EEC). This resulted in misallocation of factors not

only with respect to farm inputs but also with respect to investments in agricultural research, thus stimulating technological innovations (Schmitt 1985). The reverse, a lack of investment in research can be observed in less developed countries (Pinstrup-Andersen 1982).

These final remarks on the repercussions of institutions in formulating farm policies in a turbulent world bring me back to the role of agricultural economists within the process of framing those farm policies mentioned earlier. They have, as we would like to put it, to remind policy-makers as well as the public that very often and to a rising extent the implications of the decision-making process in farm politics are socially unacceptable. Due to the fact that these policy decisions are to a large extent determined by the institutional framework, institutional innovations have to be asked for by economists in order to come to better policy decisions. Of course, such changes will not be reached in the short run. Therefore, agricultural economists have to repeat their messages again and again. Furthermore they have to analyse the functioning of prevailing institutions in the field of agricultural policies in order to design institutional settings which will result in policy decisions better suited to the challenges of a rather turbulent world.

NOTES

[1]The basic problem whether the voting process reflects the true preferences of the constituency is questioned since the rediscovery of the *Condorcet*-Paradoxon by Arrow (1963). See especially Bernholz (1985) with respect to the present state of that discussion.

[2]'Institutions' are quite differently defined. We are following here Ruttan and Hayami (1984, p. 3f.) by defining institutions as 'the rules of a society or of organisations that facilitate coordination of people by helping them from expectations which each person can reasonably hold in dealing with others. They reflect the conventions that have evolved ... regarding the behaviour of individuals and groups relative to their own behaviour and the behaviour of others ... Institutions provide assurance respecting the actions of others, and give order and stability to expectations in the complex and uncertain world of economic (and social, G.S.) relations'. It has to be added perhaps that institutions in general and in politics especially are regulating such relations in order to prevent 'Hobbesian' anarchy. They are based, at least in democratic societies, on a general consensus of the societies' members as well as on the consent of people involved in particular institutional arrangements. Institutions are not restricted to organisations but also include the rules of interpersonal relationships either by law or conventions (traditions).

[3]See especially Ruttan and Hayami (1984) and quotations.

[4]See among others Tollison (1982).

[5]Exceptions are Rausser (1982) and de Gorter (1983).

[6]See especially North (1981).

[7]See for instance Furubotn and Pejovich (1974).

[8]See among others Mueller (1979) and Frey (1974).

[9]Sometimes governments are only backed by minorities and tolerated by parts of the opposition.

[10]See Rausser (1982), de Gorter (1983) and Haase (1983).

[11]This is discussed in more detail by Hagedorn and Schmitt (1985). See the quotations therein.

[12]See especially Tullock (1965), Downs (1967), Niskanen (1971) and Roppel (1979).

[13]See Schmitt (1972) and references.

[14]See Schmitt (1972) and references.

402   *Günther Schmitt*

15See among others Koester (1977).

16In order to be quite clear on this concept of rationality it has to be remembered that rationality is not identical with profit or utility maximising behaviour, see Schumpeter's basic paper on 'rationality in the social sciences', written in 1940, published first in 1984 (Schumpeter 1984).

17Several investigations of such a type (in the field of economic policy) are quoted by Kalt and Zupan (1984).

18See footnote 1.

19This of course is not equivalent to welfare economics which is subject to valid criticism as far as transaction costs etc. are neglected.

REFERENCES

Alchian, A. A. and Demsetz, H., 'Production, information cost and economic organisation', *American Economic Review*, vol. 62, 1972, pp. 777–95.

Arrow, K. J., *Social choice and individual values*, New York 1963.

Bernholz, P., 'Verfassung und konsistente gesellschaftliche Präferenzen: Ein allgemeines Möglichkeitstheorem', in Boettcher, E. et al. (eds), *Jahrbuch für Politische Ökonomie*, Tübingen 1985, pp. 73–89.

Buchanan, J. M., 'Positive economics, welfare economics, and political economy', *Journal of Law and Economics*, vol. 2, 1959, pp. 124–38.

Cheung, S. N. S., 'Transaction costs, risk aversion and the choice of contractual arrangements', *Journal of Law and Economics*, vol. 12, 1969, pp. 23–42.

Coase, R. H., 'The nature of the firm', *Economica*, vol. 4, 1937, pp. 386–405.

Coase, R. H., 'The problem of social cost', *Journal of Law and Economics*, vol. 3, 1960, pp. 1–44.

Demsetz, H., 'Towards a theory of property rights', *American Economic Review*, vol. 57, 1967, pp. 347–59.

Demsetz, H., 'Information and efficiency: another viewpoint', *Journal of Law and Economics*, vol. 12, 1969, pp. 1–22.

Furubotn, E. G. and Pejovich, S. (eds), *The Economics of Property Rights*, Cambridge, Mass., 1974.

Hagedorn, K. and Schmitt, G., 'Die politischen Gründe für eine wirtschaftspolitische Vorzugsbehandlung der Landwirtschaft', *Jahrbuch für Neue Politische Ökonomie*, Bd. 4, Tübingen 1985, pp. 250–95.

Hagedorn, K., 'Agrarpolitische Innovationen und wissenschaftliche Methodologie', *Agrarwirtschaft*, Jg. 34, 1985, pp. 283–47.

Johnson, D. G., *World Agriculture in Disarray*, Macmillan, London, 1973.

Kalt, J. P. and Zupan, M. A., 'Capture and ideology in the economic theory of politics', *American Economic Review*, vol. 74, 1984, pp. 279–300.

Luard, E., *Economic Relationships Among States*, London, 1984.

Mueller, D. C., *Public Choice*, Cambridge University Press, 1979.

North, D. C., *Structure and Change in Economic History*, New York, 1981.

Pinstrup-Andersen, P., *Agricultural Research and Technology in Economic Development*, Longman, London and New York, 1982.

Rausser, G. C. and Farrell, K. R. (eds), *Alternative Agricultural and Food Policies and the 1985 Farm Bill*, Berkeley, Cal., 1984.

Runge, C. F., *Instability and Flexible Response in International Agricultural Policy*, Department of Agricultural and Applied Economics, Minnesota, USA, 1984.

Ruttan, V. W. and Hayami, Y., *Toward a Theory of Induced Institutional Innovation*, Discussion paper no. 200, University of Minnesota, 1984.

Schmitt, G., 'Warum Agrarpolitik ist wie sie ist, und nicht wie sie sein sollte', *Agrarwirtschaft*, Jg., 1984, pp. 129–36.

Schmitt, G., 'Ideologien, Interessenverbände, Bürokratie und ökonomische Theorie der Agrarpolitik', *Agrarwirtschaft*, Jg. 34, 1985, pp. 10–19.

Schmitt, G., 'Agrarforschung, technischer Fortschritt und Agrarpolitik' (forthcoming).

Schuh, E. G., 'Trade and macroeconomic dimensions of agricultural policies' in G. C. Rausser and K. R. Farrell (eds), *Alternative Agricultural and Food Policies and the 1985 Farm Bill*, Berkeley, Cal., 1984.

Schumpeter, A., *Capitalism, Socialism and Democracy*, Harper-Row, New York, 1942.

Schumpeter, A., 'The increasing of rationality in the social sciences', *Journal of Institutional and Theoretical Economics*, vol. 40, 1984, pp. 577–93.

Sohmen, E., *Allokationstheorie und Wirtschaftspolitik*, Tübingen, 1976.

Turmanoff, P. G., 'A positive analysis of theory of market failure', *Kyklos*, vol. 37, 1984, pp. 529–41.

Williamson, O. E., 'Transaction cost economics: The governance of contractual relations', *Journal of Law and Economics*, vol. 22, 1979, pp. 233–62.

JOHN C. ABBOTT

Alternative Forms of Marketing Enterprise for the Developing Countries

The focus on rural development and equity in the 1970s stimulated appraisal of marketing mechanisms in terms of their contribution to these goals as well as the more immediate dimensions of marketing efficiency. They were judged not only for their ability to move produce to the best available markets with a minimum of waste and cost, but also for the consideration and assistance they gave to the smaller producers. For these farmers the main considerations are whether they are treated fairly at the local buying stage, how far the marketing system helps and protects them against larger rivals in the same production area, how far the system helps them to match their level of quality of output and to gain access to the techniques and inputs needed to achieve this and credit until sales proceeds come in.

FORMS OF MARKETING

Broadly, the following organisational systems for marketing have been used in providing marketing and associated services for farmers' produce in the developing countries:

—Independent private firms operating within some institutional framework such as assembly and central markets or exchanges, possibly with some mechanism for cushioning extreme price fluctuations.
—Transnational companies bringing processing technology, economies of scale and established market outlets.
—Farmers' associations or co-operatives.
—Marketing boards or other state agencies including special area and development authorities.

The most favourable position for the small farmer has generally been that of participant in a production/marketing contract system for a particular crop organised by an enterprise with assured market outlets for the crop after processing. He receives a full set of services on credit. The quality of the extension assistance provided far exceeds that available normally because it is tailored to the needs of the market outlet served and the processes used. It is likely to be based on specific research and be backed

404

up by the direct provision of seeds, pesticides, fertiliser on credit, etc., together with day-to-day advice on how and when to carry out production operations and the harvesting and handling of the product. Typically this kind of marketing service has been offered by the transnational – B.A.T. for tobacco, Unilever subsidiaries for oilseeds, Cadbury for cocoa in India, cotton in francophone Africa, for example.

Only a proportion of small farmers have obtained access to such contracts. For the great majority the first buyer of their produce has been a private enterprise trader in their village or at a nearby market. The tenor of many government policy initiatives has been to direct farmers elsewhere. The establishment of co-operative or state enterprise marketing systems has been their main action line. Determining factors have been the political preferences of national leaders, a desire to appear to be doing something new quickly and lack of reliable information on the realities of market performance in their own countries.

External aid agencies tended to back up these preferences for much the same reasons, and for administrative convenience; they needed an 'official' counterpart agency to which they could tie their aid or loan. International fellowships for advanced training in marketing went mostly to government officials, rarely to the sons of merchants. Aid resources were concentrated on government sponsored marketing enterprises.

Awareness of the costs of maintaining these bodies in the face of declining government revenues and aid inflows since the recession of the early 1980s has brought a new realism to the policy area. It appears timely in this context to review alternative types of marketing enterprise in terms of characteristic attributes, the advantages they offer and the support needed from governments. The goal is to show for what purposes and under what conditions each performs well. As a basis for this, case studies of enterprises that were generally recognised as successful were assembled from FAO, World Bank and university research sources. The criteria taken for success were that the enterprise had:

—operated continuously for five to ten years without external aid;
—shown little evidence of farmer or consumer complaint;
—shown little evidence of inflated costs and functional inefficiency;
—made a clear contribution to agricultural and general economic development;
—no senior officer who had been sent to prison.

The findings are not new. Together, however, with the case study summaries they constitute useful material for policy guidance and training.

Indigenous private enterprise
Individual private marketing enterprises are well adapted to provide a range of positive contributions towards marketing efficiency and economic development. They have demonstrated themselves well suited to:

1. Take advantage of and exploit unforeseen opportunities and follow up new ideas.
2. Start up and go a long way with very little capital. Private marketing enterprises are great builders of capital assets. Their operators tend to be economical, even parsimonious, in their personal expenditure, very careful in their business outlays, stringent in their requirements of performance from salaried staff.
3. Operate at very low cost. Only those staff are employed who make a positive contribution to the enterprise. Full use is made of family labour available at no cost. Outlays on equipment and other capital expenditure are commonly kept to the minimum and delayed until proved indispensable.
4. Because decision-making is concentrated, these enterprises tend to show ready initiative and a quick response to changing situations.
5. Family ties and kinship linkages can often be used to extend the marketing operation with high confidence and low risk. Where the infrastructure for marketing is at an early stage of development, reliable means of communicating information, sales commitments and financial proceeds are important.
6. A continuing sanction against inefficiency in a private enterprise is that, unless there are barriers to the entry of new firms, it will lose customers and go out of business.

Areas of marketing where private enterprises tend to perform better than others include:

1. Perishable products. Variability in quality, a tendency to deteriorate quickly if not held in special storage or processed, and sharp changes in price in response to variable supply call for rapid responses on the part of the enterprises marketing such products.
2. Livestock and meat. The variability of the product, the need for judgement in appraising quality and value and for care in handling to avoid losses give an edge to direct decision-making. The predominance of private enterprise in the marketing of livestock and meat also reflects a reluctance of many people to come close to the realities of this trade.
3. Combined purchase of produce and sale of farm inputs and consumer goods. When the quantities supplied and taken by each customer are small and varying, considerable local knowledge, patience and willingness to serve over a wide range of hours and locations is needed. Prices may have to be adjusted at each transaction and complex small-scale credit arrangements provided, if such an enterprise is to serve its clientele well. Often only a family enterprise, with a wife or child minding a shop while the husband goes out on rural purchasing and sales rounds, can provide this service economically.
4. New and highly specialised activities in marketing. Characteristically these are the outcome of an individual initiative, not a planned development by a committee or a government department. Not all such

initiatives are successful over the longer run. Nevertheless, to shut the door on the exploitation of unforeseen opportunities by leaving no legal scope for private marketing enterprise is manifestly negative to progress.

Transnationals
Potential contributions of the transnationals to marketing development and efficiency are:

1. Finance. Generally they are in a position to mobilise capital from the lowest cost sources. They can bring this into a country directly to acquire land and facilities and provide a working base. It can also be brought in as equipment, improved seeds, strategic supplies and skilled management and technology for which foreign exchange would be needed in any event.
2. Applied technology. Developing countries face the risk of selecting unsuitable designs and equipment and the problems of putting new plants into operation and maintaining them. Engaging an enterprise with demonstrated experience in applying a desired technology and in a position to keep it up to date is often the safest, and, in the long run, least expensive way of acquiring it.
3. Management. When qualified management experienced in the specific lines of product marketing comes with a transnational it is an immediate advantage. Local personnel can learn from it by working with it. The cost of maintaining expatriate managers will lead the transnational into promoting nationals into their place as soon as they are sufficiently competent.
4. Quality standards and presentation. The transnational experienced in meeting such standards can help a country overcome such barriers to successful marketing. It can also reduce quality risks to domestic consumers and help adapt domestic agriculture to produce raw materials with the required attributes.
5. Market access. In export sales a close link with an enterprise which has established outlets in major import markets is a great advantage. Experience shows that when prices turn down exporters with continuing distribution arrangements in the importing countries hold on to their market and the independents lose out.
6. Brands. These carry great weight with consumers and the wholesalers and retailers who serve them. An agreement to sell through the owner of an established brand enables the producer to share in the benefits of past outlays on its promotion.

Export marketing This is the transnational field par excellence. Here knowledge of the required technology, close familiarity with the import market's requirements and an established position there are strategic. Processed products sold by brand with substantial value added have priority, e.g. pineapple and soluble coffee. Also favoured are perishable products that can reach a distant market under integrated management and be sold by brand, e.g. bananas.

Farm supply marketing. Economies of scale favour transnationals in the development and distribution of higher yielding seeds and poultry strains, and specialised livestock feed ingredients, pesticides, etc. Fertilizer, however, is not an important product of the transnationals. Whilst they helped promote its use, most developing countries now purchase by ingredient specification and branding is not significant.

Domestic marketing. Here the main opportunity for the transnational is in the application of advanced technology and associated commercial management. This can be backed up by use of an established proprietary brand. By introducing into Pakistan their technology for extracting valuable starch products from maize Corn Products Inc., for example, expanded greatly its cultivation with attendant benefits to agriculture.

Co-operatives

The marketing efficiency of a group of farmers is increased by selling together where they can benefit from economies of scale in the use of transport and other services through increasing the volume of a commodity handled at one time and raise their bargaining power in sales transactions.

Conditions recognised as favouring co-operative marketing are:

specialised producing areas distant from their major markets;
concentration and specialisation of production;
homogeneity of production and output for market;
groups of farmers dependent on one or a few crops for their total income.

Factors favouring successful co-operative marketing are:

availability of local leadership and management;
a well-educated membership;
members all belonging to one family grouping, i.e. with strong kinship ties or integrated by religion.

In developing countries co-operatives have shown themselves well suited to undertaking the assembly of fairly standard not very perishable products, such as coffee and cotton, for sale on pre-established markets where the price risk is small; and the distribution of a fairly standard not very perishable farm input such as fertilizer where pricing is pre-established.

Thus the assembly of coffee for export has been a successful area of co-operative marketing in various African countries – generally channelled to a monopoly export marketing board as in Kenya, Uganda and Tanzania. The West Cameroun Cooperative Union exports arabica directly to France. The Windward Islands Banana Association works well as assembling agent for the Geest Company with pricing based on independent observation of the destination market. Most of these assembly arrangements are reinforced by distance from the market and by official protection.

Fertilizer distribution is a classic area of farmer co-operative activity in Western Europe, North America and Japan. In developing countries coffee, banana and other co-operative systems combine it conveniently with marketing the crop on which it is used. This then constitutes a practicable basis for distribution of inputs on credit.

Parastatals
These are autonomous in day-to-day operations but directly responsive to government instructions. They are convenient vehicles for the application of public capital, implementation of government price policies, and assignment of marketing monopolies where these are judged advantageous.

Parastatal marketing bodies have been found advantageous to:

1. Moderate supply and price fluctuations on domestic markets by buying into and selling from a buffer stock. The parastatal operating a buffer stock in parallel with other enterprises is specifically adapted to moderating fluctuations in market supplies and prices of products intended for domestic consumers. Most African, Asian and Latin American countries have established such mechanisms to implement minimum prices to producers of major food grains and to protect consumers against prices likely to cause hardship. Sharp variations in price can be caused by marginal surpluses and deficits; buying into a buffer stock some 5 to 15 per cent of the marketed supply of the product concerned is normally sufficient to eliminate wide price extremes. Confining the operation to such proportions limits the capital and subsidy required from the government. It leaves the bulk of the trade to existing marketing enterprises generally able to operate at lower cost, because they have lower overheads and can select their transactions to match their resources and convenience.

2. Operate export marketing monopolies. These can obtain higher returns for their growers if they control enough of the total volume going on to a particular market to be able to influence prices. Within its own seasonal niche in the UK market the Cyprus Potato Board has done this very well. With 40 per cent each of the export market for the long staple varieties cotton export monopolies in Egypt and Sudan manage well the markets they dominate. In Zimbabwe the benefits from maintaining high-quality standards for specific buyers have been demonstrated. Where buyer preferences are varied a monopoly board may obstruct price signals from industry seeking to adjust production to its requirements, as in Nigeria in the early 1980s. When the Commonwealth West African export monopolies were set up and sold together they dominated the main export markets for cocoa, but this is no longer the case. Export markets for coffee are subject to International Coffee Organisation quotas. It is in an exporting country's interest that its best quality coffee goes out in the quota. So some control mechanism is advantageous, but not necessarily a monopoly export board.

3. Operate monopolies in domestic marketing. These are assigned to parastatals to concentrate sales of produce through a particular processing plant to justify the investment, to facilitate collection from small farmers of credit repayments and other dues, and to implement market separation programmes whereby higher overall prices can be obtained.

There are commodity marketing situations where parastatals are common and others where for practical reasons, they have been found less convenient and effective. Major food grains – maize, rice and wheat have priority. Less 'political' grains and pulses, including those often used by lower income consumer groups, receive less attention – because of governments' needs to limit activities that might call for eventual subsidisation. Coffee, cocoa and cotton typically sold by standard quality specifications are widely handled by parastatals. Tea and tobacco requiring direct examination of samples are more often sold by open auction. Livestock and meat, perishable fruits and vegetables and relatively perishable tubers also tend to be left aside.

CONSTRAINTS AND SUPPORT MANAGEMENT

Private enterprise The classic concern about a structure of private marketing enterprises is that they will collude to keep prices down to producers and up to consumers. The remedy is the entry of new enterprise. So government policy will be to encourage the development of competing enterprises facilitating access to information and to capital and to provide local and central market infrastructure.

In various developing countries private marketing enterprises have been considered too many and too small. In an economy where small-scale producers and low-income consumers are also numerous, small marketing enterprises have a role that is strategic. They tend to operate more economically than larger enterprises and provide services that would otherwise not be available. Provided conditions are favourable, some will develop to a national scale. Building on family and religious ties, a few private enterprises in Sudan pushed their shares of some commodity markets up to 80 or 90 per cent. The capital they accumulated appears to have been ploughed back into family businesses which then diversified into agricultural and industrial production. Because this was integrated through the marketing enterprise it led to an effective economic development.

Transnationals The reservations of developing country governments *vis-á-vis* the transnationals have focused on the risks of becoming dependent on them, and so dominated by them. A recent illustration was the concern over the proposed withdrawal of Gulf and Western Inc. from its major sugar and other operations in the Dominican Republic. In fact, much of the steam has now gone out of the issue of transnational power:

1. Because of the uncertainties of foreign investment the transnationals have tended to shift from production in a developing country to the sale of technology, management services and marketing.
2. The panorama of transnationals is now much wider – no longer conspicuously USA-based with its aura of neocolonialism. It includes many with their headquarters in other countries including Japan and in some developing countries.
3. The form of transnational is becoming more varied and more flexible including banks, retailing firms, consulting firms and training agencies.
4. Transnationals have learned to accommodate themselves more to the needs of the developing countries.

Transnationals have been shown very much subject to organised labour and political pressures. Alternatives are available to take their places. The situation has become one where the government of a developing country can assess the benefits that a transnational investment or collaboration can bring to its economy and bargain over the terms.

Co-operatives. Characteristic handicaps of marketing co-operatives are (a) lack of own capital and (b) group decision-making. These follow directly from the democratic principles of the co-operative. If equal capital shares are to be subscribed by all members then they cannot be large: otherwise small farmers would be excluded. This means that most co-operatives depend on government finance for both fixed and working capital. Such capital tends to come on a standardised basis under decisions made at a distance. There is little commitment by the members themselves. Group decision-making implies less enterprise and ability in responding to changing marketing opportunities. Directing committees of farmers often lack management and marketing experience. This also reduces their willingness to offer an attractive salary and bonus to a paid manager. They can be diverted from their long-run interests by influential groups and local politicians.

Stemming also from group direction and the democratic principle is the need to maintain relatively complicated accounts. It can become a major preoccupation in environments where educational qualifications are limited, yet still not protect members against misdirection of funds.

While co-operative systems may not be able to match the cost efficiency of many private enterprises, it is often argued that they should be maintained as an alternative channel. In India some 6 million tons of fertilizer are channelled to farmers annually through a co-operative system operated in parallel with private channels. It is protected by government allocation to it of about 40 per cent of the total supply.

A protected role as handler for the government, or for a marketing board, of some standard product does provide a base from which a farmers' co-operative with the necessary leadership can undertake a range of other activities to help its members, as evidenced in Korea and Taiwan (China).

There are a number of functions for which farmer co-operatives are well suited and of situations favouring successful operation. Promotion of co-operative marketing irrespective of those parameters, particularly as a means of recouping production credit, can involve governments in high support costs for the results achieved.

Parastatals Autonomy in day-to-day operations is vital for an enterprise engaged in practical marketing. While the autonomous parastatal is certainly better suited to marketing operations than a government department, many are still tied too closely to civil service salaries and conditions of employment. While ways are found to add staff, many parastatals find it extremely difficult to terminate them. Management capacity must be sufficient to overcome traditional attitudes and competing loyalties of staff, and the depredations of politicians.

The cost to the government in subsidies for foodgrain stabilisation parastatals are often a continuing burden. These can be kept down by maintaining a wider margin between its buying and selling prices and price differentials for location, quality and storage. It can employ as local buying agents enterprises which already have an operating base and so incur lower overhead costs than direct purchasing stations. Buying costs per bag of maize in Kenya were recently estimated at 4.80 shillings for private agents, 6.15 for direct buying and 7.0 for a specialised co-operative.

If a parastatal is given a monopoly it is in a favourable position to avoid losses that must be met by government, but adequate checks on its efficiency are difficult to devise. In the absence of legal alternatives producers and consumers will be obliged to use its services. It is on them that the burden of its costs will fall. Over the years 1971–9 the costs incurred by the monopoly board of Jamaica in marketing bananas in the UK averaged $100 per ton higher than those of bananas marketed in Germany from Ecuador. Along this channel a national private enterprise was in competition with two transnationals. If a parastatal monopoly is maintained there should be a clear technical justification – that it permits a certain marketing function to be carried out more efficiently than would be feasible otherwise.

In determining the most appropriate enterprise for a particular situation local conditions can be decisive to an extent that is often glossed over. Where family allegiances are dominant and the commercial infrastructure is uncertain the more elaborate marketing organisations are handicapped.

REFERENCES

Abbott, J. C., 'Consideration of alternative marketing organisations to serve small tropical farmers', *Agricultural Administration*, vol. 9, no. 4, 1982, pp. 285–99.

Abbott, J. C., *Agricultural marketing mechanisms and institutions; their performance and limitations*. World Bank internal paper, Washington, DC, 1983.

Abbott, J. C., *Agricultural Marketing Enterprises for the Developing World*, Cambridge University Press (forthcoming).

FAO, *Report on the international expert meeting on the role of the entrepreneur in agricultural marketing development*, Berlin, November 1971, FAO, Rome, 1972.

Harper, M. and Kavura, R., *The Private Marketing Entrepreneur and Rural Development*, FAO, Rome, 1982.

Spinks, R. D. 'Attitudes towards agricultural marketing in Asia and the Far East', *FAO Monthly Bulletin of Agricultural Economics and Statistics*, Rome, vol. 19, no. 1, January 1970, pp. 1–9.

DISCUSSION OPENING I – J. NARVÁEZ-BUENO

I would first like to focus my attention on Dr Abbott's confirmation of the importance of non-economic relationships in the agricultural marketing of developing countries.

The governments of developing countries created, during the late 1950s, 1960s and 1970s, public institutions to be in charge of agricultural marketing. Those institutions had a lot of tasks ahead of them, and only a slight idea of the economic reality of their countries. In spite of this, the really successful enterprises were the ones based on family ties and other non-economic links between their members. The knowledge of this fact implies that some of the policy measures taken by the governments were wrong, and so the policy-makers seemed to have forgotten that in those developing countries the anthropological relationships are at least as important as the economic logics in the developed countries. Nevertheless, the public institutions which I have already mentioned should remain, because sometimes they are used as safety nets by individuals and the private sector. There is also a need to study whether the efficiency of the private sector is due to the lack of efficiency in the public sector.

Regarding Dr Schmitt's paper, I would like to make a clear distinction between his theoretical analysis and the final conclusions he draws through this analysis.

In the economic analysis of the political process, I would insist on the various different meanings that the word democracy could be given. More than a welfare function, which is determined by the aggregation of individual welfare functions, in my opinion the more realistic approaches of today are those which consider government policies as a function of the preferences of a group, *influenced* by the preferences of the individual voters, but not *determined* by them, and this function is imposed prior to all other possible welfare functions, due to the voting results of the democratic election.

I do not consider it completely correct to use the example of the EEC as the basis of the conclusions, mainly due to the many historical implications of the Community; because it could serve in the same way to show that, independently of the farmers' group dimension whose interests are discussed, there are many more interests engaged in the discussion, which are not connected with the farmers.

In negotiations of agricultural prices, each nation's representative seems to place the national interest above his farmers' interests and the advantages he obtains are in general part of a more complex strategy.

So I think that in practice the method used by Dr Schmitt is not the best one to study the basic aspects engaged in the elaboration of agricultural policy. Nevertheless, it is a very valuable approach, and many more efforts like his would be very desirable and fruitful for the world economy.

DISCUSSION OPENING II – OLOF BOLIN

Professor Schmitt has in a skilful manner demonstrated the need for a more holistic theory to make us understand the characteristics of present agricultural policy. His approach includes elements of the traditional market as well as elements of the political market, bureaucracy and interest groups acting together in a complex set of institutional relationships.

The main results of his analysis are that agricultural policy (favouring farmers and often not very efficient) is an ideological commitment of society to farmers and that economists have to accept that in their work what they believe are third-best solutions might in fact be first-best solutions according to the political preferences of society.

This 'new institutionalism' is a young art of economic science and many of the findings I think should still be regarded as hypotheses to be tested empirically.

Referring to my and my co-authors' post-session paper, an alternative approach might be appropriate, at least for the Swedish case. It includes elements of time (dynamics and irreversibility) as well as failures of policy and bureaucracy to correct (possible) failures of the market, or in other ways to represent the preferences of society.

This approach combining Professor Mancur Olson's theory of collective action with theories of bureaucracy and political behaviour, is based on self-interest rather than on ideological commitments of society to agriculture.

Consequently, my basic questions on Professor Schmitt's paper are:

1. What is the empirical basis for the statement that agricultural policy is an ideological commitment? Are other hypotheses possible?
2. What about the time element in the theory? Are we not today the victims of a policy that was set up in an economic and political world quite different from that of the present? Has not time in itself made it possible for different actors and interest groups to organise efficiently a strong resistance to changes? We must have in mind that today agricultural

policy is a matter of rather many interest groups and that the policy is capitalised in high land values, high salaries, safe jobs, etc., so, much money is at stake for the persons involved. It might be extremely hard to get rid of a bad agricultural policy (if it is bad).

3. If that is true, cannot economists contribute to a better state of affairs by studying failures of decision-making procedures used by politicians and bureaucracy? They might well be as fatal as the failures of the traditional markets.

While Gunther Schmitt tries to explain institutional behaviour John Abbott tries to evaluate it, according to its marketing performance for certain types of enterprises in the developing countries.

I can shortly summarise my comments in four questions:

1. Is it really possible to evaluate the performance of different enterprises and what is the empirical technique used to judge whether an enterprise fulfils its (often not very transparent) goals or somebody else's goals? Some might be profit-maximisers, others are bureaucracy controlled and still others might be lobby-oriented rent-seekers and used to organise interests etc. I do not think there exists a single norm for society to judge their performance.

2. Has not society the kind of enterprises it deserves according to, for instance, restraints in competition and monopolistic opportunities often supported by the government?

3. Is not free entry the relevant test of behaviour? Without entry barriers sound enterprises survive and inefficient ones have to go out of business.

4. Anyway, it is not enough to know how enterprises develop. To go further and make use of that knowledge we must know *why*. That means that we have to go back to Günther Schmitt's approach to see how the institutional setting works in order to be able to implement a new order of things.

GENERAL DISCUSSION – RAPPORTEUR: JOHN STRAK

It was commented, with reference to Swedish agricultural policy, that it was possible to see policy being influenced by political markets, economic factors and ideological changes in society. Another speaker felt that behind every institution there was an idea and that we could look, for example, at the Federal Reserve Board in the USA and the ideas that lay behind it. Other comments were that the paper needed a dynamic context and that we needed to involve the interaction of technology and institutions. More discussion of the role of ideology in Dr Schmitt's paper was required and the definition of institution might be questioned. Should we distinguish between market and non-market institutions? Farming should not be considered as just a business operation.

Regarding Dr Abbott's paper, the question was asked as to whether the author had used the survivor technique for evaluating marketing enterprise. It was suggested that co-operative marketing enterprise should be encouraged. Another speaker wondered if enough countries were encouraging their local entrepreneurs and what policies would the author recommend for such encouragement?

Günther Schmitt replied to the various commentators by saying that he felt market co-ordination and institutional flexibility were really concerned with the same thing. He also said that there was no difference between the self-interest of farmers and questions about ideology. He agreed that the time element was important and that we should study market failures as well as political failures.

In reply John Abbott agreed with the discussion opener that evaluation was a problem because so few enterprises were eligible over time. He also said that different enterprises had complementary roles, co-operatives worked quite well where their main selling function was undertaken by another organisation or enterprise. Finally, he agreed that even the removal of apparently trivial obstacles to transportation or production could make a large difference to the performance of the farm sector – for example, providing access to larger trucks or to bank credit.

Participants in the discussion included Ewa Rabinowicz, A. B. Lewis, G. S. Bhalla, Peter Soderbaum, Sven Holmstrom, Julian Briz, A. D. Indraratna and Barry Prentice.

JEAN CHATAIGNER AND YVES LEON

Self-Reliance or Dependence of Agricultural Economics Research in Developing Countries

The optimism which reigned at the beginning of the first 'decade of development' concerning the possibilities of growth possessed by Third World countries was replaced, little by little, by a much more circumspect attitude, justified by the numerous disappointments sustained by attempts at development. In the agricultural field, in particular, it was gradually understood that a better comprehension of these countries' realities was necessary. It was a matter of better observing their farming, in order to provide an answer which was well adapted to the problems which were faced.

One often questions the role played by the research conducted in agricultural economy in this development of attitudes. The aim of this article is to answer this question; it is based on research conducted in French-speaking Africa, the Ivory Coast in particular. We would like to describe how the idea of research devoted to the agricultural economy of countries in the process of development was conceived and the difficulties of carrying out this research. In addition, we would like to show why the autonomy of this research is henceforth an indispensable condition of its impact on development.

THE EMERGENCE OF RESEARCH IN AGRICULTURAL ECONOMY ADAPTED TO THE PROBLEMS OF DEVELOPMENT

After the Second World War, the sudden awareness of under-development was accompanied by great confidence in the technical capacities of the modern world to surmount the handicap of feeble agricultural production in under-developed countries. The spectacular successes of agricultural modernisation in the economies of countries undergoing reconstruction helped to increase this confidence. It seems that one wondered little about the real reasons behind this success. Was it a result of the diffusion of good technical models of development available to European farmers, or, rather, the reaction of these farmers to powerful incitations created by a reality of food scarcity, or was it perhaps the consequence of actions taken by the governments concerned?

417

Confident in the role of technical progress, a model of development based largely on the popularization of new techniques was diffused in Third World countries. This movement resulted in setting up an impressive number of agricultural development projects at all levels. It is now necessary to recognise that a large number of them ended in complete or semi-failure, and it was necessary to explain the cause of these failures.

For example, it was necessary to explain the variation between the results obtained by agricultural research and those obtained by the farmers who had been proposed corresponding innovations. Worse, these deviations were maintained throughout the years and even augmented, thus showing that the proposed model was ill adapted to the logic of the farmers.

This state of affairs was interpreted as the result of a great reticence on the part of the farmers regarding the innovations which were imposed on them, and exposed the conflicts of interest which existed between the different participants in agricultural development: the farmers, the state and its related associations, and exterior financiers.

It took time to respond adequately to these difficulties. They necessitated the formation and gradual mobilisation of specific competences in rural economy. In effect, it is the need for a more complete understanding of the mechanism which governs economic and social phenomena which is at the core of an important development in the activity of the agricultural economy in and around developing countries. This new activity is manifested by a summons for exterior aid, in the form of experts, the formation of national experts, and the progressive organisation of research oriented towards a better understanding of production systems.

Until a relatively recent period, the group of qualified argricultural economists in the developing countries was found at the level of national decision-making, notably in planning. At the same time, experts belonging to financial organisations or to departments of specialised studies completed diagnoses and studies concerning the realisation of operations and developmental projects during relatively short time periods. For at least a dozen years, the agro-economist has been fixed in the function of decision-making or of accompanying studies, related to or even centred on operations of development. In a country like the Ivory Coast, for example, there existed practically no agricultural economists in the structures of development in 1974, whereas they numbered more than 20 in 1982.

Another type of response to the need for agro-economists in developing countries was furnished by foundations (principally Ford and Rockefeller) which favoured the formation of national specialists under the conditions that they attend universities in the developing countries and that they help to create education appropriate to the countries themselves. In East Africa, for example, the cited foundations vigorously aided the university departments of social sciences and permitted the number of diplomas conferred to increase appreciably. With the passing of a dozen years, one can observe an analogous phenomenon in French-speaking Africa.

The contribution of foreign universities (especially American) was constantly increased, improving at the same time the qualifications of the corps of professors brought to gain a better understanding of the reality of the Third World. Europe is not absent in this movement but its means are relatively feeble and perhaps the specifics of a certain number of its structures oriented towards the developing countries have not always permitted a satisfying response in relation to the importance of the demand.

The economic and social problems of rural development have finally been taken into account in the organisation of the research itself. In international centres, such as the IITA or the ICRISAT, citing only those which intervene in Africa, it had been desired, for example, to integrate the analysis of the systems of production as a frame of reference for the introduction of innovations. In other centres, the contribution of rural economy to the formation of agronomists is considerable.

At the same time, in the restructuring or the development of an apparatus for national research there is also noted a tendency to integrate rural economy. This integration occurs generally by the creation of a central team charged with following and, if possible, anticipating the economic evolution in the agricultural sector and, finally, aiding the orientation of research, through the organisation of regional multi-disciplinary teams centred on the analysis of systems of production. Senegal, in French-speaking Africa, offers a beautiful example of the recent creation of such a device.

Through this brief view of the evolution of the growing place that rural economy takes in decision-making, up to and including the orientation of agronomic research, it can be observed that the required competences depend entirely on aid which comes from the exterior of those countries concerned. The place of the native researchers is still very weak and in the majority of the cases their formation, like those of foreign experts, still depends on the base of knowledge acquired by experience or scientific investigation completed outside their own countries. In this domain, as in many others, the dependence of almost all the developing countries is quasi-total. Even taking the considerable role of North American universities in this process into consideration, one can speak of a preponderant dependence on American education. Briefly, theories, methods, knowledge, ideologies all come from the exterior. It can be imagined, it should even be admitted, that there will only be real development with the existence of an autonomous capacity for analysis and reflection on rural development. This capacity for reflection in our contemporary world is manifested by the existence of an active research in the social sciences.

DIFFICULTIES IN SETTING UP AUTONOMOUS RESEARCH

The attempts to help construct the potential for national research have been multiplied in the recent past, but they collide with numerous difficulties related to their methods of insertion into the society. Having participated in one of these attempts we would like to try to characterise the circumstances and expose this which, according to us, still opposes full development.

In the Ivory Coast, the birth of research in rural economy was incontestably favoured by the existence of dynamic agricultural and agronomic research. But the research organised in this domain was essentially the result of political will, expressed at the time (1972–8) through a movement toward planning by the Minister of Scientific Research who had wagered on the development of a national structure.

Entering into a general process of reorganisation and of progressive control over all research, the creation and development of CIRES benefited the development of a regulated research worker status and a national finance put it temporarily out of danger of exterior excesses. The choice of programmes had been facilitated by a procedure of confrontation with the principal participants in the development, and their preparation exposed without a doubt the necessity to educate national researchers. Recourse to exterior existence for personnel had been voluntarily reduced to a minimum, but the co-ordination with the potential existing in other structures had been largely favoured. The regular publication of research results in the notebooks of CIRES played a determining role in the evaluation and the diffusion of knowledge. Finally CIRES used all available resources to educate the maximum number of researchers in the shortest space of time, and systematically supported students in various types of economy, putting their studies to work on the land.

Ten years later, CIRES has about 20 researchers of whom half are rural economists. In particular CIRES supports the creation of education at the doctoral level for all of West Africa. However, dependence still exists. It centres essentially on the difficulties faced in adapting research to the realities of development; often, they are aggravated by non-adaptation to the manner of internal administration of research and the multiplicity of forms of exterior intervention in developing countries. In developed countries agronomic research and, particularly, research in rural economy benefit from the incessant movement of ideas which are manifested between the researchers and the many organisations which animate the agricultural world. The translation from perceived needs into research apparatus at the different levels of decision-making is facilitated by the existence of numerous occasions for confrontations between researchers and producers and an improved education which furnishes the basis for communication. Finally, the multiplicity of interlocutors guarantees free expression, a principal source of efficiency.

In developing countries, the situation is principally characterised by an unequal capacity for expression on the part of those participating in social and economic activity. The researcher often has as his only interlocutor the state and its diverse branches to prepare developmental plans. In the best of cases, such as that which can be observed in the Ivory Coast, the systematic organisation of dialogue between the different decision-making levels of the state and the researchers of different disciplines has been able considerably to improve the possibilities for orientation. But in almost all cases, the absence of opportunities for the farmers to express themselves makes it difficult to take into account fundamental questions of development. In the social sciences there is no really objective scientific approach. The researcher is, himself, a part of the world which he observes and a scientific verification can only be established by examining the variety of behaviours exhibited by the different members of a society. Under these conditions the staging of research in rural economy in a large number of developing countries is confronted by a major handicap; the expression of inequalities related to development. In the majority of cases, this situation is aggravated by the precarious status of the researchers and by insufficient means for research, which explain the feeble recognition of the researchers' social utility and, unfortunately, a certain mistrust which exists. In fact, through his work, the researcher exposes social and economic mechanisms whose explanations can reflect negatively on the interests of the state or on those of individuals and groups with whom he is aligned. Thus, it is necessary to examine problems concerning liberty of expression.

When the public powers recognise the value of efforts made by those who have attempted to construct a national potential for research and when the comprehension of foreign money lenders suffices to authorise a continuation of funds, other obstacles remain to be overcome.

In fact, if this research becomes credible, it is highly probable that solicitations for studies to be completed would be numerous and more alluringly accompanied by comfortable financing. The demand can come from the interior, but still comes more often from the exterior. The young researchers or professors flattered by such a consideration, are trained in a rapid succession of disorganised operations which often only give an illusory understanding of the reality of the country. The young researchers and professors in these operations are only workers in the service of analyses which are exterior to them. Very rare are the situations which permit a study to realise a scientific accumulation which is useful to the development of a programme managed by the institution who employs these researchers.

On the other hand, fearing such compromises, or not at all enjoying the necessary esteem on the part of public powers, a young researcher can rightly consider that his actions should be oriented toward exterior education: the research should support the education, but another danger threatens him, concerning faulty articulation in development, which extends to a veritable isolation. Isolation which unfortunately characterises numerous universities in the Third World. Isolation which favours the simple repetition by the native researchers themselves of precepts conceived and received from the exterior.

The autonomy of research in developing countries, in rural economy in particular, is therefore very difficult to construct. It demands on the part of its promoters a great clearness of priorities and a great firmness in its management. It is necessary to define programmes which are well articulated to the priorities of development such that they are desired by the country, to construct or develop superior education whose principal priority is to establish this education on an effective knowledge of the country's agriculture and to respond, without letting itself be inundated, to exterior solicitations.

Before these difficulties, international co-operation contents itself with pointed but limited aid. It could be more effective if it undertook, long-term, the support of a defined programme recognised as having priority in the country receiving aid, and if it was careful to favour relations from team to team between northern and southern countries and between the countries of the South themselves.

What are in fact, the faults of international co-operation as it is practised? We notice two principal weaknesses which constitute obstacles to the construction of autonomous and efficient research in developing countries.

First of all, it seems to us that the brevity and inconsistency of aid is opposed to the long period which is necessary for the construction of efficient research. It is necessary to have at least ten years to create an autonomous research team in a completely developed country as well as under the worst conditions. However, it is rare that aid to these research programmes last longer than two, three, at most five years without severe modifications in the origin, the direction and the orientation of the work.

The inadequate formation received by the national researchers causes other problems which are extremely complicated. It would be necessary to create an education which better responds to real needs of the country concerned. How can this be done when the knowledge of these countries is still so weak? On the contrary, all is ready for veritably extroverted research when education, its programmes and financing, is defined by the exterior and often, in spite of the good will of its contributors, to the advantage of the exterior.

CONCLUSION

The experiences of the last two decades show that research in agricultural economy can make a considerable contribution to a country's development. This fact became progressively apparent and necessitated an important evolution in the demand for economic studies in order that it would be clearly established.

The development of autonomous research is necessary. This alone can conveniently integrate the actions of various economic agents. But the development of such a research in rural economy is yet confronted with many difficulties. Some are of internal origin. They will be overcome when rural economics is recognised as necessary for development. Other difficulties are of external origin. They will be resolved when the different international contributors of aid understand that their interest is to support the development and expansion of an autonomous team of native researchers.

REFERENCES

Arnon, J., *Planification et programmation de la recherche agricole*, FAO, Rome, 1976.

Arndt, T. M., Dalrymple, D. G. and Ruttan, V. W., 'Resource Allocation and Productivity', in national and international agricultural research, University of Minnesota Press, Minneapolis, 1977.

Casas, J., *Réflexions sur la recherche agronomique dans les pays sous-développés et moyennement développés*, INRA, Montpellier, 1977.

Casas, J., Labouesse, F., Devred, R. and Trouchaud, P. P., *L'Institut National de la Recherche Agronomique du Maroc*, Bilan et perspectives, ISNAR, La Haye, 1984.

Centre Ivoirien de Recherche Economique et Sociale, *Plan de développement du CIRES, 1984–2000*, Abidjan, 1984.

Contant, R. B., *Linking agricultural research and higher agricultural education: a partnership for success*, ISNAR, The Hague, 1984.

Du Plessix, D. J. et al., *La programmation de la recherche agronomique en Côte d'Ivoire*, Colloque IIP, Abidjan, 1973.

Idachaba, F. S., *Expanding and managing agricultural research in West Africa*, invited paper delivered at the 5th Biennal Conference of the West African Association of Agricultural Economists, Abidjan, 1983.

Nurske, R., *Problems of Capital Formation in Underdeveloped Countries*, 1953.

Ruttan, V. W., *Agricultural research policy*, University of Minnesota Press, Minneapolis, 1982.

MULUMBA KAMUANGA[1]

Irrigation Investment in Africa: Major Issues in the Design and Implementation of Large Schemes

IRRIGATION IN THE AFRICAN CONTEXT

Developing countries which have achieved food self-sufficiency are countries where substantial investments have been made in irrigation as a vehicle for expanding agricultural production. The World Bank has estimated that China and India, for example, contain more than half of the 160 million hectares of irrigated land in the developing world (World Bank 1982). In comparison, irrigation plays an insignificant role in sub-Saharan Africa; estimates of land under irrigation range from 1 to 5 per cent in most countries, in contrast to 30 per cent in India (Eicher and Baker 1982).

Countries and regional experiences vary considerably. Irrigation dominates the agricultural sector of the Sudan (50 to 75 per cent of cultivated land). It is important in Madagascar with 15 per cent of its cultivable land under farmer's small-scale perimeters. Irrigation also plays a significant role in Mali, Senegal and to a much lesser extent in Cameroon, Ivory Coast, Nigeria, Ethiopia, Mozambique, Somalia and Zimbabwe (World Bank 1981).

Over the last 10 to 15 years irrigated agriculture has made some advances in the Sahelien countries. This is a result of the 1968–74 drought and the optimistic view by many governments in the region of irrigation as the solution to unreliable rainfall and a means for intensifying crop production. The potential for increasing the proportion of arable land under irrigation is indeed very large in the Sahel. A 1980 CILSS/Club du Sahel study indicates that the area currently under total and partial water control represents less than 10 per cent of the 2.3 million hectares which could be developed over the next 20 to 25 years if the necessary regulating dams were built.

Despite the considerable interest and investment in irrigation development over the past decade, there has not been a substantial increase in agricultural production. The record is particularly disappointing with regard to formal large schemes with full water control such as the Office du Niger in Mali. Reviewers of large-scale irrigation projects in Africa –

e.g. de Wilde (1967), Chambers and Moris (1973), Barnett (1981), Bonnefond et al. (1981), CILSS/Club du Sahel (1980a, 1980b) and the World Bank (1981) have concluded that irrigation is not making an efficient contribution to food production. Poor performance is attributed to many factors, but the most important include:

(1) The cost of building the installations which runs from $5,000 to more than $10,000 per hectare; this compares with an average of $1,600 per hectare in South Asia (FAO 1984).

(2) Lack of maintenance and technical problems which in the case of the Sahel, has led to a situation where for every 5,000 hectares of new land put under irrigation, nearly another 5,000 hectares is taken out of cultivation.[2]

(3) Problems of recurrent costs and low rates of cost recovery; this is compounded by the fact that most rehabilitation programmes are behind schedule.

(4) Inadequate organisation capacities and generally an unfavourable socio-economic environment which provides poor incentives to farmers.

These constraints are commonly grouped into two categories – technical and socio-cultural. Technical constraints are the result of poor design and/or bad maintenance and could logically be overcome if additional investments to finance recurrent costs and rehabilitate existing installations were available. However, the successful operation of an irrigation scheme requires more than a simple injection of good money after bad money. It also requires the establishment of a socio-economic environment favourable to the farmers. In view of the importance accorded irrigation in the agricultural plans of Sahelian countries, it is essential to stress again the need for feasibility studies to account for social and cultural factors.

THE PROBLEM

For many governments and donor agencies, large irrigation schemes are still regarded as an answer to the problem of lagging food production. Irrigation, for example, represents 38 per cent of the value of the World Bank loans to the agricultural sector (Carruthers 1983). For many villagers too, the vulnerability of dryland farming to recurrent droughts and the unpredictable nature of the harvest become the main motive behind their decision to join irrigation schemes.

Irrigation benefits, however, have not been fully realised, either from governments' point of view or that of farmers. Apart from constraints of a technical nature, those associated with socio-cultural and organisational factors stem from a misunderstanding by project designers and planners of the essential nature of an irrigation scheme. As P. Vicinelli states: '... (it is) not simply a public works project but a complex socio-economic undertaking in which human relationships, in a variety of institutional forms, including legal, have to be carefully considered' (in Carruthers 1983, p. 79).

In recent years attention has been given to the need for irrigation project designers to broaden the scope of *ex-ante* feasibility studies through a more systematic analysis of the milieu, and of farmers' practices and reactions (Dey 1982). In this paper, I take the position that trade-offs between expanding crop production on irrigation schemes and improving farmers' social well-being should be negotiated beforehand, with obvious consequences for the project design and implementation phases. This is possible if enough attention is paid to two aspects which have often been neglected during the design phase. First, and perhaps of equal importance to the provision of engineering and managerial inputs, is the understanding of the functioning of local farming systems. Second, is an effective attempt to anticipate conflicts arising from the mismatch of farmers' motivations and aspirations with the government's efforts to achieve – through its supervising agency – the objective of expanding agricultural production.

I draw my arguments mainly from a case study (see below) and the results of my two-year research work at the Office du Niger in Mali (Kamuanga 1982, 1984). A short illustration of how the knowledge of local institutions and organisation of production can inspire the design of a better irrigation scheme, derives from my current experience as a member of a multidisciplinary research team in Southern Senegal. Much of the paper, however, is a discussion of a few ideas which could help improve planning techniques in the design and implementation of irrigation projects in West Africa.

CASE STUDY: PRODUCTION RELATIONS AT THE OFFICE DU NIGER[3] (MALI)

Created some 50 years ago, the Office du Niger (hereafter referred to as the Office) is a state agency with a mandate to help settle independent farmers. The settlers contract to grow irrigated rice and use the office infrastructure, equipment and services. Currently about 5,000 farm families are settled and cultivate approximately 40,000 hectares of gravity irrigated land along the delta of the Niger River in central southern Mali. The contract requires the settler to abide by the Office recommended practices, to maintain field (tertiary) level supply/drainage canals, and to deliver the harvest to the authorities. This is the means by which the Office seeks to ensure its primary objective – increasing rice production.

Settlers, however, are not willing to make the continued land improvements needed for intensive irrigated cultivation since they are not guaranteed continued access to the land and are uncertain of reaping the benefits from such long term investments.

The performance of irrigated rice in the Office is generally poor. The output it achieves today is disproportionately low, given the capital investment and the amount of experience accumulated over 50 years of trial and error (Kamuanga 1982). Acute problems of maintenance of the canals and weed infestation have crippled rice yields to an average of 1.8 metric tons per hectare over the past decade. At the same time, producer prices remained at very low levels until 1983. In 1981, for example, it cost the Office farmer 83 Malian Francs (MF)[4] to produce a kilo of rice, but the farmer level price was only 60 MF per kilo. In 1983 the price was increased to 132 MF per kilo, but inflation and subsequent increases in input prices (including paid labour) kept the farmer's revenue at an average of 734 MF a day, approximately 40 per cent lower than the daily rate for unskilled labour (Kamuanga 1984). The fixed land tax of 400 kg of rice per hectare does not reflect differences in yield potential across the scheme. A substantial number of settlers (particularly in the Office Kolongo zone) live in a permanent state of impoverishment. The authorities, however, maintain a different assessment of its settlers' well-being, despite empirical evidence in support of the farmers' view.[5]

As is the case in other settlement schemes, farmers have devised strategies to accommodate their risks and ensure their survival. For example, rice is smuggled out of the Office area and into neighbouring countries for a higher price. The recommended practice of stacking bundles in the field for mechanical threshing is implemented by farmers, but primarily to assure that enough grain is left on the ground for gleaning by family members. Farmers also concentrate on more profitable activities such as supplying off-farm labour, vegetable growing, rainfed farming and cultivation of (illegal) rice plots outside their official holdings. Off-farm revenue is often 25 per cent higher than on-farm revenue.

Other examples of strategies which demonstrate that project authorities and farmers have different objective functions are commonly noted in the literature (e.g. Bonnefond et al. 1981; Barnett 1981). The conclusion is fairly obvious: so long as the organisation and the relations of production block farmers' aspirations, the farmers' rational responses will appear irrational from the viewpoint of the supervising agency. To what extent can existing rural social organisations and actual experience from long-established irrigation schemes inspire the design and the implementation of new irrigation projects in order to avoid such unnecessary misunderstanding and confusion in the future?

PLANNING FEASIBILITY

Designing new irrigation projects
I begin with the assumption that the technical design of the scheme is adequate.[6] The decision to implement an irrigation project rests then on the premise that physical measurements (yields and outputs), monetary measurements (shadow prices and opportunity costs) and the value of non-marketed inputs and production reflect social values and costs. The flow of benefits and costs is balanced and nets out in favour of the farmer and the society as a whole, as shown by the values of quantitative

indicators – the internal rate of return (IRR), the benefit-cost ratio (BCR) and the net present value (NPV). In simpler terms project analysts demonstrate that the net value of production foregone in the traditional agricultural system (the without case) is more than compensated by the net benefits stream of the project over its expected life time (Little and Mirrlees 1974).

However, the predictive power of economic evaluation of projects should not be overemphasised. Discrepancies can exist between the values of quantitative indicators even a few years after project implementation (Franzel 1979; Weiler and Tyner 1981). The gap between *ex-ante* and *ex-post* analysis could be a question of difference in perspective, since it involves a comparison of projected and historical data. Often, however, it is a question of unrealistic assumptions, the use of inappropriate technical coefficients and the dismissal or failure to account for non-tangible and non-quantifiable benefits and costs. Some of these factors are the results of basically misguided organisation forms inherent in the components of the irrigation system the planners have built. The absence of a land tax modulated to the variation in yield potential across the Office scheme on Mali is one such example. More important, this gap exists because the current popular view maintains an approach to irrigation project planning which views change as a one time transition from an earlier state to a static (improved) state. Barnett has contrasted planning change with planning for change which, he states: '... assumes that the *ex-post* state following the planned intervention will set up and sustain its own dynamic and impetus' (Barnett 1981). Some aspects of that dynamic are discernible beforehand in view of past experiences with irrigation schemes.

The office experience in Mali is instructive with respect to several aspects of irrigation project design. The settlers' kit of survival strategies should remind planners that when an irrigation project relies on a single food crop (rice in this case), the latter should be regarded only as a part of the farmers' overall production system. Therefore production goals have to be compatible with the possibility that farmers will engage in other activities, particularly if they find it difficult to meet their consumption needs. How much supervision and extension efforts should the scheme authorities devote to these side activities is a question that needs to be addressed prior to the implementation of irrigation projects.

There is another lesson to be learned from the Office case with respect to the trade-off between settlers' management and the amount of control the scheme authorities can give up. In 1983 when the producer price of rice was increased by 120 per cent to 132 MF per kilo, smuggling of rice to private traders was drastically reduced. In the framework of the current reform of the cereal market in Mali (expansion of the role of private traders in foodgrain) there is evidence to suggest that for the Office to draw off substantial marketable surpluses of settlers' rice production, it will need not only to offer competitive prices, but also to assure a cash payment to farmers at the time of harvest (Amselle et al.

1985). Total control of production and prices has turned the Office into a supplier of cheap rice to urban dwellers and civil servants in a system that is both very constraining for the farmers and very costly to the government.

For practical purposes this discussion implies that (1) there is a demand for an approach to irrigation project design that emphasises a project realistic feasibility by bringing into the foreground the aspirations (objective functions) of the various groups of actors, including the government agency; and (2) this approach must recognise that the scheme authorities will have to cope with a situation that is dynamic and changing. This is an invitation to pragmatism and flexibility in planning the functioning of irrigation schemes. I will outline a few practical steps and draw attention to their implications.

First is the recognition that project life needs to be realistically divided into stages with moderate yield and production targets set for early years. Farmers admitted to formal irrigation schemes, particularly in Sahelian countries, do not have prior experience and lack the peculiar discipline which irrigated agriculture requires. Therefore the first phase should actually be viewed as an adjustment period. Depending on the type of agro-ecological and socio-economic setting under consideration, it is reasonable to expect that farmers will first, and of necessity, pursue production levels aimed at reproducing their farming system. This supposes that accumulation and social consumption needs are satisfied, perhaps in a way that may not be consistent with the search for economically optimal levels of production and incomes from the planners' viewpoint. Reproduction is taken here in the large sense of a safe and careful maintenance of their system with respect to its technico-economic and socio-cultural aspects (Campagne 1982). This obviously implies on the part of project designers an adequate knowledge of the social organisation of production and consumption (Dey 1982) including questions of land tenure and the transmission of property rights.

One corollary of this perspective is the need for project monitoring and evaluation to be conducted at regular intervals – every five years, for example – after project implementation. Evaluation procedures have to be broader in scope and beyond the standard concepts of technico-econo-mic efficiency (IRR, BCR, NPV), include some indicators of the improvement of the social well-being of farmers. The question of land rights, for instance, needs special consideration. It is often a peculiar one and should be addressed with regard to two groups of peoples: (1) those excluded, as a result of the scheme, from secure and regular access to the ownership or usufruct rights to improved land; (2) those in the second generation who contemplate joining the scheme. Evidence from the Gambia indicates that irrigation projects, by inviting only men's participation, have led to the establishment of land rights which virtually exclude women traditionally responsible for rice land (Dey 1982). With most large irrigation planned under the assumption of a 30–40 years' lifetime, serious attempts should be made at each stage to reconcile the rules governing traditional (local) societies with the need to build a long-lasting incentive structure for all scheme members.

Second, once an understanding of what can be possibly achieved after the initial phase is gained, attention should be directed to the question of how a surplus can be generated and maintained on the scheme, and how it will be shared between the state agency supervising the scheme and the farmers (Campagne 1982). Pricing policy remains in this regard a powerful tool, for it determines the extent to which, eventually, the share of that surplus is fair to all parties. But project designers do not set prices; they must instead explore other avenues and existing opportunities for improving the design of irrigation schemes leading to a successful implementation programme. One such avenue is the determination of optimal sizes of family holdings compatible with labour and non-labour resources available to different groups of farmers.[7] Research also needs to be undertaken in order to improve the productivity of family labour.

Third, it is necessary at later stages to begin to review the initial objectives in light of the scheme's historical development and also on the basis of similar experiences in other countries. This leads us to the subject of the next section – the rehabilitation of large irrigation schemes where substantial investments have already been made.

Designing projects to rehabilitate existing irrigation schemes
A crucial aspect in rehabilitating old irrigation schemes, which has received deserved attention, is the recovery of recurrent costs. Two complementary approaches are commonly proposed: (1) absorption of production subsidies by making the farmers pay for the actual costs of services they receive, and (2) reduction of management operating costs by redefining its tasks and reorganising these on a more operational basis. An in-depth treatment of this subject for the West African Sahel is presented in the CILSS/Club du Sahel study completed in 1980 and the proceedings of the OECD workshop (Carruthers 1983). I would like to centre my reflections on another aspect of the structural adjustment which, in my opinion, has received less attention.

In a remarkably concise diagnosis of the situation, the 1981 World Bank report on *Accelerated Development in sub-Saharan Africa* discussed the principal issues involved and outlined the required consolidation and rehabilitation measures (p. 78). Unfortunately the view that large-scale irrigation development is primarily technical in nature prevails.[8] Although the report recognises the importance of improving economic incentives for farmers and of increasing their participation in operating and maintaining the irrigation scheme, in our view it falls short of recommending concrete measures necessary to attain these objectives, namely (1) reassessment of the current production objectives, (2) streamlining or reforming the existing administration to adjust it to the revised objectives and (3) reconsideration of the social relationships between the scheme authorities and the farmers. In particular, measures are needed to concretely tackle the following issues (Kamuanga 1983):

> farmers' cumulative indebtedness and the ways and means of alleviating it;
> their lack of enthusiasm in carrying out production, now being increased at the cost of considerable inconvenience and the feeling that they are agricultural labourers disguised as smallholders;
> the low rate of information flow between the scheme authorities and the farmers which has led to suspicions around the question of money, prices and farmers' accounts;
> income disparities among farmers as a result of inappropriate and sometimes discriminatory credit policies (for instance against women);
> the provision of incentives which will help farmers participate in the life of the scheme and identify their interests with those of the whole undertaking.

Since the responsibility for the operation and maintenance of the infrastructures must somewhere along the line rest with the farmers themselves, it is necessary to involve them in the initial planning and subsequent implementation stage of the irrigation project (Goodell 1984; Dey 1982; Carruthers 1983). While there is growing recognition of the efficacy of this approach (Bonnefond 1981; Diemer and Van der Laan 1983), effective participation of farmers in irrigation projects has not been fully evaluated. It can result in changes which alter the relationship between farmers and the supervising agency and thereby raises fundamental political questions with respect to power and problems of governance (Bingen 1983).

One must recognise, however, that economic research on irrigation has left aside many important questions including (1) the benefit-cost analysis of alternative types of government versus farmers' organisation and control of production,[9] and (2) the economics of differential access to resources both between various groups of villagers and within the household.

An obvious implication of the foregoing discussion is that a successful implementation of an irrigation scheme requires a collaborative multidisciplinary effort within the team responsible for planning.

Multidisciplinary analysis and irrigation planning
As indicated earlier, knowledge of relevant aspects of the local farming system, i.e. the organisation of production and consumption, land tenure, and the roles of different status positions within the village and the household, is a prerequisite for the design and implementation of agricultural projects. A strong case should be made for economists to work with sociologists and anthropologists and use existing local capacities during the initial planning phase. Effective collaboration as perceived in this context is a two-way exchange. On one hand, it calls for our colleagues in the 'soft' social sciences[10] to move from their *ex-post*

discovery of what went wrong to more involvement with *ex-ante* socio-economic planning. It is the sociologist's or anthropologist's job to anticipate the emergence of incompatible organisational forms (Goodell 1984) and help minimise social costs (in a much broader sense including farmers' inconveniences). On the other hand, it calls for economists to begin to realise and utilise such conceptual tools as unit of production, consumption group, level of accumulation, role and status within households etc., commonly used by sociologists/anthropologists, because (1) they are helpful in capturing the structure and the dynamic of family groups as production units and (2) they can bring realism into farm budget analysis as a necessary complement and logical step to agricultural project analysis (Brown 1979).

The need for interdisciplinary interaction during the planning phase should be emphasised. Drawing from the current experience in farming systems research (FSR) in Basse Casamance (Senegal), we learned how difficult it was to find an acceptable definition of a farm (*exploitation agricole*) in the Northeastern zone without a prior knowledge of the social organisation of production among the Fogny-Diola. An irrigated project is also contemplated in that area. On the basis of our knowledge of the sexual division of labour, disparities in access to and control of resources within family compounds, the FSR team was able to recommend the following to the local extension agency: (1) women who are traditionally responsible for rice production should be able to gain access to seasonal credit for seeds, fertilizer and herbicide; (2) credit for animal traction equipment should be extended to men who allocate most of their labour to upland crops (groundnuts) but could eventually help their wives with ploughing and seeding.

CONCLUSIONS

I have tried to emphasise in this paper two main points in planning the feasibility of irrigation schemes. First, the necessity for planning teams to learn from similar experiences to avoid past mistakes. Second, the need to improve *ex-ante* benefit-cost anlysis using realistic assumptions about technical coefficients and farmers' objective functions at different stages of the implementation of the project.

Poor performance of irrigation schemes, often attributed to technical deficiencies, is also a consequence of the fact that feasibility studies have neglected social aspects which influence technical and economic feasibility. This gap can be filled if a distinction is made at the project level between (1) 'macro-planning' which takes a telescopic view of the entire life of the irrigation project to derive a quantitative index for its profitability, and (2) 'micro-planning' dealing with the practical (feasible), functioning of the project as constrained by local institutions. An important prerequisite of this is a thorough understanding of local farming systems and of the environment in which the irrigation project is situated.

The ideas presented in this paper are still too limited to do more than suggest hypotheses to guide further research in this area. Yet some implications are clearly obvious at the planning phase. The need for interdisciplinary research and for effective collaboration between economists and sociologists as equal partners in the design and planning phase of irrigation schemes is in itself a call for a methodological breakthrough. For donor agencies in particular, covering beforehand the cost of a sound long-term programme in planning and assistance to the irrigation sector of a developing country will unfortunately not improve the benefit-cost analysis; greater sensitivity may be needed.

NOTES

[1]The author extends his appreciation to Jim Bingen, Eric Crawford and Carl Eicher of Michigan State University for their comments on an early draft of this paper.

[2]C. Eicher, personal communication.

[3]For a history of the Office du Niger, see M. Guillaume, in *Agronomie Tropicale*, vol. XV no. 3, 1960; de Wilde (1967); and Jones (1976).

[4]In 1983 the exchange rate was 700 Malian Francs for 1 US $. The Malian franc had a fixed parity of 1 to 0.5 with the CFA franc.

[5]My study over the 1978–80 seasons has shown that the Office farmers did not generate a return above the financial and opportunity costs of all resources, i.e. they were not in a position to reinvest or increase their current level of consumption out of their earnings from the production of irrigated rice alone (Kamuanga 1982).

[6]This is, however, a very serious and unresolved problem for many irrigation projects.

[7]This approach was used to determine an optimal norm of land allocation at the Office du Niger. The results of a linear programming model indicated that a maximum of 5.4 hectares can be efficiently brought into cultivation by a family with 2.5 man-equivalents using no outside labour and no custom plough (Kamuanga 1982).

[8]This point is reinforced in the report by the statement that '... unless close to 6 tons of cereals are grown per hectare per year, investments of $ 10,000–$ 20,000 per hectare cannot be justified' (p. 78).

[9]I am indebted to Jim Bingen for his comments on this point.

[10]In reference to the term 'hard social science', as suggested by Kuttner alluding to the overmathematisation of economics.

REFERENCES

Amselle, J. L., Bagayoko, D., Benhamon, J., Leullier, J. C. and Ruf, T., 'Evaluation de l'Office du Niger (Mali)' – Conclusions – mimeo 13pp. MRE-CD, March 1985.

Barnett, T., 'Evaluating the Gezira Scheme: Black Box or Pandora's Box?' in *Rural Development in Tropical Africa*, Roberts, J. and Williams, G. (eds), St Martin's Press, New York, 1981.

Bingen, R. J., 'The State and Rural Development: The Case of Operation Riz – Segou in Mali', Paper prepared for the December 1983 meeting, African Studies Association, Boston, Massachusetts.

Bonnefond, Ph., Cannel, J., Lericollais, A. and Weigel, J. Y., 'La Vallée du Fleuve Sénégal et ses Aménagements', *Etudes Scientifiques*, Paris, December 1981.

Brown, M., *Farm Budgets – From Farm Income Analysis to Agricultural Project Analysis*, Johns Hopkins University Press, Baltimore and London, 1979.

Campagne, P., 'Etat et Paysan: la Contradiction entre Deux Systèmes de Reproduction', *Revue Française d'Economie et de Sociologie Rurale*, no. 147–48, Versailles, 1982.

Carruthers, I. D. (ed.), 'Aid for the Development of Irrigation', *Workshop on Irrigation Assistance*, OECD, 1983.

Chambers, R. and Moris, J. (eds), *Mwea – An Irrigated Rice Settlement in Kenya*, Ifo – Institut für Wirtschaftsforschung, Munich 1973.

CILSS/Club du Sahel, 'The Development of Irrigated Agriculture in the Sahel, Review and Perspectives – Ouagadougou', 1980.

CILSS/Club du Sahel, 'Recurrent costs of Development Programs in the Countries of the Sahel – Analysis and Recommendations', August 1980.

Dey. J., 'Development Planning in the Gambia: The Gap between Planners' and Farmers' Perceptions, Expectations and Objectives', *World Development*, vol. 10, no. 5, 1982.

Diemer, G. and Van der Laan, E. C. W., 'Using Indigenous skills and Institutions in Small-Scale Irrigation: An Example from Senegal', Irrigation Management Network, A.A.U. Overseas Development Institute, 1983.

Eicher, C. K. and Baker, D. C., *Research on Agricultural Development in Sub-Saharan Africa: A Critical Survey*, MSU International Development Papers no. 1, East Lansing, Michigan, 1982.

Food and Agricultural Organization (FAO), *Land, Food and People*, Rome 1984.

Franzel, S., *An Interim Evaluation of Two Agricultural Production Projects in Senegal: The Economics of Rained and Irrigated Agriculture*, Working Paper no. 28 AREP Michigan State University, East Lansing, 1979.

Goodell, G. E., 'Bunds and Bottlenecks: Organization Contradictions in the New Rice Technology', *Economic Development and Cultural Change*, vol. 33, no. 1, University of Chicago Press, October 1984.

Guillaume, M., 'Les Aménagements Hydro-agricoles de Riziculture et de Culture de Décrue dans la vallée du Niger', *Agronomie Tropicale*, vol. 15, no. 3, 1960.

Jones, W. I., *Planning and Economic Policy: Socialist Mali and Her Neighbors*, Three Continent Press, Washington DC, 1976.

Kamuanga, M., 'Farm Level Study of the Rice Production System at the Office du Niger in Mali: An Economic Analysis', unpublished Ph.D. thesis, Michigan State University, 1982.

Kamuanga, M., 'Réflexions sur la Politique d'Implantation des périmètres Irrigués en Afrique de l'Ouest', Paper presented at the conference of the West African Association of Agricultural Economists, Abidjan, Icory Coast, December 1983.

Kamuanga, M., 'L'Economie des Exploitations de l'Office du Niger et les Perspectives d'Intensification au Niveau du Paysan', Publication Spéciale de l'ADRAO (forthcoming) 1984.

Kuttner, R., 'The Proverty of Economics – A report on a discipline riven with epistemological doubt on the one hand and rigid formalism on the other', *Atlantic Monthly*, February 1985.

Little, I. M. D., and Mirrlees, J. A., *Project Appraisal and Planning for the Developing Countries*, Heinemann Educational Books, London 1974.

Weiler, E. M. and Tyner, W. E., 'Social Cost–Benefit analysis of the Nianga Irrigation Pilot Project, Senegal', *Journal of Developing Areas*, vol. 15, Western Illinoîs University, July 1981.

de Wilde, J., 'The Office du Niger: An Experience with Irrigated Agriculture', *Experiences with Agricultural Development in Tropical Africa*, vol. 11, Johns Hopkins Press, Baltimore, 1967.

The World Bank, *Accelerated Development in Sub-Saharan Africa; An Agenda for Action*, Washington DC, 1981.

The World Bank, *World Development Report 1981*, Oxford University Press, 1982.

DISCUSSION OPENING I – JACQUES BROSSIER

The first paper emphasises what the second illustrates: the need and the role of good socio-economic research in Africa.

I personally agree with the main opinions of the authors even if their ideas are more affirmed than proved (it is the general rule in a Congress). I will gather my remarks and questions on both papers into four topics.

1. General failure of agriculture development projects, because they are based only on technical considerations.
We all agree with that. We economists know that development is not only physical and material. But how are the agricultural economists proposing to improve the efficiency of the techniques? Have we good enough data to calculate the internal rate of return (IRR), benefit–cost ratio, net present value (NPV) and other ratios? We have, all of us, many examples of completely false figures. Are we credible? How can we increase these? Furthermore, in a turbulent world do we not need more efficient techniques?

2. Need of good economic studies on the functioning of the local society.
Farming system research is every day more prominent. In this area, the agricultural economists play a leader role. All of us approve the plea of Chataigner and Leon for a real autonomy of research and researchers, for a long-term research protection, and for the need of adapted training for scientists. I would like to ask for some more precise detail, mainly from M. Leon.

It is all right for scientists to have a good status (as pointed by Idachaba in an earlier paper) but it is essential to organise mobility (in both senses) between institutions: research, ministry, development offices, private and co-operative. How do we facilitate this mobility? How do we assure the leader role of the research institutions?

Autonomy and experiences like in-service training suggested by foreign donors in some developing countries are all right; but what does autonomy mean exactly? This concept can have several misunderstandings. Kamuanga from Zaire, realised a very good research in Mali. I would like some comments on its concept.

I appreciate that Chataigner and Leon insist on the necessary involvement of other interlocutors than the state. They recognise that it is difficult in West Africa. As Idachaba says: 'Government should provide incentives for the organisers of the private sector to participate in agricultural research', and, I add, to help the farmers to organise themselves but with autonomy. I think there is a shortage of macro-economists studying the behaviour of the farmers in Africa. Do you agree with this priority? Are there dangerous disequilibria for macro level in crisis?

3. Are economic studies sufficient to understand the functioning of the local society?
The work of Kamuanga and the questions of Chataigner and Leon are strongly related to the fields of other social sciences like sociology and ethnology. Many works show that it is impossible to understand how production occurs and what are the limiting constraints, without studying aspects like work-associations in village activities of the women, land tenure, social and family relations etc. Have economists the comparative advantage to discover the family peasant rationality? Several anthropological, ethnological and sociological studies exist, but they are under-used.

Why? Are these contributions estimated as too subjective? How can we create conceptual tools to formulate appropriate indicators of the social well-being of farmers and their family members? Following the sociological and economic analysis of the rural society in Office du Niger, do you think, Professor Kamuanga, that progress is possible in this area without a deep shift of behaviour and attitude of the ON administration?

4. Pluridisciplinarity and rapport between 'soft' and 'hard' social sciences. Kamuanga makes a plea for the collaboration with so-called 'soft' social sciences. He asks for a deeper dialogue with 'soft' social scientists. In studies on human activity we need a strong collaboration with other social sciences. How does one define 'soft'? I think that the subjective and fugitive aspects are essential. So the domain of the decisions are mainly 'soft'.

Are we clear about the theoretical and practical problems of pluridisciplinarity? Is the concept of rational thought a myth? Is economic life rational? Probably not, but each person thinks of his own affairs as if it were.

DISCUSSION OPENING II – WILFRED MWANGI

Chataigner and Leon argue in their paper that introduction of new agricultural technology failed in developing countries because economic and social aspects of rural development were neglected in the research. This was recognised and changes introduced in research methods. But they lament that the foreign theories and methods dominate.

The authors assume that autonomous research in rural development will be essential to achieve development. The major reason given is that in social science the researcher cannot produce an objective analysis since he himself is part of the system he analyses. But one finds this is contradictory with the whole argument about autonomy because autonomy will not necessarily make the indigenous agricultural economists in developing countries become objective. Inequality (between small and large farmers and between farmers and researchers) needs to be exposed in the analysis and this requires freedom of expression granted by the political rulers in a particular country.

I, on the other hand, would argue that once objectives and priorities are set for agricultural economics research on the basis of the country's own needs (and not some foreign agency's) and the work programme is implemented in a disciplined manner, research personnel can be foreign, Africans trained in Africa or Africans trained abroad, so long as they are observant, have no built-in bias and are not class-bound in a political sense. Professional qualifications, we feel, need a complement of human sensitivity.

I would furthermore be in favour of mixed teams of researchers in rural development projects (research) with sociologists always being from the country in question to ensure better understanding especially of social relationships. But one could argue that they may introduce more of a bias than the foreign expert who looks at a developing country's social systems in a more detached way! On the other hand, the foreign expert may unintentionally include objectives derived from his own cultural background into his work – for example, high value attached to efficiency at the expense of human contacts.

The paper is silent in respect of advantages and disadvantages of using foreign inputs under controlled circumstances in agricultural economics research in developing countries. I feel they should have gone deeper into this. The paper has no time perspective, just as it assumes we shall know the model that was proposed to transfer agricultural technology to developing countries.

As a way of opening the discussion to the floor I would like to hear what the authors think about international co-operation in agricultural research which might also include agricultural economics research. This now seems to be the fashion given the very serious shortage of funds and possible benefits accruing from collaboration.

The International Agricultural Research Centres (IARCs), particularly those under the aegis of the Consultative Group on International Agricultural Research, have promoted and supported many of the agricultural research networks in the developing countries since the 1960s. Incidentally those intervening in sub-Saharan Africa include the IITA, the ICRISAT, the ILRAD, ILCA, CIMMYT, CIP, CIAT, and ISNAR and not only IITA and ICRISAT as the paper indicated. All IARCs intervening in sub-Saharan Africa are teaming up with national programmes to further their research into crops and livestock. Do agricultural economists and other social scientists have anything to learn from such networks? We would like to hear the views of Chataigner and Leon on this.

In the second paper Dr Kamuanga has written very interestingly on a topical issue in sub-Saharan Africa currently faced with an unprecedented food crisis and a very rapidly growing population. My problem is that I nearly fully share the views he has expressed in his paper and I risk being repetitive.

The experience with irrigation schemes in sub-Saharan Africa has been largely disappointing and research in irrigation has been neglected. Dr Kamuanga has shown very lucidly that one major reason for the failure of irrigation schemes has been due to irrigation planners ignoring important institutional and managerial issues. He has indicated through his case study in Senegal that settlers' original farming systems and their traditional social relationships need to be analysed and used at the design stage. Taking this and the settlers' interest into account as well as involving them in the planning, construction and management of the irrigation scheme will lead to success, as the case was with the Diola of the Basse Casamance compared with those of the Office du Niger in Mali. The Office du Niger is a good example of the way large irrigation schemes are organised in sub-Saharan Africa – built on a rigid control model with the state managing every detail from production to marketing of the output but always ending up, in most instances, as dismal failures.

Understanding traditional social relationships at the design stage can be a useful starting point towards a more egalitarian society or elimination of sex bias but this should not necessarily be perpetuated.

Financial management practices in most irrigation schemes coupled with inappropriate agricultural pricing policies in a major part of sub-Saharan Africa have led to huge indebtedness of settlers culminating in underinvestment and large government subsidies.

Land tenure in most irrigation schemes creates insecurity and settlers tend to invest off the scheme, especially in purchase of extra land to take care of second generation problems.

Micro planning through multidisciplinary teams at the preparation and design stage is fine. But before we begin to urge the so-called 'soft' social science to be involved with *ex-ante* socio-economic planning we must also examine our own involvement (as agricultural economists) in multidisciplinary teams. We have definitely not solved the very many theoretical problems regarding relationships between several scientific (social) fields, nor have our interactions with physical and biological scientists made much progress.

Dr Kamuanga contends that research in irrigation should address itself to the methodological issues of formulating appropriate indicators of the social well-being of farmers, settlers and their family members in relation with the development of the project over time. I acknowledge this is important but equally important is research on improving water allocation efficiency, distributional issues and understanding the nature of institutional change, especially in the future, and how these can be accommodated.

Before concluding let me pose a few questions to Dr Kamuanga that might start off the discussion:

1. What did income distribution look like between the two schemes?
2. Were the economic rates of return on both schemes competitive with other investments that could be made in Senegalese and Malian agriculture?
3. What were the scales of operation on both schemes?
4. How did the production of rice and costs of operation compare in both schemes?
5. What was the share of subsistence food production without market exchange on both schemes?

Finally, it is important to note that circumstances and conditions in sub-Saharan Africa vary from country to country, and from society to society within each country, and hence irrigation development must be viewed in the broader context of the political and social framework of each country.

GENERAL DISCUSSION – RAPPORTEUR: ERIC TOLLENS

A speaker from the floor was concerned with the interaction between researchers and the people they study. He felt there was a difference between agricultural economics and rural economics and, as the latter includes income generation through the development of non-farm activities, such as roads and tourism, he wondered what were the trade-offs. Another contributor to the discussion considered that expensive socio-economic research was not always necessary and that the same basic mistakes were continually being made. It was felt that there were many difficulties in establishing a system of socio-economic research but what mattered was to define programmes and projects in terms of the development needs of the specific country. There was a general questionmark over the future of irrigated farming in Africa, particularly with regard to its organisational status (i.e. state, private, etc.).

There was agreement with the author of the second paper that more needs to be known about local production systems and particularly information about the traditional varieties of cultural practices, land tenure systems and the supply of factors to accompany irrigation water. Another speaker held that results from large-scale irrigation projects had been disappointing. Was small beautiful in this context?

In reply, Yves Leon agreed that the researcher was usually himself involved in the research environment, but the setting-up of mixed teams was important. Autonomy of research did not mean isolation – what was needed was autonomy of ideas. He felt that the agricultural-economics/rural-economics controversy could be dealt with through the setting-up of integrated rural development projects and programmes.

Mulumba Kamuanga stated that information on the irrigation schemes in Mali and Senegal were not presented for comparative purposes but to illustrate the main points. No comparison was made of the rates of return of the schemes nor of the costs. The concept of 'soft' social sciences was borrowed from Kuttner to make a distinction between those that used mathematical tools and those that did not (mainly sociologists and anthropologists). As agricultural economists, we tended to neglect the qualitative aspects which were very important, in order to understand the organisation of production. Regarding the Office du Niger, changes were being made under pressure from donor agencies. The assessment of operation and maintenance costs was mainly a technical issue but the economics of it were tricky: if the user charges were set too high, there was a lack of incentive fully to utilise the irrigation facilities; if they were set too low, there might be an excessive government burden. Some international donors now bore part of the recurrent costs. The large- versus small-scale controversy had not been explicitly addressed in his paper but the evidence available suggested that we should be more optimistic about small-scale irrigation projects.

Participants in the discussion included K. M. Azam, A. T. Birowo, A. K. Bhattacharya, B. M. Bakar and P. Dofonsou.

YAN RUI-ZHEN

Economic Reform in Rural China

It is an honour for me, a Chinese agricultural economist, to have the opportunity to make a presentation about rural economic reform in China to my colleagues from different countries. This reform, which started several years ago, has attracted wide attention from people in various circles all over the world.

China began the reform of its rural economy in 1978. The basic goal was to transform China's subsistence agriculture into a planned commodity economy, and traditional agricultural technology into a modern one, and thus to develop agricultural productivity.

For a long time before 1978, a series of leftist policies, including those policies with regard to the rural economy, were dominant in China. The outstanding characteristics of these leftist policies consisted in deliberately overstepping the stage of a commodity economy and attempting to distribute social goods directly. As experience has proved, the stage of commodity economy cannot be overstepped. In fact, it was with the development of a planned commodity economy that China began the reform of its rural economy, thus promoting comprehensive rural development. In general, the reform has been in four stages, as follows:

I REFORMING THE RURAL ECONOMIC SYSTEM AND INTRODUCING THE RESPONSIBILITY SYSTEM

For more than 30 years, the system of the people's commune was exercised in China's rural areas. Under this system, the means of production were owned collectively, farm work was done together, and returns were distributed in a unified way. Communes accumulated funds for agricultural development, trained a good deal of qualified managerial personnel, and they represented more powerful productive forces. While positive results were achieved, communes as an economic system had many drawbacks; namely, this system suffered from undue unification and over-concentration. By 'undue unification' I mean that we had a single model for all China. This prevented peasants from using various means to develop commodity production in the light of their specialities and advantages. 'Overconcentration' refers to the excessive decision-making power of communes in matters of enterprise management and labour allocation. This hampered efficient co-operation of labour and well-co-ordinated work, thus discouraging peasants' initiative and attentiveness to the results of production.

The Chinese government called for a new policy in 1978 to invigorate the national economy and to open China to the world. The Chinese peasants in their hundred millions, based on their own experience, found at last a new economic system – the production responsibility system, which is effective in overcoming the above-mentioned drawbacks caused by the communes.

In the collective economy under the production responsibility system, the household acts as the basic production unit. The household signs contracts with the collective, assuming the agricultural tax quota for the collective and the quota of farm products to be sold to the government. The household also contributes a percentage of funds for the collective's production accumulation and public welfare, while the remainder (both products and cash) belongs to the peasant household.

The principal features of this system can be summed up as follows:

1. It is founded on the collective ownership of the basic means of production, including land. Production is managed on the basis of separate households, each assuming sole responsibility for its own profits or losses.
2. The household is linked with the collective by contracts, the family economy of the household representing a level of management of the collective economy.
3. The collective supervises land use in a unified way and co-ordinates the use of large-scale farm machinery and drainage-irrigation facilities. In accordance with state plans, the collective deducts funds for production accumulation and public welfare and carries out agricultural capital construction according to unified planning. The peasants have the authority to choose desirable jobs on condition that they will fulfil the quotas fixed by contracts.
4. The collective regulates the distribution of returns on the basis of household contract quotas, guaranteeing to distribute the gains on the socialist principle of 'equal pay for equal work'.

As we see from the above four aspects, the responsibility system in agricultural production did not change the nature of socialist collective ownership. The thing that has altered is merely the management system.

Great changes have taken place in China's rural economy since the introduction of the responsibility system:

1. The unitary economic structure in the countryside has been replaced by a new one with varied elements, forms, and levels. The peasants are allowed to use their surplus production resources, such as funds, labour, equipment, and skills, to engage in new production activities, shifting from one enterprise to another or co-operating with others, on condition that they complete their contracts. The unitary rural economy has also

given way to a multiple rural economy embodying several elements, forms and levels. That is to say, apart from the collective-run and state-run economies, we have now the partnership economy formed on a voluntary basis, the individual economy (e.g. some specialised households), the economy of small proprietors and big contractors. There are, in turn, several different management forms within each of these economies. The collective economy, for example, in addition to the existing co-operatives, includes partnerships, corporations, and the like. These economies embrace various levels in the process of development, for instance, individual undertakings, economic combinations of new types, agricultural-industrial-commercial associations, and so on.

2. The household, as the basic production unit, has been given more decision-making power under the guidance of the state plan. The household has the authority to choose economic undertakings and arrange production according to local conditions. Egalitarianism has been rejected; the principle 'more pay for more work' is carried out instead of the previous one when everybody was equally paid regardless of his real performance. From now on, if a peasant improves his management, offers more products, and lowers the cost, he increases his income and gets more material benefits. This is a new form of economic management which creates inherent economic incentives, capable of stimulating greatly the producers' enthusiasm. Consequently, agricultural production, as well as peasants' income, has expanded at an unprecedented rate.

Initially, the responsibility system was implemented only in crop cultivation, which was therefore entitled 'land contract system'. Later, following its essential advantageous aspects, the peasants extended similar contract responsibility systems to other economic activities, including collective-owned forests, livestock, fisheries, sideline occupations, and rural industrial enterprises. A great number of specialised households have come out in rural China. Crop farming became a burden for some of the specialised households, preventing them from concentrating all resources on contracted specialities. They wanted their fields to be transferred to other peasants who were skilled at crop production. The rural economy has become more specialised. This is characterised by two opposite trends: large numbers of peasants, having left farmland, are engaged in other undertakings, such as forestry, animal husbandry, fishery, sideline occupations, rural industries and service trades; on the other hand, the land is being concentrated in the households that are more skilled in crop cultivation.

As agricultural production becomes more specialised, it is important for the peasants to have pre-production services (input supply, etc.), production services, and post-production services (marketing, processing, etc.). The peasants, however, are unable to undertake such services individually. As a result, beyond the existing co-operatives that were set up on a geographical (village) basis, the peasants have established co-operatives of a new type in the light of specialities. The peasants have founded these economic associations on their own initiative, pooling their shares of capital, products and manpower. These joint firms offer services in the following domains: input supply, technical know-how, agricultural marketing, processing, storage, transportation, and so on.

The production responsibility system is effective in stimulating the peasants' initiative to develop rural commodity production. In addition, readjustment of the economic structure is also necessary to speed up the comprehensive development of the rural economy.

II READJUSTING RURAL ECONOMIC STRUCTURE

For a long time, the Chinese government carried out an agricultural policy which paid consistent attention to grain production, but neglected other diversified undertakings. That policy was unfavourable for the development of industrial crops, forestry, animal husbandry, fishery, rural industry, and other sideline occupations; furthermore, it hampered improvement of environmental conditions for agriculture taken as a whole. It also impeded rural trade and the prosperity of rural towns. The commodity economy could hardly develop smoothly in such circumstances. The peasants' income could not increase significantly.

The ultimate purpose of the adjustment of China's rural economic structure was to transform a unitary emphasis on grain production into comprehensive development of agriculture, forestry, animal husbandry, fishery, sideline occupations, rural industry and trade. This can be understood at the following levels:

1. *Readjustment of the crop mix.* The area under industrial crops, vegetables, and feed crops should be expanded, reducing accordingly the acreage of grain crops. Meanwhile, per unit area yields should be raised.
2. *Readjustment of agriculture as a whole.* Forestry, animal husbandry, fishery, and sideline occupations should be developed vigorously, diminishing the share of crop production in the rural economy.
3. *Development of rural industry.* As rural industry grows, it supplements the market with a portion of industrial goods. Surplus manpower can be absorbed into these rural industrial enterprises, which accumulate the funds necessary for the adjustment of the rural economic structure. Rural industry provides processing facilities and pushes forward the technical transformation of the rural areas. Peasants' income thus can be increased by a great margin.
4. *Development of tertiary industry.* This includes transportation, commerce, catering trade, tourism, culture and education, science and technology, and health care.

The adjustment of the rural economic structure is to be implemented mainly in two ways: (1) Increasing the yields of grain crops per unit area and restoring a portion of cropland to its original use; because some forestry land, grassland and even lakes were reclaimed for grain production in the past. 12 million hectares of land have been withdrawn from grain production and are now used for industrial crops, trees, pasture, fishery, and other purposes. (2) Making use of wasteland, hills, waters or grassland to develop diversified undertakings.

Practice has proved in recent years that the following policies are effective in promoting rural adjustment:

Encouraging the flow of peasants' surplus manpower, capital, equipment, and technical personnel from one region to another, and from rural to urban areas. The peasants can engage in new economic activities of various forms. They are allowed to buy equipment for processing farm products, big or medium-size tractors and trucks. They are permitted to run transportation and small mining sites as well.

Supporting specialised co-operatives. The peasants can set up and manage co-operatives specialised in pre-production, production, and post-production services, because it is difficult for individual peasants to acquire new technology, input supply, and facilities for processing, storage, transport and marketing of agricultural products.

Favouring diversified undertakings. In addition to land contracts, the peasants are encouraged to sign contracts to reclaim waste and hilly land, grassland, ponds or lakes, and build up specialised households. The term of validity of the contracts is usually 15 years, and can be prolonged.

Granting preferential tax rates, loans and input supplies to newly established larger rural industries.

Developing rural market towns and small- and medium-sized cities. The peasants are permitted to move and settle there to work in the secondary and tertiary industries, urbanizing the rural areas.

TABLE 1 *Average annual growth rates of selected crops*

Crops	1953–78	1979–83
	per cent	
Grain	2.4	4.9
Oilseeds	0.8	15.1
Sugar beet	6.9	27.7
Timber	5.6	7.1
Fruits	3.9	7.6
Tea	4.6	8.4
Meat	3.6	10.4
Aquatic products	4.0	3.2
Silkworm cocoons	4.0	9.1

The diversified economy in rural China has recently developed at high speed. The average growth rates of selected crops are shown in Table 1. The gross output of rural industry grew from 38.5 billion yuan in 1978 to 103.5 billion yuan in 1984, or a 2.7-fold increase. The total value of farm and sideline products purchased by the government increased from 71.36 billion yuan in 1979 to 126.5 billion yuan, registering an average growth of 15.4 per cent annually. The commodity economy has entered into a new stage.

III REFORMING AGRICULTURAL PLANNING AND RURAL COMMERCIAL SYSTEMS

The shortcomings of agricultural planning and the rural commercial system have been revealed as the commodity economy develops in rural areas. As regards the management system of agricultural planning, the major problems were overconcentration, undue control and inflexibility and a failure to bring into play the law of value. Here are some examples:

1. The production quotas were assigned from the very top to the grass-roots production units. There were many orders issued as mandatory – what and how much to produce, which production measures to be taken, and so on. As a result, these orders tended to go against local conditions. The peasants entitled them ironically 'blind commands', 'severing everything at one blow'.

2. A state monopoly for purchase and marketing of farm produce represented the basic form of the planned purchasing system. At first, in 1953, the monopoly was confined to grain, cotton, and oilseeds, but it was extended to other farm products later on. In 1961, all farm products were classified into three categories: The *first* category referred to grain, cotton, and oilseeds, which were under state monopoly for purchase and marketing; nobody other than state-run enterprises could market these commodities. The *second* category referred to pigs, poultry and eggs, which were also under the government control, but they might be delivered to market on condition that the quotas had been met. Farm products of the *third* category were to be sold on a negotiated basis. Generally, farm products of the first and second categories made up 80 to 85 per cent of the total amount of farm and sideline products purchased in rural areas. It was very clear that the peasants had little decision-making power in marketing their products. That certainly dampened their willingness and enthusiasm for developing the commodity economy.

In order to vitalise the economy, the government has recently abolished mandatory quotas in agriculture. The new agricultural plans are ones of guidance and serve as tools for the leaders at various levels in their macroeconomic regulation. The state carries out a planned market economy, exercising its leadership in agricultural production by means of economic levers, such as contracts, prices, taxes, credits, and through government-run enterprises and co-operatives as regulative organisations. Agricultural enterprises have the right, under guidance of the state plans, to decide their farming patterns according to local conditions and on measures for increasing production, the right to determine their methods of management and operation, and the right to distribute their products and cash. The government guarantees and respects the decision-making power of grass roots units of production.

Beginning in 1985, the system for purchasing farm products is to be reformed. The State does not issue any mandatory quotas to peasants. While offering fixed prices for grain and cotton by contract purchasing, other products are allowed to float at free prices and are handled on the open market.

As for the reform of the rural commercial system, the goal is to unclog channels of circulation and promote development of commodity production. There was too much unified control of the commercial system in the past. Monopoly prevailed and channels of circulation were under strict control. That phenomenon has been changed. There are various forms of economy and management now and we have opened several channels of circulation. Ensuring the leading role of state-run commercial enterprises, we nevertheless support supply and marketing co-operatives and other collective trade enterprises. Also, individual commerce is allowed to develop in a proper way. It is necessary to break down the barriers between the urban and rural areas, raise the blockade among regions, and actively open more channels of circulation.

The responsibility system applied to the business sector, with contracts as its key point, is now vigorously implemented in the state-run trade enterprises and the supply and marketing co-operatives, linking perform ance with the economic interests of staff and workers. There are different types of the responsibility system. As a rule, small retail shops, restaurants, repair shops, and the like, are contracted to groups, occasionally to individuals. Some facilities also can be leased to groups or individuals to favour the development of planned commodity production.

IV PROMOTING TECHNICAL TRANSFORMATION OF AGRICULTURE

The progress of science and technology is the key to the success of rural commodity production. It decides whether the new enterprises can withstand market competition and become mature. Thanks to the introduction of the production responsibility system in agriculture, the millions of peasants are anxious to equip themselves with modern inputs and technology. China's countryside is experiencing a technical revolution which is to transform traditional agriculture into a modern one. During the period between 1978 and 1983, the number of large- and medium-scale tractors in China increased from 557,000 to 841,000, walking tractors from 1.373 million to 2.75 million, trucks from 73,000 to 275,000, chemical fertilizers from 8.84 million tons to 16.6 million tons, and electricity used in rural areas from 25.3 billion kilowatt-hours to 43.5 billion. The peasants are eager to study new techniques and put them into practice. Improved crop and animal varieties, compound feeds, the technique of covering fields with polyvinyl film, the techniques of greenhouse cultivation, and other scientific methods of cultivation and breeding have been extended very quickly.

The technical transformation of China's agriculture depends, first of all, upon an appropriate system of agricultural science and technology with Chinese characteristics. At present, China's agricultural science and technology have a relatively short history of development and a poor foundation. There is a huge population with scarce arable land per caput, agricultural techniques of different levels exist at the same time, and traditional agriculture still plays a dominant role. The cultural level of the peasants remains low, but they can hardly raise enough finance to make the intellectual investment. In a word, the technical transformation is carried out in a complicated setting, which requires that China's specific features be considered. The newest technology should be combined with the best traditional measures; machinery should be united with biological techniques, with focus on the latter. The techniques of intensive agriculture imply a three-dimensional use of natural resources. First, good economic performance should be viewed in the light of ecological balance and favourable circulation of nutrients. Second, we should strengthen international exchange of agricultural techniques and promote international trade of farm products. Third, the traditional agricultural technology of China traces its history back several thousand years. Some techniques, for instance dry farming, multiple cropping, pest control, by biological methods, acupuncture treatment in veterinary practice, as well as a great number of famous and rare plant germ plasm and animal resources, have attracted world-wide attention. On the other hand, it is necessary for China to adopt modern agricultural technology in its modernization drive. Exchange of agricultural techniques between China and other countries benefits both modernisation of China's agriculture and development of agricultural science and technology in the world.

In order to introduce fine varieties, advanced technology and equipment, and attract foreign investment, it is necessary to export agricultural products, raw and processed, and develop the world market-oriented agriculture which will enable us to increase foreign exchange earnings. Today, 14 coastal cities along with the special economic zones are open to the world, which play a dual role: open windows for attracting foreign capital and bases for linking the interior with the outside world. Consequently, the adjacent provinces should shift agriculture to meet export demands; in other words, they should develop the farm produce processing industry and promote agricultural production in accordance with the requirements of processing plants. In this way, agriculture is likely to provide more marketable commodities and accelerate the process of modernisation.

Next, attention should be paid to scale economies. The scale of land management by a household should be enlarged as more and more peasants cease land farming to undertake secondary and tertiary industries in rural areas. Moreover, there is a tendency for specialised production in rural China to advance from households to specialised towns, or even specialised zones. Naturally, the process of specialisation and combination in agriculture will take a long time, but this process might be speeded up, because it is possible to push forward agricultural technology only on condition that the scale of management be enlarged, and specialisation and combination of agriculture be realised.

Finally, it is very important to strengthen the development of agricultural science and technology, extension services, and intellectual investment.

The reform of China's rural economy is proceeding in an orderly fashion, step by step. The reform of the economic system in rural areas has been basically finished. The reform of the economic structure and commercial system is in full swing. The transformation of agricultural technology is just under way. Initial results have been admirable since the reform began: the total value of agriculture was 145.88 billion yuan in 1978, that went up to 288.18 billion yuan in 1983; the net income per caput of peasant households was 133.57 yuan in 1978, while it reached 355 yuan in 1984. The peasant masses are striving for realisation of the great goal of quadrupling the total value of industry and agriculture by the year 2000.

AN XI-JI*

Pricing System Reform for Agricultural Products and Price Policy Adjustment in China (1979–1984)

Since 1979 the Chinese government has initiated a broad range of economic reforms among which pricing system reform for agricultural products has been a fruitful one. The aim of the reform has been to move from a rigid quota system with government fixed prices toward a market system with government induced economic planning. In the period 1979–84 the reform went through its first stage and began the second stage in 1985 of changing the model of price formation and decision from administrative channel to market mechanism. At the same time the Chinese government has successively adjusted the price policies, mainly raising agricultural prices in relation to prices of industrial produce and modifying relative prices among agricultural products. The price policy adjustment has not only occurred at the same time as the pricing system reform but both also affected each other.

Together with the completion of the household responsibility system in the countryside, the pricing system reform and price policy adjustment have given a vigorous push to agricultural production. Between 1978 and 1984 the national total grain output increased from 304.7 million tons to 407.1 million tons at an average growing rate of 4.9 per cent per year, that of cotton from 2.2 million tons to 6.1 million tons at an average growing rate of 18.8 per cent per year and that of edible plant oil from 5.2 million tons to 11.8 million tons at an average growing rate of 14.6 per cent per year. Besides the influence on agricultural production the reforms have tremendous impact on a broad range of national economy items mainly including income redistribution among various occupations, government budget balance and the steps taken for overall economic system reform. Along with the impact mentioned above it is nevertheless not easy to differentiate the impact of pricing system reform, price policy adjustment and the household responsibility system.'In the following paragraphs I will try to focus on three problems concerning pricing reform and price adjustment:

*Presented by Professor Yan Rui-Zhen

1. The contents and processes of pricing system reform and price policy adjustment;
2. The result of the reform and adjustment in the first stage;
3. A prospect of further reform and adjustment in the coming second stage.

I   THE CONTENTS AND PROCESSES OF THE PRICING SYSTEM REFORM AND THE PRICE POLICY ADJUSTMENT

Within the past six years, China's pricing system reform and price policy adjustment for agricultural products had three aspects, namely gradually weakening the state monopoly in agricultural products purchase; gradually adjusting prices of agricultural products; and gradually strengthening the functioning of market co-ordination.

Gradually weakening the state monopoly in agricultural products purchase
The state had had a monopoly in the purchase of major agricultural and sideline products in China since 1953. The different commodities under state purchase could be as many as 180. The government set the production plan and purchase plan every year and set up the procuring price. In the 1950s when this system began, the varieties and quantities of the state procurement set by the government was, by and large, in accordance with the natural and economic endowment of different regions and production units, and procuring prices were close to market prices. So, in that period under the specific situation, it played an important role in guaranteeing an adequate supply of basic living stuffs to the people and the drawbacks were not so prominent. But, with the development of the economy and the increase of the varieties of commodities under state procurements, the state procurement plan began to deviate from the natural and economic conditions of different localities. Hence it impaired the advantage of specialisation of different regions in production, ran foul of the principles of labour division and comparative advantages. The procuring prices were often too low, far from the level determined by supply and demand, to give any incentive to the peasant for increasing production. Further, because most of the major agricultural commodities were in the hands of the government, the integral connections between commodity, money and price were vanishing, so that some commodity exchange assumed a barter form. For example, in order to encourage the hog or cotton production, the government had to sell the 'bonus grain' to peasants who were engaged in hog or cotton production as feedgrain or food. ('Bonus grain' is the grain sold back to peasants by the state at a low price). According to government documents, claims for 'bonus grain' such as raising pigs, growing cotton, etc. might run up to 210. Only 'bonus grain' alone might account for 24 per cent of the total state grain purchase at the year. Besides 'bonus grain', there was 'bonus fertilizer' etc. These further distorted prices and disturbed the adjustment of supply and demand.

As can be seen from the above, state monopoly in agricultural products purchase had many problems. It hindered the optimal allocation of resources, reduced economic efficiency and the necessary incentives for peasants to produce, and hence was one of the main sources of agricultural commodity shortage over a long period.

In order to reverse the situation, the government has done a great deal to weaken and even get rid of the state monopoly system in agricultural products purchase since 1979, which was a part of the overall economic reform. The government accordingly took several steps:

First, the varieties of commodities under state procurement were reduced. Up to the first half of 1984, the varieties of commodities under state procurement had been reduced from 180 to 39. Again, in the second half of the year, they were further reduced to 21. Beef, mutton, fresh eggs and fruit were free of the state procurement plan. From the beginning of 1985, the state procurement of agricultural products as an economic management system has ceased to function. In its place was a system of contract system and market price combination.

Second, while the varieties of commodities of state procurement were reduced, control over the commodities still under state procurement was lessened. For example, the market exchange of 'first category' crops (grain, cotton, oil-bearing crops) had long been considered illegal. But after 1979, except for cotton they could be freely sold and bought in the markets after the state quota was fulfilled. In 1982, the grain sold through market channels accounted for 10 per cent of the commodity grain in the whole country and together with the grain sold to the state at bargaining price accounted for 30 per cent of the commodity grain in that year. This largely changed the situation of state monopoly in grain markets.

Third, the quantity of state procurement was reduced for compulsory delivery at low price. Again, taking grain as example, the quantity of compulsory delivery (planned quantity) in 1979 decreased by 8.6 per cent compared with 1978. It decreased 12 per cent in 1981 from 1978. Delivery actually fulfilled also declined, actual delivery in 1981 was only 64 per cent of that of 1978. Compulsory delivery at a low price was reduced, while grain sold to the state at increased price and bargaining price increased, the quantity sold to state in total having increased. The total sales of grain to the state in 1982 increased by 86 per cent. Up to 1983, the situation of supply and demand of grain had been fundamentally changed. As for the peasants, the state purchase of grain has become a subsidy instead of a burden for more than 20 years (at an increased price and bargaining price). The implication of this change will be discussed below.

The three steps mentioned above not only reduced state monopoly system in agricultural products purchase, but also promoted the prices of agricultural products and peasant income. Hence it changed the relationship between agricultural and industry in the national economy.

Adjusting agricultural prices
The state procurement prices of agriculture and sideline products being lower than market prices (open market or black market) had been a long-term phenomenon. Peasants who solely depended on sales to the state could barely maintain their production. Since 1979, the government has increased the state purchase prices and adjusted the relative prices among different agricultural products. A multi-price system was set up for major agricultural products such as grain and cotton. There were procurement price, over-quota price, bargaining price and market price. This changed the price policy for agricultural products as follows:

First, there was a substantial increase in procurement price. Grain procurement price in 1979, for example, increased by 20 per cent from 1978, while over-quota price even rose to 50 per cent over the already increased procurement price. Procurement price for cotton increased by 15 per cent, over-quota price was 30 per cent over procurement price. In northern cotton growing regions, there were even some additional subsidies on the price. Procurement price of hogs increased by 26 per cent and those for other agricultural and sideline products increased by between 20 and 50 per cent. Since 1979 an additional increase in procurement prices or main agricultural products was enforced each year.

Second, in the total government purchase of agricultural products, the part purchased at procurement price decreased while the part purchased at over-quota price and bargaining price increased. In the years 1978–81, the part purchased at procurement price in total purchase of grain decreased from 84 to 50 per cent. Grain purchase at bargaining price accounted for only 3.6 per cent of the total grain purchased in 1978, while it rose to 19.4 per cent in 1982, and the bargaining price level was very close to that of market price. Prices of cotton and edible oil were in the same situation. Altogether, the general price index for agricultural products in 1981 increased by 38 per cent from 1978. There were successive increases in the ensuing years for grain; in 1982, 1983 and 1984, the price was increased by 2.2, 4.4 and 4.0 per cent respectively. Since 1983, the over-quota price level has risen above the local market price; that means it has become a support price.

Strengthening the functioning of market co-ordination
Free marketing had been tightly controlled in China for a long time and grain, cotton and edible oil were not allowed to be sold in the market. But the government commercial department could hardly provide adequate supply of goods for the people, especially among different regions in the countryside. This handicapped the regional division of agricultural production and specialisation, and also handicapped the economic development of both urban and rural areas. Since 1979, as an important step of agricultural price system reform, the control over the free market has been relaxed. Free markets rapidly developed within a few years. The number of free markets, in both urban and rural areas, increased from

38,000 in 1979 to 48,000 in 1983, and, at the same time, the turnover more than doubled. From 1982 to 1983, the turnover of pork increased by 36.6 per cent, those of beef and vegetables increased by 20 per cent respectively. In 1983 the total turnover of the free market already accounted for 10.2 per cent of the total turnover of the retail goods of the whole country. There were some slow increases in the free market prices which corresponded to prices in state retail markets. Generally speaking, it favours the peasants when the free market prices are higher than the state retail market price. It opened a new channel for peasants' products and hence promoted agricultural production and specialisation.

With the further development of the national economy, the free market has recently shown some new features. The major characteristics are: the size of the market continues to increase, small ones become big ones, big ones grow into towns and cities. The structure of the free market is also changing: from purely agricultural market to market for both agricultural and industrial goods; from retail market to market at both retail and wholesale; from small quantity transported on foot and shoulder to large quantity dependent on modern transportation. A new marketing system is emerging, it will share the responsibility of developing the economy with the state market.

II ACHIEVEMENTS AND PROBLEMS OF PRICING SYSTEM REFORM AND PRICE POLICY ADJUSTMENT FOR AGRICULTURAL PRODUCTS

Pricing system reform itself is not the object but the vehicle to achieve the faster and better development of the national economy and the Four Modernization. The achievements and problems are viewed from this standpoint.

The achievements of the pricing system reform and price policy adjustment
A great deal has been accomplished in the past six years. During that time the foundation has been laid for the second stage of agricultural price reform and a basis provided for overall price reform. National economy has been developed and income distribution adjusted by means which can be summarised as follows: increase of peasant income; rise of living standards; stimulating agricultural growth and re-vitalising the market economy. Generally, a new incentive system has been provided for the peasants and the rural economy, and the priority of agriculture in the national economy has been recognised.

First, the increase of peasant income. From 1978 to 1984, the net income of the average person in agriculture increased from 133.6 yuan to 355.5 yuan, an increase of 2.7 times. The sources of income increase include increasing agricultural produce; developing non-agricultural production and service industry; increase of agricultural prices and others. Among them, increase of agricultural prices is a major source of the increased income. In three years from 1978 to 1981, the net income of the average person in agriculture increased by 68 per cent, of which 65 per cent was accounted for by price increase (including procurement price, over-quota price and bargaining price). With the rapid expansion of agricultural production, the peasants depended more and more on greater production to increase their income in the years following 1981 but price increase was no longer the most important factor. In the period 1980–3, price increase still accounted for 21 per cent of the increase in peasants' income. there was even a 4 per cent increase in agricultural product prices in 1984 (current price, factors of inflation not eliminated).

Second, the peasants' living standard has risen while their income increased. From 1978 to 1981, the consumption expenditure of the average person in agriculture increased from 116.1 yuan to 190.8 yuan (living standard increased 64 per cent). In 1984 it again increased to 273.4 yuan, an increase of 2.35 times compared with 1978 (in current prices). Of the peasants' living expenditures, part was directly from their own production, such as foodgrain, vegetables, meat, eggs, cotton and edible oil. But the peasants' income structures and consumption structures are changing. From 1979 to 1983, the part directly from peasants' own production in total expenditure decreased from 57.9 to 24.1 per cent, while the part of cash spending increased from 41.1 to 75.9 per cent.

Third, investment in production was also increased. Production expanded and productivity increased. The following is the use of modern inputs in China in recent years: from 1979 to 1984, the total power of the agricultural machinery in the whole country increased from 182 million hp to 265 million hp, a rate of 45.6 per cent; chemical fertilizer increased from 10.86 million tons to 17.73 million tons, a rate of 63.4 per cent; electricity used in the countryside increased from 28.27 billion KWh to 46.2 billion KWh, an increase of 63.4 per cent. This provided the physical and technological conditions for the rapid development of agriculture in recent years.

Because of the successive good harvests and commercialisation of agricultural production, the total purchase of agricultural products in 1983 was 2.27 times that of 1978, even when inflation is allowed for, the increase is still 53.5 per cent. It provided more consumer goods in the market, easing the tension of the supply of basic living commodities, especially foodstuffs, and greatly changed the contents of the food basket. In addition, it indirectly influenced the development course of industry through multiplier effects. The economy in both urban and rural areas is thriving. Under the state monopoly system, the relation between price and production and supply was distorted. The government fixed price could not give signals of scarcity and abundance of commodities to peasants and consumers. And so, increase in price did not necessarily affect production and market supply. After the reform, price and production and supply was positively related. Taking 1978 as base period, state purchase prices of agricultural products increased reaching 141.5 in 1982, while output of major agricultural products also presented an increasing trend, agricultural product purchase index rose to 186 in 1982. It rose again in 1983 and 1984.

Problems in pricing system reform and policy adjustment for agricultural products

Agricultural price reform, as a dramatic diversion from an economic system in China, is unprecedented. It is not easy to change an old marketing system, which people have long been used to, to a new system in a short period of time. Obviously many problems will be encountered. And the price policy adjustment itself is very delicate and sensitive. Price change will affect every part of the national economy; industry v. agriculture, production v. marketing, capital accumulation v. social consumption: all of these important economic relationships are going to be adjusted in the economic movement. It concerns very much the economic relations among peasants, workers and government budget balance, concerns the interests of everyone in the country. And price policy adjustment has to be done in the process of pricing system reform, while it has in return to give a push to the pricing system reform. These dual reforms, conducted in a vast country like China where the economy is backward, natural and eco-social endowments are very different among regions, and there are so many people, cannot be expected to be perfect. According to the above analysis, the pricing system reform and price policy adjustment were successful, the process went smoothly and quite quickly. But some problems also arose, such as the emergence of some new imbalances in the agricultural production structure, increase of budgetary subsidies and government budgetary burdens, the lag between wage adjustment and agriculture price adjustment.

First, imbalance in agricultural structure. The recent adjustments in relative prices of different agricultural products affected agricultural structure. From 1978–83, crop production in total value of agricultural output (not including industries run by communes) decreased from 71.3 to 66.7 per cent, while the proportion of forestry, husbandry and fishery rose from 28.79 to 33.3 per cent. Agricultural structure began to move to a way of comprehension development. But the problem is that some economic crops, such as tobacco, cotton and oil-bearing crops, expanded too abruptly and too fast. In 1982, the planting area of economic crops had already reached 100 million mu (1/15 hectare) of grain production area and greatly surpassed the government's crop planting structure adjustment plan. Increase of intensitivity of cultivation of economic crops is also higher than that of grain crops. The result is a surplus of edible oil and cotton, especially cotton for which there is no market at home and abroad and storage is very costly. Surplus of cotton has much to do with the unreasonable price relationship between grain and cotton. In 1983 in Shandong Province, a major cotton production region, cost-profit rate was 22.7 per cent for wheat, 53 per cent for corn, and as high as 124.9 per cent for cotton. The profit in growing one mu of wheat is 16.35 yuan, corn is 24.13 yuan, while cotton is 133.74 yuan. Karl Marx said, 'If supply and demand determined market price, then on the other hand, market price ... also determines supply and demand.'[1] The high price of cotton made the cotton production increase abruptly. So, price adjustment should be flexible and state price should change with the changes in situation. If the price policy is rigid and slowly responsive, many problems will arise.

Another problem in agricultural production structure adjustment is that animal husbandry production did not develop fast enough. Husbandry was 13.2 per cent of the total value of agricultural output in 1978, but it was only 14.79 per cent in 1983. On the other hand, many regions in 1983 and 1984 had much surplus foodgrains coupled with a serious shortage of meat and eggs. The supply had to come from other regions and rationing still prevailed. Many factors are to blame for this phenomenon, but the relative prices of grain, hogs and eggs, fixed by government agencies, are the major ones. It made the hog industry a profitless business. In some regions, the hog industry stopped growing in accordance with the increase of demand, or even slowed down.

The second problem is the range of price subsidy expansion and the increased budgetary burden on government.

The price policy for agricultural products in recent years includes the price difference between state purchase and sale. Price subsidy is part of state economic planning. According to the experience, price subsidy as an expedient within a certain range for agricultural price adjustment has played a positive role. But problems arise when price subsidy lasts too long and in a wide range. When the government control gets loose some people will make use of the price differences to carry out malpractices. For example, in some places the purchase at procurement price is unreasonably reduced and purchase at over-quota price and bargaining price is over-expanded; some peasants deliver products of low quality to the State at procurement price, while they take high-quality products to market, and so forth. Government budgetary subsidies therefore faced an unexpected increase.

Another problem is that 'bonus' materials sold to the peasants at low prices are ever-increasing, as mentioned above; the low price 'bonus grain' alone accounted for 24 per cent of the total government grain purchase. 'Bonus fertilizer' is also given to some production that does not need fertilizer at all and this leads to misuse of a valuable resource. Foodgrain sold back to the countryside has also unduly increased. So, government budgetary subsidies greatly expanded, accounting for more than 30 per cent of the government budgetary revenue and seriously affecting the government budgetary balance. This is one of the main sources of inflation.

The third problem is that price adjustment is not well co-ordinated with adjustment of the workers' wage.

Workers' wages in China have been increasing in recent years. The price of foodgrain which is the most basic living stuff is unchanged; the consumption of meat, eggs and vegetables are subsidised to different degrees; the price of industrial consumer goods in daily use is either unchanged or reduced. The increase of the average wage per worker and per household are generally greater than that of the retail price index of the whole country. All of these are important in stabilising or improving the workers' living standard. But sometimes price changes are not favourable to the workers in cities, especially large and medium-size cities. Increase of the retail price of vegetables, meat, eggs, poultry and fish greatly outstrips the rise in wages. It makes a big difference in some years. For example, average wage rates of workers in 1981 increased by 1.5 per cent, while at the same time, the price of foodstuffs like vegetables, meat, eggs etc. increased by 13.8 per cent. In 1983 again, the average wage rate of workers increased by 3.5 per cent, while prices of fresh vegetables, fresh fruit and aquatic products increased by 12.7, 14.7 and 13.4 per cent respectively. These data come from the publications of the State Statistics Bureau and do not include various illegal price increases. In workers' expenditures, food accounts for a large proportion, while foodstuffs like meat, vegetables, eggs, etc. account for more than half of the expenditure on food. So, any delays between price reform and wage adjustment pose a problem for workers, especially those who have little bonus and subsidy and those whose cash wages have remained unchanged for a long time. This finally will reduce the market demand and affect production. In the long term, money, prices, wages and so on under a market economy are flexible, ever-changing and cannot be fixed at one level for ever. So, in price and wage system reforms, directly connecting workers' wages with a living expenditure index is a good way to prevent price increases and workers' real incomes from being unco-ordinated.

III   A PROSPECT OF FURTHER AGRICULTURAL PRICING SYSTEM REFORM AND PRICE POLICY ADJUSTMENT

On 25 March 1985, the Central Committee of the Party and the State Council, published 'On Ten Policies to Further Vitalize the Rural Economy'. According to this document, beginning from this year, the government will not give the peasants any compulsory delivery quota. Agricultural products will be purchased by contracts in markets. Up to this point, the state monopoly in agricultural product purchase has ceased to exist and pricing system reform has entered a new stage. The new system of contract purchase and market purchase has some new characteristics. Only three of these will be briefly discussed here: the nature and development of the new pricing system; changes and evaluations of the multi-price system; budgetary subsidies – subsidies on the difference between purchase and sales prices and general price subsidies.

Nature and development of contract purchase and market price system
Contract purchase prevails in grain and cotton marketing after compulsory delivery was abandoned. In principle, the relationship between the farmers and the state commercial departments is no longer one of giving

and taking, but one of sellers and buyers based on bilateral negotiation. Any agricultural products other than grain and cotton can be freely sold and bought in the market, price being dependent on the quality. Grain and cotton beyond the amount of purchase contract can also go to the market. This is the basic feature of the new price system. But, is this system the same as the free market system conducted by an 'invisible hand'? Of course not. This is because the government has macro-economic control of all the economic policies, including price policy, taxation policy, subsidy policy, finance policy and monetary policy, which enables the government in the macro-sense to incorporate the open market into the state economic plan.

What is the difference between this new system and the co-called 'mixed economy' of free market and government intervention prevailing in many capitalist countries? There is a difference. First, the state may make use of the weapon of economic legislation to adjust the direction of economic development, promoting economic activities that are deemed to follow the line of socialism and preventing economic activities that are considered unhealthy in China. This has already attracted some attention in recent years. Second, there is a huge commercial system in government's hand that directly participates in marketing activities. It can lead the market on to the track of economic planning by selling and buying in the free market. This agricultural product market and price system embody the principle of a socialist-planned market economy.

It takes time for this system to reach maturity. Compulsory delivery cannot immediately be completely eliminated for some commodities in some places. Some preparations are obviously necessary. The contract system can be improved only step by step. Nevertheless, contract purchase should be clearly distinguished from state monopoly in practice. The position of state commercial sectors has changed, it is doing business with farmers, co-ops, corporated and private commercial sectors. It also takes time for them to be adapted to the new environment. Moreover, the state commercial department assumes the task of market adjustment according to the economic plan after it changed into relatively independent accounting units. It plays dual roles in the course of movement of the economy. Problems certainly will arise, solutions can only be found in practice and so far there are no precedents. New commercial channels other than the government commercial system also have their own ways of development. Economic legislation should be greatly strengthened, but it may not be made perfect in a short time. And the old information system no longer exists, while new ones are yet to be set up. We mentioned above several problems that may arise in the development of the new price system. How these problems are going to be solved will have a great impact on the future of the new system itself and on the national economy as a whole.

Changes and evaluations of the multi-price system
The co-existence of procurement price and added price for over-quota

purchase in China can be traced back as early as the 1960s. But the multi-price system was configurated only after 1979. Take grain as an example. There were procurement prices, over-quota prices, bargaining prices and market prices. On the selling side, there were foodgrain rationing prices, bargaining sale prices, market prices, bonus grain sale prices (to the peasants only) and selling back to the countryside prices etc. This author pointed out in a research report about multiprice that the development of the system follows a certain process. Its basic nature is to use a special method to increase the purchase price of agricultural products, encourage agricultural production and increase peasants' income under the condition of maintaining the monopoly system and with the consumers' price in cities unchanged.[2] The difference between the purchase price and retail price (in cities) is to be covered by government subsidies.

According to the experience of recent years, this system has shortcomings as well as merits. First, under state monopoly in marketing, the multiprice system prevents the production plan from being actually practised; regional distribution of agricultural production can be discrete, social economic efficiency can be low. Second, as mentioned above, it creates pseudo supply and demand and hence increases the price subsidies. This is one of the reasons for the heavy budgetary burden on the government in recent years. This author made the following suggestions in May 1983: incorporate procurement price and over-quota price into one price; abandon bargaining price and various bonus price; gradually abandon the practice of grain sold back to countryside.

However, I do not agree with the opinion that 'Multiprice for commodities is not a success. It has negative effects on producers, traders and consumers, and is not in accordance with the law of value.'[3] It totally denies any merit of the system. Now, with the pricing system reform in its second stage, the multiprice system will finally vanish. But as a historical experience, one should try to be realistic in evaluating it. In fact, the multiprice system, as a price policy under state monopoly marketing, played a positive role, as we have mentioned above. Moreover, after 1979 the multiprice system in fact became a transitional form from the old system to the new. It follows the line of higher and higher price levels for agricultural products and looser and looser government control till enforcement of a free market with government macro-planning: procurement price – added over-quota price – bargaining price – market price. The experience of the past six years tells us that in the process of economic reform, any evaluation of price policy cannot be separated from the reform itself. How to closely connect economic reform with economic policies is still an urgent and complex problem for China and it requires constant attention.

Subsidy problem (from subsidies mainly on difference between purchase price and sale price to general subsidies)

Budgetary subsidy is a problem related to the one discussed above. With the expansion of budgetary subsidies in recent years, it has become a major concern in China's finance and economy. In particular, the subsidies on price difference between government purchase and sale of agricultural products not only distort the relative price among various commodities, conceal waste and mismanagement, add to the budgetary burden on government and impede the economic reform but might also be unavoidable under state monopoly of agricultural marketing.

Now that the agricultural pricing system is being reformed, the problem of subsidies on price difference between purchase and sale is automatically solved once for all. But it does not mean the elimination of all budgetary subsidies or price subsidies. For example, the selling prices of grain and cotton prevailing now in the open market are lower than the contract purchase prices set by the government. Hence it is a kind of price subsidy by nature, but is no longer the subsidy on price difference between purchase and sale under state monopoly. It can be called support price. And, beyond the contract purchase price, there is a guarantee price (original procurement price in compulsory delivery), at which the government is obliged to purchase grain when it is in surplus. This is a specific price policy in the new price system and it is likely to exist for a long time and no longer a mere method of transition. This subsidy can avoid the problems with the subsidies on price difference between purchase and sale and contain the range of subsidies within government planning. But as to the problems of how to subsidise, how much to subsidise and when to subsidise etc., these are new problems facing China. Flexibility and constant study is needed.

NOTES

[1]Karl Mark, *The Capital*, vol. III, p. 213 (Chinese edition).
[2]An Xi-Ji, 'A Possible Solution to Present Grain Price Problem', unpublished research report, Beijing Agricultural University, May 1983.
[3]Wu She, 'Trend, Problem and Solution of Grain Commodities', *Agricultural Economic Problems*, vol. 2, 1985.

DISCUSSION OPENING I – HAROLD BREIMYER

When I first studied economics, more than a half century ago, courses of study began with the history of economic thought and economic history and continued with what was called 'comparative economic systems'. Formal theory followed, and it was almost free of mathematical baggage.

The papers of Drs An Xi-Ji and Yan Rui-Zhen are of the category of comparative economic systems. All the Western world is fascinated by the changes in economic policy that are being made in the People's Republic of China. Dr Xi-Ji's paper of price policy and Dr Rui-Zhen's more comprehensive paper therefore interest us all.

Moreover, the papers are excellent. I like the candour. The gains made in agricultural production are recounted but also there is the warning that it is not possible to allocate accurately the credit for that performance.

Credit must be divided among pricing system reform, price policy adjustment, and changes in the household responsibility system. Elsewhere we even find a subtle suggestion that the weather may have helped. Dr Rui-Zhen's paper is less guarded in its favourable account, but it is more a descriptive than an evaluative paper.

In my country, the United States, it is fashionable to say that the People's Republic of China is moving fast towards our US style of capitalism. Our political stand is more friendly towards the People's Republic than towards a number of other socialist countries. In March 1985 the Central Committee and State Council of the People's Republic liberalised further the pricing and delivery system for a number of farm products. 'But,' Dr Xi-Ji asks rhetorically, 'is this system the same as the free market system conducted by an "invisible hand"?' His answer: 'Of course not'.

It is interesting to note two separate explanations of how the economic system of the People's Republic of China differs, both generally and in agriculture, from that of many capitalist countries. I find the first explanation not highly convincing, but the second full of wisdom.

The first explanation is that the government of the Republic – I quote Dr Xi-Ji – 'has macro-economic control of all the economic policies, including price policy, taxation policy, subsidy policy, finance policy, and monetary policy ... '. My response is that a similar macroeconomic control is held, at least potentially, by the Governments of France, Japan, Canada and the United States of America. My country practises all those economic controls, even as it suggests that it does not – or minimises what it does.

Both authors add a second explanation of differences between China and the West that is more convincing. It is that the People's Republic remains a planned economy. Open market activities are incorporated into the state economic plan. Dr Xi-Ji even uses the language of 'the weapon of economic legislation to adjust the direction of economic development ... '. Dr Rui-Zhen refers to a 'planned commodity economy' and adds that it is a 'collective economy'. Moreover, 'the nature of socialist collective ownership' has *not* changed.

All of which invites a comparison between what Dr Xi-Ji calls 'this new system' of the People's Republic of China, and the 'so-called "mixed economy" ... prevailing in many capitalist countries'. As I said above, it is refreshing that both authors tell us that their country remains socialist, and socialistically planned. Here I offer my personal comment that Western nations would be well advised to admit that their mixed economies, though not planned, include a powerful economic role for central government. That role might be played better if its players were quicker to admit they were playing it.

I make only one observation about China's new system as described by Dr Rui-Zhen. Peasant households are to be paid on the socialist principle of 'equal pay for equal work'. First of all, I did not know that to be a distinctively socialist principle. Second, that should not be regarded as identical with reward according to value of product; in farming, at any given time and place, the correlation between effort and volume of production is not necessarily close. It makes a difference whether reward be calibrated according to input or output.

Both papers are a significant contribution to knowledge about comparative economic systems.

DISCUSSION OPENING II – G. H. PETERS

In commenting on the two papers which have been so neatly presented by our single speaker my aim will be to concentrate on pricing policy for agricultural products. Before turning to that in a somewhat critical manner it should, however, be said how willing our Chinese colleagues have been both to present information and to openly reveal the nature of some of the mistakes which they have made and the problems which they still have. They have also been too modest. It is all too easy for the outside observer to fail to realise how dramatic the post-1978 changes have been, both in the reorganisation of the entire work situation of the farmer following introduction of the responsibility system and in allowing market forces to play an increasing role in the resource allocation process.

There is clearly a close relationship between the responsibility system and the pricing of products; which itself is now in a process of amendment. When the household rather than the commune assumed the responsibility for *its own* self-supply and production for the non-agricultural sector, the household was nevertheless still constrained. The contract eventually handed down to it through a complex administrative process ultimately directed from the centre, specified *quotas* for delivery. There was, however, a complication over prices mentioned by Professor Xi-Ji (see page 452). I will very quickly summarise and raise queries as I proceed.

(a) The procurement price was a state-fixed price for *quota* governed output.
(b) To encourage effort an over-quota price was also available at which additional output could be sold, the proceeds from which would accrue to the household.
(c) There was then a further opportunity to use the 'free markets' (which are essentially *locations* at which products can be sold by farmers to the community at large) at a price determined by the local forces of supply and demand. The 'free markets' provided what Westerners would describe as a 'free market' and I put it that way simply to emphasise what can often be a confusion between single and plural usage.
(d) This appears simple until one realises that a 'bargaining price', dependent on the state purchasing agencies rather than the 'free market' has also been mentioned. With the new change in the

system this appears to be of growing importance. The question essentially is – *who* bargained and *with whom*?

The changes of March 1985 then appear. As a linked development between the responsibility system and the market system *compulsory delivery* is to be abolished. On pp. 457–8 it is stated that the relationship between farmers and the state commercial departments is no longer one of giving and taking, but one of buyers and sellers based on bilateral negotiation. This is hard to understand. Apart from difficulty in grasping the way in which a *state* can *bargain* with a farmer (unless the farmers are grouped into co-operatives of large scale) I am confused by the denial that the 'invisible hand' is at work because the *government* has macrocontrol of price policy. I could understand a system of state *fixed* prices, with the decision of *how much* to contract at those prices being left to the farmer as a means of further developing household responsibility rather than being in part governed by a compulsory quota. Additionally it is easy to see how the state fixed prices under macrocontrol could be *altered* from time to time to reflect both needs and farmers' willingness to supply. Unfortunately the discussion becomes even more difficult on p. 459 where the author disagrees with the view that the 'multiprice' system is *not* a success and by the admission that 'to closely connect economic reform with economic policies is *still* an urgent and complex problem' (my emphasis). When I had the opportunity to visit China two years ago I was impressed by the sheer ingenuity of the multiprice system – and I felt that I understood it!. What I cannot *now* grasp is the way in which it will 'vanish' and be replaced by a bargaining system. It will be recalled that I mentioned this in connection with my query about the role of bargaining in the multiprice situation, and here it appears again. The speaker would perform a great service to us if he could, perhaps, elaborate on these issues in greater detail.

GENERAL DISCUSSION* – RAPPORTEUR: AKE ANDERSON

Q. Please discuss inflation in China. What has been the rate of inflation?

A. The inflation rate during the last two years has been between 2 and 3 per cent but has recently increased considerably. The inflation is caused by holding down state-fixed consumer prices while raising prices to producers, hence raising their incomes. One result is a large budget deficit in China of 3 billion yen.

Q. What do you mean by the term 'household'?

---

*Much of the general discussion on the two papers from China was in the form of question and answer. In view of the interest in the subject and thanks to the careful recording of the rapporteur, this is reproduced verbatim (Ed.).

A. It is the same in China as elsewhere. It is the members of an immediate family living in the same residence, usually a mother, father, their children, and often grandparents.

Q. You talk of growth rates. Are you using physical or monetary terms?
A. In the papers the terms are identified as physical or monetary when they are used.

Q. Some regions in China are richer or poorer than others. As a result of the rapid growth in your agriculture since 1979, have these regional differences increased or decreased? Why have some regions developed less rapidly? What are you doing to help the poorer regions?
A. While income has risen in all regions since 1979, the income gap between richer and poorer regions has increased. Generally the regions nearer the urban areas in the east have had the greatest income growth. This is because of the higher value of the products they produce (including high-valued fruits and vegetables for urban markets) and greater opportunties for shifting excess labour to production of industrial and consumer goods. The poorer regions are those furthest inland, away from urban areas, and producing lower value goods.

Q. The rapid change in agriculture must be creating stress on farm families. Are excess workers being forced from traditional agriculture that they know and like into other occupations? Are they being forced on other regions? What is being done to ease this adjustment stress on families?
A. Families have not been broken up or moved. Usually they remain in the same village. The co-operative initiates new activities, such as manufacture of consumer products or industrial parts, to employ the workers freed from agriculture.

Q. As you have moved to the 'household responsibility system' has the number and role of collectives declined? How many collectives are left?
A. The rural reforms have not changed the number of collectives. It is simply that within them, family households now have more individual responsibility and more opportunity to reap the rewards of their efforts.

Q. You point out that food price subsidies in China have been growing and are now quite large. Why is this? Is the objective one of using food price subsidies to redistribute income to urban consumers?
A. The food price subsidies have created a large budget deficit, which contributes to our inflation. These subsidies are being re-examined. Urban wage rates have not increased as rapidly as rural incomes,

therefore the subsidised food prices have helped to equalise the situation of urban peoples.

Q. How does the State make policy decisions regarding taxes, producer prices, etc. What is the decision-making process and who is involved?

A. Since 1979 the government has increased the state purchase prices and adjusted the relative prices among different agricultural products such as grain and cotton. It is a result of taking into account reports from the collectives during earlier years. Earlier we had four prices: procurement price, over-quota price, bargaining price, market price. This system did not work well and was abolished from the beginning of 1985. Now the government has strengthened the functioning of the market. I refer to the paper by An Xi-Ji, presented today.

Q. You speak of China moving to a 'market' economy, yet you still refer elsewhere to China having a 'planned' economy. How do you use these two concepts, and is it consistent to speak of having both a 'planned' and a 'market' economy?

A. Yes, it is consistent. The 'market' is a part of the planning process and an element in the framework of the plan.

Final remarks: Some participants in the general discussion have asked about the possibility of China becoming self-sufficient in food. We are not there yet but moving steadily in that direction. I refer to the figures in the presented papers. Our big problem is the shortage of cultivated land and overpopulation in agriculture. Only when a large number of people gradually separate themselves from land and engage in a variety of specialised types of production outside farming, will it be possible to improve our standard of living considerably.

Participants in the discussion included J. B. Wyckoff, N. Westermarck, J. Klatzmann, Todor Popov, Azai Shankar, Per Pinstrup-Anderson, Robert G. F. Spitze and Solomon Belette.

D. P. CHAUDHRI*

Human Capital, Structures of Production and the Basic Needs

INTRODUCTION

The role of human capital formation through education, nutrition and public health in economic development has been examined in the literature from the point of view of rates of return approach, income share approach, and social welfare approach.[1] Schultz (1980) considers human capital formation as an important means for dealing with the problem of persistent poverty which is largely concentrated in the rural areas of developing countries.[2]

Sen (1981) while examining the nature of poverty and occurrence of famines has articulated the role of 'entitlements' in meeting one of the absolute basic needs, namely food and nutrition, for bare survival. He draws a sharp distinction between 'need' and 'demand'. In this way we are forced to view a market system based on economic organisation as a 'democracy of dollars'. If dollars are equally distributed, claims on production will be equitable and need will get translated into demand, otherwise not.[3]

The distributional questions cannot be separated from the structure of production. Thus the 'causes' which lead to persistent poverty are rooted in the structure of production and the value added shares. The poor are poor because their value added shares in the production system are low. This can be illustrated through a simple model.[4]

STRUCTURE OF PRODUCTION AND INCOME SHARES

We begin by assuming that the economy is divided into three sectors: agriculture, industry and services, and the population is equally divided into three income groups: rich, middle and poor. Let X be a (3×1) vector of outputs from the three sectors, and Y a (3×1) vector of incomes accruing to the three groups. There are two types of relationships between X and Y. On the one hand there is the process of income generation showing how the income generated in each sector is distributed among the different groups, shown by the equation

*Presented by D. M. Etherington

$$Y = AX \tag{1}$$

where A is a (3×3) matrix of elements a_{ij} representing the income accruing to the i-th group from a unit output of the j-th sector. On the other hand there is a pattern of consumption showing how the income of each group is spent on the output of the various sectors shown by the equation

$$X = BY \tag{2}$$

where B is a (3×3) matrix of elements b_{pq} representing the demand for the output of the p-th sector arising from a unit increase in the income of the q-th group.

In practice not all the output of any sector is available for final consumption and not all the value of output is distributed as income to the factors of production, as each sector may be buying part of its output from other sectors. For the present simple exposition we shall assume away the existence of such inter-industry transactions and assume instead that all incomes in each sector are derived from the value of production in that sector, and are fully spent on final output. Thus we get

$$X = BAX \tag{3}$$

a homogeneous set of equations which completely determine the structure of outputs up to a scale factor. Also we have

$$Y = ABY \tag{4}$$

another homogeneous set of equations which completely determine the distribution of incomes, again up to a scale factor. So long as the co-efficients of the A and B matrices are fixed the structure of production and the distribution of incomes are completely determined. The only levers for changing the distribution of income are the co-efficients of these matrices.

The model may be illustrated by a simple numerical example. The co-efficients of matrices A and B have been chosen to reflect a low share of the bottom groups in the incomes generated in each sector, especially the agricultural sector, and the high propensity to spend on agricultural products by the bottom group. These values correspond roughly to those prevailing in India, and seem quite realistic for other parts of Asia with high land concentration and high rates of rural landlessness.

		Agr.	Industry	Services	
(Value	A =	.12	.20	.15	poor (bottom ⅓rd)
added		.40	.33	.25	middle (middle ⅓rd)
shares)		.48	.47	.60	rich (top ⅓rd)

and,

		Poor	Middle	Rich	
(Expen-	B =	.80	.51	.40	Agriculture
diture		.13	.29	.36	Industry
shares)		.07	.20	.24	Services

With these values of matrices A and B the structure of output and the distribution of income are given by

$$
\begin{array}{ll}
\text{(Sect-} & \\
\text{oral} \quad X = z \begin{bmatrix} .5 \\ .3 \\ .2 \end{bmatrix} \begin{array}{l} \text{Agric. Sector} \\ \text{Industry, and} \\ \text{Services Sector} \end{array} & Y = z \begin{bmatrix} .15 \\ .35 \\ .50 \end{bmatrix} \begin{array}{l} \text{Poor (bottom } \frac{1}{3}\text{rd's share)} \\ \text{Middle (mid. } \frac{1}{3}\text{rd's share)} \\ \text{Rich (top } \frac{1}{3}\text{rd's share)} \end{array} \\
\text{output)} &
\end{array}
$$

where z is total output.

In this example the structure of production and the distribution of income are completely determined by the A and B matrices; therefore the only way to alter the distribution of income is to change these co-efficients by policy. Note that we have also assumed away supply constraint in this simple illustration.

ROLE OF THE STATE

As demonstrated by Sinha *et al.*, (1979) for a 77 sector model for India, attempts at income transfers from the rich to the poor, with serious inequalities in the value added shares left untouched, the outcomes would accentuate inequality further and would benefit the rich *more* than the poor. Booth, Chaudhri and Sundrum (1980) through the illustrative model of the type given above, show that policy attempts dealing with greater emphasis on a particular sector of income transfer from rich to poor would benefit the rich more than the poor as long as the inequality of value added shares and therefore income shares *within* the agricultural sector stays as high as assumed in the numerical example.

Thus attempts at meeting the basic need for food of a section of the population through food stamps, free midday lunches or food for work programmes would indefinitely keep the poor dependent on their welfare payments unless such transfers influence the structure of production in favour of the poor. Historical experience shows that such transfers do not influence the structure of production.

Since the time of Adam Smith the role of the state as an initiator and facilitator of economic development has been increasing. This may be termed the 'late development effect'. This is partly due to technological advance and partly because the list of the duties of the sovereign is getting longer. This is not because of welfare reasons alone. In fact, it is mainly because our understanding of the role of public goods, infrastructure and education in the development process has considerably improved.[5] Schultz (1963) drew the profession's attention to the economic value of education. In his Nobel lecture drawing on his own work and that of others in this field, Schultz concluded by quoting Alfred Marshall – 'knowledge is the most powerful engine of production: it enables us to subdue nature and satisfy our wants'.

Production and distribution of knowledge of which schooling is an important component is one of the important duties of the sovereign partly because one of the peculiarities of the knowledge industry is that both its demand and supply are positively sloped with respect to individual's and society's income. It is both a cause and consequence of economic progress. One of the most important attempts at social engineering in recent history has been provision of free and *compulsory* school education in present-day developed countries. This has resulted in occupational and geographical mobility of labour within the country and went a long way towards improving the value added shares of the poor in these countries.

However, education is never neutral in content or consequence. Different types of educational policies affect different socio-economic groups differently. In most of the 'low income' countries education of the poor and particularly the rural poor is sadly neglected in their public education policies.

EDUCATION IN AGRICULTURAL PRODUCTION

We developed a conceptual breakdown of the effects of education of agricultural output and productivity in Chaudhri (1968) and elaborated on it in Chaudhri (1972). Essential argument is that a farmer's education could be relevant because it enables him to acquire:

(a) Ability to decode new information – know what, why, where, when and how.
(b) Ability to evaluate costs and benefits of alternative sources of economically useful information.
(c) Ability to establish quickest access to newly available economically useful information.
(d) Ability to choose optimum combinations of crops, new inputs and agricultural practices in least number of trials.
(e) Ability to perform agricultural operations more effectively in economic sense, i.e., ability to produce more from a given amount of inputs.

Conceptually, we can think of the educational impact, if any, as comprising the following components:

(1) Innovative effect – this would consist of (a), (b) and (c) described above.
(2) Allocative effect – according to the above description (d) would belong here. This can be seen to consist of two parts, namely (i) business activity and (ii) production activity.
(3) Worker effect – quality of labour as described in (e) above.
(4) Externality – neighbouring farmers and other producers in the vicinity who are in direct contact with educated farmers would be able to consult the educated farmers without paying any price for it and being able to copy (without paying any price) his sources of information, crop and input combinations and related production and business techniques of proven success.[6]

The following chart depicts various components of educational impact.

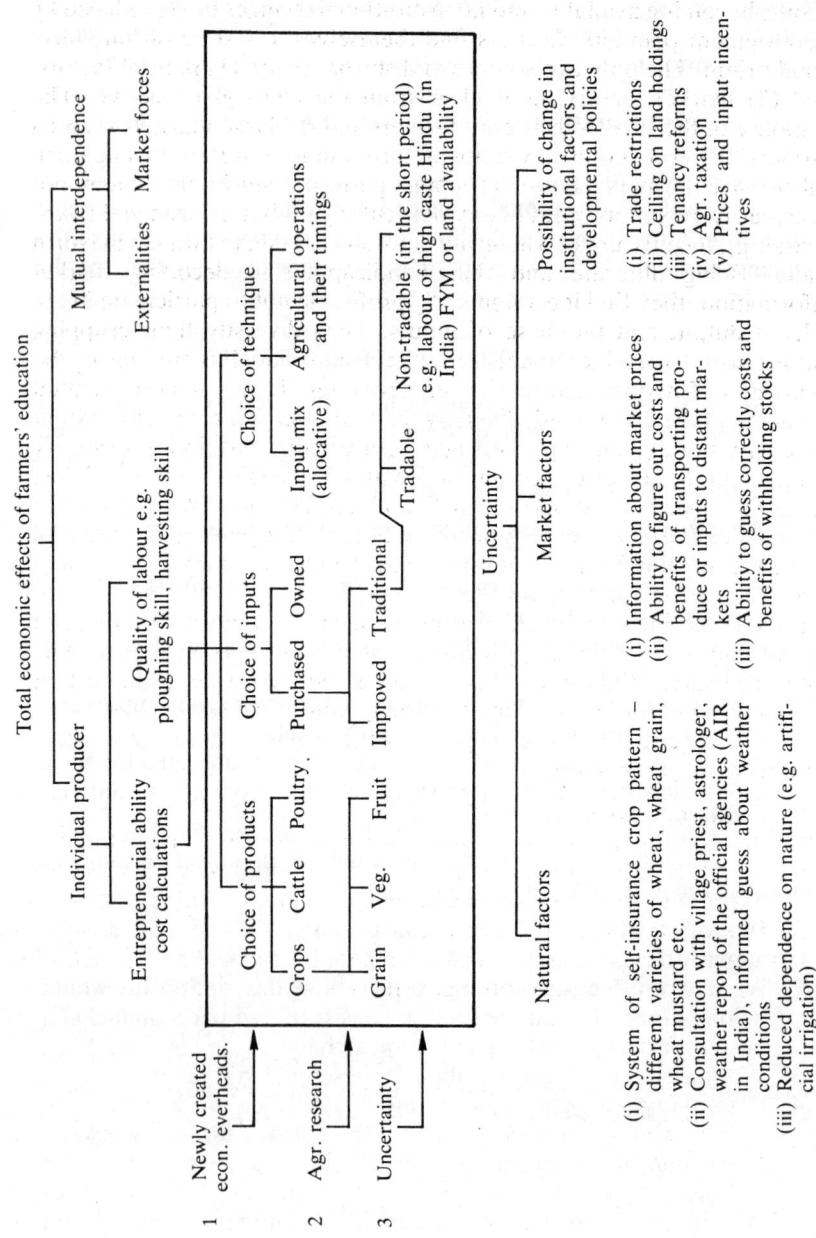

Figure 1

In a situation of traditional agriculture as defined by Schultz (1964) when there are no additional economic overheads, no additional research results becoming available and no institutional changes being induced by development planners, farmers find themselves in a state of long-term equilibrium. The only two sources of disturbance are (1) natural factors, and (2) market factors, as is clear from the chart given above. The response of the small-subsistence farmers and the large market-oriented farmers, being economically rational, turns out to be different. The small subsistence farmers choose cropping patterns which give them not necessarily maximum yield in any particular year but assured yield each year, e.g., the mixture of wheat and grain sown by small farmers in North India. Being illiterate and thus handicapped in decoding market information, they find it economically profitable not to participate in the sale of output and purchase of inputs. They diversify their cropping pattern so as to produce mainly for self-consumption thus minimising the twin risks of natural and market uncertainties. Large market-oriented farmers, on the other hand, diversify their cropping pattern to the extent necessary to safeguard against vagaries of weather but find it necessary and useful to acquire market information decoding ability.[7] Thus, economic dualism as described by Sen (1966) emerges. We get a set of subsistence farmers, economically rational, but having a different objective function (maximisation of utility) and a set of market-oriented large farmers, maximising profit.

Functional literacy or education in such a situation of long-run equilibrium in traditional agriculture would be of very little economic value to small, utility maximising farmers but would be an important economic input for farmers largely participating in the market system.

Now let agents of change appear on the scene in the form of state authorities wanting to provide:

(a) Economic overheads.
(b) Market regulations in terms of economic incentives/restrictions.
(c) Changes in the institutional structure, e.g., provision of agricultural credit through co-operatives in an attempt to replace high-cost moneylenders.
(d) Agricultural research information about high yielding varieties of seed and new inputs through extension agents, radio and printed leaflets.[8]

The sources of information of two sets of farmers would be different. Small utility maximising subsistance farmers would be passive involuntary recipients of information through local sources, e.g., other farmers and occasionally extension agents or a radio if they have equal access to the latter two sources in the village; while the market-oriented large farmers would have more cosmopolitan sources of information, including printed leaflets.

The use of extension agents is obviously inconvenient and inefficient when compared to the potential of printed media.[9] Unless the administrators of development strategy specifically take corrective steps, one would inevitably find that farmers with greater access to economically useful information and ability to decode it (education) and greater access to required capital would be early adopters of new technology and thus termed as innovators.[10]

If this change is once for all, e.g., extension of an artificial irrigation facility to some regions for the first time, the subsistence farmers would also be found adapting to change with a lag, probably through the 'externality' caused by the demonstration effect of the market-oriented large farmers. But if the contemplation is for a continuous change, which has to be in a dynamic agriculture, the role of externality cannot continue to be large.

Contrary to the expectations of the development planners, the rest of the subsistence farmers are not likely to follow, even with a lag, as long as their twin handicaps of restricted ability to decode new information and limited access to the capital market exist. To the extent that they are able to overcome these handicaps they would be found to be imitating the innovators. Some empirical evidence in this connection is reported in Chaudhri (1979).

The information decoding ability of the farmer is also crucial in establishing a two-way process of communication between the researchers and the farmers, otherwise the research results may not be directly relevant to the immediate problems of the farmers. It is this ability which education provides among its other benefits. In principle, it is always possible to think of alternatives to farmers' education, for example, the use of television. But these have to be evaluated in terms of their relative costs and effectiveness.

Public provision of education for the small farmers on an equitable basis with appropriate market integration can go a long way towards improving the value added shares of the poor small farmers.

BASIC NEEDS AND RURAL EDUCATION POLICY

Considerable difficulty remains in defining a basket of basic needs goods. A decision at the national level in respect of the components of the bundle of goods will be arbitrary. On the other hand, as Burki and Streeten (1978) p. 414 put it:

> We cannot ask the individuals to order these items according to the priority they attach to them because all actual choices are incremental – more or less extra food compared with more or fewer clothes – and individuals do not assess and compare the total value to them of food and clothes. The problem is rendered even more difficult by the consideration that individual ordering would be an inappropriate indicator in the presence of consumption externalities.

This applies to the purchased consumption basket only. Provision of free and perhaps compulsory public education along with appropriate policies minimising the opportunity cost of participation of the children of the poor in the schooling process is perhaps the most important means of changing the magnitudes of the co-efficients of the value added matrix in favour of the poor. The policy, like land reform, is bound to be opposed by the vested interests and we can easily cheat the poor by providing them with poor quality education as is done in some market-oriented high-income countries today. We hope that Keynes was right in pointing out that the power of vested interests is grossly exaggerated and that of ideas (i.e. knowledge) must prevail.

NOTES

[1]See Sen (1966) and Chaudhri (1979) for the underlying theoretical assumptions and implications of these approaches.

[2]See IBRD (1975) for statistical magnitudes and the procedures.of measurement.

[3]See Chaudhri (1974) and Sen (1981) for elaboration of this point.

[4]This model is from Booth, Chaudhri and Sundrum (1980).

[5]Despite a lot of contradictory empirical estimates the direction of causation seems clear and is cogently summarised in Schultz (1975, 1980).

[6]The industrial sector innovations are patented and thus can be copied only at a price through market interdependence; but in agriculture this takes the form of externalities.

[7]This probably explains why it is highly respected in these communities, but is mainly accessible to large farmers only. Apart from having higher ability to pay, its economic utility also seems to be higher for the large farmers in traditional agriculture.

[8]Assume that all this information about new technology is scale neutral and the developmental authorities are benevolent (and not short-period production results conscious) and want to help small farmers as much as large farmers.

[9]See Wharton (1965) pp. 208–11.

[10]See Rogers (1971).

REFERENCES

Booth, A., Chaudhri, D. P., and Sundrum, R. M., 'Structure of Production and Income Distribution', unpublished paper, Department of Economics, Research School of Pacific Studies, Australian National University, 1980.

Burki, S. J., and Streeten, P. P., 'Basic Needs: Some Issues', *World Development*, vol. VI, no. 3, 1978.

Chaudhri, D. P., *Education and Agricultural Productivity in India*, Ph.D. thesis, University of Delhi, April 1968.

Chaudhri, D. P., 'Education in Production in Modernising Agriculture in Asian Under Developed Countries', *Research Quarterly*, vol. 1, no. 2, January 1972.

Chaudhri, D. P., 'Rural Education and Agricultural Development – Some Empirical Results from Indian Agriculture' in Foster and Shiefield (eds), *International Year Book of Education 1974 – Education and Rural Development*, Evans, London, 1974.

Chaudhri, D. P., *Education, Innovations and Agricultural Development*, Croom Helm, London, 1979.

IBRD *Assault on World Poverty*, Johns Hopkins University Press, Baltimore, 1975.

Rogers, E. M., and Shoemaker, F. F., *Diffusion of Innovations*, New York, Free Press of Glencoe, 1971.

Schultz, T. W., *Economic Value of Education*, Colombia University Press, 1963.

Schultz, T. W., *Transforming Traditional Agriculture*, Yale University Press, New Haven, 1964.

Schultz, T. W., 'The Value of the Ability to Deal with Disequilibria', *Journal of Economic Literature* 13, September 1975, pp. 827–46.

Schultz, T. W., 'Economics of Being Poor', Nobel Lecture reproduced in *Journal of Political Economy*. August 1980, vol. 88, no. 4, pp. 639–51.

Sen, A. K., 'Economic Approach to Education and Manpower Planning', *Indian Economic Review*, April 1966.

Sen, A. K., 'Peasants to Dualism With or Without Surplus Labour', *Journal of Political Economy*, September 1966.

Sen, A. K., *Poverty and Famines: An Essay on Entitlement and Deprivation*, Oxford University Press, 1981.

Sinha, R., Pearson, P., Kadekodi, G., and Gergory, Mary, *Income Distribution, Growth and Basic Needs in India*, Croom Helm, London, 1979.

Wharton, C. R. Jnr., 'The Role of Education in Early Stage Agriculture', *Education and Economic Development*, in Anderson, C. Arnold, and Bowman, Mary Jean, (eds), Aldine Publishing, Chicago, 1965.

JULIO A. PENNA[*]

Sources of Growth of Argentine Agriculture and Prospects for the 1990s

INTRODUCTION

In the middle of the 1960s, Argentina was referred to as 'the sleeping giant', a term which corresponded to the title of a paper written by North American economists, where it was pointed out that the stagnation of the agrarian sector from the 1930s onwards was nothing but the result of a series of technological and economic policies of little – not to say scarce – incentive for the country. Nowadays, in the middle of the 1980s, we can confirm that the country has overcome that productive stagnation, even though, during the course of the years, there was no evidence of a sufficiently *stable* and *coherent* economic policy which could be responsible for the development of the sector.

In Table 1 it may be observed that between the quinquenniums 1968/9–1972/3 and 1963/4–1967/6 the average production of cereals and oleaginous crops increased 9.8 per cent, whereas its area increased 7.5 per cent. In the sub-period 1973/4–1977/8 production continued growing to 21.8 per cent. But it is in the last quinquennium, 1978/9–1982/3, where a steady increase in productivity is observed, since production rose by 22.9 per cent, while the area increased by 6.0 per cent. At present, in the middle of the 1980s, we are already near the amount of 44,000,000 tons.

However, throughout this period the real prices of these leading products became lower. In addition, between 1974/5 and 1982/3 the variability of these prices was much greater than that observed in relation to the previous decade. That is, the producer was more subjected to the variations of prices in the last ten years than in the period between 1963–74. Argentina developed within a context which was, in a certain way, turbulent.

How could this apparent contradiction be settled? On the one hand, Argentine producers saw that the real prices of their products declined through the passing of time and with more variability from one year to the

*The author acknowledges the valuable technical collaboration and opinions of Sarah Dingle. As it is customary, any errors or omissions are the exclusive responsibility of the author.

TABLE 1 ARGENTINA. Sowed Area and Production of Cereals and Oleaginous Crops.[1]

QUINQUENNIUM	Sowed area ('000s ha)	Increase or reduction in relation to the previous quinquennium (%)	Production ('000s tons)	Increase or reduction in relation to the previous quinquennium (%)
1963/64–1967/68	19.023		20.009	
1968/69–1972/73	20.443	7.5	21.964	9.8
1973/74–1977/78	19.887	−2.7	26.749	21.8
1978/79–1982/83	21.089	6.0	32.885	22.9
Years 1983/84–1984/85	22.000	4.3	42.000	27.7

Source: Department of economy-INTA on the basis of data from SEAG and Cereals Exchange.
[1]Cereals: wheat, corn, sorghum, barley, rye, canary grass, rice, oat and millet. Oleaginous: soybean, sunflower, flax and peanuts.

other, and on the other hand that there was a substantial increase in land productivity. In a country where the expansion of the pampean agrarian frontier stopped at the end of the 1930s such increase in productivity cannot be associated with the incorporation of highly fertile lands. More precisely, what the growth of productivity indicates is that there was either an intensification of already-known techniques, or an incorporation of new techniques, or a combination of both.

In the subdivision of cattle-raising, significant technological changes have also taken place. However, as the relative prices of cattle-raising-agriculture were unfavourable for this sector, and besides the new techniques employed in agriculture received a more favourable economic response in a short term, from 1977 there began a sell-out process of the cattle stock which extends to the present day. Thus, according to general opinion, those technological ways have been left 'concealed' by the strong decrease in stock.

Nevertheless, lately it has been commonly heard that 'cattle-raising is moving to marginal zones', which is a very popular opinion, but which, in our view, has not been authentically proved. In addition, it is maintained that in mixed production areas which are very important for Argentine agriculture, such as the north of Buenos Aires and the south of Santa Fe, a large part of the cattle area has been substituted for agriculture. This assertion should also be analysed in more detail.

AIMS OF THE STUDY

The aims of the study are the following:
1. To divide the production growth of the pampean region main crops according to three factors: area effect, yield effect and location effect, for each productive area.
2. To describe the main technological changes observed in agriculture and associate them with the yield increase.
3. To evaluate, in an introductory manner, the supposed movement of cattle-raising to 'marginal' zones.
4. To put forward some hypothesis of production for the 1990s.

SEPARATION OF SOURCES: A SIMPLE MODEL

The production growth of the main crops (which will be mentioned later on) will be separated into three effects: (a) area effect (AE), yield effect (YE) and location effect (LE). The model is the following. The amount produced Q of a product X is defined as:[1]

$$Q_{tj} = \sum_{i=1}^{m} \alpha_{itj} A_{tj} Y_{itj} \qquad \begin{array}{l} i=1...m \text{ (counties)} \\ j=1...n \text{ (zones)} \end{array} \qquad (1)$$

where
A_{tj} = total harvested area of crop X belonging to all the countries within zone j, in the year t.

α_{itj} = dimensions of A_{tj} devoted to X, corresponding to the county i, in the year t.

Y_{itj} = yield for each harvested hectare of crop X in the county i, of zone j, in the year t.

Similarly, the amount produced in a base year (b) may be estimated.

$$Q_{bj} \sum_{i=1}^{m} \alpha_{ibj} A_{bj} Y_{ibj} \tag{2}$$

Now, let us suppose that from the base year only the area devoted to crop X is changed, leaving the constant α_{ibj} and Y_{ibj}. A new equation is obtained:

$$Q_{tj}^* = \sum_{i=1}^{m} \alpha_{ibj} A_{tj} Y_{ibj} \tag{3}$$

Therefore

$Q_{tj}^* - Q_{bj}$ is the effect of increase (reduction) of *area* (AE) in the zone.

Now, if A_{tj} is kept and at the same time the yields Y_{itj} are added, we have:

$$Q_{tj}^{**} = \sum_{i=1}^{m} \alpha_{ibj} A_{tj} Y_{itj} \tag{4}$$

The difference $Q^{**} - Q_{tj}^*$ is the *yield* increase effect (YE).
Finally, the geographic *location* effect (LE) is measured by the difference.

$$Q_{tj} - Q_{tj}^{**}$$

In short,

$$Q_{tj} - Q_{bj} = \underbrace{(Q_{tj}^* - Q_{bj})}_{\text{area effect}} + \underbrace{(Q_{tj}^{**} - Q_{tj}^*)}_{\text{yield effect}} + \underbrace{(Q_{tj} - Q_{tj}^{**})}_{\substack{\text{location} \\ \text{effect}}} \tag{5}$$

The division of both sides of formula (5) by Q_{bj} gives as a result the participation of each source in the percentile increase of production between two points of time.

ZONES UNDER STUDY AND THE SELECTED CROPS: SOME RESULTS

Buenos Aires province was divided into seven zones and four further zones were considered: south Sante Fe, south-east Córdoba, east La Pampa and central La Pampa. The following crops have been selected due to their economic importance in pampean agriculture: wheat, corn, sorghum, sunflower and soybean. The separated effects are shown in Table 2. (For space reasons, only the main zones will be discussed.)

Although technology has played a significant role in the increase of yields, the variations in the areas devoted to the growth of the pampean region leading crops (wheat, corn, sorghum, sunflower and soybean) have also had a fundamental participation in the growth or decline of

TABLE 2 *Division of the rate of production growth, into each crop (1971/73–1981/83)*

ZONES	Buenos Aires I				Buenos Aires II			
CROPS	Rate of Annual Growth (%)	Area Effect (%)	Yield Effect (%)	Location Effect (%)	Rate of Annual Growth (%)	Area Effect (%)	Yield Effect (%)	Location Effect (%)
CORN	3.0	-0.22	3.46	-0.24	0.17	-0.41	2.07	-1.49
WHEAT	1.53	-2.24	0.58	0.13	2.55	1.15	1.21	0.19
SUNFLOWER	7.04	0.56	6.32	0.16	3.54	-1.07	6.58	-1.97
SORGHUM	37.00	31.96	13.12	-8.05	-1.56	-3.08	1.08	0.44
SOYBEAN	n.d.	---	---	---	n.d.	---	---	---

n.d.: non-available data for 1971/73.

ZONES	Buenos Aires III				Buenos Aires IV			
CROPS	Rate of Annual Growth (%)	Area Effect (%)	Yield Effect (%)	Location Effect (%)	Rate of Annual Growth (%)	Area Effect (%)	Yield Effect (%)	Location Effect (%)
CORN	-0.94	-3.40	2.35	0.11	35.52	11.83	22.83	0.86
WHEAT	23.71	13.13	10.60	-0.02	11.23	5.95	5.03	0.25
SUNFLOWER	-5.64	-7.34	1.77	-0.07	19.44	7.57	10.59	1.28
SORGHUM	-4.22	-5.31	1.28	-0.19	18.58	3.09	12.95	2.54
SOYBEAN	4340.17	2866.75	1512.25	-38.83	n.d.	---	---	---

TABLE 2 *Division of the rate of production growth, into each crop (1971/73–1981/83) cont'd*

ZONES	Buenos Aires V				Buenos Aires VI			
CROPS	Rate of Annual Growth (%)	Area Effect (%)	Yield Effect (%)	Location Effect (%)	Rate of Annual Growth (%)	Area Effect (%)	Yield Effect (%)	Location Effect (%)
CORN	7.32	3.83	5.20	-1.71	30.99	11.33	23.17	-3.51
WHEAT	11.37	5.99	4.92	0.46	15.19	10.69	3.97	0.53
SUNFLOWER	3.98	-2.63	6.63	-0.02	22.44	9.38	11.29	1.77
SORGHUM	3.55	-0.73	4.41	-0.33	-2.61	-3.91	-0.11	1.41
SOYBEAN	n.d.	---	---	---	n.d.	---	---	---

n.d.: Non-available data for 1971/73.

ZONES	Buenos Aires VII			
CROPS	Rate of Annual Growth (%)	Area Effect (%)	Yield Effect (%)	Location Effect (%)
CORN	12.44	2.54	7.37	2.55
WHEAT	2.22	0.45	1.53	0.24
SUNFLOWER	53.03	32.54	11.73	8.76
SORGHUM	40.06	16.63	14.68	8.75
SOYBEAN	n.d.	---	---	---

ZONES	LA PAMPA I				LA PAMPA II and III			
CROPS	Rate of Annual Growth (%)	Area Effect (%)	Yield Effect (%)	Location Effect (%)	Rate of Annual Growth (%)	Area Effect (%)	Yield Effect (%)	Location Effect (%)
CORN	18.19	0.49	17.91	-0.21	16.64	0.82	15.33	0.49
WHEAT	6.65	2.75	3.85	0.05	8.90	2.08	6.13	0.69
SUNFLOWER	895.54	450.32	420.80	24.42	171.47	89.14	83.58	-1.25
SORGHUM	42.51	12.19	34.45	-4.13	59.58	25.67	34.34	-0.43
SOYBEAN	n.d.	---	---	---	n.d.	---	---	---

n.d.: non-available data for 1971/73.

ZONES	SOUTH SANTE FE				CORDOBA			
CROPS	Rate of Annual Growth (%)	Area Effect (%)	Yield Effect (%)	Location Effect (%)	Rate of Annual Growth (%)	Area Effect (%)	Yield Effect (%)	Location Effect (%)
CORN	-2.01	-4.70	2.44	0.25	11.08	2.33	9.37	-0.62
WHEAT	14.36	12.37	3.86	-1.87	11.10	10.00	1.40	-0.30
SUNFLOWER	-7.64	-8.63	0.82	0.17	17.83	5.63	12.21	-0.01
SORGHUM	1.15	-3.80	3.63	1.32	15.04	1.52	13.64	-0.12
SOYBEAN	665.29	446.29	214.10	4.90	n.d.	---	---	---

production. Therefore, in the case of corn in the 1970s, the effect of the yields has been relatively more important in the west and south-west zones of Buenos Aires province than in those known as the corn centre (south of Sante Fe and north of Buenos Aires). Moreover, harvested areas in the former zones were considerably enlarged, whereas those in the latter were reduced.

In the case of wheat, genetics have made a substantial contribution to the rise of yields, *but in relative terms the area effect was more important than the yield effect on most zones.* However, in the south and southeast zones of Buenos Aires and in the east and centre of La Pampa the yield effect had a relatively greater participation. This fact must be emphasised because in the previous decades the yield of this cereal, in these zones, was stationary or mildly growing.

The situation of sunflower is similar to that of corn.

In the present decade, the rise of output is evident in zones such as the central-west and south-west of Buenos Aires province, where both the yield effect and the area effect had considerable participation. On the other hand, in the south of Santa Fe and the north of Buenos Aires the positive yield effect could not make up for the reduction of area.

Graniferous sorghum presents an area reduction in certain zones as the south of Santa Fe and north of Buenos Aires, but it spreads in most of the other zones. The yield effect was very important in the west of Buenos Aires and in the southwest of Córdoba.

Finally, the growth of soybean production, which concentrates mainly in the north of Buenos Aires, south of Santa Fe and southeast of Córdoba, is relatively more due to the area effect than to the yield effect.

As a summary, in Table 3 it may be observed that the zones of south-southeast Buenos Aires and east-central La Pampa have contributed *relatively more* to the growth of pampean agricultural production during the seventies than the zones to the south of Santa Fe, north of Buenos Aires and southeast of Córdoba. The former zones evidence not only a space replacement of production but also a further speed in the growth of yields per hectare than that experienced by the three traditional zones of local agriculture. Obviously, soybean is the exception to this tendency.

TECHNOLOGICAL CHANGE AND THE USE OF LAND: TOWARDS AN INTENSIVE AGRICULTURE?

In general, the high yields of pampean agriculture are produced by an important change: the massive introduction of wheat with germ plasm of Mexican origin, which allowed an even greater expansion of the secondary soybean and the continuous increase in the yields of corns and hybrid sunflowers. Moreover, soybean reached the average yields of the United States. But, in addition, there was a fairly widespread incorporation of tractors of higher power and of a series of innovations in machinery for tillage, which aimed at: first, preserving the soil resource; second, saving

TABLE 3 *Participation of different pampean zones in the increase of agricultural production between 1971/73–1981/83*

ZONES	CORN (tons)	%	WHEAT (tons)	%	SUNFLOWER (tons)	%	SORGHUM (tons)	%	SOYBEAN (tons)	%
					CROP					
-Increase of all the zones.	1630559	100	4140928	100	817145	100	2399783	100	2939935	100
-Bs. As. III South Santa Fe, South Córdoba.	376763	23	2038737	49	−7407	0	1161182	48	2747198	93
-Bs. As. I, II,IV,V,VI, VII; La Pampa I,II,III	1253796	77	2102191	51	824552	100	1238601	52	192737	7

labour; and third, saving energy due to the minor requirements of tillage. These new implements, together with the genetic change, account for the high increase rate of the yields of pampean agriculture in the decade under analysis.

Therefore, there seems to be a tendency to pass from mixed production systems to systems of agriculture over agriculture; if this inclination persists, it may give rise to future problems in soil fertility. Besides, the increasing participation of contractors in farm work should be carefully evaluated as regards the preservation of the resource.

Nitrogenous wheat fertilization rose, even though its levels per hectare are comparatively low in relation to the optimal levels. Such rise was caused by two factors: a fall of the fertilizer real price (in comparison with the 1960s) and, in addition, a genetic change in the varieties of wheat (of Mexican origin) which show greater relative responses to the use of fertilizers. The use of agrochemicals also showed signs of increase, which arose from the decline in their real price and the fact that the greater response of crops in more fertile or fertilized lots is also accompanied by an increasing growth of weeds.

With respect to cattle-raising, there is not enough empirical evidence to conclude that 'there is an approach to marginal zones'. In fact, the data indicate that there was simply a big stock sell-out. Neither do the available data confirm that between 1971/3–1981/3 there was a great expansion of the agricultural area over the cattle area in North Buenos Aires and South Santa Fe. This fact would imply a significant reduction of cattle numbers. This first conclusion should be the object of further investigation so as to explain in more detail the effects attributed to the expression 'agriculturisation of the humid pampas'.

However, in the regions of central-west and south-southeast of Buenos Aires there was an enlargement to a certain extent of the argicultural area over the cattle area; this fact is consistent with the preceding conclusions which state that, in these zones, the increase in agricultural output relies, largely, in the horizontal expansion of production. Consequently, the respective cattle stocks decreased but, presumably, this was more due to a substitution effect than to a cattle-head-effect. Obviously, all these conclusions require another deeper study.

'THE SLEEPING GIANT REVISITED': TOWARDS 60,000,000 TONS IN A TURBULENT WORLD

The democratic Argentine government has fixed as its objective to reach up to 60,000,000 tons of cereals and oleaginous crops in the medium term. There are some technicians and economists who also believe that this is an attainable objective. There is an implied assumption that most producers would adopt the agricultural techniques of the advanced producers, in which case production could increase from the present 42,000,000 tons to 56,145,014 tons (an increase of 33.6 per cent).

However, if besides the modern agricultural techniques, new genetic varieties and hybrids which are being put on the market were incorporated, Argentina would be able to attain a production level of 62,264,000 tons (an additional increase of 11 per cent). Finally, if wheat and sunflower were fertilized, total output could increase again to 66,582,000 tons (the additional increase would be of 6.9 per cent).

The reader may see that the greater impact would occur in the first case, if the techniques of more advanced producers became generalized.

Nevertheless, the previous objectives are strictly agricultural. Argentina would be able to attain them only if the economic policy reached the following aims: (a) improvement of the relation of input-output prices which, from the last economic measures (June 1985), remained extremely unfavourable; (b) avoidance of the *aleatory* fluctuations of relative prices, since they restrain many producers from adopting new techniques (let us remember the risk-aversion character of farmers); (c) fostering of a supervised credit system for the generalisation of new technologies, so that money would not be diverted to other purposes.

Twenty years ago, agricultural economists were divided into two positions: the 'structuralists', who maintained that the productive stagnation was caused by problems of land tenancy, and, on the other hand, those who considered that the unfavourable relative prices during the 1940s and 1950s were the principal cause of such stagnation. Today, this controversy seems to have been overcome in a certain way because production rose considerably in spite of the fall of relative prices through the passing of time.

However, the temporal fall of relative prices should not be regarded as *causative* factor in relation to the technological change. Simply, and in the case of Argentina, it is a matter of a statistical association between a decline in international prices and technological improvements which *took place many years later*. In other words, the lowering of relative prices does not necessarily imply a technological change. On the contrary, this may produce a decapitalisation of the sector.

Argentine agriculture developed in spite of a turbulent context: sudden changes of government, instability in the economic policies, high inflation rates, lack of protection of the food exporting sector, and so on. Now our country is trying to reconstruct its political and economic life. We are faced with a frontal attack against inflation and, above all, we are faced with a struggle to consolidate our political system. However, our scope of a future 'turbulent' world is based on the following facts:

(a) An excessive interventionism of the countries of the Northern hemisphere in international trade by means of export subsidies. We are, perhaps, in the outcome of a 'war' of international prices between the USA and the EEC which will significantly affect our exports.

(b) On the other hand, there is a very strong protectionist economy on the part of markets which in the past have been important purchasers of our products.

486   *Julio A. Penna*

(c) Even though our substantial foreign debt is refinanced, it may go on
     being a serious problem as long as the prices of our export products
     continue to fall in real terms.
May a worse 'turbulence' exist in our country?

NOTE

[1]For a more detailed analysis of the Shift-Share Analysis model, see Curtis, Wayne C.,
'Shift-Share Analysis: a Technique in Rural Development Research', *American Journal of
Agricultural Economics*, vol. 52, pp. 267–70, May 1972.

DISCUSSION OPENING I – DAVID SUMNER

First, let me thank Professor Renborg for the opportunity to open the
discussion relating to these two papers by Professors Penna and
Chaudhri. But let me apologise in advance for my lack of deeper
preparation. As a 'last minute' substitute I may not have done justice to
the work done by our authors. I will be quite brief and perhaps contribute
to keeping us on our schedule. This will provide additional time for
general discussion.

The session itself is an odd one with two very different papers.
Therefore I will comment upon them separately, beginning with the
analysis of recent changes in Argentine agriculture by Professor Penna.

I much enjoyed reading this paper. Since my knowledge of the factual
base is scanty I leave it to the audience to press the author on the
description he has prepared.

In Argentina the growth in area and especially yield for cereal and oil
crops in the last two decades is impressive. Against the background of the
'stylised fact' that Argentina agriculture had grown but little during the
previous period, this recent record cries out for explanation.

The breakdown of the recent changes into yield, total area and location
helps to isolate where the growth has come from, but it leaves aside the
more basic question of why there were changes at all.

Professor Penna does allude briefly to a few potential changes that
encouraged growth in Argentina. Wheat varieties became available that
were useful in Argentina. But, of course, previous decades saw many
technical changes that paid off elsewhere but were less used in Argentina.
The author tells us little about adoption rates and how these may have
increased. Use of fertilizers increased and combined with fertilizer
sensitive varieties this has increased yields. But corn and other yields
went up more than wheat. In mentioning that relative prices of fertilizer
had fallen the author may have given us a clue about where to look for
what has caused the dramatic change in Argentina.

So we have a puzzle about what will happen in the decades ahead. The
basic question in interpreting recent history is, what was the change in
incentives facing Argentina farmers in the late 1960s, 1970s and early
1980s relative to the more distant past?

The author at first seems to suggest that low prices encourage farm output growth, but then he backs off. He does briefly indicate what is really needed to understand agricultural change in Argentina; but this requires a careful quantitative analysis, with due recognition to the lags involved (the dynamics), of the changes in both the potential *supplies* of new ways of doing things and of *demands* for new techniques. Growth occurs both because there are available changes and also because people find such changes profitable to implement. Cavallo and Mundlak (1982) have provided a dynamic analysis of policy that will help in studying productivity growth in this context.

The second paper is a rather oddly placed one for this session on land and location. I suppose it really belongs in the *human capital* session but it is here and I will discuss it on its own terms. Both papers are concerned with the development of agriculture. Professor Chaudhri puts the emphasis on farm people while Professor Penna looks to land and technology. I hope that this is simply a matter of emphasis and that they agree that in the dynamics of development all the factors must come together.

Professor Chaudhri's paper is general but his geographic context is clearly South Asia. So let us shift our minds now to that part of the world with quite a different economic and agricultural history from Argentina.

Professor Chaudhri concerns himself with distribution as well as growth and sets out for us a framework to decompose income by income group and sector (regions could, I suppose, also be used here). But the major emphasis of the paper is: what does schooling do? Chaudhri lists the major roles of the schooling of farmers that he introduced several years ago in his path-breaking Ph.D thesis.

Here let me only add an illustration. Many of us have arrived here in Spain with little ability in Spanish. We have been much like the farmers with low education. We find it costly to search for bargains and find ourselves in a followers' role. We pay higher prices and are less innovative than our neighbours with better education.

Let me add a couple of bits of evidence on the pay-off to human capital. For US evidence I recommend Huffman's recent survey. Among many open findings he cites Petzel (1978) who looks at the value of schooling in improving the adjustment of farmers to price changes. More schooled farmers more quickly adjusted to profitable opportunities in soybean production in the US.

A major pay-off to schooling of farm people may also be in the non-farm sector both easing the transition out of farming and by making part-time farming a profitable alternative. Returns to schooling in non-farm jobs have been often documented. For part-time farmers several of us have shown the higher wages due to schooling in the US (see Huffman for a review). Results also show that farmers can gain from schooling used off the farm in less developed countries (Sumner 1981). In panel-data from Guatemala we have found that higher wages are *not* associated with schooling for hired farm workers. But when workers can move across occupations, schooling helps them to gain better wage rates (Sumner)

The pay-off to schooling used off the farm does raise an interesting but troublesome issue. When we observe the behaviour and incomes of farmers in any economy we are looking at a self-selected sample where the sample selection process is one of occupational choice. Schooling raises the opportunity cost in other occupations of potential farmers. Therefore more schooled farmers have foregone higher wages than farmers with low schooling levels. Thus, even if schooling had *no* direct pay-off in farming we would observe higher incomes by farmers with more schooling.

This selection bias adds to the observed relationship between schooling and farm success. It means we must be careful in measuring the impact of schooling in farming *per se*. The key to this is attention to the impact of schooling on the choice to farm. In many economies we have seen a real change in human capital in agriculture. Older farmers have below average schooling but young entering farmers are above average in schooling and other general human capital attributes. These farmers have high opportunity costs and to remain in farming they must attain a large size of operation and high rates of return.

Let me finish by seconding the strong plea made by Professor Chaudhri for redoubling the efforts to make high-quality schooling available to the rural poor in such a way that they can and will take advantage of this investment.

REFERENCES

Cavallo, Domingo and Mundlak, Yair, *Agriculture and Economic Growth in an Open Economy: The Case of Argentina*. Research Report no. 36. International Food Policy Research Institute, Washington DC. 1982.

Huffman, Wallace E., 'Human Capital for Agriculture' presented at the 1985 meetings of the American Agricultural Economics Association, Iowa State University.

Petzel, Todd E., 'The Role of Education in the Dynamics of Supply', *American Journal of Agricultural Economics*, August 1978, pp. 445–51.

Sumner, Daniel A., 'Wage Functions and Occupational Selection in a Rural Less Developed Country Setting', *Review of Economics and Statistics*, November 1981, pp. 513–19.

Sumner, Daniel A and Frazao, Elizabeth, 'Wages, Specific Human Capital Using Retrospective Data from a Rural Less Developed Area', North Carolina State University (in progress).

DISCUSSION OPENING II – DONALD OSBURN

Professor Chaudhri provides us with an input-output model and highlights the proposition that only through policy manipulation can the coefficients that influence income distribution be changed. I was expecting, therefore, to find the remaining part of the paper dealing with some empirical observations associated with the role of education in changing these distributions. Rather, however, he addresses some of the benefits associated with education from the micro perspective.

Professor Chaudhri states: 'Education is never neutral in content or consequence. Different types of educational policies affect different socio-economic groups differently.' I would like further clarification on this statement. What are the implications for educational policies and how can they in turn influence income distribution?

What comes to my mind from a policy point of view is what should be the mix in the educational delivery system? That is, the trade-off among the following alternatives:

(1) Formal v. informal education
(2) Primary v. secondary
(3) General v. vocational
(4) On-job or experience v. the other alternatives in various socio-economic situations.

Professor Chaudhri notes some of the characteristics of subsistence and larger farms under long-run equilibrium conditions. He concludes with the statement that 'functional literacy or education in such a situation of long-run equilibrium in traditional agriculture would be of very little economic value to small, utility maximising farmers but would be an important economic input for farmers largely participating in the market system.' I disagree. I believe there is economic value associated with education for all of the rural people. Education enables one to exercise options – this could be the move to off-farm employment opportunities. And, in fact, education may enable the occupation of part-time farming that appears to be becoming more prevalent in many countries.

A second point I want to make is that perhaps we should be concerned with the distribution of assets rather than focus solely on education. Education (both level and quality) is, I suggest, tied to asset levels. Many of the observations that Chaudhri makes with respect to subsistence farmers are not because of low educational levels, but because of the low asset levels that farmers have to work with. They are often, as Schultz points out, efficient resource allocators. The problem then, in part, lies with their resource base, and schooling impacts must be investigated from a multi-variate context.

GENERAL DISCUSSION – RAPPORTEUR: ROY FAWCETT

Dr Penna was asked if he had considered the effect of the real rate of interest on cattle farming. Grain fed systems require a lot of capital and a lot of time. Could the declining trend in beef production be explained by real interest rates alone?

Another participant noted that in the paper Dr Penna discussed relative prices. One can distinguish three distinct terms of trade. The ratio of product prices to input prices, the ratio of farm to non-farm prices and finally the external terms of trade as influenced by export taxes and import duties. How, Dr Penna was asked, did he explain productivity increases when inputs were so expensive?

Dr Penna was also asked if he would agree that the spectacular performance of Argentinian agriculture stems from educated and talented farmers. Whilst price policy does not exactly favour farmers the current position is more favourable than in the 1960s.

In reply, Dr Penna said that in the last eight to ten years new entrepreneurs were different. Technical innovation had occurred. Hybrid corn came in the 1960s but the present genetic material came from France. The Mexican varieties of wheat produced a high response to fertilizer. Well-educated farmers made rapid adoption possible and as a consequence there was a better growth of productivity. The whole country needed increased production because of foreign debt.

There were no comments from the floor in the general discussion on Dr Chaudhri's paper and in reply to David Sumner's comments.

Dan Etherington said that regarding the trade-off between formal and informal education Dr Chaudhri did not mean formal education in the sense of Western schooling but formal in the sense of being properly organised and getting through to the poor. The issue of functional literacy had been raised. Dr Chaudhri suggested that without other agents of change, functional literacy was not important to profit maximising farmers. It was only when there were external factors that functional literacy came into its own.

On the question of distribution of assets, land reform in India had never really occurred. There was the possibility through the creation of human capital that migration to better opportunities could take place. Redistribution could occur as a consequence of this migration. The creation of human capital was a less disruptive and more powerful engine of growth than the forced redistribution of assets.

Participants in the discussion included Philip Raup, Marshall Martin and David Sumner.

SECTION VI

Structure of Agriculture and People in Rural Societies

HOWARD NEWBY*

The Changing Structure of Agriculture and the Future of Rural Society

INTRODUCTION

Since the Second World War, rural society in most of the advanced industrial nations has been transformed by a process which is often referred to, with pardonable hyperbole, as the second agricultural revolution. Essentially this has involved the increasing application of scientific and technological principles to the pursuit of profit in the production of food. It should be emphasised that, in itself, the commercialisation of agriculture is nothing new. Farming has been organised around the principle of profit in most nations for a century or more and therefore long ago became disciplined to the exigencies of the market. All that has occurred in recent decades has been a transformation in the technology of most branches of food production, accompanied by state intervention in agriculture, which has granted farmers the conditions of production under which they could embark on a programme of increasing productivity and cost-efficiency. The most visible consequences of these changes have involved the mechanisation of agriculture and the 'drift from the land' of a large proportion of its former labour force. Elsewhere, advances in genetics have produced unprecedented increases in output from both plant and animal breeding, while the application of nutritional science has also resulted in immense benefits from the scientific application of animal feed and fertilisers. Husbandry management has also been improved by the introduction of complex forms of vaccine and pesticides. In these ways agricultural production *has* been revolutionised to the extent that any sense of technological continuity has been shattered within the lifetime of most of today's farmers. As a result agricultural entrepreneurship has followed the precepts of rationalisation apparent in other industries and farms have become bigger, more capital intensive and more specialised in their production. Farmers in turn have partaken in the gradual 'disenchantment' of agriculture – the replacement of intuition by calculation, and the progressive elimination of the mysteries of plant and animal husbandry

*Presented by John Marsh

493

by exposing them to scientific appraisal. Such changes have involved, to use a cliché often employed to summarise them, a move 'from agriculture to agribusiness'.

Without wishing to subscribe to any naïve form of technological determinism it is nevertheless possible to trace a chain of causality from these transformations in farming technology and management to the significant social changes which have occurred in rural society since the Second World War. It is worth noting, however, that the economic exigencies of contemporary agriculture owe little to the workings of the free market in agricultural commodities. Individual farmers may indeed act *as if* they were governed by market rationality, but over the last three decades the state has intervened decisively and continuously as the midwife of technological change and the guarantor of profitability (Newby 1979). The technological transformation of agriculture, then, is not a product of 'the hidden hand' of the market, but of quite deliberate policy decisions, consciously pursued and publicly encouraged up until the present day. In this sense, agriculture in all advanced industrial societies is deeply politicised and in many countries agricultural policy is regarded as much a branch of social policy as it is a policy concerned with the economics of a particular industry. This at least suggests why technologically determinist accounts of social change in rural society are inadequate.

The state regulation of agriculture has, therefore, profoundly altered both the structure of the industry and the day-to-day nature of life and work in the countryside. The encouragement of fewer, larger and more capital intensive farms has resulted eventually in all of the catalogue of changes which we associate with rural life today: the mechanisation of agriculture, the declining numbers of workers employed in the agricultural industry, the growth of an 'adventitious' rural population which has replaced the former agricultural inhabitants of the countryside, widespread changes in the rural landscape and other environmental aspects of change in the countryside. These changes have not been the result of some immutable natural law, but of policy decisions made by individual national governments and – increasingly – by transnational organisations such as the European Economic Community. Individual governments, for example, have promoted technological change both directly through their grants and subsidies for farm capitalisation and amalgamation, and indirectly through their complex manipulation of commodity price supports and guarantees which have protected farmers from the consequences of chronic overproduction. Most governments also provide direct assistance through various advisory services to agriculture and through the funding of research establishments. A large and complex network of institutions has thus been erected in the public sector in order to effect the technological transformation that post-war agricultural policy ordained. An adherence to the 'technological fix' in the drive towards cost-efficiency has been almost universal. We can now see, however, that these policies have been almost too successful in their principal aim –

increasing production at lower real levels of cost – so that now, in Western Europe at least, the major policy problem is how to manage a *decline* in agricultural production rather than a continuing increase. What was known in the 1950s as the 'farm adjustment problem' is now back on the political agenda with a vengeance.

Debates on the 'changing structure of agriculture' have tended to follow this familiar path. When one looks back over the last 30 years or so, one is indeed struck by the increasing concentration and capital intensification of production on fewer, larger farms. In this paper I do not wish to go over this ground yet again, except to make one or two brief observations. We are now aware that while there is a general tendency towards an increasing concentration of production, this is by no means a simple unilinear process. By this I mean that, although in most countries there is a persistent tendency for an increasing proportion of agricultural production to be concentrated on a declining percentage of holdings, this has not been accompanied by the disappearance of the family farm, small farm or peasantry (depending on which kind of society we are discussing) to the extent that many commentators believed. For example, the last rites have been uttered over the disappearance of the peasantry for more than a century now and yet the peasantry persists. Even in some of the most technologically advanced agricultural societies (e.g. the United States) the number of small farms has actually increased over the last decade, rather than declined as some would have predicted. We can now see how small farmers have proved to be remarkably adaptable to changing economic circumstances. The forms of adaptation are many and varied, involving such matters as the growth of pluri-activity and part-time farming, the ability to find niches in the market which have not been or cannot be penetrated by the larger agricultural producers, the specialisation in production which is not amenable to economies of scale, the dependence upon local and/or specalised markets, etc. In many countries, therefore, we are witnessing the *slow* emergence of a dual farming economy, with the bulk of the production taking place on large-scale holdings in a highly capital intensive manner, while a large number of small farms continue to exist even though they account for only a small amount of overall production. If we look to the future then it seems to me that something like this kind of dualistic structure is likely to become more apparent. What will become an important policy issue in most advanced industrial societies will be concerned with the ways in which this dual structure is spatially allocated – i.e. the extent to which small farms are clustered into particular localities where they will present an important policy issue for those concerned with rural development and/or rural deprivation. It is certainly quite likely that the policies directed towards the large-scale capital intensive farms will be inappropriate for the small farm sector and will be unlikely to offer direct help to those areas in which they are concentrated. A greater flexibility of policy response – which takes account of the social implications of agricultural policy as well as the economic aspects – is therefore an important necessity.

THE GROWTH OF AGRIBUSINESS

These introductory remarks provide the context for the main subject matter of this paper. I wish to draw attention to other, less well researched, ways in which the structure of agriculture is changing and to speculate on what some of the effects of this might be on the nature of rural society. For the increasingly capital intensive nature of modern agriculture has had one further effect which deserves serious attention: it has made farmers more and more dependent upon non-farm inputs (machinery, agro-chemicals, etc.) while also drawing them into the embrace of a much wider complex of industrial companies involved in food marketing, processing, distribution and retailing. Agriculture is being slowly incorporated into sectors of the engineering, chemical and food processing industries which collectively we may call 'agribusiness'. The rise of agribusiness therefore, implies not only the increasing rationalisation of agriculture, but the growth of a food production system only a small proportion of which may actually take place on farms. The 'structure of agriculture' therefore changes from a relatively simple chain of processors linking production and consumption, to a highly complex integrated system of food production which begins with the manufacture of seeds, machinery, fertilisers, pesticides, etc. and ends in a complex chain of food manufacturing, processing, wholesaling, distribution and retailing: – in sum, from seeds to fast-food outlets. Within this context formally free farmers represent merely one link in an increasingly vertically integrated chain which links seed manufacturers with super-market retailers or fast-food franchises. The implications of this for the structure of rural society have barely been explored, yet there is little doubt that in promoting a highly capitalised farming industry, recent agricultural policy has also promoted the interests of agribusiness companies in the agriculture of advanced industrial societies (and indeed in many Third World countries too).

In a paper of this length it is obviously impossible to offer a comprehensive and detailed account of the growth of vertically integrated corporate agribusiness in Europe and North America. (For the most comprehensive account, see The Report of the United Nations Centre on Transnational Corporations, 1980.) We should note, however, that multinational agribusiness companies are often in the vanguard of multinational organisation (the most notorious is arguably Coca Cola) and, particularly in the Third World, pose acute problems of national sovereignty and market power. Under these circumstances it becomes tempting to weave conspiracy theories around the exercise of oligarchical corporate power, but there is no need to invent the conspiracy theories in order to discern the lack of public accountability embodied in many agribusiness conglomerates. They are actively involved in changing dietary habits, the structure of agriculture, food marketing and retailing, and wield enormous market power – and yet remain impervious to control by politicians and consumers.

Sociologically agribusiness corporations are of more than passing interest. Along with the state they represent one of the most important agencies involved in the restructuring of rural society. The processes involved are often incremental and indirect but are nonetheless effective and far reaching. There is, however, an increasing tendency for agricultural multinationals to work their transformation by proxy, abjuring large-scale involvement in farming itself but controlling the conditions under which farmers operate. There is therefore becoming a persistent tendency for farmers to become the 'domestic outworkers' of major agribusiness companies, receiving inputs from them *and*, having transformed them, supplying their output back to them. It seems likely that agribusiness influence over the structure of agriculture is likely to continue to proceed in this indirect manner with agribusiness companies seeking out highly market-oriented agribusinessmen farmers with whom to place contracts, thereby exacerbating the tendency towards a dualistic farming structure. Sufficient numbers of farmers have, indeed, proved sufficiently flexible to the needs of agribusiness companies for the latter not to feel the necessity to vertically integrate and take up farming themselves. This has enabled them to avoid the high cost and political risk of land purchase and to avoid the cost of purchasing managerial expertise in agriculture. It is, for example, surely not coincidental that agribusiness companies have been quite willing to integrate vertically overseas (principally in the ex-colonial parts of the Third World) where these conditions do not, or have not, applied. In Western Europe and North America, by contrast, contract farming has usually sufficed. In this manner agribusiness companies have accelerated the trend towards the rationalisation of agriculture and the concentration of the industry on fewer larger farms. Smaller farmers, who do not participate in such contractual arrangements, find themselves becoming increasingly marginal, while the larger farmers find their enterprise gradually transformed by the relentless 'industrial' logic of agribusiness. The latter are encouraged to become specialised in order to make the maximum possible use of their specialised technology and skill. As a result agriculture has become organised according to non-agricultural criteria, on the assumption that agriculture is merely a disguised form of manufacture. This has implications not only for farming entrepreneurs, but also for farm workers, the employees of food processors and ultimately all of us as consumers.

The general public is largely unaware of these trends – and, for that matter, rather uncaring. What counts primarily to the consumer is the price of food. Agribusiness companies themselves certainly believe they are performing a public service by implementing the consumer demand for cheap food. The changing pattern of consumer demand for food is also encouraging the growth of agribusiness. More of the food that we purchase is processed food and, given current trends such as the increasing proportion of females participating in paid employment, the demand for convenience food is likely to increase, quite aside from the encouragement given by the agribusiness company's own advertising campaigns. Since the value added from processing food is much greater than that which is accrued from growing it, agribusiness domination of food production seems likely to increase in the foreseeable future. However, it is on the implications of the rise of agribusiness for the changing social structure of society that I wish to concentrate in my concluding remarks.

AGRIBUSINESS AND THE FUTURE OF RURAL SOCIETY

It is apparent that the 'changing structure of agriculture', in both of the senses in which I have used this term above, has been responsible for major transformations in the structure of rural society. The agricultural indsutry now forms such a small part of economic and social activity in the rural areas in Western Europe and North America that it has led to a reconsideration of what is understood by the term 'rural' in the first place. It is now apparent that the relationship between 'urban' and 'rural' society has changed so dramatically in the post-war period, and even in the last decade, that the nature and content of contemporary 'rural communities' are themselves a necessary topic for discussion. For example in many parts of Europe and North America it is now necessary to dissociate 'rural' from 'agricultural'. Only in terms of land use is rural society now an agricultural society in many countries. In all other senses – economically, occupationally, socially, culturally – rural society has already been comprehensively 'urbanised'. It also follows from this that the assumption that there is a natural tendency for economic activity to gravitate to towns and cities must also be questioned: in the last two decades many Western economies have manifested pronounced centrifugal tendencies, even though this decentralisation of economic activity has been accompanied by a continuing centralisation of decision making and control. Furthermore we have witnessed a 'population turn-around' in many areas, with a pronounced flow of population back into even some of the most remote rural areas. All these and other factors mean that many of the conventional definitions of 'rural' have been rendered obsolete. Apart from anything else this means that we cannot predict the future of rural communities on the basis of a straightforward extrapolation from the past. If we care to look at the *history* of rural communities it is clear, with a few minor qualifications, that the very far reaching social changes which have overtaken rural society in recent decades have been rooted first and foremost in changes within agriculture. Since rural society is no longer entirely, nor even predominantly, an agrarian society, however, it is very doubtful indeed whether any future changes in agriculture will have the kind of impact upon the social fabric of the countryside that they have had in the past. Harsh though it may be, agriculture now has only a residual significance in many rural areas and it is to other forms of economic activity that we must look if we are to analyse the future of rural society in such localities. This is not to deny the importance of agriculture in other respects, but to acknowledge that its future direct contribution to such matters as, say, rural employment growth, is likely to be negligible.

In Britain, for example, the great majority of villages today, in both upland and lowland areas, are no longer agricultural communities. Except in a few very remote areas the village and agricultural settlement has been transformed by the twin assaults of the drift from the land of agricultural labour and creeping urbanisation. As the rural working population moved to the towns in search of jobs, so they have been replaced by an urban, overwhelmingly middle class, professional and managerial population which was attracted by a combination of cheaper housing (until the late 1960s) and by an idealised view of rural life, which the ownership of a car at last allowed them to indulge. Since the railways allowed a commuting population to inhabit the rural parts on the outskirts of London since before the First World War, the transformation of rural villages into non-agricultural settlements has taken place in a series of ways out along the lines of transportation from the major urban centres. By the end of the 1960s a network of motorways and electrified railways had linked up most of the commuting areas between the major conurbations and the infilling of commuter villages between such road or transport routes had virtually been completed. Only a few rural areas, isolated by bad roads or non-existent railways, remained relatively untouched; but even these, by virtue of their isolation were often gobbled up by the equally voracious demand for holiday homes and weekend cottages. Rural Britain, which was once agricultural Britain, had now become middle-class Britain. Similar patterns can be observed elsewhere in Western Europe and North America, although clearly the precise nature of these changes varies considerably according to local and economic circumstances.

If we superimpose on to these social changes the kind of changes in the organisation of agriculture to which I have alluded, what do we find? Rural areas have long been familiar with the notion of 'jobless growth' through the experience of technological innovation in agriculture, whereby massive increases in output and productivity have been accompanied by an equally dramatic fall in employment opportunities. It is doubtful if we can look to agriculture, including forestry, to provide anything other than marginal prospects for employment growth in a few localities. Indeed continuing technological change in agriculture is likely to create further downward pressure in employment, not merely through the further economies of scale which can be gained from amalgamation and further mechanisation, but for the potentially much more extensive effects of new innovations in biotechnology. To deal with these fully would require another paper and would be more than a little speculative, but among those just over the horizons include such factors as genetically engineered protein for human, but more especially for animal consumption which could lead to a good deal of the production of animal feedstuffs, which now takes place on farms, being moved to industrial processing plants using technologies somewhat similar to gas and oil production. One could continue with further examples, some more speculative than others, but in any case there is little to suggest that those concerned with rural economic development will be looking to agriculture to provide employment growth in the countryside of the future. On the contrary, it seems that an increasing proportion of food production will take place off the farm and a great deal will depend, as far as the future of rural society is concerned, on where this production will be located.

The second agricultural revolution, then, is far from complete. The increasing concentration and vertical integration of agricultural production is not going to fade away. None of this is to suggest an apocalyptic vision of the future of agriculture, for the changes which will occur will largely be the extrapolation of existing trends. Farmers are likely to retain their nominal independence, but their share of retail food prices seems destined to decline further and they will find themselves even more vulnerable to the agribusiness company's marketing policies. So the countryside of the future will contain fewer farms, fewer people occupied in agriculture, a more industrialised system of production, and a rural social structure – and even a rural landscape – which takes all of these factors into account. Since, however, the social significance of agriculture in rural areas is likely to decline still further then some fundamental rethinking is required over the links between agricultural policy and rural development policy. There is, however, little sign yet that such fundamental rethinking is taking place.

REFERENCES

Newby, H. *Green and Pleasant Land? Social Change in Rural England* Penguin Books, London, 1979. (second edition published by Wildwood House, 1985.)
United Nations Centre on Transnational Corporations, *Transnational Corporations in Food and Beverage Processing*, United Nations, New York, 1980.

DISCUSSION OPENING – ALAN MATTHEWS

Arising from Professor Newby's paper I would like to distinguish three themes for the discussion: changing agricultural structures, changing structures in rural societies, and changing interest structures in rural areas. The first two themes are treated in the paper, and I feel the third might also profitably be considered in the discussion.

Professor Newby discusses the changing structure of agriculture in the first part of his paper and highlights three trends: the growing commercialisation of farming and its increasing integration with the rest of the economy; the changing size distribution of farms and the concentration of production on the larger farms; and the growing complexity of the food chain and marketing system. Each issue suggests a question for current research or policy.

First, the growing dependence of agricultural production on purchased inputs has substantially eroded a fundamental justification for government intervention in agricultural product markets, namely, to promote stability in farmers' expectations of their future returns. In the past, input markets were relatively stable, and purchased inputs were anyway a small proportion of total input, so that the stabilisation of product prices could be defended as a way of stabilising expectations of future returns. This is no longer the case. During the 1970s input markets, including those for fertilizer, energy products and credit, have been very unstable. Furthermore, purchased inputs are now a much more important item in farmers' budgets, so contributing significantly to the destabilisation of their incomes and expectations. Agricultural price policy as traditionally conceived makes less and less contribution to the stability goal.

Second, Professor Newby points out that despite the growing concentration of production on large farms in industrialised countries, small farms survive and indeed their number in some of these countries is increasing. We thus witness the slow emergence of a dual farming economy. The apparent contradiction is explained largely by the possibility on smaller farms of combining part-time farming with off-farm employment. Often average total household income on smaller farms is greater than that on commercial farms for this reason. Thus to focus on farm labour income alone to identify areas of rural disadvantage in industrialised countries, as suggested by Newby, can be quite misleading – Bavaria in southern Germany provides an example of this point. Newby's conclusion that the way in which the dualistic farm structure is spatially allocated has important policy implications must be severely qualified on this ground.

The third identified structural change is the growing complexity of the food system. In the 1970s this led some researchers and institutions to talk of the need for a food policy rather than just an agricultural policy to ensure consistency in decisions taken at various points along the chain. It is my impression, however, that this notion of a food policy has made little practical impact. If this is the case, I want to raise the question whether this reflects a failure at a theoretical level by agricultural economists to establish that there are real gains to be had by thinking in food policy rather than just agricultural policy terms, and/or to provide a satisfactory theoretical framework within which such a food policy might be articulated.

I now turn to the second theme in the second half of Professor Newby's paper, the changing structure of rural societies. Here he draws attention to two main points. The first is the influence of agribusiness on changing agricultural structures. The second is that rural society is no longer an agrarian society, and that some fundamental rethinking is required on the links between agricultural policy and rural development policy. In my view both points as developed in the paper are overstated.

The discussion of the influence of agribusiness provides a most illuminating example of methodological differences between sociologists and economists in addressing a similar problem issue. It might be more correct to make the distinction between sociologists and institutional economists, on the one hand, and neoclassical economists on the other. The sociological account, quite legitimately, focuses on the actors, whether institutions, political parties or interest groups, in any situation. But occasionally there is a tendency, observable in places in Professor Newby's paper, to lapse into what I will call a sociological determinism. By this I mean ascribing causal influence and motivations to these agencies where economists (with perhaps an equal determinism) would see them as merely vectors for more fundamental forces.

For example, we know that agribusiness companies are involved in the delivery of fertiliser to farms. From that the jump is sometimes made by the sociological or institutional determinist that the increase in fertiliser consumption is explained by the marketing activities of these companies. To the economist, however, (more precisely, the neoclassical economist), the increase in fertilizer consumption is to be explained by a favourable movement in relative prices, while the marketing activities of the fertilizer companies may alter their market shares or at most have a transitory influence on overall demand. Examples of such sociological determinism in Professor Newby's paper include the suggestion that changing dietary habits are brought about by the marketing activities of agribusiness firms (where economists would explain them in terms of the changing relative value of time within the household), and the suggestion that agribusiness has accelerated the trend towards the rationalisation of agriculture and the concentration of the industry on fewer larger farms through its contracting activities (where economists would explain this in terms of economies of scale and the changing returns to resources in on-farm and off-farm uses).

Now I know I have drawn an exaggerated dichotomy here. Nonetheless, I hold that there is an important difference of substance which can be summarised crudely in the slogan 'For sociologists actors matter, while for economists they don't'. To avoid misunderstanding let me make it clear that I know economists would fully accept that institutions can affect the structure of incentives and thus the pattern of resource allocation in both the short and long run. But this is different from suggesting that actors have the power to create their own environment, which is the essence of what I have called sociological determinism. I also recognise that political actors are in a special category and do have this ability, at least in the short run, to rig the market environment.

The question is, does it matter that we have different models of explanation. I think it matters profoundly. The purpose of an explanation is to provide an ordered sense of how the world works. If the explanation is a good one, we can use this knowledge to avoid unpleasant outcomes and to achieve more desired ones. Sociological determinism provides explanations which are 'voluntaristic' in character. That is, it stimulates political activism by offering the tempting possibility of one or many alternative scenarios if only the influence of malignant actors can be removed. Economics leads to a political passivity with its message that eliminating unpopular actors will do nothing to alter the impersonal and inexorable movements in relative costs and returns which underlie their behaviour. The implications for the discussion of the influence of agribusiness on agricultural structure should be clear. In general, it would be worth pursuing the possibility of a methodological exchange between agricultural economists and rural sociologists at some future conference.

Returning to the paper proper, Newby argues that the agrarian basis of rural society has been eroded to the extent that some fundamental rethinking of the relationship between agricultural policy and rural development policy is now required. Newby, of course, is talking about the United Kingdom, where the proportion of the labour force employed in primary agriculture is only round 2 per cent, and for other countries even in Western Europe his remarks may represent more an indication of a likely future state than present reality. Even for the UK, however, I wonder if there is not a methodological flaw in his reasoning which leads him to understate the continuing importance of agriculture.

The relevance of agriculture to rural development policy does not depend on a counting of heads but on its economic significance. Now the economic significance of primary agriculture can best be measured using economic base methodology. This approach distinguishes between those activities whose levels are exogenously determined by export demand, and those activities whose levels are derived from the export of basic activities. Basic activities in rural areas have become more diversified, and now include rural industry, tourism, and the sale of labour services by urban commuters living in rural areas as well as agriculture itself. The economic importance of agriculture is measured by taking its size and the size of its induced multiplier effects relative to the size of other basic activities and the size of their induced multiplier effects. Because of the greater linkages between agriculture and the local economy, this measure will suggest that primary agriculture remains considerably more important for rural development even in the UK than the author suggests.

Nonetheless, his point that the trends in the structure of agriculture are inevitably diminishing the social significance of agriculture in rural areas can be granted. This may well require some rethinking of the appropriate instruments for rural development in particular areas, but it is unclear to me why this should necessarily imply the rethinking of agricultural policy, the rhetorical flourish on which the author ends his paper. Is it Professor Newby's intention to suggest that we should be trying to reverse current structural trends in primary agriculture in order to facilitate rural development, for example, by emphasising employment rather than production growth within the sector? Without a clearer indication of what might be required the suggestion remains a rather empty one.

The points contained in the Newby paper, finally, might usefully be complemented by considering the changing structure of interests in rural areas. Until recently, land was seen primarily as a rural resource for the production of food and timber. But urban interests are increasingly demanding that the role of land as an input in the production of values such as visual amenity and recreational services of interest mainly to them should be recognised. The creation of national parks, the designation of areas of outstanding beauty where planning controls are applied more strictly, the opening of national trails and walkways, and the formulation of a countryside code, are some of the ways in which society is responding to this conflict. Environmental interests are also becoming more vocal. Resolution of these matters is fundamentally a question of recognising and affirming a particular set of property rights with respect to land and other natural resources, and the conference might wish to consider what such solutions might look like in the future.

GENERAL DISCUSSION – RAPPORTEUR: VILJO RYYNÄNEN

The discussion concentrated mainly on three topics: the changing agricultural structure, the changing structure in rural societies, and the methodological differences between sociologists and economists. Discussion concerning the first two topics followed loosely the contents of Professor Newby's paper, either accepting his model of rural development or disputing it as a misunderstanding caused by methodological differences between sociologists and economists.

Some of the participants considered the development of vertical integration between farms and agribusiness as a threat to independent agriculture and even rural societies, though opposite opinions were presented. The increase in the number of large farms connected with the changing structure of land use and the establishment of new industries may cause big structural and environmental problems in certain societies. Multidisciplinary rural policy making and planning were recommended, because the rural societies in industrialised countries are no longer agrarian societies.

The discussion touched also on the prevailing agricultural crisis, the rise in the cost of farm credit and consequences for agricultural and rural structures. Some participants saw the only way to understand the role of both agricultural and economic policies was to have a clear macroeconomic understanding, because no agricultural or economic policies would be able to change the trends of society.

The discussion dealt with differences between the development of rural societies in the North (industrialised countries) and those in the South (developing countries). Terms of trade, restrictions on trade, competition from overproduction and changing consumption patterns of agricultural products were seen by some participants as partial reasons for the decline of agricultural and rural societies in various parts of the world. Policies should be devised to remove the restrictions and to promote the harmonic development of agricultural and rural areas.

The Discussion Opener, A. Matthews, drew attention to the contradiction between sociological determinism and neoclassical economic explanation. This emphasises the importance of interdisciplinary dialogue and importance of opportunities provided by Conferences such as those of the IAEE.

Participants in the discussion included J. Berthelot, R. D. Bollman, F. de Casabianca, L. Drake, E. K. Ireri, H. S. Kehal, A. B. Lewis, T. Palaskas, D. Roldan and J. T. Scully.

TADEUSZ HUNEK

Farmers and Rural Societies in Uncertain Food Production Systems

The uncertainty, interpreted as 'not being dependent on', that is to say, situations and conditions independent of the agricultural producer, is, undoubtedly, a factor of change in farming; it 'feeds' those changes. It means that specified changes in agricultural management are a protection from the menace brought by the category of uncertainty. On the other hand, dynamics and development, while introducing agriculture in new areas, in new technical-economic and social conditions, confront it with new uncertainties and new threats.

The subject of these observations is the problem of uncertainty in the process of change and evolution of categories such as the farmer and the local rural societies. It means that our aim is to show conditions of signs of uncertainty, and the reaction of agricultural producers and rural societies to the uncertainty in the sequence of thinking, formulated in the phrase: change and continuity or transformation and continuity.

In short, we can speak of four types/areas of reasons for uncertainty of farmers and local rural societies.

CLIMATIC CONDITIONS; BIOLOGICAL PROCESSES OF AGRICULTURAL PRODUCTION

This type of uncertainty has accompanied agriculture since it developed as man's activity. The fluctuation of climatic conditions, susceptibility of cultivated plants and animals to diseases and pests account for the effects of farming and the volume of agricultural production obtained being always risky and hard to predict precisely. These features are the foundation of the frequently raised specific character of agricultural production.

With the development of agriculture there takes place the process of becoming independent from natural conditions. Present-day agriculture in countries of developed economy has far exceeded in its production level the natural fertility of soil or the production efficiency of animals. Agricultural output, supported in its production process by fertilizers, pesticides and herbicides, is able not only to reach a high productivity per unit of land or livestock, but also to limit effectively or simply eliminate fluctuations in the production level due to geo-natural conditions.

We may say, in conclusion, that the natural conditions of agricultural production are, nowadays, a factor, which brings about, in a small degree only, the uncertainty of farming.

ECONOMIC AND SOCIAL ENVIRONMENT OF AGRICULTURE

Contrary to natural conditions, the economic and social environment, in which agriculture is functioning, is the basic sphere of reasons causing conditions of uncertainty. One may say that the development stages of agriculture and agricultural uncertainty are determined by the three following factors:

(i) *The economic market*, which we define as the whole of supply processes, transformation and regulation of agricultural production, food production. Thus, the economic market reflects the technical and economic aspect of farming. It is obvious that the economic market is run by its own order rules, which allow the provision of agriculture with optimum assumptions for achieving both dynamics of development processes and the rationality of transforming reserves and supplies in production effects. The content of the economic market, of the economic side of agricultural production, are relations, trends and also driving forces of the agricultural development mechanism.

The variability of those relations and of driving forces and mechanisms of agricultural development makes an endless chain of reasons for uncertainty in farming. It should be emphasised that the position of a single agricultural producer towards the market economy is weak. The supply of information he has in the sphere of business trends, of new elements of the economic situation, is, necessarily, inconsiderable. This knowledge of his becomes dramatically clear on the market, after the production cycle is ended. Therefore, making decisions in advance is extremely restrained by the scale of an individual farmer. That is the reason for so frequent an inconsistency between the volume and structure of agricultural production and the expectations formulated in this respect by the national economy or, in a wider sense, by the world market of agricultural products.

(ii) *The ideology market*, covering the system of ideas, conceptions and evaluations, concerning the shape of agriculture in the form of production techniques, economic and social structures. We may speak of a specified revaluation of the technical-economic aspect of agricultural production from the viewpoint of the criteria of a given system of ideology, and of giving a new, ideological qualification to technical and economic aspects of farming. The market of ideology seems to be determined by two basic factors namely, the prevailing doctrine and the social interest, in the broadest sense of the word; to put it more precisely, by a specified articulation of the social interest by the social governing group.

I believe that the viewpoint can be formulated that the ideology market gives rise to particular assumptions of uncertainty conditions, actually for all forms of agriculture, peasant, farmers', collective, state or agribusiness. If, however, the economy market is a place of reasons for uncertainty for the given production cycle, then the ideology market brings uncertainty for long periods of time; so to say, secular development trends for a given form of agriculture. These are the ideological assumptions, which often 'decree' whether the specified forms of agriculture have any future or not. Considering the fact that ideological systems have their own development logic, in the sense of creating forces, slow rates of change, threats and uncertainties may be coming from those systems, almost entirely independent from the leading actors of farming, i.e. agricultural producers.

The example of Poland, for practically the whole of the past four decades, may prove that the ideology market can be the source of acute conditions of uncertainty. When peasants had full possibility of articulation of their demands, in the years 1970–81, the demand for constitutional permanence of peasant farming was a universal demand, made much more definitely than, for example, the ensuring of profitable conditions for agricultural production.

(iii) *The policy market* is reduced to a system of legal and economic instrumentation, in the sphere of orders and bans, rules, principles of organisation, management and administration of agricultural affairs. The policy market is, on the one hand, an executive apparatus of the ideology market, and on the other hand, it implements directly the interests of social forces, which are in control in the country.

The policy market owing to its direct executive character, is considered to be the most important source of uncertainty in the agricultural process. The uncertainty created by this market can be of an economic, legal and administrative nature. Moreover, it may concern both the farming and the life of the agricultural producer's family. Referring to the example of Poland, peasants' demands addressed to the agricultural policy, come down to its being lucid, readable and stable.

The inside functioning of the markets of economy, ideology and policy, and, moreover, their mutual conditionings and relations, are not in the least incidental, but are the effect of specified reasons and results, which produce in consequence a specified condition of economic, ideological and political forces. It seems certain that all the above named markets exist and function in each agriculture, regardless of the degree of its technical development, modernisation level or structure of social organisation. The viewpoint that some agriculture is the effect of the influence of only one market, cannot be maintained.

According to the subject of this paper, we have presented single markets as sources of uncertainty in farming. This is, however, only one side of the functioning of the named markets. There is no denying the other, favourable side, that is to say, the creative role of markets in agricultural and farming development as well as in the functioning of local rural societies. If we consider the process of transformation of traditional agriculture into a modern one to be a very special achievement of agriculture, we have to say that, undoubtedly, this process is a sort of product of those markets.

Meanwhile, the attitude of agricultural economists to the single markets is highly differentiated. It seems that the most common attitude of agricultural economists is the underestimation or simple disregard of the market of ideology, less frequently of the market of policy, in formulating the strategy rules for agricultural development. Most agricultural economists tend to retire to the sphere of purely economic phenomena, i.e. the market of economy, both in formulating the theory of agricultural development or in postulating the specified strategy of agriculture, or even the actual planning-programming tasks. They assume that the power of arguments in the real/economic sphere, the logic of technical and economic development will find their way to implementation regardless of the market of ideology or policy. I wonder, if this attitude is not the main reason for poor 'implementation force' for concepts of solutions of agricultural development problems submitted by economists.

The functioning and evolution of single markets set specified forces in motion. Therefore, they can be recognised as determinants of agricultural condition and development in the long evolution from natural to market agriculture, from traditional to modernised, from stagnant/balanced to dynamic, from peasant to farmer's agriculture. It is characteristic that the evolutionary process of agriculture shows many common, universal causalities. It is especially conspicuous if we use the concept of turning points of trends of production factors in agriculture.

If we consider the evolutionary turning point of the factor labour as the moment when the numbers of the agricultural population/manpower reserves, after having reached the uppermost volume, begins to show a downward trend, with further relative decrease of labour reserves in agriculture in comparison to non-agricultural sectors, the consequences for agriculture are essential, and can be formulated as follows:

The turning point 'opens' agriculture to the expansions of non-agricultural sectors. There starts the process of subjecting agriculture to the national economy, and mainly to its most dynamic sectors – primarily industrial production and then service activity.

This point originates modernization of agriculture, both by sucking in new techniques and technology by agriculture, and by extracting manpower from agriculture.

The turning point in manpower reserves starts the era of economization of agriculture. The economic calculus becomes the basic assumption for making production decisions instead of tradition, routine and custom.

As a turning point of the evolution of the factor land in the process of farming there can be assumed the condition of the uppermost volume of that reserve, and the beginning of the process of arable land reduction.

The reaching of the turning point by the factor land is also of vital consequence for farming and for food production.

The turning point introduces the substitute calculus to farming – land can be replaced by the capital factor, the consequence of which is the arising of the land market, on which land occurs as a regular commodity. The land, by becoming a commodity, becomes de-mythologised, loses the quality of supreme value, value as such, which, for a long time, has been creating social stratification of local agricultural societies.

The scale of agricultural production volume becomes, to an ever higher degree, independent from the area of land possessed. This provides conditions furthering its far-reaching mobility as a production factor, with an evident trend to match the manpower magnitude, mainly in the individual system of farming.

Substitution of the land mainly by capital, and by labour as well, opens agriculture to the expansion of non-agricultural sectors.

Finally, the reduction of arable land reserves originates the process of shifting food production outside agriculture, and is, at the same time, a result of this shifting, to some degree. This process is revealed both in the production increase of food additives, and in the attempts to render agriculture fully independent from production of so essential an element of food as protein.

In the process of capital evolution as a production factor in agriculture, the turning point is reached when there occurs the balancing of capital profitablity in agricultural production and in non-agricultural sectors. This situation also brings about many consequences:

The turning point means full opening of agriculture to the penetration of non-agricultural sectors of economy. The effect of this penetration is an intensive inflow to agriculture of non-agricultural production factors such as technique, chemistry, biology, as well as taking over from agriculture specified operations and organising them either in the system of industrial production or in the system of services. The turning point in the evolution of the capital factor in agriculture starts an increasing process of 'melting' of agriculture and food production in the scale of the entire national economy, and also through import and export on a world scale.

The turning point of the capital evolution in agriculture provides conditions furthering the equalising of effectiveness of agricultural and non-agricultural production. This offers to agricultural producers, to the agricultural population, a chance of equalising many parities, primarily income parity.

The turning point, while offering through the abundance of capital possibilities of a wide substitution of land and labour, introduces in agricultural production technical and biological advance, in the wide sense of the word, the scale of which is so great that it creates the so-called intellectual factor, that becomes the fourth independent production factor in agricultural production.

It is easy to prove that the process of evolution of agriculture, of reaching by it the turning points in developing production factors, is, simultaneously, a series of sources, assumptions of uncertainty and threats in farming. A characteristic is some evident shifting of the sphere of uncertainty from climatic, natural conditions to uncertainty in the sphere of economy, trends of business and ideology, as well as of agricultural policy.

THE FARMERS' PARTNERSHIP IN SOCIAL LIFE

Undoubtedly, an essential factor accounting for conditions of uncertainty in farming is the underestimation of agricultural producers and of rural societies in social stratification. Unfortunately, the situations are still common when agricultural producers feel they are 'second-class' citizens, when the economic position of their farms is easily sacrificed to the interests of non-agricultural sectors of national economy. This occurs, when the economic strategy is implementing, often on a drastic scale, the process of accumulation of means in agriculture in favour of industrial development, or in countries which artificially maintain a policy of low food prices.

The phenomenon of social underestimation of agricultural producers, lack of their subjectivity in social stratification, brings about the major threat for agricultural producers and rural societies by bringing into operation the mechanism of unfavourable selection in the process of migration from agriculture to non-agricultural jobs, from villages to towns. The feeling of being a citizen of the 'second class' in the social or political stratification is most acutely experienced by gifted individuals and the way of solving these problems most frequently leads to abandoning agriculture and abandoning the countryside.

TRANSFORMATION OF LOCAL RURAL SOCIETIES AND DISTORTION OF THEIR IDENTITY

The process of transformation of agriculture does not only essentially change local rural societies. There occurs the vanishing of economic functions of the local society, which shows in a reduction of common economic initiatives, of neighbourly aid. In effect there appears the process of economic atomisation, when, in the course of production, single farms establish connections with the 'outside' institutions and are not involved in neighbourly co-operation. The thesis can be confirmed that modern, prosperous agriculture is no longer the same as a prosperous local society.

Similarly dramatic changes occur in the cultural sphere. The traditional value system, typical for traditional stratifications of local rural societies, the role of local authorities and of local opinion are gradually eliminated. They are superseded by universal value systems, considered to be urban ones, containing, of course, new determinants in the value system of categories such as leisure time, privacy of home and family, and the like. All that brings about changes in the peasant model of life, from the model, in which the farm and the land were supreme values, and farming was a way of life, to the model of living for the sake of oneself, which is typical of non-agricultural professions and societies.

TYPES OF REACTION OF FARMERS AND LOCAL RURAL SOCIETIES TO CONDITIONS OF UNCERTAINTY

The types of reaction of agricultural producers to conditions of uncertainty actually indicate the way of the evolution of agriculture from its natural and traditional state towards a modernised agriculture, fully open to the market.

The basic reaction of traditional agriculture to conditions of menace and uncertainty was retiring in the scale of the farm and reducing the consumption level of the peasant family, absorbing of unfavourable impulses of the outside world, expressed in unfavourable prices for agricultural produce, increase of taxes and other burdens. Frequently, a peasant's reaction to worsening business conditions was to increase the production offered to the market, which led to further aggravation of business outlooks and which allowed the economists to formulate a thesis on 'irrational' behaviour of the peasant with respect to the market.

The uncertainty and the conditions of menace in traditional agriculture also led to consolidation of local rural societies. This rural society was the first and often the only instance which helped survival under uncertainty and conditions of menace, and which allowed the organisation of specified forms of self-aid and common protection. Those were the conditions of uncertainty and menace that created the category of local rural society, which category played a vital role in agricultural development for many hundreds of years. Nowadays still, in countries such as Poland, Yugoslavia, and elsewhere, it is constantly an important imperative for the behaviour of agricultural producers in the way of agricultural production, in the way of life.

In modernised agriculture the reaction of agricultural producers to the conditions of uncertainty shifted from the scale of a farm and the producer's family to a wider scale, namely to specified activities on the market of agricultural policy. This state is a simple consequence of the 'sinking' of agriculture into the national economy when the general business outlook determines the opportunities of farming.

Present-day agriculture has developed two specific forms of reactions to the conditions of uncertainty and menace, which are: organisations, farmers' unions, and the agricultural lobby. Their instruments of activity are, primarily, of a political activity character on the policy market. That is so, although the share of agriculture in the national economy is decreasing drastically, the number of farmers keeps declining, and their percentage compared with that in other professions amounts to a few points only in many countries.

The above observations allow one to raise the final problem, which we would like to present in the sphere of uncertainty in farming namely:

EVALUATION OF THE UNCERTAINTY AND MENACE IN AGRICULTURAL PERFORMANCE

The opinion of many agricultural economists, especially those interested in farm economics, as well as the view of many rural sociologists, concerning the sphere of uncertainty in farming, can be resolved into the following statement. The uncertainty, often changing into a condition of menace, is explicitly an unfavourable state, whereas the situation without any uncertainty in farming, or with as minimal uncertainty as possible, is ideal. I dare express some doubts as to full correctness of such views, and I will formulate my doubts in the following questions:

Is there a possibility of separating uncertainty in farming from the evolutionary process of transforming traditional agriculture into a modern one?

Is advance in agriculture, in a wide sense of the word, possible without uncertainty?

Is, then, uncertainty the price paid for advance?

Is the uncertainty a prerequisite for a Darwinian concept of development in the area of agriculture, through the evolution from simple to more complex forms, from less to more efficient forms of farming?

Consequently, does it make economic and social sense to eliminate excessively conditions of uncertainty in farming?

Does not the excessive elimination of uncertainty in farming result in supporting, as production goes, poor farms that are economically and socially ineffective, in short, is not this a blockade of progress?

Would not the reduction of subsidy systems in European and the US agriculture, actually the limiting of uncertainty conditions in farming, improve in effect the world agricultural market, providing a chance for agricultural development in the developing countries?

Finally, a somewhat paradoxical question: Would not the limitation of excessive elimination of uncertainty in farming give in effect a greater economic power to the agricultural sector, a greater breakthrough ability in making bargains with other sectors?

HIROYUKI NISHIMURA

The Rural-Urban Balance in Rural Development

INTRODUCTION

This paper is primarily concerned with a critical examination of the nature, extent, and causes of rural poverty as well as the consequent impact on urban society in several developing Asian countries.[1] To clarify a number of points, a relative comparison is made between the experience of Japan and the developing countries included here. Since the Industrial Revolution the world has witnessed two centuries of urban growth, but over the last three or four decades, this growth has taken a different form. Formerly, the city was a dense complex which grew out from its centre. However, there has been a much greater and irregular use of land, and a considerable increase in the population within and surrounding the cities. These changes have created serious problems for these countries.

Regarding the development of the rural areas, many Asian countries have maintained a considerable urban bias in their development plans. One result of such a bias has been an increasing imbalance in the planned changes between rural and urban areas. Although the majority of the population in the developing countries live in rural areas, these areas have not received their proportionate share of development resources. In some cases, they have even experienced a net outflow of resources, resulting in their gradual impoverishment. In many developing countries, the rural areas suffer from poverty, mal- and under-nutrition, poor medical, health and educational facilities and a lack of proper infrastructure facilities. Farming, which is the main occupation of the rural people, remains poorly developed with a low level of technology without proper linkages with the growing urban sector except as suppliers of food and raw materials. Furthermore, other farm and non-farm facilities, such as credit, extension, marketing, transportation and storage remain undeveloped, and the opportunities for the development of technology, knowledge and training in the rural areas remain severely limited.

In contrast, the urban areas in many countries have grown at a high rate. Both income and the modern amenities of life have increased similarly. While such facilities are still inadequate compared to the standards of developed countries, they show relatively considerable advances compared with those in the rural areas. Poverty and deprivation in rural areas are still causing a continuous exodus of rural people to urban areas. Unfortunately the urban sector cannot create enough job opportunities for these people. These migrants usually get petty jobs and they cannot hold down steady employment. Their inflow only tends to increase poverty and the numbers of squatters in urban areas. These trends often lead to serious socio-economic and political problems. Unlike the historical experience of the developed countries where the process was slow and transformation gradual, the change in the developing countries is occurring very rapidly.

CHARACTERISTICS AND NATURE OF THE RURAL-URBAN DIFFERENTIAL

There are many countries with an income per caput below US$ 300. These countries are predominantly rural with a moderately high growth rate of population (see Table 1). Agriculture is the main sector contributing to their national income and working opportunities (see Table 2). The relative level of poverty varies among developing countries (see Table 3) and it is estimated, for example, that in the Philippines about a third of its population live below the poverty line. Moreover, in both Bangladesh and the Philippines, the extent of poverty has increased over the last two decades.

Various indicators of the socio-economic imbalances between rural and urban areas may be considered. Practically, the following indicators are adopted:

(a) Economic indicators: (i) per caput income differential, (ii) its intrasectoral distribution and the extent of poverty in the rural and the urban sectors (percentage population below poverty line), (iii) level and nature of employment and employment opportunity, and

(b) Social indicators: (i) literacy, (ii) health (infant mortality rate), (iii) medical, health, education, infrastructure facilities etc.

The per caput income differential (measured by urban income as a percentage of rural income) is within the range of 228 (Nepal) and 126 (India). The percentage of people below the poverty line varies between the rural and urban areas. In Bangladesh, the incidence of poverty is considerably higher in the rural areas than in the urban areas. In addition, the degree of poverty has increased in both rural and urban areas in some countries.

In many developing countries, the majority of the labour force is engaged in agriculture. In the rural area the predominant occupation is farming, but some portion of the labour force are landless labourers (partly non-agricultural). In the urban area, the predominant occupations are petty trading, industrial and construction. The average wage per worker in urban areas is higher than in rural areas. There is a considerable amount of disguised unemployment in the rural areas, especially in Bangladesh, India, and Pakistan. Productivity is also relatively low in the

TABLE 1 *Area and national product*

Country	Area (1,000 km²)	GNP per caput			GDP Distribution (%) 1980		
		US$ 1980	Average annual growth (%) 1960–80	Average annual growth (%) 1970–80	Agr.	Ind.	Ser.
1. Low-income economies:							
Bangladesh	144	130	(.)	3.9	54	13	33
Nepal	141	140	0.2	2.5	57	13	30
India	3,288	240	1.4	3.6	37	26	37
Sri Lanka	66	270	2.4	4.1	28	30	42
Pakistan	804	300	2.8	4.7	31	25	44
2. Middle-income economies:							
Indonesia	1,919	430	4	7.6	26	42	32
Thailand	514	670	4.7	7.2	25	29	46
Philippines	300	690	2.8	6.3	23	37	40
Malaysia	330	1,620	4.3	7.8	24	37	39
3. Industrial market economies:							
Japan	372	9,890	7.1	5[a]	4	41	55
United States	9,363	11,360	2.3	3	3	34	63
France	547	11,730	3.9	3.5	4	36	60
Germany, Fed., Rep.	249	13,590	3.3	2.6	2	44	54
United Kingdom	245	7,920	2.2	1.9	2	35	63

Notes: [a] Figures are for 1970–79, not 1970–80.
 .. Not available.
 (.) Less than half the unit shown.
Source: World Development Report 1982, World Bank.

TABLE 2 *Population, distribution and growth rate (urban and rural)*

Country	Population		Percentage of labour force in agriculture 1980	Distribution of total population (%)		Average annual growth rate of urban population (%) 1970–80
	Number mid-1980 (millions)	Average annual growth rate (%) 1970–80		Urban 1980	Rural 1980	
1. Low-income economies:						
Bangladesh	88.5	2.6	74	11	89	6.5
Nepal	14.6	2.5	93	5	95	4.9
India	673.2	2.1	69	22	78	3.3
Sri Lanka	14.7	1.6	54	27	73	3.6
Pakistan	82.2	3.1	57	28	72	4.3
2. Middle-income economies:						
Indonesia	146.6	2.3	58	20	80	4
Thailand	47	2.5	76	14	86	3.4
Philippines	44	2.7	46	36	64	3.6
Malaysia	13.9	2.4	50	29	71	3.3
3. Industrial market economies:						
Japan	116.8	1.1	12	78	22	2.1
United States	227.7	1	2	77	23	1.5
France	53.5	0.5	8	78	22	1.4
Germany, Fed., Rep.	60.9	(.)	4	85	15	0.4
United Kingdom	55.9	0.1	2	91	9	0.3

Note: (.) Less than half the unit shown.
Source: World Development Report 1982, World Bank.

(...income differentials, income differential and poverty *(urban and rural)*)

Country	Year	Percentage share of household income by percentile group of households (%)			Urban income as percentage of rural income		Percentage of the population below poverty line[c]			
		Lowest 20%	Second quintile	Highest 20%	Year	%	Urban Year	Urban %	Rural Year	Rural %
1. Low-income economies:										
Bangladesh	1973/74	6.9	11.3	42.4	1976/77	178.4[a]	1976/77	70	1976/77	81
Nepal	1976/77	4.6	8	59.2	1978	228.3[a]	..	..	1977	37.2
India	1975/76	7	9.2	49.4	1967/68	126.3[a]	1968/69	50	1977/78	43.5
Sri Lanka	1969/70	7.5	11.7	43.4	..	..	..	..	..	..
Pakistan	..	..	..	..	1971/72	153.8[a]	1975	23.3	1975	35.1
2. Middle-income economies:										
Indonesia	1976	6.6	7.8	49.4	..	..	..	..	..	..
Thailand	..	..	..	..	..	..	..	..	..	..
Philippines	1970/71	5.2	9	54	1971	208.2[a]	1971	51.6	1971	76.1
Malaysia	1973	3.5	7.7	56.1	1979	190.1[a]	1976	15.1	1976	42.8
3. Industrial market economies:										
Japan	1969	7.9	13.1	41	1983	175.9[b]				
United States	1972	4.5	10.7	42.8						
France	1975	5.3	11.1	45.8						
Germany, Fed. Rep.	1974	6.9	11	44.8						
United Kingdom	1979	7.3	12.4	39.2						

Notes: .. : Not available.
[a] Household income
[b] Farm income in the rural area compared to non-farm income in the urban area. Concerning comparison of per caput living expense the percentage is 90.1 in 1982.
[c] The definition of poverty line varies from country to country and hence strict comparison cannot be made across countries.

Source: 1. *Rural–Urban Balance Study*, CIRDAP, Bangladesh, 1982, p. 16.
2. *World Development Report 1982*, World Bank.

Original: 1. *Country Papers*, CIRDAP Study Series no. 1 through 7.
Source: 2. *Socio-Economic Indicators of Bangladesh*, Bangladesh Bureau of Statistics, September 1981.

rural areas and despite various public works programmes in the rural areas, especially in Bangladesh, Pakistan and India, the conditions of landless agricultural workers have deteriorated. This is because the high growth rate of population and increasing number of small farmers have created less favourable conditions for the rural labour force. There are no opportunities for new employment and under- and unemployment are common features of the local economy.

TABLE 4   *Literacy rate (urban and rural)*

Country	Literacy rate (%) Age of 15 and over (Year)	Percentage of literate population (%)		
		Year	Urban	Rural
Bangladesh	25.8 (1974)	1974	37.7	18.5
Nepal	19.8 (1975)	1974/75	14.2[b]	5.1[c]
India	36.2 (1981)	1971	59.7	27
Pakistan	20.7 (1972)	1972	41.5	14.3
Philippines	82.6 (1970)	1970	86.6	71.5
Malaysia	58.5[a] (1970)	1980	69	56

Notes: [a] Figure is for West Malaysia, not including Sabah and Sarawak.
        [b] The literacy rate of the Central region.
        [c] The literacy rate of the Far Western region.
Source: 1. *Country papers*, CIRDAP Study Series no. 1 through 6.
         2. Shrestha, B. P. and Jain, S. C., *Regional Development in Nepal*, 1978.
         3. *World Development Report 1982*, World Bank.

Literacy rates may be used as an indicator to illustrate substantial rural-urban differentials. In general, literacy rates of the rural population are way below that of the urban areas. In Pakistan the urban literacy rate was 42 per cent compared to only 14 per cent in the rural areas in 1972 (see Table 4). The distribution of educational facilities also shows a marked imbalance. The rural educational institutions lack facilities compared to their urban counterparts, and the quality of both teachers and teaching is poor in the rural areas. There is also a higher drop-out rate in rural educational institutions. In India, however, the rural sector has a favourable ratio of primary schools. In 1976/77, the number of primary schools per ten thousand population was 8.4 in the rural areas and only 3.2 in the urban areas.

The differentials between the rural and the urban areas in terms of medical facilities, sanitation, health are also noteworthy. In Bangladesh, at present there is approximately one doctor per 65,000 rural population compared to one doctor for 900 urban population. Similarly, there is one bed for 28,000 rural people and only 600 urban people. The quality of service in the urban areas is also much better than in the rural areas. In terms of infrastructural facilities, consumption of energy and consumer goods, basic-need items, potable drinking water, etc., one can also observe substantial differences in favour of the urban areas.

IDENTIFICATION OF THE CAUSES OF IMBALANCE

The rural-urban imbalance may be classified into two categories, relating to economic imbalances and social imbalances.

The general causes of the economic imbalance seem to be (a) resource endowment, (b) growth-biased development policies, (c) ineffective implementation of the development plans and programmes, (d) lack of proper and adequate institutions to plan and execute development policies and programmes of the governments, and (e) lack of political stability.

Most of the countries are characterised by severe resource constraints. This is due to the fact that a large portion of the natural and human resources remain untapped and underutilised. Insufficient land use planning by the government is mainly responsible for this. Moreover, the distribution of land which is the most productive asset for the great majority of population and other productive assets are disproportionately allocated. This has caused an increase in the number of landless workers in the rural areas through time, accentuating the process of migration to urban areas. The migration flows which drift into the informal urban area have ensured that very low levels of income have been maintained. It has continued to add to the number of the urban poor, with its consequent effects on the productive and social service sectors.

In the past, countries have tended to adopt growth-biased development strategies but there has been little consideration of the social consequences of distribution. The financial allocation made in the various plans for rural development has not increased through time. Indeed, in some countries it has even declined. Even in the case of rural development, various government policies such as irrigation, credit etc. have favoured the large farmers. The benefits accruing from the various development plans of the government have not been equitably distributed. These have made the rich richer and the poor poorer.

In the event of the failure to mobilise enough resources (locally and through external resources), the rural sector of the economy has to bear the main burden in resource use for development purposes. There is a lack of proper and adequate institutions both at the national, regional and village level needed to carry out the various development policies and programmes. Planning has been carried out from top to bottom by officers who may not be very interested in or are unaware of the development needs in the rural sector. Although some institutions at the lower levels, such as local government and co-operatives exist, these are under the control of rural élites and, therefore, are unable to work in the interest of the rural people. It is also observed that local officials are not always sufficiently motivated. Most of these Asian countries have established village governments or committees in the recent past, but many of these bodies are controlled by the richer peasantry and do not serve the needs of the common villagers.

It is crucial to have political stability to ensure the success of prevailing policies and programmes. However, most countries are characterised by an absence of political stability which is the *sine qua non* for rural development.

The social imbalances between the rural and urban areas have been reduced in various fields. In the case of the Philippines, Nepal and Pakistan, the declining trend of differentials (between the rural and urban areas) in health and education appears to be due to the increased spread of facilities in the rural areas as compared to the urban areas. Existing rural-urban differentials in education are due to several factors: (a) better motivation and the needs for literacy in urban areas, (b) absence of active literacy programmes in rural areas, (c) poor quality of teachers, teaching materials etc., and (d) high rates of drop-out (caused by the need to supplement family income).

In the case of health, the factors responsible for the widening rural-urban differentials in India and Bangladesh seem to be the result of: (a) limited facilities of the primary health centres and absence of proper transportation facilities for access to the centre, (b) absence of facilities for the supply of safe potable water, and (c) lack of proper pre-natal and post-natal care.

It is argued that urbanisation and the rural-urban imbalance is a necessary adjunct in the process of development. In many developing countries which had a colonial past, urban centres have gradually developed their predominantly agrarian economies in response to the efforts of the colonial rulers to integrate the export sector of these economies with the needs of industrial development in the ruling countries. In order to facilitate centralised administration and transportation of exportable surpluses, small towns and other facilities were created. Unfortunately, however, the rest of the economy was left behind without much effort being devoted towards its development. After the independence of these countries urbanisation has accelerated along with industrialisation policies and urban facilities such as industries, commerce and business have developed. Nevertheless, it is true that the concentration of economic activities at urban centres has been established by economic and social motivations.

BIASED POLICY IN DEVELOPMENT PLANNING

It is undeniable that a certain urban bias does exist in the formulation of policy and development planning in the developing countries and that such a bias has been maintained through various direct and indirect policy measures which favour the urban sector. The urban bias in development planning is revealed in the allocation of development expenditure between the urban and the rural sector. Experience of development planning shows that agriculture receives only a small share of development expenditure. In Bangladesh, successive Five Year Plan documents allocated about 35–42 per cent of total development expenditure to the rural areas (defined to include expenditure on agriculture and parts of expenditure on the other sectors which have some impact on rural areas). However, in terms of actual expenditure, the agricultural (rural) sector received about 35 per cent of total development expenditure in 1972 and it gradually declined to about 27.5 per cent in 1978.[2]

While the government can control and guide public sector investment, their control on private sector investment is not very effective. The private sector largely invests in industry, commerce, business and the transportation sector in urban areas. The various indirect policies which favour the urban (industrial) sectors and the urban population more than the rural (agricultural) sector and the rural population include these: (1) pricing policy and intersectoral terms of trade; (2) intersectoral resource flows; (3) food rationing and various subsidy programmes; and (4) government credit and loan policies.

In most developing countries, the intersectoral terms of trade remain against the rural (agricultural) sector. Although, in some cases they show some improvement, the benefits of this improvement usually accrue to those limited farmers having strong links with the urban centres. Improvement in the agricultural terms of trade is usually the exception rather than the rule, and the terms of trade, price and banking policies cause a net outflow of resources from the rural to the urban sectors. Indirect policies like food rationing and credit distribution require subsidies, and the benefits of such programmes are usually enjoyed by urban residents.

The institutions established for local level planning and development through local resource mobilisation become rather ineffective in the developing countries mainly because of (1) favourable grants to the urban municipalities; and (2) the controlling power of the rural élites. Thus, through time the local bodies fail to reduce the rural-urban disparity.

CONSEQUENCES OF THE RURAL-URBAN IMBALANCE

The existence of excessive rural-urban imbalances may result in various undesirable social, political and economic consequences. Poverty and deprivation in the rural areas, lack of education and technical skills and the paucity of other services gradually prevent the potential of the rural sector to increase its productivity and employment. The continuous exodus of the rural destitute to urban areas causes a severe strain on urban life and living conditions. The slow growth and even decline of the marketable surplus necessary to sustain an increment in the urban labour force and the growth of the industrial sector may ultimately be a severe constraint on the overall growth rate of the economy through various adverse linkage effects. The urban sector may expand at a rapid rate in the initial stages of development, but it may face increasing problems to sustain the growth rate through time. In most developing countries, the urban (industrial) sector becomes dependent on foreign aid and imported technology. But this does not always contribute the vital economic linkages necessary for harmonious and complementary rural-urban growth.

One of the socio-economic implications of the persistence of excessive rural-urban differentials is the exodus of people from the rural to the urban area in response to various pull and push factors. Recently, it has been argued that three predominant migration flows exist: rural to urban, rural to rural, and urban to metropolitan areas. In the Philippines rural to rural migration is the most prominent stream, but rural to urban flows, especially to Manila and its suburbs are becoming bigger. The rural-urban differential is undoubtedly one of the main causes of migration but the composition and characteristics of migrants depend on whether push or pull factors operate. If the urban pulling factor is the major determinant of migration, then it is the more enterprising, skilled, and educated persons who migrate to the urban areas. In this case, the rural-urban differentials tend to be aggravated with time. If the push factors operate due to poverty in the rural areas, then it is usually the rural destitute who are forced to leave the countryside. They are absorbed into the informal urban sector leading to an increase in urban poverty, squalor and slums. In reality, such migration only tends to accentuate rural-urban differentials. Even if the push factor becomes the predominant force in causing rural-urban migration, the pull factor arising out of the existing imbalance continues to operate.

Two points can be noted about the slowing down of rural-urban migration in recent years in some countries.

(a) The lower rate of migration may be due to the high differential between the rural and urban sectors. The technological advances in the urban centres make it difficult for new entrants in urban areas to find employment. Besides, the severe strain on urban facilities pushes the new entrants to live in urban slums. Some may get absorbed in informal sectors, but such migration does not promise immediate employment, income nor minimum living standards.

(b) Various development policies, especially new settlement schemes may have diverted the rural-urban migrants to become rural-rural migrants, for example, in Malaysia, the Philippines and Indonesia. Settlement schemes like those in these countries promise to be an effective policy in the short run to weaken the rural-urban migration movement. In the case of countries where land scarcity still remains a problem, like Bangladesh where there is hardly any scope for new settlement, the obvious answer would be to reduce both the push and pull factors through improving the conditions of the rural people in the rural areas themselves.

EFFORTS TOWARDS REDUCING THE RURAL-URBAN IMBALANCE

Planners and policy-makers are usually aware of the existence of rural-urban imbalances, and their awareness is often reflected in planning, such as Five Year Plans. However, there is a gap between intention and concrete policy actions. Various policies and programmes which are relevant to the rural-urban imbalance can be grouped into four categories: (a) policies on urbanisation or de-urbanisation, (b) regional development policies with special emphasis on the development of less developed areas, (c) local level planning, and (d) rural development policies – both growth and poverty-oriented approaches.

Policies for regulating the growth of urban centres through the development of peripheral areas of towns and cities have been undertaken, but such policies have had only limited success. The policies developed to promote balanced regional development have some relevance for moderating the rural-urban imbalance. This is mainly because it is usually the more developed regions which have the largest concentration of urban centres. In the Philippines and Indonesia, rural settlement schemes were put into action and settlers were encouraged to move in. Despite a number of policies and programmes in all the countries to achieve a better regional and spatial balance in their development, the effectiveness of such policies to attain their objectives and the indirect objective of reducing rural-urban differentials is subject to serious question. The resettlement programme seems to have contributed very little to rectifying disparities between the urban and rural areas. The failure of the resettlement programme may be attributed in part to paternalism and the lack of infrastructure support.

Other policies which may help reduce the rural-urban imbalance include the decentralisation of administration; planning through developing local bodies; and resource mobilisation. These policies have been undertaken in response to the belief that the centralised administration often lessens local initiatives and hence the development potential. The proper implementation of locally developed schemes and programmes, which in many countries are at an early stage, may lead to a reduction in the rural-urban disparity, but the effectiveness of the management will depend on the socio-economic and political structures of each country. It will take a long time to improve such imbalances.

In most countries the rural development policies which benefited the rich in the 1950s and 1960s were primarily growth-oriented. Although some of the programmes did have a significant impact on the condition of the rural sector in a specific area, attempts to replicate such programmes on a nation-wide scale have not met with success. Policies and programmes for overall rural development, therefore, continue to be changed, modified and revised. The real constraint, as before, was the inadequate provision of financial resources to deal with such massive and challenging problems. The growth-oriented policies, which included

some welfare-oriented objectives, have led to growth where such policies
have been pursued dynamically but the benefits of such growth have been
confined to particular areas and to a particular section of the population.

In response to the rather modified policies and programmes in the 1960s
in South Asian countries and their rather limited success in terms of
generating growth along with equity, the integrated rural development
approaches were encouraged in the early 1970s. The integrated rural
development approach has been introduced as a multi-faceted programme
which includes a variety of development activities and seeks to provide a
packaged solution to problems covering technology, institutions, poverty
alleviation, and so forth. In this integrated approach to rural development,
various new programmes are being devised and service organisations are
being developed. It is rather difficult to ensure that various rural
development policies are effective in lessening the rural-urban differentials. One of the main reasons is that the policies are being continually
introduced, modified and changed. Some programmes have been
successful in reducing the rural-urban imbalance but they are generally too
expensive to replicate on a nation-wide scale.

RELEVANCE OF JAPANESE EXPERIENCE

The Japanese economy after the Second World War, at its early stages of
development, was like many developing countries in Asia today with a high
density of population, small-scale farming, and so forth. Yet, in a rather
short time span (compared to the Western developed countries), Japan
attained a high level of development in its rural sector which enabled it to
achieve a balance between the rural and urban areas in terms of such
indicators as income, level of living, and consumption of consumer durable
goods. The most significant developments in Japanese agriculture can be
attributed to the impacts of the Land Reform, activities of modern
agricultural co-operatives, establishment of agricultural extension systems, the farm land consolidation programme, introduction of farm
mechanisation and other advanced technologies, farmers' motivation and
efforts, and various subsidy programmes offered by the government. The
prices of many agricultural commodities were stabilised at a high level and
the average income of farmers in comparison to that of urban labourers
increased from 83 per cent in 1965 to 132 per cent in 1983. In terms of
consumption of consumer durable goods like televisions and refrigerators,
the rural areas perform well in comparison with urban areas and sometimes
even surpass them.

Compared with the rapid expansion in the industrial sector, agriculture
was not far behind. The latter was supported by complementary industrial
growth and the two sectors supported each other. During the 1950s and the
early 1960s, the rapid growth in the industrial sector exacerbated the
rural-urban imbalance. However, since 1972 this position has been
transformed by the farmers taking advantage of increasing non-farm
sources of income and by taking non-farm job opportunities.

The imbalance between the rural and urban sectors could be partially solved by the rural population taking non-farm job opportunities in the nearby urban areas and by accepting the extraordinarily high selling price of farm lands induced by the rapid urbanisation. Japanese agriculture still has difficult problems of overproduction and inefficiencies in resource uses. Many farm products, at present, have lost their competitiveness with foreign farm products.

The crucial points in the Japanese experience are as follows:
The complementarity and mutually supporting growth of both the rural and urban sectors were essential. Indigenous techniques were developed, refined and used to raise agricultural production. In this context the industrial sector provided valuable support in terms of necessary equipment, technology and know-how. Further, the backward linkages of industrial growth resulted in an increase in non-farm sources of income to farmers.

CONCLUSIONS

In order to examine the nature and degree of imbalance between the rural and the urban sectors among the developing Asian countries, reference was made to Japan's rural development which attained fairly balanced performances. Within a quarter of a century Japan had realised a high level of development in its rural sector which enabled it to achieve a balance between the rural and urban areas. The problems of imbalance there between the rural and the urban sectors arose from the dynamics of growth rather than stagnation. Both sectors grew rapidly and the process of adjustment was reached by the farmers' efforts and sympathetic government policies. The imbalance could also be partially solved by the rural population taking non-farm job opportunities. Meanwhile, farm income could not increase similarly with the income for non-farm jobs, although productivity in farming had certainly progressed, and there has been little success in controlling land prices and preventing the contamination and deterioration of human environments. This paper signifies that in order to overcome these drawbacks it is crucial to have a comprehensive area development policy aimed at achieving an integrated and effective use of space for both the rural and the urban sectors.

NOTES

[1] The contents of this paper are based on the results of the Workshop on The Rural-Urban Balance which was held by The Centre on Integrated Rural Development for Asia and the Pacific. I designed this research project, presented an overview paper, presided over the workshop, and compiled the final report. Although this paper is based on the results of the workshop I have revised the approach and materials for this paper. I have also added my own personal views and extended the discussions to include other regions. I owe special thanks to Dr Atqur Rahman, Programme Officer of the Research, CIRDAP, for editing the original workshop report.

[2] *Rural-Urban Balance Study*, CIRDAP, Bangladesh, 1982, p. 24 and notes.

Hiroyuki Nishimura

DISCUSSION OPENING I – EARL. R. SWANSON

These two papers deal with the important problem of the welfare of people in rural societies. Mr Hunek provides a useful classification of the sources of uncertainty for farmers in terms of three markets –economic, ideological and policy. He correctly points out that agricultural economists are apt to neglect the ideology and policy markets in their analysis of agricultural development. His ranking of the relative importance of these three markets as a source of uncertainty (first, policy, second, ideology and third, economic) does not appear to me to be universally applicable. It would seem that in countries where (1) the prevailing ideology has been fairly stable over long periods, (2) government intervention in the agricultural sector is minimal or moderate and (3) the economy is reasonably open to international trade, the economic market might well rank first as a source of uncertainty for farmer decisions. Further, in the absence of price and other controls, at least a portion of the neutral (biological) uncertainty, which Mr Hunek dismisses as a minor contributor, would be reflected in the economic market. Thus, although Mr Hunek's classification provides an important perspective, the relative importance of the sources of uncertainty may vary from country to country.

Mr Hunek introduces an interesting 'turning points' doctrine for agricultural development. Among other things, he indicates that one of the consequences of the introduction of technology which substitutes for land is the emergence of a land market. It seems to me that the land market (or some other institution) is a prerequisite, rather than a consequence for making the necessary calculations (under either a centralised or decentralised system of decision-making) regarding the adoption of technology which substitutes for land.

What is the primary method by which farmers react to uncertainty? Mr Hunek points out that this takes the form of group activity in the policy market. Although outside the scope of Mr Hunek's paper, an analysis of how the various interest groups (farmers' unions, agricultural lobbies, etc.) interact in the policy market would have been of substantial interest. There are several hypotheses about which of several groups' interests will prevail in the political market. As a logical extension of Mr Hunek's view of this process as a market, one might assume that the formation and support of the various organisations depends on expected benefits and costs for the individual members. For the reallocation of a fixed amount of benefits, one would expect benefits per caput to decline with group size and also that the total cost of organising and articulating group interests would increase faster than group size because one can gain without joining the group (the free rider problem). Thus one hypothesis which needs empirical testing is that small groups will be more effectively organised than large groups. In any event this might be considered as a topic for the Twentieth International Conference of Agricultural Economists.

Mr Hunek, in good pedagogical style, concludes his paper with eight yes-no questions. My responses are 'no' to Questions 1, 2, and 5 and 'yes' to questions 3, 4, 6, 7 and 8.

Mr Nishimura's paper shifts our attention to the equity question in the form of the nature, extent, and causes of rural poverty. He asserts that it is necessary to meet the basic needs of the disadvantaged with certainty. Clearly such a goal has its base in the ideological and policy markets referred to by Mr Hunek.

Mr Nishimura has provided an excellent summary of both the economic and social indicators of rural-urban differentials. It is of interest to note that Japan has now reversed the usual rural-urban income differential and has exceeded the parity goal in that rural incomes now exceed urban incomes (Table 3).

Mr Nishimura cites severe resource constraints as one of the primary causes of economic imbalance. I am puzzled by the apparent inconsistency of listing natural and human resource constraints as a cause of imbalance and at the same time noting that a large portion of these resources remain untapped and underutilised. This apparent anomaly implies that there is a more fundamental cause of the rural-urban imbalance than the physical supply of resources. I suggest that a major part of the cause lies in the structure of incentives generated by the existing institutions. I hasten to add that Mr Nishimura's list of causes also includes the importance of institutions but in their restricted role of policy formation and programme implementation.

We should especially note that Mr Nishimura appears to be far from optimistic regarding the success of even the more comprehensive or integrated rural development approaches. He indicates that the successful ones are too costly for widespread use.

In a session titled 'People in Rural Societies' I must express a mild disappointment that we have not had papers that disaggregated to the household and sub-household level. This is not a criticism of the two excellent papers that we have heard. The authors have been faithful to the titles of their individual papers. An example of what I expected is in the book by Ronald P. Dore, *Shinohata: A Portrait of a Japanese Village* (Pantheon Books, New York, 1978). Shinohata is a village with a fictitious name that Dore visited over a period of 20 years. It has 49 households and is located about 100 miles from Tokyo. Dore's description based on detailed interviews illustrates at a micro-level the transformation in rural Japan that Mr Nishimura has presented in macro terms.

DISCUSSION OPENING II – E. SEVILLA GUZMAN

The two papers on which I am commenting to set up a framework for discussion in this session differ strongly. In spite of this they both have in common something which I wish to emphasise since I regard it as a very positive point, not only for this session, but in general for this

International Conference, namely the interdisciplinary nature of these presentations. The fact that people like myself and Professor Howard Newby (both strongly labelled as rural sociologists) have been invited to participate in a conference of agricultural economists is something very worthwhile and atypical of this sort of meeting.

Given the differences between the two papers I shall make some comments on them separately, but mainly on that of Professor Tadeusz Hunek.

This is a very attractive work in which an interesting presentation of agriculture in the process of economic development introduces uncertainty as the independent variable. However, although I believe such a presentation is quite valid in general terms, it does not analyse the differential character of uncertainty in terms of the character of the small- or large-scale production of agricultural enterprises. I believe that to put this theme forward for discussion can be of great interest, given that since Kauski and Lenin characterised in their classic and parallel works, the development of agriculture, predicting the disappearance of the small-holding, the theme constitutes an important problem still not yet solved.

Another point which I think is of interest to debate is as follows: Professor Hunek has developed a brief theoretical outline of the impact of uncertainty in the step from traditional to modern agriculture. This has been done by considering the global tendencies of change both in a free market economy and a planned economy. I think it would be very positive to lower his level of abstraction to bring out the differences themselves produced during the processes of change in one or the other type of economic system.

The last point I wish to comment on in this paper is about the interesting differentiation he establishes between economic, ideological and political markets as being three aspects which introduce uncertainty for farmers in rural societies. I think such a concept is a very fertile analytic tool and it would be useful to cross this with a typology of political systems according to the way in which the farmers organise themselves in syndicates and also with the power of negotiation these have in each type of political regime. I will dare put the following question in the context of the current economic crisis in developing countries: if we consider the three dimensions of market which Professor Hunek defines, is the present policy of corporate pacts between syndicates of owners and workers and government administration really a solution for the present crisis, or would it not be on the contrary a solution exclusively of the market ideology so that the least favoured sectors of the population bear the brunt of the crisis? I will not dare attempt an answer to this question, but I think that the conceptual framework which Professor Hunek puts forward enables us to get into the problem.

The presentation of Professor Nishimura sets out to characterise the rural-urban inequalities in different countries with distinct standards of living in the context of the capitalist world, and proposes programmes of rural development as a means of mitigating these differences.

I will limit myself to making a general comment on his paper. Social theory, from whatever disciplinary focus (economic, sociological, anthropological etc.) has for a long time been questioning the rural-urban concepts as a means of theoretical approximation to explain reality. In spite of this the empirical characterisation of urban-rural differences made here is of great interest. However many radical social scientists maintain that the very nature of capitalism has as part of its internal intrinsic logic the need to generate inequalities – inequalities between national economies, inequalities between regions within a nation and inequalities between social classes. I ask myself if it is possible that rural development can break into this dynamic function without first altering the existing model of world development.

GENERAL DISCUSSION – RAPPORTEUR: D. A. G. GREEN

Topics raised in discussion are grouped into those addressed to (1) Hunek's paper, (2) Nishimura's paper, and (3) general observations on both papers.
1. It was felt that the first paper was very useful in assessing the socio-economic issues of uncertainty in the subdivision between 'realpolitik' and 'apparent' situations since the professed intentions of political leaders frequently differ from real intentions in order to retain a position of power. Funds can be diverted from rural development despite a leader's nominal support.
2. Regarding the second paper it was pointed out that some two to three decades have elapsed in seeking to understand the role of agriculture in economic development which suggests that not all imbalances between the rural and urban sectors are undesirable. Perhaps the analysis could be sharpened by a classification of imbalances into healthy/desirable and unhealthy/undesirable to facilitate structural change in the economy. Second, in the Japanese experience, how crucial and therefore how desirable for replication are: (a) population homogeneity, (b) the post Second World War land reform (c) a strong rural lobby, and (d) modest urban welfare expectations?
   The reduction of rural-urban disparity may not be the most relevant question but rather to focus on the most relevant of the Japanese experience to other countries today. By the mid 1950s, income per caput in Japan already exceeded that of most developing Asian countries. More relevant comparisons would be with Japan's experience in the late nineteenth century to the mid 1930s, when rural-urban disparity was widening, which is similar to developing countries today.
3. The 'rural-urban balance' has various interpretations since this must be a dynamic phenomenon according to the nature and pace of development, i.e. a world perspective. Are there criteria to determine when the relationship is balanced or imbalanced, or when rural-urban migration should either be stopped, or reversed?

The rural-urban balance must be judged according to individual welfare criteria which differ according to rural and urban values. Rural values appear to be determined on the basis of a man v. nature relationship, in contrast to urban values determined by man v. machine. Indeed, with increasing access to individual information, society may well be moving toward a value system determined by individuals v. individual relationships. Is it possible to diversify value generation more favourably for rural people?

In their response to the discussion, Professor Swanson's suggestion that planned economies were ideologically oriented was accepted but a useful debate could well ensue from the proposition that market economies were also ideologically based. Professor Sevilla Guzman's criticism that the approach to uncertainty was essentially small-scale was also accepted although the approach also had application to the large-scale situation, because it was essentially a general approach. The emphasis of the analysis was primarily a general one to be adapted through differentiation. It appeared doubtful that either co-operation or collective organisation were adequate for handling uncertainty; other means of analysis must be sought. The generation of different value systems was important but incorporating this into the analysis was very difficult. Finally, there was a world market perspective but all could not be included in ten pages.

Professor Nishimura replied that Japan's economy, in which current technology was good, was now developing problems. The relatively favourable position for the rural sector resulted from the fact that many farmers could not expand their sizes of farming operation, due to the restriction of land and its ownership structure, and they had to seek the off-farm jobs which were easily accessible to them. The reference to the Japanese experience was only relevant to explain the dynamic adjustment process between rural and urban sectors after the war. The suggestion of looking at the conditions which led to take-off, when the rural and urban sectors were in balance, rather than at the 1960s and 1970s, was helpful. The paper underlined the importance of considering the two sectors together; their separation created much difficulty.

Participants in the discussion included Richard L. Meyer, Yujiro Hayami, Petri Ollila, A. D. Indraratna, and K. M. Azam.

JEAN-MARC BOUSSARD*

Changing Environment and Structural Heterogeneity in Agriculture

Heterogeneity is a striking feature of agriculture. This is obviously true of farm sizes, ranging from the Cuban 'Agrocombinat' (over 100,000 ha and 1,000 workers) to the small plot of the Senegalese woman, growing paddy for her family, of less than 0.5 ha. The technical heterogeneity is not less remarkable. Even without considering the variety of production, from pork and poultry to grain, the same commodity, rice for instance, at the same competitive international price, may be produced almost without capital in Africa or almost without labour in Texas.

Now, if there exists something like an optimal firm size, competition should select it as the only feasible one. If there exist different input/output ratios, one of them should imply a lower cost than the others, and should emerge as the only feasible technique after the competitive adjustment of prices to costs. Since this kind of equalising process does not occur, something must be very peculiar in the agricultural production function.

It is the purpose of this paper to seek plausible reasons for this situation, and consider their practical consequences from a policy point of view. First, the absence of optimal size and the existence of an optimal structure will be demonstrated in a static framework. Then, the dynamic implication of this situation will be examined. Finally, consequences on structural policies will be drawn.

FARM SIZES AND STRUCTURES IN STATIC

The absence of optimal farm size
In the classroom, the size of a production unit is unambiguously defined by the quantity of the unique output. A great advantage of this definition is that the size is then completely independent of prices. The optimal size is more difficult to assess, because it depends upon the criterion chosen for optimality. In that respect, economists are accustomed to minimise

*I am greatly indebted to Denis Bergmann for helpful comments on a previous version of this paper. He does not share my views, however.

unit costs, not so much on the ground of some metaphysical creed in the virtue of cheap production, but simply because competition will automatically select the associated techniques in a liberal organisation of the society, whatever the goals of individual producers.

Even so, with several inputs, the optimal size will in general remain price dependent, because the unit cost is the sum of input quantities weighted by their prices. However, in this context, the optimal size is not always defined. Let us consider a production function, $q = f(y)$, where q is the quantity of output, and y is a column vector of input quantities. If $f(y)$ is homogenous and of degree 1, i.e., $f(\lambda y) = \lambda f(y)$, whatever the real valued scalar, λ, then it is easy to show that there is no value of q minimising the unit cost xy/q, where x is any row vector of input prices. Thus, in this case, any size of firm is feasible in a competitive economy, whatever the price system.

In the more realistic case of a multiproduct firm the above properties remain; it is impossible to define the size of a farm out of price considerations, because the size is then a weighted sum of outputs or of inputs. Two farms can eventually be ranked differently by two different systems of weights. But if the production function (now expressed as $f(q,y) = 0$, where q is a vector of output and y of input quantities) is homogenous and of degree 1, then it is impossible to find any vector q minimising xy/pq, whatever the price vector (p, x).

The considerations outlined above are restricted because the absence of optimal size depends upon one special criterion of optimality, and also, upon the idea that actual production functions can be linearly homogeneous. But at the same time, they are fairly general, because the criterion in question imposes itself very naturally as the only feasible one in a competitive situation, and which is more, because the degree of homogeneity is an intrinsic property of the production function absolutely independent of prices. For these reasons, in a competitive economy, unless the production functions are homogeneous and of degree 1, all firms disappear, except those which, by chance or skill, can stay in the vicinity of the optimal size. For instance, in car manufacturing industries, economies of scale quickly pushed out individual producers, without leaving them any chance of recovery. Clearly, the situation is quite different in the case of agriculture. Even artificial regulations, such as preventing small farms having access to government subsidies, do not discourage small and part-time farming.

The fact that several farm sizes can coexist for a long time within a common economic environment is an indirect proof of the linear homogeneity of the production function in agriculture. The direct proof is more difficult to bring about, because it needs a particular analytical specification of the production function. The pitfalls[1] of this kind of exercise are numerous. The most serious studies show that increasing returns to scale and indivisibilities are not, strictly speaking, absent, but they are counterbalanced by decreasing returns in other fields, and statistically negligible. We shall refer to other authors (for instance,

Boussard 1976) for details, and turn here our attention towards the consequences of this situation.

Without economies of scale, there are no incentives to the homogenisation of farm sizes. Thus, the heterogeneity of farm sizes derive straightforwardly from the specificity of the agricultural production function. What about farm structures?

THE EXISTENCE OF OPTIMAL STRUCTURES

If there exist no optimal farm sizes, there exist optimal farm structures. However, for this statement to be valid, it is necessary to define precisely the term 'structure', the meaning of which is really too vague in ordinary language. Let us call structure the ratio between the various quantities of fixed factors: If $z = \{z_1 \ldots z_k \ldots z_K\}$ is the vector of the K available quantities of fixed factors, the structure is a vector s of dimension $K - 1$, the current element of which is z_k/z_K, the Kth factor being conventionally taken as reference. Thus, land (or a certain quality of land) being the reference factor, the elements of the structure are the number of fixed permanent workers of such or such qualification per ha of that type of land. If it is possible to define structure in that way, then the existence of optimal structures is a direct consequence of the elementary theory of production.

Consider a farmer maximising his income, $F = pq - xy$, under a production function constraint : $f(q, y, z) \leq 0$, where the column vector z with K elements denotes the quantities of fixed factors, and f is a function increasing with each element of q, and decreasing with each elements of y and z. f is homogeneous of degree one, and the constraint is convex. Then, there is no optimal value for z : by the convexity of f if any triplet (q, y, z) is feasible, the triplet $(\theta q, \theta y, \theta z)$, where θ is any positive scalar, is also feasible, so that F is unbounded for infinite values of θ.

But if one element of z, say z_K, is fixed, at the level z_K^*, F is actually bounded. Since the feasible set is convex, this means that there exists a finite unique maximum for F with respect to q, y, and the $K - 1$ other elements of k. Let us denote the solution by $\hat{q}$, $\hat{y}$, $\hat{z}$. The vector $\hat{s}$, with $K - 1$ elements, given by $\hat{s}_k = \hat{z}_k/z_K$ is called the optimal structure.

An optimal structure is linked with optimal production plans; in effect, the examination of the solutions of the maximizing problem above shows that all farms for which $k = \lambda(\hat{s}, 1)$ will produce the same outputs, and need the same inputs in the same proportions, because they are making use of the same techniques. They will be homothetic. At the same time, it is obvious that, in reality, agricultural firms are seldom homothetic. It is therefore necessary to explain why, despite the existence of optimal structures, farms are still technically heterogeneous.

This is a consequence of a second peculiarity of optimal structures, their dependence on prices. Actually, the solution of the maximisation problem stated above depends upon the price system, so that $\hat{s}$ is price-dependent. This is the reason why one speaks of several optimal structures. Each variation of the prices of outputs or of variable inputs will imply a corresponding change in the optimal structure.

Again, there is a strong difference between structures and sizes : the absence of optimal size was a consequence of the specification of the production function f, which, it must be recalled, is perfectly free of any price consideration. On the contrary, $\hat{s}$ cannot be defined before the price system is known. Therefore, it is not surprising that two firms, in two different price contexts, for instance, in Senegal and in Texas, have two different structures. However, observation shows that even firms placed within the same price environment may differ in structure. How can this happen? For answering this question, dynamic considerations must enter the analysis.

THE DYNAMIC HETEROGENEITY OF AGRICULTURE

When considering a dynamic version of the static model which has been sketched above, it is necessary to distinguish between the situation of the individual producer and the behaviour of the industry as a whole.

The individual producer in dynamics and the turnpike theorem
The basic phenomenon here is that structures, which were fixed in the short term, are now variable, at least to a certain extent, because fixed factors can be produced or purchased. The idea of buying a certain quantity of fixed factor may seem self-contradictory. The contradiction vanishes if one recalls that a factor is not fixed once and for all. It is fixed when its marginal value product falls between its acquisition price and its salvage value (Johnson 1959). When saving is abundant, its opportunity cost becomes lower, so that it may be profitable to buy new units of previously fixed inputs. In that way, it is possible to modify the vector z, and to consider it as endogenous.

Obviously, such modifications of z are not random, but directed toward the necessity of narrowing the gap between the actual and the optimal structure. Since the available resources in saving or in own produced capital items are limited, it will not always be possible to reach at once the optimal structure. Nevertheless, after a few years, repeated increments of the quantities of the most productive factors should enable any producer to stay on the optimal expansion path defined by the optimal structure. This is the basic meaning of the famous 'turnpike theorem'.

It is beyond the scope of this paper precisely to state it (or rather them, because there is a variety of different formulations).[2] Let us only say that, under fairly general conditions, the individual producer, if his planning horizon is long enough, will be dynamically led to an optimal structure which is independent of his own utility function U, and is determined by the production function alone.

The fact that the optimal structure is independent of U is important for our discussion, because, whatever the tastes of a farmer, provided that he is interested in something which is an increasing function of output, he should come to the optimal structure. Such a result contradicts the arguments of Tchajanov and others, who relate the heterogeneity of farms with differences in objective functions. By contrast, the optimal structure is not independent of prices, because the production function f incorporates now the possibility of purchasing inputs by selling outputs. There is therefore a deep difference between the static production function, which could be considered as purely technical, and the dynamic production function. In addition, the prices in question are not observed, but expected: thus, two farms in the same situation may have two different optimal structures only because the first farmer is pessimistic, and the second optimistic. Now, variations in prices are frequent, for inputs as well as for outputs, and are not purely random, but market driven. The consequences of this fact must be drawn.

The interactions between optimal structures and markets
Thus, reaching the 'turnpike' for a given system of prices, means producing a certain set of commodities, and requiring a certain set of inputs, all in the same proportions. Nothing guarantees that the market is ready to absorb these commodities and provide these inputs. For instance, the optimal structure may require that 50 per cent of the cash receipt of farms be made from grains, and, at the same time, consumers are ready to spend only 25 per cent of their food budget on this kind of commodity. In such a situation, if the market is re-equilibriated by a change in prices, this will also, in general, change the optimal structure, so that the situation after adjustment can be no better than before. Even more, since the reaction of farm production systems may take several years, there is a possibility that the reaction of the market be far larger than that which should in principle be necessary to reach an equilibrium: for instance, the price of one specific commodity can fall far under the level for which the optimal structure meets consumers' wants. In that case, firms will be misled, because they will have to direct their adjustments towards a structure which cannot warrant market equilibrium.

An additional complication arises because farmers are not immortal; at each generation, newcomers have to buy again all existing assets to continue to produce. Since they start from scratch, they are free to choose the current optimal structure at prevailing prices. But since these prices are bound to change, the structure of the newly acquired farms quickly become out of the optimal expansion path. This element of perturbation is essential, as we shall see now, to understand if not how heterogeneity perpetuates itself, at least how it can be generated from an initially homogeneous farm population.

It would be difficult, in this paper, to develop a formal model embodying the preceding considerations. Rather, let us examine the results of a simplified, computable version of such a model. Assume a sample of N farms and a Cobb Douglas production function, with two inputs, K and L, in quantities k_i and l_i for farm i. q_{it} being the quantity of the one output produced by farm i, at time t, $q_{it} = k_{it}^{\alpha} l_{it}^{1-\alpha}$. K is a variable, non-durable factor, supplied at fixed price p. L is a durable factor, which can be purchased or sold in quantity i_{it} ($i_{it} > 0$ if L is purchased, and $i_{it} < 0$ if it is sold). The price of L is p_{lt} if L is purchased, and $\theta\, p_{lt}$ if it is sold : thus, θ is an index of the fixity of L, with this factor perfectly liquid if $\theta = 1$, and perfectly fixed if $\theta = 0$. p_1 is determined in such a way that : $\Sigma_i i_{it} = 0$. The output is sold at price p subject to a demand curve specified by : $p_{qt} = a(\Sigma_i q_{it})\,\beta$ where $\beta < 0$ is the elasticity of output demand with respect to price, and $a > 0$, a scale factor.

Farmers' incomes are given by : $m_{it} = p_{qt}\, q_{it} - p_k k_{it}$.

A fraction c of this income is consumed, so that at the beginning of each year, a farmer is endowed with a quantity of money, $e_{it} = p_{qt-1} q_{it-1} - c\, m_{it}$ and a quantity of L given by : $l_{it} = l_{it-1} + i_{it}$ k_{it} and i_{it} are subject to a liquidity constraint :

$$P_k\, k_{it} + P_1\, i_{it} = e_{it}, \text{ if } i_{it} > 0, \text{ or}$$
$$P_k k_{it} + \theta p_1\, i_{it} = e_{it}, \text{ if } i_{it} < 0.$$

Finally, each year, a number n of farmers are removed from the sample. Their assets are sold (which increases the supply for L) to the same number of newcomers, each of them being endowed with an exogenous fixed quantity of money e^*. Thus, the total quantity of L is fixed, but its distribution among farms can vary. The set of equations just presented, and the assumption according to which the income m_{it} is maximised, determine each year the set of endogenous variables (q_{it}, k_{it}, l_{it}, p_{qt}, and p_{lt}) from the situation of the preceeding year, and the parameters α, β, θ, N, n and e^*.

In fact, these equations represent a dynamic general equilibrium model, endowed with a Walrassian 'tatonement' process. Thus, the successive solutions should converge toward a steady state from any feasible starting point. The steady state itself can be readily computed, by the two conditions that the total quantity of money flowing out the system through consumption should equate the quantity of money flowing into it, through the e^*s, and that all farms should have the same optimal ratio $k/1$. Actually they do so, but the convergence is not necessarily quick : it is well known that the Walrassian tatonement is a poor algorithm for the search of general equilibrium solutions.[3] In the meanwhile, the sample remains heterogeneous if it was so at the origin, and, even more, becomes heterogeneous if it was not, as shown on Figures 1a to 1f.

The corresponding results were obtained with $N = 50$, $n = 2$, $\alpha = \theta = C = 0.5$, $\beta = -0.5$, $e^* = 100$, and all farms identical in period 0, with $l_i = 50$, and $k_i = 5$, but similar results were derived from other values of these parameters. Heterogeneity within the sample is measured at each time by the coefficients of variation of the relevant variables, y_{it}/l_{it} for techniques (this variable is an index of 'intensity'), and y_{it} for sizes. It

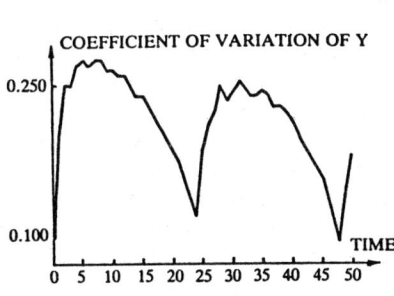

Figure 1a Coefficient of variation of farm output.

Figure 1b Coefficient of variation of the ratio output/land.

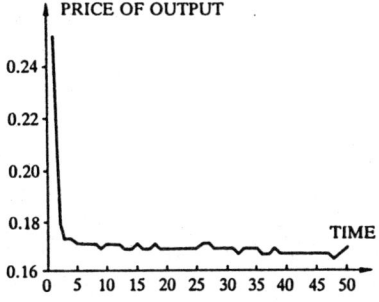

Figure 1c Price of output.

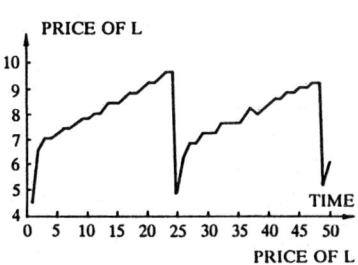

Figure 1d Price of fixed input.

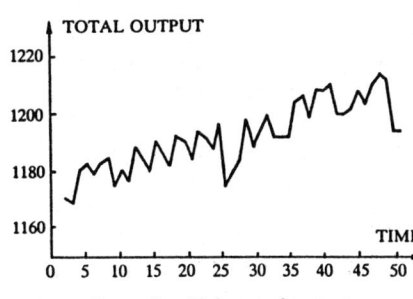

Figure 1e Volume of output.

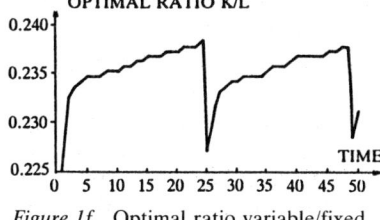

Figure 1f Optimal ratio variable/fixed input.

FIGURE 1 *Results of the simulation of a sample of 50 farms over 50 years*

is significant for both variables, (Figures 1a and 1b), although greater for sizes than for techniques. This is not surprising, for at equilibrium, techniques should be homogeneous, but not necessarily sizes. Anyway, equilibrium, in that case, is very far reached, and, because of that, hetereogeneity introduces itself into the sample, despite the absence of any random event but the starting point, and despite the fact that this starting point is itself completely homogeneous.

This process of heterogenisation is driven by oscillations of prices and quantities, as pictured on Figures 1c to 1e. They swing up and down in a cobweb style, although the origin of the cycle is quite different from what it is in the traditional cobweb model : instead of being produced by errors in expectations, the cycles are triggered by the liquidity constraint, which is tightened when prices are low, and loosened when they are high. For that reason, cycles are less regular than those of the cobweb, and eventually, their periods are longer.[4]

Whatever their sources, these cycles introduce, even at period 1, an element of difference between the newcomers and the other farms, because the former can invest in the optimal proportions, whereas the latter cannot, as they are tied by the liquidity constraint and the difficulty of selling their fixed inputs. But since the optimal proportions vary with prices (Figure 1f), each new farm is different from the others. Thus, once the process of differentiation is triggered, it cannot end before the equilibrium is reached, very far away from the fortuitous initial disequilibrium.

In a real-life situation, the behaviour of the system would be complicated by three additional considerations:

(i) The existence of technological change : since the equilibrium is far reached, technology can vary exogenously during the adjustment process, with the consequence that the convergence can be delayed indefinitely.

(ii) The existence of several outputs, and of more than two inputs : it is dubious that their introduction could change significantly the behaviour of the system, but it can considerably complicate the time path of the variables, thus increasing the degree of heterogeneity.

(iii) The existence of a risk averse behaviour of farmers : although it is difficult to assess exactly the consequences of explicitly introducing risk in this matter, I would hypothesise that it would lead to a smoothening of the curves pictured in Figure 1. In fact, risk will lead to more cautious investments and, perhaps, induce farmers to hoard at least a fraction of their liquidities. In that case, they would react less fiercely in response to market incentives. The adjustments would take a longer time. It is likely (but not proved), that this would result in less dramatic accidents than those which are observable with the model without risk. This is a reason for heterogeneity being reduced. At the same time, by widening the wedge between the price at which an asset can surely be bought and that at which it can be sold, uncertainty increases the degree of fixity of any factor; in that way, heterogeneity is increased. Which of these two contradictory tendencies supersedes the other is a matter of discussion, and of further empirical as well as theoretical research.

Anyway, no complete study of the mathematical properties of the model described above has been attempted, as far as I know, although some references could be the point of departure of such an investigation.[5]

A wide, non-conventional field of research is thus open, and will probably be the object of developments in the next few years.

CONCLUSION : POLICY IMPLICATIONS

Thus, farm size heterogeneity is a consequence of the absence of economies of scale. Farm structure heterogeneity is a consequence of the interactions between a dynamic process of adjustment toward optimal price dependent structures, and of market constraints which perturb this adjustment, through pseudo-random historical events. In both cases, it is a consequence of deeply rooted natural mechanisms, which are not easily modified by policy measures. This may be a reason for the failure of 'structural policies' in agriculture.

A first rationale for such policies is that increasing their size would make small farmers in a position to increase their incomes, by benefiting from economies of scale. This is two inconsistencies in one statement. First, the existence of economies of scale is problematic, as we have seen. Second, small farmers' income is not the difference between the value of outputs and that of inputs. With a production function homogeneous and of degree 1, this difference is simply zero. Actually, a farmer's income is the cost of own supplied inputs, evaluated at implicit prices if they are fixed, and at market prices if they are variable. In that context, if additional factors are given to farmers as a gift, it is possible to increase their income by an amount exactly equal to the value of the gift, computed at reference price, after suitable adjustment to convert capital stocks into income flows. This is perfectly tautological. But subsidising them, or giving them credit facilities for acquiring such or such input is not likely to produce any increase of income in excess of the opportunity value of the subsidy. In fact, since opportunity costs for fixed inputs are always less than the market price, the value of the subsidy for the farmer is always less than the nominal cost for the government, so that the latter would make a more efficient use of its money by distributing it without conditions.

A second rationale for structural policies is sounder. Since, because of delay in adjustments, the market is likely to keep a large number of farms very far from the optimal structure, and, even more, from the optimal structure which should balance supply and demand, it may be wise to try to correct this inefficient situation. Thus, the structural adjustment could be speeded up or slowed down in order to avoid forecasted detrimental disequilibria. Actually, this should be the role of the government agencies. Unfortunately, this is not the way they usually operate. There are a number of reasons. Setting up a true contracyclical policy requires reliable long-term forecasts which are not available in the present state of the science. It would also require that governments be free of short-term pressures, which is not true.

Moreover, these policies would be extremely costly. Actually, by Euler's theorem (and contrary to common creed), it costs just as much for a government to buy or sell production factors in excess or in short supply as to buy or sell commodities on unbalanced output markets. In fact, there are reasons for the opinion that these interventions on factors are even more expensive than interventions on output markets; since the demand for a particular factor is relatively elastic (because of substitution), whereas the demand for output is rigid (because of the properties of Engel's curves), it is likely that the total sum of government money required for a given effect is greater on the factor side than on the output side (this is not always true, however, and the statement deserves a number of qualifications, which could be the object of further research). In any case, the cost of structural policies is large. It is the basic reason for the failure of the PIK Program in the US (where excess land was hired by the government in order to be 'frozen' and removed from production), which did not resist the cut in budgetary expenditure of the Reagan administration. Another example is the farm retirement programme in France (IVD), where old farmers are offered a pension in exchange for their commitment to leave, in the avowed purpose of decreasing the man/land ratio ; this programme is still in action, but to keep its cost within reasonable limits, pensions are so meagre that it is dubious if they had any significant influence on actual retirement decisions (Klatzmann 1981). Other similar examples could easily be found.

What remains, then, of the ambitious structural policies which should furnish governments with the possibility of influencing production decisions and income distribution at low cost? I am afraid the answer is almost nothing, except the faculty for a number of local notabilities to claim for their skill in pushing administrative cases through the bureaucratic labyrinth. Actually, all the beneficial effects of structural policies can be achieved by a sound output price policy. This is why, in general, the so called 'structural policies' are extremely efficient in wasting government money. They have at least the advantage of providing safe positions to a large number of civil servants who, otherwise, would have to seek more productive employment – a difficult task in the present situation of the world economy.

NOTES

[1]See, for instance, Zellner et al. (1966).

[2]The best article on the question is probably McKenzie (1976). The first version of the theorem was published by Dorfman, Samuelson and Solow (1958), inspired themselves by Von Neumann. On agricultural applications, see Boussard (1971).

[3]See, for instance Ginsburg and Walbroeck (1981).

[4]This is the kind of result which has been published by Day in a large number of references (for instance, Day 1982, or Day and Tinney 1969). I am greatly indebted toward this author, most of the theoretical ideas exposed in this paper having been drawn from his work.

[5]For instance, Aubin and Cellina (1984).

REFERENCES

Aubin, J. P. and Cellina, A. *Differential Inclusions*, Springer Verlag, Berlin, 1984.

Boussard, J. M. 'Time horizon objective function and uncertainty in a multiperiod of firm growth', *American Journal of Agricultural Economics*, Vol. 53 no. 3 1971, pp. 467–77.

Boussard, J. M., 'The concept of economies of scale in a multiproduct industry, and its implications for the future of agriculture'. *European Review of Agricultural Economics* vol. 3 no. 1, 1976, pp. 53–70.

Day, R. H., *The complex dynamic of farm growth*, mimeo, Paris, 1982.

Day, R. H. and Tinney, E. H., 'Cycle phases and growth in a generalized cobweb theory', *Economic Journal*, Vol. 79 no. 313, 1969, pp. 90–108.

Dorfman, R., Samuelson, P. A. and Solow, R. M. *Linear programming and economic analysis*, McGraw-Hill, New York, 1958.

Ginsburg, V. and Waelbroek, J. L., *Activity analaysis and general equilibrium modelling*, North Holland, Amsterdam, 1981.

Johnson, G. L., 'Agricultural supply functions : some facts and notions', in Heady, E. O. et al. (eds), *Agricultural adjustment problems in a growing economy*, Iowa State University Press, Ames, 1959.

Klatzmann, J., 'Les conséquences économiques de l'indemnité viagère de départ', *Economie Rurale*, Vol. 146, 1981, pp. 30–36.

McKenzie, L., 'Turnpike theory', *Econometrica*, Vol. 44, September 1976, pp. 841–51.

Zellner, A., Kmenta, J. and Dreze, J., 'Specification and estimation of Cobb Douglas production function models', *Econometrica* Vol. 34, October 1966, pp. 784–94.

LUTHER TWEETEN

Agricultural Structure in a Service Economy

INTRODUCTION

Highly developed market economies have been described variously as affluent, technocratic, and urban-industrial (see Ruttan 1969; Tweeten 1979, chs. 1, 2). Such economies may also be characterised by *service* economies because a large portion of jobs are in service industries, such as, trade, finance, insurance, and government (see Table 1). Approximately three out of five jobs in the United States were in service industries in 1982. If service jobs in transportation, communications and public utilities are included, then nearly two out of three jobs were in service industries. Perhaps more important, as many as nine out of ten *new* jobs were in service industries. Non-metropolitan counties (essentially those not having a city of 50,000 or more) did not differ sharply in structure from metropolitan communities; the major difference was relatively lower employment in service industries and higher employment in extractive (agriculture and mining) industries in non-metropolitan counties (Table 1).

As buying power expands, consumers seek self-fulfilment and self-realisation as opposed to simply meeting basic needs for food, shelter and clothing. Income elasticities tend to be high for entertainment, health care, education, eating out, finance and insurance. Thus, normal workings of the price system cause advanced market economies to become service economies. The thesis of this paper is that transformation of nations into post-industrial service economies has pervasive implications for agriculture and rural communities. A number of such implications are explored herein.

SERVICE INDUSTRIES

Service industries and servcie employment are too diverse to be easily classified. On the one hand are low-paying jobs in fast-food chains, jobs often filled by teenagers and secondary family breadwinners. On the other hand are jobs in scientific research, education, medicine, and finance that are well paid and tend to be capital intensive, especially human capital intensive.

TABLE 1 *Structure of employment in metropolitan and non-metropolitan counties in the United States*

Item	United States		Metro		Non-Metro	
	1973	1982	1973	1982	1973	1982
	(per cent)					
Wage and Salary						
Agriculture and mining	2.2	2.6	1.1	1.5	4.7	4.9
Construction	4.9	4.2	4.8	4.1	5.3	4.4
Manufacturing	24.3	19.9	24.2	19.7	24.5	20.1
Transportation, communication, and public utilities	5.4	5.4	5.8	5.7	4.4	4.8
Services: trade, finance, insurance, government	53.6	58.3	57.1	61.4	45.5	51.5
Self-employed and family workers						
Agriculture	2.6	1.9	0.7	0.7	6.9	4.8
Other	7.0	7.7	6.3	6.9	8.7	9.5
TOTAL	100.0	100.0	100.0	100.0	100.0	100.0

Source: US Department of Agriculture, September 1984, p. 38.

Features of service industries include:

Service industries are dynamic. Firms and jobs change so rapidly and many industries are so new and competitive that organised labour has made few inroads.

Service industries are basic as well as non-basic. Traditionally, service industries have been viewed as secondary or tertiary industries existing only to serve basic industries such as agriculture. Modern service industries such as finance, scientific research and development, and government frequently are basic 'export' industries, however, in that they draw revenue from outside the area in which they are located.

Some service industries, frequently basic service industries noted above, are characterised by agglomerative economies. They can reduce costs or increase revenues per unit of output by bunching several firms together to realise economies in finance, communication and skilled labour markets. Thus, many of the more progressive and well paid service industries and workers are in metropolitan areas.

On the whole, service industries are more footloose and less tied to specific locations than are extensive industries such as agriculture, mining, forestry and fisheries.

Compared to other industries, service industries less often entail 'traded goods' competing with imports or for export markets.

Service industries are often characterised by high human resources investment per worker but not necessarily by high material capital resources per worker.

Finally, service industries have made slower gains in productivity than

have other industries, such as, agriculture and transportation, but many
are benefiting from automation of operations through emerging microcomputer and telecommunications technology.

SOME IMPLICATIONS FOR AGRICULTURAL AND RURAL AREAS

The implications for agricultural and rural areas from operating in a
service economy are far-reaching, as noted in the following:

1. By the very nature of the development process, advanced industrial
nations lose their comparative advantage in labour intensive industries
such as textiles to emerging industrial economies. Fairly capital intensive
industries such as steel and autos also may lose their comparative
advantage, especially if organised labour has won outsized wage
settlements. The process of adjusting from an industrial to a service
economy is traumatic to displaced workers and industries. Rural areas
particularly feel the impact in textile and mining industries. Displaced
workers and industries understandably resist change with the tools
available. One such tool is the political system used to erect barriers
against 'cheap' imports. Although agriculture may not be directly
affected by quotas and other barriers imposed on imports, it indirectly
feels the impact in paying higher prices for imports and realising lower
prices for exports because developing countries buy fewer farm products
when they are shut out of US markets.

2. Traditional traded goods industries in service economies survive
high labour costs and intense foreign competition only by increasing
productivity to offset high labour costs. Agriculture is a notable example
of an industry which has survived by unrestrained adoption of the
products of a service economy – science and technology produced by
education and research. The demands are great, however, by large
numbers of farmers to retreat from world competition behind a wall of
high support prices protected by tariffs, import quotas or export
subsidies. Farmers in many advanced industrial nations have won such
protection. Success of American agriculture in following the high price
support-protectionist route would have serious implications not only for
American farmers but for farmers and consumers around the world.
However, the world-wide impact would be quite different depending on
whether the strategy is to (a) use subsidies to export surpluses generated
by higher support prices or (b) abandon the world market to other
exporters of farm products.

3. As noted earlier, the highest-paying service industries tend to locate
in metropolitan areas to achieve agglomerative economies. High-tech-
nology communications partly offset the comparative disadvantage of
rural locations for such industries, but high technology is unlikely to be
decisive. Growing awareness of costs of pollution and congestion and
internalisation of such externality costs brought considerable decentrali-
zation of firms and workers in the 1970s. The demographic transition or

rural turn-around in the 1970s was probably a transitory digression from the longer-term pattern of urbanisation – a trend again manifest in the 1980s with faster rates of population and employment growth in urban than in rural areas.

4. Rural areas have reduced underemployment by attracting manufacturing firms which would be unable to compete with foreign imports at urban wage rates. These manufacturing industries, while a boom to many farmers who survive only by off-farm employment, are part of an overall declining industry and do not constitute the long-term economic future of rural areas. Not that farmers have entirely missed the attractions of service economy employment – the largest single source of off-farm employment is government.

5. Farms have adapted in unique ways to economic forces characterising a service economy. Some of the most notable accommodations include off-farm employment, part-ownership and leasing of assets, incorporation, vertical co-ordination, and greater reliance on debt capital. A problem is that these arrangements frequently compromise the family farm. On family farming units the operator and family ideally provide more than half of the labour, management, and equity capital and derive most of their income from farming. The following data reveal some of the departure from the family farm ideal in US farming (see Tweeten 1984):

Over 90 per cent of all farm families have at least one source of off-farm income and two-thirds of all income of farmers come from off-farm employment.

Part-owner operators accounted for one of eight acres operated in 1900 but for over half of all acres operated in 1978. The gains were accompanied by a decline in the full-renter class of operator–full-tenant operators accounted for only one-tenth of land operated and of all farm operators in 1978.

Larger than family size farms accounted for 6 per cent of all farms but for nearly half of all farm output in 1978. Most of these farms were considered 'larger than family size' because they hired over 1.5 person years of labour rather than because they were non-family corporations. If farms with crop and livestock sales of $20,000 or less are not classified as family farms because most of their income is from non-farm sources, then family farms accounted for only 30 per cent of all farms and 45 per cent of all output in 1978.

The proportion of crop and livestock output produced under vertical co-ordination increased from 20 per cent in 1960 to 30 per cent in 1980. Most of the vertical co-ordination was production contracts (23 per cent of farm output in 1980) rather than vertical integration (7.4 per cent of farm output in 1980), the latter a much more ominous threat to the family farm structure than the former.

Farmers have resorted to more debt financing to control assets required to form an economic farming unit, defined as an operation large enough to realise economies of size and a labour-management return comparable to that in the non-farm sector. Real debt per farm increased 350 per cent between 1960 and 1984! This rate well exceeded the real gain in assets, hence the debt-asset ratio went from 12 per cent in 1960 to 21 per cent in 1984. Although real volume of assets in the US farming industry has remained almost unchanged for two decades, real assets per farm have increased substantially.

6. Many of the above changes are inseparable from the pervasive substitution of capital for labour in agriculture. Because the price of capital was low relative to the price of labour, the proportion of all farm inputs accounted for by labour fell from just over 50 per cent in 1940 to 14 per cent in 1981. The proportion of inputs accounted for by labour was even less on large farms. Risk increases with these greater capital-labour ratios and farmers have made adaptations to cope.

7. These above adaptations by farmers to cope with economic instability and cash-flow problems while catching up in income with their city cousins irreversibly changed the countryside. One notable change has been evolution towards a dual farm economy. The US *commercial sector* is comprised of a comparatively few large farms accounting for the majority of farm output. For example, 5 per cent of all farms account for half of US farm sales. The *non-commercial* sector, increasingly dominated by part-time small farms, accounts for a minor proportion of farm output but for most farm numbers.

Each of these sectors has accommodated to cash-flow and instability problems in its own unique way. The commercial sector thrives by exploiting market and production economies of size, by utilizing diverse sources of debt and equity capital and of earnings, and by sophisticated management and technical assistance. In short, large farms utilise the best products of a service economy to survive and even to prosper. In 1983, farms with sales of $500,000 or more on average earned an 18 per cent return on assets while smaller farms on the average lost money (Melichar November 1984). The small-farm sector thrives despite low returns on resources by extensive use of off-farm employment and income. Although the sector is not very efficient measured by earnings relative to opportunity cost, it provides families with a valued way of life and sizeable tax advantages.

Squeezed between these sectors and at risk is the mid-sized family farm which accounts for a declining share of farm output and numbers. It is often too large and demanding of time to allow the operator to find security in off-farm employment and too small to utilise sophisticated management, marketing, and financial arrangements common among large farms. The mid-size family farm, long the backbone of American agriculture, remains unsurpassed for operational efficiency – getting the crops in on time, overseeing farrowing, and executing cost control. But the value of operational management is increasingly being overshadowed by the value of organisational management apparent in sophisticated investment portfolio management, use of microcomputers or paid consultants to help make marketing and management decisions, and access to diverse debt and equity capital on a corporate basis not subject to family farm life cycle problems. It is too strong to say that the once magnificent species known as the mid-sized family farm is obsolete and soon headed for extinction – generous parents will ensure that the heritage is passed to future generations. However, family farmers will be a continuing source of political agitation because in equilibrium the average mid-size family farm will not earn a return covering opportunity costs of resources. Even in normal economic times, family farms will engage in protest movements and political lobbying efforts to raise earnings. If large, medium and small farms receive the same higher commodity price, receipts will not cover all costs on medium-size and small farms after land prices are bid up. In short, society will have to determine whether to let the family farm fade away under a market-centred policy or preserve the family farm by income transfers targeted to mid-size and smaller farms.

8. If preserving family farms is deemed important, affluent service economies can afford to pursue such policies. The decision whether to follow such policies is ultimately political but the terms of debate can be informed by social and economic analysis. My results (Tweeten 1984, p. 49) indicate that mid-size family farms are much more efficient (measured by opportunity resource cost per dollar of farm output) than small farms but slightly less efficient on the average than larger farms. Mid-size farms practise better soil conservation than small farms but slightly poorer conservation than large farms. Farm operators do not differ significantly in quality of life among farm sizes – given the same income, education and age. Having many small farms as opposed to large farms creates more social activity in nearby communities. 'In strictly economic terms, however the gain to rural communities from a system of small farms is more than offset by higher food and other commodity costs to consumers due to lower economic efficiency on small farms' (Tweeten 1984, p. 50).

Some contend that unbridled operation of markets would lead to concentration of farm economic activity into so few hands that farm and food prices could be raised to arbitrarily high levels. That contention is groundless for the foreseeable future. Valid arguments might be assembled for the public to provide some protection against acute economic distress on farms (such as in the current financial crisis) to avoid a large and disorganised wave of family farm failure and out-migration with attendant real wealth losses, dislocation and personal trauma. But such arguments are more difficult to validate for avoiding longer-term farm adjustments to economic incentives – including adjustments towards more larger farms and fewer mid-size family farms. Perhaps the strongest argument for preserving the family farm is that it is a part of the national heritage.

9. Efforts to survive economically in a service economy have created a farm structure not well equipped for the pressures imposed on it by macroeconomic policies in the 1970s and 1980s. The major drama of American farm policy in the past decade has been the role of

macroeconomic policy in creating economic hardship for an economic sector increasingly ill-equipped to cope with that hardship.

Money supply was overly expansive and erratic in much of the 1970s. Resulting high inflation created cash-flow problems for farmers. Since 1981 money supply has been well managed – perhaps as much by luck as design. Since 1982 the problem has been large structural (full employment) deficits. Teamed with restrictive money supply, such deficits have brought high real interest and exchange rates. American farmers have been especially disadvantaged because they (a) have approximately double the capital per worker as other industries, and interest is a major cost of capital; (b) are net debtors, with only $23 of financial claims on others for each $100 of claims on them; and (c) depend much more heavily on export markets than do other sectors on the average. Agriculture, with about 3 per cent of the nation's national income, accounts for about 20 per cent of the nation's exports. Creditors gain from high real interest rates; consumers gain from a strong dollar. Consumer-oriented service sectors that dominate the US economy are less concerned than is agriculture about the high value of the dollar.

10. The incidence of farm financial stress was much higher on mid-size than on large or small farms in 1983. The proximate cause of the stress was high real interest and exchange rates stemming from large structural federal deficits, but the more basic cause was a breakdown of the political process. It is not possible to tightly link unfavourable macroeconomic policies to the service economy. But under normal circumstances an affluent service economy might be committed to goals of justice, democracy, and security. Perhaps these commitments underlie Congressional reforms which enhanced the power of subcommittees and staffs and diminished the power of Congressional leaders and political parties. Whatever the intended impact of the 'democratisation' of Congress, the result has been a decline of *encompassing* institutions which have interests coinciding with the public interest, and a rise in power of special interest groups which aggrandise themselves at the expense of society. As noted earlier, service industries are often 'non-traded goods' which are not exported and also do not have to compete with imports, and are not material capital intensive. They tend not to be hurt by current macroeconomic policies. The result is that industries such as agriculture are relatively isolated in their call for sound macroeconomic policies.

11. A service society characterised by generally high income and wealth is especially concerned about security. Food security is near the top of the list. Such a society is especially responsive to calls by farm groups to maintain the family farm and maintain reserves of idle acres or commodity stocks to guard against food shortfalls and high food prices. A service economy is almost certain to subsidise agriculture. One result is international trade problems because subsidies frequently lead to dumping of surpluses on foreign markets and to depressing international food prices. Thus a service economy world is likely to be a protectionist economy world. A case can be made that heavy subsidies to farmers and

protectionist trade policies in aggregate diminish world food security. When world food supplies are short and prices high, the developed service economies protecting their agriculture with high price supports and variable levies receive no signal for their producers to increase output and for their consumers to decrease consumption. Receipt of such signals could reduce world price fluctuations. The burden is great on multilateral trade negotiations attempting to maintain more open markets in an international service economy.

12. As governments have undertaken larger interventions in agricultural markets, a growing proportion of the economic problems confronting farmers in the US and elsewhere may be traced to those interventions. As governments in service economies seek security for people, government failure has been as pervasive as market failure was once thought to be. Clearly, a government role is essential in dealing with long-term farm problems of instability, family farm demise, environmental degradation, poverty and financial stress. But it appears that the advice to service economies is the same as the advice to developing countries: utilise markets to the extent possible to make decisions of what, when, and where to produce; ration scarce public decision-making and administrative resources by directing them to relatively few key areas where markets do not function well or at all.

SUMMARY AND CONCLUSIONS

The United States and several other nations can now be classified as service economies. Although other industries are frequently driven out by service industries in such societies, agriculture need not necessarily fare badly. It survives by using service industries, such as science, education and information to improve technology and overall efficiency, thus remaining competitive despite cheaper labour in other countries. It also survives by appealing to political instincts of a service economy to seek security through protecting agriculture from international competition. This drive for food security in world perspective is probably counterproductive.

American farms have adapted to a service economy in numerous ways. Through part-time farming, part-ownership of land, extensive use of debt capital, and substitution of capital for labour, many American farm operators have survived. Some have prospered. Income from all sources per farm has become more evenly distributed among farm sizes. Pursuit of the above strategies to save the family farm is giving rise to a dual farm economy with a relatively few large industrial farms producing most of the output and with a large contingent of part-time smaller operators accounting for most farms. Fewer and fewer mid-size units conforming to the family farm ideal remain.

NOTE

Comments on the paper by Daryll Ray and Dean Schreiner are much appreciated.

REFERENCES

Melichar, E., *The Incidence of Financial Stress in Agriculture*, Board of Governors of the Federal Reserve System, Washington, DC, November 1984.

Ruttan, V. W., 'Agricultural Policy in an Affluent Society' in Ruttan, V. W. et al. (eds), *Agricultural Policy in an Affluent Society*, W. W. Norton and Company, New York, 1969.

Tweeten, L., *Causes and Consequences of Structural Change in the Farming Industry*, National Planning Association Food and Agriculture Committee Report no. 207, Washington, DC, 1984.

Tweeten, L., *Foundations of Farm Policy*, University of Nebraska Press, Lincoln, 1979.

Tweeten, L. and Brinkman, G., *Micropolitan Development*, Iowa State University Press, Ames, 1976.

US Department of Agriculture, *Chartbook of Nonmetro-Metro Trends*, Rural Development Service Report no. 43, Washington, DC, September 1984.

DISCUSSION OPENING I – FERNANDO B. SOARES

I will try to follow Ulf Renborg's advice to place before the Conference the main issues to be discussed from the floor as well as making some personal remarks on the papers presented. I must confess however that my task is quite difficult given the limited time at my disposal. The main reason for this is because both papers undoubtedly contain an above average content of new provocative ideas.

My first comment on my friend Dr Boussard's paper is to support his statement that the absence of economies of scale, or to put it in another way, the quick vanishing of economies of scale for the generality of agricultural production, is at the core of the reason for heterogeneity of farm sizes. In this respect Denis Britton and others have already provided us with sufficient empirical evidence.

Now let me comment more closely on the dynamic model presented. For obvious reasons the model must be a simplified one. Thus this is not the criticism I have in mind. What I think could have enriched the analysis and may or may not have given additional support to the author's conclusions would have been to perform some simulations considering prices as exogenously determined. Of course the general equilibrium framework must, in my opinion, remain the reference scenario for sound economic analysis, but if, as it is well known, price fixing is a permanent temptation for policy-makers, my suggestion may not be completely inadequate.

Another type of simulation would have been on the value of the parameter in order to approach the question that markets for durable factors are not in general of the perfect competition type.

My last remark on this paper pertains to what I view as his fundamental implicit conclusion: traditional structural policy, understood as land consolidation, farm size enlargement, land retirement plans, etc., is self-defeating because one easily can find oneself back to square one; not to speak about its costs. Let me, if I may, be also a little provocative on going along with Dr Boussard's conclusions: if we want to improve farmers' incomes, we had better address our attentions to credit and fiscal policies, including direct income compensation schemes, and leave half of the job to be done by markets.

This I think is a good bridge to start my few comments on Professor Tweeten's paper. One of his first statements is, and I quote: 'Farmers have adapted in unique ways to economic forces characterising a service economy. Some of the most notable accommodations include off-farm employment, part-ownership and leasing of assets, incorporation, vertical co-ordination, and greater reliance on debt capital.'

Although US agriculture is quite different from agriculture in Western Europe, they used to have a common feature: the overwhelming importance of the family farm despite the fact that they could not compare in size.

What I think could be some interesting questions to discuss from the floor in regard to Tweeten's paper are:

1. Is it foreseeable that the process of becoming service economies, that Western European countries are going through, will have the same disruptive effect on the importance of the family farm as happened in the US?

2. In what concerns EEC countries, the Treaty of Rome clearly states the objective of maintaining that importance (of the family farm). The question then is what is the least costly way of doing so if that political decision is to be maintained?

3. Why not put fewer eggs in the basket of structural policies and handle with more care macropolicy decisions which Tweeten so rightly emphasises in his paper and which unfortunately have not received attention in accordance with the effects they have on the agricultural sector?

DISCUSSION OPENING II – J. A. GROENEWALD

These two papers are, as anyone who has previously read publications of Dr Boussard and Dr Tweeten would expect, of a high quality. High quality does not necessarily imply full agreement. There are overlapping domains in these two papers, but they also differ considerably in nature, in main thrust and to a certain respect, in reasoning.

All the causes which according to Dr Boussard, cause heterogeneity, should in effect be accepted as such. But some ruled out, also induce heterogeneity. There is at least one respect, however, in which this particular discussion opener has to disagree with Dr Boussard. This is concerning his assertion of lack of economies of scale in agriculture, thus the lack of optimal size and hence its role in explaining heterogeneity. Whilst most empirical production functions do not show anything but constant returns to scale, this is largely because over the short and medium term, management is a fixed resource, and any bundle of the other resources will therefore obey the Law of Variable Proportions.* This then implies that since it varies among farmers, each manager has his own particular optimum size, depending on his own management. Neither will he, if he is a profit maximiser, strive towards minimum cost per unit product. He will expand as long as his expected marginal returns exceed marginal costs, provided he can gain control over needed finance.

Dr Boussard is correct in stating that optimal farm structures exist. These, however, are extremely heterogenous, as each farm is probably unique with respect to natural resources endowment, economic location, access to loan capital and, especially, management as well as committed resources in, particularly, fixed plant. As stated by Dr Tweeten, farmers' ability to manage funds are also variant. If one adds to this differences in relative prices, then much heterogeneity is to be expected. In a dynamic world, uncertainty or risk prevails. There is as shown by Dr Boussard, uncertainty concerning prices. There are in addition other sources of risk. Risk aversion (at varying degrees) and differing desires to maintain liquidity, provide another source of heterogeneity. In such a framework, use of the turnpike theorem is still useful, but one may picture it differently, like a man trying to catch up with and board a moving vehicle. Economic conditions also change. Farmers do leave agriculture. But n farmers' assets are sold to fewer than n farmers, particularly with full-time operators. One cannot, with all these various factors, really expect convergence. We rather have continuous disequilibrium.

Dr Tweeten convincingly argues that the continued development of already highly developed market economies renders adjustment in agriculture necessary. His exposition of the whole process is both interesting and stimulating. Different farmers do have different perceptions of what would benefit them most, thereby causing adjustments to differ and increasing heterogeneity. Neither can different objectives for large commercial units, medium-sized family farms and part-time operators in the small farm sector be ruled out. There has obviously, at least lately, been a movement toward drastic change in the whole socio-economic nature of farming. One can be certain that the patterns already identified in the USA, will over time, also become evident in the other service economies.

However, if it is the desire of farm legislators to preserve medium-sized family farms, the question of appropriate policy measures becomes a very difficult one. Dr Boussard argues convincingly that structural policy is both ineffective and expensive. But, also, that price policy will be completely inappropriate. It will be of disproportionate benefit to the

*In one study a scale of managerial inputs, based on farmers' future image, record systems, office organisation, maintenance and labour organisation (Burger 1971) was included in Cobb-Douglas functions. After inclusion, increasing returns to scale was evident, unless other factors such as farm size were limiting. When the same functions were fitted but the management scale was omitted, results indicated constant returns to scale (Jansen et al. 1972).

very large farms relative to medium-sized farms. Then the large units will also increasingly be able to bid resources, particularly capital, away from the others. Benefits are often also capitalised in land and quota prices, thus increasing opportunity costs. Windfall gains to one generation become a cost to the next.

Therefore the protectionist tendencies, which according to Dr Tweeten, go hand in hand with development of service economies, is disturbing. Larger intervention does not succeed in solving these socio-economic structural problems. In fact they even do worse. They remove the necessary economic signals. They distort agricultural prices away from those which would be efficient and which would clear markets. Through import controls and export subsidies they also weaken the agricultural sector – and hence, also the industrial sectors – of developing countries. They retard development where it is most needed. We should heed the words of Dr T. W. Schultz (1982): 'No government which has abolished markets has been successful in modernizing agriculture'.

REFERENCES

Burger, P. J., 'The measurement of managerial inputs in agriculture – III: The construction and evaluation of a scale', *Agrekon* Vol. 10. no. 4 1971, pp. 5–11.
Jansen, A. A., Swanepoel, G. H. and Groenewald, J. A. 'The measurement of managerial inputs in agriculture – IV: Application with business results', *Agrekon* Vol. 11 no. 2 1972, pp. 5–14.
Schultz, T. W., in Hill, Lowell D. (ed.), *Role of government in a market economy*. Iowa State University Press, Ames, 1982.

GENERAL DISCUSSION – RAPPORTEUR: J. GORECKI

The two papers created a great deal of interest and there were many who commented on the contents, as well as raised some points including questions related to them and the discussion openers' remarks. Some participants asked also for clarification of the figures presented by M. Boussard and related to the reasons for decreasing and/or increasing the output.

One participant discussed and questioned the relationship between value and size from the point of view of economic theory. In his opinion we should give more attention to the division of labour and management which may influence growth of farm business through duplication of technical units. A participant from the United States asked – does reliance on gross value of products sold as an indicator of farm size distort interpretations of economies of size? Value added tends to be inversely related to sales volume. The same participant noted that increasing specialisation in grain farming is creating part-time farms with large sale volumes but unable to employ resources fully through the year. What does this do to our concepts of part-time farming? Regarding the paper of Professor Tweeten, one participant asked that if subsidies are given to agriculture in the USA and in the EEC, can he explain why the IMF insists on removal of subsidies on fertilizer before Third World countries can qualify for IMF loans?

Another participant referring to the dangers of linking farm income via farm size to incomes in non-agricultural sectors, stressed that farm size is an important parameter in the planning process, especially as executed in LDCs.

M. Boussard in reply, thanked the discussion openers and the participants for their comments and questions.

On the question of subsidies in agriculture in the United States and the EEC countries he said that this mistake cannot be afforded by developing countries. In his opinion, in the process of farm planning too much attention was given to the size of the farm but too little to other factors influencing farming. He agreed that the volume of production was important but prices were also created by supply and demand.

Professor Tweeten also thanked the participants for their comments and questions. He stressed that the reasons for subsidies in the United States and the EEC were different. In his opinion many factors influenced the efficiency of farming, size was only one of them and many others should be taken into account. However net farm income was the most important measure of the effectiveness of farming.

Participants in the discussion included James Akinwumi, Philip M. Raup, Aidan Power, John Strak and Toman Von Roogen.

SECTION VII

Markets and Trade

JAIME LAMO DE ESPINOSA*

International Markets and Price Policy: The Instability of Agriculture

INTRODUCTION

At times we agricultural economists appear to be divided between what our knowledge teaches us and what we are offered by practical reality. Is it that we are incapable of convincing the politicians, or are our answers so theoretical that they cannot be put into practice without provoking major traumas in the economic systems we aim to modify? This question hits the nail on the head, probably because in no other field are there as many important contradictions as in price policy.

A major review of the American agricultural economics literature (Gale Johnson 1976) indicates a clear contradiction between the liberal policy of agricultural foreign trade and the programmes applied at national level, which is a fact that is found both in the United States and in Western Europe, as well as in other groups of developing countries. There are few disciplines such as this one where there is such contrast between what the theory offers and what agricultural policy takes for its use. One of these contradictory fields is the connection between agricultural price policy followed in the developed countries and its indirect effects upon agricultural markets and the insecurity of the developing countries.

In this paper I shall make a reflection, in the first part, on agricultural policies, particularly directed at the regulation of markets and prices, their growing importance, and their unwanted effects on surpluses and international markets. I shall then examine the international markets which are not, then, a reflection of the comparative advantages, neither do the production guidelines respond to these prices. Nevertheless, as we shall see later, protectionist tendencies, far from being reduced, are becoming more accentuated, and this accentuation does not improve the opportunities of the developing countries, but on the contrary limits their possibilities. Finally I shall examine the relationship between the

*I am grateful to Professors Luis Gamir Casares, Julian Briz, Carlos Tió and Tomás García Azcárate for their advice and opinions, which have served to improve the text. Also to Julian Briz for his direct collaboration in the preparation of statistics. Any possible errors may only be attributed to the author.

instability of world markets and the food insecurity of that group of countries.

I should remark that not all the issues surrounding the topic dealt with have been touched upon in the text. Limitations of space have made this impossible. The discussion will probably provide an opportunity to resolve this question.

PRICE POLICIES

Agriculture is not characterised by stability of markets. Quite the reverse. There can be little doubt that the weather and also some policies make agriculture an adventure difficult to predict, in which governments attempt to intervene, to a greater or lesser extent, to stabilise production, prices and incomes within fixed limits. And it is no use that the new technologies applied to production have allowed the developed countries to stabilise their supply a little more, as the developing countries pass their price fluctuations on to the markets of the developed countries through their exports.

Hardly anyone appears to doubt the need for a certain degree of intervention in agricultural markets at national level to prevent this instability of prices or to ensure a certain level of incomes. At times, these objectives become confused and it is believed that action on prices will inevitably lead to the stabilisation of incomes. But prices are not incomes, and the instruments for acting upon the former sometimes have no direct connection with what should be done for the latter.

It is the special characteristics of the agricultural sector, with regard to the factors conditioning its supply, which have traditionally motivated state intervention. This justifies and explains the various forms of intervention which Watson separates when dividing growth or development agricultural policies from incomes policies. One still frequently comes across texts where the latter are simply assimilated into market management and price regulation policies, including among the measures sustaining incomes all those affecting prices of products (price subsidy, compensatory payments, standard prices, double price systems, stabilisation mechanisms, intervention purchasing, measures at frontiers etc.) (OECD 1983). But it is a well-known fact that these policies may have different aims, such as increasing production deficiencies, reducing overproduction, increasing exports, improving nutrition, etc. And on occasion they cause inadvisable secondary effects such as restricting consumption, giving greater rigidity to the structure of production, accumulating surpluses, removing incentives for technological change or upsetting international markets.

Despite this, in one way or another, the developed countries have gradually established a thick network of government interventionism which nowadays protects, at high cost, the agriculture of their countries or communities. The model offered, from the EEC for instance, is based on few but considerable interventions: internally, by stockpiling, purchasing, denaturing etc., and externally by import levies or duty. With this the result is evident: the prices of protected products are higher than those outside and public spending is destined for raising prices and not reducing them (Bergmann 1970).

The agricultural policy thus achieves stability of agricultural prices inside the intervened area, which provokes as an undesired secondary effect, the generation of overproduction, which must later be sold abroad by subsidies. (Later we shall see its effect upon the possibilities of outside countries expanding their foreign food production and their role as suppliers of raw materials and fruit to the developed countries.)

Levies to raise domestic prices and protect them from external instability, and export subsidies which accentuate this instability, are the two sides of the coin of the new agricultural protectionism, which recalls the paradox of Bastiat of protecting candle manufacturers by bricking up windows in homes, to assure the sale of their production.

One may ask what the balance is of the various protection measures of agricultural policy at world level, from the point of view of common welfare. But, as has been noted (Gale Johnson 1976), despite the high financial costs and sacrifices which in many cases are required from taxpayers and consumers by some of these policies, there are not many studies measuring their repercussions in terms of a benefit-to-cost ratio. This has been no impediment to the repeated affirmation that no economic justification may be found to this agricultural protectionism and that the price policies are not very coherent with the principal components of social welfare (Tarditi 1985). Well, if this is so, it would seem logical that a policy of protection which makes the end consumer pay more for food and also finance, by taxes, its increased cost should be questioned and rapidly replaced by an economy based on greater freedom and relation with the market.

AGRICULTURAL PROTECTIONISM

Nevertheless, agricultural protectionism has grown in the last few years as the undesired fruit of the economic crisis. More products have been protected, more spending has been earmarked for this function, more countries have applied these techniques. To support domestic production, by cutting off imports, is too great a temptation for a politician to resist, if the decisive votes in an election depend on it. Therefore it is true that the world foodstuffs economy is dependent upon the political decisions in each country more than ever. (Koester 1984).

Why this situation? The figures for demographic growth, rates of income and food production speak for themselves. The developing countries have increased their populations by rates (2.1–2.4%) higher than the developed countries (0.7%). The growth rate of the GDP in real terms has also been considerable (4.6–5.6%). And the growing demand for food, especially with high income elasticity, has not been able to be met by the domestic supply and must be satisfied in foreign markets. One of the reasons for the insufficient level of growth of the food supply, both in absolute terms and in comparison with the developed countries, lies in the technological differences (as indicated earlier) but also in the protection policies applied. Because, even in areas where protection should be less by reason of their fundamental principles, as in the case of the EEC, it is clear that the result of the integration of various countries has given a mean level of protectionism which is higher than that of each of the member countries taken separately (Koester 1984). Therefore we should not be surprised that the concern of economists and experts for the quantification of levels of protection and the effects of the distortions on international trade, has been a constant for years (Dardis and Learn 1967).

They have even proposed a model at world level (UN 1971), taking into consideration the principal producing and consuming areas, which would make it possible to know the natural trade flows and consequently the positive and negative effects of the various distorting measures.

The new agricultural protectionism, measured through the equivalent *ad valorem* duty (FAO 1984) shows growing increases in Japan, the EEC and USA, as subsidies to producers have also risen. And though it is true that world agricultural trade grew between 1960 and 1980 at a rate of 4.3 per cent (OECD 1983), as against a world increase in agricultural production of only 2.5 per cent, it is no less true that only for three groups of products, sugar, fruit and tropical beverages, did the developing countries supply in 1980 over 50 per cent of the world's exports. On the contrary, the developed countries were at the origin of exports of meat, dairy products, cereals for human consumption, fodder grain, and oleaginous grains.

One of the most suggestive studies of the strategic change that would be revealed in an alteration of the obstacles to trade is that of A. Valdés (1983), which establishes a new scene, taking as the point of departure that if a reduction of 50 per cent were operated in the tariff protection of prepared foodstuffs and fodder in the OECD countries, it would result in an increase of near $3,000m in the yearly exports of the 57 most populated developing countries, with an important incidence in Brazil, Argentina, Colombia, India, the Philippines and Thailand, and 60 per cent of this income would go to Latin America. One should note that in that case, the percentage increase in value would be 339 per cent for pork, 134.4 per cent for refined sugar and 78.2 and 76.7 per cent for barley and wine respectively.

The above figures show that:

1. Although the effects of this liberalization may seem modest, they are not negligible, at the income levels and volumes of exports of these countries and areas at the present time. For some countries the increase of income obtained from agricultural exports would be 40 per cent for Chile, 33 per cent for Afghanistan, 28 per cent for Argentina, 23 per cent for South Korea and Turkey, etc.

2. The increases produced in these countries will back production structures which at present find no justification in a reduced market.
3. It would give back to the international market part of the principle of comparative advantages, at present heavily sequestered by restitutions and subsidies.
4. It would be a source of employment and in many cases make rural life more dignified.

In the contrary sense, it must be stated that if governments were to continue to give in to the protectionist pressures derived from the crisis, their consequences would certainly be capable of estimation. In an old, yet significant example, made using the Brussels world model, it can be clearly deduced that an increase of protection of 15 percentage points, would generate a reduction in the GDP, both of the developed and developing countries, affecting most gravely the low income petroleum importing countries (BIRF 1983).

Price and other policies of a protectionist nature, both new and traditional, are therefore generating a broad curtain of isolation of the agricultures protected with regard to outside, and in particular with regard to the developing countries.

MARKET INSTABILITY AND FOOD INSECURITY

The need to improve the stability of agricultural markets led Keynes in the 1940s to launch the idea of international regulation stocks under the direction of a general council. Since then to the present time, there has been a succession of attempts to harmonise and stabilise markets. Thus we have the UNCTAD Integral Products Programme, the International Product Agreements, the International New Economic Order, with its provision for establishing two funds for stockpiling and promotion, and so many other multilateral formulae for tackling the problem.

Nevertheless, despite all attempts, the degree of instability of agricultural markets has always been high. An analysis made for the period 1954–73, although distant in time, shows a variation running from 13 per cent for bananas to 68 per cent for coffee. (Labys 1978). And the higher the degree of concentration of international trade, the more necessary market stability is to countries; as over 50 per cent of exports of sisal, cocoa, palm and coconut oil, tea, bananas and coffee are effected by the six principal exporting countries of each product.

More recently, over the last years, the trade in agricultural products of non-petroleum producing developing countries has accounted for approximately one-fourth of the world total of agricultural products exported, although in the first years of the 1980s their real value did not rise owing to the worse conditions of exchange.

Between 1979 and 1981 the balance of trade of the non-petroleum producing developing countries as a whole, referring to agricultural products, gave a negative balance of $13,400m, whereas the developed countries as a whole gave a positive balance of nearly $15,000m. The situation for the non-petroleum-producing developing countries would not be serious if there had been improvements in their trading in non-agricultural products, but this was not so (FAO 1983). On the contrary, their imports of agricultural products rose, especially grain, which accounted for approximately half of the increase. The exportation of 'grain culture' to these countries conditions in a clear and serious manner their food future, among other reasons because their capacity for importing agricultural produce is also highly conditional upon their exchange rates, the lessening of income from exports, the burden of foreign debt and the difficulty in obtaining new international loans. Furthermore, as the FAO pointed out in its report for the two-year period 1982–3, the depression of international markets in basic products and the fall in income this represented for some developing countries, obliged them to reduce the funds allocated for the importation of indispensable means of agricultural production, which has of course had an effect on production levels.

For the developing countries exporting raw materials or foodstuffs, the reduction of external protection in the developed countries would benefit their economies. And for others characterised by penury and food insecurity, that protection at the present time helps them to purchase food in a world market at prices kept artificially low by subsidies. And in the same way as remunerative prices made possible the development of farming in South Asia in the 1960s, depressed international prices are an impossible obstacle to the generation of sufficient incentive to motivate investment, the transformation of agriculture and the growth of its degree of self-sufficiency. Therefore the protection of these countries also seems necessary to generate a first impulse of development, prior to greater food security.

The negative effects many of these policies have had in the developing countries have been analysed by various specialists; for example, in the case of Brazil (Schuh 1968) it is clear how local agricultural production and the situation of the farmers themselves have been harmed by a series of measures such as forcing industrialisation to substitute possible imports, excessive protectionism to reduce imports without sufficiently stimulating exports, taxation and credit policies with a mistaken approach and insufficient putting into practice. And, on the contrary, if those in favour of agricultural free trade at world level expound a series of arguments which are in force at certain times and in certain circumstances, it is no less true that if these are put into practice without the due safeguards and considerations, they may lead to critical situations, which has been the case in some countries of southern South America. The unfair competition to which agriculture in this situation may be subjected is aggravated by the fact that surpluses, often heavily subsidized, are dumped in that market. Furthermore, the line separating them is not that clear, as developing countries with food insecurity problems are permanent or temporary exporters of some agricultural products. Thus, the countries of the Sahel exported 15 million kilos of vegetables during the drought of 1971 to the developed countries, and irrigation transformations were made in the desert to produce aubergines and mangoes for consumers in the developed countries (FAO 1979).

This duality, which is typical of the developing countries, leads to the co-existence (as is well known) of two completely different agricultural models: the traditional one, which is aimed at covering the minimum nutritional needs of their populations in basic products (grain, rice, pulses, ...) and the export model (occasionally technologically advanced), which provides them with the foreign exchange needed for their balances of payments. The problem is that frequently the developing countries with a dual economy reserve the best part of their land for exportable crops and increase these greatly at the expense of basic foodstuffs. For example, in Africa the production of coffee, tea, cocoa, cotton and sugar cane has multiplied, whereas the basic food crops have fallen alarmingly (FAO 1979). At the general level, 24 developing countries obtain mean calorific stocks, per caput, equal to or less than 90 per cent of their needs and of these countries, 16 are in Africa and seven in Asia.

In these cases, food security depends to a large extent on the short-term stability of the food supply and the connection of the market with the international market. But here it is not so much a case of exporting raw materials from these countries and therefore operating in a stabilised market for these products, but of the internal supply of basic foodstuffs purchased in stable markets.

A. Valdés (1983) has indicated that the food insecurity of these countries with regard to the equilibrium of their consumption, by recourse to the international market, has at least three causes: (a) the risk of them being denied a reliable access to external supply (b) the short-term instability of world markets not offering reliable directives for the planning of imports, and (c) the capacity of the developing countries to finance increasing and fluctuating food imports.

I shall stress, for these effects, cause (b). Who can plan imports in a reliable way when many of them depend upon restitutions decreed by the pressure of a temporary surplus or the proximity of a harvest which is foreseen to be surplus? Who can reliably plan food supply operations when the supply may be subjected to an embargo resulting from a simple political change? Is not the instability of markets on occasion the result of political instability?

U. Koester (1984) has pointed out very clearly four causes of the rise in prices of world markets in agricultural products: the creation of the EEC; state commerce; the trend towards concentration and the trend towards bilateral agreements. These clearly show the incidence of protectionist policies on international markets. And, taken together, they all mean that the markets get further away from the principle of free trade and accentuate the lack of confidence.

In the light of these facts, it is not surprising that the developing countries should increasingly look to themselves in search of solutions for their problems (Espinosa 1984). Thus Latin America focuses on the problem from the so-called 'enlarged autarky', which tries to find solutions within the region itself, even in the form of barter, to combat the obstacle they meet in the protectionist measures of the industrialised countries to exports of agricultural products, one of the aims of which is obviously the provision of foreign exchange to reduce the foreign sector gap in a 'hostile and uncertain' world context (IICA 1984).

FINAL CONSIDERATIONS

The topic dealt with above, as indicated at the outset, is sufficiently polemical and suitable for an analysis by the contradictory method, to attempt to close it with precise conclusions. Humility obliges me to simply present some final considerations.

Food, even today, is the great challenge of mankind. The developed countries cannot be insensitive to the penury and needs of others. But if this is a moral responsibility of a political nature, it is we economists who have the scientific responsibility of recommendation and analysis.

Prices play a central rôle in the allocation of resources and protection prevents them from correctly reflecting the relative scarcity of these resources. Price policies created to re-orient production to ensure agricultural incomes and prevent the deterioration of farm incomes, have had a history as dense as it has been discussed. And since the 1970s, when energy prices, interest and exchange rates became upset, agricultural price policy took on considerable importance.

The developed countries carry out agricultural, particularly price and market protection policies, which are all the healthier the more they make possible a growing supply of food for the developing countries and the more they give fair competition to the market.

However the problem at the present time, 1985, is that the food situation has been complicated as a result of:

1. A sustained and generalised economic crisis with low growth rates and increasing unemployment.
2. High and increasing energy costs for food production.
3. The appearance of neoprotectionist tendencies.
4. Foreign indebtedness which makes difficult the purchase of fertilizers or machinery necessary for production.

The crisis has reinforced an extension of the agricultural price and protection policies to a greater number of products in the developed countries, with the appearance of surpluses and the application of heavy budget spending for sustainment. This neoprotectionism which requires subsidized exportation as a necessary instrument to float its domestic market, depresses international markets, generates a lack of confidence in them and although it does provide cheaper food, it does not facilitate the development of food production in the developing countries, nor does it facilitate the exportation of food and raw materials to the developed countries, as a measure necessary to finance their development and improve their balances of payments. It only consolidates 'Food Aid', and perhaps not for altruistic reasons.

Attempts to stabilise the markets in certain basic products by multilateral agreements have not offered the expected result and the system of generalised preferences does not seem sufficient. Furthermore, Food Aid cannot and should not be either a permanent or structural solution.

Probably as 'the facts are very obstinate' and the teachings of agricultural economics continue to appear to be correct to us, only a lower degree of protectionism in the developed countries, with greater degrees of freedom in international markets and a certain protection (even though this may appear contradictory) in developing countries, could give greater stability to the food markets and greater food security to insecure countries. Not forgetting the beneficial effects on budget deficits ... but that is another matter.

REFERENCES

Bergmann, D., Kaldor, N., Krohn, J. B., Marsh, J. S., Rossi-Doria, M., Schnittker, J. A., Thomsen, C., Wilbrandt, J. 'Un avenir pour l'Europe Agricole', *Cahiers Atlantiques*, 1970.

BIRF, *Informe sobre el desarrollo mundial 1983,* Washington, DC, 1983.

Dardis, R. and Learn E., *Measures on the Degree of Protection of Agriculture in Selected Countries*, USDA Technical Bulletin 1384, 1967.

Espinosa, J. Lamo de, (a) 'Considerations about food security with special attention to Latin America', IICA, 1984.

　　　　　　　(b) 'Reflexiones sobre la política de precios agrarios en la agricultura', *Rev. de Estudios Agro-Sociales*, 1970.

FAO, *Actas del periodo de sesiones correspondientes a la XIX Conferencia*, Rome, 1979.

FAO, Serie estudios, *El nuevo proteccionismo y los intentos de liberalizar el comercio agricola*, Rome, 1983.

FAO, *Situación y perspectivas de los productos básicos 1982–83*, Rome, 1983.

IICA-OEA, *Examen del estado de la Agricultura y el Desarrollo Rural en América Latina y el Caribe*, Costa Rica, 1984.

Johnson, Gale, 'Postwar Policies Relating Trade in Agricultural Products' in *A survey of Agricultural Economics Literature*, vol. 1. American Agricultural Economics Association, 1976.

Koester, U., 'L'intervention sur le marché agricole et le commerce international' IV CEEA, Kiel, 1984.

OECD. *Les implications des différentes méthodes de sostien des revences agricoles*, Paris, 1983.

OECD, *Echanges agricoles avec les pays en développement*, Paris, 1984.

Schuh, E., 'Effects of some General Economic Development Policies on Agricultural Development', *Journal of Farm Economics*, vol. 50, December 1968.

Tarditi, Secondo, 'Prix et revenues dans le secteur agricole', IV CEEA. Kiel, September 1985.

United Nations, *A world price equilibrium model*, CCP 72/Wp 3, Rome, 1971.

Valdés, A., 'La seguridad alimentaria. Un problema de estabilización para los países en desarrollo', *Comercio Exterior*, vol. 33, no. 12, December 1983.

JEAN-CLAUDE DUFOUR, GÉRARD GHERSI AND
ROBERT SAINT-LOUIS

New Types of Multinational Firms in the Agribusiness Sector: Implications of their Emergence in the Least Industrialised World

'First and foremost the food and feed industries, more concerned with low cost and high quality than country of origin for their raw materials, have shown an impressive facility for searching out foreign sources of supply. They have forced agricultural interests to play 'catch-up' taking advantage of new trade opportunities until they become an embarassment to domestic farm policy', Tim Josling

INTRODUCTION

Who would dare to predict that by the turn of the 1980–90s, national governments in the least industrialised world might receive more and more significant project proposals from MNFFCs to build in their countries important first stage or even second stage food processing plants and firms, with or without the help of local investment capital? Is there anybody who would dare to go further and predict that these firms will be exporting most of their output? Such predictions are likely to cast serious doubts and/or stir up waves of controversy. This is one of many scenarios which tend to become likely, because MNFFCs seem to reveal significant signs of their increased flexibility in setting up their investment strategies throughout the world. One might think that the probability of this particular hypothesis being confirmed as being less than that of other scenarios is even more surprising.

This tentative paper brings forward the following hypothesis: it may be that the best interests of MNFFCs are coming to rest more and more upon their ability to act as oligopolies seeking consenting partners rather than on their stubbornness to keep on behaving as fiercely competing ones, at least for the remainder of thiŝ decade.[1] Three sets of features are presented on this issue. The first one throws in to relief a few recent trends in international trade of food and feed products. It raises questions concerning their suitability from the perspective of national food and/or nutrition strategies in some countries.[2] The second deals with selected

566

structural changes of MNFFCs during the 1980s. Finally, the third one deals with their 'new' ways of doing business deals.

INTERNATIONAL TRADE OF FOOD AND FEED PRODUCTS: PROTECTED MARKETS UNDER THE INFLUENCE OF FLOATING EXCHANGE RATES

The outstanding importance of the highly industrialised world in international trade of food and fibre products is already well known.[3] Less evident are the roles and the importance of specific firms supplying agricultural inputs, as well as that of those transforming raw food and feed products, despite the fact that more and more research is being conducted on them.[4]

Rates of growth of volumes of food and feed products traded on international markets during the 1980s, which were apparently fostered by newly emerging solvent national markets ever since 1960, have been somehow surprising. Indeed, they seem to be if one accounts for a parallel surge of sometimes vicious non-tariff trade barriers between the most relevant countries. These seem to become more and more efficient trade impediments.[5]

Authors, such as Schuh (1979) and Ruttan (1980), have stressed the relationships between various degrees of changes in exchange rates between national currencies of some countries, the flows of international funds and the changes in the respective national food and fibre sectors both in the industrialised world and in the LICs ever since the system of floating exchange rates has been restored.[6] In other respects, Ruttan also documented the extreme weaknesses of economic situations in LICs, and in particular those which import a high proportion of cereals to meet their consumption needs.[7]

One may wonder who cares much about the growth of international trade of food and feed products in such a world environment. There is one promising hypothesis that is currently being tossed around on this matter. The alleged ability of most major corporations, including those that do not belong to the MNFFCs' group, to take advantage of highly fluctuating exchange rates, to get to grips with the changing cost of living throughout the world, and finally to make the best out of selective trade barriers between countries, is put in the forefront by various authors.[8] Others argue that MNFFCs stand to gain or lose the most by making wise decisions regarding the geography of their new investment capital and its congruence with various international trade patterns. There seems to be a more and more noticeable intention on their part to match their self-interest with national objectives even in countries more deeply committed to their own agricultural and/or food policies.[9] Beyond these trends stands the real possibility that new types of MNFFCs might be in the making. More specifically, this paper suggests that significant structural changes in MNFFCs, some of which have a lot to do with the ways they spread out their investment capital throughout the world and in the LICs in particular, have been taking place. It also suggests that, in the meantime, MNFFCs have enhanced their ability to adapt their marketing strategies to world-wide changes as well as to local characteristics of the LICs, where perennial and rationally consistent food and feed policy objectives are sometimes wanting.

STRUCTURAL CHANGES OF MNFFCs: SOME PAST TRENDS RECONFIRMED

Growth and concentration of the leaders
Exceptionally rapid growth of MNFFCs is deemed surprising by some and troublesome by others. In 1981, the top hundred leaders that operated in market economies (according to AGRODATA), reported a cumulative sales value of 333 billion $ US.[10] This is close to one-third of the total production value of hundreds of thousands of firms operating in the food, feed and beverage sector. Their dominant importance can also be depicted by comparing them with the size of some national economies where they are present.[11] For instance, in 1981, 17 out of 24 South American countries, and 36 out of 40 African countries displayed a GNP (gross national product) a little different or even much smaller than the yearly sales of Unilever.

Since the turn of the century, leaders among MNFFCs have gained increased importance. In the last 20 years, cumulated sales volume of the top hundred has increased the most rapidly, going up at a rate of about 7 to 8 per cent a year. This is, on average, from 2 to 3 per cent more than the comparable growth rate of the industry throughout the world. Moreover, our own calculations show that, despite the recent crisis, the proportion of world-wide production which is accounted for by those leaders has gone from 28 per cent in 1978 to a little more than 33 per cent in 1981.[12] This trend is likely to continue in the near future, in parallel with greater concentration, as well as with increased volume of production in some socialist countries and in LICs which are emerging as the new markets of the 1990s.

Stable and praiseworthy way through the crisis
According to recent trends, greater concentration may lead to the top hundred MNFFCs gaining world-wide control of about 40 per cent of the whole sector by the turn of the 1980–90s. The main reason for this is the outstanding performance of the mammoth firms. Indeed, there is some kind of a cumulative impact which is going on and that takes either one of the following forms. On the one hand, fiercely competing firms with exceptionally good self-financing capacity swallow up smaller and weaker ones and/or merge with kins. On the other hand, the tops among the top seem to attract other giants outside MNFFCs' groups, mostly because of the stable performance of the former (Table 1).

Apparently, however, only the leaders were capable of such perform-ances, which may explain the growing gap between the top and the bottom groups. Although significant changes are not expected in the membership club of the chosen few at the top,[13] it is felt that market penetration by a second generation of firms of mixed breeds (Europe, Japan, Canada and eventually from LICs experiencing rapid growth), as well as the dynamic behaviour of specific firms,[14] combined with the impact of research and development (R&D) efforts, may cause shifts in the order of firms appearing on the list as well as in their relative dominance in the MNFFCs' group.

Growth focused on specific targets
Research conducted in the last decade indicates some loss of enthusiasm by MNFFCs for the fluid and the industrial milk, as well as for the feed subsectors. By 1981, however they were showing increased interest in cereals and cereal products, as well as in high value-added items such as brewery products. But the most striking change in this trend towards diversification is undoubtedly the highly significant entry of giants in bakery and fishery products. Despite this, it is not in the food and feed processing sectors that trends towards diversification in downstream direction seem to have been the most significant in the MNFFC sector. Wholesale trade and restaurants, caterers and tavern operations seem to attract the greatest share (13 per cent) of new investments made by the leaders. In contrast, entry of MNFFCs in food retailing is perceivable but much quieter. It goes on mostly by way of food retailers integrating food processing.

In the restaurants-caterers-tavern subsector, fast food was undoubtedly the fastest growing area in the Western world in the past decade. Some 20 MNFFCs appearing in the AGRODATA catalogue are deeply involved in fast food outlets. Their activities also stretch out to management of chains of hotels and/or restaurants. This type of diversification sometimes leads to the development of very large conglomerates, within which the food and feed divisions are no longer dominant.

REGIONAL STRATEGIES: LOOKING OUT FOR DEVELOPING SOLVENT MARKETS

Along with diversification, the tendency for food and feed sectors to become multinationalised is growing. According to our own statistics, numbers of firms under the control of MNFFCs but not located in the same country as the head office, has gone from 2070 (in 112 countries) in 1978 to 2330 (in 127 countries) in 1981.

From the early 1900s until the mid-1940s, multinational firms were mostly transforming raw materials in colonies, exporting raw food and feed materials to European and North American markets. MNFFCs such as Swift-Esmark (1885), Brooke-Bond (1892), Castel and Cooke (1894), United Fruits (1899) and UNILEVER (1929) were born during that period. One may rightfully call this period the golden age of *input supply strategies* by MNFFCs.

TABLE 1 *MNFFCs compared to other industrial sectors on the basis of four indicators of performance*

	TOP FIVE HUNDRED AMERICAN CORPORATIONS		TOP FIVE HUNDRED OTHER CORPORATIONS IN THE REST OF THE WORLD	
	1981	1982	1981	1982
GROWTH OF SVBT (%)				
Food and feed	8.5	2.0	5.6	1.1
Beverages	6.8	6.7	12.7	0.2
Average of all sectors	7.5	5.7	4.7	2.6
GROWTH OF PROFITS (%)				
Food and feed	10.6	7.1	13.4	-1.8
Beverages	15.1	8.5	11.6	-15.1
Average of all sectors	3.7	-27.1	-24.0	-39.0
SVBT/NUMBER OF WAGE-EARNERS ($)				
Food and feed	114979	128834	103154	86414
Beverages	139272	120016	168208	55556
Average of all sectors	86381	90837	103048	99692
SVBT/EQUITY CAPITAL ($)				
Food and feed	4.33	4.88	1.69	1.36
Beverages	2.89	3.00	2.37	0.81
Average of all sectors	2.97	2.74	1.16	1.21

SVBT: Sales value before tax
Source: Our calculations from *Fortune*

From 1945 to 1960, MNFFCs extended their zones of influence to LICs with the greatest agricultural development potential. MNFFCs kept increasing the volume of their most basic activities but they gradually appeared also interested in supplying LICs' urban markets with high value-added products with strong demand. The golden age of *input supply strategies* became overlapped by the age of *marketing strategies*. Competition did not seem to be as fierce in these infant markets as it was in already established ones. Moreover, the fact of being there first, together with the cumulative process of learning how to operate in these countries, somehow hid the first comers from the sight of competitors.

During the 1970s, MNFFCs' presence in national economies then became more dominant and more integrated, by way of diversified local investments. Use was made of local financing and of subsidies of various types. They even complied with nationalisation of some of their activities. It seems as if they were following a two-pronged strategy: on the one hand, they set up *marketing strategies* based on production in both *autonomous plants* and *assembly-line plants*, but on the other hand, they tried to improve their *production strategies* by better linking some of their strategic factors as multinational producers.

Nowadays, most giant firms display high proportions of multinational activities. AGRODATA statistics indicate that one-third of the leaders do more than 30 per cent of their activities in foreign markets, and a little more than 40 of them operate plants in more than ten countries. Notwithstanding these trends, production rationalisation built into marketing strategies remains a regional management technique for MNFFCs. Indeed, in 1981 three plants out of four, among the 4,200 branches operated under the control of the top hundred MNFFCs, were located in North America or Europe. The trend towards across-the-border ventures in countries of the northern hemisphere has thus significantly increased. But MNFFCs seem to favour countries or regions with high population growth rates, with the least abated economic growth rates and with stable social environments.

MNFFC: NEWEST TRENDS

Facing world-wide crisis and unpredictable political environments, some MNFFCs may already be in the process of changing somewhat drastically their management processes. The terms '*Third Type*' have been used in a rather loose sense to qualify firms which are openly trying to eliminate plant breakdowns, delays in filling orders, construction defects, stocks of products and red-tape. Centralisation is a key word but open-mindedness, flexibility, sharing in new ideas and looking out for relevant and critical facts and figures also come into prominence. Top executives get along with that by connecting themselves with quality circles, think-tank sessions, project partnerships as well as through their various links with other firms. Taylor-type organisations tend to become superseded by more daring, more open and perhaps even more competitive ones. Dominance by access to materials, technology and/or financial power is replaced by new forms of business intelligentsia. Intertwining of information and grouping of interests become closer and closer. Except for such things, however, firms stubbornly cling to their independence. The linking rings are chief executives, technical innovation channels and human know-how transfers. Those aspects seem to outweigh control of capital in cementing the newest groups.

In the manner of Japanese firms, infant international groups encompassing large, average as well as small organisations may have taken a substantial lead over non-linked firms in keeping in the closest touch with the various moods of a rapidly changing world-wide environment. Information systems of such groups are exceptionally rich. Highest-level executive meetings on linking matters strengthen their efficiency in fact-finding roles. Long-term objectives (within time horizons of about 15 years) then tend to fit in nicely both with overall market trends as with the group's self-evaluated capacity to successfully meet challenging opportunities.

Chief executives attend, more and more often, 'linking' meetings where long-term objectives are scrutinised whereas staff management personnel is led to think of practical strategies with other members of the group. Product lines marketed by these firms can therefore be viewed as the result of forward looking and strategically planned (not to say pruned) goals set up by the group, and having to do with financing, technical services, group image, merchandising and foreign investments.

A suggested taxonomy for those newest groups already exists. It breaks them down into three sub-groups: (1) merger types of traditional international consortia (Unilever, Nestlé); (2) types of groups highly supported by major banking institutions (DKB in England); (3) types of groups specialised in highly industrialised product lines (Nissan, Komatus, Nippon Steel). All of them have at least two things in common: *diversification* into new product lines and/or in technological changes is the first; selection of an *optimal basket* of lines of products conducive to the group's development, from input supply all the way to retailing, is the second.[15]

Links between firms within a group are fathered by highest-ranking executives. Integration may be two-pronged: it takes place either on a horizontal scale between chief executives of top MNFFCs and/or on a vertical scale. Networks of sequential meetings are institutionalised. Various levels of staff convene in such meetings episodically. There are of course some structural financial links which are woven within the group. In rare instances though, some firms are totally owned by others. The average degree of control by the leading firms is in the vicinity of 20 to 30 per cent. Degrees of control tend to be the highest in those groups supported by major banking institutions, extending them from 40 to 80 per cent. Lastly, other strong intermingling links exist between members of these groups, such as for availability of short-term and intermediate-term financing under special conditions, for shared access to input suppliers and/or to chains of buyers, for market prospection circles and/or lobbying services.

The building pressure for LICs to pay much greater attention to the structural changes that are going on in MNFFCs must be reckoned with. The choice of determining whether or not LICs ought to join in by ways of lobbying groups and/or by using other linking rings will be a crucial one. LICs declaring themselves out of such groups might be deprived of some degree of power in making MNFFCs espouse their long-term objectives.

THE NEWEST TECHNOLOGICAL PROCESSES: NEW SOURCES OF POWER?

R&D budgets allocated to research in the food and feed sectors indicate that discovery of new processes is of the utmost importance for MNFFCs. It is felt that structural changes will undoubtedly result from further major technological steps forward if capacities of MNFFCs to compete with one another are then intruded upon or impaired. For instance, bio-industry and the production of food and feed from non-agricultural materials might create a still greater dependence of agriculture and/or of food and feed industries production processes from progress in bio-engineering, chemistry, enzymetics and genetics (Table 2). Recent analysis of MNFFC strategies with regard to bio-engineering and to the newest food and feed production processes indicates that the dividing lines between relevant sectors are becoming more and more shallow. Sectoral stratification is coming to rest upon technological processes which are closer and closer akin. The food and feed sector, pharmaceutics, chemistry and energy tend to become almost every man's land from the point of view of the previously more specialised MNFFCs.

Recent studies have revealed the degree of interest of top multinationals for biotechnology.[16] Some 225 uses of such processes, either under testing and/or under normal conditions, were recorded out of a relevant sample of 95 leading corporations operating in the food and feed, in the chemistry, in the pharmaceutic and in the energy sectors in 1983 (Table 2). The food and feed sector is on top of the list according to declared number of applications. Production of food and feed from unicellular organisms, of food additives and of sweeteners is also reported. More than a third of all items made known by sampled firms enter in these specific categories of uses. Chemistry and energy also seem to attract much attention. Peculiarly, some of the utilisations discovered thereon are no full strangers with food and beverage production. Indeed some of these firms extract various components out of food and feed by-products and/or from biomass.

AGRODATA statistics tend to corroborate such findings. However top MNFFCs display a noticeable restraint by limiting themselves to the most

TABLE 2 *Number of uses made of biotechnology by multinationals*

FIELD OF USE	Food and feed technology	Chemistry	Pharmaceutics	Energy	Total number of uses recorded	Firms reporting
	NUMBER OF APPLICATIONS					(number)
SECTOR						
Food and feed	47	14	13	10	84	28
Chemistry	22	13	13	1	49	28
Pharmaceutics	31	7	27	3	68	25
Energy	2	5	1	4	12	7
Other sectors	5	1	3	3	12	7
TOTAL	107	40	57	21	225	95

Source: Our calculations from data collected and reported by CFCE (Centre Français du Commerce Extérieur).

traditional applications of biotechnology. Biotechnology-related production processes accounted for 36 production activities of the top hundred MNFFCs. Makers of cereal products and of fats are frequent users of enzymes in processing sweeteners and yeasts. Brewers of alcoholic beverages take the keenest interest in fermentation processes. The newly developed techniques with the latest uses are for production of dehydrated proteins and amino-acids. According to these figures, a few new trends are in the making. First, significant attraction seems to emerge in chemistry, energy and pharmaceutic sectors for MNFFCs, especially for those under Japanese control. Perhaps of still greater interest is the fact that multinationals which were aliens to the food and feed sector are finding their way into it.

Tomorrow's food and feed production processes will undoubtedly come to rest more heavily upon innovative technology. That will bring along deeper changes in MNFFCs. Considerable matters are at stake for MNFFCs and for countries, some of which are not even aware of their consequences. Both the apologists and the fiercest denunciators of these trends tend to agree about at least one thing: what might otherwise become a promising stream of hope for a significant part of the world, it is feared, might make a large contribution to placing a few already dominant and highly diversified MNFFCs, endowed with the most advanced technology, in fuller control of world production of food and feed.

SUMMARY AND CONCLUSION

International capitalism has proved its capacity to adapt to local conditions. MNFFCs have played an active role in this matter. This paper suggests that the birth of the so-called 'third type' of firm has already been set going in the food and feed sector. Increased demand, which stirred up new flows of international trade particularly between countries of the western hemisphere, has lead MNFFCs to seek new ways of making profits. Established strategies are being adjusted to or substituted for by new ways for firms to compete with one another, which are overall less aggressive and which come to rest more and more on technological advantage. LICs that are confronted with firms of this new generation might court serious disappointments, such as those of becoming still more deprived and/or more dependent, if they fail to co-ordinate their efforts right now. The case is pressing for scientific questioning of the likely impacts of new strategies which are being put forward by dominant MNFFCs on national policies, at least to the extent that food and nutrition programming remains a high-priority issue in most countries of the world.

NOTES

[1]Leopold, M. and Ghersi, G., 'La performance des firmes multinationales agro-alimentaires et leurs perspectives de croissance', and Maddoff, M., 'L'extension des firmes multinationales américaines' in *Firmes multinationales et autonomie nationale*. De colloque de l'Association d'économie politique, under the direction of Jorge Viosi, Editions Saint-Martin, Montreal, 1983. See also Archier, Georges and Hervé Serieux, *L'enterprise du troisième type*, Editions du Seuil, 1984.

[2]Ruttan, Vernon W., 'Food strategies for grain deficit poor countries' in E.W. Tyrchniewicz, (ed) *The New Era in World Agricultural Trade: Perspectives for the Prairies and the Great Plains*, occasional papers no. 12. Department of Agricultural Economics, The University of Manitoba, September 1980. See also Thoburn, John T., *Primary Commodity Exports and Economic Development: Theory Evidence and a Study of Malaysia*, John Wiley, 1977.

[3]*Problèmes des échanges agricoles*. OCDE, Paris, 1982. See also Simantov, Albert., 'Où sont les marchés mondiaux accessibles et solvables' in *L'agro-alimentaire québécois et son développement dans l'environnement économique des années 1980*, published under the direction of Jean-Pierre Wampach, Laval University, Quebec, 1983.

[4]Simantov, Albert, op. cit.; Simantov suggests that, among other things, because of the great importance of these markets, it is mainly those countries and/or firms which can supply clients with large quantities of products on a regular basis that will gain a privileged access to state trading countries (p. 331). See also Ghersi, Gérard, Padilla, M., Allaya, M. O. and Allaya, M., *Les cent premiers groupes agro-industries mondiaux*, Institut agronomique méditerranéen de Montpellier, December 1983.

[5]Hillman, Jimmye S., *Nontariff Agricultural Trade Barriers*, University of Nebraska Press, 1976. See also Schuh, G. E., *The Lesser-Developed Countries and the Multilateral Trade Negotiations*, University of Minnesota, 1979 and Schuh, G. E., and Cleveland, H., *North American Grain Production in World Affairs*, University of Minnesota, 1984.

[6]Schuh, G. E., 'Fluctuations in Foreign Exchange Rates: Implications for Agricultural Trade', published in *The New Era in World Agricultural Trade: Perspectives for the Prairies and the Great Plains*, op. cit. See also Ruttan, V. W., *Food Strategies for Grain Deficit Poor Countries*, op. cit.

[7]Ruttan, V. W., ibid.

[8]Josling, Tim., 'Agricultural Trade among Friends: the Parlous State of U.S. Trade Relationship with the Industrialized West', in *United States Agricultural Policy: 1985 and Beyond*. A series of Seminars compiled and edited by Jimmye S. Hillman, University of Arizona and Resources for the Future, May 1984.

[9]Mayer, Leo V., 'Agricultural Policy in a Changing Domestic and International Environment', in *United States Agricultural Policy: 1985 and Beyond*, op. cit. See also Simantov, Albert, op. cit. and Pisani, E., *Réflexions sur une politique agricole et alimentaire commune et ses liens avec une politique structurelle de développement régional*, SEC (83), 616, 12 April 1983.

[10]Padilla, M., Ghersi, G., Allaya, M. C. and Allaya, M., *Les cent premiers groupes agro-industriels mondiaux*, I.A.M., Montpellier, December 1983.

[11]Ghersi, G. and Rasioin, J. L., *Firmes multinationales et systèmes agro-alimentaires dans les pays en voie de développement*, Centre de Développement de l'C.C.D.E., Paris, 1981.

[12]Calculations made from AGRODATA, a bank of data compiled by the Groupe de Recherche Agro-Alimentaire of the Institut Agronomique Méditerranéen (I.A.M.) and by the Groupe de Recherche en Economie Rurale de l'Université Laval in Quebec (G.R.A.A.L.).

[13]Vernon, R., 'Influence of National Origins on the Strategy of Multinational Enterprises', R.E., vol. XXIII, no 4, July 1972, in Rainelli, M., op. cit.

[14]Hymer, S. and Rowthorn, R., 'Multinational Corporations and International Oligopoly: the non-American Challenge', in Kindleberger, C. P., *The International Corporation*, MIT Press, Cambridge, 1970.

[15]Burns, Jim., McInenvey, John and Swinbank, Alan, *The Food Industry, Economies and Policies*, Commonwealth Agricultural Bureau, 1983.

[16]C.F.C.E., *Analyse de l'activité de 95 firmes industrielles étrangères dans la bio-industrie*, Centre Français du Commerce Extérieur, Direction des produits alimentaires, Paris, February 1983.

DISCUSSION OPENING I – GUILHERME DIAS

A required background to any argument about neoprotectionism, export subsidies and price instability is the financial crisis, that has gone on for more than fifteen years.

Much of the strategy adopted by developed and less industrialised countries, with extensive protection in the agricultural sector and industrial sectors such as steel, do suggest a disguised system of multiple exchange rates to cope with the crises in the international monetary system. The main objective being the segmentation of the capital market from the real sector of the economy.

The protectionist policy to reduce price instability, together with a coherent income policy on the domestic side and an investment programme in the agricultural sector, combine themselves in an objective policy to take advantage of technological progress never available before in such magnitude.

This environment suggests that we are much closer to a second-best situation on theoretical grounds. Prices do not reflect comparative advantage but they stand for trade opportunities for a much longer period than expected, requiring from each country an appropriate strategy.

There is no alternative to developing countries than to insulate the domestic market from international price instability. Widespread protection to the agricultural sector may not be possible due to its costs but are also not recommended if the burden is going to fall on low-paid wage earners.

A variable levy system should be put into effect whenever international prices fluctuate widely along a medium-run trend. Nowadays what is done to protect domestic market is a discretionary use of non-tariff barriers introducing another set of uncertainties that upset investment and the adoption of new technology.

Concerning the second paper, mutation on multinational firms strategy has much to do with taking advantage of this constantly changing environment of trade barriers and industrial growth policy in developing countries. They have shown a very flexible structure to different forms of regulation, from what was called in the text 'marketing structures' (requiring capital control and entrepreneurial dominance) together with the import-substitutions period of industrial policy, to the 'production strategy' (autonomous plants-control over strategic factors) with export-drive oriented industrial development in less industrialised countries.

On the latest trends revealed by the MNFFCs, the size and the amplitude of R&D investment do significantly establish a minor role for future associations or joint ventures. Together with high levels of indebtedness of the more industrialised middle-income countries there is a strong case for an unprecedented control of world production of food and feed.

A recent trend over less industrialised countries has been revealed by the multinationals stressing as a precondition for new investment on biotechnology-related production, a fully developed legislation on patent rights that would assure them of restricted competition by domestic enterprises. Although in Latin-America the first reaction was negative, further investment in a joint effort by countries that are facing the same problem in planning the future development of their industrial sector may lead them to a new pattern of regulation that could be enforced on multinationals.

Otherwise the quest for a food and nutrition programme, a high-ranking political demand in the domestic scenario, may well be frustrated, as predicted in the paper, due to this unforeseen concentration of capital and technological knowledge.

DISCUSSION OPENING II – PETER M. SCHMITZ

The focus of both papers is on market power or market distortions in international agricultural markets; due to governmental protective trade policies of large trading countries in the first paper and due to monopoly power of private multinational firms in the second paper. In addition the papers aim at giving advice on how to cope with these market imperfections from the developing countries' point of view.

Needless to say, both aspects are of growing importance, have been ignored by agricultural economists for a long time, and demand further research for revealing, evaluating and overcoming market imperfections in the future. However, both papers are rather descriptive in nature and they do not contribute very much to an analytical understanding of some of the issues raised; nor do they give much empirical evidence of the hypotheses developed. What is missing is a clear formulation of a theoretical framework from which one could derive some of the conclusions the authors have drawn on proposals for policy or which could serve as a guideline for evaluating certain structural developments on international agricultural markets from the developing countries' point of view. Unfortunately both papers promise more in their introductions and titles than is met with in the text. Nevertheless they come to far-reaching conclusions for policy adjustments without discussing alternatives and the opportunity costs of such alternatives.

Going into more detail, I would like to pose some questions and to make some comments with respect to the individual papers separately. May I draw your attention to the first paper of Professor Espinosa. First of all, I would like to stress that I fully agree with one main conclusion of this paper, namely that a lower degree of protection in the developed countries with greater degrees of freedom in international markets would decrease instability and would improve food security in developing countries. However, I am not in accordance with the author's demand for a so-called 'soft protection' of the developing countries' agricultural sectors. This seems to be a contradiction to what the author has elaborated in the rest of his paper. I would like to hear from the author some more details about what is meant by 'soft protection'. Before discussing new protection measures in developing countries it might be worthwhile to look for possibilities of reducing the negative protection in most of the developing countries which seems to be very significant. In addition, the proposal of an 'enlarged autarky' of some developing countries is not derived logically from the text and lacks a careful elaboration of the conditions under which regional integration is superior to general integration.

The next point I would like to stress is the author's explanation for growing protection. de Espinosa focuses on the economic crises as the main cause. However, the economic crisis might also be the consequence of new protectionism which itself is a result of the political decision-making process influenced by different interest groups as we heard from Günther Schmitt's paper during the Saturday session. Hence, explaining growing protection and a new quality of protective measures seems to be more complex and interdependent than de Espinosa suggests. Let me now pose some further questions concerning details of the paper:

(a) What is your definition of the need for a certain degree of intervention in agricultural markets on page 557? What is your objective function and do you not consider income policies or intervention in risk markets as alternatives to direct intervention in commodity markets?

(b) Are these quoted degrees of instability on pages 561–2 those of prices or of export earnings?

(c) On page 562 you claim that agricultural free trade in developing countries may lead to critical situations, due to unfair competition. Would you agree with me that protective trade policies also induce critical situations and that an evaluation should include the shortcomings of both alternatives?

Let me now draw attention to the second paper by Dufour/Ghersi/ Saint-Louis which gives a complete and interesting overview of the growing importance of multinational firms in the agribusiness sector, especially of the third type of multinationals. The authors describe in detail the processes of diversification, of multinationalisation, of centralisation, and of co-operation of multinationals in international agricultural markets. However, what is missing is a treatment of the implications of multinationals' activities in LDCs as promised in the title. The authors confine themselves to some very brief conclusions that LDCs confronted with firms of this new generation might be deprived and/or more dependent if they fail to join in by means of lobbying groups or by using other linking rings. An extended impact analysis concerning price, trade, and welfare effects of increased market power as well as a comparison of different policy responses to this new development would have been helpful for the reader.

Without discussing possible alternatives, for instance a supranational strategy, and without defining a clearcut objective function for the LDCs it is hardly possible to derive strategies or policy proposals which lead to something which the authors called a 'favourable situation' or 'suitability' for the LDCs.

Finally it would be very interesting to have some more information on the impact of the ongoing market power concentration on uncertainty in international agricultural markets. Economies of scale in acquiring and disseminating information on the one hand and a tendency towards unequal distributed information on the other, might be the counteracting forces in determining the net effect on world market uncertainties. Could you please give a very brief comment on this aspect because I think this issue is very important from the developing countries' point of view.

GENERAL DISCUSSION – RAPPORTEUR: LIONEL HUBBARD

Discussion from the floor was opened by a general attack on the developed countries' exploitative trading position *vis-à-vis* the developing countries. Whilst some sympathy with this view was evident most points were clearly more political than economic. In this same vein it was suggested that since consumers in the developed countries were spending only 20 per cent of their income on goods and that less than half of this was finding its way back to producers, it was not unreasonable to ask them to pay more for their food. This would ensure a larger return for the world's food exporters. However, it was not made clear how such a change would occur.

On a less emotive level general concern was expressed regarding the distortions in international trade resulting from the various protectionist policies around the world. One way for the developing countries to tackle this situation was for them to insulate their own domestic economies. An alternative was to try to persuade the developed countries to reduce their protection so as to achieve freer international trading. However, it was agreed that there was no easy or obvious way in which the developed countries of the world could be persuaded to change their existing policies in favour of more open trading. It was also pointed out that the injured party in distorted world markets was not only the developing countries. Australia is an example of a low-cost producer heavily reliant on agricultural exports.

The question was posed as to why the teachings of agricultural economists were used so little and so badly by politicians. Was this the fault of economists or politicians or both? Some techniques were being used successfully, but there was obviously something of a gulf between the two parties. To improve the situation it was suggested that more agricultural economists should become Ministers of Agriculture!

Some concern was expressed over the multi-nationals' increasingly aggressive strategies regarding developing countries. These firms are now more adaptive and are responsible for moving large amounts of capital from country to country. This is causing greater uncertainty throughout the world and it was suggested that more research be undertaken into their financial activities. One option might be the development of international financing institutions to regulate these capital flows.

SECTION VIII

Theoretical Developments

ALEXANDER H. SARRIS

Uncertainty in Market Analysis

INTRODUCTION

Uncertainty has always been a factor in agricultural markets and an important attribute of agricultural market analysis. In fact, uncertainty is a major factor in economic life in general.

An uncertain event is usually defined as one which has several possible outcomes. By this definition uncertain events are not only those which will occur in the future and have different possible outcomes, but also those for instance which have already occurred and whose state is difficult to observe, such as the exact size of a crop. It is thus crucial to define clearly what is meant when one speaks about uncertainty.

In this paper the aspects of uncertainty that are important in agricultural market analysis will be emphasised: The effort will be to clarify the ways in which uncertainty modifies the standard models of market analysis, and to pinpoint current gaps in our knowledge and frontier research issues.

THE NATURE OF UNCERTAINTY IN MARKET ANALYSIS

Before we proceed it might be useful to distinguish between what will be termed analysable uncertainty versus non-analysable uncertainty. Consider a random variable. Suppose we identify what we or others think are the possible outcomes of that random variable, namely those states that have some probability of occurrence (which might even be zero), irrespective of whether this probability is objectively determined or subjective. Analysis using this random variable will then be based on the underlying definition of the state space which probability theory considers as given before analysis proceeds. Analysable uncertainty will be defined as the union of underlying state spaces of all random variables that enter the analysis.

The conclusions and predictions of the analysis will be conditional on the analysable uncertainty. In economics, however, where the human factor is an important element in the system, the underlying states of nature cannot be considered fixed. A good example might be the 1973–4 world food crisis. Analyses of those events abound, but a key element in the evolution of the grain market in these years was the drastic change in

585

the economic behaviour pattern of an important market participant, the Soviet Union, a change that was not thought probable before 1973, namely was not considered as a member of the state space of the underlying market related uncertain variables. As such this event belongs to the group of what will be termed here non-analysable uncertainty.

In economics, as well as in other sciences, the definition of the appropriate state spaces of the relevant random variables is an empirical and many times subjective matter. When the state spaces of these random variables change, the whole analysis on which a market model is based must be changed to accommodate the new possible states. Hence, we have what might be termed a structural change of the uncertainty in the model. Notice that this is quite different from mere changes of the probabilities assigned to some fixed outcomes in the state space, e.g., via Bayesian updating. Here, the membership of the state space is itself altered.

While it seems clear that the only kind of uncertainty that can be studied is what has been termed here analysable uncertainty, an important question that arises is whether in market analysis uncertainty enters largely in an analysable or a non-analysable fashion. A second important question is whether the analysis made based on analysable uncertainty is robust in the face of structural changes as alluded to above. Finally, a third question relates to the speed and ease with which structural change in the underlying uncertainty can be identified and hence brought into the analysis.

Identification and estimation of structural changes are very difficult tasks. Econometricians have made some attempts to deal at least with time varying and random parameters in models (for a review see ch. 10 of Judge *et al.*) but very little work has been done on identifying structural changes in the uncertainty of the system, of the type alluded to above.

Market analysis usually comprises examination of demand, supply, inventory and government behaviour. Uncertainty enters in the analysis of all these aspects but in different forms. What can be classified as uncertainty (whether analysable or not) depends on the particular viewpoint examined and might not be termed uncertainty if looked at from a different level of analysis. For example, when one looks at the farm level, the uncertainty facing an individual farmer might be mostly environmental, with an ensuing yield variability for given land, farming practices etc. However, if we examine aggregate supply, which entails a large number of farmers, uncertainty is not only environmental. If, for instance, the aggregate land cultivated to the crop stays constant, but its distribution among the geographically feasible production land changes, e.g., because of farm changes of product mix, then from the aggregate viewpoint uncertainty of yield might increase. Thus, uncertainty is closely related to the scale of analysis and to the information assumed available about the underlying variables.

The last observation, also brings up the distinction between informational uncertainty about the present versus uncertainty related to the future. Suppose that in a particular year we try to analyse the production of a particular crop. After the harvest is completed the size of the crop is theoretically known. From the particular viewpoint, however, of an agency trying, for instance, to order imports, the size of the crop might be an uncertain variable and might stay so throughout the year albeit with decreasing bounds of ignorance. The uncertainty at that level of analysis is an informational one. Suppose, on the other hand, that there is perfect information about the size of the crop as soon as the harvest is complete. It is, nevertheless, impossible to predict accurately the crop in the next period, no matter how much information about the present state of the world is available.

Finally, uncertain future events can be split among those that occur only once and those that recur in a fashion that permits the estimation of actuarial tables. The effects arising out of the construction of an irrigation project are uncertain only until the completion date, while the size of rainfall in September in a region is a variable that permits the construction of frequency tables.

From the above discussion it seems that we can say in summary, that uncertainty relates to the state of knowledge about particular events, whether in the present or the future. At each point in time and for each problem, uncertainty can be defined as the extent of ignorance about the underlying variables of the problem.

SUPPLY AND DEMAND UNDER RISK

All market analysis models contain equations for supply and demand. Yet, while substantial amount of research has been done into behaviour under risk there is still no agreement as to the most appropriate ways of incorporating uncertainty into these models.

Modelling decision-making under uncertainty is by now old art. There is an array of hypotheses about behaviour, such as maximisation of expected profit, or expected utility, the safety first or maximin principle, stochastic dominance rules and others (for a good review, see Anderson 1979). Much effort has also been devoted to measuring people's attitudes toward risk and whether one or the other model, especially the expected utility model, fit well with people's behaviour (for reviews, see ch. 7 of Newbery and Stiglitz, 1981 and Arrow, 1982). The results have been mixed and useful in the sense that they have led to the statement of even more new theories and hypotheses about decision-making under uncertainty such as Kahneman and Tversky's (1979) prospect theory.

However, most of this research has not had significant impact on market analysis models. Most currently used market models still use supply and demand curves that are functions of only the price level. The only mildly significant evolution seems to have been the modelling of market supply curves with multiplicative versus additive disturbances. This, however, has not added too much to what we already know about uncertainty in market analysis.

It seems that a fruitful way in future research would be to attempt to incorporate explicitly higher order moments of the probability distributions of uncertain variables in specifications of aggregate supply and demand curves. A simple example below will illustrate the potential effects.

Assume a closed economy market model for one commodity, where the supply and demand curves are linear with additive disturbances. Assume that supply is negatively influenced by the variance of price. Assume, as in a rational expectations world, that the underlying average price and the price variance are known by market participants. Suppose a government agency decides to stabilize price by instituting a buffer stock that is based on a rule which is based on a buy–sell formula symmetric about the known mean price. Such a stock rule, however, will accumulate supplies forever. The reason for this somewhat unexpected result is that when the price variance is reduced by the operation of the stock, producers will increase their average production, thus leading to a decline in average market price *ceteris paribus*. If the stabilizing authority has not considered this higher moment effect it will eventually be forced either to stop or to modify its rule.

Research in this area is still young, but a good start has been made by the work of Just and Pope (1979).

NATURAL VERSUS INDUCED UNCERTAINTY

How is uncertainty in a market affected by different policies? What are policies that reduce uncertainty and should they be pursued? Should markets be left uninterfered with or should they be controlled in order to reduce uncertainty? Answers to these questions are not easy and they are sometimes ideologically charged.

Before, however, any attempt is made to answer these questions it seems logical to assess the degree to which what is classified as uncertainty is induced by policies or is natural and irreducible in the sense that it would occur in the absence of any intervention. To answer this challenge is not easy, as almost any policy meant to affect a certain aspect of a market will usually have some unintended side effects.

For instance, much research has been done in recent years to investigate the impact on price variability of restrictive trade policies, Josling (1977), Shei and Thompson (1977), Bale and Lutz (1979) and more recently Sarris and Freebairn (1983) have shown, theoretically and empirically, that many restrictive trade policies have adverse impacts on world price variability.

All these models, however, dealt with the side effects of policies primarily intended to affect the volume of trade. Similarly policies affecting farm size, input markets, income distribution etc. will all have some side effects influencing the uncertainty of a market model. It is useful to assess the size of these effects. However, if none of these policies were meant to affect the variable of interest, then they should be considered as part of the background of the problem and attention should be concentrated on the policies directly affecting the market variables of interest.

The idea will be illustrated through a discussion of price stabilization. The concern with undue price instability in many primary commodity markets is long-standing and the literature that has evolved around the issue of price stabilization is large and growing. Most of the discussion, however, (for an early survey, see Turnovsky, 1978), has concerned the benefits from price stabilization. Issues such as the feasibility of price stabilization, the costs of price stabilizing policies, the implementation of price stabilization policies have received secondary attention (a notable exception is the comprehensive book of Newbery and Stiglitz, 1981).

The questions relevant to the discussion here are the following. First, starting from a market where many other policies are present, is it always possible to reduce price variability with buffer stocks or other policies aimed directly at this purpose? Second, will it be more efficient or cheaper to remove or alter other policies designed for other purposes?

In almost all the literature there has been a presumption that stabilization is feasible. Sarris (1982), however, as well as Newberry and Stiglitz (1981), have shown that in the presence of well functioning private arbitrageurs, price stabilization is infeasible. It is imperfections in private markets that make price stabilization feasible and desirable. If this is the case, then the question arises whether it is less costly and more efficient to aim policies at indirect price stabilization via, for instance, improvements in the marketing system rather than institute costly buffer stocks.

Related to this issue is the question of whether it is possible that because of natural market uncertainties, price stabilization policies could lead to opposite effects. Turnovsky (1978b), in fact, has shown that when observation errors are present, it is quite possible that a price stabilization policy can have destabilizing effects. In such a case of course, the best action would be to do nothing.

Related to this issue is the question of behaviour modification by policies. For instance, if a risk insurance programme for farmers is instituted then it might make farmers more careless about their crops hence modifying the underlying supply behaviour and making it more risky (this and several other related issues are discussed in Binswanger 1985).

MARKET IMPERFECTIONS AND UNCERTAINTY

The issue of market imperfections has a long history in the economics literature. Every discussion of market imperfections, however, must necessarily start from a definition of what constitutes a perfect market. The age-old textbook model of a perfectly competitive market under certainty, namely one with many small market participants none of which can influence price has been extended in recent years to include issues of uncertainty. Two key elements have been introduced in the traditional model, a complete set of contingent markets and perfect and equal information about the current state of nature by all market participants.

A perfect market of the type envisaged above would not, of course, be without any fluctuations. Unpredicted events would always occur but market participants would almost instantaneously adjust to them. A market operating under the above assumptions would be efficient in the sense that all information about the present state of nature would be incorporated into current market variables such as price.

Enormous amounts of research in the last 20 years have gone into investigating whether markets are efficient (see the early survey of Fama, 1970, for capital markets and Labys and Granger, 1970, for commodity markets) with mixed results. By and large the markets that have been analysed are the large organised ones for which data is readily available. This, of course, immediately biases the analysis in favour of efficiency. Even for these markets, however, recent research shows that there is ample room for imperfections (see, e.g., Kyle, 1984).

That real world markets depart from the theoretical ideal is no news, especially since it is well known that complete sets of contingent markets do not exist and information is costly to acquire and not universally available. It is of great practical interest, however, to decide how close real world markets are to the theoretical ideal and whether policies to intervene in some market aspect are worth the cost.

For instance, is it less costly and more efficient for the government to provide more and better information in order to stabilize a market or is it better to intervene directly? In many developing countries the latter course has been chosen. This could be due to the fact that markets in those countries are not as well organised and are strewn with marketing imperfections, such as local monopolies, inadequate transportation and communication facilities etc. In countries with a developed infrastructure, on the other hand, market intervention is likely to be more efficient if it is done indirectly via, for instance, introduction of more contingent markets, better information etc.

Research in the relation between market imperfections and uncertainty is rather scant, but the subject is fairly ripe for intense study. An *a priori* hypothesis that could be studied is whether residual (as opposed to government induced) uncertainty and instability in a market is a decreasing function of the development of market infrastructure. Answers to such questions would then provide the basis for evaluating alternative policies. For instance, the building of food security stocks in a remote region might be a cost-efficient policy if the road and communication network were very rudimentary and any production shock would have to be absorbed locally. Similarly the efficacy of provision by the government of satellite-based information to the market about world-wide crop developments would depend on the general development of the market information network.

EXPECTATIONS AND MARKET UNCERTAINTY

Expectations formation is a significant part of market analysis. Many years of research have produced essentially two types of general hypotheses about aggregate expectations formation: the well known adaptive expectations model (of which naïve expectations is a special case) and the rational expectations model. While most models of market analysis use one or the other hypothesis, not much has been done to clarify which model is more relevant and under what market conditions. The assumption of rationality while theoretically convenient has rather drastic implications about the effectiveness of market intervention policies. In fact, under most cases it can be shown that when expectations are rational, market stabilisation policies are ineffective. This line of research, of course, has developed mostly in the macroeconomic literature on the effectiveness of monetary policy (see the volumes by Fischer, 1980, and Lucas and Sargent, 1981), but the arguments apply *a fortiori* to market analysis research.

It is not easy to assess empirically whether expectations follow one or other major models. It is not even easy to assess conclusively whether different expectations hypotheses theoretically reduce or not the variability of market variables such as prices (for a comparison of a market model with rational v. adaptive expectations, see Turnovsky 1979).

An interesting and as yet untackled question is whether the development of a more organised market changes the structure of expectations formation. Another question also unresolved but interesting for market analysis is whether the evolution of more organised markets and more efficient expectations formation in one part of the world helps or not the markets in another part of the world. Finally, the issue of whether different expectations hypotheses reduce or not market uncertainty should be further investigated within more complete market models.

INFORMATION AND MARKET UNCERTAINTY

The issues surrounding market information raise extremely interesting research questions many of which are still not resolved.

To begin with, does improved market information reduce market uncertainty? The answer is not clear because while one could argue that improved information to all market participants would make their trading strategies more rational, it would also make traders much more alert to changes in market conditions and the ensuing rush to capitalise on market news could lead to overreactions and increased market instability.

Does differential access to information lead to informational monopolies? Kyle (1981) has shown that indeed such things are possible. What is the impact of informational private monopolies on market uncertainty? Is there an informational externality and what is the best way to correct it? Interesting work along similar lines by Figlewski (1978) points out that a market with traders possessing diverse information will lead to wealth redistributions and might not be efficient. On a different line Grossman (1976) investigates how information from informed traders is 'revealed' to uninformed ones through the market.

Research in this area is very young. As markets evolve, however, and technological developments make information cheaper and more accessible, issues such as the above are bound to receive increased attention.

MARKET INSTITUTIONS AND UNCERTAINTY

Markets evolve over time and different institutions are introduced to account for technological developments and market needs. The institutions most analysed in the recent literature have been the organised futures markets, perhaps because data is most readily available for these and also because they provide examples of contingent markets of which there exist very few.

There is, nevertheless, a fairly extensive literature analysing the efficiency of the marketing system (for a survey see French 1977), but it has not dealt very much with the issue of uncertainty. This is unfortunate because uncertainty in a market is directly related to the efficiency of the marketing system. It seems that renewed effort in coming years should go in this area as it is related to general development policies. It is this author's belief that there is a significant trade-off between policies designed to deal directly with uncertainty and policies designed to improve the functioning of the marketing system. These trade-offs have not been analysed at all until now.

Returning now to the institution of futures markets, the literature is enormous and growing to the point where there is now a specialised journal devoted only to futures markets studies. The growth in futures trading is probably not unrelated to the technological revolution in information processing and communications. However, one of the basic questions concerning the impact of futures markets on price stability of the cash markets has not been conclusively resolved. While theoretical work has advanced to the point where under certain assumptions one can show that futures markets stabilize the cash markets (Sarris, 1984; Kawai, 1983), empirical work has lagged. However, much more needs to be done before one gives the green light for the enactment of more futures markets. Furthermore, it seems that all work regarding futures markets has dealt with closed models. However, the existence of futures markets in a developed country while influencing the world market of a commodity can have unknown impact on a developing country which for instance has currency controls and hence cannot allow its traders to participate.

SUMMARY AND CONCLUSIONS

The brief discussion above has highlighted the many unresolved questions that exist in the field of uncertainty in market analysis. While much progress has been made in recent years, uncertainty remains a clouded and important issue. In fact the onset of the 1973 world food crisis led many people to believe that market uncertainty was growing. This is certainly probable, although not much work has been done to corroborate it.

The perusal of the huge literature and the diverse aspects that have been examined leave one somewhat uneasy, in the sense that not many solid policy recommendations are forthcoming. Introducing uncertainty in market models is an art of positive economics that has not as yet been perfected, and hence the policy conclusions are not very solid. One of the major questions that remains is whether policies designed to deal with some issues under certainty are relatively robust when uncertainty is introduced. The answer to that question seems to be a well qualified yes. Thus, price supports, trade restrictions etc., while influenced by and in turn influencing the system's uncertainty, are not seriously modified in their qualitative impact (albeit the quantitative impact might be large) on the economic system. It is policies directly designed to deal with uncertainty, such as price stabilizing buffer stocks, commodity agreements, futures markets etc., that are heavily influenced by the precise nature of the uncertainty and how it is introduced in the system. This area of research has only recently started and it appears that since the need for these policies has increased, it is an area of much promising future.

REFERENCES

Anderson, J. R., 'Perspective on Models of Uncertain Decisions' in Roumasset, J. A., Boussard, J. M., and Singh, I. (eds), *Risk, Uncertainty and Agricultural Development*, Southeast Asian Regional Center for Graduate Study and Research in Agriculture, and Agricultural Development Council, 1979.

Arrow, K. J., 'Risk Perceptions in Psychology and Economics', *Economic Inquiry*, vol. 20, no. 1, January 1982.

Bale, M. D. and Lutz, E., 'The Effects of Trade Intervention on International Price Instability', *American Journal of Agricultural Economics*, vol. 61, 1979, pp. 512–16.

Binswanger, H. P., 'Risk Aversion, Collateral Requirements, and the Markets for Credit and Insurance in Rural Areas' in Hazell, P., Pomareda, C., and Valdes, A. (eds), *Agricultural Risks and Insurance: Issues and Policies*, International Food Policy Research Institute (forthcoming), 1985.

Fama, E., 'Efficient Capital Markets: A Review of Theory and Empirical Work', *Journal of Finance*, vol. 25, no. 2, May 1970.

Figlewski, S., 'Market Efficiency in a Market with Heterogeneous Information', *Journal of Political Economy*, vol. 86, no. 4, August 1978.

Fischer, S. (ed.), *Rational Expectations and Economic Policy*, University of Chicago Press, 1980.

French, B. C., 'The Analysis of Productive Efficiency in Agricultural Marketing: Models, Methods and Progress' in Martin, L. R. (ed), *A Survey of Agricultural Economics Literature*, vol. 1, University of Minnesota Press, 1977.

Grossman, S., 'On the Efficiency of Competitive Stock Markets where Traders have Diverse Information', *The Journal of Finance*, vol. 31, no. 2, May 1976.

Josling, T., 'Government Price Policies and the Structure of International Agricultural Trade', *Journal of Agricultural Economics*, vol. 28, 1977, pp. 261–78.

Judge, G. G., Griffiths, W. E., Hill, R. C. and Lee, T. C., *The Theory and Practice of Econometrics*, John Wiley, New York, 1980.

Just, R. E. and Pope, R., 'Production Function Estimation and Related Risk Considerations', *American Journal of Agricultural Economics*, vol. 61, no. 2, May 1979.

Kahneman, D. and Tversky, A., 'Prospect Theory: An Analysis of Decision under Risk', *Econometrica*, vol. 47, no. 2, March 1979.

Kawai, M., 'Price Volatility of Storable Commodities under Rational Expectations in Spot and Futures Markets', *International Economic Review*, vol. 24, no. 2, June 1983.

Kyle, A. S., 'An Equilibrium Model of Speculation and Hedging' Unpublished Ph.D. dissertation, University of Chicago, 1981.

Kyle, A. S., 'Market Structure, Information, Futures Markets, and Price Formation', ch. 2 in Storey, G. G., Schmitz, A. and Sarris, A. H., (eds), *International Agricultural Trade: Advanced Readings*, Westview Press, Boulder, Colorado, 1984.

Labys, W. C. and Granger, C., *Speculation, Hedging and Commodity Price Forecasts*, Lexington Books, 1970.

Lucas, R. E. and Sargent, T. J. (editors), *Rational Expectations and Econometric Practice*, vols 1 and 2, University of Minnesota Press, 1981.

Newbery, D. M. G. and Stiglitz, J., *The Theory of Commodity Price Stabilization*, Clarendon Press, Oxford, 1981.

Sarris, A. H., 'Commodity Price Theory and Public Stabilization Stocks', ch. 5 in Chisholm, A. H. and Tyers, R. (eds), *Food Security: Theory, Policy, and Perspectives from Asia and the Pacific Rim*, Lexington Books, 1982.

Sarris, A. H. and Freebairn, J. 'Endogenous Price Policies and International Wheat Prices', *American Journal of Agricultural Economics*, vol. 65, no. 2, May 1983.

Sarris, A. H., 'Speculative Storage, Futures Markets and the Stability of Commodity Prices', *Economic Inquiry*, vol. 22, no. 1, January 1984.

Shei, S. Y. and Thompson, R. L., 'The Impact of Trade Restrictions on Price Stability in the World Wheat Market', *American Journal of Agricultural Economics*, vol. 59, 1977, pp. 628–38.

(a) Turnovsky, S. J., 'The Distribution of Welfare Gains from Price Stabilization: A Survey of Some Theoretical Issues' in Adams, F. G. and Klein, S. (eds), *Stabilizing World Commodity Markets*, Lexington Books 1978.

(b) Turnovsky, S. J., 'Stabilization Rules and the Benefits from Price Stabilization', *Journal of Public Economics*, vol. 9, 1978, pp. 37–57.

Turnovsky, S. J., 'Futures Markets, Private Storage, and Price Stabilization', *Journal of Public Economics*, vol. 12, 1979, pp. 301–27.

GORDON C. RAUSSER, JAMES A. CHALFANT, AND KOSTAS
G. STAMOULIS

Instability in Agricultural Markets: The US Experience

INTRODUCTION

Governments continue to play a major role in agricultural markets throughout the world. As argued at some length in Rausser and Farrell (1984), the only market-failure justifications for governmental intervention are *excessive* uncertainty or unanticipated instability and an incomplete set of risk markets. In the United States prior to 1972, the common explanations for instability were the inelastic nature of aggregate food demand; the low-income elasticity of demand; and, on the supply side, weather patterns, rapid technological change, atomistic behaviour (and in some treatments naïve price expectations), and asset fixity. These characteristics were viewed as existing in a closed, insulated representation of the US agricultural sector. Without governmental intervention, the inherent and unanticipated instability resulting from these characteristics was regarded by many to be unacceptable to all actors in the food and agriculture system: input suppliers, producers, assemblers, processors, distributors, and consumers.

Keynes (1938), Houthakker (1967), and others have argued that, because inherent instability in storable commodity markets would lead to insufficient private stockholding, some government intervention is warranted. Since 1972, however, conventional wisdom has placed increasingly less emphasis on the inherent instability in commodity markets and more emphasis on instability due to external linkages with other markets. During this period, deregulation of the credit and banking system resulted in a greater exposure of agriculture to conditions in domestic money markets. Also, because international capital markets have become increasingly integrated, agricultural commodity markets are more sensitive to international monetary events, capital movements among countries, etc.

Government behaviour has also played an important role in commodity market instability. After the Soviet grain deal, the absence of government-held stocks contributed to large price increases, With the Food and Agriculture Act of 1977, changes in commodity programmes were introduced which permitted a wider fluctuation in prices. The

595

export embargo in 1980, variations in the rules of the Farmer-Owned Reserve Program since 1980, and the Payment-In-Kind (PIK) Program of 1983 suggest that policy uncertainty can be a major contributor to private commodity market instability.

Another source of instability is increased dependence on export markets. In the late 1970s, US agricultural exports accounted for almost 40 per cent of total output. This greater dependence on foreign trade has left US agriculture more vulnerable to shocks from foreign markets. In addition, the Soviet Union has emerged as a major importer, making the effects of its unstable agriculture felt in the United States.

The linkage of commodity markets with US money markets occurs through both demand and supply effects. Because farming in the United States is extremely capital intensive and debt-to-asset ratios have risen dramatically during the last ten years, movements in real interest rates have significant effects on the cost structure facing agricultural production. In addition, grain stocks held and the level of livestock breeding inventories are interest rate sensitive. Finally, the influence of interest rates on the value of the dollar can lead to reduced foreign demand for US grain. Thus, rising interest rates at once increase the cost of grain production and depress demand. Therefore, monetary and fiscal policy changes, through changes in real interest rates, also affect the stability of agricultural markets.

Along with these interest rate effects, there appear to be differential effects of monetary policy between agricultural and non-agricultural markets. If agricultural commodity markets behave as 'flex price' while other markets behave as 'fixed price', 'macroexternalities' will be imposed on the agricultural sector. Different speeds of adjustment in the two types of prices following changes in monetary policy mean that overshooting in agricultural prices will occur even if expectations are formed rationally. This overshooting is analogous to the exchange rate overshooting, first studied by Dornbusch (1976), and amounts to either a tax or a subsidy for agriculture through relative price changes. Thus, overshooting can introduce further instabilities into a sector that is already inherently unstable.

RECENT US MONETARY EFFECTS

The combination of US fiscal and monetary policies has driven real interest rates to all-time highs. The management of money supply in the United States and the relatively high interest rates in this country have reversed the decline of the US dollar that occurred throughout the 1970s. Possibly because of the dominant role of the Federal Reserve in world money markets and the rapid appreciation in the value of the dollar, other central banks also maintained a tight rein on their money supply in an attempt to manage the value of their currency. This has led to a decline in foreign demand for US agricultural exports.

The deflation in agricultural commodity markets over the 1980s, along with the increasing attractiveness of financial assets, has resulted in some rather dramatic decreases in agricultural asset values, particularly land prices. Due to the role of land resources as collateral for agricultural loans and credit lines, the debt-absorption capacity of US agriculture has fallen markedly. This is evidenced by the increased frequency of bankruptcies in the agricultural production sector and by what has come to be called the agricultural financial crisis of 1984.

In the decade of the 1970s, conditions in the US general economy and the international economy were almost the exact opposite of the conditions that exist in much of the 1980s. In 1972–3, the magnitude of increases in farm product and food prices surprised even the most informed people within the public and private sectors. The move to flexible exchange rates, the rapid expansion of international markets, the emergence of a well integrated international capital market, and the decreasing barriers between the agricultural economy and other domestic economic sectors all resulted in significant changes in the agricultural sector. During this period, the Federal Reserve expanded the US money supply with the effective objective of holding the real price of energy at basically the same level; other countries attempted to 'inflate their way out' of the energy price shocks by increasing their money supplies. They also attempted to manage their exchange rates with the US dollar by selling their currencies and buying dollars and, thus, indirectly increasing their money supplies even more.

The increases in relative commodity prices which resulted along with the rapid rate of inflation experienced in 1972–4 and again in 1978–80 resulted in a dramatic increase in the valuation of the major resource input in agricultural production, namely, land. US agricultural land prices increased at a more rapid rate than the rate of inflation during much of the 1970s. Once again, due to the role of this resource input in agricultural credit markets, viz., its use as collateral for agricultural loans and credit lines, the total absorption capacity of the US agriculture for debt appeared to be augmented by leaps and bounds during the decade of the 1970s.

Thus, since the early 1970s, the US agricultural sector has been subjected to a vicious roller coaster ride, the valleys and peaks of which have been defined in part by the external linkages to the US macroeconomy and the international economy. These external linkages have made it crystal clear that timing, in terms of entry and exit from US agricultural production, is indeed critical. More important, they show that, in large part, the inherent instability in the agricultural sector has been augmented by instability caused by factors outside that sector.

DYNAMIC MARKET ANALYSIS

The experience in the United States, as well as in numerous other countries, makes it clear that the conventional microeconomic analysis of commodity markets is inadequate. The dynamic path of agricultural commodity markets cannot be explained on the basis of private market demand and supply functions alone. In fact, the appropriate characterisations of such dynamics can only be obtained by specifying (1) the real supply and demand forces for a particular market; (2) the influence of governmental intervention; and (3) the linkages between domestic agricultural markets, exchange rates, and domestic as well as international money markets. Most observers would agree with the need for (1) and (2), but few have explicitly recognised the importance of (3).

Any attempt to characterise the dynamic instability of agricultural markets should address itself to at least three major sources of instability: inherent instability emanating from natural supply and demand forces, uncertainties and risk emanating from political or governmental failure (Rausser and Foster 1984), and overshooting of storable commodity prices resulting from linkages with financial markets. The first two sources of instability are reasonably well known and need not be addressed here. The new source of instability, namely, overshooting, is not widely known by agricultural economists and is generally neglected in agricultural price analysis.

As shown in the Appendix, overshooting of flexible prices, such as exchange rates or storable prices, arises because some markets in the general economy are fixed-price markets. This results in short-run non-neutrality of money because relative prices are affected (Stamoulis, Chalfant and Rausser 1985). Over time, as fixed prices adjust, relative prices are assumed to return to long-run equilibrium levels; but the interim effects can be thought of as macroexternalities.

As shown in the Appendix, as the share of flex-price markets rises, the extent of overshooting falls. This suggests, of course, that, *ceteris paribus*, the larger the number of flex-price markets, the less instability in storable commodity markets resulting from overshooting. In the case of the US agricultural sector, the introduction of flexible exchange rates in 1973 and, more recently, the introduction of flexible interest rates in late 1979 imply less overshooting for a given shock. Of course, the amount of observed instability may be greater, even though more markets become flex price, if the shocks in money markets are larger.

In the case of storable commodity markets, the overshooting phenomenon requires that the economy be a mixture of fixed and flex-price markets. Without this specification, money will not assume non-neutral effects over the short run. In the following section, we present a formal test for the fixed price, flex-price specification of the US economy.

FIXED/FLEX PRICE SPECIFICATION

We conducted a simple test for the presence of overshooting by examining the sensitivity of prices to anticipated money growth. We estimated money growth using a fairly *ad hoc* mechanism which we treat as the reaction function of monetary authorities. As in the series of studies by Barro (1977, 1978) and the recent paper by Enders and Falk (1984), predicted values from this regression (MFIT) are treated as anticipated money growth. Fitted residuals are thought of as unanticipated money growth.

The anticipated money growth rate was used to explain the price level response in the fixed and flex-price sectors of the economy. The rate of change of the non-food Consumer Price Index (CPINF) is taken as the growth rate of prices in the fixed-price markets, while a calculated growth rate of the US Department of Agriculture Index of Prices Received by Farmers (FOODINF) was used to measure growth in flex prices. An equation is also estimated for the percentage change in the Consumer Price Index for food and beverages (CPIF).

To explain variation in these rates of change, we used as independent variables our anticipated money growth variable, distributed lags of the gap between potential and actual income (INCGAP), oil price inflation (OILINFL), the differential of wage and productivity growth rates (WPRODIF), and a lagged dependent variable. The following equations were estimated using instrumental variables (standard errors are given in parentheses, and we report only the sums of lag coefficients):

$$
\begin{aligned}
\text{FOODINF} = \ &\underset{(2.608)}{1.891} + \underset{(0.128)}{0.0319}\ \text{FOODINF} - \underset{(0.380)}{0.188}\ \text{WPRODIF} \\
&+ \underset{(0.0238)}{0.00003}\ \text{OILINFL} + \underset{(0.0113)}{0.0286}\ \text{INCGAP} + \underset{(1.319)}{1.641}\ \text{MFIT}
\end{aligned}
$$

$$
\begin{aligned}
\text{CPINF} = \ &\underset{(0.321)}{0.0117} + \underset{(0.144)}{0.366}\ \text{CPINF} + \underset{(0.044)}{0.070}\ \text{WPRODIF} \\
&+ \underset{(0.0039}{0.0115}\ \text{OILINFL} + \underset{(0.0014)}{0.003}\ \text{INCGAP} + \underset{(0.169)}{0.329}\ \text{MFIT}
\end{aligned}
$$

$$
\begin{aligned}
\text{CPIF} = \ &\underset{(0.588)}{0.9826} + \underset{(0.127)}{0.3778}\ *\ \text{CPIF}_{t-1} + \underset{(0.074)}{0.0018}\ *\ \text{WPRODIF} \\
&+ \underset{(0.00597)}{0.0052}\ *\ \text{OILINFL} + \underset{(0.0028)}{0.0067}\ *\ \text{INCGAP} + \underset{(0.250)}{0.2144}\ *\ \text{MFIT}
\end{aligned}
$$

$$\bar{R}^2 = 0.242$$
$$\text{DW} = 1.91$$

Comparing the coefficients across the equations for FOODINF and CPINF, we see that the lagged dependent variable has a large and significant coefficient in the non-food inflation equation compared to the food equation. In addition, anticipated money growth causes a much greater response in food inflation than for non-agricultural goods. In fact, the estimated coefficient exceeds one – corresponding to overshooting of food prices following money growth. By contrast, the coefficient in the CPINF equation is significantly less than one, indicating sluggish response to anticipated money growth. Presumably, this is because some of the factors causing stickiness of non-food prices, say, contracts, were already in place in the preceding quarter. These results support the assumption that prices in the non-food sectors adjust more sluggishly than food prices to changes in money growth. Coupled with the theoretical model presented in the Appendix, this provides a basis for assuming that there are spillover effects from monetary changes in US agriculture.

The results from the CPIF equation strongly indicate that the use of a Consumer Price Index for food is an inappropriate way to represent commodity prices, especially in the context of an asset-market equilibrium. The significance and magnitude of the coefficients of the lagged dependent variable and the income gap suggest an adjustment pattern that strongly resembles the industrial (non-food) price index adjustment. This is not surprising once we recognize that, from the farm gate to the food store, a lot of 'industrial contamination' occurs that increases the degree of 'stickiness' of the farm prices.

The test presented above for the fixed/flex-price specification of the US economy will be investigated for a number of other countries as well as worldwide agricultural markets. We are in the process of collecting the data for the three equations presented here for major exporting countries of food and feedgrains. We also propose to make the same sorts of tests for world-wide food and non-food prices. Ultimately, the latter empirical investigation will admit currency substitution; reaction functions on the part of central banks; and, indirectly, the influence of international monetary linkages on storable commodity market prices.

CONCLUSION

To the extent that money is non-neutral in the short run, analysis of agricultural market dynamics must take into account not only real demand and supply forces and the effects of sectoral governmental intervention but also the macroeconomic policies of the federal government. The fixed/flex price dichotomy of the US economy implies that money is, in fact, non-neutral. Because some goods and services do not respond to changes in demand in the short run, namely, the 'customer' goods defined by Okun (1975) or the fixed-price goods defined by Hicks (1974), analysis of commodity markets requires an explicit treatment of monetary factors and the linkages with the macroeconomy. The prices of most other goods are sticky while the prices of agricultural commodities, in the absence of governmental intervention, are free to respond to fluctuations in demand and supply.

Since the general price level is not free to respond fully in the short run, changes in nominal money supply are also changes in the real money supply and, therefore, induce changes in the interest rate which, in turn, induce changes in relative prices. As a result, changes in the money supply will lead to overshooting in flex-price markets. Through much of the 1970s and 1980s, exchange rates have been flexible; hence, changes in the money supply will lead to changes in the value of the dollar that are more than proportionate to the change in money supply. Only when the dollar is 'overvalued' ('undervalued') will investors rationally expect a future rate of depreciation (appreciation) that is sufficient to offset the interest rate differential so that the interest rate parity condition holds and investors are willing to hold foreign currency. In the short run, the exchange rate overshoots its long-run equilibrium. This quite obviously happened from 1980 to 1982 when the Federal Reserve adopted a stringent monetary policy. Unlike the 1970s, the resulting higher nominal interest rates did not reflect higher expected inflation but, rather, represented higher real interest rates. As a consequence, the dollar appreciated sharply.

The overshooting is a direct implication of the fixed/flex price framework. This framework was formally tested and the empirical results corroborate the differential response of nonfood market prices and food market prices to changes in anticipated money growth. Factors affecting commodity price overshooting are shown in the Appendix to be the number of fixed-price markets, the speed of adjustment of those prices, and the interest rate elasticity of money demand.

Non-monetisation of large federal government deficits can be interpreted as a restrictive monetary policy. Such a restrictive monetary policy leads to increases in the real rate of interest and the exchange value of the dollar and to decreases in the long-run equilibrium feedgrain and wheat commodity price path. Because of slower adjustment in other segments of the macroeconomy, commodity prices in the short run also overshoot the new long-run equilibrium commodity price. With an expansionary monetary policy, all of these factors run in the opposite direction.

Results reported in Rausser (1985) demonstrate that macroeconomic policies can easily dominate the short-run effects of agricultural policies on the price and income paths for US agriculture. The implicit taxes resulting from overshooting that are imposed on US agriculture are modified by the current form and shape of US agricultural policy. In particular, price supports imply downward inflexibility of some commodity prices which, in turn, cause the incidence of the macroeconomic policy tax on agriculture to show up as an unexpected increase in the cost of maintaining price supports and the various forms of government stockholding. Overshooting of agricultural commodity prices in the downward direction places some of the implicit tax on the private sector and some on the public sector. Due to the form and shape of current US agricultural policies, the overshooting effects of expansionary monetary policies are asymmetric. Much, if not all, of the subsidy accrues to the private sector.

In the long run, because money is neutral, agricultural sector policies have a more significant influence on resource allocation to the US agricultural sector than do macroeconomic policies. The sector policies that provide incentives for overallocation of resources to agricultural production quite obviously make the sector especially vulnerable to macroeconomic policies that impose implicit taxes via overshooting. Such sector policies, when combined with macroeconomic policies that 'subsidise' US agriculture, must, by definition, lead to a financial crisis for both private and public sectors if and when macroeconomic policies begin to impose 'taxes' via overshooting on agriculture. The dynamic path composed of a subsidy period followed by a tax period during which sector policies provide incentives for overallocation of resources to agricultural production can be expected to create crises.

APPENDIX

Overshooting in commodity and exchange rate markets

Assume that uncovered interest parity holds which require that

$$i - i^* = x,$$

where i and i* are domestic and foreign nominal interest rates, respectively, and x is the expected depreciation of the domestic currency. This expectation, in turn, is assumed to be a function of the extent to which the exchange rate (domestic currency per foreign currency units) deviates from its long-run equilibrium level,

$$x = \theta(\bar{e} - e),$$

where θ is directly related to the flexibility of non-agricultural prices. It ranges from zero (fixed prices) to one (perfectly flexible prices).

An equilibrium condition in the money market is expressed in natural logarithms:

$$m - q = \phi y - \lambda i,$$

where m denotes the nominal money supply, q the price level, y income, and i the interest rate. All are measured in logarithms except the interest rate. Purchasing power parity is assumed to hold for the agricultural commodity,

$$e = P_a - P_a^*.$$

If each price P_a is expressed in logarithms, the assumption that the foreign price is one allows this expression to be rewritten as

$$e = P_a.$$

Note that this is simply a choice about the units in which to express the price of the agricultural commodity.

The domestic price level is Q, and its natural logarithm q appears in the money market equilibrium condition. Initially, let Q be a Cobb-Douglas price index so that

$$q = \alpha P_n + (1 - \alpha) P_a$$

or

$$q = \alpha P_n + (1 - \alpha) e,$$

where P_n is the natural logarithm of the fixed-price good. The money market equilibrium condition can therefore be expressed as

$$m - \alpha P_n - (1 - \alpha) e = \phi y - \lambda i.$$

Combining the uncovered interest parity assumption and the expected depreciation of the currency, the money market equilibrium condition becomes

$$m - \alpha P_n - (1 - \alpha) e = \phi y - \lambda[\theta (\bar{e} - e) + i^*].$$

This expression summarises equilibrium in financial asset markets.

A long-run version of the expression for asset market equilibrium, one in which money supply is taken to be at its long-run equilibrium level, is

$$\bar{m} - \alpha \bar{P}_n - (1 - \alpha) \bar{e} = \phi y - \lambda i^*.$$

Note that the expected depreciation of the currency is now zero.

Combining the last two expressions and expressing the nominal interest rate differential $(i - i^*)$ as expected depreciation or appreciation of the home currency,

$$m - \alpha P_n - (1 - \alpha) e = -\lambda \theta(\bar{e} - e) + \bar{m} - \alpha \bar{P}_n - (1 - \alpha) \bar{e},$$

where $y = \bar{y}$ is assumed for convenience. By taking $m = \bar{m}$ as well, we find that

$$e - \bar{e} = -\alpha[(1 - \alpha) + \lambda \theta]^{-1} (P_n - \bar{P}_n).$$

The equilibrium exchange rate deviates from its long-run equilibrium rate ($\bar{e}$) by an amount proportional to the deviation of the price in the fixed-price sector from its long-run equilibrium level. The proportion is increasing in α and decreasing in λ and θ.

The persistence of expected appreciation or depreciation does not mean that unexploited profits exist. The expected capital gain or loss on bonds denominated in the home currency will be consistent with both the uncovered interest parity assumption and the rate of return available through storing commodities. For instance, when the domestic interest rate falls below the foreign rate following an increase in money growth, the currency depreciates instantly as the prices of foreign assets are bid up. The more the interest rate falls, the greater this immediate overshooting response of the exchange rate must be. Depreciation continues until the expected revaluation plus the (lower) nominal interest rate just equals i^*, the rest-of-world interest rate. Then expected depreciation falls over time as the fixed-price P_n moves towards its long-run equilibrium and i returns to i^*.

In addition, there is no advantage to holding commodities instead of currencies. Frankel and Frankel and Hardouvelis (1983) develop this latter point in more detail, but a brief summary is in order. To compensate the holders of grain inventories for foregoing present consumption, the grain price must rise at the interest rate in between harvests once convenience yields, storage costs, and a risk premium are taken into account. If an unanticipated growth in the money supply occurs so that the liquidity effect causes a fall in the interest rate, a better return is available for storing grain than dollars and investors compete to hold grain inventories. This causes an immediate jump in the price of grain so that an asset market equilibrium of equal rates of return is restored. All commodity prices are, therefore, expected to rise at the now lower interest rate.

Recall that we took P_a to be equal to the exchange rate by normalising the rest-of-the-world price of agricultural output. This means that there is an equivalent amount of overshooting in the agricultural goods markets. Also, note that the proportion by which e deviates from e is increasing in α or decreasing in $(1 - \alpha)$, so this illustrates the importance of the number of fixed-price markets. As the share of fixed-price markets rises, the extent of deviation of e from e is greater; and, as that share falls, it is less.

Both e and P_a overshoot their long-run equilibrium levels in the manner directly related to deviation of P_n from its long-run equilibrium level. The upshot is that there are relative price changes during the adjustment period. This is a source of macroexternalities. In the short run, relative price changes occur so that, after monetary growth, there is a period in which agriculture is subsidised; conversely, after a contraction, the change in relative prices acts as a tax on agriculture until the fixed-price has fully adjusted.

REFERENCES

Barro, Robert J., 'Unanticipated Money Growth and Unemployment in the United States', *American Economic Review*, vol. 67, 1977, pp. 101–15.

Barro, Robert J., 'Unanticipated Money Output and the Price Level in the United States', *Journal of Political Economy*, vol. 86, 1978, pp. 549–80.

Bosworth, Barry P. and Lawrence, Robert Z., *Commodity Prices and the New Inflation*, Brookings Institution, Washington, DC, 1982, ch. 4.

Dornbusch, Rudiger, 'Expectations and Exchange Rate Dynamics', *Journal of Political Economy*, vol. 84, 1976, pp. 1161–76.

Enders, Walter and Falk, Barry, 'A Microeconomic Test of Money Neutrality', *The Review of Economics and Statistics*, vol. 64, 1984, pp. 666–9.

Frankel, Jeffrey, A., 'On the Mark: A Theory of Floating Exchange Rates Based on Real Interest Differentials', *American Economic Review*, vol. 69, 1979, pp. 610–22.

Frankel, J. A. and Hardouvelis, G. A., 'Commodity Prices, Overshooting, Money Surprises, and FED Credibility', Working Paper no. 1121, National Bureau of Economic Research, Cambridge, Mass., May 1983.

Hicks, John R., *The Crisis in Keynesian Economics*, Basil Blackwell, Oxford, 1974.

Houthakker, H. S., *Economic Policy for the Farm Sector*, American Enterprise Institute for Public Policy Research, Washington, DC, 1967.

Keynes, John Maynard, 'The Policy of Government Storage of Food Stuffs and Raw Materials', *Economic Journal*, vol. 48, 1938, pp. 449–60.

Okun, Arthur, M., 'Inflation: Its Mechanics and Welfare Costs', *Brookings Papers on Economic Activity*, 1975, pp. 351–401.

Rausser, Gordon C., *Macroeconomics and U. S. Agricultural Policy*, Occasional Paper, American Enterprise Institute for Public Policy Research, Washington, DC and Department of Agricultural and Resource Economics, University of California, Berkeley, 1985.

Rausser, Gordon C. and Farrell, Kenneth R. (eds), *Alternative Agricultural and Food Policies and the 1985 Farm Bill*, Giannini Foundation of Agricultural Economics, Division of Agriculture and Natural Resources, University of California, Berkeley, 1984.

Rausser, Gordon C. and Foster, William E., 'Agricultural Policy: A Synthesis of Major Studies and Options for 1985', paper presented at the National Conference on Food, Agriculture, and Resources: Policy Choices, 1985, Washington, DC., 4–6 December, 1984.

Stamoulis, Kostas G., Chalfant, James A. and Rausser, Gordon C., 'Monetary Policies and the Overshooting of Flexible Prices: Implications for Agricultural Policy', Department of Agricultural and Resource Economics University of California, Berkeley, 1985.

DISCUSSION OPENING I – H. E. BUCHHOLZ

Two quite different papers have been presented. The first is a review of problems connected with uncertainty in market analysis. The second paper deals with a specific approach to analyse the increased instability which results from the linkage of commodity markets with other markets in the economy at large. I will comment on these papers in the order in which they have been presented.

The paper by Sarris contains a rather extensive review of literature which shows on the one hand the importance that the notion of uncertainty has for many aspects of market analysis and, on the other hand, indicates some of the methodological concepts and approaches to deal with uncertainty in market analysis. Among the topics discussed are uncertainty with respect to supply and demand, stabilization problems, market imperfection and uncertainty, the role of expectations and of information and market institutions to deal with market uncertainty. This presentation concentrates on problems of empirical investigation. The methodological foundations and theoretical framework are touched upon only briefly. With this the paper conveys, in my view, an unnecessarily cloudy picture of the state of the art. This impression is emphasised by the concluding remarks which leave the impression that not very much has been achieved yet by way of analyses and, more importantly, that whatever has come out of such research has had even less of an impact on policy recommendations. In what follows I want to state briefly why I do not share this view. First of all, I think it is the *theoretical foundations* that should be stressed more than has been done. It is to be remembered, therefore, that there are at least three areas of basic research where solid progress has been achieved and is established firmly. These are:

probability theory as a base of statistical inference;
decision theory which is concerned with the optimisation of decisions under uncertainty;
the use of stochastic simulations in econometric model building and testing.

It is wellknown that minimising uncertainty is the central research objective of analytical statistics. Statistical sampling requires a measure of probability and inferences from sample results are valid only within certain bounds. Methods of statistical inference are standard knowledge. Also, it became evident that economic uncertainty is closely related to the statistical uncertainty problem. The combination of both has nowadays resulted in a number of different concepts and methods that allow the analysis of economic decision-making when it is known that the objective variables are subject to probability distributions. In this respect such analyses go beyond the scope of deterministic models. They do not lead, however, to easy and unique results. The answers are more complex and not easily, if at all, to be generalised. They require on the one hand more empirical effort and emphasis, on the other, the conditional character of policy recommendations. So far they correspond closely to reality, since in the real world, too, there are no easy answers to complex problems. I would like to point out two recent studies where research along these lines has been applied to analyses of price uncertainty in the wheat market and the coffee market, respectively, by Kirschke (1985) and Hermann and Kirschke (1985), both at the University of Kiel.

The Rausser et al. paper deals with the increasing complexity of agricultural market analysis in a highly industrialised open economy. The specific problem is the increased importance of money markets for the farm sector and the additional source of instability that opens up thereby. The authors succeeded in identifying and providing quantitative estimates for an overshooting of storable commodity prices resulting from linkages with financial markets. This analysis takes into account the traditional two other sources of instability: natural supply and demand forces and government intervention.

To appreciate fully the originality and I may even say ingenuity of their approach would require one to go rather deeply into the details of the model and also into the literature cited. This is not possible here. Therefore it may only be said that the arguments developed are of a convincing logic and the estimated values of the model parameters show plausible magnitudes. An open question still is how far the results of the analysis are actually suited to reduce instability and how they can be incorporated in real world decision processes. In these respects some doubts may be expressed because evidently only a small proportion of total variance of the dependent variables seems to be explained by the model variables. In the paper that was available to me, R^2 was given only for one of the equations. This one was very low (0.25) and its seems likely that the other equations fared no better. With about three-quarters of total variance unexplained the degree of uncertainty naturally remains high. Also the model presented so far is a deterministic analysis. Probably some work should be done to exploit the stochastic properties of the approach. Perhaps the authors could comment on their intentions in these respects.

Finally, it may be a question how successfully this approach can be applied to the situation in other countries or regions, as the authors intend. It may well be that the flex-price behaviour of storable commodity prices is rather an exception and restricted largely to the US markets. Elsewhere such prices are probably more of a fixed-price quality. What comes to mind here are the low price policies of developing countries, price setting procedures of centrally planned economies as well as the price stabilization policies of the EC. The EC in this regard is a special case since even the consequences of currency revaluations among member states are smoothed out by monetary compensation amounts (MCAs). The EC on the other hand is a good example of the fact that despite all stabilization efforts farmers cannot indefinitely be protected from market uncertainty. Recently the risk of policy changes has been greatly enhanced. But this is a different story.

REFERENCES

Herrmann, R. and Kirschke, D., *The analysis of price uncertainty: Theoretical issues and empirical measurement on the world coffee market*, Diskussionsbeiträge no. 57, Institut für Agrarpolitik und Marktlehre, Universität Kiel, 1985.
Kirschke, D., *Agrarmarktpolitik bei Unsicherheit*, Kiel 1985.

DISCUSSION OPENING II – BRIAN S. FISHER

Professor Sarris has outlined a number of important areas where he believes that there are gaps in our current knowledge of the impact of uncertainty in agricultural commodity markets. I have made some similar observations elsewhere (Fisher 1985) and I am in strong agreement with many of Professor Sarris's points. There is much research yet to be done in the area of commodity market uncertainty.

Perhaps more important from an empirical point of view than the distinction drawn by Professor Sarris between analysable and non-analysable uncertainty is the notion that the level of uncertainty in agricultural commodity markets is subject to significant change. There is strong evidence that the level of uncertainty has increased over the past decade. This observation was made earlier at this conference by Ed Schuh and is consistent with that made by Professor Rausser and his colleagues. At this stage there appears to be no satisfactory way of modelling such changes. Although, as Professor Rausser has observed, we now have a better understanding of the importance of linkages between the agricultural sector and the rest of the economy and of international linkages.

As Professor Sarris has pointed out, perhaps one of the most difficult things to accomplish in research in the area of stabilization policy will be to properly account for the effect of any scheme on existing market institutions and *vice versa*. For example, the existence of an active futures market for a commodity for which prices are stabilized is likely to seriously complicate the analysis. Newbery and Stiglitz (1981), pp. 190–1, show that under some conditions farmers may prefer to use futures markets rather than to participate in a price stabilization scheme. An additional complication is that the existence of a buffer stock scheme will almost certainly lead to the substitution of institutional stocks for private stocks. Assuming that both groups are equally efficient in the storage operation, this is likely to have little consequence for the global expected gains from a given level of stabilization. However, if this effect is ignored, there is a danger of underestimating the levels of stocks required by the buffer authority, for a given reduction in price variability.

As Professor Sarris has noted, to model the effects of a stabilization scheme properly, it is necessary to recognise that producers are likely to respond to the scheme by changing supply. In contrast to Professor Sarris I believe that most of the econometric models of supply response which include risk variables are *ad hoc* in nature (see, for example, Just 1974; Traill 1978; Brennan 1982). There is a need for such models to be derived from first principles using the theory of decision-making under risk. A useful starting point may be to attempt to integrate the mathematical programming and econometric literature on the subject. In addition to the problem of accounting for the effects of a reduction in risk, it is also necessary to model expectations.

Uncertainty about the way expectations are formed has important implications for policy and policy research. In the case of stabilization policy, Scandizzo, Hazell and Anderson (1983) show that the estimated gains from stabilization are sensitive to assumptions about the way in which expectations are formed. Professor Sarris has called for more research into the way in which expectations are formed. There is a limited agricultural economics literature on this subject. I suspect the reason for this is that research in this area is notoriously difficult. It is important to distinguish between the gains from reducing the losses due to incorrect forecasting and other benefits from stabilization, such as its effects on risk reduction.

Professor Sarris has asked the question whether it is more cost-effective for a government to provide better information to stabilise a market rather than to intervene directly. If there are large gains arising from the use of improved information then it may be more efficient to provide the information rather than attempt to compensate for bad forecasting by agents by the establishment of a stabilization scheme. As pointed out by Newbery and Stiglitz (1981) the market will not supply the optimal amount of information if information has a public-good element. There may therefore be a case for governments to supply additional information or to ensure that futures markets, for example, operate effectively. However, care should be taken to assess whether the benefits from an attempt to improve market information outweighs the costs. Newbery and Stiglitz (1981, pp. 144–8) present an example in which the gains from improved information make producers better off, consumers worse off and there is little net gain in welfare. In other words, there may be strong distributional effects from such policies. The nature of such distributional effects will depend, among other things, on assumptions about how expectations are formed.

Professor Rausser's thesis that overshooting in agricultural commodity prices will occur as a result of the different characteristics of agricultural and non-agricultural markets, even if expectations are formed rationally, is an important one. To date, much emphasis in research into agricultural commodity markets has been placed on traditional demand and supply forces and on trade linkages. Linkages with financial markets are less well understood. However, there is a vast literature on commodity futures markets.

Most economies can be characterised as having a mixture of 'fixed' and 'flex' price markets and it may therefore be reasonable to presume that money will be non-neutral in the short run. However, fixed price markets do not only occur in the non-agricultural sectors of economies. In many countries there is also extensive government intervention in agriculture. Such intervention may restrict the movement of farm prices. As Professor Rausser points out, the result may be unexpected increases in the cost of maintaining price supports. However, the effects may be more far-reaching if stocks are accumulated in an attempt to offset the effects of price overshooting. The existence of such stocks is likely to have an impact on future prices. The dynamics of models of this type are therefore well worth studying.

The two papers presented this morning have highlighted a number of important challenges in modelling agricultural commodity markets. Models in which full account is taken of uncertainty, future expectations and government intervention are likely to be highly non-linear and to present major computational problems. As a result, relatively simple analytical models of commodity markets will continue to be used in policy analysis for some time to come. It is therefore important to determine just how robust such models are.

REFERENCES

Brennan, J. P. 'The representation of risk in econometric models of supply', *Australian Journal of Agricultural Economics*, vol. 26, no. 2, 1982, pp. 151–6.

Fisher, B., 'Frontiers in agricultural policy research', *Review of Marketing and Agricultural Economics,*, vol. 53, no. 2, (forthcoming).

Just, R. E., 'An investigation of the importance of risk in farmers' decisions', *American Journal of Agricultural Economics*, vol. 56, no. 1, 1974, pp. 14–25.

Newbery, D. M. G. and Stiglitz, J. E., *The Theory of Commodity Price Stabilization: A Study of the Economics of Risk*, Clarendon Press, Oxford, 1981.

Scandizzo, P. L., Hazell, P. B. R. and Anderson, J. R., 'Producers' price expectations and the size of the welfare gains from price stabilization', *Review of Marketing and Agricultural Economics*, vol. 51, no. 2, 1983, pp. 93–107.

Traill, B. 'Risk variables in econometric supply response models', *Journal of Agricultural Economics*, vol. 29, no. 1, 1978, pp. 53–61.

GENERAL DISCUSSION – RAPPORTEUR: EWA RABINOWICZ

In the discussion from the floor of A. H. Sarris's paper the question was asked, who pays the costs of turbulence, claiming that traditionally shocks have been absorbed by farm families. Another issue raised was that differences between analysable and non-analysable uncertainty are of degree rather than of kind. Furthermore, it was suggested that the 'electoral/political cycle' was another uncertainty related subject for research in agricultural economics. A question about the possibility of endogenising policy behaviuor was also asked. Finally, a point was made about using general equilibrium models in the uncertainty analysis.

In reply to Dr Buchholz, Professor Sarris disagreed that his paper should have been more theoretically oriented. He claimed that the stated purpose of the paper was to see how much theoretical developments in probability theory, optimisation theory etc. have influenced policy analysis and/or recommendations. Furthermore he stated that statistical uncertainty is different from economic uncertainty. On the issue of who pays the risk, he mentioned that distributional implications of risk are not well researched and deserve futher study.

On the issue of the difference between analysable and non-analysable uncertainty Sarris stated that those are of different kind, non-analysable uncertainty not being included in the state space.

Commenting on endogenising of policy behaviour Sarris pointed out that attempts have been made by some authors with mixed success because it is quite difficult to describe the policy process. The political cycle is and has been analysed in the general economic literature. Related to it is a question of administering the policy.

Ending his remarks Professor Sarris pointed out that many recent contributions in uncertainty analysis have been made in the context of general equilibrium theory and many interesting cases from our world of incomplete markets and imperfect information can be analysed in this context.

In the discussion from the floor on the paper by G. C. Rausser et al. the point was made that the instability can be created not only by an inapropriate economic policy but also by the inefficient administration of a 'right' policy. The role of expectations for economic model building and forecasting and the possibility of endogenising policy behaviour in models were discussed as well. Scepticism was expressed about the applicability of the model for LDCs with badly developed credit markets. Furthermore it was pointed out that the risk premium in financial markets had effects on agrticultural markets. Finally the question was asked in which way overshooting was non-optimal.

In reply to the remarks of Dr Buchholz on goodness of fit of the equations, Professor Rausser stated that the equations reproduced were a part of a large system, which has been estimated simultaneously. Furthermore, *ex ante* forecasting and *ex post* comparison with the data showed a high degree of correspondence. However the main point in the paper was to test if the coefficient (of anticipated money growth) was significant, i.e. to test the theory.

Commenting on the applicability of the model to other countries (Western Europe, LDCs) Rausser pointed out that the approach could be used for other countries as well. On the issue of the role of expectations in modelling, he stated that in large-scale models we had to be cautious and that policy variables had been separated in the model. For policy modelling we were still looking for evidence.

Commenting on the risk premium Rausser agreed that it was an important factor which was not included in the model. He believed, however, that overshooting would still be present, even if risk premium was included.

In reply to the issue of non-optimality, Rausser stated that if people did not adjust to the overshot prices, non-optimality would be present. Since not everyone, however, would realise that prices were overshot, the resource allocation would be affected causing non-optimality.

Participants in the discussion included G. Jones, F. Soares, H. Breimyer, J. Viaene, I. Elbadawa, A. Salazar, J. Kitchen and H. Mahran.

YAIR MUNDLAK

Agricultural Growth and the Price of Food[1]

INTRODUCTION

In discussing the price of food in the context of growth, food is usually associated with agriculture. Thus the problem becomes that of determining the price of agriculture relative to that of non-agriculture along the growth path. This however does not reveal the whole story since food purchased by the consumer contains non-agricultural inputs such as processing, packaging, transportation, refrigeration, as well as food consumed in restaurants. The quantity of the non-agricultural inputs and their prices affect the consumer price of food. The non-agricultural inputs of food are not forced on the consumer, but rather demanded by him. Consequently, it is of interest to analyse the determinants of the agricultural and non-agricultural inputs of food. To simplify the discussion all the non-agricultural inputs of food are aggregated. The utility function of a representative consumer is written as

$$u = U[F(A, Q), N] \tag{1}$$

This function is weakly separable in food (F) and non-food (N). Food has an agricultural component, A, and a non-agricultural component, Q. The ratio $q = Q/A$ can serve as a measure of quality of food. The expenditure on food is decomposed according to the two components, that received by agriculture $P_A A$ and that received by non-agriculture $P_N Q$, where P_N is the price of the non-agricultural product. Thus, the food budget is:

$$B_F = P_A A + P_N Q \tag{2}$$

The average price paid by the consumer for food, per unit of A, to which we refer as the consumer price is:

$$P_F = B_F/A = P_A + P_N q \tag{3}$$

and its ratio to the price received by farmers is

$$R_A \equiv P_F/P_A = 1 + pq \qquad (4)$$

where $p \equiv p_N/p_A$.

This is also equal to the ratio $B_F/P_A A$, the reciprocal of the share of the farmer in the consumer's dollar. The price of food in terms of the non-agricultural product is:

$$R_N \equiv B_F/p_N = \frac{1}{p} + q \qquad (5)$$

It is clear that R_A and R_N both increase with the quality of food but are affected differently by the price ratio p. The remainder of the analysis will examine the behaviour of p, q, R_A and R_N in the process of growth. That requires an analysis of the product market along the growth path.

We begin by providing some empirical evidence. The share of agriculture in the retail cost of food in the US is published by the USDA. The value for 1983 was 33 per cent. Dunham places this value in a perspective by stating that it '... was trended down gradually since the mid forties when the share was nearly 50 per cent.'[2] A casual review of the time series of this share indicates considerable fluctuation. The trend can be attributed, at least in part, to a positive income response of q which implies that the income elasticity of Q is larger than that of A. The fluctuations can be attributed to fluctuations in prices. A study by Houston (1979) for the UK covering 1963–75 concludes that 'The relative stability of these marketing costs, despite the trend towards increased consumption of processed and convenience foods, suggest that improvement in marketing techniques and advances in food technology have to some extent offset the cost of additional services provided by services and manufacturing.'[3] This conclusion can be interpreted as an increase in q and a decline in p, thus leaving R_A fairly stable. Some scattered information is provided by Mittendorf and Hertag (1982) for developing countries. The information shows a wide spread across countries and the sample is small. Nevertheless the conclusion is suggestive: 'the data indicate that the share of marketing costs in relation to the consumer price is higher in the developed countries (due to considerable higher labor costs and higher levels of processing packaging and presentation of food items)'.[4] Again, a suggestion of an increase in p and q with level of economic development.

An analytic formulation of the farm-retail price spread was provided by Gardner (1975). The essence of his model consists of a production function for food consisting of two inputs, A and Q in terms of our notation. There is a demand function for (aggregate) food which depends on the price of food and a shifter. The model is closed by assuming supply functions for A and Q and imposing the competitive conditions. In this framework the composition of food is determined by the producers, and the consumer has to buy the food provided at the profit maximising combination of A and Q. This assumption is restrictive and as indicated above it is alleviated in the present analysis. Besides this, we deal with developments along a growth path.

The discussion begins with the derivation of the demand functions for the two components of food as well as for non-agriculture. The supply side is the standard two sector model. The short-run equilibrium is determined within a competitive framework of a closed economy. We deal with a closed economy, although food is tradable, because the world is a closed economy, and this fact determines the major developments in the variables of interest. The growth path is then generated by treating individually and exogenously some of the major determinants of growth: capital accumulation and different kinds of technical change. This is followed by some consequences of removing the assumption of competitive factor markets. In view of the space limitation, the analysis is largely graphical, based on some general known properties and concentrates on essentials.

DEMAND

The problem of the representative consumer is to maximise (1) subject to the budget constraint: $B = [p_A A + p_N Q] + p_N N \equiv B_F + B_N$

Using obvious notations, the first order conditions are:

$$U_A = U_F F_A = \lambda p_A, \quad U_Q = U_F F_Q = \lambda p_N, \quad U_N = \lambda p_N \tag{6}$$

The utility function is weakly separable, so that the composition of food is independent of the level of N. This is seen from

$$\frac{U_Q}{U_A} = \frac{F_Q}{F_A} = \frac{p_N}{p_A} \equiv p \tag{7}$$

Thus the demand for A and Q conditional on the food budget are:

$$A(p_A, p_N, B_F) = A(p, B_F/p_A)$$

$$Q(p_A, p_N, B_F) = Q(p, B_F/p_A) \tag{8}$$

The expression to the right of the equality sign utilises the homogeneity property of the demand functions. The solution is illustrated in Figure 1. Point E indicates the optimal choice at the budget level $B_F/p_A = F_1$. The income consumption curve ICCF is drawn to illustrate two assumptions: (1) Both components, A and Q are normal; (2) the income elasticity, with respect to B_F, of A is smaller than one and that of Q is larger than one. Thus, the quality of food q, increases with the food budget. Turning to (4) and (5) it is seen that under (i) increasing expenditure on food, and (ii) constant prices, both R_A and R_N increase.

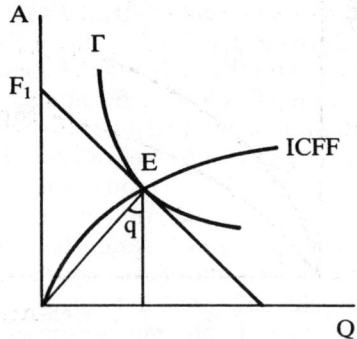

FIGURE 1   *The composition of food*

The increase in the price of food, either in terms of A or N, reflects the consumer preference for quality.

The unconditional demand functions can be obtained by finding the optimal food budget and using it in (8). Alternatively, they can be obtained directly. Those are presented below in the Hicks compensated form with the signs of the partial derivatives attached:

$$
\begin{aligned}
&(p_A \ p_N \ u) \quad (p \ u) \\
A&(- \ + \ +) = (+ \ +) \\
q&(\ ? \ \ ? \ +) = (? \ +) \\
N&(+ \ - \ +) = (- \ +)
\end{aligned}
\tag{9}
$$

Since all the three components are normal goods, each of these functions is monotone increasing in u. Thus we can substitute A for u and write

$$
Q(p, A), \quad N(p, A)
\tag{10}
$$

These functions are drawn in Figure 2. They represent the loci of optimal points achieved at price ratio p and increasing levels of expenditures. The income effects are summarised in the first two columns of Table 1.

Changes in prices have inter and intra group effects. A decline in p_A reduces the price of F relative to N and thus the intergroup substitution effect is in favour of F. A decline in p_N decreases the prices of F and N but the price of F declines less because Q is only one component of F. Therefore the intergroup substitution of a decline of P_N is in favour of N. The sign of the intergroup price effect is shown in Table 1 in the first two lines and last two columns.

A decline in p calls for an intra food substitution in favour of Q(F), where Q(F) is the quantity of Q used in F. This intra food substitution is summarised in line Q(F) of Table 1. Lines Q and A are the sum of the

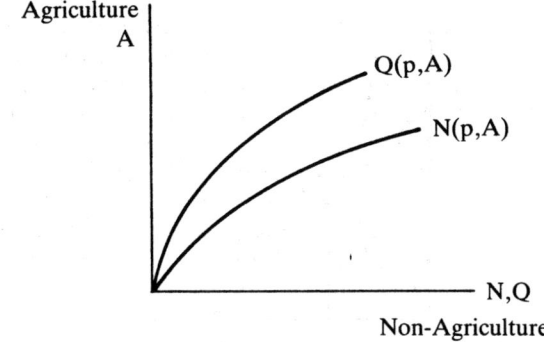

FIGURE 2   *Unconditional income consumption curves*

TABLE 1   *Signed changes in various demand components*

Endogenous \ Exogenous	B	B_F	p_A	p_N
F	+	+	−	+
N	+	..	+	−
A	+	+	−	+
Q(F)	..	..	+	−
Q	+	+	?	?
q	+	+	?	?
R_A	+	+	?	?
R_N	+	+	?	?

Note: .. means irrelevant here.

inter and intra group substitutions. While A is signed, Q is not because of the contradicting signs in the response of F and Q(F). Consequently, the price effects of q, R_A and R_N are also ambiguous.

It is possible to place some boundaries on the effects. Since the price of Q and N is the same, we can view $Q + N = \bar{N}$ as a compositive good, and write the utility function as $U(A, \bar{N})$, resulting in demand functions.

$$A(p, u), \bar{N}(p, u) \tag{11}$$
$$+ +\quad\ -\ +$$

and those are clearly signed.

THE ECONOMY IN THE SHORT RUN

Under the space limitation, it is most efficient to analyse the process within a neoclassical framework of a two sector model of a closed economy and thereby build on some known results. The model consists of constant returns to scale sectoral production functions:

$$Y_i = F_i (K_i, L_i, T_i) \qquad i = 1, 2$$

where K_i and L_i are sectoral employment of capital and labour respectively and T_i is a measure of technology. Sector 1 is agriculture and 2 is non-agriculture. It is assumed that factors are fully employed and their supply is exogenously given. This latter assumption only simplifies, but does not modify the qualitative results. Finally, it is assumed that the competitive conditions are met in that factors of production are paid their value marginal productivities. Under these assumptions, the production possibilities of the economy are given by the transformation curve in Figure 3a. The relationship between the (supply) price and points on the transformation curve is summarised by the supply function for agriculture in Figure 3b. Note that $p = p_N/p_A$, hence, when the economy specialises in agriculture ($y_1 = \bar{y}_1$) p is at its minimum level ($\underline{p}$) and conversely, when the economy specialises in non-agriculture ($y_2 = \bar{y}_2$) the price is at its maximum, $\bar{p}$. Also, p increases with y_2 and declines with y_1.

Next we turn to the demand functions. Combining the two equations in (11), the demand can be summarised by:

$$x_1 = D(p, x_2) \tag{12}$$
$$+ \quad +$$

where x_1 is demand per caput of A, and x_2 is demand per caput of $\bar{N}$. It is assumed that $D(p, 0) = 0$, as $p \to 0$, $D \to 0$, and as $p \to \infty$, $D \to \infty$.

Under these assumptions there is a unique stable short-run equilib-

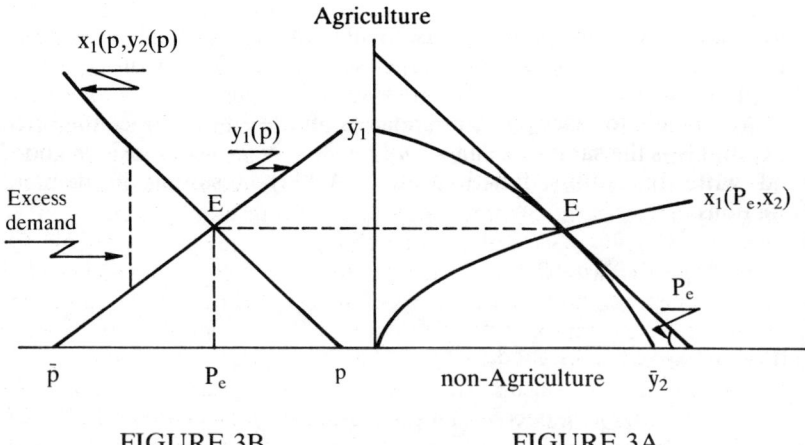

FIGURE 3B   FIGURE 3A

The economy in the short run

rium. That is, there exist a price p_e such that $x_1(p_e, y_2(p_e)) = y_1(p_e)$. This is illustrated by point E in Figure 3. The determination of the equilibrium can be demonstrated in Figure 3b. For this, we evaluate x_1 only at points $[p, y_2(p)]$, where $y_2(p)$ is the production per caput at price p. At $\bar{p}$, $y_2(\bar{p}) = \bar{y}_2 > 0$ but $y_1(\bar{p}) = 0$, hence $x_1[\bar{p}, y_2(\bar{p})] - y_1(\bar{p}) > 0$ implying an excess demand for x_1. The opposite occurs at p where $y_2(p) = 0$ and therefore $x_1(p, 0) = 0$, hence excess supply. As $\partial y_1(p)/\partial p < 0$, $\partial y_2(p)/\partial p > 0$, $\partial x_1/\partial p > 0$, $\partial x_1/\partial x_2 > 0$, the excess demand declines with p, and E is achieved where the excess demand is zero. Having determined p, A and $\bar{N}$, the demand functions facilitate decomposition of $\bar{N}$ into N and Q and thus the determination of food, F(Q, A). This outline of a graphical proof can be repeated in each of the following cases to determine the displacement in the equilibrium position.

The analysis can be generalised to the case where the factor supplies in the economy are increasing functions of their prices. Such an extension will add technical details but will not affect the qualitative results.[5]

CAPITAL ACCUMULATION

By capital accumulation is meant an increase in the capital labour ratio for the economy as a whole. An accumulation facilitates an expansion of the production possibilities of the economy and thereby causes a positive effect for all the commodities.

The evaluation of the price effects of accumulation requires an assumption on the capital intensity. It is assumed here that agriculture is the labour-intensive sector. That is, at any price regime, $k_1 < k_2$, where $k_i \equiv K_i/L_i$. Under this assumption, the Rybezyneki proposition indicates that under constant prices capital accumulation leads to an expansion of the output of the capital-intensive sector and to a decline of the output of the labour-intensive sector. Thus, at the initial prices capital accumulation causes an increase in the demand x_1 due to the increase in income, and a decline in the supply y_1, hence excess demand. A new equilibrium is achieved at a higher price for y_1, that is a decline in p. Consequently the equilibrium output of y_1 will increase if the income effect is stronger than the substitution effect and will decrease if the converse holds. The decline in p supplements the income effect for $\bar{N}$ and its equilibrium output will increase. Finally, in view of the price change, the quality of food, q = Q/A is likely to increase. This reflects two effects, a stronger income elasticity for Q than for A, and a substitution in favour of Q due to the decline in p. However, the total quantity of Q depends on the equilibrium consumption of food. If A does not decline, then Q will increase. If A declines, it is possible that food consumption will decline even through its quality will improve. Still it is expected that the income effect will dominate.

The foregoing analysis shows a decline in p, the price of the capital-intensive product. How does it affect the relative price of food? By (5) R_N, the price of food in terms of N, increases. However, by (4) the change in R_A, the price of food in terms of A, is ambiguous. Since p declines and q is likely to increase, the outcome will depend on the relative changes. If the income effect is weak, it is possible that the change in price will dominate and R_A will decline. The change in p depends on the supply and demand elasticities and will not be discussed here. It is however likely that the income effect on q is strong and dominant and R_A will increase.

TECHNICAL CHANGE

Technical change (TC) is basically the engine of growth. However it is not a simple concept. It takes various forms and at least in part is endogenous in the economic system. The best we can do in the limited space is to illustrate some leading cases. Such cases are selected to illuminate the importance of the income and price elasticities of demand. We begin with Hicks neutral technical (HNTC) of equal rates in the two sectors. Figure 4 presents transformation curves for two technologies, 0 and t. Point E is the initial equilibrium. Under HNTC of equal rates in the two sectors, the supply price at H, located at the intersection of the outer transformation curve and a ray through E, is the same as at E. However, at this price and the new production possibilities the demand is given by point C. Thus, there is an excess supply of A and p increases until a new equilibrium point E_1 is reached. It can be shown that this point is located between H and C. The location of C, and therefore E_1 to the right of H reflects the fact that the income elasticity of A is less than 1.

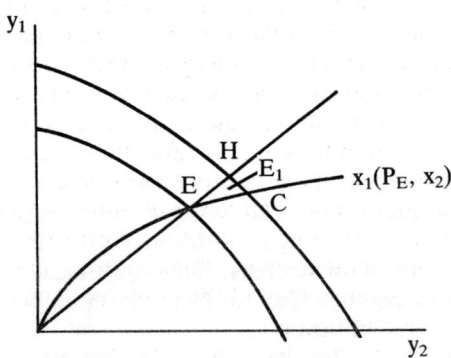

FIGURE 4   *HNTC of equal rates*

The increase in p makes food cheaper relative to N. Hence, the consumption per caput of food increases due to the income and price effects. Yet, both effects are not sufficient to increase consumption of A at the rate of the TC. Consequently, the consumption of N + Q increases by more than the rate of the TC and the income effect

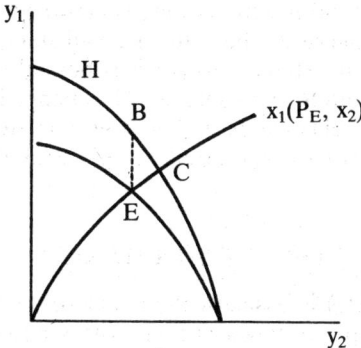

FIGURE 5 *HNTC in agriculture*

dominates the price effects. This is also true for the two components, N and Q, individually, implying an increase in q. The final outcome is an increase in pq and therefore an increase in R_A. On the other hand the sign of the change in R_N is ambiguous. But again, the increase in quality may dominate the change in price thus leading to an increase in R_N.

Another extreme case is that of TC in one sector only, say in agriculture. Figure 5 illustrates HNTC in agriculture alone. At point B the resource allocation is the same as at the initial point because it produces the same quantity y_2 under constant technology. However, due to the TC the relative price of agriculture declines (p increases) and hence point H representing the initial price p_E is to the left of B. The demand under the initial price is at C. The new equilibrium point will be in the segment BC when the price elasticity of demand for A is less than 1. It will be in the segment BH if the elasticity is larger than 1. Empirically, such elasticity is smaller than one. In this case HNTC in agriculture alone leads to an increase in p and in the consumption of both commodities. The increase in the consumption of non-agriculture reflects the income effect, since the economy becomes more affluent due to the TC. It can produce a larger output of food with fewer resources and the resources saved can be diverted to non-food production. Note, however, that this result depends crucially on the demand elasticity, for if the demand for A were elastic, such a change would have reduced the equilibrium consumption of non-agriculture.

The effect of this change on q depends on the strength of the intrafood substitution between A and Q. Since p increases, such a substitution reduces q. However, this may be dominated by the income effect on q. If q does not decline then R_A increases and if q does not rise R_N declines. The other possibilities are ambiguous.

The foregoing two cases of HNTC facilitates a more general analysis. To show this, let T_1 and T_2 be the rates of the HNTC in the two sectors, then the consequences of such a change can be analysed in two steps: (1) Equal rates: Assume that $T_1 > T_2$, then analyse first the system under the assumption of $T_1 = T_2$. (2) Differential rate: Now analyse under the assumption of TC in agriculture alone at a rate $T_1 - T_2$. Over a long swing, it is likely that even if the rates are not the same, the common part is dominating and therefore the results obtained for equal rates of HNTC are more relevant.

DISEQUILIBRIUM ANALYSIS

The foregoing analysis dealt exclusively with equilibrium points. When dealing with the growth of agriculture, the assumption of equilibrium might be too restrictive for the analysis to be empirically pertinent. The low income elasticity for A forces resources to flow out of agriculture as the economy expands. For reasons not discussed here, this flow particularly in the labour market, is not fast enough in order to equate wages across sectors and consequently the agricultural wage is lower than that of non-agriculture.[6] In this sense the economy is not operating efficiently. This is illustrated in Figure 6 by point H, which is not on the frontier. The demand curve that passes through H determines the price which clears the product market at H.

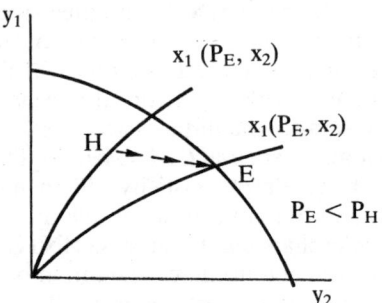

FIGURE 6   *Convergence to equilibrium*

Assuming that labour migrates to the sector with the higher wage, there will be a flow of labour out of agriculture. This will cause a decline of A and an increase of $\bar{N}$ as shown by the arrows in Figure 6 which illustrates convergence to E on the transformation curve. Note that such a process of convergence to the frontier increases the consumption possibilities and as such has a positive income effect on A, Q and N. In addition to the income effect there is also a price effect. The partial effect of the off-farm migration is to narrow the wage gap and thereby to increase the cost of production in A and to decrease it in $\bar{N}$. Assuming that competition prevails within each sector, the average cost is equal to the product price (zero profit) and therefore p declines. Such a decline in p facilitates the absorption of the expanding production in non-agriculture. Note that such a convergence to the efficiency frontier shows negative relationships between sectoral outputs and their prices.

The positive income effect and the price effect increase Q whereas A declines and therefore q increases. However, the sign of the change in R_A is ambiguous whereas R_N increases.

The foregoing analysis assumed constant resources and technology. Once this assumption is removed, we will have a simultaneous movement toward the transformation curve and a movement of the curve itself. This is the reason that the process takes so long to complete.

AN EMPIRICAL ANALYSIS

The foregoing analysis suggests positive relationship between q, R_A, R_N and between income and it is somewhat less definite on the net effect of p. Thus, the empirical analysis can test the qualitative results and supplement them. The analysis is of the US data for the period 1946–82. Such data were readily available.[7] It would be interesting to repeat the analysis on other data.

The analysis consists of computing regressions of ln q (Lq) and ln R_A on ln p(Lp), lny (Ly) where y is disposable income per caput deflated by the consumer price index, and an interaction term (Lp) (Ly). The average compounded rates of change of these variables are: $p = 0.0116$, $q = 0.00295$, $y = 0.021$ and $p_A A/B_F = -0.0035$. Thus, the terms of trade of agriculture deteriorated at an annual rate of about 1 per cent whereas q increased at the rate of about 0.3 per cent. In terms of Table 1 it means that the effect of the TC dominated that of capital accumulation and of flow of resources in its effect on the terms of trade. This statement should be qualified to allow for the role of the US as an exporter of food. However, this qualification is not that simple and conspicuous and is avoided here. In terms of q we see that its growth is consistent with the HNTC of equal rates and not inconsistent with the others.

The regressions are summarised in Table 2. Two regressions are presented for each of the two dependent variables, with and without the interaction term. The contribution of the interaction term is particularly important for the Lq regression where it improves the fit and eliminates the serial correlation. The price elasticities were positive at the low income level. They gradually declined and became negative at about the mid-point of the sample. The average for the period was -0.047 whereas the extreme values were -0.30 and $+0.24$.

Recall that an increase in p reduces the relative price of food and thereby affects positively Q and A. This is the intergroup effect. It can be shown to be proportional to the income elasticities of Q and A and therefore, by our assumption it increases q. The intrafood substitution due to an increase in p leads to a decline in q. Since we obtain positive price elasticities for the low income years it implies that at such income levels the intergroup effect dominates the intrafood substitution. That is, the main effect of an increase in p, which implies a lower price for food, is

TABLE 2

Regression no.	(1)		(2)		(3)		(4)	
Dependent								
Variable	Lq		Lq		LR$_A$		LR$_A$	
R^2	.38		.66		.96		.976	
DW	.78		1.46		1.02		1.59	
Constant	.70	(3.7)	−.88	(7.2)	.786	(8.5)	.254	(3.7)
LP	−.014	(.2)	2.25	(5.7)	.56	(18.4)	1.55	(7.0)
Ly	.15	(3.5)	.35	(7.6)	.088	(4.0)	.173	(6.7)
(Ly) (LP)	—		−.80	(5.8)	—		−.350	(4.5)
EP: average	−.014		−.047		.56		.544	
SD	0		.19		0		.08	
Ey: average	.151		.12		.088		.074	
SD	0		.13		0		.059	

Notes:
Numbers in parentheses are *t* ratios of coefficients to the left.
DW: Durbin-Watson statistic.
EP: Elasticity of the dependent variable with respect to price.
Ey: Elasticity of the dependent variable with respect to income.
Average: Average for the period.
SD: Standard deviations of the computed elasticities.

to increase food consumption. The change in the quality due to intrafood substitution is less important. The situation is reversed as income increases.

The income elasticity of quality was stronger in the early period and declined gradually and become negative in the last three years. This trend reflects the increasing price of quality (p) and indirectly the increase in income. Thus, at high income and high price of quality, the intra food substitution dominated and that called for a decline in q.

The second set of regressions reports the response of R$_A$ to changes in p and y. In this set, the interaction, though significant, contributes less to the simpler regression (3), but still as in the previous case reduces the serial correlation. Nevertheless, there is little difference in the average elasticities between the two regressions. Thus, the elasticity of R$_A$ is about 0.55 with respect to p and 0.075 with respect to income. That indicates that R$_A$ increased with p and y. Recall that R$_A$ is the reciprocal of the share of agriculture in the food budget, and this declines with p and y. This of course reflects the changes in q.

NOTES

[1] I am indebted to Bruce Gardner, Dennis Dunham and Ulrich Koester for assistance in locating the empirical evidence. The study was supported by the International Food Policy Research Institute and by a grant from BARD – The United States-Israel Binational Agricultural Research and Development Fund.
[2] Dunham, p. 10.
[3] Houston, p. 59.

[4]Mittendorf and Hertäg, p. 31.
[5]In this case, the slope at the transformation curve is not equal to the supply price. However, the supply function is still positively sloped and the equilibrium determination according to Figure 3b is still valid (Mundlak 1984).
[6]Cf. Mundlak 1979.
[7]Sources of data: R_A was derived from Dunham. The remaining variables are obtained from USDA, *Agricultural Statistics*, different volumes.

REFERENCES

Dunham, D., 'Food Cost Review 1983', *Agricultural Economic Report*, no. 514, USDA, Washington DC.

Gardner, B. L., 'The Farm-Retail Price Spread in Competitive Food Industry', *American Journal of Agricultural Economics*, vol. 57, pp. 399–409, 1975.

Houston, George, 'The Behavior of Prices and Margins of Selected Food Products in the United Kingdom', OECD, Paris, July 1979 (mimeograph).

Mittendorf, H. J. and Hertäg, O., 'Marketing Costs and Margins for Major Food Items in Developing Countries', *Food and Nutrition*, vol. 8, FAO pp. 27–31, 1982.

Mundlak, Y., *Intersectoral Factor Mobility and Agricultural Growth*, International Food Policy Research Institute, Washington DC, 1979.

Mundlak, Y., 'Lectures on Agriculture and Economic Growth, Theory and Measurement, 1984 (mimeograph).

ALBERTO VALDÉS

Exchange Rates and Trade Policy: Help or Hindrance to Agricultural Growth?*

INTRODUCTION

In attempting to diagnose the causes of the current 'troubles' in agriculture, symptoms of which are excess capacity in developed countries and the disappointing performance of agriculture in many less developed countries (LDCs), trade and exchange rate policies are receiving increasing attention. Intervention in agricultural markets is widespread and is practised in rich and poor countries alike. To guide such intervention, incentive policies are a matter of concern for policy-makers and economists because economic incentives are perceived to be a basic determinant of production performance. Various types of policy interventions are used to modify the structure of economic incentives for agriculture. Many of these policies are directed at agriculture alone and include government expenditures (on roads, irrigation schemes, storage, agricultural research and extension systems, and so forth) – that is, the 'shifters' of supply – and explicit price policies (price controls and subsidies on inputs and outputs).

But there is, however, another set of policies directed at the macroeconomic management of the economy (e.g., on nominal exchange rates, interest rates, wages, international capital flows, fiscal and trade policy) which are of the utmost importance to agriculture. The consequences of these policies can reinforce or neutralise the policies directed solely at agriculture. This paper presents a simplified version of a framework to estimate the combined effect of trade and exchange rate policies on the structure of relative prices for agriculture. This framework is then applied to several LDCs. Emphasis is put on defining and measuring the 'implicit' protection or taxation of agriculture, in a long-term perspective, which results from the linkages between it and the rest of the economy. In many LDCs it is argued that import-substitution-based industrial growth pursued through tariffs and other import restrictions can be presumed to have a strong bias against agriculture, and

*The analysis for this paper was done during 1984 while the author was a visiting research fellow at the United Nations Economic Commission for Latin America in Santiago, Chile.

results in a structure of incentives that could have deleterious effects on production and as such on long-term growth of agriculture.

The real exchange rate, defined as the ratio of the price of tradables to non-tradables, is portrayed as playing a central role in the profitability of tradables in agriculture – import-competing (such as cereals) and exportables; and it is through the real exchange rate that the macroeconomic management of the economy affects agriculture.[1]

It is a well accepted argument in theory that a tariff on imports also taxes the production of exports, and that a subsidy for exports also subsidizes the production of import-competing activities. A policy that protects industry directly raises the cost of importable inputs such as fertilizers, machinery and other materials used by farmers. More importantly and indirectly, through its effects on the real exchange rate, such a policy affects the relative profitability of other tradables. The exchange rate that maintains a balance in the external account at a 'higher' rate of protection to industry is below the rate at lower rates of protection. The result is that the domestic prices of tradable goods from agriculture are lower relative to the prices of protected tradable goods from industry and of non-tradable goods. This drives up the prices of labour and other inputs to agriculture relative to the output prices, reducing the profitability of producing tradables in agriculture. It is postulated that most products in agriculture are tradables, and thus the main force behind real exchange rates will be intersectoral resource flows, essentially labour and savings, toward the non-traded (in and outside of agriculture) and import-competing activities outside agriculture. The real exchange rate can also be influenced by exogenous factors, such as a drastic shift in external terms of trade and oil or mineral discoveries (so-called 'Dutch disease'), and by policies affecting capital movements (including foreign aid). If they appreciate the real exchange rate, these phenomena reduce the profitability of farming on tradable products.[2]

It is hypothesised that one of the most dramatic manifestations of the combined effects of a Dutch disease phenomenon and the implicit and presumed strong bias against agriculture resulting from the trade and exchange rate policies in LDCs in the 1950s throughout the 1970s, is the massive flow of labour out of agriculture during this period. This suggests that the severe production constraints emanating from rural labour shortages, for example in sub-Saharan Africa, may not be independent of real exchange rate phenomena. But labour also flowed out of agriculture in developed countries, even in those that protected agriculture. What we suggest is that the rate of out-migration in LDCs was higher than it would otherwise have been, other things being equal. It is an empirical question which could be tested.

THE APPROACH AND BROAD CHARACTERISTICS OF THE MODEL

The analysis of the incidence of trade regime and exchange rate policy presented here for a 'small' open economy is based on a simple three-sector model, with the three sectors being importables, exportables and home goods. General equilibrium is implied by equilibrium in the home goods market and assumed equilibrium in the balance of payments (BOP) and in the monetary sector. Such an approach helps identify which sector loses and which sector gains. It also suggests that the effects of trade and exchange rate policies on resource allocation and income distribution could be quite different from what the policy-makers intended, as suggested, for example, by a profile of nominal rates of protection.

Theoretical and methodological advances in recent years have elucidated the nature of some of the relationships involved. These include the work of Dornbusch (1974) and Sjaastad (1980). Empirical research on foreign trade regimes in LDC economies has generally emphasised the consequences on domestic industry (Little *et al.* 1970; Balassa 1971; Krueger 1978; and Bhagwati 1978), but little has been done on agriculture.[3] However, industrial policies, it is hypothesised here, often have unintended economy-wide repercussions which are particularly strong in agriculture.

A simple framework that examines the effects on relative prices quantitatively, and was initially suggested by Sjaasted (1980) for three sectors, was extended and applied to examine the effects on agriculture in several LDCs. A sketch of the reduced form follows.

The excess demand for importables (Me), excess supply of exportables (Xe), and excess demand for home goods (He) are assumed to depend only on relative prices (Pm/Ph, Px/Ph) and real income, where Pm, Px, and Ph represent the domestic prices of importables, exportables, and home goods. The domestic relative prices can be expressed as a function of world prices (Pm* and PX*), the nominal exchange rate (E), tariffs (t), and export subsidies (s). Then:

$$Pm/Ph = (E/Ph) Pm^* (1 + t), \tag{1}$$

$$Px/Ph = (E/Ph) Px^* (1 + s), \text{ and} \tag{2}$$

$$Pm/Px = Pm^*/Px^* (1 + t)/(1 + s), \tag{3}$$

where E/Ph represents the real exchange rate. In the short run, of course, the existence of large domestic stocks could alter this relationship, such as in (1) after a devaluation. Equation (3) shows that the domestic relative prices of importables (in terms of exportables) are functions of trade policy, that is, tariffs and subsidies (t and s, respectively), and of world prices. Tariffs (subsidies) in the model include tariff (subsidy) equivalent of quantitative restrictions applied at the border.

As policy-makers attempt to affect resource allocation by imposing a protective tariff on importables that compete with domestically produced goods, the relative price of home goods will rise relative to exportables (the real exchange rate will fall) and the unprotected tradables (including exportables) will be taxed. As a sector sheltered from trade, the home goods market adjusts, as required, to maintain general equilibrium, absorbing and spilling resources to the traded sectors as relative prices change.

Assuming that expenditure equals income and BOP equilibrium, equilibrium in the home goods sector implies that $H^d = H^s$, where the demand (H^d) and supply (H^s) of home goods is given by

$$H^d = H^d \,(Pm/Ph, Px/Ph, I), \text{ and} \tag{4}$$

$$H^s = H^s \,(Pm/Ph, Px/Ph, K, L, T) \tag{5}$$

where K, L, and T represent the productive capacity of the economy, determined by existing capital (K), labour (L), and technology (T). After displacement from equilibrium, and holding I, K, L, and T constant, a new equilibrium is reached where

$$\hat{H}^d = \hat{H}^s = (\eta m - \varepsilon m)\, Pm\hat{/}Ph + (\eta x - \varepsilon x)\, Px\hat{/}Ph = 0, \tag{6}$$

where $\hat{}$ represents a percentage change and ηm and ηx represent the demand elasticities for home goods with respect to price of importables and exportables, respectively, and εm and εx are the corresponding supply elasticities.

Given world prices, the incidence of a change in trade barriers on exportables is given by

$$\hat{P}h - \hat{P}x = \omega(\hat{P}m - \hat{P}x), \tag{7}$$

where $\omega = \eta m - \varepsilon m/(\eta m - \varepsilon m) + (\eta x - \varepsilon x)$, with $0 \leqslant \omega \leqslant 1$, represents the incidence parameter, which consists essentially of substitution relationships. Let d represent the change in the price of home goods, then, as shown by Sjaastad,

$$d = \omega t + (1 - \omega)s. \tag{8}$$

The nominal distortion introduced by trade policy consists of $(t - s)$, where $(t - s) = (t - d) + (d - s)$, where $(d - s)$ represents the proportion of the 'distortion' shifted in the form of an implicit tax on producers of exportables. Government policy determines the size of $(t - d)$ but cannot determine how this is allocated between import-competing activities and exports.

After some algebraic manipulations and assuming constant ω, after integration, the basic equation for the estimation of ω becomes

$$\ln (Ph/Px) = a + \omega \ln (Pm/Px), \tag{9}$$

which is estimated using ordinary least squares.

Garcia for Colombia (1981) and Bautista for the Philippines (1984), in order to capture the effect on agricultural exports, disaggregated equation (9) to

$$\ln Ph/Pxa = a + \omega_1 \ln Pm/Pxa + \omega_2 \ln Pxna/Pxa \qquad (10)$$

where a represents agricultural and na represents non-agricultural products. To distinguish between agricultural importables (Pma essentially food) and other importables, in his work on Peru, Valdés also disaggregated importables, into

$$\ln Ph/Pma = a + \omega_1 \ln Pmna/Pma + \omega_2 \ln Px/Pma \qquad (11)$$

Expressing $\hat{P}h$ as a weighted average of $\hat{P}m$ and $\hat{P}x$, after some transformations, the real exchange rate (E/Ph) is shown to relate directly to world prices and trade policy (t and s):

$$E/Ph = [(Pm^* (1 + t))^{\omega} \cdot (Px^* (1 + s))^{1-\omega}]^{-1} \qquad (12)$$

A fall in the real rate (E/Ph) implies that prices of tradables fall relative to those of home goods, therefore diverting some resources from tradable to home goods (in and outside of agriculture), on the reasonable assumption that intersectoral resource flows are sensitive to changes in relative price. Under industrialisation policies (that is, an increase in t), Pm rises and, in turn, raises Ph, depending on the value of ω. If importable and home goods are close substitutes (in consumption or production), higher tariffs will not influence Pm/Ph much but they will lower Px/Ph and Px/Pm. That is, part of t becomes a tax on exportables. This implicit export tax argument applies as well to other importables, like food, when they are given less protection than industrial products.

SOME EVIDENCE

The incidence of the protection parameter (ω) aggregates the net effects of a country's trade restrictions to show how the burden of the changes in relative price is shared by the sectors. The value of ω reflects the proportional change in the price of home goods relative to exportables as a function of the proportional change in the price of importables relative to exportables. Three-sector studies for the 1960s and 1970s by Sjaastad and by IFPRI staff give the following figures for ω:

Argentina (Sjaastad)	0.4 to 0.5
Chile (Sjaastad)	0.5 to 0.6
Colombia (Garcia)	about 0.9
Nigeria (Oyejide)	0.6 to 0.9

Peru (Valdés)   about 0.7
Philippines (Bautista)   about 0.8
Zaire (Tshibaka)   about 0.8

The results suggest a high degree of substitution between home goods and importables. A clear implication from these results is that at least one-half of the burden of protection is borne by exportables. Since the exports of many LDCs are predominantly agricultural, an import-substitution strategy taxes agriculture substantially more than a comparison of the nominal rates of protection would suggest. For example, the values of ω for Chile and Argentina indicate that a uniform tariff on imports of 20 per cent – which is not high by LDC standards – represents an implicit tax on exports of approximately 10 per cent. If exports are taxed directly, say at a rate of 15 per cent (as beef exports in Argentina were in the past), the total tax rate on exports is 15.6 per cent. Similarly, only part of the tariff is a tax on consumers of importables and protection to producers of import-competing goods. The rest is an implicit tax on producers of exportables (and of import-competing activities with lower protection, such as food) and an implicit subsidy to consumers of exportables and of those importables (like food). The implications of these results for economic policy are strong.

It is necessary to recall, however, that the discussion above is based on comparative statics, assuming that total production capacity, total expenditures and technology remain constant and that there is no surplus in the current account. Several tests were performed by the authors to establish whether the exclusion of these variables could affect the estimated value for ω. In all cases the results showed that the value of ω was highly stable for the sub-periods, indicating the robustness across different specifications.

In an effort to disaggregate the analysis further and capture the same type of incidence parameter for subsectors of agriculture (m_a and x_a), the same approach used here was applied to Peru for the period 1940–83 (see Table 1).

The results in Table 1 indicate that, using 1966–83 data, if the uniform tariff on non-agricultural importables is raised by 10 per cent and tariffs on agricultural goods did not change, an implicit tax of 5.6 per cent (with respect to home goods) is imposed on import-competing agricultural activities (such as rice) and an implicit tax of 6.6 per cent is imposed on exportable agricultural goods (such as cotton and sugar). When prices are compared to the prices of non-agricultural importables, the implicit tax on both types of agricultural goods is 10 per cent. In contrast, similar calculations made with respect to an increase in protection of agricultural importables (Pma) resulted in a much lower incidence on the price of home goods. That is, during the same period in Peru, changes in the prices of non-agricultural importables had a much greater effect on the prices of home goods than changes in the prices of agricultural importables. This was unexpected, given that food items dominate the

630   *Alberto Valdés*

TABLE 1   *Implicit tax on agriculture resulting from a 10 per cent increase in protection[a] to non-agricultural imports, Peru, 1949–1983*

	With respect to the price of	
Agricultural	Home goods	Non-agricultural Import-competing
Importables[b]		
1940–63	3.8	10.0 If Δt applies
1966–83	4.6	10.0 to Mna
Exportables[c]		
1940–63	6.4	10.0 If Δt applies
1966–83	6.1	10.0 to all imports
		(Mna and Ma)

Notes: [a] Increase in the uniform tariff equivalent.
  [b] Includes cereals, oil crops, beef and dairy.
  [c] Includes sugar, cotton and coffee.
Source: Alberto Valdés (1985).

last item. Similar computations for agricultural exportables indicate that an increase of 10 per cent in the price of agricultural exportables raises the value of home goods by 2.6 per cent, compared to 0.6 per cent resulting from a rise in the price of non-agricultural exportables. This was to be expected, as the former are partly consumed in the domestic market while the latter are practically all exported.

As part of an industrialisation strategy through protection, the real exchange rate falls consistently through time. That is, the higher average tariff implies a fall in the equilibrium real exchange rate. The evidence for Peru is consistent with this presumption. In fact, the evolution of the uniform tariff equivalent (Table 2) suggests that during the 1960s and 1970s, the Peruvian economy became more closed, with increases in restrictions on trade. The real exchange rate underwent a major and persistent decline after the 1960s, reducing the profitability of producing tradables *vis-à-vis* non-tradables. Preliminary evidence suggests that this decline began in the mid 1960s.

Such declines in the long-run real exchange rate have been particularly harmful for the production of agricultural tradables in LDCs, slowing their production and speeding up increases in the domestic consumption of tradables (imported cereals and exportables), reducing the contribution of agriculture to growth and to the balance of payments, and making LDCs more dependent on imported food. It is important to recognise, however, that a falling real exchange rate is not necessarily a sign for a devaluation. The external accounts of a country could be in equilibrium at a low real exchange rate, because of restrictions on imports or larger inflows of capital, including foreign assistance. A result would be that agriculture, together with exportables in general, would be taxed implicitly. This penalty on agriculture is inherent and lasts as long as

TABLE 2   *Evolution of the level of protection and of the real exchange rate in Peru, 1949–1983*

Uniform tariff equivalent[a] (percent)		Real exchange rate (E/Ph)			
1949–53	5.3	1966	100.0	1975	70.8
1954–58	29.9	1967	96.6	1976	57.1
1959–63	71.2	1968	122.7	1977	66.3
1964–68	133.0	1969	118.6	1978	86.1
1969–73	256.0	1970	109.7	1979	80.7
1974–78	181.7	1971	102.0	1980	65.3
1979–82	91.3	1972	96.2	1981	55.8
		1973	89.6	1982	47.4
		1974	78.9	1983	52.4

Note: [a] Uniform tariff equivalent represents the hypothetical value of tariffs and subsidies which, in replacing the prevailing structure of trade barriers, would result in the same volume (but not composition) of trade, without adjustments in the nominal exchange rate nor in the price of home goods. Calculations based on methodology suggested by Sjaastad (1981).
Source: Alberto Valdés (1985).

industry is highly protected. It cannot be eliminated by better management in other areas of economic policy.[4]

In an analysis of the effect of the foreign trade regime on Philippine agriculture between 1950 and 1980, Bautista found that it discriminated heavily against agricultural exports and favoured import-competing products. This was true not only during the 1950s, when import and foreign exchange controls were imposed, but also, rather surprisingly, during the 1970s when the official stated policy was to promote exports. The combined effect of exchange rate policy and industrial protection substantially reduced the incentive to produce agricultural exportables, relative to producing either home goods (including services) or, most strongly, import-competing industrial goods (Bautista 1984).

Garcia observed that in Colombia a uniform tariff of 30 per cent on all imports constituted a tax equivalent of 27 per cent on all exports, which implied that exports with high supply elasticities would be unable to compete in international markets. In the 1970s, sugar, coffee, barley and rice showed negative nominal rates of protection. The estimated 20 per cent overvaluation of the peso in the 1970s was in effect another tax that should be added to the tax on exports. Colombia recently broadened the coverage of its export subsidy scheme (previously restricted to manufactured goods) to include some agricultural products. This offset at least partially this implicit taxation of agricultural exportables. Garcia concludes that during the 1960s and 1970s, the implicit overvaluation of the peso resulting from the combined effect of exchange rate and trade policy in Colombia more than offset the nominal protection given to import-competing agricultural products, such as corn. But this was not true with milk, vegetable oils and wheat, the nominal protection of which has consistently been above the measured rate of overvaluation of the peso (Garcia 1981).

CONCLUDING COMMENTS

The effects of policies directed at the macroeconomic management of the economy on agriculture can more than offset the sector-specific policies, in terms of its incidence through effects on the relative price signals guiding producers and consumers. This can be particularly influential for agricultural tradables. Observations from several South American countries and the Philippines show that agricultural tradables are usually discouraged across-the-board, whether they are import-competing commodities or exportables. This penalty on agriculture is inherent and lasts as long as industry is highly protected, but could apply as well following a heavy influx of capital.

It is postulated that in LDCs most products in agriculture are tradables. But home goods are important as sources of traditional food products, particularly in sub-Saharan Africa. The analysis and empirical evidence submitted in this paper indicates that producers of home goods can benefit indirectly from industrial and exchange rate policies, if the prices of home goods increase relative to tradables. However, the possibility that 'home good' foods (such as pulses, root crops, etc.), and tradable foods (such as cereals, oilseeds, milk, etc.) can be close substitutes in consumption puts a ceiling on the market prices of the home goods. This ceiling is determined by the effects of the foreign trade and exchange rate policies on the prices of the tradables. Furthermore, it is likely that foreign trade regimes in LDCs contributed considerably to their growing dependence on imported food, by taxing production and implicitly subsidizing consumption of tradables.

The disappointment shown in much of the current literature with the performance of agriculture in LDCs is centred on the production of tradables. It is usually associated with poor export performance and the growing foreign exchange requirements of food imports. This is particularly true of sub-Saharan Africa. However, the risk of a trade-oriented policy for agriculture is often cited as grounds for rejecting it (Valdés and Siamwalla 1984). This is essentially the risk as perceived by governments, with their own concerns about world price-related risks, fluctuations of government revenues and food security. As a result of these concerns, some governments have followed a variety of risk reduction policies. A warning is needed in an environment in which the production of agricultural tradables has been taxed rather heavily in many LDCs, usually implicitly and unintentionally. Policies to explicitly 'close' the economy more could dampen the very subsector with the highest potential growth.

NOTES

I am especially grateful to Romeo Bautista, F. Javier Leon, and Maurice Schiff for their helpful comments.

—

Exchange rates and trade policy 633

Home goods (or non-traded goods) are those goods where internal prices are not directly deduced from world prices plus the tariffs. These include services and in agriculture, in addition to perishables, could include many traditional food crops in tropical areas such as cassava, yams, potatoes and some types of beans, where transport costs and preference for local varieties are a real barrier to trade.

[2]These issues were developed further in Valdés and Siamwalla (1984).

[3]A remarkable exception is Cavallo and Mundlak (1982).

[4]There is more than one concept of the equilibrium exchange rate. What people usually have in mind when they describe rates as 'overvalued' or 'undervalued' corresponds to a rate that would clear the market in the absence of official intervention, given the country's average level of protection. In contrast, the equilibrium real rate of exchange referred to here relates to the exchange rate effect of trade policies. In another context, however, one could speak also of the protectionist impact of an overvalued currency, such as in the United States in early 1985, that is, when prolonged deviations of exchange rates from equilibrium can generate protectionist pressures.

REFERENCES

Balassa, Bela, *The Structure of Protection in Developing Countries*, Johns Hopkins University Press, Baltimore, 1971.

Bautista, Romeo, *Effects of Trade and Exchange Rate Policies on Export Production Incentives in Philippine Agriculture*, International Food Policy Research Institute (mimeograph), Washington DC, December 1984.

Bhagwati, Jagdish, *The Anatomy and Consequences of Exchange Control Regimes*, Ballinger, Cambridge, for the National Bureau of Economic Research, 1978.

Cavallo, Domingo, and Mundlak, Yair, *Agriculture and Economic Growth in an Open Economy: The Case of Argentina*, Research Report no. 36, International Food Policy Research Institute, Washington, DC, 1982.

Dornbusch, Rudiger, 'Tariffs and Non-Traded Goods', *Journal of International Economics*, no. 4, 1974, pp. 177–85.

Garcia, Jorge, *The Effects of Exchange Rates and Commercial Policy on Agricultural Incentives in Colombia: 1953–1978*. Research Report no. 24, International Food Policy Research Institute, Washington, DC, 1981.

Krueger, Anne O., *Liberalization Attempts and Consequences*, for the National Bureau of Economic Research, Ballinger, Cambridge, 1978.

Little I., Scitovsky, T. and Scott, M., *Industry and Trade in Developing Countries: A Comparative Study*, Oxford University Press, 1970.

Sjaastad, Larry, A., 'Commercial Policy, True Tariffs, and Relative Prices', ch. 3 in Black, John and Hindley, Brian (eds) *Current Issues in Commercial Policy and Diplomacy*, St Martin's Press, New York, 1980.

Sjaastad, Larry, A., 'Proteccion y Volumen de Comercio: La Evidencia' in *Cuadernos de Economia*, no. 54–5, August-December 1981, Santiago.

Valdés, Alberto and Franklin, David L., *Trade and Exchange Rate Policies: Implications for Peruvian Agriculture: 1950–1980*, International Food Policy Research Institute, Washington, DC, (forthcoming).

Valdés, Alberto and Siamwalla, Ammar, 'Foreign Trade Regime, Exchange Rate Policy, and the Structure of Incentives for Agriculture: Issues and Policies', Paper presented at the Agricultural Price Policy Workshop, Elkridge, Maryland, 29 April – 2 May 1984.

DISCUSSION OPENING – GERRIT MEESTER

The two papers we are discussing now deal with the impact of factors from outside the agro-food sector on price formation and supply and demand in this sector. In particular, the methodological aspects of the papers are of course of interest in this session on 'Theoretical development of market and price analysis'. However, I will also give some comments about the relevance of the analyses for agricultural policy.

The Mundlak paper, which is rather technical, aims at analysing 'the determinants of the agricultural and non-agricultural inputs of food'. A central issue in the paper is the separation of food supply and demand, and of food prices into what Mundlak calls an agricultural component and a non-agricultural component. The hypothesis then is that the income elasticity of demand of the non-agricultural component is larger than that of the agricultural component. This means that economic growth generally will increase the volume as well as the price of the non-agricultural component relative to the agricultural component in food. This in its turn leads to a situation where, in general, demand for food increases more rapidly under economic growth than demand for agricultural products.

It seems to me that the proposed separation of food into two components is a rather interesting way of analysing the impacts of growth on the sector. The only question I have is about the hypothesis that the price of the non-agricultural component in food is in all circumstances equal to that of the non-food sector. This seems both from an empirical as well as a theoretical point of view rather unrealistic. It seems empirically unrealistic, for instance, for the EC, where one can conclude – from a simple interpretation of changes in recent years in prices of agricultural products, food and non-food prices – that prices of the non-agricultural component in food must have been different from those in the non-food sector. Moreover, the hypothesis seems theoretically unrealistic because the price formation as well as the rate and kind of technological change and the capital–labour ratio need not be equal in the food sector and in other economic sectors. Would not it be better therefore to distinguish separate prices for the non-agricultural component in food and the non-food sector?

The Valdés paper deals with another impact of economic growth on the agro-food sector, namely the consequences for agricultural prices and output of a tariff or similar protective measures in other economic sectors. The paper contains a very interesting and for policy-makers important analysis of the relevance of interdependencies between economic sectors. In general, I fully agree with the paper and have only some minor questions.

The first question concerns the level of the measured protection parameters for various countries. These levels seem rather high. One reason could be the open character of the economies of the countries that have been analysed. But is there not also another reason, namely the dual economy situation in some of these countries? Such a situation could mean that the market economy part of the home good sector is rather small and hence the impact of international trade on that sector rather large. The same occurs, as Dr Valdés mentions in his paper, for parts of the agricultural sector.

My second question is how far the unexpected relatively small effects of price changes of agricultural importables (in relation to price changes of non-agricultural importables) on the price of home goods in Peru, mentioned in the third part of the paper, can be explained from the different kinds of imported goods. Changes in import prices of special consumer products for rich people, like condensed milk, cheese and wine, will probably have a much smaller effect on the price for home goods than changes in import prices of, for instance, transport means and other investment goods for the domestic processing, trade and retail sector. My question is: have there been any additional analyses in these respects?

My third question concerns the estimated equation (9). I presume that there is a time lag between the price change of imported goods and of home goods. What time lag is used in this estimation?

My fourth question, and maybe an item in the discussion on the food problem in some of the developing countries concerns the relative importance of the phenomenon discussed in the paper as an explanatory variable for this problem in comparison to other explanatory variables.

These are my questions on the paper presented by Dr Valdés and I repeat my already mentioned view about the importance for economic policy-making of the phenomenon that has been discussed in the paper. That is the case for import tariffs as well as for other exogenous factors, of which Dr Valdés mentions in his paper the effects of an oil or mineral boom, policies affecting capital movements and food aid. Many other examples can be added. One of these is the system of so-called monetary compensatory amounts in the Common Agricultural Policy of the EC. These MCAs compensate in the short run the effects for agriculture of an exchange rate change between EC member countries, but create in the longer run a relatively favourable position for the agricultural sector in countries with an appreciated currency, and a relatively unfavourable position for the sector in countries with a depreciated currency. The causal relationships for these changes in the relative position of agriculture are similar to those described in the paper. The MCA phenomenon explains partly why the West-German, Dutch and recently British self-sufficiency ratios for agricultural products increased more than those of France and Italy. It partly explains, too, why the so-called 'Dutch disease' did not affect the agriculture in the country where this disease was diagnosed for the first time after the natural gas boom at the beginning of the 1970s, nor in the UK agricultural sector after the North Sea oil boom at the end of that decade.

REFERENCE

Corden, W. M. *Inflation, Exchange Rates and the World Economy* (second edition), Clarendon Press, Oxford, 1981.

GENERAL DISCUSSION – RAPPORTEUR: EWA RABINOWICZ

The discussion of the Mundlak paper centred on the assumptions made in the paper (in particular income elasticity of q and identity between p_Q

and p_N), and on additional factors which could be included in the analysis. The factors which were mentioned were: market conditions, share of women in labour force, age of housewife, new kitchen equipment, structural movements (drop of auto-consumption on farms) etc.

It was claimed that prices of agricultural products on the world market are determined by developed countries and that prices for developing countries are deteriorating. Furthermore the issue was raised about the substitution within agriculture (from grains to meat) as a result of increasing incomes. Such a substitution did not necessarily increase the service input.

In reply, Dr Mundlak stated that some assumptions were made for convenience and nothing in the results depended crucially on the assumptions. The price of service of food was equal to the price of non-food for the sake of simplicity. The assumption of income elasticity of q was of an empirical nature and could be replaced if other evidence were available. On the issue of additional factors, he agreed that the empirical analysis could be further elaborated by introducing demographical attributes such as age distribution or share of women in labour force, and market conditions. This would make the analysis more realistic without changing it qualitatively. On the issue of optimal strategy for developing countries with deteriorating terms of trade for agriculture, Mundlak pointed out that this problem was outside the scope of the paper but that the principle of comparative advantage should not be forgotten. Concluding his remarks, he emphasised that the major point was that the change of the share of agriculture in the expenditure on food was not only a function of income but also depended on prices.

In reply to the comments of the discussion opener (G. Meester) on the explanation of the high value of estimated incidence parameter (w) Dr. Valdés stated that value of w depended on the degree of substitutability between home goods and tradables and that he expected w to be lower at relative high levels of economic development. Furthermore he highlighted the role of the institutional setting of the country – in particular wage readjustment *vis-à-vis* changes in nominal exchange rate for the value of w. On the issue of time lag in estimating w, he pointed out that value of w had proved to be very robust with respect to different specifications of the time lag structure.

In reply to the question about the relative importance of trade regime/exchange rate phenomena, Dr Valdés stated that the importance of the factor studied would change according to the specific country situation and that an empirical test of the relative weight required an overall theory of agricultural growth which we still did not have. Efforts in this direction included work in this field at IFPRI.

In the discussion from the floor, scepticism was expressed about using world market prices as the opportunity costs. Furthermore it was questioned if more liberal trade regimes were advisable for LDCs and a point about industrial protection in India was made. The impact of trade/exchange rate regimes on the income distribution was also mentioned. Finally a question about the implication of the author's analysis for IMF recommendations for devaluations and a question about empirical evidence on consumption effects were put.

In reply, Dr Valdés stated that for small countries which were 'price takers', there was really no alternative but world market prices to express opportunity costs, in spite of existing distortions. On the issue of appropriate trade regimes for LDCs, he pointed out that his prescription was one of more neutral trade (not necessarily free trade), as compared with the present situation where agricultural exportables were often taxed and agricultural importables were subsidized. The example of India, a country with a large domestic market was, he believed, a questionable one for most small LDCs' economies.

In reply to the question about income distribution, Dr Valdés observed that there was not much empirical evidence on long-term effects of alternative trade regimes. Concerning the IMF's recommendations, he pointed out that his analysis concerned long-term, real exchange rate phenomena while the IMF dealt with short- medium-term, nominal exchange rate problems. He mentioned also that a study on the consumption effects was on the way.

Participants in the discussion included K. Hassan, G. Jones, S. Simons, J. Berthelot, E. Grigshy, I. Elbadawi and E. Rabinowicz.

JOCK R. ANDERSON, JOHN L. DILLON AND J. BRIAN HARDAKER

Farmers and Risk

INTRODUCTION – RISKS FACED BY FARMERS

Farmers everywhere face risks emanating from their natural, economic and socio-political environments. Most overtly, the natural environment features risks associated with climate, particularly in terms of precipitation and temperature. Other risks from the natural environment – notably pests and diseases – may be influenced by climate. The economic environment features many uncertainties with variable product prices reflecting variations in factors underlying demand, such as incomes, and factors influencing supply, such as climate. Some of these uncertainties can be modified by forms of intervention such as stabilisation schemes or other more heavy-handed government measures. The final broad source of risk is the socio-political environment. Agriculture is increasingly subject to unforeseen interventions by government and in many countries there is a high degree of uncertainty built into the socio-political environment which has its origins in changing power structures or other influences on policy.

In summary, the conjunction of uncertainties from natural, economic and socio-political sources leads to a plethora of risks for farmers. Seldom are these uncertainties amenable to precise prediction and so, while the farmer's environment is unstable, it is inherently risky and, overall, might well be described as turbulent.

THEORETICAL ADVANCES AND RETREATS

The decision analysis paradigm
Agricultural economists have been striving for adequate modelling of the risky environment and decision-making processes of farmers for several decades. Many ideas have come and gone; universal agreement on the framework that is most appropriate is yet to be realised. Our preferences in this matter are clear with our stated choice and exploitation of the modern paradigm of decision analysis in which the decision-maker is seen as choosing so as to maximise subjective expected utility (Anderson, Dillon and Hardaker 1977). While one can be critical of the elements of this paradigm, as we are in what follows and as others such as Allais

638

(1984) have been, we have yet to encounter a more satisfactory framework for considering farmers and risk.

A sketch of the paradigm. Decisions under uncertainty, i.e., practically all decisions in real life, involve the choice by an individual (or group) of one option from a set of alternative actions. The consequences of the selected action depend on the outcome of relevant uncertain events. Decision-makers are assumed to hold beliefs about the chances of occurrence of the uncertain events bearing on their choices as well as preferences for the possible consequences. The beliefs are encoded as subjective probabilities (thereby implying a probability distribution for the consequences associated with each possible choice) while the preferences can be captured via a suitably elicited function as utilities. A rational decision is one that is consistent with the decision-maker's beliefs and preferences and thus corresponds to choice of the action whose probability distribution of consequences maximises the decision-maker's subjective expected utility. Though developed mainly as a normative model, decision analysis (as discussed below) has also been seen as having positive or behavioural relevance.

Normative relevance of the paradigm. Normative use of decision analysis is based on the presumption that the decomposition of at least some important decision problems into their components, followed by analysis that integrates the components into a choice consistent with the elicited beliefs and preferences of the decision-maker, is better than wholly intuitive choice. The procedure does not guarantee correct choice. Where chance is involved, some decisions will turn out well and others badly. Decision analysis can only lead to decisions that are 'good' in the *ex ante* sense of being consistent with expressed beliefs and preferences, not decisions that are 'right' in the *ex post* sense of being regret free.

A considerable portfolio of methods has been developed to put the deceptively simple ideas of decision analysis to work in the normative analysis of a wide range of choice problems. Little use has been made, however, of these in the context of everyday farm decision-making. From a farmer perspective, the reasons for non-adoption would seem to be difficulty with the concepts involved, the apparent complexity of the approach, the cost of data gathering and the possibly limited benefit for all except significant decisions. From an extension perspective, these difficulties are compounded by the personal nature of the approach which implies, in principle, separate analysis for each farmer. Like mathematical programming, farm-level use of decision analysis would seem likely to be confined to larger scale, if not corporate, farms.

Probability
Probability is the language of uncertainty. We find it impossible to conceptualise any analysis of the risks that farmers face without using this language. Unfortunately, the language has problems when it comes to

elicitation of the decision-maker's subjective probabilities. Despite some decades of practice, procedures are still anything but standardised.

The nature of subjective probabilities as statements of belief makes them essentially personal judgements. Their personal nature emphasises the sovereignty of decision-makers in choices that affect their welfare. There are no right or wrong probabilities, but they should reflect the decision-maker's true feelings of uncertainty, taking account of all the information to hand about the uncertain events of concern. A rational person will thus strive to make subjective probability judgements that are as 'objective' as possible.

Considerable evidence exists that these worthy ideals in probability elicitation are not easily achieved (see, e.g., Hogarth 1975 and Kahneman, Slovic and Tversky 1981). It is disappointing that there has seemingly been little development on this front, especially in agriculture. We believe that the reference lottery technique (Spetzler and Stael von Holstein 1975) is under-utilised in applications as a means of keeping respondents 'honest'. We also look for studies with peasant farmers, analogous to those of Binswanger (1981) in eliciting preferences, where money prizes are used rather than hypothetical rewards. We recognise, however, that bias in subjective probability judgements is likely to be difficult to eliminate, suggesting a need to provide more extension information for farmers in a sensible probabilistic framework.

Utility

As noted by Anderson, Dillon and Hardaker (1977, p. 108), though only developed in recent decades, the major ideas involved in utility or the encoding of decision-makers' preferences have been around for centuries. The Dillon (1971) article might be regarded as a convenient watershed marking the start of the active exploitation of the concepts in agricultural economics. This year of the mid 1980s is not, then, the time to be elaborating on the methodology of utility assessment which is widely exposited in convenient sources such as Anderson, Dillon and Hardaker (1977, ch. 4) and Farquhar (1984). Rather, the emphasis here is first on some pragmatic procedures which economise on resources used in applying the utility concept and then on a brief review of the continuing difficulties in the theory.

Risk aversion and pragmatism. The essence of using utility concepts to capture non-neutral attitudes to risk is that, if choices can be made in relatively simple situations, the inferences from these choices can be formalised and used to appraise complex situations that it would be too difficult to resolve consistently otherwise. Procedures for capturing risk preferences are now well known and more or less tried. However, it is also established that psychological difficulties intrude into expression of risk preferences, even in simple situations (Machina 1981).

If a farmer's risky decision problem involves very significant changes in wealth, a full-blown formal risk analysis may be unavoidable, requiring complete encoding of preferences over all relevant ranges of potential consequences. However, many risky decisions do not involve such sweeping changes. In these situations, more pragmatic procedures deserve careful consideration. One such procedure is based on the notion that, over restricted ranges of risk, measures of risk aversion may be approximately constant. The two main measures of risk aversion, absolute and relative, are defined as

$$r_A = - U_2(W)/U_1(W) \quad \text{and} \quad r_R = Wr_A,$$

respectively, where the numerical subscripts denote the derivatives of $U(W)$, the univariate utility function with respect to wealth.

Speculations as to likely values of r_R (which is measured in dimensionless units) have ranged from about unity to two. Sample data from Nepal suggest that, in extremely resource poor farming situations, it may even reach values as extreme as four and greater (Hamal and Anderson 1982). A value for r_R can be adopted for use in an analysis, the value used depending on how the analyst perceives the decision-maker. The value presumed might, for instance, be unity if the individual is regarded as being 'normal', two or three if considered fairly risk averse, and four if extremely risk averse. On the other side, values as small as 0.5 might be presumed if an individual were regarded as hardly concerned with risk.

The coefficient of absolute risk aversion is also commonly used in both theoretical and empirical work. Unfortunately, this measure is not unit free and its magnitude depends critically on the units in which wealth is measured. However, if a value for r_R can be presumed, then – given an estimate of wealth (including the present value of future net earnings) – r_A can be estimated as r_R/W. Once estimated, r_A can readily be incorporated in various sorts of analysis. It is most simply applied to those decision problems that are linear in uncertain quantities that are normal in distribution (Freund 1956). Thus, for instance, if risky farm income can be regarded as approximately normal, the certainty equivalent C (which serves as a surrogate for expected utility) for a particular option can be calculated as $C = E - 0.5r_A/V$ where E and V are respectively the mean and variance of farm income under the option being assessed. This result is fairly robust with respect to departures from normality since it can also be regarded as a second-order approximation to the certainty equivalent.

It is the experience of many analysts that accounting for risk aversion in a full-blown manner leads in many cases to very modest adjustments in the optimal quantities (i.e., utility maximising rates are often similar to expected profit maximising rates). This is bound to be the case at modest levels of risk aversion as would often be associated with relatively high levels of wealth. It also implies that if adjustments are rather small, the consequences of using more pragmatic methods to assess them are robust.

Criticisms of the subjective expected utility model. The axiomatic basis of subjective expected utility (SEU) has been the subject of much criticism as documented in, e.g., Allais (1984) and Bouyssou (1984). There is mounting evidence that decision-makers often violate some of the axioms that underlie the SEU model. Schoemaker (1982) points out that, from a positive perspective, the interpretation of the evidence counter to the model is complicated. From what he calls a 'postdictive' perspective, it is possible to argue that apparent violations of the SEU model in studies designed to test its predictive power occur because improper account is taken of the costs and benefits influencing the decision-maker's choice. The trouble with this argument, however, is that it makes the SEU model impossible to falsify. Schoemaker argues that it would be appropriate to examine the kinds of behavioural anomalies being documented with a view to developing a model of choice more in tune with observed cognitive processes. While we accept this view as reasonable, we note that no such alternative model, attracting widespread acceptance, has yet been developed.

For normative applications, the observed violations of the axioms are somewhat less worrying. The fact that people do not always make the most rational choices under uncertainty is a necessary condition for the SEU model to have prescriptive power. Nevertheless, there are some worrying aspects. Most obviously, decision-makers are unlikely to accept prescriptions from analyses based on assumptions that depart appreciably from their actual view of the world. Furthermore, persistent violations of some axioms may make the model inoperational, for instance, through the impossibility of eliciting utility functions that adequately capture the decision-maker's real preferences. Thus, following a reappraisal of his well-regarded work in deriving utility functions for Indian peasants, Binswanger was forced to conclude that his results were inconsistent with the SEU model (Quizon, Binswanger and Machina 1984).

The accumulating evidence against the SEU model, whether for positive or normative application, is certainly not to be dismissed lightly. Nevertheless, as Schoemaker (1982, p. 556) concludes:

> ... until richer models of rationality emerge, expected utility maximization may well remain a worthwhile benchmark against which to compare, and towards which to direct, behavior. On the other hand, it is likely that today's paradoxes and persistent expected utility violations hold the seed of future normative as well as descriptive theories of choice.

We take a somewhat stronger position than this in arguing that, despite its imperfections, the SEU model is likely to remain for some time as the best operational framework for considering risk in agriculture. It has proved its worth not only in numerous overt applications, but in more subtle ways, for example by sensitising farmers, their advisers, scientists and the makers of agricultural policy to the importance of risk in farm decision-making and to the need to recognise the effects on farmers' behaviour of the widespread existence of risk aversion.

Stochastic efficiency

The idea of stochastic efficiency appraisal is to proceed as far as possible in decision analysis without having to elicit decision-makers' preferences. The implementation of the maker's procedure involves comparison and some manipulation of probability distributions of uncertain consequences expressed as cumulative distribution functions. The procedures, which are elaborated for the cases of first, second and third degree stochastic dominance in Anderson, Dillon and Hardaker (1977, ch. 9), are reasonably straightforward. The main difficulty is that the resultant efficient sets of options may not be definitive as guides to decision-making in the sense that too many actions may remain for decision-makers to choose amongst according to their individual preferences. However, as exemplified by Quiggin (1983), there have been useful applications to the appraisal of policy options for risk mitigation.

More recently, there have been applications based on the development by Meyer (1977*a*, *b*), of the concept of stochastic dominance with respect to a function. This concept has many potential interpretations. One that is of relevance to the analysis of farm decision-making involves bounding more closely the efficient sets according to any designated degree of stochastic efficiency. Of most practical importance is the second degree since this allows for risk aversion and it is widely agreed that farmers generally are risk averse. The additional complexity of third degree stochastic efficiency, which is implied by the existence of decreasing absolute risk aversion, seems hardly worthwhile.

Meyer's concept amounts to putting limits on the degree of absolute risk aversion over which the set of decision-makers is defined. Unqualified second degree stochastic efficiency implies a range of r_A from zero to infinity. On the lower side, this borders on risk indifference, which is probably true only for extremely wealthy individuals, and on the upper would amount to pathological levels of risk aversion. Intuitively, any designated group of farmers will fall into some limited range of attitudes towards risk. All that needs to be done to implement the approach is to pin down these ranges approximately, perhaps by a purposive survey of the group directed to the individuals expected to be extreme in their risk attitudes. Once the empirical range of r_A is established, limits can be invoked in applying stochastic dominance with respect to a function. These ideas were used insightfully by King and Robison (1981) and have since been exploited widely in US farm-level applications of the procedures. Kramer and Pope (1981) have used the ideas in an analysis of alternative policy options in US commodity programs, as have Anderson and Griffiths (1982) in analysis of risky input use in a multi-factor production function context.

Amongst other potential applications of these notions are enhanced comparative statics of the risk-averse firm. For example, some policy-oriented applications have been explored by Quiggin and Anderson (1979). A promising line is the recent work of Meyer and Ormiston (1983) dealing with the particular changes that can be made to distribution functions which cause risk-averse decision-makers to adjust choice variables in the same direction. Such ideas will add both relevance and complexity to the traditional models of firm behaviour that agricultural economists so heavily rely on.

Another growth point in application of such ideas may be in the valuation of information. This can be thought of as a rather special aspect of comparative statics but it need not necessarily be just statics. Indications of the ways to go are indicated by Byerlee and Anderson (1982). The concepts are applicable in any attempts to value information on any source of uncertainty.

Multi-attribute considerations
The definition of utility over more than one attribute is making slow but steady progress in the practice of decision analysis. The procedures have been elaborated for some time, notably by Keeney and Raiffa (1976). A farm application is provided by Herath, Hardaker and Anderson (1982). Application is easier if some simplifying assumptions can be made about the nature of trade-offs amongst attributes, as described in part in Anderson, Dillon and Hardaker (1977, ch. 4).

An obvious further development would be to generalise the concept of stochastic efficiency across multiple attributes. There have been a few such attempts – see, e.g., Levhari, Paroush and Peleg (1975) – but these deal only with the straightforward concepts of one-way stochastic efficiency of pure form. The problem is difficult but progress may well be made if simplifying procedures analogous to those above are invoked as well as the simplifying trade-off assumptions that are built in to most multi-attribute applications.

ONGOING DEVELOPMENTS

In this short review there is very limited scope for exploring such a rapidly growing field of application. Our selections are thus idiosyncratic and surely biased but befitting the personal orientation of the decision analysis paradigm.

Risk and farmers' behaviour
Modern decision analysis has provided a framework for gaining a better understanding of how risk considerations affect the choices that farmers make. The SEU model may be given a direct behavioural interpretation with scope for applications to the analysis of farmers' behaviour under risk. Some relevant issues are considered in the first subsection below. In the second subsection, more econometrically-oriented attempts to assess farmers' risk behaviour are noted.

Behavioural decision theory. Although the SEU model was developed as a normative model of choice, a number of positive applications to agriculture are to be found in the literature. For example, there have been several studies using the paradigm to explore the important question of farmers' adoption of new but presumably subjectively very risky technology (e.g., Feder and O'Mara 1981). Likewise, applications have been made in agricultural sector modelling (e.g., Hazell 1982).

Direct tests of the predictive power of the SEU model for farmers' behaviour have given mixed results (e.g., Officer and Halter 1968; Lin, Dean and Moore 1974). Certainly, the evidence is clear that farmers, on the whole, are risk averse and do respond as theory predicts to changes in riskiness. All else equal, therefore, any model that accounts for risk and risk aversion is likely to predict behaviour better than one that ignores these phenomena.

There are, however, at least two difficulties with the use of expected utility analysis as a model of behaviour. The first is the accumulating evidence already referred to of violations of the axioms of the theory. The psychological literature – see, e.g., Bouyssou (1984) – suggests that, at best, the model will predict behaviour very imperfectly, and the empirical evidence from agriculture confirms that a gap often exists between prediction and farmers' actual behaviour. Second, as evidenced by the theoretical criticisms and/or alternative models presented by Allais (1984), Kahneman and Tversky (1979), Machina (1982) and Quiggin (1982), there is much dissatisfaction with the SEU model *per se*. As Dillon (1979, p. 36) notes, it will require far more robust tests than have been used to date to select the more plausible of the models of behaviour under uncertainty. Meantime, use of the SEU model in behavioural applications must rest largely on its operational appeal *qua* model and on the richness of the insights it can give into so many important questions involving risky choice.

Risk responsiveness. There has been a long tradition of including variables that capture changes in the riskiness of environments in aggregate models of producer behaviour. In the ealier versions this was done mainly on an *ad hoc* basis (e.g., Freebairn and Rausser 1975). The pioneering work of Just (1977) added a more formal dimension to such work by introducing a Bayesian rationalisation that allowed riskiness, as measured by a time series concept of variance, to be estimated econometrically. Such models are demanding of data for reliable estimates and are computationally challenging since they are inherently non-linear. Applications have proliferated but there seems to be a swing away from the formality of Just's models back to more *ad hoc* specifications since the results seem robust across forms of specification.

One thing is clear from such work: farmers are indeed responsive to changing riskiness. If their economic environment becomes less risky through, say, the operation of a stabilisation scheme, they will respond by increasing production. The significance of this finding in policy analyses can be considerable, as MacLaren (1983) demonstrates. It is particularly important to account for risk responses in analyses of stabilisation schemes since ignoring such effects will seriously undermine the accuracy with which gains and losses can be measured.

Policy-induced uncertainties

Often, the policy environment is another source of uncertainty for farmers. Governments can intervene in many ways, from shielding or exaggerating the impact of international price fluctuations and trade distortions back to producers, through market operations under the banner of stabilisation, to more directly intruding into input markets to modify prices faced by producers. The need of politicians to trade for votes can lead, especially at election time or at times of rural crisis as may be induced by drought, to interventions which, with hindsight, can be seen as less than fortunate. However, such seems to be the nature of life in democracies, and implies the need for agricultural economists to develop frameworks for analysing the political market. The pioneering work of MacLaren (1980, 1983) in this regard is most insightful. The surface has, however, hardly been scratched and there remains much to be done by careful analysts to incorporate formal concern for policy uncertainty. Unless such unpredictability is accounted for, any policy analysis will be potentially flawed in its assessment of producers' response to designated incentives.

CONCLUSION

Although the analytical challenges of understanding the nexus between the farm and its risky environment are considerable, the rewards are likely to be great. It seems inevitable that the environment of farmers will be forever more or less turbulent and thus urgent progress must be made on both matching and applying analytical frameworks to this reality. Useful starts have been made in several directions. Much, however, remains to be done. This is particularly true in terms of policy analysis, the provision of guides to agricultural scientists in their search for appropriate new technology and the institution of mechanisms to enhance farmers' information about the risks they face. We hope that some of this unfinished business will be done before the next International Conference.

REFERENCES

Allais, M., 'The foundations of the theory of utility and risk', in Hagen, O. and Wenstrop, F, (eds), *Progress in Utility and Risk Theory*, Reidel, Dordrecht, 1984.
Anderson, J. R. and Griffiths, W. E., 'Production risk and efficient allocation of resources', *Australian Journal of Agricultural Economics*, vol. 26, no. 3, Dec. 1982.
Anderson, J. R., Dillon, J. L. and Hardaker, J. B., *Agricultural Decision Analysis*, Iowa State University Press, Ames, 1977.
Binswanger, H. P., 'Attitudes towards risk: theoretical implications of an experiment in rural India', *Economic Journal*, vol. 91, December, 1981.
Bouyssou, D. 'Decision-aid and expected utility theory: a critical survey' in Hagen, O. and Wenstrop, F. (eds), *Progress in Utility and Risk Theory*, Reidel, Dordrecht, 1984.
Byerlee, D. R. and Anderson, J. R., 'Risk, utility and the value of information in farmer decision making', *Review of Marketing and Agricultural Economics*, vol. 50, no. 3, December, 1982.

Dillon, J. L., 'An expository review of Bernoullian decision theory', *Review of Marketing and Agricultural Economics*, vol. 39, no. 1, March, 1971.

Dillon, J. L., 'Bernoullian decision theory: outline and problems' in Roumasset, J. A., Boussard, J. -M and Singh, I. (eds), *Risk, Uncertainty and Agricultural Development*, SEARCA, Laguna, 1979.

Farquhar, P. H., 'Utility assessment methods', *Management Science*, vol. 30, no. 11, November, 1984.

Feder, G. and O'Mara, G. T., 'On information and innovation diffusion: a Bayesian approach', *American Journal of Agricultural Economics*, vol. 64, no. 1, February, 1982.

Freebairn, J. W. and Rausser, G. C., 'Effects of changes in the level of U.S. beef imports', *American Journal of Agricultural Economics*, vol. 57, no. 4, November, 1975.

Freund, R. J. 'The introduction of risk into a programming model', *Econometrica*, vol. 24, no. 2, April, 1956.

Hamal, K. B. and Anderson, J. R., 'A note on decreasing absolute risk aversion among farmers in Nepal', *Australian Journal of Agricultural Economics*, vol. 26, no. 3, December, 1982.

Hazell, P. B. R., 'Application of risk preferences estimates in firm-household and agricultural sector models', *American Journal of Agricultural Economics*, vol. 64, no. 2, May, 1982.

Herath, H. M. G., Hardaker, J. B. and Anderson, J. R., 'Choice of varieties by Sri Lanka rice farmers: comparing alternative decision models', *American Journal of Agricultural Economics*, vol. 64, no. 1, February, 1982.

Hogarth, R. M., 'Cognitive processes and the assessment of subjective probability distributions', *Journal of the American Statistical Association*, vol. 70, no. 350, June 1975.

Just, R. E., 'Estimation of an adaptive expectations model', *International Economic Review*, vol. 18, no. 3, October, 1977.

Kahneman, D. and Tversky, A., 'Prospect theory: an analysis of decision under risk', *Econometrica*, vol. 47, no. 2, April, 1979.

Kahneman, D., Slovic, P. and Tversky, A., (eds) *Judgement under Uncertainty – Heuristics and Biases*, Cambridge University Press, 1981.

Keeney, R. L. and Raiffa, H., *Decisions with Multiple Objectives: Preferences and Value Tradeoffs*, John Wiley, New York, 1976.

King, R. P. and Robison, L. J., 'An interval approach to measuring decision maker preferences', *American Journal of Agricultural Economics*, vol. 63, no. 3, August 1981.

Kramer, R. A. and Pope, R. D., 'Participation in farm commodity programs: a stochastic dominance analysis', *American Journal of Agricultural Economics*, vol. 63, no. 1, February 1981.

Levhari, D., Paroush, J. and Peleg, B., 'Efficiency analysis for multivariate distributions', *Review of Economic Studies*, vol. 42, no. 1, January 1975.

Lin, W., Dean, G. W. and Moore, C. V., 'An empirical test of utility vs. profit maximization in agricultural production', *American Journal of Agricultural Economics*, vol. 56, no. 3, August, 1974.

Machina, M. J., '"Rational" decision making versus "rational" decision modelling?', *Journal of Mathematical Psychology*, vol. 24, no. 2, June, 1981.

Machina, M. J., 'Expected utility analysis without the independence axiom', *Econometrica*, vol. 50, no. 2, April 1982.

MacLaren, D., 'Agricultural policy uncertainty and the risk averse firm', *European Review of Agricultural Economics*, vol. 7, no. 4, December, 1980.

MacLaren, D., 'The output response of the risk averse firm: some comparative statics for agricultural policy', *Journal of Agricultural Economics*, vol. 34, no. 1, January 1983.

Meyer, J., 'Choice among distributions', *Journal of Economic Theory*, vol. 14, no. 2, December 1977a.

Meyer, J., 'Second degree stochastic dominance with respect to a function', *International Economic Review*, vol. 18, no. 2, June 1977b.

Meyer, J. and Ormiston, M. B., 'The comparative statics of cumulative distribution changes

648   *Jock R. Anderson, John L. Dillon and J. Brian Hardaker*

for the class of risk averse agents', *Journal of Economic Theory*, vol. 31, no. 1, October 1983.

Officer, R. R. and Halter, A. N., 'Utility analysis in a practical setting', *American Journal of Agricultural Economics*, vol. 50, no. 2, May 1968.

Quiggin, J. 'A theory of anticipated utility', *Journal of Economic Behavior and Organization*, vol. 3, no. 4, December 1982.

Quiggin, J., 'Underwriting agricultural commodity prices', *Australian Journal of Agricultural Economics*, vol. 27, no. 3, December 1983.

Quiggin, J. and Anderson, J. R., 'Price bands and buffer funds', *Economic Record*, vol. 57, no. 156, March 1979.

Quizon, J. B., Binswanger, H. P. and Machina, M. J., 'Attitudes towards risk: further remarks', *Economic Journal*, vol. 94, no. 1, March 1984.

Schoemaker, P. J. H., 'The expected utility model: its variants, purposes, evidence and limitations', *Journal of Economic Literature*, vol. 20, no. 3, September 1982.

Spetzler, C. S. and Stael von Holstein, C-A. S., 'Probability encoding in decision analysis', *Management Science*, vol. 22, no. 3, March 1975.

JOHN KERR AND K. KALIRAJAN

Measuring Production Risk Using a Modified RCRM Model

INTRODUCTION

Fluctuations in agricultural output are considered to be associated primarily with the following three factors:

1 decision input variables which are under the control of the producer;
2 stochastic input variables which are not under the control of the producer and have unknown values at the time of decision; and
3 context input variables which are also not under the control of the producer but have known values at the time of decision (Anderson, Dillon and Hardaker 1976).

In production risk analyses the question often asked is what is the effect of the stochastic variables on production for given specified levels of decision and context input variables? This means that individuals differ greatly in their behaviour and the diversity of individual decision units implies parameter variation across units. In such cases the model of fixed coefficients may not be predicting the outcome with significant degree of accuracy.

The random coefficient regression model (RCRM) popularised by Swamy (1970) allows for some heterogeneity in the existing functional relationships among the cross-section units. A slight modification to RCRM facilitates examining production risk analysis more meaningfully using panel data. Recently, Young and Mount (1979) used one such variant of a RCRM with apparent success. However it has several restrictive assumptions. The objective of this paper is to consider a variant of a RCRM to examine production risk in a Southern Indian district without imposing these restrictive assumptions.

THE MODEL

A production risk model which takes into account fixed location effects and stochastic temporal effects may be written as follows.

$$Y_t = X_t a + Z_t b_t + u_t \quad t = 1 \dots T \quad (1)$$

where Y_t = dependent random variable

X_t = matrix of independent variables
Z_t = matrix of regressors
a   = vector of fixed location parameters
b_t = vector of stochastic temporal effects.
u_t = vector of random disturbances

$E(b_t) = b \quad Var (b_t) = \Delta \quad u_t \sim N(0, \sigma^2_t)$
$Cov(b_t, b_s) = 0 \quad Cov(b_t, u_s) = 0 \quad V\ t,s.$

This model corresponds closely to the model evaluated by Just and Pope (1978) as having the best properties in relation to reasonable risk criteria. When the X matrix is equal to zero, then equation (1) corresponds to Swamy's specification of the RCRM, and to Young and Mount's model.[1] This study deviates from these earlier models and assumes that $X \neq 0$.

Estimation
   Let $b_t = b + e_t$ where e_t is a vector of random effects with zero mean and variance Δ, and $E(b_t) = b$.
Hence, in equation (1), we have

$$E(Y_t) \quad = X_t a + Z_t b$$
$$\qquad\qquad\qquad\qquad\qquad t = 1 ...T$$
$$Var (Y_t) = Z_t \overset{*}{\Delta} Z'_t + \sigma^2_t I_n = \Sigma_t$$

The system of equations given by (1) can be written conveniently as

$$
\begin{bmatrix} Y_1 \\ Y_2 \\ \cdot \\ \cdot \\ \cdot \\ Y_T \end{bmatrix}
=
\begin{bmatrix} X_1 : Z_1 \\ X_2 : Z_2 \\ \cdot \\ \cdot \\ \cdot \\ X_T : Z_T \end{bmatrix}
\begin{bmatrix} a \\ ... \\ b \end{bmatrix}
+
\begin{bmatrix} Z_1 & 0 & ..... & 0 \\ 0 & Z_2 & ..... & 0 \\ & & \cdot & \\ & & \cdot & \\ & & \cdot & \\ 0 & 0 & ..... & Z_T \end{bmatrix}
\begin{bmatrix} e_1 \\ e_2 \\ \cdot \\ \cdot \\ \cdot \\ e_T \end{bmatrix}
+
\begin{bmatrix} u_1 \\ u_2 \\ \cdot \\ \cdot \\ \cdot \\ u_T \end{bmatrix}
\qquad (2)
$$

or

$$Y = w\theta + \varepsilon \qquad\qquad\qquad\qquad\qquad (3)$$

Swamy (1973) has suggested a number of alternative estimators for RCRM with parametric constraints. In this study, we consider the generalised least squares (GLS) estimator of θ which is given by

$$\hat{\theta} = (w'v^{-1}w)^{-1} \quad w'v^{-1}y \qquad\qquad\qquad (4)$$

where $v = diag (\Sigma_t)$

i.e.,

$$
\begin{bmatrix} \hat{a} \\ \hat{b} \end{bmatrix} = \begin{bmatrix} \Sigma X_t' (Z_t \Delta Z_t' + \hat{\sigma}2_t I)^{-1} X_t & \Sigma X_t'(Z_t \Delta Z_t' + \sigma^2_t I)^{-1} Z_t \\ \Sigma Z_t' (Z_t \Delta Z_t' + \hat{\sigma}2_t I)^{-1} X_t & \Sigma Z_t'(Z_t \Delta Z_t' + \sigma^2_t I)^{-1} Z_t \end{bmatrix}^{-1}
$$

$$
X \begin{bmatrix} \Sigma X_t' (Z_t \Delta Z_t' + \hat{\sigma}2_t I)^{-1} Y \\ \Sigma Z_t' (Z_t \Delta Z_t' + \hat{\sigma}2_t I) Y \end{bmatrix} \tag{5}
$$

In practice, Δ and $\hat{\sigma}2_t$ ($t = 1, 2, \ldots T$) are usually unknown, and one would normally substitute,

$$
\hat{\sigma}2_t = [(Y_t - w_t \hat{\theta}_t)' (Y_t - w_t \hat{\theta}_t)]/(n - p - q) \tag{6}
$$

where $\hat{\theta}_t = (w_t'w_t)^{-1} w_t'Y_t$ is the ordinary least squares (OLS) estimator from regressing Y_t on w_t which is equal to $(X_t : Z_t)$.

Let $(w_t' w_t)^{-1} = \begin{bmatrix} w^{11} & w^{12} \\ w^{21} & w^{22} \end{bmatrix}$,

then an unbiased estimator of Δ is given by

$$
\hat{\Delta} = \frac{1}{T-1} \left[\Sigma_t (\hat{\theta}_t - \bar{\theta})(\hat{\theta}_t - \bar{\theta})' \right] - \frac{1}{T} \Sigma \hat{\sigma} 2_t w^{22} \tag{7}
$$

where $\bar{\theta} = \dfrac{1}{T} \Sigma \hat{\theta}_t$.

It may be noted from equation (7) that the estimator $\hat{\Delta}$ is composed of two factors. The first factor on RHS is the observed variance covariance matrix of the computed $\hat{\theta}$ and the second is the average computed sampling variance of $\hat{\theta}$. Thus the advantage of working with the model is that the effects of sampling errors are removed from the observed variability of the estimated slope coefficients so as to obtain the true variability which alone influences the decisions made by producers. Equation (7) further reveals that there is nothing to ensure that $\hat{\Delta}$ will be either positive definite or positive semi definite; and unless at least $\hat{\Delta}$ is positive semi definite the slope coefficients cannot be estimated. A number of methods have been suggested to ensure that $\hat{\Delta}$ is positive definite (Schmalensee 1972; Lee and Griffiths 1979). The property that the characteristics roots of non-negative definite matrices are equal to or greater than zero has been used in this study (Schmalansee 1972).

Data
The data were collected during an extensive 4 years study in a rainfed rice culture in the Southern Indian District of Ramnad (Tamil Nadu State), covering the period 1978 to 1981. Data collection was based on a system

of daily record keeping of production activities of 30 farmers, all residing in the same village.

Empirical analysis and discussions

From the viewpoint of production theory, the transcendental production function was selected which incorporates all the three stages of production.[2] Following our analysis of the model in the paper, it is assumed that labour (L) has only fixed effects on the output and does not have any stochastic effect.[3] Fertilizer (F), chemicals (Ch) which include pesticides and weedicides and land areas operated (A) are assumed to have stochastic effects on output. The intercept term is also assumed to have random effects on rice production. Thus in the fixed effect set, there is 1 element and in the random or stochastic effect set there are 4 elements.

$$\ln Y = b_0 + C_0 + a_1 \ln L + (b_1 + c_1)\ln F + (b_2 + c_2)\ln Ch$$
$$+ (b_3 + c_3)\ln A + a_2 L + (b_4 + c_4)F + (b_5 + c_5)Ch \qquad (8)$$
$$+ (b_6 + c_6)A + u$$

where Y means rice production measured in tons per farm, and u is a random disturbance term with $N(0, \sigma^2)$.

TABLE 1 *Yearwise estimates of transcendental production risk functions*

Variables		Years			
(parameters)		1978	1979	1980	1981
constant	(b_0)	4.5943	3.8762	4.6301	4.4832
labour	(a_1)	0.2159	0.2089	0.2102	0.2126
	(a_2)	−0.0001	−0.0001	−0.0001	−0.0001
fertilizer	(b_1)	0.2726	0.1986	0.2523	0.2183
	(b_4)	−0.0002	−0.0003	−0.0002*	−0.0003
chemicals	(b_2)	0.1683	0.1248	0.1589	0.1496
	(b_5)	−0.0003*	−0.0002	−0.0003*	−0.0002
area	(b_3)	0.6157	0.6783	0.5892	0.6201
	(b_6)	−0.0421	−0.0536*	−0.0329	−0.0493*
$\bar{R}^2$		0.64	0.59	0.68	0.65

Note: All coefficients are statistically significant at the 5% level except where marked with an asterisk.

Table 1 presents the OLS estimates of the individual year regressions without assuming any stochastic effects for inputs and the intercept. The production parameters associated with fertilizer, which is basically nitrogen, and land area operated vary substantially across years.

At the outset, the null hypothesis that the response relationships are similar in each year was tested. This means examining whether the random effects associated with input variables are zero. This is equivalent to testing the following hypothesis:

$$H_0: \theta_t = \hat{\theta} \qquad t = 1978, 79, 80 \text{ and } 81.$$

If the hypothesis holds, then $\hat{\theta}_t$'s are independent estimators of the same parametric vector. Then it may be assumed that $(\theta_t - \hat{\theta})$ follows a normal distribution with zero mean and variance–covariance matrix $(w_t'w_t)^{-1}\sigma^2_w$.

The observed variance–covariance matrix of the estimated θ_t's which represents the first term of RHS of equation (7) is first calculated. This matrix is a combination of both the true variability and the sampling variability. The average sampling variability across the periods which is the second term on RHS of equation (7), is calculated and then is subtracted from the earlier calculated matrices to obtain the unbiased estimator of the true variability of the coefficients which are given in Table 2. Inspection of Table 2 reveals that one diagonal element is negative. It is then adjusted by substituting the negative characteristic roots to zero as explained earlier.

TABLE 2 *Estimates of true variability of the production risk coefficients*

	const	ln L	L	ln F	F	ln Ch	Ch	ln A	A
const	269								
ln L	9.4	196							
L	25	12.3	18						
ln F	7.3	1.9	3.4	25					
F	42	3.0	7.2	2.7	−36.6				
ln Ch	8.9	0.5	0.9	1.1	1.1	3.0			
Ch	17	0.5	1.2	2.9	1.6	1.2	0.3		
ln A	2.1	0.8	3.6	6.8	7.1	9.5	2.4	120	
A	82	1.1	0.5	1.6	2.7	2.2	2.3	1.4	53

Using these estimates of the true variability of the coefficients, the mean coefficient vector of the GLS estimates with random parameters are calculated (Table 3). In general, the GLS estimates appear to be somewhat higher than the corresponding OLS estimates. The higher GLS estimates for the linear fertilizer term (F) implies a steeper response surface. This indicates that the year to year variability in production response is an important factor in fertilizer response analysis and suggests that this heterogeneity should be taken into account while estimating the response function to avoid erroneous predictions.

TABLE 3 *GLS estimates of the mean slope coefficients of the production risk equation*

Variables (parameters)		Units of Measurements	GLS Estimates
constant			5.1286 (6.92)
labour	(a_1)	man days	0.2193 (3.23)
	(a_2)		−0.0001 (2.92)
fertilizer	(b_1)	kg	0.2812 (3.43)
	(b_4)		−0.0002 (3.10)
chemicals	(b_2)	kg	0.1501 (3.75)
	(b_5)		−0.0002 (2.56)
area	(b_3)	acre	0.6210 (4.12)
	(b_6)		−0.0475 (3.00)

Note: Figures in parentheses are the absolute t values.

CONCLUSION

The foregoing analysis demonstrates that it is rational to use a model involving both fixed and random effects to analyse production risks more meaningfully. As an exercise, the fertilizer response variability was derived valuing other inputs at their mean levels. The empirical results show that output variability increases exponentially, and it increases rapidly even at low levels of fertilizer application. This means that interactions between fertilizer and stochastic factors should not be neglected in production risk analyses.

NOTES

[1] In Young and Mount's model, $Y_t = Z_t b_t + u_t$ where b_t is stochastic effect with $E(b_t) = a$.
[2] Though the theory also insists that the economic optimum decisions lie only in the second stage of production function, this is true only under perfect competition. The assumption of transcendental function thus does not impose the assumption of perfect competition in both input and output markets.
[3] This assumption is statistically tested at a later stage.

REFERENCES

Anderson, J. R., Dillon, J. L. and Hardaker, B., *Agricultural Decision Analysis*, Iowa State University Press, Ames, Iowa, 1976.

Just, R. E. and Pope, R. D., 'Stochastic Specification of Production Functions and Economic Implications', *Journal of Econometrics*, vol. 7, 1978, pp. 67–86.

Lee, L. and Griffiths, W. E., 'The Prior Likelihood and Best Linear Unbiased Prediction in Stochastic Coefficient Linear Models', University of New England Working Papers in Econometrics and Applied Statistics no. 1, Armidale, Australia, 1979.

Schmalensee, R., 'Variance Estimation in a Random Coefficient Regression Model', Department of Economics, University of California, San Diego, (mimeo), 1972.

Swamy, P. A. V. B., 'Efficient Inference in a Random Coefficient Regression Model', *Econometrica*, vol. 38, 1970, pp. 311–23.

Swamy, P. A. V. B., 'Criteria, Constraints and Multicollinearity in Random Coefficient Regression Models', *Annals of Economic and Social Measurement*, vol. 2, no. 4, 1973, pp. 429–50.

Young, R. and Mount, T. D., 'An Econometric Analysis of Uncertainty in Rice Production', Department of Agricultural Economics, Cornell University, (mimeo), 1979.

W. L. NIEWUWOUDT AND J. B. BULLOCK

The Demand for Crop Insurance

INTRODUCTION

It is universally common that farmers receive some state support during natural disasters such as severe drought or floods. Disaster assistance is costly and it may encourage production in high risk areas if payments are made frequently. In the USA, disaster assistance was phased out in 1982 and the official view is that farmers must insure their crops (US Congress). Hail insurance is provided adequately by the private sector in many countries as the occurrence of hail is more random than droughts. Crop insurance, however, only enjoys sufficient acceptance by farmers in countries where it is highly subsidised such as in Canada or where it is compulsory as in Sweden. In the USA, only 16 per cent of potential cropland is insured in spite of a 25 per cent subsidy on premiums. In South Africa, crippling droughts during the past years (1983, 1984) again focused attention on crop insurance, while the Australian Bureau of Agricultural Economics is at present considering providing incentives to farmers to insure their crops. International interest is shown in crop insurance by the conference on agricultural risk, insurance and credit held in San José, Costa Rica, in February 1982 (Binswanger, Hogan Gardner and Kramer).

The demand for crop insurance, even at a subsidized level, appears low. The purpose of this paper is to measure empirically factors explaining farmer participation in a crop insurance programme with a view to assist policy-makers. Welfare redistributional impacts of insurance as simulated within a simultaneous equations model, are also presented.

THEORY

Crop insurance is a contingent contract, an agreement in which a farmer pays a price, the premium, after which his crop output determines a payout or indemnity. The contingency is that only certain (low) yields result in indemnities, and yield is a random variable whose value is unknown when the insurance contract is purchased. Due to lack of information the insurer cannot separate farmers into risk classes leading to adverse selection. The lower risk within each group will always opt out, raising the loss ratio (Binswanger 1982) and there may be no equilibrium in the insurance market (Rothschild and Stiglitz 1975).

The demand for crop insurance depends on (a) the farmer's utility function of income, (b) his current income, (c) his subjective frequency distribution of future income, (d) the change in the frequency distribution of future income generated by the contract and (e) the premium of the contract. Regarding (a), Friedman and Savage show that if marginal utility of income decreases as income increases then the maximum insurance premium an individual will pay depends on the extent that $U(\bar{I}) > \bar{u}$ where $\bar{I}$ = expected income and $\bar{u}$ = expected utility. Regarding (b), Arrow suggests that the cost an individual attaches to risk is a declining function of profit (wealth) i.e. decreasing absolute risk aversion. Items (c) and (d) determine the returns from insurance and (e) its cost.

Previous empirical research on the demand for crop insurance is limited. Gardner and Kramer, because they could not find empirical research on the demand for crop insurance, undertook a 'pilot' study of a cross-section of 57 counties (1982).

ANALYTICAL PROCEDURE

In the subsequent empirical estimates of the demand for crop insurance, percentage potential acreage insured for a specific crop in a given year was taken as the dependent variable while the price of insurance was derived from premiums paid and indemnities received. Other variables included are risk, crop diversification, farm size, part ownership, etc.

The demand for crop insurance was estimated from state data on insurance participation in major crops for the years 1960–81. More than 700 cross-section time series observations on participation rates are utilised. While probability distributions of yield vary significantly amongst farms, producers in an area essentially face the same price distribution. Thus, an aggregate demand function should provide a good estimate of the price parameter. A preliminary analysis indicated that substantial variation in regional data existed, for instance, during 1981, the percentage of wheat acreage insured varied from 4 per cent in Illinois to 48 per cent in Montana. Data on indemnities, premiums, liability and acreage insured were obtained from the Federal Crop Insurance Office in Kansas City, Missouri.

The insurance 'price' variable was specified in returns form. Two alternative price variables were used, namely the indemnity/premium ratio lagged one year and a variable slightly modified from the one suggested by Gardner and Kramer. The latter variable expresses the rate of return for year t as follows:

$$\left\{ \frac{\text{Indemnity/liability as moving average of recent period}}{\text{Premium/liability ratio for year t}} - 1.0 \right\} * 100 \qquad (1)$$

The denominator expresses the premium as a ratio of liability which is analogous to expressing the cost of a lottery ticket as a percentage of the maximum price (Gardner and Kramer 1982).

At the time when the farmer enters the insurance contract the premium rate and liability coverage (denominator) are known. Future indemnities are unknown. Thus the numerator reflects farmers' expectations of the proportional 'payout' of the contract.

The risk expectation variable, based on immediate past experiences of the farmer, was derived from yield per acre data as suggested by Ryan.

EMPIRICAL RESULTS

Findings presented in Table 1 indicate that both return variables (X_1 and X_2) were highly significant and positive implying that participation in crop insurance does respond to economic forces. The return variable X_1 was derived from Gardner and Kramer's specification (refer equation 1 text) while X_2 is a ratio of actual indemnity payments/premium payments, lagged one year.

Positive and highly significant coefficients for the risk variable (X_3) are in accordance with expectations because if producers are risk averse,

TABLE 1 *Demand functions for crop insurance. Dependent variable: percentage of acreage insured (t ratios)*

Independent Variable (Y)	(1)	(2)	(3)	(4)	(5)
Expected rate of return (Gardner) = X_1			0.0139 (3.9)	0.0194 (5.3)	0.0114 (8.1)
Indemnity/Premium for year t$-$1 = X_2	0.951 (12.0)	0.798 (9.16)			
Expected risk = X_3	3.161 (3.7)	5.723 (4.5)	4.864 (4.2)	4.217 (3.8)	2.23 (5.1)
Diversification (Entropy index) = X_4				-10.30 (-7.6)	
Diversification (Herfindahl index) = X_5			22.11 (7.1)		
Crop dominance = X_6			9.740 (9.1)	9.973 (9.5)	
Part owners = X_7			0.237 (8.5)	0.283 (10.4)	0.023 (2.5)
Farm Size = X_8				-0.0355 (-5.8)	
Disaster payment dummy 1974–1981 = 1 X_9			-1.047 (-2.1)		
Lag Y = X_{10}	1.032 (91.1)	1.031 (91.3)			0.998 (70.1)
Constant = X_{11}	-0.972 (-5.9)	-0771 (-6.1)	-17.60 (-16.6)	13.18 (4.2)	-0.84 (-2.0)
R^2	0.92	0.92	0.51	0.53	0.92
df	740	740	692	684	694

658   *W. L. Niewuwoudt and J. B. Bullock*

more insurance will be purchased the greater the risk experienced. The variance of returns from a portfolio of crops and insurance is reduced by the purchase of insurance. In model 1 (Table 1) risk (X_3) was measured as reflected in both shortfalls and increases in production while in models 2 to 5, only production shortfalls are considered.

The diversification indexes (X_4 and X_5) were highly significant with expected signs implying that producers insure more in specialised cropping areas. The entropy index of diversification (X_4) approaches zero when a farm is completely specialised while the Herfindahl index (X_5) approaches unity when a farm is specialised. The sign of the entropy index should thus be negative and that of the Herfindahl index positive as in Table 1. Crop specialisation is a dimension of risk as shown in portfolio theory and it is expected that in areas where farmers tend to specialize, for instance where a single crop has a clear comparative advantage, producers would insure more. This may explain why in intensive wheat areas included in the model such as Montana and North Dakota percentage acreage insurance in recent years reached between 40 and 50 per cent. As a contrast only 4 per cent of wheat acreage was insured in Illinois and Indiana during 1981.

The 'percentage of part owners variable' (X_7) was positive and significant. This may be due to a higher leverage position of part owners compared to full owners with creditors requiring crop insurance as a security on loans. Hogan showed that an increase in debt/equity ratio will increase the overall riskiness of the income stream if assets are held constant.

The negative sign on X_9 indicates that an increase in farm size was associated with a decline in percentage acreage insurance and that the risk premium declines as farm size increases. If large farmers are wealthier and can more readily secure loans they may have less incentive to insure their crops. The small farmer who does not own land may insure as a substitute for collateral due to the non-price rationing of credit (Binswanger 1982).

The R^2 in models could have been increased substantially by inclusion of regional dummies. Regional dummies account for regional differences captured by variables studied and were consequently not included.

Variable X_9 estimates that the Disaster Payment Program (DPP) of 1974–81 had a negative influence on participation in crop insurance. The DPP covering feedgrain, wheat and cotton paid indemnities but charged no premiums.

EVALUATION

Actual data for 1982 on insurance participation were not incorporated into the model but will be used to test the predictive performance of model parameters. Rather than comparing model predictions with actual data, turning points (+ or −) in percentage acreage participation (Y) for 1982 compared to 1981 are studied which is a rigorous test. A comparison is made for each crop in each state studied.

Correct turning points in percentage acreage insured were correctly predicted in 32 out of 36 cases if returns variable X_2 and risk variable X_3 are used while 29 correct predictions were obtained if returns variable X_1 instead of X_2 is used. Risk and return variables were equally successful in predicting increases as well as decreases in percentage acreage insured; for instance 11 out of 13 changes were correctly predicted when insurance increased, while 21 out of 26 were correctly predicted when it declined. The exceptionally good results are attributed to economic rationality on the part of producers and strong annual signals emitted by the returns and risk variables. Insurance experts confirm this finding, that after a crop failure, such as 1980, acreage insured increases.

DISASTER PAYMENTS AND SUBSIDY ON PREMIUMS

Model 3 (Table 1) estimates that had the Disaster Payment Program (DPP) not existed, participation in crop insurance would have been 19.5 per cent more. This percentage appears small, given the magnitude of the DPP, but it agrees with Gardner and Kramer's observation that the DPP apparently did not discourage participation in crop insurance as much as expected.

Using the returns specification of Gardner and Kramer (Table 1) it is estimated that a 1 per cent subsidy on the premium rate would be expected to increase acreage insured by 0.429 per cent. This suggests that the percentage acreage insured is not very responsive to changes in the premium rate. The low 'price elasticity' indicates that some farmers will still insure at higher premium rates in situations of high risk arising from crop specialisation, yield related risks etc.

The question arises, what would be the impact on acreage insured if farmers pay the full cost of crop insurance? The farmer contribution to the total cost of crop insurance is estimated as 54.2 per cent. In this calculation, administration cost, the extent to which indemnities exceeded premiums in the past and the 25 per cent subsidy on premiums were considered. If the previously determined price elasticity of −0.429 is used, it is estimated that percentage acreage insurance will decline from the present 16 per cent (1983) level to 10.2 per cent if farmers pay the full cost of insurance.

While it is comforting that an estimated 10 to 11 per cent of farmers will insure even if they pay the full cost, one would have liked to see the subsidy having a greater expansionary effect on acreage insurance. It points out that a fairly large subsidy may be required to achieve the participation in crop insurance that the Federal Crop Insurance Corporation is aiming at and that the appropriate attention should rather be given to problem areas such as moral hazards or adverse selection.

WELFARE REDISTRIBUTIONAL EFFECT OF RISK REDUCTION

In a separate study the welfare effects of risk reduction were simulated by incorporating a risk specification in the corn and soybean supply functions of the simultaneous equation modelling system of the University of Missouri, Columbia. Since a variance-covariance risk specification was used, interrelationships between corn and soybean markets are recognised within the demand and supply system as well as in the risk specification. Variances and covariances were derived using Ryan's procedure. The risk averse coefficient was significant when included in supply functions of both soybeans and corn. Risk and no risk solutions were simulated by changing the variable cost of corn and soybeans in supply functions of the modelling system by a constant proportion. This adjustment in variable cost was derived from the risk aversion factors estimated. It was simulated that 'removal' of risk would lead to an expansion of corn and soybean acreage respectively of 0.453 million acres and 0.159 million acres. The social cost of risk as a percentage of the value of the crop was estimated for corn and soybeans respectively as 0.36 and 0.35 per cent.

In the case of the corn market a substantial welfare redistributional effect between consumers and producers was estimated. The gain in consumer surplus as a result of lower corn prices is estimated at $464 million while producer loss is $392 million. The redistribution in welfare is expected because the demand for corn, as incorporated in the modelling system was inelastic. For instance, elasticities of corn demand components included were; feed (-0.311), commercial export (-0.441) and food (-0.275). Welfare redistribution is estimated to be relatively smaller for soybean producers and consumers because the demand for soybeans, as incorporated in the model, is elastic. The gain in consumer surplus for soybeans is $54 million and the loss in producer surplus $11 million. A loss in producer surplus was simulated for soybeans, in spite of the elastic demand, because the demand for soybeans shifted backwards as a result of a decline in corn prices.

For this analysis risk removal had a greater impact on corn acreage planted than on soybeans. This agrees with expectations of extension specialists, since corn is considered as more 'risky' than soybeans. A subsidy on crop insurance could provide an incentive to expansion of more risky products and to expansion of production in 'riskier' areas.

CONCLUSIONS

Several countries are presently looking at crop insurances as a programme for protecting farmers against yield and income losses. The demand for crop insurance, however, appears low even at a subsidized level.

The following factors were significant in explaining the demand for crop insurance; expected rate of return in insurance, expected risk, crop specialisation, part ownership, disaster payments and farm size. The risk and returns variables were found to be excellent short-run predictors of turning points in acreage insured, as in 32 out of 36 state/crop comparisons the change (positive or negative) in percentage acreage insured between 1981 and 1982 was correctly predicted by these variables. A better understanding of these economic forces may aid programme administrators in understanding why certain areas will always have lower participation rates and why participation in some years may decline.

The welfare distributional impact of risk reduction was simulated in a separate study by including a risk variable in the corn and soybean supply functions of the University of Missouri, Columbia simultaneous equation modelling system. The social cost of risk was estimated as 0.36 and 0.35 per cent of the corn and soybean crops. Risk reduction was estimated to lead to a loss in producer surplus but gain in consumer surplus. Simulations indicate a loss in producer surplus for soybean producers, in spite of an elastic demand. The reason being that demand for soybeans shifted backward as a result of decline in corn prices.

REFERENCES

Arrow, K. J., *Essays in the Theory of Risk Bearing*, Markham Publishing Co., 1971.
Binswanger, H. P., 'Risk Aversion, Rural Financial Markets and the Demand for Crop Insurance', Paper presented at Conference on Agricultural Risk, Insurance and Credit, San José, Costa Rica, 8–10 February 1982.
Friedman, M., and Savage, L. J., 'The Utility Analysis of Choices Involving Risk', *Journal of Political Economy*, vol. 56, 1948, pp. 279–304.
Gardner, B., and Kramer, R. A., 'The U.S. Experience in Crop Insurance Programs', Paper presented at Conference on Agricultural Risks, Insurance and Credit, San José, Costa Rica, 8–10 February 1982.
Hogan, A. J., 'The Role of Crop Credit Insurance', Ph.D. thesis, University of Wisconsin, 1982.
Rothschild, M., and Stiglitz, J., 'Equilibrium in Competitive Insurance Markets: An Essay on the Economics of Imperfect Information', *Quarterly Journal of Economics*, vol. 15, 1975, pp. 629–50.
Ryan, T. J., 'Supply Response to Risk: The Case of U.S. Pinto Beans', *Western Journal of Agricultural Economics*, vol. 2, 1977, pp. 35–43.
US Congress, *Review of Federal Crop Insurance Program*, Hearings before the Subcommittee on Conservation, Credit and Rural Development of the Committee on Agriculture, 98th Congress, 1st Session, 20 April 1983.

DISCUSSION OPENING I – R. J. HILDRETH

This session deals with risk aspects of decision-making. Such a focus is appropriate as risks are pervasive in farming and the intellectual concepts and methods of dealing with risk are complex, confusing and difficult. To the degree that agricultural economics can make use of theory and add to the development of theory of decision-making with risk, farmers, policy-makers and consumers will benefit.

662   *W. L. Niewuwoudt and J. B. Bullock*

The Anderson, Dillon and Hardaker paper sketches, criticises, reviews ongoing developments and supports the use of the paradigm of subjective expected utility. The approaches of the other two papers are not in conflict with subjective expected utility but do not use the approach directly. One reports research measuring production risks and the other measures empirical factors explaining farmer participation in a crop insurance programme. My assigned function is to place before the conference some issues and questions that could be discussed. I now proceed to state some issues and questions which you may wish to explore further.

At a July 1985 conference on ethics and economics in the United States, serious questions were raised about the logical fundamentals of utility identification and measurement. If it is not possible usefully to measure or identify utility, much less subjective expected utility, then the usefulness of models which optimise utility for explanation, prediction, or prescription is in doubt.

The Anderson, Dillon and Hardaker paper points out difficulties with the subjective expected utility model. Clearly models and paradigms which do not incorporate risk are not very useful. But are there alternatives to the subjective expected utility model in dealing with risk? Schoemaker lists nine variants of expected utility models in his 1982 *Journal of Economic Literature* article. If we were to apply a subjective utility analysis to an issue involving risk for economists, using subjective utility analysis, would we focus on subjective utility analysis, other expected utility models, or explore other paradigms such as mean-variance models?

The valuable papers on measuring production risk and the demand for crop insurance do not add greatly to a better understanding of the subjective utility analysis paradigm. Should research in this area focus on the development of the theory as an end in itself, or deal with questions of use to individual farmers or policy-makers as the measuring production risk and the demand for crop insurance papers do? In other words, will we move ahead further by dealing with problems perceived as important by the users of our efforts, or problems perceived to be important by the profession of agricultural economics itself? Perhaps the situation to be desired is to deal with questions and problems perceived to be important by the users of our work and at the same time add to the theoretical development.

A less significant issue, but one that causes confusion, is the use of the words 'normative' and 'positive'. It seems to me to be more useful to use the word 'prescriptive' rather than 'normative' and to use the word 'predictive' rather than 'positive'. An alternative is to use prescriptive and normative together and predictive and positive together. Misunderstanding of the use and meanings of words may impede progress in understanding.

The elegant paper on measuring production risk reports that by holding other inputs at their mean level and varying the level of fertilizer input, output variability increases exponentially for a village in India. Hazel reports increased variability in world cereal production and suggests that increased use of improved seed fertilizer-intensive technologies may have been an important factor. He suggests that price effects rather than higher sensitivity of new technologies to environment stress may be the cause of variability at the world level. But the evidence reported in the Kerr–Kalirajan paper is strong, for a much smaller area. Are these situations for farms where increased fertilizer use will reduce yield variability, say by increasing moisture efficiency? More analysis in measuring production risk would be valuable.

The application of risk models to macroeconomic phenomena, such as international trade or agricultural policy, is relatively new. This issue is mentioned or implied in all three papers. It would appear that we will require improvement in our ability to measure values (welfare) in an interpersonally valid way in order to make progress. Can the understanding in the macroeconomic area be increased at the same time as understanding is increased in the micro area? Or does the micro understanding have to come first before progress can be made in the macro area? Where should the relative emphasis be placed?

Many challenges and opportunities exist for economists in the area of risk analysis. The papers presented here are suggestive for further work.

REFERENCES

Hazel, Peter, B. R., 'Sources of Increased Variability in World Central Production since the 1960s', *Journal of Agricultural Economics*, vol. 36, no. 2, May 1985.
Schoemaker, P. J. H., 'The Expected Utility Model: Its Variants, Purposes, Evidence and Limitations', *Journal of Economic Literature*, vol. 20, no. 2, September 1982.

DISCUSSION OPENING II – JEAN-MARC BOUSSARD

We have just heard three very interesting and stimulating papers, although the scope of each is quite different.

I shall begin with the Kerr and Kalirajan paper, on which my own contribution will be poor, because, in fact, I am not very qualified to discuss a sharp econometric matter. I shall make only three points:
1 In some cases, this paper uses a restricted vocabulary, which makes its understanding for the non-initiated difficult (e.g. the three stages of the production function).
2 This is a pity, because this contribution is important, on an important subject. Another paper in this conference tackled the same subject, with apparently quite different conclusions (the paper by Antle, on *Technology and Uncertainty: evidence from Egypt*). It would be very useful to compare both in detail.
3 Why are these estimates measured in absolute rather than in relative values (i.e., 'per ha')? It would have made the estimation easier, without loss of generality.

The paper by Nieuwuwoudt and Bullock is also a pioneering one. Few studies have been undertaken to elicit the determinants of crop insurance. This one is therefore specially welcomed, the more so as it is two papers in one, with the measurement of crop insurance elasticity on the one hand, and the effects of risk reduction on the other.

On this second point, the paper is perhaps rather too short. The question of the welfare effects of output variability is intricate. For instance, the conclusions may differ widely if the risk is additive:

$$\text{i.e.:} \quad y = \bar{y} + \varepsilon, \quad E(\varepsilon) = 0, \quad E(\varepsilon^2) = \sigma^2$$

or multiplicative:

$$y = \varepsilon\bar{y}, \quad E(\varepsilon) = 1, \quad E[(\varepsilon - 1)^2] = \sigma^2.$$

Since nobody knows which of these alternative models holds, one should be careful with firm conclusions in this field.

On the crop insurance market, on the contrary, the paper is new and informative. It is interesting to know that the price demand elasticity of crop insurance is small: this makes highly questionable the policy of subsidizing it, a classical example of an inefficient 'structural' measure. I would have appreciated also a comment on the difference in the values of the R^2 between models 4 and 5, and the others. This is a consequence of the omission of the lagged variable, but why?

Nevertheless, I am not in full agreement with the authors when they say that the ability of their model to react to changes in the rate of return on insurance is a good mark. In fact, when the return on insurance is high, it is because of a large number of crop failures which induces many farmers to revise their expectations when they should not. Thus, this factor means essentially that expectations are not free of contingent considerations. This is an illustration of the irrationality of the decision to subsidize an insurance contract, as shown by various authors, including Kunreuther. And this leads me to the discussion of the paper by Anderson et al.

This is, of course, a superb piece of literature, devoted to what could be called the classical theory of farmers and risk. In particular, they give a useful bibliography which will occupy my thoughts and my leisure time this winter. But I am a heretic, and I do not think this theory is really useful.

From a normative point of view, its usefulness is a matter of faith, we all agree, and the faith is far from being widely spread. Therefore, the real potential of the theory is descriptive. It gives a better understanding of farmers' behaviour, in their choices of techniques and, of course, this is essential.

Nevertheless, it seems to me that two major problems are ignored by this theory:

1 *The expectation problem.* Expectations are often inconsistent, and, in any case, seldom expressed in terms of probability. This is the sense of my previous remark. It is therefore important to set up a theory of

expectations pertaining to random events. This is a challenging task, that Marc Ne Love could perhaps undertake.

2 *The risk aversion coefficient problem*. Of course, the pure theory of expected utility does not *require* that the risk aversion coefficient be constant, and a permanent characteristic of each farmer. But all practical applications admit it. Now, it is simply wrong to say that 'within a reasonable range of values for wealth', the risk aversion coefficient may be approximately constant, especially when wealth can be negative as well as positive. An immediate proof of what I say is that many people buy at the same time fire insurances and horse-race betting tickets: such behaviour would be perfectly inconsistent with a constant risk aversion coefficient.

Therefore, the main problem, when building a descriptive model of farmers' behaviour, is precisely to determine the relevant values of the risk aversion coefficient in each element of the set of feasible actions. The debt equity ratio, which varies considerably over this set, plays an important part here. Elsewhere I had occasion to explain how to incorporate the previous considerations in actual models, by expressing the consequences of risk through a set of constraints, rather than by choosing a different utility function. I suspect Jock Anderson will not agree with me, although I do not understand why. Thus, it is better to stop here, and let him explain.

GENERAL DISCUSSION – RAPPORTEUR: S. C. THOMPSON

The question was asked whether decision analysis, as described in the Anderson et al. paper, could be applied on small as well as on large farms. Another question on this paper concerned the period between a decision and its payoff – does a gap exist between *ex ante* and *ex post* risk parameters? It is assumed that probabilities of states of nature are independent of the size of rewards; but is this a fair assumption when we know that the high prizes in life are rarely won? Does the model link risk aversion with money flexibility of consumption income well enough to allow analysis of farmer welfare?

A participant in the discussion on the same paper noted that even in multi-attribute utility models of the type referred to, the final index of utility was unidimensional – is risk itself multidimensional? For example, is survival risk different from the risk of losing social prestige? Another speaker felt that it might be more profitable to study aggregate group behaviour under risk in order to draw policy implications, rather than developing more detailed theoretical models.

A question was asked about the best dependent variable to use in empirical studies of demand for crop insurance – does income level or wealth influence demand; can wealthier farmers bear more risk? It was suggested that crop dominance and diversification should be included in measures of risk associated with crop insurance. A further question asked how subjective mean and variance should be assessed in supply response analysis and how is it possible to distinguish between a quadratic price response and a linear response plus a quadratic variance term? Another question concerned the use of climatic variables and the importance of cyclical effects. It was also wondered if the crop insurance model could incorporate political and administrative changes over time.

Dr Anderson was then asked if he would accept that there were limitations to the concept of probability in forming expectations. Can the Subjective Expected Utility model be expressed in a dynamic rather than a static formulation?

Dr J. R. Anderson replied as follows:

I think there is something circular about Dr Hildreth's suggestion to use Utility Theory to select among competing utility models. Surely some external viewpoint would be needed. I. M. Boussard and I differ in our views on utility functions, which I view as concave rather than sigmoid. In response to Mr Agrawal I have stated in my paper that the model has application for both small and large farms. George Jones expressed a head-on confrontation with the very notion of subjective probability. Certainly if preferences are not independent, then the model will fall apart. He is right that estimating subjective probabilities for rare or calamitous events remains a most challenging task.

I agree with Burger that econometric models which use only mean and variance effects to represent risk can be very limited in their application – but does a better methodology yet exist? I agree also with Parton that our model does not do justice to combining different dimensions of risk in one analysis. In response to Michel Petit, the SEU model is not explicitly static and can be as dynamic as the imagination of the analyst. The use of probabilities is a great simplification of our risky environment, but what I do not see is why you cannot believe in them more readily! Lastly, I hope I have demonstrated my pragmatism to Alexander Sarris. I too am interested in robust results applicable over groups of farmers.

Dr Niewuwoudt replied:
J. M. Boussard asks whether risk is additive or not, and I agree we do not yet know. In response to his question on R-squared values, there are substantial regional differences and using a log term, like bringing in regional constant terms, will dramatically increase R-squared. In answer to Agrawal, we captured risk in the model from past yield data in each region. Kada asked what was the best dependent variable. We looked at past indemnity and premium values. I agree with him that the merit of crops insurance will change as income level changes. In answer to Burger's question, we did include crop dominance measures. Farmers tend to insure the crops from which they earn most income, regardless of whether it is dominant or not.

We dealt with Lumayag's question in our model by taking a

North-South slice in order to maximise diversity in our data. Sonka's observation on political influences on crop insurance is quite accurate. Different payments in different states actually create distortion rather than stability!

Participants in the discussion included R. C. Agrawal, G. T. Jones, R. Kada, K. Burger, K. Parton, M. Petit, S. Sonka, E. Lumayag and A. Sarris.

MICHAEL BOEHLJE AND J. LOWENBERG-DEBOER

Integration of Production and Financial Theory in Analysing Farm Firm Behaviour

INTRODUCTION

Important changes have occurred in the financial and economic environment facing agricultural producers world-wide. Increased price volatility for both inputs and products has resulted in significantly higher risk. Price changes on land and other inputs have created capital gains and losses that have sometimes overshadowed current income from production in agricultural decision-making. High interest rates on borrowed funds combined with the increased use of leverage or debt capital in many farm businesses have increased the financial vulnerability of a number of firms. Government policy in the form of subsidized credit, price supports or constraints for agricultural commodities, and tax treatment of farm investments in agricultural production have become a significant dimension of the environment in which farmers must make their production, marketing and financial decisions.

Given these significant changes in the production environment for agriculture, the theory of the firm, which is used as the conceptual base for most production economics studies of farm firms, must be re-examined. As traditionally developed in most microeconomic or farm management textbooks, this theory does not encompass some of the major dimensions of the farm firm's decision environment including financing strategies, capital gains and losses, liquidity problems, risk, and tax considerations. A more complete theory of the firm that integrates production theory and investment-financial theory is necessary to explain producer behaviour and the adjustment processes of the farm firm.

The purpose of this paper is to develop a broader theoretical framework of farm firm behaviour that encompasses production, financing, and investment-disinvestment decisions with explicit recognition of cash flow, liquidity, capital gains and losses, rate of return, and tax considerations. The discussion will proceed by first identifying the important characteristics of the farm firm decision environment. Then an explicit model of an integrated theory of the firm will be developed. Implications of this integrated theory of the firm for optimal input use, optimal product mix, optimal investment and disinvestment behaviour, optimal financing strategy, and optimal firm size will be discussed. Finally, policy considerations will be reviewed.

THE DECISION ENVIRONMENT

The modern decision environment for the farm firm includes some important new dimensions as well as a renewed awareness and focus on 'old' dimensions that have been previously recognised, but not adequately reflected in farmers' decisions in recent years. The old dimensions include the multiplicity of enterprises or products that can be produced and inputs that can be used in the production process. This basic and well recognised dimension of the decision environment is increasingly important for two reasons. First, the focus of much of the expansion of agriculture in the developed countries during the 1970s has been on specialised agriculture which required capital-intensive technology resulting in capital-labour substitution and reduced diversity. Higher capital charges and increased financial and business risk in agriculture attributable to more price volatility and higher leverage ratios suggests that the trends to more specialisation and capital-labour substitution should be re-evaluated. The conceptual framework must be sufficiently robust to evaluate the benefits in terms of efficiency compared to the cost in terms of higher risk and reduced flexibility or adaptability to a changing environment of specialization and technology that embodies a high capital-labour ratio.

A second dimension of the production response phenomena that must be tractable in any theoretical model and should be recognised in empirical work is the twofold response function for such production inputs as fertilizers, chemicals and growth stimulants of various forms. These 'non-traditional' inputs generate two important outputs, a 'good' in the form of increased yield of grain or livestock products, and a 'bad' in the form of a residual that may result in environmental degradation. Most farm management-production economics studies have not recognised these residuals or have treated the residual response function as an externality. With increased consciousness of the environmental degradation and social cost of such residues, these externalities must be internalised and response functions that explicitly recognise both products (the agricultural commodity as well as the environmentally degrading residual) must be included in the empirical analysis of optimal enterprises choice and input combinations.

A third important dimension of the modern decision environment is that returns can be obtained in the form of annual flows of income (losses) *and* in the form of capital gains (capital losses). The capital gains or losses have typically occurred in the form of price appreciation or declines on farm real estate, but such gains or losses could be associated with any asset. Various researchers have speculated about the impacts of capital gains on production decisions. Bhatia argued that in a world of perfect capital markets and equal taxes on all types of income, unrealised capital gains would be a perfect substitute for current income in wealth of the individual, and hence there is justification for including at least a part of the capital gain in the current income stream of an individual. Plaxico and Kletke (1979) formalised this wealth approach by recognising a fraction of capital gain as income, while deferring the remaining gain and the taxes on the gain to the end of the holding period.

Another approach to the value of unrealised gain is to argue that unrealised gain is a substitute for equity in the financial negotiation – unrealised gain increases the financial base for acquiring credit and reduces risk for borrower and lender. Thus, Lins and Duncan argue that because appreciated value of land holdings provides a base for additional purchases, capital gains have resulted in incentives for farm expansion. They also suggest that rising land prices encourage greater reliance on debt financing; in an attempt to reap the benefits of capital gains, farmers buy sooner and go further into debt than they would in a stable price environment. Davenport et al. (1982) suggests that the preferential tax treatment of capital gains has exacerbated the farm expansion trend by offering high income land owners tax shelter incentives for purchasing more land. Castle and Hock argue that farm land capital gains reduce incentives to adopt land saving practices and technologies and may help explain the increase in acreage per farm, the use of larger machinery and the relatively low growth of land productivity in the 1970s. Thus, a complete theory of farm firm behaviour must explicitly recognise capital gains and losses as well as annual income flows as important dimensions of the decision environment.

Taxation is one of the irritants of the real world that has become increasingly important in the decision environment of the farm firm. Numerous recent studies indicate that the optimal product mix and input utilisation is substantially altered by the tax treatment of various inputs and products. Differential tax treatment of capital compared to labour under the US tax law, which reduces the cost of capital but increases the cost of labour, would be expected to alter the utilisation of these two inputs. Investment credits and rapid depreciation allowances have also contributed to adoption of capital intensive technologies and capital-labour substitution (Davenport et al., 1982). Differential tax treatment of 'capital gains' compared to 'ordinary income' have encouraged the production of those products that will generate the more favourably taxed capital gain income. Tax sheltering which is part of the tax code in the United States and many other countries whereby income can be sheltered from taxation through judicious use of deductions, exemptions and credits has significantly affected investment behaviour and expansion as well as contraction strategies. The institutional structure of the tax rules cannot be ignored in analysing farm firm behaviour – in fact, it would appear to be a major determinant of individual production, investment-financing, and marketing strategies for many farmers.

A fifth dimension of the decision environment is the significant impact that financing has on the optimal input mix and product choice. The traditional thoery of the firm assumes that adequate financing is available to purchase inputs in the optimally desirable quantities and that the financing institutions will not implicitly or explicitly differentially ration funds for different enterprises. But Vickers and Baker have clearly indicated that financing arrangements do affect optimal firm behaviour. Through differential interest rates or credit constraints for various inputs and products, which are more a function of cash flow rather than net income considerations, lenders can alter the relative net prices (market price plus or minus implicit finance charges) of various products and inputs, and thus optimal input mix and product choice. Explicit recognition of finance charges and the money capital constraint must be part of a robust theory of firm behaviour.

Furthermore, recent innovations in financing the production process, in addition to the traditional funds sources of retained earnings and debt, suggests that the choice of a particular financing arrangement is much more complex than has traditionally been the case. The theoretical model must include alternative equity sources including retained earnings, family transfers and non-farm equity, as well as non-equity sources of debt and lease capital with various terms and maturities. In fact, in the current high interest rate, high risk environment, the optimal financing arrangement may be as important as the optimal enterprise choice and input mix for the successful farm business, and these two decisions are clearly interrelated.

A final dimension of the current decision environment which must be explicitly recognised in the conceptual framework and empirical work is the significant element of risk in agricultural production and the interrelatedness of the financial characteristics of the farm business and new concepts of risk in agriculture. Most previous analyses have utilised the widely accepted concept of risk as the variation in income that results from variable prices and yields. Consequently, the results traditionally have been represented in the framework of expected income and the standard deviation, variance, absolute deviation or coefficient of variation of expected income. More recent studies have focused on cumulative probability distributions for income and evaluated those distributions using stochastic dominance techniques (Barry). But the financial stress of recent times has focused attention on a second concept of risk – that of the probability of firm survival as an entity. For a large number of producers, the focus of risk management is not on controlling or managing the variability in income, but protection from failure or termination of the firm.

This concern about financial failure has stimulated a new emphasis on the cash flow and liquidity characteristics of the firm and its asset base. Each asset or input in the farm business has five financial characteristics of importance in economic analyses. Four of these – net income, net cash flow, capital gains, and collateral value – have been commonly recognised. Furthermore, the uncertain nature of the first three of these is frequently acknowledged, but the uncertain nature of the collateral value has seldom been considered in modelling the farm firm. The fifth characteristic, which we will refer to as the asset's liquidity value, has typically been overlooked because models have seldom considered the possibility of asset liquidation as a survival strategy. These liquidation losses, which may be larger and more variable for some assets than others, have had an important effect on the economic viability (including survivability) of farm firms. A more complete understanding of farm firm behaviour is possible if these important and significant dimensions of the decision environment are explicitly recognised in the conceptual framework.

AN INTEGRATED THEORY OF THE FIRM

A theoretical model that encompasses most of the characteristics of the modern production environment for the farm firm is summarised in the following set of equations. Ideally the model should maximise expected utility considering price, production and financial risks. This approach has been used elsewhere with a specific focus on survival (Robison and Lev). The approach used here is a simpler lexicographic model which maximises the expected value of the firm subject to a probabilistic constraint on firm continuance.

As suggested by Vickers, the entrepreneur is assumed to maximise wealth, which can be stated as:

$$V = \frac{E[\pi]}{\rho} - K = \left\{ \sum_{t=1}^{\infty} E[\pi]/(1 + \rho)^t \right\} - K \qquad (1)$$

where V is the expected value of the firm, $E[\pi]$ is the expected annual stream of income and capital gain, and ρ is the capitalization rate. The expected annual stream of income and capital gain is specified as:

$$E[\pi] = E\left[\left\{ Pf(X, L) - \gamma_1 X - \gamma_2 L - r\left(\frac{D}{K}\right)D \right\} \right.$$
$$\left. (1 - \tau) + \phi_1 \delta_1 L + \phi_2 \delta_2 X \right] \qquad (2)$$

where P is a vector of output prices; X denotes non-durable inputs or products that contribute to production and are consumed or sold during the production period; L denotes durable inputs that contribute to production over time and may increase (decrease) in value resulting in capital gains (losses); $f(X, L)$ is a strictly concave multiproduct production function with $f_X, f_L > 0$, $f''_X, f''_L < 0$ for all products; γ_1 and γ_2 are the cash prices of inputs X and L respectively (the price of non-durable inputs is easily determined; the price of durable inputs is calculated as the annualised cost of the services rendered and is frequently estimated as the explicit or implicit rental cost per unit of service); D is debt funds used to finance the production process; K is equity funds; r(D/K) is the debt supply function with $r' > 0$ and $r'' > 0$; τ is the average tax rate; δ_1 and δ_2 are the rate of capital gain or loss on non-durable and durable inputs; and ϕ_1 and ϕ_2 are the portion of unrealised capital gain or loss on non-durable and durable inputs substitutable for income. The formulation of equation (2) does not explicitly recognise the differential taxation of capital gains compared to ordinary income, although such a distinction has been accommodated elsewhere (Lowenberg-DeBoer).

The capitalisation rate is specified as a function of firm size and financial leverage:

$$\rho = a - \theta_1 (K + D) + \theta_2 \left(\frac{D}{K}\right)^2, \tag{3}$$

where a is a constant, θ_1 is the firm size parameter of the capitalisation rate function, and θ_2 is the leverage parameter of the capitalisation rate function (Vickers). The specification of equation (3) recognises that as firm size increases the marginal productivity of capital and thus the capitalisation rate declines, but that increased leverage and thus higher financial risk results in an increase in the capitalisation rate.

The value of the firm is maximised subject to the financing and survival constraints. The financing constraint is specified as:

$$K + D - \alpha X - \beta L \geq 0 \tag{4}$$

where α and β are the amount of financial capital absorbed in the acquisition of the non-durable and durable inputs respectively; these parameters may not be equal to the purchase price of the input if special financing arrangements reduce the capital absorbed in the acquisition process. For example, leasing arrangements or concessionary financing used as a sales tool by farm equipment manufacturers can reduce the capital required to acquire such equipment. Equation (4) indicates that the acquisition of inputs requires and is constrained by the availability of equity (K) and debt (D) capital. Equity capital is comprised of proprietor's contributions and retained earnings, as well as equity funds contributed by outside investors. Thus, the equity capital base is not presumed to be constant since the entrepreneur's equity can be augmented with outside equity.

The final constraint is a liquidity or survival constraint. It recognises that assets have a net cash flow and/or a liquidity component that can be used to meet the firm's minimum requirement for cash. Given the uncertainty associated with the cash and the liquidity components, this is specified as a constraint which must be met with a specified probability:

$$PR\left[\left\{Pf(X, L) - \gamma_1 X - \gamma_2 X - r\left(\frac{D}{K}\right)D\right\}(1 - \tau) + \lambda_1 X + \lambda_2 L - C \geq 0\right] \geq Z \tag{5}$$

where λ_1 and λ_2 are the after-tax liquidity coefficients per dollar of nondurable and durable inputs (which is one minus the liquidity loss), respectively, C is operator withdrawals and Z is the minimum probability with which the constraint must be met. Equation (5) might be termed the 'survival function'. It reflects the cash flow requirements that the firm must meet to continue in business. Production inputs and capital assets typically contribute cash earnings; while others, such as stored grain awaiting sale, commonly contribute cash through liquidation. However, the constraint recognises that durable and non-durable inputs can be liquidated to meet cash needs, even though such sales are expected to significantly impair the long-run income-generating capacity of the firm. The formulation specified here assumes that assets are liquidated only at the end of the production cycle; however, such an assumption is not essential if the model included a more detailed time specification. In a dynamic context, with changing debt and equity levels, the liquidity constraint could include a more detailed specification of financial plans, including principal payments.

The decision variables in the model include non-durable inputs (X), durable inputs (L), debt, and equity (K). The multiproduct nature of the production function [f(X, L)] implies that the optimal values of these decision variables will result in an optimal product mix as well as an optimal size of farm.

IMPLICATIONS

The comparative statics properties of this model are complex to develop analytically, particularly given the probabilistic nature of the survival constraint (equation (5)). Lowenberg-DeBoer has derived comparative static properties for the model excluding the survival function. As a step in the development of a more general model, the discussion here will draw upon and augment that earlier work by examining the implications of adding the survival function to the model.

The implications of this integrated model for optimal input use and product mix are significant. Lowenberg-DeBoer indicates that ignoring the survival constraint the optimal mix of durable and non-durable inputs is not only a function of the relative prices (γ_1 and γ_2), but also the finance charge coefficients (α and β) and the capital gains parameters ($\phi_1\delta_1$ and $\phi_2\delta_2$). Using his approach, the marginal rate of input substitution is defined as:

$$\frac{f_X}{f_L} = \frac{[\gamma_1 + \alpha \ (r + r' \ (D/K))] \ (1 - \tau) - \phi_1\delta_1}{[\gamma_2 + \beta \ (r + r' \ (D/K))] \ (1 - \tau) - \phi_2\delta_2} \quad (6)$$

where f_X/f_L denotes the ratio of marginal products of durable for non-durable inputs.

As is typical of the Vickers' formulation, the marginal rate of substitution is equal to a factor or input cost ratio which includes after-tax relative input prices, plus relative 'finance charges'. These relative finance charges reflect the interest payments on funds borrowed to buy the inputs, as well as the implicit or explicit collateral constraints imposed by lenders as reflected in specific lending limits that restrict the use of credit in acquiring various inputs. Because these lender-imposed collateral and funding constraints are more a function of cash flow and liquidity characteristics of various inputs rather than relative prices, it is typically the case that the relative finance charges will not be equal to relative input prices.

Unlike the usual Vickers' model, the input cost ratio also includes an argument reflecting differential capital gains or losses on durable and non-durable inputs. Typically, capital gains or losses on durable inputs will exceed those on non-durables; in fact, the capital gains or losses for non-durables will frequently be zero. Assuming that capital gains on non-durables are zero ($\delta_1 = 0$), but that capital gains on durables are positive ($\delta_2 > 0$) and that part of these gains are substitutable for current income ($\phi_2 > 0$), the capital gains will tend to offset part of the cost of acquiring the durable inputs. Capital losses would have the opposite affect; they would tend to increase the cost of durable inputs. Thus, the optimal input mix is not only a function of relative factor prices, but also relative finance charges and relative capital gains or losses.

The recognition of capital gains and losses and finance charges will also have an impact on the choice of outputs. Lowenberg-DeBoer introduces two production functions [g(X, L) and f(X, L)] into the model, and when input prices are the same for both enterprises the marginal rate of substitution equation is as follows:

$$\frac{f_X}{f_L} = \frac{g_X}{g_L} = \frac{\{\gamma_1 + \alpha[r = r'\ D/K]\}\ (1 - \tau) - \phi_1\delta_1}{\{\gamma_2 + \beta[r + r'\ D/K]\}\ (1 - \tau) - \phi_2\delta_2} \tag{7}$$

Both the marginal rate of substitution for the f production function (MRS$_f$) and marginal rate of substitution for the g production function (MRS$_g$) will be larger than is traditionally the case because of the presence of capital gains on durable inputs. But, if one production function has a lower marginal product of durable inputs than the other, the output and use of durables in the production of that commodity will be curtailed. For instance, assume g describes the production of fruit and vegetables such that at some relatively small amount of land g_L becomes small compared to g_X, that is the marginal product of land becomes small compared to the marginal product of other inputs such as fertilizer, labor, pesticides, etc. Assume f describes the production of grain; the marginal product of land in grain production can remain relatively high even if substantial amounts of land are already in use. Under these conditions MRS_g would be equal to the input cost ratio at some low level of land input, but a much larger level of land input would be required to equate MRS_f and the factor cost ratio.

As capital gains increase, the input cost ratio increases and the output which lends itself to land-extensive production assumes a larger share of the output mix. It may be the case for some levels of capital gain and some production functions, that the land input for g must be made so small to achieve equality (7) that the production of output g drops to zero. It should be noted that this does not suggest that the most land extensive output is always favoured. Rather it indicates that the favoured output in the presence of capital gains is one in which the production process is relatively land-extensive and the marginal product of land remains relatively high even when the firm uses large amounts of land. For capital losses the opposite effect occurs and enterprise choice tends toward land-intensive options.

The discussion thus far has not recognized the impact of liquidity and cash flow differences in the choice of optimal durable and nondurable input use as encompassed in the survival function of equation (5). If the lender's perception of cash flow and liquidity characteristics of durable and non-durable inputs as reflected in the finance charges are an accurate reflection of the actual values of these coefficients as experienced by the farmer, then explicit recognition of these characteristics as in equation (5) will have little impact on the optimal input mix. However, if cash flow and liquidity characteristics as actually faced by the farmer differ from those of the lender, then the addition of these parameters will influence optimal input use. Specifically, non-durable inputs are typically more liquid and generate more cash flow on a per unit basis than durable inputs, which would suggest a larger quantity of nondurable inputs in the optimal input mix.

With respect to investment behaviour, the optimal mix of durable and non-durable inputs as well as the optimal type of durable input to acquire is influenced by the net income, net cash flow, capital gains, collateral value, and liquidity parameters in the fashion noted earlier. The disinvestment behaviour, as noted elsewhere (Boehlje and Eidman 1983) is a function of the same parameters; the owner would prefer to sell those assets that possess the characteristics of high liquidity, low net income and cash flow, low capital gains, and limited collateral value.

Ignoring the survival constraint, the financial structure of the firm can be characterised by solving the first-order conditions for equity and debt to yield an expression in the discount rate and leverage ratio as:

$$\rho - r' \left(\frac{D}{K} \right)^2 = r + r' \left(\frac{D}{K} \right) \tag{8}$$

The left-hand side of this equation is the marginal cost of equity capital, and the right-hand side is the marginal cost of debt capital, which generates the common financial result that in the optimal financial structure the marginal cost of all sources of capital are equal. Lowenberg-DeBoer indicates that if equity is not fixed, capital gains and losses do not affect the financial structure or the optimal debt-equity mix. However, if equity is fixed, the optimal use of debt must be found simultaneously with input levels. The result in this case is that capital gains or losses do impact debt utilisation; debt use increases (decreases) with higher levels of capital gains (capital losses).

In a more detailed specification of the model, D may be a vector of debt with various maturity and principal repayment characteristics. The optimal composition of debt is then a function of the cost of each debt source and its impact on the survival constraint through the debt servicing requirements. Debt servicing requirements are typically lower for current compared to long-term debt because of lower interest rates and scheduled principal reductions (assuming normal inventory financing). Consequently, with increased financial stress and cash flow problems, the optimal debt composition will include a larger quantity of long-term and a smaller quantity of short-term (current) debt. Equation (5) also suggests that, because of relative liquidity and cash flow characteristics as noted earlier, an input mix that contains a higher proportion of non-durable inputs will improve the probability of survival. Clearly lower levels of withdrawal and the substitution of entrepreneural and investor equity for debt will reduce the cash requirements for debt servicing and also increase the probability of survival.

In summary, the implication of incorporating capital gains or losses and finance charges (including liquidity and collateral coefficients) in the analysis for the use of durable and nondurable inputs and organisation of the farm firm are important. Since real estate is the most important durable input used in most farming operations, the farm size implications are also significant. In essence, the larger the capital gain on durable inputs (for example, the land price increase) or the smaller the finance charges, all other parameters constant, the greater the optimal use of durable inputs (farmland). Use of nondurable inputs is reduced if capital gains are larger or the fraction of capital gains substitutable for current income is greater. Capital losses and higher finance charges have the opposite effect; they tend to increase the cost of durables (land), reducing the factor or input cost ratio and hence reducing the use of durables (land) in the optimal solution while increasing use of nondurable inputs. Thus, in an environment of capital losses or higher relative finance charges, the decision-maker would tend to economise on durables (land) to avoid those losses or costs.

With specific reference to capital gains or losses, it is important to separate the effects of the price level of durable inputs compared to the rate of change in durables' prices. If the price of durable inputs is higher, the annualised cost of durables' ownership will be higher and there will be

678   *Michael Boehlje and L. Lowenberg-DeBoer*

a tendency to use fewer durables. The price change in durables can, however, either offset or add to the cost of owning durable inputs, depending upon whether the price is rising or falling.

The analytical results suggest that at least part of the increase in the use of durable inputs and farm size in the United States in recent years may be a result of the almost continuous capital gains that have occurred. It also indicates that, all other things being equal, if capital gains during the period had been smaller or if those unrealised gains had been less substitutable for wealth, farmers would have invested in more non-durable inputs such as labour, fertilizer, pesticides, and improved seed. The analysis also suggests that farm size and the use of non-durable and durable inputs can be significantly affected by government policy. For instance, it is frequently argued that land prices are the capitalised value of expected future income from land ownership. If this expected future income is rising, capital gains are likely to occur. If a price support programme increases the rate at which future income from land is expected to rise, the analysis suggests that there will be a tendency for farm size to increase and for land use to become more extensive. Conversely, a weakening of government price support commitments which reduces income expectations, resulting in a lower rate of land price change, would tend to reduce the optimal farm size and encourage more intensive farming. Government tax and credit policies that have a differential impact on income, capital gains and finance charge coefficients for durable and non-durable inputs will affect the optimal input mix in like fashion.

REFERENCES

Barry, Peter (ed.), *Risk Management in Agriculture*, Iowa State University Press, Ames, forthcoming.
Bhatia, Kul, 'Capital Gains and the Aggregate Consumption Function', *American Economic Review*, vol. 62, no. 5, December 1972, pp. 866–79.
Boehlje, Michael and Eidman, Vernon, 'Financial Stress in Agriculture: Implications for Producers', *American Journal of Agricultural Economics*, vol. 65, no.. 5, December 1983, pp. 937–44.
Castle, Emory and Hoch, Irving, 'Farm Real Estate Price Components, 1920–1978', *American Journal of Agricultural Economics*, vol. 64, no. 1, February, 1982, pp. 8–18.
Davenport, Charles, Boehlje, Michael and Martin, David, *The Effect of Tax Policy on American Agriculture*, USDA, Economic Research Service, Agricultural Economic Report 480, February 1982.
Lins, David and Duncan, Marvin, 'Inflation on Financial Performance and Structure of the Farm Sector', *American Journal of Agricultural Economics*, vol. 62, no. 5, December 1980, pp. 1049–53.
Lowenberg-DeBoer, J., 'The Impact of Farmland Price Changes on Farm Size, Debt Use and Enterprise Choice', Ph.D. dissertation, Iowa State University, Ames, Iowa, forthcoming.
Plaxico, James and Kletke, Darrel, 'The Value of Unrealized Farm Land Capital Gains', *American Journal of Agricultural Economics*, vol. 61, no. 2, May 1979, pp. 327–30.
Robison, Lindon J. and Lev, Larry, 'Distinguishing Between Initial and Final Impact

Variables to Predict Choices under Risk, or Why Woody Chip Went to the Air', Michigan Agr. Exp. Sta. Journal article.

Vickers, Donald, *The Theory of the Firm: Production, Capital and Finance*, McGraw-Hill, New York, 1968.

CARLOS E. CUEVAS AND DOUGLAS H. GRAHAM

Rationing Agricultural Credit in Developing Countries: The Role and Determinants of Transaction Costs for Borrowers

INTRODUCTION

Transaction costs in financial intermediation are a measure of the 'friction' existing in the functioning of financial markets. The higher the costs of intermediation, the less efficient the performance of the financial sector in resource allocation and distribution. Transaction costs frequently increase as a result of regulations imposed on financial markets, such as interest-rate restrictions and selective credit policies. Financial intermediaries circumvent interest-rate regulations through non-price mechanisms that generate transaction costs for lenders and borrowers, whereas selective credit policies usually carry built-in cost-increasing procedures and requirements.

In this paper we investigate the role of transaction costs of borrowing as a rationing mechanism in the agricultural credit markets of five less-developed countries. We show that borrowing transaction costs become an effective non-price rationing device in these markets. We further argue that the results of these rationing practices are regressive, despite the intended distributional goals of low-interest rate credit policies and small-farmer credit allocations schemes. We also investigate the main determinants of borrowing transaction costs, and show that an inverse relationship exists between the level of the explicit interest rate charged on loans and the magnitude of these transaction costs. Our findings indicate that both development banks and private banks pass on transaction costs to borrowers as an implicit-pricing mechanism to ration out undesired clients. Private banks are generally more effective in doing this than development banks and, at the same time, more responsive to changes in the interest-rate structure.

We first present a summary and discussion of recent evidence on the levels and degree of regressiveness of borrowing transaction costs in agricultural credit. The next section deals with the main determinants of these costs borne by farmer borrowers, emphasising the trade-off between transaction costs and interest rates on the one hand, and the differences between private bank and development bank behaviour on the other hand. Major conclusions follow.

COSTS OF BORROWING TRANSACTIONS IN LDcs: A REVIEW OF RECENT RESEARCH

This section draws upon results from field surveys reported in five different studies of agricultural credit programmes undertaken between 1981 and 1983. Four of these studies relate to Latin-American countries: Honduras (Cuevas), Ecuador, Panama and Peru (Inter-American Development Bank), while the fifth study was undertaken in Bangladesh (Ahmed). These surveys document the explicit and implicit non-interest costs incurred by farmer-borrowers in the process of securing and repaying loans. Explicit costs consist primarily of transportation, lodging and meal expenses associated with trips to the bank's office, and fees and other cash payments for documents and legal procedures. Implicit costs correspond to the opportunity cost of time spent by farmers in negotiating and securing their loans.

The most important common characteristic of all five case studies is a low nominal interest rate to provide subsidised credit to small and medium-sized farms. These rates implied negative real interest rates in three cases: -3 per cent in Bangladesh, -0.5 per cent in Ecuador, and -22 per cent in Peru. In the other two cases the resulting real interest rates were positive (3.3 per cent in Honduras, and 2 per cent in Panama) though still clearly subsidised when taking into account the opportunity cost of capital in these societies.

Table 1 summarises the results reported in the five country-studies. Panel A presents the magnitude of transaction costs as a percentage of the

TABLE 1   *Borrowing transaction costs at the farm level in selected countries, by loan size*

Transaction costs by loan size	Bangladesh	Ecuador	Honduras	Panama	Peru
	%	%	%	%	%
A. Transaction costs as percentage of loan amount					
Sample average	21.7	2.8	3.0	5.2	1.2
Small loans	29.4	5.3	5.9	5.7	3.9
Medium loans	17.5	2.0	1.6	3.0	1.3
Large loans	7.0	0.6	0.2	2.0	1.0
B. Transaction costs as percentage of explicit-interest charges[a]					
Sample average	180.8	22.9	23.1	46.4	4.0
Small loans	245.0	47.7	45.4	50.9	13.0
Medium loans	145.8	17.3 ,	12.3	26.8	4.3
Large loans	58.1	4.1	1.5	17.9	3.3

Sources: Bangladesh, Ahmed; Honduras, Cuevas; Ecuador; Panama and Peru, Inter-American Bank.
[a]Computed based on the levels of explicit interest rate reported in the different sources, e.g., for Bangladesh the average transaction costs in panel A is 21.7 per cent and the explicit rate reported by Ahmed is 12 per cent; therefore $(21.7/12)*100 = 180.8$ per cent.

loan amount. In Panel B, these transaction costs have been expressed as a proportion of the explicit-interest charges documented in the case studies. This proportion indicates the relative importance of transaction costs *vis-à-vis* explicit interest charges. In both panels we report the sample average of each measure and the results for three loan-size categories.

Transaction costs per cent of the loan amount vary between 1.2 (Peru) and 21.7 (Bangladesh), and the magnitudes across countries and loan-size categories range from 0.2 to almost 30. There is a striking contrast between the results shown for Bangladesh and those reported for the Latin-American countries. This contrast is accounted for by the unusually small loan sizes characteristic of the Bangladesh survey in comparison to those recorded in Latin America. This contrast is also reflected in panel B, where transaction costs are expressed as a percentage of explicit-interest charges. Here transaction costs for Bangladesh are on average almost twice as large as the explicit interest charged on loans, whereas in the Latin-American cases they represent between 4 and 46 per cent of explicit interest. With the exception of Peru, the findings suggest that borrowing transaction costs play an important role as implicit prices in these credit markets. Their magnitude certainly cannot be ignored by prospective borrowers. Loan procedures established by lenders create these transaction costs and should be interpreted as rationing or screening devices. These mechanisms substitute for explicit prices (i.e., interest rates) that are constrained under the regulatory schemes prevailing in these markets.

The figures in Table 1 also highlight the distributional effects of credit rationing through this implicit pricing. In all cases the incidence of transaction costs by loan-size categories is clearly regressive with small loans bearing high costs and large loans entailing the lowest borrowing transaction costs as a percentage of the loan. In relative terms, transaction costs for small loans in Honduras are almost 30 times as high as those associated with large loans, 8.8 times as high in Ecuador, 4.2 times in Bangladesh, 3.9 times in Peru, and 2.9 times in Panama.

We conclude that the intended effect of credit policies promoting a low and relatively uniform interest rate among borrowers is not attained in practice. Instead, a skewed, regressive structure of total credit costs (interest rate *plus* transaction costs) is obtained. Even when the administered rates are set so that small loans are charged a lower rate than medium or large loans, as is the case in the Ecuador study, transaction costs more than offset the explicit interest-rate differential (two percentage points in the Ecuador case).

SOME DETERMINANTS OF COSTS OF BORROWING TRANSACTIONS:

Interest rates and lending institutions

The Honduras case provided information on transaction costs borne by clients of the development bank, private banks and credit unions.

Lenders were constrained by a narrow range of explicit interest rates they could charge on loans, therefore they used selective and discriminatory application of their loan procedure to screen and ration out loan applicants. Transaction costs were passed on to borrowers in direct proportion to the perceived risk involved in the different loan operations.

A trade-off equation was estimated between borrowing transaction costs and the explicit interest rate charged on loans. In this estimation a generalised power function was specified with transaction costs as a function of the explicit interest rate, the area of the farm, the loan amount, a set of dummy variables to account for loan source (development bank, private banks, credit unions), and another set of dummy variables that captured the effect of loan end-use.[1]

As expected, transaction costs as a percentage of the loan amount were a decreasing function of the loan amount. Transaction costs *per loan* are an increasing function of loan amount; however, the elasticity of this function is less than one, therefore transaction costs per loan increase at a decreasing rate as loan size increases. As a result, transaction costs *per unit of money borrowed* decrease as the loan amount increases.

The results obtained for the effect of the interest rate on transaction costs were also significant and stable across different specifications. Overall, the coefficient associated with the direct effect of the interest rate on transaction costs was not significantly different from -1. This finding indicates that there is a trade-off between transaction costs of borrowing and the nominal interest rate charged on loans, such that a one per cent increase in the interest rate will bring about a one per cent decrease in borrowing transaction costs.

The foregoing general results for the overall sample are broken down in Table 2, controlling for both the loan source and the loan-size. For simplicity, only two loan sources (development bank, private banks) and two loan-size categories are defined here. The first column of Table 2 indicates the estimated transaction costs as a percentage of the loan amount. It is evident from these figures that borrowing from private banks is about twice as expensive as borrowing from the development bank, a finding that suggests a greater ability of private banks to pass on transaction costs to borrowers. The skewed, regressive incidence of transaction costs by loan size is clear in Table 2, regardless of the lending institution involved.

Column two of Table 2 reports the elasticity of transaction costs with respect to the interest rate for different combinations of loan source and loan size. Borrowing transaction costs are very elastic to changes in the interest rate in the case of private banks. For these loans the absolute value of the elasticity is three to five times as large as the values obtained for the development bank. In the latter, large loans show a unitary elasticity whereas for small loans the response of transaction costs to changes in the interest rate is inelastic (significantly less than zero and greater than -1). For small-loan operations, the absolute value of the elasticity is lower than the values obtained for large loans, denoting a less flexible response. This is expected, since smaller loans are associated with more rigid and cumbersome targeting schemes.

TABLE 2   *Borrowing transaction costs as percentage of loan amount (t), elasticities of t with respect to changes in the explicit interest rate (i), and changes in t with increases in i, by lender and loan size*

Lender/Loan Size	Estimated value of transaction costs (t)[a] %	Estimated value of elasticity[b] e(t, i)	Change in t with a one-point increase in the interest rate (i) pct. points
Development Bank			
Small Loans	2.85	−0.5551	−0.123
Large Loans	0.38	−0.8425[c]	−0.025
Private Banks			
Small Loans	5.77	−2.6692	−1.184
Large Loans	0.77	−2.9566	−0.175

Source: Cuevas. Details results of the estimated function available from the authors. See note 1.
[a] Estimates evaluated at geometric means of farm area and interest rate.
[b] All estimates significantly different from zero.
[c] Not significantly different from −1.

The response of transaction costs in percentage points to a one-point increase in the interest rate were calculated based on the elasticities discussed above. These are presented in the last column of Table 2. This response is considerably larger for private-bank loans. A one-point increase in the explicit interest rate will lead to a larger compensatory decline in borrowing transaction costs in private-bank loans than in the case of loans from the development bank. This result shows that private banks are more responsive and flexible in adjusting their loan procedures and requirements to changes in the regulatory environment.

In both lending institutions the compensatory change in borrowing transaction costs as a result of an increase in the interest rate is considerably larger for small loans than for large loans. This implies that a one-point increase in the interest rate will be almost fully translated into a corresponding increase in total borrowing costs (i.e., interest rate *plus* transaction costs) in the case of large loans, since the compensating effect of reduced transaction costs is very small. For small loans however, this offsetting response of transaction costs is far more important. Thus an increase in the explicit interest rate will be partially compensated by the resulting reduction in borrowing transaction costs. Since this offsetting effect occurs for increases as well as decreases in the level of the interest rate, it follows that further reductions in the interest rate on loans will benefit primarily borrowers of large amounts, instead of farmers borrowing small loans. In this sense, cheap-credit policies will not attain their intended distributional goals in the rural sector.

SUMMARY AND CONCLUSIONS

In this paper we have investigated the role of transaction costs of borrowing as a rationing mechanism in agricultural credit markets in less developed countries. Results of recent research in five LDCs suggest that the intended effect of credit policies involving a low and relatively uniform interest rate is not attained. Instead, a skewed, regressive structure of total credit costs (interest rate *plus* transaction costs) is obtained.

The estimation of a transaction-costs function based on data from one of the case studies above indicated that loan amount, interest rate, and loan source are significant determinants of the level of transaction costs. Transaction costs as a percentage of the loan amount decrease with loan size, decline with increases in the interest rate (i.e., the trade-off relationship), and are higher for private-bank loans than development-bank loans, at given loan sizes and interest rates. The trade-off (negative elasticity) is larger in private banks than in the development bank, and is more significant for small loans than for large loans. We conclude that, under interest rate restrictions, private banks are more effective in passing on intermediation costs to borrowers than development banks. At the same time, private banks are more responsive to changes in the interest-rate structure, and more flexible in adjusting their loan procedures and requirements to a changing regulatory environment. Finally, contrary to conventional wisdom, an increase in the explicit interest rate on loans would have a progressive impact, since it would reduce transaction costs more for small loans than for large loans.

NOTE

[1]The transaction-costs function estimated here is:

$$\ln T = a_0 + a_1 \ln A + a_2 \ln L + a_{30} \ln(i) + a_{31} S \ln(i) + a_{32} D_1 \ln(i)$$
$$+ a_{33} D_2 \ln(i) + a_{34} F \ln(i) + b_1 D_1 + b_2 D_2 + c_1 U_1 + c_2 U_2$$
$$+ c_3 U_3$$

where,
  T is the borrowing (non-interest) transaction costs per loan,
  A is the area of the farm,
  L is the loan amount,
  i is the explicit interest rate that can be charged on the loan by the lender,
  S is the dummy variable for loan-size category,
     $S = 1$ if the loan amount is less than or equal to L. 2,000, $S = 0$ otherwise,
  D_1 and D_2 are dummy variables that account for deviations of T in private banks and credit unions with respect to the development bank, that is used as the base or level of reference,
  F is a dummy variable for farm-size category,

F = 1 if the area of the farm is less than or equal to 20 hectares, F = 0 otherwise, U_1, U_2, and U_3 are dummy variables defined to capture the effects on transaction costs of different loan-uses: basic grains, export crops, and livestock, as deviations with respect to a miscellaneous end-use category conformed by all other end-uses in agriculture (land purchases, trade, vegetable crops, and others).

REFERENCES

Adams, Dale W., Graham, Douglas H. and Von Pischke, J. D., *Undermining Rural Development with Cheap Credit*, Westview Press, Boulder, Colorado, 1984.

Ahmed, Zia U., 'Transaction Costs in Rural Financial Markets in Bangladesh: A Study of a Rural Credit Market', Ph.D. dissertation, University of Virginia, 1982.

Cuevas, Carlos E., 'Intermediation Costs and Scale Economies of Banking Under Financial Regulations in Honduras', Ph.D. dissertation, Ohio State University, 1984.

Inter-American Development Bank, *Banco Nacional de Fomento: Evaluacion de Programas Globales de Credito Agropecuario: Ecuador*, Operations Evaluation Office, 1983.

Inter-American Development Bank, *Agricultural Development Bank (BDA): Evaluation of Global Agricultural Credit Programs in Panama*, Operations Evaluation Office, 1983.

Inter-American Development Bank, *Banco Agrario del Peru: Evaluation of Global Agricultural Credit Programs: Peru*, Operations Evaluation Office, 1983.

DISCUSSION OPENING I – MARK DRABENSTOTT

Financial stress is the leading problem of agriculture in many countries around the world. Thus, as economists grapple with the complex set of forces that are producing that stress, it is appropriate that we re-examine many questions of finance as they relate to farm firms. This session serves a very useful role in highlighting some of these pertinent questions.

Boehlje and Lowenberg-DeBoer provide a well-constructed theoretical model of the farm firm incorporating some useful financial dimensions. Their treatment of capital gains and losses helps to explain farm behaviour. The decade of the 1970s supports their conclusion that rapid capital gains will induce producers to become more land extensive. The emphasis on finance charges is appropriate, particularly the delineation of liquidity value. One might ask, however, if the collateral and liquidity value do not come close to equalling one another when asset values are declining rapidly, as they have recently in the United States. A thorough treatment of taxes, both income and capital gains is certainly also welcome.

The firm survival constraint is perhaps the authors' best contribution. The current financial strains on highly leveraged farm firms certainly underscore the need for this constraint.

Their model is a robust framework for some possible improvements in even better explaining farm firm behaviour. I offer the following suggestions. First, the *externalities of inputs* are still not internalised. The authors mention externalities in their introduction, but then do not include them in the model. Second, *financial risk management* is more than just survival. While survival is an overriding goal, firms that are liquid will still manage their financial risk in other ways. For example, the model does not account for interest rate risk within decision periods. What effect would volatile interest rates have on the firm? What is the value to the firm of interest rate risk management techniques such as financial futures and options?

Finally, the model seems to ignore the effects of positive *real* interest rates. With deregulated financial markets in many developed countries, real interest rates are likely to remain positive, and highly positive if price inflation accelerates. Firms will alter their financial structures in response to the increase in real rates. The authors conclude that debt use increases with higher levels of capital gains. But with deregulated financial markets, interest rates will rise in step with accelerating inflation (if not faster), thus removing the incentive to purchase farm real estate with borrowed capital.

The Boehlje-Lowenberg paper stimulates a number of important policy questions. Faced with an eroding credit reserve of unrealised capital gains, how do farm firms behave? The answers can serve as useful guides to policy-makers who may try to assist such farmers. The authors conclude that government policies that raise farm incomes will, by creating capital gains, tend to increase farm size and make land-use more extensive. That conclusion prompts the question: can farm policies which improve farm income have neutral effects on farm structure? The answer appears to be no, unless the policy is very carefully targeted. Finally, as farm borrowers re-order their financial positions due to positive real interest rates, what innovative means will arise to bring off-farm equity into agriculture? The markets currently are poorly developed at best. Cuevas and Graham provide some results that can be very useful to policy-makers. Their conclusion that transaction costs, compared with either the loan amount or the interest rate, often more than compensates for the subsidized interest rate is a striking one. The conclusion that transaction costs are regressive is not surprising, but useful to the policy-maker. And that private lenders pass on more transaction costs than do development banks is also not surprising, but certainly worth documenting.

While the authors could not fully develop their analysis within the pages allowed, I offer some suggestions to improve their worthwhile study. First, the paper does not delineate transaction costs. What components were most critical: perceived credit risk, transportation costs, or administrative fees? The answer will have great bearing on any policy attempts to reduce transaction costs. Second, it was not clear what credit risk, if any, was assumed by the national governments. If the government does guarantee the loan, then private lenders ought to reduce their 'fees'.

Third, the analysis could be strengthened by comparing transaction costs for farm loans with costs for other types of loans in the various countries. Are farm loans special, or is there a more general credit problem that must be addressed? Finally, the authors imply that development banks are more benevolent in passing smaller transaction costs on to borrowers. A strong case can be made that private lenders simply understand their costs better.

The Cuevas and Graham paper prompts some important questions about government programmes to supply low cost loans to farmers. How can governments supply subsidized credit to farm borrowers while minimising regressive side effects such as high transaction costs? If transportation is a major portion of transaction costs, then the loan programme can be made more effective by creating more field loan offices. But if credit risk is the problem, then other tools must be used. What role can fixed term federal loan guarantees play in supplying credit to farmers through commercial lenders? If private lenders are attaching large administrative fees to subsidized loans, then the government can overcome this by guaranteeing the loans for a fixed period of time, during which the credit risk would gradually revert back to the commercial lender. This partnership makes the loan more palatable for the lender when the loan is extended, but does not leave the government to bear all of the loan servicing costs and possible loan losses.

Finally, how ought farm credit and farm income support policies complement one another? Or, in the context of the Cuevas and Graham paper, do high transaction costs simply reflect low profitability for the sector? Subsidized credit can only be substituted for income so long. Eventually, either cash flow is sufficient to service the loan, or the lender must foreclose. In the United States, the Farmers Home Administration is currently under the cloud of a multi-billion dollar loan portfolio that will never be fully repaid if current market conditions continue.

DISCUSSION OPENING II – MADHUKAR GADGIL

Being an economist working in a bank, I must admit that I had a banker's bias when I read the two papers. I propose therefore to comment on both the papers from the viewpoint of policy and action in credit institutions financing agriculture.

The paper on 'Integration of Production and Financial Theory' has obviously been inspired by the recent developments in US agriculture. The rising farm land prices in the US during the pre1984 period were caused by a variety of factors pointed out by the authors, but easy access to credit for speculative purchases of land was probably an important contributory factor. The basic policy issue for the financing banks therefore is: should they finance the purchase of farm land at all, especially when land prices increase far beyond the level indicated by their intrinsic productive value? In India, formal credit for the purchase of land has been taboo for the last 15 years, mainly for avoiding financing of transfer transactions. Since almost every farmer inherits his land, this provision has basically curbed speculative land purchases.

The next question is the basis for the valuation of land when it is considered as a collateral for loans. If the market price of land is higher than its capitalised future income, valuation with reference to market price will produce over-financing and over-capitalisation of the farm. In India, where the supply of land is inelastic and where, for that reason, the market price of land is always higher than its intrinsic value, banks have been advised to estimate the collateral value of land on the basis of the income capitalisation method to avoid over-financing of those investment loans which require land as a collateral.

The paper refers to higher capital charges and increased financial and business risk in agriculture attributable to greater price volatility and higher leverage ratios and hence the need for re-evaluating specialised farming and capital-labour substitution. Is the new financial environment economy-wide or is it a change in the environment for agriculture relative to other sectors? Steps for corrective action would depend upon an answer to this question.

Is farm survival related to financial failure really a new risk? To what extent is it caused by fluctuating interest rates and other financing terms? Apart from their impact on input-output mix, changes in financial arrangements are frequently used to influence the viability of a farm enterprise and should therefore be built into the survival constraint equation. The larger question that arises here is the financial strategy to assist farmers in distress.

A complete theoretical explanation of the behaviour of farm firms should also recognise differential changes in market prices of land across regions not related to differences in real productive values but to exogeneous factors. Farmers in India are known to respond to such a phenomenon by selling their lands in one region and acquiring larger lands in other regions to maximise their annual income stream.

One last question: is it theoretically possible to anticipate all externalities and internalise them into a model to explain farm firm behaviour?

I shall now turn to the second paper entitled 'Rationing Agricultural Credit in Developing Countries'. The basic argument of this paper is that because credit institutions in most developing nations charge low interest rates on agricultural lands, the borrowers' transaction costs are higher and since the incidence of such costs is higher on small lands than on big lands, charging of low interest rates and small farmer credit allocation programmes turn out to be regressive. Let us examine this argument. The costs of borrowing transactions consist of the explicit expenses on transport to and from the bank office, lodging and boarding expenses etc. Implicit costs equal the opportunity costs of time spent by a borrower on securing a loan. I suggest that, other things being constant, both the explicit and the implicit costs are more or less fixed in absolute terms and it is but natural that the proportion of such costs would be inversely related both to the amount of loan as well as to the interest rate. A change in the bank's lending rate is not likely to reduce the distance between the borrower's village and the bank office, nor is it likely to reduce the formalities associated with securing a loan. What matters to the farmer is the sum of transaction costs and interest charges and not the relative changes in the two components. The mathematical relationship pointed out by the authors (1 per cent increase in interest rate is associated with 1 per cent decrease in the borrower's transaction costs) appears to me to be questionable unless a satisfactory explanation of why transaction costs decrease with an increase in the interest rate is provided. While studying borrowing transaction costs, one must distinguish between production credit, which has to be borrowed for each crop season, and investment credit which a farmer may borrow once or twice in his lifetime. In India, the documentation associated with a production loan does not have to be repeated each crop season. A farmer may also have several options for borrowing such credit but the common practice is to borrow from the village co-operative. Thus, the explicit and implicit transaction costs associated with production credit are both low and non-repetitive. The transaction costs associated with investment loans are relatively high, but their annual incidence is low due to infrequent borrowing of such loans by farmers and long loan maturities (five to fifteen years). The paper does not tell us whether farmers in the five countries had borrowed both types of credit or only one and how many of them were borrowing for the first time.

An additional but important component of the implicit borrowing transaction costs is the time spent by a farmer on securing a loan and its effect on the input-output relationship of the farm. For instance, if a farmer is unable to obtain credit for buying fertilizer at the right time, his output and income may be reduced and the cost of the foregone output/income may overshadow other transaction costs. The paper does not recognise such costs.

In most developing nations, formal credit is used as an instrument for promoting agricultural development by increasing the rate of on-farm investment. The effectiveness of this instrument depends on several endogenous and exogenous factors – adequacy and timeliness of credit, extension service, land tenure system, input supply, product market prices and location-specific technology, to mention only a few. The priority for research by agricultural economists on developing agriculture should therefore be the impact of credit on agricultural development and the steps required to raise its marginal productivity.

GENERAL DISCUSSION – RAPPORTEUR: URS GANTNER

Regarding the first paper it was commented that many farmers had loans which their present and expected incomes could not service. One option which these farmers had was to liquidate their assets in order to reduce the debt. This meant selling land, which in turn reduced net revenue by much more than the interest saved and hence income goes down. The result was a smaller business with the same problem and indicated that it was almost impossible to get out of a debt problem through contraction.

Comments on the second paper included one of surprise at the small value of transaction costs shown – in Africa differences in rates of interest between traditional moneylenders and commercial banks is of the order of 200 per cent; thus 20 per cent is almost negligible. Another speaker asked how was it that transaction costs between 1981 and 1983 (Table 1) went up more than five times.

In reply, Professor Boehlje stated that:

1 collateral and liquidity coefficients would become the same under financial stress;
2 the model did not explicitly encompass externalities but the specification allowed for it;
3 parameters like income and cash flow could be stochastic;
4 he agreed with the policy issues raised and added a few additional ones;
5 the study was US-inspired but was not unique to a US environment;
6 income capitalisation was appropriate but it ignored the supply side which was an important additional determinant of land values.

Replying to discussion on the second paper, Dr Cuevas stated that ways of reducing transaction costs included the reduction of targeting requirements associated with loan programmes; having a more flexible interest rate structure; and reliable guarantees to commercial banks. He agreed that a flexible interest rate structure would not change the distance to the bank; but it might change the number of times a borrower had to go. The loan procedure is a risk reducing mechanism, therefore if part of the risk was accounted for by the explicit interest rate, procedures could be simplified and, thus, transaction costs reduced.

In his reply to comments from the floor, he pointed out that the reported transaction costs related only to those borne by *borrowers*. To get total costs one would have to add those incurred by lenders, which were considerably higher.

Participants in the discussion included M. Boussard, P. A. Sow and G. E. Dalton.

CLARK EDWARDS

The Role of Natural Resources in Regional Agricultural Growth

INTRODUCTION

World food production increased 1.96 per cent per year during 1974–83 (Economic Research Service 1984). Population increased more slowly, 1.75 per cent per year. This resulted in an increase in food consumption per caput of 0.21 per cent per year. During the 1970s, the amount of cropland in the world increased 0.27 per cent per year (Urban and Vollrath 1984). If we use the measure of cropland as an indicator of natural resources used, this implies that the productivity of resources increased 1.69 per cent per year.

Some look at these trends with a sense that food production per caput is not rising fast enough and seek ways to accelerate it. And some look with a fear that food production per caput may decline; that the population may outrun the food supply. Beneath the trends is the relationship that the supply of food per caput increases with increasing resource availability and with increasing technology but decreases with increasing population. This relationship suggests three strategies for ensuring that food supplies per caput continue to increase and for averting a food crisis: reduce demand by slowing the rate of population growth, increase supply by increasing the rate of technological advance, and develop the natural resources.

These three strategies are supported by economic theory and by successful applications of the theory to regional and world food problems. This paper takes the position that the three strategies, while both empirically and theoretically correct, are inadequate because they oversimplify a many-sided problem. They do this in two ways. First, even when demand, resource availability/and technical advance are explicit in the analyses, other bases for growth are often omitted, such as regional variations and institutional arrangements. Second, the level of analysis is often too aggregative and thereby fails to consider resource or commodity substitution within any one of the heterogeneous categories, to consider changes in the structure of agriculture.

All too often, a single strategy is proposed to deal with a regional or world food crisis. One group may recommend: reduce the birth rate and limit population growth. Another says: develop the natural resources,

692

and conserve what we now have. And yet another proposes: introduce new technology. But economics tells us that a multidimensional problem requires a multidimensional solution, because one strategy may attain the goal defined in one of the dimensions, but it will probably widen the gap with respect to goals in other dimensions. Each basis for growth when taken alone as a basis for policy is found to bestow mixed blessings, but policies which bring into balance the several facets of agricultural growth can avert unintended side effects when dealing with future food crises. At the other extreme, the principle that everything is related to everything else can lead to multidimensional strategies so complicated that no-one can understand them, much less implement them. That will not do, either. In this paper, I emphasise two bases for agricultural growth in addition to the conventional demand, resource and technology bases. These are also found in the literature but do not receive as much attention as they deserve. The additional bases for growth are geographic and institutional. I also explore the benefits of further disaggregation within the heterogeneous categories. The objective of this paper is not to arrive at a new and more comprehensive growth theory, but rather to emphasise the multidimensional complexity of agricultural growth and to suggest some things one needs to think about as one tries to focus on the problem.

RESOURCE AVAILABILITY

The quantity of resources is considered the basis of growth by a number of economists; the idea is firmly embedded in the classical and neoclassical economic literature. Additions of land, labour and capital are what Kindleberger called 'the ingredients' of economic development.

Natural resources that are not reproducible are sometimes considered more important for growth than other resources. One can trace several threads in the literature on the role of natural resources in economic growth. One is the pessimistic view based on Malthus's concern that population is limited by the capacity to produce food, and that food is limited by diminishing returns to the fixed supply of land. Another is the optimistic view that the spectre of diminishing returns can continue to be sidestepped through science and innovation. A third view is one of silence and neglect: the role of natural resources has received little or no mention in several books, articles and models that purport to cover the field of economic growth.

The importance of natural resources relative to other farm inputs varies among regions and over time. Let me recount the experience in the United States during the past half century. The area of US cropland is about the same as it was 50 years ago, yet output has doubled. The potential to convert other lands to cropland has always been there, but during the past half century there was insufficient economic incentive to do so because there were other, more efficient ways to increase output. Production became more intensive on the same land area. Much of the expansion depended on irrigation of arid areas, but that is no longer a

major source of growth; the United States could double exports and feed
its growing population during the next three decades without additional
irrigation of arid areas but assisted instead by higher yielding varieties,
supplemental irrigation in humid areas, double cropping, changes in
management and ownership patterns, regional shifts in location of
production, resource substitution, and institutional change. This is not to
say there will be no resource problems; there will. But the emphasis
appears to be on maintaining the resources now in use, conserving them,
and replacing them as we can so that we are sure to have at least as much
in several decades as now. The country is large, and losses in capacity in
some regions probably can be offset by gains in others. The natural
resource base is an important determinant of regional growth but a
considerable amount of growth and change can be derived from a fixed
resource base.

US farmers are using more purchased farm inputs and less labour than
they were on about the same amount of land, although there has been a
high degree of labour retention during the past decade. Output increases
are associated not with more land and labour but with more purchased
farm inputs. These purchases, in turn, are associated with new
technology, and their supply is relatively elastic. As the added cost of
using a scarce resource rises, other, less scarce resources are substituted
for it. This principle of substitution is well understood in economic
theory, but it is not well represented in most of the models economists use
to describe and analyse prospective growth in food production because
the models are too aggregated or because they assume fixed proportions.
Lutton (1984) illustrates how important the principle of substitution can
be in avoiding a food crisis.

TECHNOLOGY

Technology and innovation are often seen as the source of growth.
Kaldor and Mirrlees (1962) captured the view of many, both in and out of
economics, when they said 'technical progress ... is the main engine of
economic growth'.

Among the benefits of technical advance are: increased income to the
first farmers in a country to adopt successfully new ways of doing things;
comparative advantage in international trade to the agricultural exporting country that develops and adopts new farming ideas; and the
possibility of feeding more people from the same natural resources. But
technology is not an unmixed blessing. Cochrane said 'technological
advances puts farmers on a treadmill' (1965, page 66).

Once enough farmers have adopted an output increasing practice and
the produce is sold into inelastic markets, the increase in profits
envisioned before the technology was adopted can be more than offset by
falling prices received (Van Chantfort 1985). The long-run advantage is
to the consumer who buys more food at a lower price, or to the natural
resource owner who realises capital gains from rising resource values.

Technical advance can widen the gap between rich and poor regions by working to the disadvantage of those who continue to use traditional practices. It puts agriculture in a cost/price squeeze that hurts most those who do not adopt the new and more efficient techniques – even subsistence farmers eventually face higher opportunity costs for the resources they use. The widening gap has been observed both among nations and among regions within a nation (Todd and Simpson 1983).

Capital intensive technology is appropriate for some regions, including parts of the United States, but does not necessarily serve the needs of others (Fern and Cooke 1982). When high technology is inappropriate it is likely to inhibit economic development in the long run. It will be inappropriate, for example, if it is geared to large-scale production and the local region is suited to a smaller scale. It may fail to use indigenous resources. The multiplier benefits of inappropriately high technology are likely to ripple through economic space to other regions, not through geographic space within the region. It thereby induces leakages for imports of both production and consumption goods with the result of fewer domestic jobs and worsened balance of payments. It tends to skew the income distribution by helping some but not others. The products of 'high-tech' agriculture sometimes do not meet local needs, they are consumed by the local wealthy or are for export. There are social consequences to technical change – social disruption and institutional breakdown – that disenfranchise people both from production and from consumption. At the other extreme, appropriate technology is not necessarily 'low-tech'. For example low technologies are inappropriate which merely take advantage of low-wage labour and make the local region dependent on a distant place (Ndongko and Anyang 1981). The difficulties which accompany the loss of local control over natural resources are considered below in the section on regions.

While adoption of appropriate technology – whether high or low-tech – is an important determinant of agricultural growth, considerable growth and change can be generated in a region even when technology is held constant.

DEMAND

Expansion in the markets for the products of a region was an important aspect of the classical economic model, but it was never really understood as a basis for growth until Keynes set aside Say's Law and considered demand-side economics. Now, from a mixture of macro, micro, and regional economics we get several ideas about demand as a basis for economic growth; regions grow through mutual exchange based on comparative advantage; regions grow through income associated with export multipliers; regions grow through local inducements to autonomous demand as a result of, for example, expansionary monetary and fiscal policies; and regions grow through demand originating in a single, driving sector (or growth pole), which may or may not be agricultural.

A substantial portion of total growth in world food demand in coming decades will be associated with population growth in the rural sectors of the less developed countries (Schutjer, Stokes and Poindexter 1983). However, effective demand depends not only on population but also on purchasing power per caput. Regions with faster growing, lower-income populations tend to have food deficits while those with slower growing, higher-income populations tend to produce agricultural surpluses.

The development of natural resources has been found to affect not only the supply of but also the demand for food. Schutjer and others found that population fertility increases: with more access to land because larger families can lease and work larger farms; with less ownership of land because children substitute for land as a source of security; with less adoption of labour-saving technology because, again, larger families are needed to work larger farms; with more dependence on urban labour markets because some members of the family can bring in off-farm income while others care for the farm; and, with lower family income because another child is not looked upon as another mouth to feed in the short run, but as another source of family income in the long run. In this way, natural resource development can affect the demand for farm products by contributing to increased income per caput and to reduced population growth.

REGIONS

Siebert (1969) said, 'growth occurs in space; it is influenced by the spatial structure and it has a feedback upon the economic landscape'. There are severe food shortages in some regions while surpluses are produced in others. How a region and its agriculture grow depends on what kind of region it is and where it is relative to other regions.

The idea of regional analysis caught hold in many professions during the 1960s. In the United States, it resulted in several new agencies to implement social programmes. These agencies included the Economic Development Administration (EDA), the Appalachian Region Commission (ARC) and other regional commissions, and the Office of Economic Opportunity (OEO). The US Department of Agriculture applied regional analysis to its rural development programmes and regional ideas were introduced into political programmes: growth centres, growth poles, base multipliers, plant location and job creation in depressed areas, and trickle down progress, to name a few. But because of oversimplification of complex ideas and because of false political hopes, the enthusiasm for regional thinking waned during the 1970s and 1980s, at least among the easy converts. The regional agencies were either closed or scaled down. Fewer questions originating with programme administrators were addressed to regional analysts; fewer books and articles were written on regional economics; and fewer students enrolled in regional economics classes. Analysis of spaceless regions as trading partners continued to be important, but analysis of geographic regions, with natural resource endowments that affected location and growth, slowed.

Let me give one example of how the oversimplification of valid and complex ideas in regional economics led to the unfortunate de-emphasis on regional analysis as a basis for public policy. The example is taken from Higgins (1983). Consider the idea of a growth pole. Growth poles are defined in economic space and innovation ripples through economic links that need not be spatially contiguous. Contrast this with the idea of a central place. The hierarchy of central places and their hinterlands is defined in geographic space. Economic change in the central place ripples through geographic links to places lower in the hierarchy and to the periphery or hinterland. Programmes based on a confusion of these two ideas can be expected to fail to attain their intended goals; the gains intended for the local hinterlands were received instead by distant central places.

Despite the loss of faith in the regional programmes of the 1960s, regional perspective on natural resource use and food production still makes a difference. Every economic event happens in some place and where it happens affects how it happens. Regional problems abound in agriculture with respect to access to markets, to natural resources, and to regional governments. Regional analysis still has much to say about growth, development, and progress. This applies both to less developed nations relative to more developed ones, and to less developed parts of either kind of nation (Todd and Simpson 1983).

There are two major threads weaving through regional economics: one focuses on the economics of the geographic location of an activity, the other on the influence of regionalisation on economic activity. Location economics, for example, explains the relocation of some corn production in the United States during the seventies. Export markets for corn were burgeoning and the Corn Belt was supplying all it efficiently could. The favourable prices induced increased corn production in the South where yields were lower but the location was closer to shipping ports. This had two effects on aggregate performance indicators: first, more corn was produced and shipped and farm income increased; second, efficiency appeared to lessen because average US yields decreased as output from the faster-growing but lower-yielding South was averaged in with output from the more stable but higher-yielding Corn Belt.

As an economy grows, each of its functional economic areas can be expected to grow (or decline) differently. Regional variations in natural ·features such as arable land, water, and shipping ports are enough to guarantee that. In addition a number of economic forces differentiate regions even when natural features are equal. Some of these forces are cohesive and lead to formation of central places and to urban-oriented functional economic areas. These cohesive forces include transportation costs, risk avoidance, economies of scale, externalities, and agglomerative efficiencies. Schultz pointed out that agriculture thrives when it is affected by these cohesive forces. Other forces are dispersive and lead to formation of hinterlands to central places and to rural-oriented functional economic areas. These dispersive forces include access to scattered resources or markets, access to amenities, avoidance of high rent, diminishing returns, and personal preferences. The agriculture in such areas tends to be relatively extensive. The interplay among a diversity of regions helps to determine the growth of economic activities, including the production, distribution, and consumption of the world's food supply.

INSTITUTIONS

Group behaviour for setting regional goals and resolving conflicts creates an institutional framework that affects regional growth. North and Thomas (1973) said, 'efficient organization is the key to growth'. A number of economic situations call for explicit institution building. Among them are: 1 Competitive market forces may result in inequities and society becomes dissatisfied with the *status quo*. 2 The economy may not be converging on an equilibrium but may be observed, in fact, to be diverging. 3 Monopoly power may override competitive forces. 4 Uncertainty, or imperfect knowledge, may interfere with competitive choice. 5 Market failure may arise for public goods that are not distributable by the same institutions that distribute private goods. 6 Conflicts related to disagreements on goals and on distributive justice among individuals may not be resolved by market forces.

Henry George (1929, pp. 126–8) was one of the first to note that recognition of institutional arrangements explained a major difficulty in the Malthusian view. In reviewing Malthus's explanation of the Irish potato famine, George pointed out that in an earlier period there were only half as many people on the same land using the same technology of food production. They therefore had the capacity then to feed twice as many people as there were, yet they had a famine then also. George attributed the famine not to the limitations of land and technology, but to the institutional arrangements for distributing food. The landlords always took as much food from the tenants as they could, leaving the tenants close to subsistence. Under this arrangement, there was no incentive, says George, for a tenant to produce more than the minimum that would keep the landlord from evicting the tenant's family. One or two years of adverse weather would deplete reserves and induce famine regardless of the rate of population growth or of advance in resource productivity.

Institutional arrangements affect the allocation of natural resources among alternative uses. Bromley and Chapagain (1984) examine economic growth which involves moving community control functions from the hinterland to the central place. As a consequence, decisions affecting the hinterland no longer met local needs and objectives. They give the example of the nationalisation of all forest lands in Nepal in 1957. This upset centuries of traditional patterns of resource control and shifted control to the government from the village so that there were different priorities, objectives, and means taken. Central policies threatened not only people but also natural resources. However, Barker (1984) questions whether the village can effectively control and manage resources. These authors disagree about what institutional arrangement is best, but they agree that an appropriate institutional arrangement is essential for using natural resources in the context of economic growth and change.

Growing regions need to compete succesfully in open, interregional or world markets. These markets are expanding and provide a basis for growth for some regions. In general, the market institutions are not free. They incorporate non-price barriers and government intervention. Government intervention can be intermittent and is subject to policy reversals. Consequently, government intervention has become a major source of price volatility in international food markets. Market volatility induces risk-averse farmers to curtail production. This decreases the supply of food, influences the allocation of natural resources, and reduces the use of productive capacity. As a region grows, exposure to markets adds risks not experienced by farmers in a self-sufficient agriculture. These risks are increased when the country becomes an open economy dependent on world markets. Shortrun concerns for productivity and income that overlook longrun concerns for stability and sustainability do not serve the needs of farmers; particularly smaller farmers (Johnson 1984).

Even when farmers' commodity markets function competitively, their factor markets may not. For example, allocation of water among various farm and nonfarm uses in the United States is determined by laws, regulations, and customs affecting water rights, and the resulting institutional allocation of water among alternative uses is different than would obtain under free markets. Institutions need to be developed to share risk and to help regions grow.

STRUCTURE

Global and regional analyses tend to focus on aggregates. We talk about numbers of people without reference to changes in the demographic composition of the population. We talk about food consumption without distinguishing crop products from livestock products. We talk about the level of resource use without distinguishing among land, labour, and capital resources. We talk about area of cropland without reference to changes in soil quality, or to regional location of land development relative to land retirement.

Changes within heterogeneous aggregates can be important in understanding and dealing with food problems. Natural resource limitations can induce substitution of other inputs. Food shortages can induce changes in the mix and location of commodities consumed. Increases in production from a given quantity of cropland are different when farms are increasing in size and concentration, as they were in the United States after the Second World War, than when the size and

700   *Clark Edwards*

distribution are relatively stable, as they have been during the past decade. Changes within the aggregates can be more important than changes of the aggregate levels in explaining changes in performance of the farm sector.

Changes in productivity are usually associated with technology. At the firm level, this is a natural way to think about productivity. However, in aggregate analysis, measures of productivity can change even when technology does not. The measures change when the proportions of farms in alternative technological situations change. For example, changes in the commodity mix toward more livestock and less crop production tends to increase aggregate measures of productivity even though technology does not change in either enterprise because of the higher input requirements per unit of crop output. More high yielding wheat on irrigated land in Arizona increases the national average wheat yield even though technology does not change either in Arizona or Kansas. Corn yields in the United States are higher on larger farms than on smaller ones, and on farms with a higher volume of sales. Tenant and part owner farms have higher yields than full owner farms. Incorporated farms have higher yields than unincorporated ones. Farm operators between the ages of 35 to 44 have higher yields than those who are older or younger. And farms specialising in cash grain production have higher grain yields than farms in other industrial classifications. The flow of output and income for the farm sector is, in part, a function of structure, of the composition of the aggregates. Highly aggregated models fail to describe or explain adequately the interplay of natural resources, technology and demand with other factors affecting regional agricultural growth.

CONCLUSIONS

World and regional food problems are multidimensional. Too often, the proposed solutions are one-dimensional. One group calls for conservation and development of natural resources. Another promotes invention and dissemination of new technology. A third seeks decrease in demand for food through population control. Each view has sound theoretical and empirical support and each has been found workable for specific situations. Yet each oversimplifies. However, even reconciling and co-ordinating the views of all three could still result in oversimplification because there are yet other, less frequently heard dimensions to the problem. Agricultural enterprises can relocate among regions, or induce modifications in the structure and character of the region in which they are located, as limits are approached within existing regional patterns. New institutions, including government policies and trade relations, can change limits to growth. Agriculture is a flexible and resilient industry which, when it approaches a limit to growth, can, through resource and product substitution, or through regional and institutional change, grow in a new direction. It can continue to grow on a fixed natural resource base by substituting reproducible resources for non-reproducible ones. There is a great diversity of agriculture beneath the aggregate indices we usually examine, a diversity of people, places, resources, and technical and social ways of doing things. Changes beneath the aggregates are recognised in aggregative models as changes in the structure of the farm sector. Food crises continue to occur. Perhaps we can discover better ways to deal with them if we can find ways to incorporate structural changes in regional and institutional patterns into the more usual analyses of markets, technology and natural resources to describe and explain world and regional food problems.

REFERENCES

Barker, Randolph, 'Renewable Resource Management in Developing Country Agriculture: Discussion', *American Journal of Agricultural Economics*, vol. 66, no. 5, December 1984, pp. 885–87.

Bromley, Daniel W., and Chapagain, Devendra P., 'The Village Against the Center: Resource Depletion in South Asia', *American Journal of Agricultural Economics*, vol. 66, no. 5, December 1984, pp. 868–73.

Cochrane, Willard, W., *The City Man's Guide to the Farm Problem*, University of Minnesota Press, 1965.

Economic Research Service, *World Indices of Agricultural and Food Production, 1974–83*, US Department of Agriculture, Statistical Bulletin no. 710, July 1984.

Fern, J. and Cooke, Philip, 'Dependency, Supply Factors and Uneven Development in Wales and Other Problem Regions', *Regional Studies*, vol. 16, no. 3, June 1982, pp. 211–27.

George, Henry, *Progress and Poverty*, Random House, New York, 1929 (First edition, 1879).

Higgins, Benjamin, 'From Growth Poles to Systems of Interactions in Space', *Growth and Change*, October 1983.

Johnson III, Sam H., 'Temporal Land Resource Concerns and Farming Systems Research: Chiang Mai Valley, Northern Thailand', *Land Economics*, vol. 60 no. 2, May 1984, pp. 202–10.

Kaldor, N. and Mirrlees, J. A., 'A New Model of Economic Growth', *Review of Economic Studies*, vol. 29, 1962, pp. 174–90.

Keynes, John Maynard, *The General Theory of Employment, Interest, and Money*, Harcourt, Brace, New York, 1936.

Kindleberger, C. P., *Economic Development*, McGraw-Hill, New York, 1958.

Lutton, Thomas, 'The Elasticity of Substitution and Land Use in Agricultural Production: A Cause for Optimism?' *Agricultural Economics Research*, vol. 36, no. 3, Summer 1984.

Malthus, Thomas Robert, *An Essay on Population*, Dutton, New York, 1914 (first edition, 1798).

Misra, R. P., (ed.), *Humanizing Development; Essays on People, Space, and Development, in Honor of Masahiko Honjo*, Maruzen Asia, Singapore, 1981.

Ndongko, Wilfred A., and Anyang, Sunday O. 'The Concept of "Appropriate Technology": An Appraisal from the Third World', *Monthly Review*, vol. 32, no. 9, February 1981, pp. 35–43.

North, Douglass C and Thomas, R. P., *The Rise of the Western World: A New Economic History*, Cambridge University Press, 1973.

Schultz, T. W., *Agriculture in an Unstable Economy*, McGraw Hill, New York, 1945.

Schutjer, Wayne, A., Stokes, C. Shannon and Poindexter, John R., 'Farm Size, Land Ownership, and Fertility in Rural Egypt', *Land Economics*, vol. 59, no. 4, November 1983. pp. 393–403.

Siebert, H., *Regional Economic Growth: Theory and Policy*, International Textbook, Scranton, Pa., 1969.

Todd, Daniel and Simpson, Jamie A., 'The Appropriate Technology Question in a Regional Context', *Growth and Change*, October 1983.

Urban, Francis and Vollrath, Thomas, *Patterns and Trends in World Agricultural Land Use*, FAER-198, United States Department of Agriculture, Economic Research Service, April 1984.

Van Chantfort, Eric, 'Technology: The Treadmill of Agriculture?', *Farm Line*, US Department of Agriculture, vol. 6, no. 6, June 1985, pp. 12–14.

SCOTT SIMONS

Land Fragmentation in Developing Countries: The Optimal Choice and Policy Implications

INTRODUCTION

In this paper, a model is developed which interprets configuration of farmlands (fragmentation/consolidation) as an economic phenomenon. Many previous studies considered configuration of farmlands as a socio-cultural characteristic with individual farmers powerless to alter configurations. In fact, farmers frequently are able to make adjustments in their land holdings. In such cases, the persistence of fragmented lands represents a decision by farmers that the benefits to consolidating lands are less than the costs incurred by farming scattered plots.

The model presented here considers possible production advantages as well as disadvantages with fragmented land but focuses on farms facing disadvantages. Consolidating lands thus raises short-run farm profits. The model breaks consolidation costs into capital and transaction cost components. Farmers maximising wealth over time will choose optimal quantities of land to consolidate in each period moving them to optimal levels of land fragmentation/consolidation. Optimal levels of fragmentation may differ across farms since individual economic conditions affect each farmer's costs.

Fragmented farmlands are often considered an impediment to agricultural development. Thus several countries have initiated public consolidation programmes. This paper discusses the efficiency of such programmes in light of the optimisation model presented. Alternative policies which affect individual costs and benefits of consolidation are also examined.

The first two sections of this paper provide some background to the fragmentation problem. Section 1 describes how it originates and why fragmentation is a problem. Section 2 identifies the relevant benefits and costs of consolidating fragmented parcels. The model which yields the farmer's decision on consolidation is presented in section 3. This section also summarises how economic factors influence optimal consolidation levels. Section 4 discusses the public role in influencing land consolidation.

703

1. THE FRAGMENTATION PROBLEM

Land fragmentation is not unique to any specific region of the world. For countries as diverse as Pakistan, Peru, and Syria, the average farm consists of at least four separate land parcels. The FAO's 1970 World Census of Agriculture reported 80 per cent of agricultural holdings worldwide were fragmented (FAO 1981). How farmlands initially became fragmented remains an open question. Many cite the influence of external factors in explaining fragmentation (e.g. Binns 1950, Srivastava 1970). The best received among such factors is an equity oriented inheritance custom where land parcels of differing qualities in the original farm are divided equally among heirs. A second source of fragmentation is a settlement pattern where as families expand, they acquire new plots on the fringes of cultivated lands. Over several generations, a considerable number of parcels could accumulate as available lands become more distant.

The literature dealing with land scattering in medieval Europe focuses on benefits which may lead farmers to fragment lands (Fenoaltea 1976; McClosky 1975). By producing on lands with varying characteristics, farmers may lower exposure to risk or enable a more intensive use of family resources. This is possible if inputs are required at different times. In such cases, farmers gain with fragmentation. However, a farmer who later switches crops or production techniques may no longer obtain benefits and still be left with scattered holdings.

For whatever reason it arises, farming on fragmented lands introduces additional production costs compared to production on contiguous lands. A principal source of extra cost is the need for additional labour and land. Labour time is consumed in travelling and in transporting inputs and outputs to and from scattered plots. Extra labour may also be necessary to supervise crops and livestock adequately on scattered land. More land may be required to compensate for greater 'wastage' in boundary hedges and corners with scattered land.

A second source of greater production expense is that some cost reducing or more productive techniques are not feasible on small and scattered plots. Irrigation and drainage, for example, involve large fixed costs per parcel and are not justified financially on small parcels. Fragmentation also complicates pest control since successful control becomes dependent on the activities of neighbouring farms.

This paper, being concerned with the consolidation issue, focuses on instances where the costs of fragmentation outweigh any benefits. Only fragmentation imposing net costs on farmers is considered. The intention here is not to imply that possible benefits are insignificant but to simplify the discussion for analysis of consolidation policies. Thus, the effective point of departure for this paper is that a large number of farmers are producing on fragmented lands and incurring the consequent added costs.[1]

2. LAND CONSOLIDATION

Exogenous sources of fragmentation such as those mentioned above only initiate the fragmention of land. To explain its persistence, obstacles to consolidation must be examined. Obstacles give rise to adjustment costs which inhibit the consolidation of land. Without these costs, landowners would immediately consolidate to eliminate the fragmentation induced costs. Two characteristics of the economic environment which permit the persistence of fragmentation are the scarcity of farm land and thin land markets. Scarcity of land impedes consolidation by limiting farm expansion in any one year while thin markets restrict opportunities for exchange of parcels. These characteristics are typical of many developing economies.

The 'effect of land scarcity is that prices for both fragmented and contiguous land are high. Fragmented land represents a valuable asset even with its associated higher production costs. Land scarcity also precludes the possibility of acquiring inexpensive contiguous lands in a frontier settlement area.

The high price of land, in turn, restricts expansions of total acreage in any year. Land acquisition is particularly difficult for small farms with limited capital stocks and limited access to capital. This problem is compounded by land being the principal long-term store of wealth in many regions. The alternative of wealth holding in livestock is complicated on small scattered plots since surrounding farmers' plots restrict access. Also, with high rates of physical depreciation, storage of farm output is only feasible in the short run. The combined effect of high land prices and limited capital means that total farm acreage is relatively stable. Though some farmers may have significant non-land assets and some farms may be expanding, incorporating these features into the model does not alter the conclusions.[2]

Since expansion possibilities are limited, land is most readily consolidated through the simultaneous sale and purchase of fragmented and contiguous parcels. Sales must finance all purchases. In such cases, the total land stock remains fixed except for compensations for variation in land characteristics. For the consolidating farmer, however, since production costs are lower on contiguous land, the exchange represents an improvement in land 'quality'. Note that this quality characteristic is associated with land configuration only. It is tied to how the land is used and thus differs from other features such as drainage, topography, and soil nutrients that are quality characteristics physically linked to a given parcel.

The two types of land, contiguous (A^c) and fragmented (A^f), can be represented in a production function:

$$y = f(x, A^c, A^f) \qquad (1)$$

where y is farm output and x is a vector of non-land inputs. The first and second partial derivatives of f(.) with respect to its arguments are positive, and negative respectively. Each input has a positive but decreasing marginal product. If farm sizes are held roughly constant, the consolidation actions increase A^c by reducing A^f.

The growth in contiguous land acreage (A^c) can be described with a transformation function:

$$\dot{A}^c = g(T) \quad T \geqslant 0 \tag{2}$$

where T is the quantity of fragmented land sold and is the farmer's choice variable. The first partial with respect to T (g_T) is positive and will be greater than, less than, or equal to 1 depending on physical quality characteristics of the parcels exchanged. If the fragmented parcel is superior to the contiguous parcel in terms of soil quality, for example, $0 < g_T < 1$. If the contiguous parcel is superior then $g_T > 1$.

The second important feature of rural economies in many developing countries is that land markets are extremely thin. With infrequent transactions of land and with a static rental market, it is difficult to acquire the appropriate contiguous plot and to sell a fragmented plot in any single period. This transaction difficulty is captured by introducing a premium per unit of land transformed, $\alpha(T)$. Larger transactions aggravate the difficulty, thus, the transformation premium is increasing, $\alpha'(T) > 0$. Increasing transaction costs may take the form of incurring higher search costs, paying a cash premium to transactors, or buying a broker's services. To summarise, the local economic environment may impose constraints on consolidating fragmented land. Consequences of these constraints are illustrated in the two components of consolidation costs. In an environment of land scarcity with little non-land wealth, direct capital costs of acquired acreage are paid for by liquidating fragmented parcels. This is shown in the transformation function above. Additional indirect costs, which accrue due to thin land markets, enter as a premium for market transactions. Unlike the capital cost, the premium is paid out of current farm income.

Consolidation costs are presented here in the context of private land ownership with a market for land. This does not imply that the following model is irrelevant for countries with differing economic structures and ownership patterns. However, the costs of consolidation would then have to be redefined in light of those economic conditions. Policy implications, of course, will differ also.

Aside from the monetary costs described above, a wide range of non-monetary elements may enter the consolidation decision. Farmers may feel emotionally attached to land they have worked for many years or may be reluctant to sell inheritances. Such non-monetary attributes of given parcels of land are omitted from the profit maximising objective presented below. A broader objective function may be employed to capture non-monetary components of utility. The intention of using a profit maximising model (below) is not to subordinate these non-monetary considerations but to demonstrate that there may be financial advantages to fragmented holdings.

3. OPTIMAL LAND CONSOLIDATION

Farmers make two types of decisions regarding their farms. First, farmers maximise current profits by choosing an optimal vector of variable inputs given input and output prices and a fixed land input:

$$\pi(p,w,A^c,A^f) = \max_x pf(x,A^c,A^f) - wx \qquad (3)$$

where p and w are the output and input price vectors. The profit function (π) has the usual properties with respect to p and w. Also, π is increasing and concave with respect to A^c and A^f from the earlier assumptions of f(.). The solution to (3) is the vector of optimal inputs $x^*(p,w,A^c,A^f)$ for that period. As stated in section 2, attention is directed in this paper to farms experiencing net costs of fragmentation. Thus, the predetermined level of land fragmentation affects profits principally by raising production costs. For two farms A_0 and A_1 equal in sizes of total farm lands, but differing in configuration, $A^f_0 > A^f_1$ and $A^c_0 < A^c_1$:

$$\pi(p,w,A^c_0,A^f_0) \leq \pi(p,w,A^c_1,A^f_1) \qquad (3)$$

indicating that short-run farm profits are greater with higher levels of contiguous land.

The second type of decision concerns the stock of land. In the long run, the fixity of land configurations is relaxed and farmers choose the rate of land transformation which maximises wealth over all future time periods. An optimal control framework is used here to convert stock benefits to flow benefits and derive optimising conditions for both types of decisions. The value function in each period is current maximised profits less current consolidation expenditure. The discounted value function is maximised over time subject to the equation of motion for the stock of consolidated land:

$$J(p,w,r,\bar{A}^c,\bar{A}^f) = \max_T \int_0^\infty e^{-rt}[\pi(p,w,A^c,A^f) - \alpha(T)T]dt : \dot{A}^c = g(T) \qquad (4)$$

Equation (5) is the Hamiltonian of (4) with λ as the co-state variable. Equations (6) and (7) are necessary conditions for maximisation (notation for time periods is suppressed):

$$H = e^{-rt}[\pi(p,w,A^c,A^f) - \alpha(T)T] + \lambda g(T) \qquad (5)$$

$$\frac{\partial H}{\partial T} = e^{-rt}\left[\pi_{Ac}\frac{\partial A^c}{\partial T} + \pi_{Af}\frac{\partial A^f}{\partial T} - \alpha - \alpha_T T\right] + \lambda g_T = 0 \qquad (6)$$

$$\frac{\partial H}{\partial A^c} = e^{-rt}\pi_{Ac} = -\dot{\lambda} \qquad (7)$$

Equation (6) written as (6') is the decision rule for selecting T:

$$-\lambda = e^{-rt} \left[\pi_{Ac} \frac{\partial A^c}{\partial T} + \pi_{Af} \frac{\partial A^f}{\partial T} - \alpha(1 + \varepsilon(T)) \right] (1/g_T). \qquad (6')$$

The bracketed term is the net marginal cost of transforming land. Transformation adds to A^c stock but reduces A^f. The net effect on current profits is positive due to lower production costs. The transaction premium is expressed in elasticity form: $\alpha(1 + \varepsilon(T))$, where $\varepsilon(T)$ is the elasticity of the transaction premium and is positive. The bracketed marginal cost is discounted by e^{-rt} and scaled by $1/g_r$. The scaling factor accounts for varying physical qualities of land in the exchange of A^f for A^c. If land qualities are equal, $g_T = 1$. Thus, the left hand side of $(6')$ is the present value of the cost of adding to the stock of A^c.

The farmer selects the path of T so that the present value of cost equals $-\lambda$ where λ is the marginal benefit of adding to the A^c stock. This marginal benefit is the present value of all future benefits to be obtained due to an increase in A^c. This is analogous on the benefit side to the concept of user cost.

Equation (7) states that gain in current benefits due to increases in the stock of A^c must equal $-\dot{\lambda}$, the negative change in benefits, in each period. With a given rate of $\dot{\lambda}$, (7) is a choice rule for the optimal level of A^c. Solving necessary conditions $(6')$ and (7) simultaneously yields the optimising condition for the wealth maximisation problem (4):

$$\pi_{Ac}/r = - \left[\pi_{Ac} \frac{\partial A^c}{\partial T} + \pi_{Af} \frac{\partial A^f}{\partial T} - \alpha(1 + \varepsilon(T)) \right] (1/g_T). \qquad (8)$$

Benefits derived from adding to the A^c stock are set equal to the costs of additions, thus, (8) is a decision rule stating that in each period the farmer should choose a rate of transformation so that the marginal benefit, which is constant in any one period, equals the marginal cost of transformation, which is increasing in T. Solving (8) for T gives the decision rule:

$$T = h(A^c, A^f, p, w, r).$$

Equation (8) may also be solved for the optimal level of consolidation. Benefits to consolidation fall and costs rise with increasing A^c. This can be demonstrated by differentiating the benefit side and the cost side of (8) with respected to A^c:

$$\pi_{AcAc}/r \text{ and } - \left[\pi_{AcAc} \frac{\partial A^c}{\partial T} + \pi_{AfAc} \frac{\partial A^f}{\partial T} \right] (1/g_T) \qquad (8')$$

$$(-) \qquad\qquad (-) \quad (+) \qquad\qquad (+)$$

where the level of A^c does not affect the transformation function, the rate of change of A^c and A^f, nor the transaction premium and its elasticity:

$$g_{TAc} = \frac{\partial^2 A^c}{\partial T \partial A^c} = \frac{\partial^2 A^f}{\partial T \partial A^f} = \frac{\partial \alpha}{\partial A^c} = \frac{\partial \varepsilon}{\partial A^c} = 0.$$

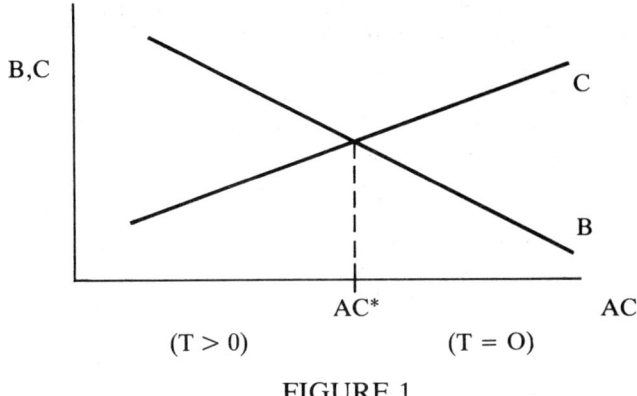

FIGURE 1

The terms in (8') can be signed as indicated noting that the profit function is concave in A^c. The sign of the cross partial $(\pi_{A_cA_f})$ is ambiguous but it can be assumed to be zero.

The optimal level of consolidation (A^{c*}) is attained when marginal benefits equal marginal costs as shown in Figure 1. The marginal benefit and marginal cost curves (B, C) are the left and right hand sides of (8) respectively. To the left of A^{c*}, benefits of consolidating exceed costs and it pays the farmer to invest in land consolidation; $T > 0$. To the right of A^{c*}, the farmer abstains from transforming fragmented lands; $T = 0$. The relevant region for consolidation is limited to $A^c \leq A^{c*}$ since costs of consolidation exceed benefits when $A^c > A^{c*}$. Consolidation will not be observed beyond A^{c*}. However, if the initial stock equals or exceeds A^{c*}, that initial A^c is optimal and no land adjustments occur.[3]

The model above indicates that fragmented land holdings may be an optimal configuration of land for farmers given the economic environment. With high costs of consolidation and relatively low benefits, the efficient decision is to forego consolidation. A number of factors in the economic environment may influence these costs and benefits and thus affect levels of farm fragmentation. Several factors which lead to higher levels of optimal fragmentation and which characterise the economic environment in some developing countries are described here:

1. The first factor is the tendency to underprice agricultural outputs. Low prices suppress marginal profits of the farm sector and benefit urban consumers. Low marginal profits of land reduce both benefits and costs in equation (8); however, the net effect of low output prices is a fall in benefits which in turn increases fragmentation. ·

2. Marginal profits are also suppressed by weak transportation and marketing infrastructures, and by unavailability of inputs which are not locally produced. Such constraints increase the costs of producing any given level of output. Low output prices and high costs also diminish incentives to invest in other productivity boosting activities. Foregone investment then lowers marginal profits in future periods.

3. A third factor raising fragmentation levels is the high interest rates typically faced by small farmers in developing countries. High r lowers consolidation benefits on the left-hand side of (8). Governments frequently set low interest rate ceilings on institutional lending causing available credit to be rationed among demanders. Credit institutions often lend first to large farmers and non-agricultural borrowers, forcing small farmers who obtain credit to pay considerably higher rates in a secondary credit market. Small farm lending is assumed by credit institutions to entail higher administrative costs and collection risks.

4. A final factor increasing fragmentation in the small farm sector is the thinness of land markets which is typical in rural areas. Thin land markets give rise to higher transaction premiums in consolidation costs and greater premium elasticities. Each serves to increase consolidation cost in (8).

4. PUBLIC LAND CONSOLIDATION POLICIES

The optimal levels of land consolidation established in section 3 are for private farmers who maximise individual wealth. Government planners operate with a wider mandate and maximise social welfare to obtain the socially optimal consolidation level. The social optimum may be higher than that chosen by individual farmers due to positive externalities of private consolidation. Externalities may include: (1) social benefits to higher output such as increasing supply or reducing demand for foreign exchange and (2) social benefits to raising earnings of low-income farmers.

Agricultural output may produce benefits which are not reflected entirely in market prices. If the output is exported, an added benefit is foreign exchange earnings. More important, many developing countries must import food to make up for stagnant production. Output gains may conserve scarce foreign exchange by reducing these food imports. In either case, greater land consolidation adds to a country's production potential.

Consolidation can reduce income disparities if public consolidation programmes are aimed at poor farmers with fragmented lands. Recipient farmers will increase consolidation obtaining higher income streams. In areas where fragmented farms are concentrated among low-income farmers, consolidation need not be aimed to reduce inequalities.

Social optima may also exceed private optima if the social discount rate is lower than private discount rates. Substituting a lower discount rate raises the net present value of consolidation which in turn leads to higher equilibrium levels of land consolidation.

Several governments have initiated public land consolidation programmes to reduce high observed levels of fragmentation. However, most programmes appear to overlook the fact that positive levels of fragmentation may be optimal and that pre-programme land configurations may not be grossly inefficient. The result is consolidation programmes which maximise land transformations rather than maximising net social returns. Post programme equilibria may be then characterised by both over and under consolidation. Farmers not affected directly by the programme will remain at private optima below the social optimum while recipients of government assistance will often have more contiguous land than it was optimal to invest in.

An alternative approach to move consolidation levels toward the social optimum is to use government resources to relax some of the constraints which inhibit private consolidation. Government actions could include policies to raise prices of farm outputs and to lower interest rates in the agricultural sector. Financial resources could be devoted to improving physical infrastructures in the country. Lower transportation costs raise returns to producers through both output and input prices. Supply of inputs can also be increased and standardised. The government can also finance research institutions concentrating on small farm needs. Finally, policies to strengthen land markets could stimulate private consolidation. Government actions could include clearly defining and enforcing property rights to land and improving the quantity and quality of information about land and land exchanges.

Each of the above policies has been proposed in the development literature as a tool to attain other farm sector goals. For example, higher output prices and land security improve production incentives. Also, infrastructural and research investments can increase farm output and incomes. The policies mentioned here influence consolidation only indirectly by altering the economic environment of farmers. Thus, the goal of increasing private consolidation can be achieved simultaneously with other agricultural development objectives.

CONCLUSION

This paper uses an optimal control approach to model choices of land consolidation by farmers. Given decreasing benefits and increasing costs the optimal level of consolidation could be less than total consolidation of land holdings. This optimal level is sensitive to a number of characteristics of the economic environment.

The fact that socially optimal levels of consolidation may exceed private optima justifies public policies to stimulate private consolidation decisions. This study identifies several policies which help to move private optima closer to social optima by altering the farmer's economic environment. By encouraging consolidation with policies based on a model of maximising behaviour by farmers, governments could move toward the social optimum without introducing new inefficiencies. Such an approach differs significantly from that of traditional consolidation programmes which ignore possible benefits to fragmentation.

NOTES

[1]A broader model whhich jointly considers benefits and costs of scattered lands is

presented in Simons, 'Optimal Land Adjustments: A Dynamic Model of Fragmentation and Consolidation' (1985). The broader model yields a decision rule without the asymmetric property described above.
[2]Actually, marginal expansion of land is another origin of farm fragmentation. When contiguous parcels are unavailable, expansion is only possible by increasing the number of parcels per holding.
[3]The broader model in Simons (1985) endogenises fragmentation as well as consolidation and thus is not limited to unidirectional adjustments.

REFERENCES

1. Binns, B. O., *The Consolidation of Fragmented Agricultural Holdings*, FAO Agricultural Studies no. 11, Washington, DC., 1950.
2. Fenoaltea, S., 'Risk, Transaction Costs, and the Organization of Medieval Agriculture', *Explorations in Economic History*, vol. 13, 1976, pp. 129–75.
3. Food and Agricultural Organization of the United Nations, *1970 World Census of Agriculture: Analysis and International Comparison of the Results*, Rome, 1981.
4. Kamien, M. I. and Schwartz, N. L., *Dynamic Optimization*, North Holland, New York, 1981.
5. McClosky, D. N., 'The Persistence of the English Common Fields' in Parker, W. N. and Jones, E. T. (eds), *European Peasants and their Markets*, Princeton University Press, 1975.
6. Simons, S., 'Optimal Land Adjustments: A Dynamic Model of Fragmentation and Consolidation', unpublished paper, 1985.
7. Srivastava, S. K. (et al.), *Agricultural Economics and Cooperatives: With Special Reference to India*, S. Chand, New Delhi, 1970.

DISCUSSION OPENING I – ANDRÈ BRUN

I have four main points to make on the first paper by Clark Edwards.
1.   First, I will mention and emphasise the central problem Edwards is tackling. In fact it goes much beyond the role of natural resources in regional agricultural growth. The modesty of the title hides what seems to me an attempt to grasp the whole food problem in a world where surpluses accumulate in some places and malnutrition is endemic in others, if not in the same places. The paper addresses itself to the main challenge that we have to face as agricultural economists. Having such a dramatic situation before us, we are not allowed to make errors. Edwards tries to demonstrate the main sources of misleading considerations that are often made when we try to grasp the world-wide situation of population and food. Even if we all know the limitations of too global figures and measurements, I am pretty sure that at times we forget them and I think we must congratulate the author for reminding us of the necessity to leave the comfort of global judgements.
2.   Edwards also indicates directions towards which we have to go in order to face, if not to solve, the growing contradiction between growth problems and distributional ones. The different paragraphs of his paper indicate different sets of variables which it is necessary to consider. Each set of factors individually is fully recognised by the different facets of our discipline; but he demonstrates that we must take them together. We

know that what is simple is wrong and what is complex is of no use. But I think that Edwards, by classifying the different types of oversimplification that we are led to make, shows a way to surmount this uncomfortable position.

3. Going a bit further I would say, from my own experience, that it is probably more useful, when we try to tackle the food problem or regional agricultural growth, to broaden our models by introducing new variables, by articulating different knowledge and theories inside social sciences and beyond, rather than to refine one dimension analysis. If science is progressing by more and more specialised fields and tools, it is urgently necessary to make sciences progress also by synthesis, by enlargement of fields under consideration. To my way of thinking, it is also urgent to introduce institutional considerations, welfare, natural resources and regional economics between these fields and to link them with production and markets, even if the tools and data that we have in the different threads of economics are rather sketchy. This is the lesson that I personally draw from the Edwards paper with which, as you can perceive, I quite agree, since it meets my own experience.

4. I have just one question, I need some clarification on the role he reserves to demand for explaining growth. I certainly recognise the role of multipliers through demand in regional or national economic development. I fully recognise the gap between potential and effective demand. But less clear is the role of natural resources development. If, by natural resources development, we mean more access to land, sustainability of embedded equipment, preventing soil erosion etc., it may generate increased income, but what is the effect on population fertility and effective demand? It depends on one hand on the sharing of the income increment and then on land structures and tenure regulations and on the other hand on the relation between income distribution and effective demand. In other words, how does income distribution, born with natural resources development, affect effective demand and then economic growth? The statements made by Edwards on these questions seems to me a bit contradictory and not convincing, probably because resources development is too broad a concept.

Let me now turn to Scott Simons' paper.

1. The question presented, despite its appearance of being an exercise, is of obvious importance particularly where redistribution problems are concerned. From the French situation where we have nearly 100 million parcels, I can see that it concerns not only tropical countries. Since there are not many analyses on that problem of consolidation, I think we may exchange views in the discussion on the different experiences that we may have about consolidation analysis.

2. Concerning the internal logic of the model, I have nothing with which to disagree. It seemed to me quite coherent, as far as I could judge from a short presentation. Perhaps some questions on the model itself may come in the discussion. For myself, I have only a question on the assumptions, on what seems to me the cornerstone of the model. I mean

the introduction of that premium supposed to reflect the main individual cost of consolidation. It appears to me as an artefact impossible to evaluate. I wonder how the author would do such an evaluation of this premium and its rate of variation with the scale of operations. The results are in fact highly dependent on this rate.

3.   I question the possibility for this premium and the function attached to it, to reflect correctly the situation to be analysed. From the experience of France, where consolidation schemes have been applied for decades, I get the impression that consolidation is a collective action or is not. Individual cost of transaction is too short and too Pandora's-box-like a concept to be operational in this kind of situation. From the French experience consolidation simply will not occur significantly – setting aside amalgamation, as the author does – without two elements: First, a collective initiative which can be taken by an agreement between public administration and a significant proportion of landowners. Only in this case, facilitating circular exchanges, transaction costs, which are in fact co-ordination costs, will be sufficiently low to induce exchanges of dispersed parcels according to farming efficiency. Second, in land property matters, the complexity and emotionality are such that without some specific institutional regulations, nothing occurs, even if a collective initiative is taken. Some specific rules of the game are necessary which cannot come through market forces only, all the more so if, as the author mentions, land market is thin, land values are high, and holdings are small.

I would be glad to know the reactions of Simons to this statement and on the sub-optimality equilibrium which can easily be predicted from welfare economics.

4.   I would like to thank Simons for obliging us to consider both individual and social costs and benefits – in the French case I am not sure that social costs and benefits have ever been formally compared. This leads me to mention that the benefits are vanishing rapidly from one generation to the next. Fragmentation delays rebirth and the work has to be done again, except if measures are simultaneously taken to prevent a new fragmentation; which, once more, leads us to consider institutional regulations and not only to rely on market forces.

DISCUSSION OPENING II – ERWIN STUCKI

I enjoyed very much reading this interesting paper by Clark Edwards. The author tries to fit together three different aspects of economic growth: natural resources, population growth and technology.

  In addition to these classical factors, the author emphasises the need to extend the viewpoint to other major aspects, in particular to the structural and the institutional aspects regarding economic growth. I agree with the author's views. The questions I am going to raise are more likely to complement and refine the theme we are discussing. So one would expect, even in such a short paper, to become more specific, for instance through a case study which would show how this enlarged concept actually becomes operational in the decision-making process.

Further, I want to raise the question of how the two concepts of 'natural resources' and of 'regional' are defined.

Natural resources: In the paper, natural resources are mainly viewed as a potential for economic production. But as we know, natural resources mean something quite different to a botanist, an agronomist, an ethnologist or to the common citizen. Natural resources have also different functions to achieve. Besides the productive function, natural resources play an important part in conserving other natural resources and for recreational purposes.

Regional: As I understand it, Clark Edwards uses regional on a large-scale basis but we have to take into account that an equilibrium between economic growth and natural resources must be attained locally. This requires an information system which will relate local concerns and observation about natural resources with national and world-wide concerns. Together with the author I want to emphasise that one of the key issues on the topic we are dealing with remains that of combining the short-run concerns for productivity with the long-run concerns for stability and sustainability. Finally, we also have to devote our thoughts to the managing of natural resources in a declining regional economy.

Turning now to the second paper, I agree that land consolidation policies are important, and often controversially handled policies in Third World countries. We must be grateful to the author for trying to tackle this question through a rational, economically based theory. However, Scott Simons' paper raises some questions which I want to share with you.

I am not going to discuss the terms of the equations and the way they are handled. The author introduces the important time factor related to such fundamental decisions as land consolidation by splitting the decision process of farmers into a current profits maximisation and a long-run scale over all future time periods, as he calls it. I believe one has to go further in taking into account the dynamic aspect of the question. As we know, the relative value set for input and for farm output prices varies over time. So how can one take this into account in the optimisation process? Simply by introducing some kind of uncertainty term in the equation, or is the uncertainty so great it cannot be correctly modelled?

The author briefly mentions that there also exists a socially optimal consolidation which in most cases differs from the farmer's individual optimum consolidation. It would be interesting to examine the mathematical formula of this socially optimal consolidating equation and to bring it into relation with the individual optimum equation. Beyond these issues, I would like to raise the following questions:

– How does one handle the question in the numerous rural areas in developed countries where land titles are still missing?
– How can one quantify properly the terms of the equation over a long period of time?

Finally, we have to be aware of the fact that the maximisation behaviour of the farmers in developing countries, as in many rural areas in developed countries, is not a single monetary profit maximisation equation but a multidimensional and complex one.

GENERAL DISCUSSION – RAPPORTEUR: K. L. SHARMA

Questions were raised mainly on the paper by Simons. It was pointed out that the scope of the paper was limited by mentioning developing countries in the title. There was hardly any difference between developing and developed countries as far as collective action for consolidation was concerned. Both faced similar problems in land consolidation actions. Considerable work had been carried out in European countries – particularly in Belgium, West Germany and Eastern Europe – where considerable collective and private funds were invested in land consolidation schemes. In the East European countries there were some indications that the private optimum level of consolidation could exceed the social optimum, mainly due to problems of surplus.

It was brought out in the discussion that land was considered in the paper as a capital asset and not as a socio-cultural asset. The approach used by Simons could not capture the socio-cultural features of land. Also, fragmentation was not merely an accident or simply due to economic factors. It was also the result of past institutional structures which must be considered. The treatment of capital costs in consolidation posed serious problems since their effects were realised over generations. It was noted that equity and income distribution aspect were not discussed in the paper. Concern was expressed on the need for more case studies on land consolidation under different climatic zones and socio-cultural and economic conditions.

In reply Simons pointed out that his paper was intended as a partial analysis focusing mainly on economic factors influencing land fragmentation. But there were also non-economic factors which certainly affected land consolidation decisions.

Participants in the discussion included L. Martens, D. Bromley, L. Drake, C. Arnade, P. M. Raup, G. M. Norton and H. S. Kehal.

STEVEN T. SONKA

Computer-Aided Farm Management Systems: Will the Promise be Fulfilled?

The topic of computer-aided farm management is very broad and a discussion of it should encompass the contributions of experts in several scientific disciplines. Even in the framework of the agricultural economics profession, there are numerous factors that one could consider when addressing this topic. Given the constraints of length imposed, however, this paper will not survey the broad range of topics possible. Instead the limited scope of the direct use of microcomputers on commercial farms will be the paper's focus. Doing this does not imply that other issues, such as the use of mainframe computers for provision of information or the use of microcomputers by advisors of limited resource farmers, are not also important.

POTENTIAL ON-FARM USES OF THE MICROCOMPUTER

The introduction and phenomenal growth of the capability of microcomputers has vastly expanded the potential number of individuals and small businesses who can afford to become computer owners. Commercial farm operators now can purchase microcomputers with significant computing capacity for less money than many of the farm machinery and equipment items they routinely buy.

In the few years since microcomputers have become available, this technology has been applied in numerous farm management applications. In the planning and control functions, the potential for microcomputer use has been exploited on a few farms. Simulation programmes have been used to help producers clarify the trade-offs between conflicting goals. The information acquisition capability of the computer has helped some producers forecast prices and production. Programmes to aid operational planning, investment analysis and whole farm planning have assisted in formulating long- and short-term plans. Accounting and physical production record programmes are available to enhance the control function. Similarly software exists which allows the producer to automate many administrative duties, such as payroll, tax reporting and activity monitoring.

717

Although computers have been used for the previously mentioned applications, the vast majority of commercial farmers do not own microcomputers for business use. Probably no more than one in ten commercial US farmers uses a microcomputer for business purposes. And there is indication that the rate of computer adoption may not be increasing among farmers. Therefore in the following sections, a number of management-related impediments to effective microcomputer implementations on farms will be discussed.

FACTORS AFFECTING FURTHER ADOPTION

The appropriate role of computers in society and the ultimate effect of markedly increased levels of computer use are issues of growing concern (Turkle 1984). These are legitimate issues and are worthy of analysis and debate. Those discussions, however, are outside the scope of this paper. Therefore, as a working hypothesis, let us assume that microcomputers have potential value in improving the farm management process. Using this hypothesis, the remainder of this discussion will consider a limited number of factors which appear to be significant impediments to the future adoption and effective utilisation of microcomputers on farms.

The following discussion will intentionally not include predictions of technological change with respect to computer hardware. Continual improvement is assumed.

ASSESSING THE VALUE OF A NEW TECHNOLOGY

One of the appropriate activities for agricultural economists is to assess the value of a new technology. Our profession has contributed many useful analyses to this end. At times we have estimated the pay-off to the individual producer for being an early adopter of an innovation. In other situations the perspective considered was that of a region, nation or the world. Despite this long and valued tradition, there is very little in our literature which addresses the economic value of computers and specifically the value of the on-farm microcomputer.

Farm decision-makers, however, are vitally interested in knowing the economic pay-off from investing in a computer. On numerous occasions I have spoken to farm groups about computer use and am invariably faced with questions such as, 'Will this machine make me any money? Will investing in a computer have a higher rate of return than applying more fertilizer?' My replies to such questions have been uniformly unsatisfactory. There are only so many ways to essentially say, 'It depends'. It is of little comfort to suspect that my colleagues also have little to offer in reply to these questions.

This issue is raised not to point out a shortcoming of our profession. Instead prior research suggests that the perceived relative advantage of an innovation affects the rate of adoption of that innovation (Rogers 1971). Therefore the lack of a rigorously determined answer to these questions is likely to be an impediment to the successful application of computers in agriculture. Because of this, it seems warranted to discuss alternative approaches to assessing the value of the computer innovation. In addition, a framework for addressing the issue of economic valuation will be proposed.

ANECDOTAL EVIDENCE

The most common approach to defining the value of microcomputers to the farmer seems to have been to rely on anecodotal evidence. Testimony from actual farmers has the important attribute of establishing credibility for the technology, which was an important factor when microcomputers were new and unusual. This expert testimony relied totally on that individual's experience. Acquisition costs and the process of learning how to utilise a limited number of programmes often were defined. The 'value' of the technology was expressed in subjective terms. In some cases, the role of the computer in changing a major decision was described. For these latter cases, the gain from that one decision always seemed to 'more than pay for the computer'.

FOCUSING ON COSTS

A second and more quantitative approach has been to focus only on the cost side of computer use (Sonka 1983). In a few cases, it is possible that the introduction of the microcomputer would not affect the amount or quality of information available for farm decision-making. For example, computerising the farm payroll or implementing a computerised farm accounting system which duplicated the previous system would result in no information gains for decision-making. In those instances a partial budget framework would be appropriate. We could compare:

Additional costs of the computerized system	versus	*Reduced costs of the manual system*
Search costs		Transactions processing
Learning costs		Calculation costs
Hardware acquisition cost		
Software acquisition cost		

In most instances, however, the farm information system expands with the addition of microcomputer capabilities. Focusing on the cost side provides no indication of the value of the enhancements to the information system. Quantifying the total costs, however, may provide a useful reference point for the potential computer adopter.

AN APPROACH TO VALUING THE BENEFITS OF COMPUTER USE

Valuing the benefits of computer adoption is directly related to the computer's impact on the farm information system. The benefits of computer use will be derived from the information obtained by utilising that technology. Although quantitative estimation of the value of information is not a trivial process, frameworks do exist which can help us conceptualize the problem (Chavas and Pope 1984). Further, application of innovative research approaches could lead to quantitative estimates if the problem area is recognized as one worthy of investigation.

The farm decision-making problem has several important attributes. Among these are that it is dynamic and that interrelated decisions are made sequentially. The presence of time in the process implies that the outcome of today's decision will be affected by stochastic future events. A helpful framework in which to consider this setting is that of a stochastic, dynamic programming problem. Applying the principle of optimality results in the following recursive objective function:

$$V_t(X_t) = \max\left[r_t(X_t, D_t) + (BEV_{t+1})(X_{t+1})\right] \tag{1.1}$$

where X_t = a state variable describing the state of the farm decision process at stage t,

D_t = the decision chosen by the decision-maker at stage t,

$V_t(D_t)$ = expected optimal outcome from following an optimal policy from the current stage t to the final stage (T) for a decision-maker currently at state X_t,

r_t = a valuation process for stage t which is a function of state X_t given the decision D_t (if the farmer is a profit maximiser, r_t is a function which computes profits; if the producer is a utility maximiser, r_t is a utility function)

B   = discount factor,

E   = expectation operator,

max   = maximisation operator.

The recursive equation in (1.1) is maximised subject to the following transition equation:

$$X_{t+1} = t_t(X_t, D_t, Z_t, O_t) \tag{1.2}$$

where t_t = a transformation function from stage t to t + 1.

Z_t = exogenous variables at stage t, and

O_t = the stochastic events occurring at stage t.

The presence of O_t implies that the transition equation is stochastic (i.e. we can think of the transition relationship in terms of probabilities).

What do the two equations (1.1) and (1.2) attempt to represent? In words, we have a farm decision-maker striving to maximise some goal structure. The producer's current situation is the product of past decisions, exogenous forces and stochastic events. Similarly the future circumstances of that producer will be a result of decisions made today, stochastic events that will occur and exogenous influences. This framework can be defined very generally. Let the possible decisions include financial, marketing and production decisions. Further the stages could be short, i.e. daily, or relatively long, i.e. annually.

If we could quantify the relationships of (1.1) and (1.2), then an estimate of the value of information resulting from adoption of a microcomputer could be obtained. That value would be the difference between $V_t^c(X_t)$ and $V_t^o(X_t)$ where $V_t^c(X_t)$ is the value of the expected optimal outcome using a microcomputer and $V_t^o(X_t)$ is the analogous value without the microcomputer. Later we will speculate on some approaches to quantitative estimation. Now let us focus on how the presence of a computerised information system might affect the parameters of (1.1) and (1.2).

One of the uses of a microcomputer is to access external information. Indeed the 'electronic cottage' concept supposes that individuals will readily adopt and utilise electronic communication networks. Accessing external information would affect the terms $EV_{t+1}(X_{t+1})$, O_t, and Z_t. Producers with improved access to futures market quotations, or weather forecasts may have subjective probability distributions which are more accurate than do producers without that capability. Here there must be some attribute of using the electronic communication system which differentially affects expectations. If the microcomputer user receives the same information but through a more 'modern' medium, the evaluation issue is one of comparing costs of acquistion. It is possible, however, that the near real time access of electronic communications and the enhanced capability to analyse electronically received data may result in differing expectations and decisions.

The term t_t is analogous to a production function. An enhanced information system could affect this term in two ways. One is by changing the coefficients because of increased efficiency. Remember that all the activities of the farm are considered here so that more efficient operation would include improvements to monitoring and administrative activities. A second avenue by which the transition function could be altered is if the producer developed a more accurate perception of those coefficients. For example computerised production records might indicate that the firm's technical performance was not as efficient as the producer relying solely on memory might have believed.

Occasionally the agricultural economics literature has contained discussions which debate the value of accounting and/or recordkeeping systems (Hardaker and Anderson 1981). If computerised versions of those monitoring activities are to have value for decision-making, that value will result because those activities provide better estimates of the current state of the process, the X_t variable. Remember again that we have defined the decision set very broadly, so that financial and marketing activites are included. If use of a computer for monitoring purposes does not alter the producer's knowledge of X_t, then it is likely that this use will have minimal value for managerial purposes.

The final term which seemingly could be affected by the information system available is the r_t term. Let us consider a producer who uses the computer solely for forward planning purposes. When evaluating a decision, the computer is used to compute expected outcomes, i.e. net cash flows or profit. In addition to the most likely outcome, possibly a range of outcomes or a sensitivity analysis, is computed. It is possible that the producer with the microcomputer could reach a different decision even though the coefficients used (the expected prices and technical relationships) were identical whether a computer was used or not. In this situation, the contribution of the computer is to increase the producer's understanding of the relationship between the goals being maximised and the decision situation currently being considered.

Given that general formulation of the decision situation, how might we approach empirical analyses? The likely first step would be to narrow the scope fo the analysis to a specific computer application and a limited set of decisions. Observation of the effects of computer use in actual decision situations probably will be unsatisfactory. Too many other factors will be influencing the decisions selected, in addition to the use of computers, to isolate the computer effect. Note that case studies or surveys describing actual computer use can be quite valuable to producers and to researchers. The point here is that such investigations are not likely to generate estimates of the economic value of the innovation.

Two other approaches may provide insights into the valuation issue. These are the uses of simulation and experimental analysis. Both techniques have shortcomings because they abstract from the real world decision setting. Yet the careful use of these techniques may contribute to our understanding of the economics of the microcomputer technology and information use.

In the simulation approach, the basic concept would be to predict decision behaviour with and without information items derived from computer use. In essence the researcher would systematically alter parameters in the decision model to reflect with and without information scenarios. The goal of the analysis would be to determine if the producer's predicted behaviour would be altered by the presence of information. Major problems with the approach revolve around specifying the decision rules (the relationship between the value of a variable and the decision selected) and quantifying how specific parameters are altered because of the presence of information.

Actual decision-makers could possibly be part of the analysis but in an experimental setting. For a very structured situation, producers would be given differing levels of information and the decisions they select recorded. Given sufficient resources, the interaction of information, the producer's current financial position, and future expectations could be examined. This method suffers because the decision-maker is not operating in an actual decision environment. If producers are presented with unfamiliar information, their experimental response may differ from what their actual behaviour would be once they were familiar with using the information. Further the producer in actuality may be affected by factors which cannot be replicated in the experimental setting.

As one contemplates construction of a simulation model to evaluate the effect of computer-generated information, our lack of understanding of actual decision making behaviour becomes more apparent. In one sense, conducting an experimental analysis or examination of actual behaviour are means to generate the needed coefficients for the decision model. The previous discussion has been directed towards the economic valuation of computer use. An additional implication of that discussion is that we need to know much more about actual decision processes if we are to provide increasingly realistic evaluations for many of the problems faced by producers.

CAPTURING INTERNAL DATA

In terms of production, a farm firm is very similar to a manufacturing firm. Inputs are combined and after time has elapsed, a new product is produced. Just as in a manufacturing firm, a substantial number of activities are often required before production is completed. The historic capability of the farm firm to monitor those activities, however, has been quite limited. There are several reasons for this. When farms are small and the number of production practice alternatives are limited, the benefits from formally monitoring activities are minimal. In addition the physical environment of farming is not conducive to accurate measurement and recording. And finally a farmer prefers farming to being a clerk.

Microcomputer systems which are purchased to provide better estimates of the farm's current state variable (the X_t of the previous section) are often constrained by the availability of high quality data on internal transactions. In some cases, microcomputer systems have been judged unsatisfactory even though the hardware and software were adequate. The 'failure' in the system was the producer's internal data capturing system, which did not produce the observations required for the microcomputer to be effective. In economic terms, the farmer perceived that the cost of obtaining the data exceeded the potential benefits.

Innovative application of microelectronics promises to reduce these data capture costs. Already the transponder for dairy animals has received considerable testing. Additional electronic advances are likely to make the data capturing process more accurate and less of a burden for the farmer or the farm worker. Such innovations could greatly alter the farmer's perceived cost/benefit ratio for enhanced information systems. Also it appears that management researchers could contribute significantly to the development of these innovations.

DIVERSE NEEDS OF INDIVIDUAL PRODUCERS

Although we are not certain to what extent management is an art or a science, the management process followed on any two farms is not likely to be identical. In a recent project a small number of farmers cooperated with university researchers to rigorously identify their financial accounting needs (Schnitkey 1984). Although these producers were fairly homogeneous in terms of size and enterprises, the number of separate accounts they specified as needed varied from 63 to 222. Clearly a single microcomputer system would not be equally satisfactory to each of these producers.

Research relating to the information of individual producers is likely to document differing management styles on farm firms. Many alternative categorisations of those management approaches will be possible. One which has been hypothesized recently is that of the information age farm versus the industrial age farm (Sonka 1985). The basic distinction suggested is the extent to which information is used in the management process. On the industrial age farm, strategies which are perceived best under average conditions are routinely employed. Conversely the management approach of the information age farm strives to implement flexible management strategies.

A flexible management strategy allows for continual re-evaluation of plans as the producer's decision environment changes or is expected to change. The role of information is to document and/or predict those changing conditions. Microcomputers can play a part in this process if their use leads to more efficient provision of the needed information.

A major impediment to the development of flexible management strategies is the lack of appropriate production coefficients. Systems simulation models of physical and biological processes can be a means of quantifying coefficients in a manner which is meaningful to managers. Bioeconomic modelling efforts which combine or integrate physical and economic systems will allow researchers to test flexible strategies in varied settings. Such research efforts would seem to have value for the producer striving to be more efficient. As the capacity of microcomputers continues to expand, it also is realistic to envisage producers independently utilising such models. Rather than expecting these models to produce 'optimal' solutions which the producer religiously adopts, a more realistic use of such models would be to allow the producer to develop a better understanding of the physical and economic systems with which the producer is working.

EXPERT CONSULTATION

The farm decision environment is becoming increasingly complex. Often the input of relatively specialised expertise is desirable. However, the geographic dispersion of agricultural production and the relatively small scale of the farm firm has traditionally made it uneconomic to acquire the services of the expert. A limited set of evidence suggests that innovative farm producers have attempted to overcome these barriers and to utilise the outside consultant. Effective use of that expertise is often a function of the availability of internal firm data. The value of computerised systems may be enhanced if there are significant advantages to the use of external consultants.

Advances in the area of artificial intelligence suggest that computerised delivery of expert consultation is currently possible and will be increasingly so in the future. As these capabilities become more powerful, the value of using the farm computer as a learning tool may exceed that associated with current applications of the technology. Development of expert systems will require considerable resources. This will be a particularly challenging task for farm management researchers. A major component of that task will be to define what the 'rules' are in farm financial and business management.

COMPUTER LITERACY

Computer literacy is the subject of intense debate today. As typically phrased, the issue revolves around the instruction needed to allow current and future decision-makers to effectively utilise the computer technology. But that typical debate seems to have the emphasis exactly backwards. Rather than focusing on how people have to change to use computers, should not the proper question be, 'How do computer systems have to change to be most appropriate for use by people?'

With respect to management of the farm, farm management researchers and educators have much to contribute to the development of more effective software. In the past few years, individuals in these areas have often provided leadership in software development and review. But it appears, probably by necessity, that we have been quite willing to utilise informal criteria for programme evaluation.

Now that we are beginning to have an actual experience base to examine, part of our focus should shift to more rigorous analysis of the effect of computer systems on decision-making. These investigations could examine the characteristics of computer systems that seem to contribute to more effective decision-making. For example, a recent study of a limited sample of pork producers suggests that producers who design and implement their own record system using general purpose software tend to make more extensive use of the resulting information (Schroeder 1984). If this finding is valid in general, it has important implications for the need for software which can accommodate very flexible designs, implementable by individual users. There are numerous other system design issues of importance. Careful research which focuses on the management needs of producers is needed. In essence, computer system design may be too important to be left to computer professionals.

SUMMARY

Our limited experience with microcomputer use in farm management gives several reasons for the optimistic belief that this technology can be an aid to effective farm decision making. Enough experience has been

726   *Steven T. Sonka*

accumulated, however, to indicate that implementation of this technology can sometimes be a painful and frustrating experience. Many of the impediments to successful use relate to interfacing existing management practices and needs to the capabilities of the technology. In many of these instances, the input of farm management researchers and educators could be of valuable assistance.

REFERENCES

Chavas, J.-P. and Pope, R. D., 'Information: its Measurement and Valuation, *American Journal of Agricultural Economics*, vol. 6, 1984. pp. 705–710.
Hardaker, J. R. and Anderson, J. R., 'Why Farm Recording Systems are Doomed to Failure?', *Review of Marketing and Agricultural Economics*, vol. 49, 1981, pp. 199–202.
Rogers, E. M., *Communication of Innovations*, The Free Press, New York, 1971.
Schnitkey, G. D., 'Accounting Systems for Farms: Design and Selection Methods', unpublished M.S. thesis, University of Illinois at Urbana-Champaign, 1984.
Schroeder, R. C., 'Computerized Production Records for Swine Producers: An Evaluation of Current and Potential Uses', unpublished M.S. thesis, University of Illinois at Urbana-Champaign, 1984.
Sonka, S. T., 'Information Management in Farm Production', *Journal of Computers and Electronics in Agriculture*, 1985.
Sonka, S. T., *Computers in Farming: Selection and Use*, McGraw-Hill, New York, 1983.
Turkle, S., *The Second Self: Computers and the Human Spirit*, Simon and Schuster, New York, 1984.

S. B. HARSH, F. KUHLMANN AND F. BURG

Farm Level Information Systems as an Aid to Decision-Makers

The popular press has made us more aware of the microelectronic revolution and the projected impacts it will have on society. One of the products of the microelectronics revolution is the microcomputer. The newest generation of microcomputers has the computational capacity of the mid-size mainframe computer of only a decade ago at a small fraction of the cost. This breakthrough in computation power and availability has prompted some to become enthusiastic about the potential of micro-computers. Berge (1984) suggests that microcomputers can do:

> ... project scheduling, resource allocating, fund accounting and decision analysis. Such sophisticated operations as cost-benefit analysis, financial projections, food policy modeling, cattle herd optimization and general farm management programs can now be done by managers with little previous experience in these 'speciality' areas.

Such enthusiasm seems to stem from a narrow focus on capabilities of the computer hardware and not realizing that the hardware is only one aspect of a computer-based information system. A computer-based information system has at least five components: (1) hardware, (2) software, (3) supporting databases, (4) the end user's analytical ability and (5) the sales, service, and training support system. Through time the relative importance and capabilities of these components have been greatly altered. In the following sections the history of computer utilisation in agriculture at the farm level will be reviewed. Attention will then be directed to the challenges and opportunities ahead if more effective use of this technology is to be achieved in the future.

HISTORICAL PERSPECTIVE

Use of computers to address actual problems of farmers began in the mid-1950s with the advent of general purpose digital computers. The dairy production records and farm accounting systems were among our first applications. These systems used batch-operated computers and utilised the mail service for delivering information to and from the data processing centre. Many of these projects still function and operate today. Although improvements have been made in the format of the records the method for processing data remains basically unchanged.

Although these production records and accounting systems could identify the strengths and weakness of the farm business, their capabilities for planning purposes were limited. For predictive information, a new and different approach was deemed necessary. Farmer workshops were first used as a technique to deliver computerised planning models to farmers. However, this approach had problems because of the limited number of farmers that could be serviced and the time delay between completing the input form and the return of the computer output.

With the availability of timesharing computers in the mid 1960s, several groups began developing software and delivery systems for farmer and farm advisor use. Based on data from the TELPLAN timeshare system, nearly 70 per cent of the usage was related to the execution of models addressing routine (or structured) problems (Harsh 1980). Routine problems are defined as those commonly faced by farm managers – ration balancing, scheduling of livestock facilities, pedigree evaluation, irrigation scheduling, etc. Since these problems are frequently faced by managers, they often have a good understanding of the analysis process necessary to make a management decision. Models used to a lesser degree on the TELPLAN system were those designed to analyse problems that are not routine in nature. Problems of this type are usually more complex. Examples include evaluating the impact of a major business expansion, adopting new technology or forming a partnership. Since these problems are generally more complex and occur less frequently, managers needed substantial assistance in utilising the models that addressed these questions. To provide assistance, agricultural advisors often worked directly with farmers. The use of timeshare systems broadened the audience reached but it still remained fairly small. Furthermore, the link between the descriptive information (e.g., the accounting system and production records) and the planning models is generally a manual process.

Advancements in microelectronics resulted in the development of programmable calculators in the early 1970s. Farmers had available to them a low cost, portable and personalised computer capacity. Many decision aid models were developed for this technology. Acceptance of the programmable calculator by farmers was initially encouraging. Because of size and speed limitations and the new microcomputer technology that developed later, the use of programmable calculators has declined.

To follow the programmable calculator in the mid 1970s was the mass merchandised microcomputer. Suddenly, farmers had available to them substantial computer processing capacity and data storage capacity at a very low cost. Many have hailed it as the revolution which will place computerised data processing capacity in the hands of nearly all commercial farming operations. Faced with this startling reality, there has been a heavy emphasis on developing software for farm based microcomputers (Strain and Simmons 1984).

CURRENT ASSESSMENT

In examining the development of these problem-solving systems, several observations can be made. As new and more sophisticated computer hardware has emerged, there have been major efforts to apply it to the problems of agriculture. Also, there has been a conscientious effort to move the data processing closer to and place it under the control of the end user (i.e., the farmer).

Anderson (1982) has classified information systems by the type of functions performed. His classification of systems is as follows: (1) Transaction Processing System (TPS) – pure data-processing programs for gathering, updating, and posting information according to predefined procedures; (2) Management Information System (MIS) – a system with predefined aggregation and reporting capabilities, often built upon a TPS; (3) Decision Support System (DSS) – an extensible system with intrinsic capability to support *ad hoc* data analysis and reduction, as well as decision-modelling activities.

Most of the software for firm level usage are either of the TPS or MIS nature. A recent study by Hepp (1984) of commercially available microcomputer software indicates that accounting packages by a large margin are the most common form of software. Other applications relate mainly to decision aids (e.g., ration balancing, irrigation scheduling, etc.) and crop and animal production records. Software of the DSS nature remain to be built and tested.

Although progress has been made in applying computer technology to agricultural problems, the proportion of the potential audience reached remains small. Harsh (1980) discovered one of the major problems in getting the TELPLAN system utilised was the training of the end user. The analytical skills of the end users were weaker than anticipated and a major educational effort was required to get farmers and farm advisors to feel confident in using computer models. This was particularly the case with the more complex models.

The supporting databases for agricultural software are currently inadequate. Many of the problems faced by farmers require data they generally do not have available to them. This includes data from their own operations as well as external data such as commodity prices and weather forecasts. Some of the software available for on-farm use exceeds the manager's ability to accurately supply the necessary data needed to support these models.

If decision makers are going to make effective use of a computer based information system, they need an adequate suport system to assist them. The support system for agriculture is currently very weak. As a rule, farmers feel that the computer salesmen generally do not know the subject of agriculture and likewise cannot visualise which software packages might be useful to them and/or how to apply them to their particular situation.

FUTURE CHALLENGES AND OPPORTUNITIES

The potential for improving the decision making process of farmers in the future is encouraging. Few would doubt that the current computer hardware is capable of supporting a fairly sophisticated farm-level information system. Increased attention must be given to the other component of the information system. This will involve several aspects including the development of decision support systems, use of expert systems and optimum control models, development of technology to automate the data collection, and enhancing the support system.

TABLE 1 *A framework for information systems*

| Type of Decision | Management Activity | | | Support needed |
	Operational control	Management control	Strategic planning	
Structured	Inventory control	Least cost rations	Choosing enterprise mix	Clerical or Man. sci. models
Semi-structured	Restructuring the farm's debt	Set production goals for the business	Expanding the business	Decision support systems
Unstructured	Hiring farm employees	Delegation of business responsi-bilities	Major re-structuring of the business	Human intuition

Source: Adapted from Keen and Morton (1978) to reflect agricultural examples.

The framework suggested by Keen and Morton (1978) can provide guidance for developing information systems for the future and identifying potential problem areas (see Table 1). The on-farm information systems of the future should concentrate on addressing the structured and semi-structured decisions. Structured decisions are those which require very little involvement on the part of the manager in using management skills to reach a decision. For such decisions a number of computerised decision aids have already been developed (e.g., least cost rations, irrigation scheduling, etc.). However, more models from management science are needed to address these decisions. This is particularly the case for structured decisions which relate to strategic planning. Furthermore, Kuhlmann, et al. (1984) has indicated, the need for more extensive use of adaptive optimum control models to address structured decisions. In many cases these control models could be of the closed loop type. Closed loop control models are particularly powerful tools for monitoring and controlling certain aspects of the business (Fischer 1982; Rausser 1979). However, the applications of these models in agricultural production has been very limited.

The potential for improving the efficiency of farms with structured decision models is very encouraging. However, in developing these models, greater attention must be given to integrating them into an overall decision support system (DSS).

One of the problems currently confronting farm managers in using models to address structured problems is the lack of farm specific data. The information system of the future must be designed so that it captures the farm specific data (e.g., field performance rates) needed by models that address structured decisions. If the data-capturing process can be automated (e.g., collecting daily milk production figures on individual cows), priority should be given to achieving this goal. Otherwise, the data capture process will divert time from other management tasks.

The analytical skills of the manager will have an influence on acceptance of models to address structured decisions. Experience indicates that once the concepts underlining these models are understood, farmers are very willing to utilise them in their business. However, teaching these concepts to a large number of farmers is potentially a major problem. One possible solution is to develop software that is capable of teaching the manager these concepts. Software with these attributes should explain to the user upon command why a given item of input information is important in the analysis, what is a reasonable or acceptable input value, the analytical procedures used in the analyses, why these procedures are used, and how to interpret the results of the analysis. This is a level of support and information far greater than the 'help' command that is found on some agricultural models.

The semi-structured decisions faced by farm managers are more complex. Although analytical models can be used to assist the manager in the decision-making process, a fair amount of discretion is required of the manger in reaching a decision. To assist the manger in addressing semi-structured decisions a decision support system is needed. DSSs currently do not exist for agriculture although a few are in the planning stage or under development. Building a DSS is a long-term and multi-disciplinary project. The DSS, being a flexible system which can support *ad hoc* analysis and modelling activities, will need to be tailored to different types of farming operations. The DSS required for a dairy farm will be different to one for a vegetable farm. Although some components of the DSS can be shared, others will be unique to type of farm operation.

Unlike structured decisions where management science models often suggest the appropriate decisions to make, the DSS supplies the manager with selective information depending upon the scenario being analysed.

Also, the decision-making process is geneally heuristic in nature. Some farm managers have good heuristic skills, but many do not. Furthermore, a significant proportion of the managers do not have the expertise to know which analytical procedure is appropriate for the problem. One approach to address these problems is to use experts to advise the manger on semi-structured decisions. Unfortunately, qualified experts are scarce in supply and their services can be expensive. These problems are not unique to agriculture. Other areas (e.g., medicine, and mineral exploration) are using the new science of expert systems (ES). An ES integrated into a DSS would be able to guide the manager through the decision making process in much the same fashion as an expert advising the farmer directly. ES has three main parts: (1) a user interface; (2) an inference engine, and; (3) a knowledgebase. Currently, there is microcomputer software that addresses the first two components. (Hayes-Roth et. al. 1983). Therefore, the most difficult aspect of developing an ES will be the generation of the knowledgebase. The knowledgebase is extracted from the experts and the process can be time-consuming and costly depending upon the problem and the experts' ability to relate their knowledge.

Finally, a better support system will be needed if more sophisticated information systems are going to be implemented on farms. These support systems will need to supply the manager with better technical support and training. In some European countries, the agriculture co-operatives are starting to assume this responsibility. Hopefully, this trend toward increased support will continue to grow.

REFERENCES

Anderson, David R., Sweeney, Dennis J. and Williams, Thomas A., *An Introduction to Management Science, Quantitative Approaches to Decision Making*, 3rd edition, West Publishing Company, St Paul, Minnesota, 1982.

Berge, Noel, 'Some Trends and Implications in the Use of Microcomputers in Development Management: A Report to USAID Science and Technology Bureau, Office of Multisectoral Development' in *Micros in Management: A Report from the Microcomputer Clearinghouse*, Thunder and Associates, Alexandria, Virginia, 1984.

Fischer, T., 'Kontrolltheoretische Entscheidungsmodelle – Ein Beitrag zur Abstimmung von Produktion und Lagerhaltung auf unsichere Nachfrage, Wirtschaftskybernetik und Systemanalysis', Bd. 7, Berlin, 1982.

Harsh, S. B., 'The Use of Operations Research Tools as an Aid to Farm Decision Making – The TELPLAN Experience', *Operation Research in Agriculture and Water Resources*, ed. D. Yaron and C. S. Tapiero, North-Holland, Amsterdam, 1980.

Hayes-Roth, Waterman, D. A. and Lenat, D. B. (eds), *Building Expert Systems*. Addison-Wesley Reading, Mass., 1983.

Hepp, Ralph, E. and Mu'min, Ridgely A., *Michigan Agricultural Microcomputer Software Directory Private Sector*, Agricultural Economics Report no. 448, Department of Agricultural Economics, Michigan State University, East Lansing, 1984.

Keen, P. G. W. and Morton, M. S. S., *Decision Support Systems: An Organizational Perspective*, Addison-Wesley, Reading, Massachusetts, 1978.

Kuhlmann, F., Burg, E. and Harsh, S. B., 'On Decision Support Systems Using Adaptive Control Procedures', paper presented at the fourth European Congress of Agriculture Economics, Kiel, Germany, 1984.

Rausser, Gordon C. and Hochman, Eithan, *Dynamic Agricultural Systems: Economic Prediction and Control*, Elsevier North Holland, New York, 1979.
Strain, J. Robert and Simmons, Stephanie, (The Cooperative Extension Service) *Updated Inventory of Computer Programs*, Circular 531–A, Institute of Food and Agricultural Sciences, University of Florida, 1984.

YOSHIHIKO SUGAI AND A. R. TEIXEIRA FILHO

Impact on Farmers' Decision-Making by Farm Management and Computer Sciences in the Turbulent Economy*

INTRODUCTION

The basic concept of agricultural development means getting more production of agricultural products with the existing resources. This process is satisfied by increasing the productivity of the production factors through the application of scientific knowledge. The high productivity is based on new technology which is created by the research institutions, as well as by capable people and competent agricultural producers. It is of fundamental importance to use the new knowledge, materialising it in the form of modern inputs that can be treated with adequate skills.

The farmer is the principal agent of changes in agriculture. He materialises the available knowledge and combines the available resources to increase the efficiency of his farm. Increasing producer capacity for using the modern technologies in order to be efficient is a fundamental prerequisite of development. Agricultural development requires availability of the technological knowledge that removes physical and social restrictions imposed by nature and society respectively.

Useful knowledge is incorporated into the human component of the productive process. It defines the production characteristics of land as basic inputs; the characteristics of the mechanical factors of production, ·machinery and equipment; the reproductive properties of the various species, seeds and varieties (in the case of plants) and breeds and races (in the case of animals).

Possible innovations from the new knowledge depends on farmers' actions. In administering the farm business the characteristics of the productive inputs which limit production growth are shown. These become the targets of new scientific investment and technological progress. Man as receiver of the benefits and agent of changes that characterise development, converts himself into the fundamental actor in

*This paper was presented by Philippe Lambrecht.

734

the process and becomes the convergency of the knowledge that makes development possible.

THE PROCESS OF TRANSFORMATION OF THE FARMING SYSTEM

In the adjusting procedures of dynamic agricultural development, rural producers show wide ranges of performance in adapting to the new conditions that technological progress and the market present to them. Those more sensible to signs of progress appear in front. They capture economic rent, incorporate new resources, capitalise the change and materialise progress. Others leave changes without great distortions, they compose the middle status group. The third group release their resources to be absorbed by the growth of their partners. They leave the sector and change activities.

The following scheme introduces some evaluations where the objectives of growth and equity in the sector bring up some questions:

1. What is the efficient utilisation of the production resources of the lower-income stratum, whose stability can be more intimately affected by progress, that will be able to bring up substantial increases in production and income?

2. Which factors of production are mainly responsible for the great differences in the behaviour of rural producers?

3. In which conditions can agricultural investment compete with other investment options?

4. How does the technology prescription to promote underdeveloped agriculture differ from that which is attractive from the viewpoint of the progressive producer?

The answer to the first question permits one to verify if a farm, or a group of similar farms, is accompanying or absorbing the dynamic context of the equilibrium-disequilibrium that the economic transformation imposes on the agricultural sector, through the decision-making processes of farmers.

The second question points out the direction of the different capacities of the producers as the important factor to explain the differences in total and in the rate of production growth with which each group of producers contributes to the global production increase. To what extent can the agility given to the decision-making process be the important component of these differences?

The third and fourth questions look for the identification within various groups of the producer population of the elements that make up their decision scheme or their utility function. The identification of these elements will allow an evaluation of the components of the progress which interests the various types of producers. It shows also the way to make a more accurate evaluation of the business with which the producers are involved.

Progress within the agricultural sector will depend on the improvement of capital, on the possibility of use of the land and fundamentally on the capability of the producers to use these modern factors adequately.

Acknowledgement of the importance and necessity of making investments in the physical elements that generate increases of productivity and economic progress in agriculture has been registered in the developed countries. Farmers' capacities for use and hire of new productive factors has received less attention and resources from the agencies of development. The work of the technological agricultural research agencies generates the various components of the progress that express itself in better seeds, more efficient machines, more appropriate techniques, more productive animals, etc. All these changes will be adopted by the producer. These decisions on the productive process will require complete knowledge about all these techniques. While the farmer acts according to economic criteria, his knowledge about the market forces acting on what he buys and sells becomes crucial.

While progress in the various technical fields that deal with agricultural production is reached through specific actions, its final utilisation in production demands global knowledge by the farmers in the administration of their business. This characterisation shows the necessity for specific investments in the preparation of the farmer for his decision making process. The refinement of the ability of the farmers for business administration depends on his education and cultural characteristics. These dimensions will affect the composition of technologies that he will be willing to learn and use. Knowledge of all these components as well as their interrelationships is reached through research on farm management, which is taken as the process of combining known techniques of production under defined market conditions related to the basic arrangement of resources, and it has made substantial progress with the utilization of the electronic computer.

THE FARM MANAGEMENT SYSTEM

In the process of choosing and combining technological resources and economic factors which characterise the farm business, the farmer will detect at any moment the factors that restrict technical behaviour and the profits generated by the farm. These technical constraints and the farm environment are sketched in Figure 1.

The farm management system considered three main inputs: Natural Environment variables, Price and Policy variables and Existing Farm Resources. After these are combined, the results are shown in terms of cost and profit structures, technical constraint evaluations through shadow prices and technical activity structures. Once farmers obtain these results and analyse them, the needed changes are made through feedback to the three main input variables. In Brazil the proposed procedure can be performed by 'PROFAZENDA'.

Showing this procedure for individual farmers with specific agroclimatic conditions, this system assists the farmer's decision making process

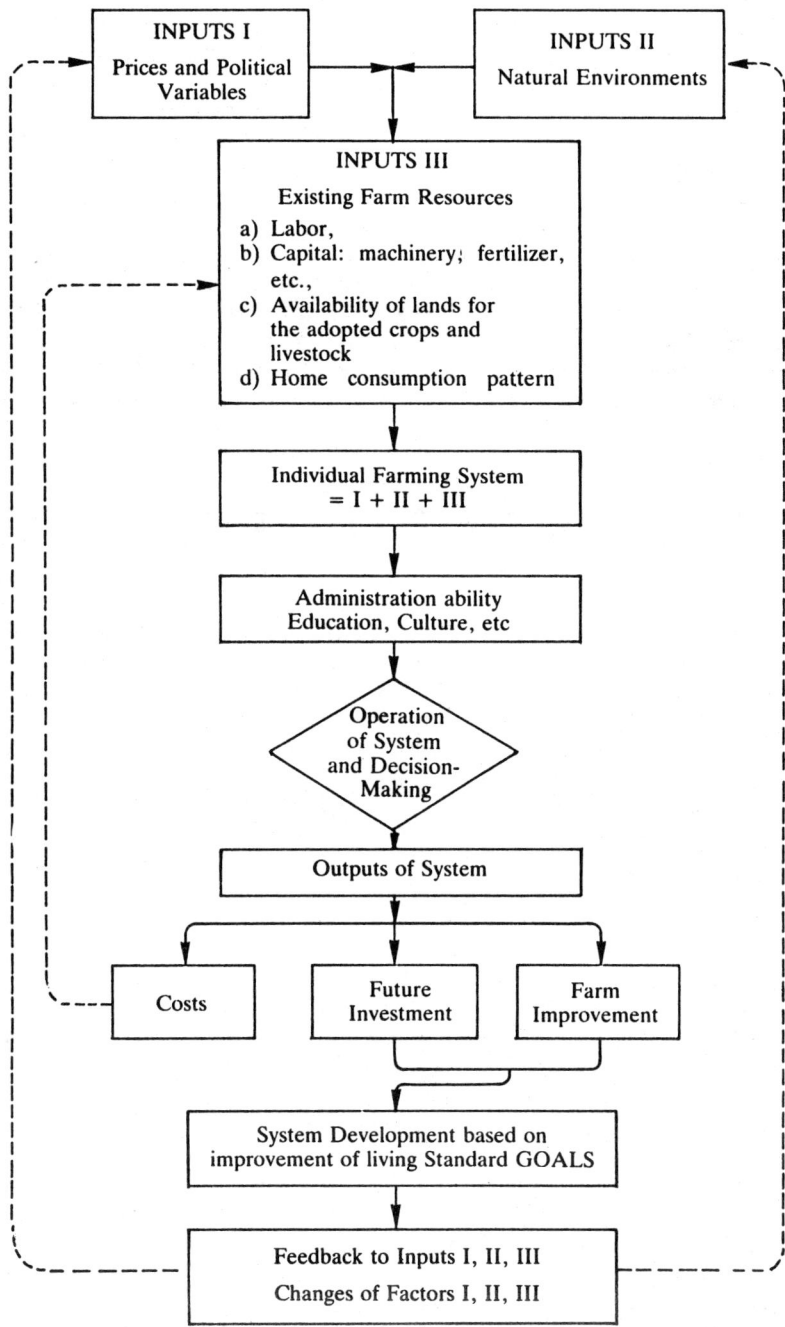

FIGURE 1   *The PROFAZENDA system*

TABLE 1   Result of the sample of the farms participating in the PROFAZENDA, by stratum of the area and by state, 1983–84

Farms (ha)	Equilibrium/ disequilibrium	Present plan net return Ad (Cr$) A	Optimum PLAN net return Ad (Cr$) B	Total area (ha)	Increased percentages B/A* 100(%)
I – Less than 100					
1.	DF	3,563,428	3,712,304	2	4
2.	DF	2,439,359	6,583,350	7	170
3.	DF	7,052,079	11,823,455	26	67
4.	DF	50,973,312	73,006,416	31	43
Subtotal		64,028,178	95,125,525	66	48.6
Average of Class I		16,007,045	23,781,381	17	–
II – 100 to 1000					
1.	PR	18,741,400	190,178,000	312	915
2.	PR	669,680,630	839,224,564	782	25
3.	PR	177,557,072	319,467,776	950	80
4.	PR	362,055,000	385,688,000	720	9
5.	PR	–148,252,624	–132,450,176	260	11
6.	PR	125,595,232	214,198,000	280	71
7.	PR	87,868,100	129,000,000	708	47
8.	PR	8,904,310	76,986,500	582	765
9.	PR	–32,322,400	–28,760,500	150	11
10.	PR	179,727,829	196,513,344	328	10
11.	PR	–12,035,327	–5,946,627	296	51
12.	PR	4,101,841	5,189,839	162	27
13.	DF	–1,702,096	1,354,000	420	180
14.	DF	37,775,056	49,472,000	121	31
15.	DF	–352,129	892,717	315	354
16.	DF	721,369	8,529,202	525	1,082
17.	DF	4,966,824	8,413,172	370	69
18.	GO	–46,327,584	–17,281,782	350	63
19.	SP	–2,207,504	34,115,056	241	1,645
Subtotal		1,434,494,999	2,274,783,085	7,872	58.8
		75,499,737	119,725,426	414	–

III – 1000 to 10000

1.	SC	-8,176,656	11,740,320	1,626	244
2.	PR	704,579,072	1,417,529,090	7,194	101
3.	PR	120,028,976	350,472,960	4,714	192
4.	PR	382,869,760	509,565,696	1,535	33
5.	PR	732,987,136	1,042,316,290	4,034	42
6.	PR	194,374,000	306,244,000	1,087	58
7.	PR	146,752,944	570,558,720	1,000	289
8.	PR	-15,841,024	217,374,176	15,761	1,472
9.	PR	193,964,096	399,241,984	1,020	106
10.	PR	108,400,000	132,247,000	1,085	22
11.	PR	-61,062,400	29,558,900	2,352	147
12.	PR	-80,918,463	-80,918,463	1,000	0
13.	PR	6,147,646,540	6,194,376,700	2,844	1
14.	DF	235,706,128	235,793,376	1,057	0.04
15.	DF	26,486,656	68,243,648	1,054	158
16.	MS	40,787,280	61,272,368	4,371	50
17.	MG	146,014,848	157,867,504	1,404	8
Subtotal		9,014,598,893	11,623,424,259	53,138	28.9
Average of Class III		530,270,523			–
TOTAL		10,513,122,070	13,993,392,879	61,076	33.1
Average of Total		202,228,052	349,834,222	1,527	

through a concrete farm operation system. Further, the shadow price analysis points out the bottlenecks of the whole farming system.

The characteristics of the electronic computer make possible quick and repeated runs for the farm analysis as well as for simulation analysis. This facilitates the analysis of the changing agricultural sector for both the price system and technologies.

RESULTS OF THE UTILISATION OF THIS SYSTEM

Preliminary results are shown by survey samples from the farms participating in the 'PROFAZENDA' system.

The sample of around 40 farms distributed in six states of Brazil was processed and analysed with the use of the 'PROFAZENDA' system. All these farms have had utilisation of their resources calculated at the optimum level. These, compared with the situation in which the farmers were adopted, made possible an increase in the net income of 33.1 per cent for all groups, as shown in Table 1. This could be reached with the same level of available resources and the same level of technology, permitting only the change characterised by the introduction of the electronic computer that executes the quick and precise calculation printing the comparison of results with various levels of input uses.

These results, even though taken only superficially, give an idea of the investment impact that the electronic computer can have as a tool in the agricultural sector for the change of attitude of the farmer decision-making.

The potentiality of 'PROFAZENDA', as a technological device to be incorporated into farm management practice, can be estimated by the volume of requests received from various parts of Brazil.

CONCLUSIONS

The use of the electronic computer makes it possible to realise detailed and quantitative analyses for farm management activities with quick and precise procedures, especially repeated uses. The characteristics of the electronic computer (high velocity and precise calculation) have shown it to be very useful for analysis in a turbulent economy, just like Brazil which is living with around 200 per cent inflation. Furthermore, there are increasing opportunities for farmers to face a variety of technologies. A computerised system makes easy the problems of technology choices in the whole farming system context.

The concrete results of the farm management analysis help to change the farmer's behaviour. The electronic computer with adequate utilisation has made possible a system for repeated uses as well as various simulations within a short period of time.

REFERENCES

Dillon, John L. and Heady, Earl O., *Theories of Choice In Relation to Farmer Decisions*, Department of Economics and Sociology, Iowa State University, Research Bulletin 485, Ames, Iowa, 1960.

McCarl, Bruce and Falck, Jurene, *Documentation Model B–9*, Station Bulletin No. 98., Department of Agricultural Economics, Purdue University, West Lafayette, Indiana, 1975.

Magalhães, Carlos Augosto de and Nathall, Peter, *Linear Programming for Repeated Use in the Analysis of Agricultural Systems*, Department of Agricultural Economics, Purdue University, West Lafayette, Indiana.

Sugai, Yoshihiko and Tsuruta, Jaime H., *Profazenda, Farm Management and Computer Sciences*, EMBRAPA/DEP, Brasilia-DF, 1983.

Sugai, Yoshihiko and Costa, J. M. and Teixeira Filho, A. R., *Computer System for the Decision Making on the Farm*, EMBRAPA/DDM, Brasilia-DF, 1982.

Sugai, Yoshihiko, Horiuchi, K. and Scolari, D. D. G., 'Goal Programming and Farm Management', *R. Econ. Rural*, Brasilia-DF, vol. 20. no. 2, April–June 1982, pp. 213–26.

DISCUSSION OPENING I – PHILIPPE LAMBRECHT

I would like to split up my presentation in two parts, first concentrating on the papers of Professors Sonka and Harsh which are largely supportive of one another and, secondly, give some comments and some food for thought in relation to Professor Sugai's paper.

The papers by Professor Sonka and by Professor Harsh provide an excellent synoptic view of the present situation of computer applications in agriculture and of the state of the art developments and challenges for the future. It can not be denied that computers, and especially microcomputers and the available software packages, have contributed to the development of agricultural economics by providing us with a powerful tool for the storage, processing and analysis of data sets. The very rapid evolution of computer technology in the last decade has considerably increased the computational power and has put it within reach of large numbers of people. This evolution, however, underlines the divergence in agricultural development between industrial countries, where agriculture has entered the high tech world, and the LDCs, where agriculture is still predominantly traditional.

When looking closer at the evolution of computer applications in agriculture, several observations can be made, and have been made to some extent by the authors.

1. The lower than anticipated adoption of computers in US commercial agriculture points at the uncertainty about the investment returns that can be obtained, as was explained by Professor Sonka, but this is probably less important than the uneasiness of potential land-users with this modern tool. Professor Sonka wonders whether we did not miss the point when calling for more and better training of people on how to use computers rather than designing computers to be more appropriate for use by people. This is a very pertinent question but when we look in both papers at developments and challenges, we are confronted with:

the development of ever more sophisticated and complex computer

systems, such as Expert Systems and Decision Support Systems, which are likely to narrow even further the potential audience;
the need for computer information systems adapted to the widely varying and specific conditions of individual farms. This requires flexible systems that can be tailored to the particular situation of the end user by that very person; self flexible systems are inherently more difficult to use though and narrow the potential audience.
My question then is, does not this defeat the very objective of making computer information systems more manageable?
2 A second consideration relates to database quality. The importance of good reliable databases is well established, and so are the specific problems of agricultural databases. The automation of data recording could prove an excellent solution to the tedious and costly manual recording. Whilst this seems at the experimental state in animal husbandry, automated recording systems for crops are still remote. Is there not a danger that automated recording will raise expectations too high since the margin of error introduced during analyses would largely exceed the margin of error contained in the database which may be very costly to establish.
3 Third, computer models tend to lack transparency. With statistics, nearly anything can be proved by selecting the appropriate database and time horizon, but at least, the rules of the game are known. Computer models usually include one or more parameters that are arbitrarily valued or simply estimated. Moreover, model builders often provide only scant documentation reducing the usefulness of the model by making it next to impossible to adjust the model and its parameters to ever changing economic and environmental conditions. This should furthermore be linked to the lack of deep understanding of the many factors that influence the physical production process and their interactions. The use of incorrect models may prove more damaging than the advantage of speedy and repeated calculations. Our Elmhirst lecturer, Professor Sen, has already warned us against blind faith in computer systems because of this lack of deep understanding of agricultural processes and because of the limitations of models that are not only technical but also the result of the imagination and comprehension limits of the model builders and of their communicative skills to transmit the message. It is our task to assure a widespread understanding that computer information systems and models, and the solutions to problems they provide us with, are merely decision aids but that people have to make ultimate decisions, be they right or wrong.
Let me turn now to the paper presented by Professor Sugai, taking into consideration the above comments. Professor Sugai presents the application of a computer-aided farm management system in a developing country, where even more care has to be taken in providing solutions to problems since farmers do not have a cushion against risks or failing innovations. The limited time and space available for the presentation of the

'PROFAZENDA' system made it impossible to go into detail and therefore the following questions should not be seen as questioning or minimising the value of this system but rather as a concern in view of what was said before, a concern that should be shared by the model builders themselves.

1. Does the database utilised justify the analyses performed (enterprise budgets)?

2. Can one model optimise resource utilisation for as wide a range of farms with sizes ranging from 1–100, 100–1000 and 1000–15000 ha and most likely different enterprise mixes and technology levels, or 'have aggregation rules been adhered to'?

3. There exists a gap between research results and farmers' results when introducing new technology. It is unclear how new technologies have been evaluated and there is a contradiction between the statements on page 740: 'This percentage of net income could be reached maintaining the same level of technologies' and 'The computerised system utilisation made easy the problem of technology choices'.

4. What optimisation objective is the most appropriate? Production, income or resource allocation?

Let me give two examples of computer model utilisations I came across during this conference and which show a lack of commonsense in the interpretation of results, that as such are rather unrealistic.

The first was a two-year simulation model based on recall labour use data collected after the agricultural season and where results indicated a decrease of labour inputs from year one to year two of 2 per cent.

The second was a LP model to identify the optimum farm size and enterprise in a developing country where the solution recommended involves an increase in farm size by factor 5, an increase in fertilizer use by a factor of 12 and to hire 350–400 additional man days per year in a country where fertilizer availability is limited and labour supply is scarce during the peak operation periods.

I would like to conclude with a slightly modified quotation from Dr Sen's address: 'Agricultural economists should be careful when using and developing computer-aided farm management systems to avoid being found with their boots dangling in the air and their heads deeply buried under piles of computer printouts.'

DISCUSSION OPENING II – GERHARD SCHIEFER

The papers by Sonka and Harsh, Kuhlmann and Burg provide a comprehensive introduction into the field, together with an overview of current problems and suggestions for future research activities. Instead of discussing individual aspects of their presentations I would like to complement the discussion by focusing attention on two issues which I believe are important for getting the papers and the discussion about the use of computers into a proper perspective:

(a) Computers as tools for administrative v. managerial tasks,

(b)   The intergration of computer-oriented research and traditional farm management research.

There is a general agreement in both papers that 'the introduction of computers has the potential to enhance management efficiency', but that the potential is not adequately reflected in the limited success of computers on farms. This prompts the question asked by Sonka: 'Will the promise be fulfilled?'. Both papers deal, in principle, with this question and answer it with a definite 'no – at least if we don't do something'. It is argued that for farms the perceived advantage of using presently available microcomputer-based data processing systems is not high enough to initiate a widespread acceptance. From this common ground, the authors discuss potential areas for research and development efforts aimed at facilitating the realisation of the perceived potential.

Computers as tools for administrative v. managerial tasks
It must be noted, however, that both papers concentrate on the utilisation of computers for management purposes (e.g., planning, control, etc.) and not so much on their use for administrative purposes (e.g., accounting, payroll, etc.). This is in line with the fact that for farms the administrative duties are of less importance than for non-farm business firms. But we should keep in mind that the success of computers is usually initiated by their capability to automate administrative tasks, i.e., to reduce manual labour input. These are areas where the advantage of computer use is usually obvious.

With regard to the use of computers for management purposes we cannot draw on much experience in the farm or non-farm business sector. A successful realisation will depend on the development of new and innovative approaches for the interaction between the farm manager and the computerised data processing system. This communication aspect is the crucial element in the development of computer-based farm management systems as it is the principal new aspect as compared to the use of management models on off-farm computer systems. Its consideration, however, will require a redesign of traditional planning procedures.

Traditional farm management research and computers: a need for integration
Both papers attempt to outline a framework for the development of computer-based farm management systems but use a different approach for their discussion. Sonka uses a dynamic stochastic programming problem to represent the planning problems of a farm and to identify areas where the value of computer use could be improved by appropriate research activities. Harsh, Kuhlmann and Burg, on the other hand, seem to have a more extensive software development background and discuss a broader range of issues related to the realisation of approaches. However, despite these differences they arrive, in principle, at quite similar recommendations which support the need for intensive research efforts.

However, for a discussion in this audience I missed more specific proposals about how to integrate those recommendations into ongoing traditional farm management research activities. If we consider computers as important tools for farm management, their introduction will affect all areas of farm management research. It will require the development of integrated data and information processing systems (see Figure 1) for farms which include as elements:

– data flow and data processing systems (which are open for computerisation),
– non-data information flow and processing systems (which depend very much on the farmer's capability) and
– procedures for the communication between farmer and computer, i.e., between the data and the (non-data) information processing elements (which depend on the design of appropriate interfaces).

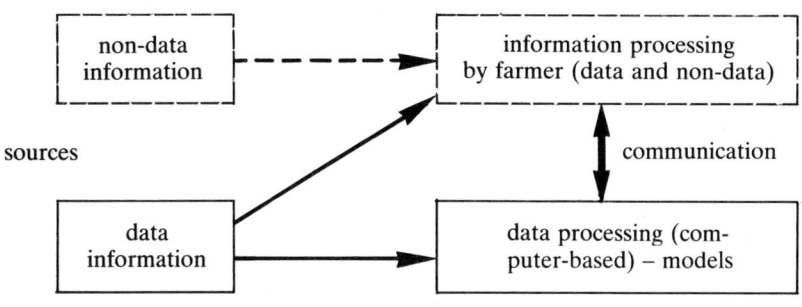

FIGURE 1

The discussion about the use of computers and their integration into farm management activities must then be part of a wider discussion which does not focus on what has to be done around computers but which focuses on new directions and priorities from computer-oriented researchers to farm management economists who integrate these data processing tools into their research framework as they integrated mathematical modelling approaches around 20 to 30 years ago.

GENERAL DISCUSSION – RAPPORTEUR: VINUS ZACHARIASSE

In answer to the discussion openers the speakers Steven T. Sonka and Stephen B. Harsh agreed with the statement that there might be a difference in the use of the microcomputer in developed compared to developing countries. By applying expert systems, the negative elements for adoption in the developing countries might be avoided however, and their advantage in using the new technology could be even greater. Both speakers supported a request for establishing new research programmes in this field of new technology. Another speaker asked for the authors' assessment of the likely consequences of farm microcomputers on the availability of farm-level data for the agricultural research institutes. Many farmers are willing now to pass their financial data to them because the data can be processed. The current development might bring them more autonomy and certain farmers might become more reluctant to pass on their data, besides having the fear of possible links with a central database. The speakers stated that it was necessary to return highly valued information to the farmer, otherwise the statement could be right. An important link with the central systems is the presence and capability of an adviser, who analyses the farmer's data and compares them to those of other farmers in the central data system. Another speaker wondered if the economists' conventional framework for the valuation of a new improvement is relevant to study the uptake of microcomputers. Sonka stated that for all types of new technology our framework of evaluation has proved to be an appropriate one. He also pointed at the challenge to defend this framework of valuing the new technology in answer to a comment that two theoretical approaches might be applicable, such as the use of diffusion models and the concept of returns to better farm management through better information. Bad management will replicate itself as the computer does not overcome the need for discipline in data management.

To several questions concerning the importance of the use of micro-computers, the speakers answered that software for microcomputers was becoming more sophisticated. The present software had to be improved by co-operating with other (agro-) disciplines. The software improves in the sense that the farmer is going to understand the science behind it, that is the science incorporated in the model used in the software. The role of extension officers must be that farmers are going to believe in the relevance of their (own) processed information, so their task is to help farmers to analyse the data, etc. Both speakers disagreed with the statement that the role of agricultural universities was to test and not develop software and held that the universities should develop prototypes in a continuing process in order to improve and so to move forward to the 'ideal' software in agriculture.

Participants in the discussion included Philippe Lambrecht, Gerhard Schiefer, Laurent Martens, Tahir Rehman, Bill Kinsey and Ulf Renborg.

SECTION IX

*Implications for Policy and Research**

*These papers were given on the last day of the Malaga Conference and represent the impressions of the individual authors regarding the content of the various sections (themes) of the conference and their views on the consequences for policy and research.

VIJAY S. VYAS

Balancing Overproduction and Malnutrition – Implications for Policy and Research

Even a decade back it would have been difficult to visualise a situation where on a global basis supply of food per caput would not only be adequate but progressively increasing. This increase in food supplies has come about without any measurable slackness in population growth or incomes. In spite of severe droughts in some regions, particularly Africa, global supplies are outpacing the demand for food in the market place. Increment to production has principally come from the developed food exporting countries, although some parts of the developing world, e.g. South Asia and Southeast Asia, have also contributed to the increase in food production.

An equally important feature of the current situation is that the relative abundance of food at the global level has not proved a sufficient condition to abolish hunger or malnourishment from the world. Available evidence suggests that during the last decade or so the proportion of people below the poverty line, which is usually drawn on the basis of calorie intake, has declined; yet the number of such people has increased. There are major concentrations of malnourished people in South Asia and sub-Saharan Africa but other developing regions, as well as some developed countries, have also not resolved the problem of poverty-induced malnourishment.

How does one reconcile these two features: abundance of food at the global level and existence of large number of malnourished people in different parts of the world? The answer can be provided by looking carefully into the aspects of (i) overall availability of food at the country level; (ii) effective demand, i.e. adequate purchasing power to buy foods; and (iii) adequate distribution mechanisms to shift more supplies from surplus areas to areas where market for food exists, in a cost-effective way. In the following discussion, we shall be concentrating on the first two aspects. A qualification may be added 'at the outset; we are not considering here the aspect of self-provisioning; this, though important, is a factor of declining importance in the world food system.

OVERALL AVAILABILITY

While food production has increased at the global level, the bulk of the

749

increases has come from the developed countries whose share in world food supplies is progressively increasing. A part of the increased surpluses is absorbed in these countries as cattlefeed, as the demand for animal products rises relatively more sharply compared with the near inelastic demand for foodgrains. However, the increased demand for cattlefeed is not sufficient to cope with the rapidly growing food surpluses. This has important repercussions for the trade and aid policies of the developed countries.

Among the developing countries three distinct patterns are discernible. The first group comprises the rapidly growing countries (e.g. Asian NICs), where food imports have increased in face of a satisfactory growth in domestic food production. These economies are at a stage characterised by an expanding demand for livestock products, relatively stable demand for foodgrains and shift of resources from agriculture to the non-agricultural sector. Because of the high productivity level in agriculture and despite resource transfer (i.e. labour transfer), the rate of growth of food production is high; but growth in demand for food and feed outpaces incremental supplies. The phenomenon of high rate of growth of domestic agricultural production coupled with high rates of growth of imports can be clearly observed in these cases.

The second group of countries comprises poor countries which are emerging as 'surplus' countries, due to satisfactory growth in food production but less satisfactory growth in domestic demand. India stands out as an important example of this group but other countries, particularly in Asia, are likely to join in the near future. While public stocks are accumulating, the number of malnourished people continues to be large.

We have a third group of countries where food production per caput has declined in recent years. Because of foreign exchange constraints they are not in a position to import adequate quantities of foodgrains to compensate for the loss in food production. Most of the countries of sub-Saharan Africa and a few in Asia (e.g. Nepal) fall into this category.

It is quite clear from the foregoing description that the problem of overproduction is complex, as also are the ramifications for future policy. At the global level, supply prospects seem to be bright. For developed countries as a whole production potential clearly exceeds their domestic demand. With the available infrastructure and technological advantages, they can easily step up their production further and augment the food surplus. The same cannot be said for the poorer countries. The engine of growth for food production is the technology which has a high capital, skill and organisation content. If significant transfer of technology, accompanied by adequate resources and favourable economic environment for the producers is not ensured, the poor countries may be faced with growing deficits.

There has been substantial rise in world trade in foodgrains, and the amount of food aid has also increased significantly. These developments have softened the impact of food scarcities in a number of countries, particularly in the countries facing natural or man-made calamities/ emergencies. However, the pricing and timing of these deliveries have many a time exacerbated the food problem. For some commodities, e.g. dairy products and sugar, so-called trade could hardly be distinguished from dumping of the surpluses of the developed countries, which in turn ruined the incentive structure for the domestic producers in the developing countries.

More than trade, the international scene in recent years has been dominated by capital movements. These capital flows, though enormous in quantitative terms have not been directed, to any significant extent, to relax the capital constraints on agricultural development in poor countries. The international aid as well as commercial investment in agriculture has not kept pace with the requirements of the developing countries' agriculture.

The likely results, of these developments are: (a) the tempo of growth in agricultural output in the developing countries may further slacken down, and (b) the concentration of food surpluses in developed countries may further accentuate. Thus, a global increase in food production by itself does not ensure adequate availability of foodgrains in the poor countries unless they augment their domestic production or create the wherewithal to import food from food surplus developed countries. Given the aid and policy regimes, the latter is not an easy option.

EFFECTIVE DEMAND

The availability of food in a country or a region by itself is not likely to resolve the problem of hunger or malnutrition. The access to the available supply is a function of effective demand. Wherever the rate of growth in an economy is substantially high generally the impact is felt by large sections of the society. Even in those circumstances certain sections of population are bypassed, or do not benefit from the 'percolation effect'. These belong to the households who do not have productive assets and the members do not possess skills or physical stamina. The situation is worse in the economies where the growth rate is modest – a more common occurrence. If the slow growth is occurring in economies where the asset distribution and earning opportunities are highly skewed, the number of 'bypassed' households will be large and their plight will be worse. The problem of removal of malnutrition cannot be disentangled from the problem of rate and pattern of economic growth.

Faced with acute disparity in purchasing power a number of countries have attempted to provide subsidized food to poorer households. In a much larger number of cases such attempts are made to cover food-insecure households during periods of drought, flood or other natural calamities. While there are several examples of successful interventions during emergency situations, the state interventions in more normal times have seldom proved comprehensive or cost-effective. This has given rise to a series of questions on target-group specific actions for providing food to poor malnourished people. These range from identification of target groups to the design of the delivery systems.

RESEARCH AND POLICY ISSUES

The theme papers submitted for this topic by John Mellor, T. N. Srinivasan and others, and subsequent discussion in the plenary sessions and group discussions have thrown up a number of researchable issues. It is not my intention to present a fully fledged research agenda on over-production and malnutrition. My purpose here is to highlight some of the conceptual and the policy issues on which the agricultural economic profession should provide guidance. These issues would include:

1. To what extent can we equate malnutrition with poverty? T. N. Srinivasan has raised serious doubts on the calorie-linked poverty measures. However, no one has come out with a better indicator of poverty. Although we need not spend too much time on 'head-counting', in any discussion on poverty alleviation proper identification of the group for which the remedial measures are suggested is the first step.

2. Why does not 'percolation effect' of growth cover all segments of population and generate adequate demand for food? Why are certain sections 'by-passed' in the growth process? Is asset redistribution the only alternative for ensuring wide response to economic stimuli?

3. What are the relative costs and benefits of target-group oriented public interventions, such as

(a) subsidized employment,

(b) subsidized distributions of foodgrains,

(c) direct feeding programmes?

4. How to strike a balance between food self-sufficiency and the trade-oriented self-reliance. Are these strategies relevant at different stages of growth (i.e. when 70 per cent of the labour force is in agriculture, compared to a stage when 20 per cent is in agriculture), or depend on the composition of output-mix (i.e. single commodity orientation of agricultural exports versus diversified export-crops sector), or predicted on available 'slack' in the food and non-food sectors?

5. What role should be assigned to price and non-price factors in augmenting food production? Should reasonable stability in food prices be considered an important goal of agricultural policy? What are the costs and benefits of such policy?

6. How does international trade in agricultural commodities affect domestic agricultural production in developing countries? To what extent should considerations be given to the 'border' prices in allocation of resources for different crops?

7. Should poor countries which have reached 'self-sufficiency' in foodgrains production pursue a deliberate policy for diversification of

their agricultural and rural sectors? What are the relevant models for such diversification (Japan, Western Europe)?

This does not exhaust the list of researchable topics or the issues which have policy significance but reflect, in our view, the over-riding concerns of the policy makers both in the developed and the developing countries.

GÜNTHER WEINSCHENK*

Pressure on Natural Resources — Implications for Research and Policy

Environmental concerns and problems of pressure on limited natural resources have been familiar to classical economists like John Stuart Mill or Malthus. However, forgotten during a long period of relatively undisturbed technical progress and economic development, they are relatively new to modern economists. Environmental problems pose principal theoretical issues, operational questions and problems of implementing an adequate environmental policy.

PRINCIPAL THEORETICAL ISSUES

Principal problems arise from the simultaneous consideration of ethical and economic principles and from the vague determination of the ecological equilibrium. Both problems are interdependent.

The ethical issue
The two following quotations from Rawls and Schweitzer characterise the two dimensions of the ethical issue involved in environmental problems:

If the world were fair, we would willingly enter it randomly

with respect to location at a given point in time, to time at a given location.[1]

I am life, which wants to live among life, which wants to live ... Hence ethic demands to pay the same reverence to all kinds of life which I pay to my own life.[2]

The ethical core of the environmental problem is the answer to the question: What is a fair distribution of limited natural resources (renewable or not) with respect to time at a given location and with respect to the division among the needs of the different kinds of life?

Need for a multidimensional objective function
Both quotations make clear, that what could be considered as fair is

*In co-operation with Rolf Brauch, Peter Maier and Rolf Werner determined by ethical rather than by economic principles. Consequently environmental policy has to consider ethical and economic principles simultaneously. In order to determine the objective function, one has to replace the one-dimensional approach of the classical cost–benefit analysis by the multidimensional approach of institutional economics,[3] since it is impossible to find a common denominator for the substitution of ethic demands and material welfare.

Value biased economics
The introduction of a multidimensional objective function is only a first step. It makes the problems evident, but it does not solve them, since rational behaviour under a multidimensional objective function requires the determination of priorities in some way or another.

At this point we enter the field of values which has caused so many discussions among economists. Certainly Popper's statement applies to environmental policy that one cannot take away value judgement from a social scientist without taking away his personality. I firmly believe, that there is not value-free economics in dealing with environmental problems.

Lack of a general accepted ethic
However, accepting a value biased approach (of course only if the values are made explicit) is only a precondition. It is necessary but not sufficient to determine the principles of finding an acceptable solution.

One of the remaining problems is the lack of a generally accepted ethic which includes future generations and nature in the responsibility of present mankind.

Nature as subject of human responsibility is certainly a novelty with which ethic theory has to deal.[4]

Jonas who has identified the problem and who has investigated it thoroughly did not find a *general* solution:

The concrete new obligations cannot be brought in a system because they just begin to appear in the reflection of the new facts of technological progress.[5]

. Let us see how far we can get if we use a more pragmatic approach and consider the different categories of resources described in Figure 1.

Non-renewable resources reduced by consumption
We are not even able to define the characteristics of a fair distribution in time for non-renewable resources which are reduced by consumption.

Economic models concerned with the problem follow mostly the attitude: 'Why should I care for wife and children? Let them beg if they are hungry.' They maximise the utility of the present users in taking into account technical progress or neglecting it. Most models which I know are typical textbook models of little if any operational value.

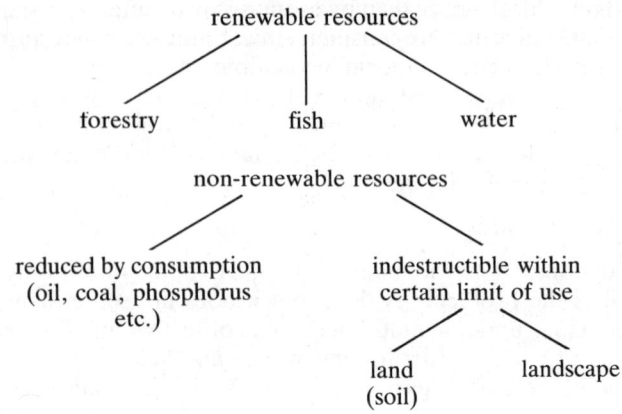

FIGURE 1   *Classification of natural resources*

Here is certainly an unresolved problem. However, I hesitate to say it is a problem for future research because it is hard to imagine that a satisfying operational solution exists.

Renewable resources and land   The ethical problem here is the problem of a fair distribution between human generations. The use of both – renewable resources and land – have in common that an upper limit for the intensity of their use exists. Observing that limit guarantees the stability of the system. Hence in both cases common sense limits the intensity of resource use. One must not cut off the branch one is sitting on. The use has to remain within the limits which preserve the long-term stability of the system.

Evidently this is a generally acceptable ethic (with the exception discussed below). Thus maintaining the stability of renewable resource and land use systems is not a problem of determining proper limits of use but a problem of defining and implementing a policy which makes people observe these limits. It will be briefly discussed in the next major section.

Ethical problems arise if the intensity of resource and land use required to satisfy the basic needs of the population, exceeds the limits which guarantee the long-term stability of the system. The exploitation of forests for the use of fuel wood[6] and the increasing intensity of land use endangering the continuous fertility of the land are typical examples which have been presented at the conference.

In these cases the 'skirt is closer than the coat' ethic will decide in favour of the existing generation. However, at the same time it demands a reduction of consumption to the lowest possible level, intensification of the search for substitutes and drastic measures which will prevent further increase of the basic needs.

Landscape   John Stuart Mill was the first economist who was concerned over the possible demolition of the landscape by technical progress and economic development. He added an aesthetic component to the objective function of environmental economy.

> Nor is there much satisfaction in contemplating the world with nothing left to the spontaneous activity of nature, with every rood of land brought into cultivation which is capable of growing food for human beings, every flowery waste or natural pasture ploughed up, all quadrupeds or birds which are not domesticated for man's use exterminated as his rivals for food, every hedgerow or superfluous tree routed out, and scarcely a place left where a wild shrub or flower could grow without being eradicated as a weed in the name of improved agriculture. If the earth must lose that great portion of its pleasantness which it owes to things that the unlimited increase of wealth and population would extirpate from it, for the mere purpose of enabling it to support a larger, but not a better or a happier population, I sincerely hope, for the sake of posterity, that they will be content to be stationary, long before necessity compels them to it.[7]

His warnings passed unnoticed as one can see if one drives through the most fertile plains in almost any part of the world. Even now the maintenance of the beauty of the landscape and the diversity of natural life is a subject which economists hesitate to approach. To my great surprise it was mentioned only in the discussion groups of this conference and one subsequent poster session.[8] In the section *Forces Shaping the Future* and even in the reaction to *Pressure on Natural Resources* the subject was completely ignored. Nevertheless, I am convinced that the problem of determining an optimal or at least an appropriate use of the landscape will become a major research area, especially of regional and interregional economics. In particular the poster session 7, 'Crise des agricultures paysannes', which has emphasised the problems of mountain farmers in the EC and in Switzerland has confirmed my conviction. It cannot be the answer of the affluent industrial societies to their structural and environmental problems in the agricultural sector, that they obey like slaves the law of comparative cost advantages promoting an increase of agricultural production in the already over-exploited horror landscapes of John Stuart Mill, while agriculture is displaced in the marginal regions where it plays an important role in maintaining the equilibrium of the existing ecological system.

The difficulty of observing adequately the appropriate intensity of the use of the landscape arises from the fact that the ecological equilibrium is not clearly defined. Ecological principles call for the stability of existing systems, generally including the demand that human use of the open landscape is kept within the limits which guarantee the maintenance of the local maximum diversity of natural life.

However, stable ecological systems can be also maintained at a low level of diversity of natural life. The horror landscape of John Stuart Mill in which every bush and tree and most of the wildlife is displaced by agricultural production can be found all over the world, mainly in the most fertile plains. Nothing indicates that the stability of these poor eco-systems is endangered as long as adequate cultivation methods assure the fertility of the land, avoiding soil erosion and destruction of the basic fertility and keeping the use of fertilizer and pesticides within certain limits.

Apparently the appropriate intensity of the use of the landscape is to be found within a (possibly wide) range of which at the one end the intensity of use allows for maintaining the maximum diversity of natural life, while the other end is determined by the stability of land fertility even at a low diversity of natural life. Economic requirements, ethical demands and aesthetic considerations will determine the adequate intensity of use in a given case, depending among others on population density and income per caput and food production.

We had two examples in the plenary session on natural resources:

the case of Java, presented by Birowo and Prabowo[9],
the case of the United States, presented by Farrel and Capalbo.[10]

There is little doubt that the adequate intensity of the use of the landscape is different in both cases, taking into consideration ecological and economic objectives simultaneously. In densely populated Java observing the ecological equilibrium at the lowest possible level of diversification seems unavoidable. Erosion control and appropriate irrigation management are major measures of environmental policy. They guarantee at least a temporary stability of the production system though on a poor ecological level. In the long run there is no solution to the environmental problems of the densely populated developing countries of the tropical world without a drastic decline of the growth of the agricultural population.

Seeing agriculture creeping up the hills of what once has been tropical rain forest one can hardly imagine that the environmental stability can be maintained another 25 to 30 years, when the population will have doubled again. Daniel Bromley[11] has added to the title of his paper the question: 'Is conflict inevitable?'. I am afraid, in many regions the answer is 'No'. Bromley sees the increase in the pressure on natural resources caused by population growth exaggerated by mistaken policy measures and by mechanised production of export crops.

Seeing the disaster coming I ask myself whether we can remain satisfied with the hope that 'agriculture is a flexible and resilient industry when it approaches a limit to growth'.[12] Is it not our job to illustrate drastically the way into the disaster if prevailing trends continue? This kind of economic analysis has been discredited as 'doomsday economics' since the Club of Rome model. However, doomsday economics is not necessarily 'measurement without data' for which the Club of Rome model was criticised. Based on well identified trends within realistic time horizons it is possible to highlight existing dangerous characteristics and enlarge them to a scale so that they become visible to everybody. Carefully used, this is one of the most important tools economists have to influence future developments in critical situations.

The low level of the ecological diversity accepted in Java is certainly not acceptable in developed countries. In many industrialised countries of the Western world the problem is not how to satisfy the basic needs of a dense population under a minimum of ecological stability but how to contain production in order to find and maintain an equilibrium of supply and demand. Two basic alternatives exist from a pure logical point of view, given the present and probably lasting trend of surplus production: either release land and labour from the agricultural sector or use the surplus of factor potential to improve the ecological performance of agricultural production. Once this choice has been made it is possible to design the framework of a rational policy.

OPERATIONAL PROBLEMS

Operational problems of environmental research and environmental policy have been described by Farrell and Capalbo,[13] by Kramer[14] and in case studies presented in contributed papers and poster sessions. We distinguish the following categories of cases in order to give a survey.

Possibilities of producing energy in the agricultural sector
The prospect of producing energy from alcohol (ethanol) has given wings to the hopes of agricultural politicians and farmers in the Western industrial countries. Alcohol means a new, almost infinite market for the agricultural sector, releasing the pressure on structural change which results from technical progress and limited markets. The main concern is that the production is not or at least not yet profitable with the possible exception of producing ethanol from sugar cane. Sugar cane has a clear comparative advantage with respect to the production of ethanol. Rask[15] has therefore proposed to increase the production of ethanol from sugar cane in Brazil and exchange it for corn from the United States. The profitability of the production of ethanol even from sugar cane seems to be a critical problem if one takes social costs into consideration. Da Rocha Ferreira and Tourinho[16] found that the Brazilian Alcohol Programme has induced substantial increases in the prices for food, thus causing an increase in the social costs which are neglected in most calculations. The opportunity costs of the production of alcohol might increase especially if increasing prices of energy cause an increase in food prices. The conclusion is: More research is necessary before one can recommend to start or increase the production of alcohol.
Economic research has to take into account:
  the social costs and the effects on income distribution,
  environmental aspects, considering not only that ethanol is 'clean alcohol' but also that its production might have negative environmental effects,

the relation between food prices and the prices of energy.

There was a second proposal for the production of energy in poster session 14. Martin[17] and Mayeux and Martin[18] from the IRHO [Institut de Recherches pour les Huiles et Oléagineux] propose to use non-edible vegetable oil as a local source of energy for small farms. They give the best chances to semi-perennial oil crops like castor beans and Jatropha curcas, which can be used as hedges protecting the land from wind erosion and also providing fuel wood. Their proposal has the charm of small-scale production directly addressed to small farmers in semi-arid areas with a limited production potential for food. I believe that further economic investigation would be worthwhile.

The use of renewable resources within stable limits

The determination of the optimal use of renewable resources is no longer a research problem if it ever was one. The problem is the implementation of a proper policy given the problem of externalities.

In many cases in the densely populated developing countries the use of renewable resources has passed the limits of long-run stability under the pressure of basic needs. The degradation of forests is one of the best-known examples showing that densely populated developing countries are about to make the same mistakes which industrial countries, especially around the Mediterranean, made a few hundred years ago.

Srivastava[19], presenting India as an example, shows that there is no hope of adapting the use of fuel wood to the existing limits of the stability of forests which have already been surpassed in many parts of the country. The developing disaster can be prevented only if one succeeds in establishing new limits of stability in which the basic needs of the population for fuel can be met.

Logically there exist two kinds of measures:
– measures to decrease the basic need for fuel wood;
– measures to increase the production potential of fuel wood without exceeding the limits of stability.

Since by definition it is impossible to decrease the basic needs of a given population, the demand for fuel wood can be decreased only by the supply of substitutes. Srivastava shows that the increase of the use of substitutes is not only a technical but also an economic and social problem. Fuel wood is cheap for farmers considering that the opportunity costs of labour for gathering it are zero or close to zero while the substitutes require either investment and social co-operation (biogas) or at least investment (solar cookers, etc).

Here is a field for economic and social research, besides technical research, needed to improve the quality of substitutes. The economic and social conditions under which rural households are likely to accept substitutes need clarification. The improvement of the integration of livestock in the farm is part of the problem to make use of energy from biogas.

The better integration of livestock into the farming systems is also a requirement to meet Ackello-Ogutu's[20] demand for a 'new approach to fertilizer use and food production in the developing countries'. The problem is known to economists. However, I doubt whether sufficient attention has been given to it so far.

Agriculture and environmental quality
The relations between agriculture and environmental quality are as complex as the field of environmental quality itself.
Three major problems are involved:
- soil erosion;
- ground water pollution;
- the diversity of the landscape.
The conference has concentrated most of its attention on problems of soil erosion, following the research of recent years. The almost exclusive concentration on land erosion is not justified in my opinion, but it is explicable for several reasons:
- land erosion is an irreversible and the most visible damage which can occur in a landscape;
- farmers are aware that there is a relation between land erosion and the stability of yields;[21]
- serious disasters have occurred in the recent history of industrial countries like the USA and the USSR and ecologists continue to warn that similar disasters might happen again, particularly in developing countries.[22]
These are reasons enough to conclude that economic research on soil erosion will remain an important research problem. Economic research in this field is still at its beginning and might gain importance but the other two fields should also attract the attention of economists, especially the problem of ground water pollution, which has not been discussed at this conference.
The basic structure of the operational problem is similar in all the three fields. The following subproblems have to be solved:
1. Measurement of environmental quality.
2. Determination of the 'environmental production function'.
3. Determination of the costs of measures.
4. Quantifying an optimal or at least satisfying policy.
5. Implementation of the chosen policy.

Measurement of environmental quality
The measurement of environmental quality requires:

(a) Criteria for environmental quality – Environmental quality can be measured:
- *with respect to land erosion* by absolute or relative losses of soil in a given period,
- with respect to water *pollution* by the content of nitrogen or other waste,

– with respect to the *diversity of the landscape* operational objectives are difficult to determine. One of the basic objectives is to guarantee survival of the possible maximum of species in a given region. However, whether the percentage of the actually living in relation to the possible maximum of species could be used as a criterion to measure environmental quality needs clarification.

(b) Transformation of ethic demands in operational measures – The transformation of the ethical consideration of the first section into operational objectives requires an answer to questions such as:
– Which time horizon has to be chosen for a tolerable or optimal solution with respect to soil erosion?
– Which is the level of ground water pollution which can·be tolerated?
– How many species should be given a chance to survive in a given regional unit?
Naturally the final answer to these questions has to be given by politicians. However, the job of scientists to ask clear questions and to insist on answers might become all the more important the more politicians prefer to 'agitate with a stick in the fog' because they are afraid of the consequences of a clear answer.

Determination of the 'environmental production function'
Determination of the environmental production function means determination of the relations between environmental quality and measures to influence it. Imperfect knowledge of these relations is one of the most important operational problems considering environmental questions from an economic point of view.[23]

The erosion model designed to compute average soil losses from water erosion is a good example of the kind of information needed for economic research. The 'Universal Soil Loss Equation' (USLE) provides an estimate of 'soil moved off the particular slope segment represented by the selected topographic factors'[24] under specified land use and management systems. It determines soil losses as dependent on: (a) the natural factors (kind of soil, length and inclination of slope precipitation); (b) the 'man-made' factors (use of the land, use and managing practices on agricultural land).

However, the specification of the function which determines soil losses is only a first step. Economic research requires a second step namely the determination of a function which explains the relationship between yields and soil fertility. The general form of these functions has been described by Lanzer and Mattuella[25] and demonstrates the complexity of the problem. The authors seem to have succeeded in specifying the coefficients of their model.

Research in other fields is less advanced. There is little hope that the coefficients for sophisticated economic models can be specified in the near future. Thus economists might find themselves confronted with the need to base at least part of their conclusions on research models with a less sophisticated data basis.

Determination of the costs of measures
The determination of the costs of measures to improve environmental quality is one of the major occupations of present research in environmental economics. One has to distinguish between costs at the micro and macro level, considering the disequilibrium in the agricultural sector of many countries.

The costs at the micro level consist of direct costs and of opportunity costs. Representative farm models are needed for the determination of opportunity costs. These models have static or dynamic character depending on the subject. Research needs extension. It is in the stage of pilot studies in most countries if it has begun at all. The knowledge of size and regional structure of costs at the farm level is essential for the successful implementation of an environmental policy based on incentives (see below).

Knowing the costs at the macro level is needed to determine social costs of environmental policy. Farrell and Capalbo[26] have rightly emphasised the need for better knowledge of the trade-off between productivity gains and improvement of the environmental quality.

A sector is productively efficient if it is producing as much as possible of every good and service given the amount or resources used. The neglect of the environmental quality components from these measures is a serious mis-statement of the economic performance of the sector and thus total factor productivity is inadequate for assessing economic efficiency and the tradeoffs between environmental quality and economic growth.

They view the process as an adjustment on the input side. Define the production function of a sector as:

$$Y = F(v, x, \dot{x}, t)$$

which represents efficient combination of the conventional inputs v, and the environmental inputs x that can be used to produce output Y at time t. 'If the level or quality of the environmental inputs declines ($\dot{x} \neq 0$), output falls for any given amount of the other inputs because of the necessity to devote inputs to changing the stock of x rather than producing output.' This diminution in output constitutes an internal cost of adjustment. The apparent inverse relationship between environmental quality ·and increasing productivity leads to several implications concerning public policies to raise agricultural productivity. Obviously, it is not enough that such policies should simply encourage individual farmers to become more efficient. Equally important is ensuring a high rate of gross investment in both the capital stock and the environmental stock. The relation described above in principle is the basis for an intertemporal model in which capital and environmental resource accumulation ties the different time periods to each other.

It seems doubtful if economists will succeed in the implementation of such a model in the near future considering the difficulties in determining technical coefficients at the present state of the arts. One must therefore ask whether less sophisticated measurements of the trade-offs would not be sufficient to justify the formulation of an environmental policy, especially in the western surplus countries which suffer rather than benefit from an accelerated growth of productivity.

Models for the determination of optimal strategies
Model building has become the playground for agricultural economists since Dantzig, Heady and others laid the basis for the rapid expansion of quantitative research which we have witnessed in the past 25 years. The principal capacity of the most advanced and complex models in production economics exceeds considerably the possibilities of specifying the corresponding coefficients taking into account the available data.

In environmental economics the playground is still waiting for cultivation. I am sure that it will attract the attention of model builders very soon. Maybe we will then face the same situation as in general production economics. Model builders will surpass data research and we will be confronted with general models for which we cannot specify the coefficients.

The general structure of the problem to be 'modelled' may be described as follows.
Given are:
1. The (dynamic) production function, which relates agricultural production of a given aggregate (farm, region or sector) to
   (a) traditional input factors land, labour, capital,
   (b) the environmental factors like quality of soil (depending on soil losses, the diversity of the landscape, etc).
2. The environmental function which relates environmental quality to factors or measures which influence it positively or negatively.
3. The quantity of fixed factors available.
4. The prices of products and inputs.
One wants to find a solution which maximises profit from production subject to the following restrictions:
   (a) Minimum given requirements for environmental quality (reflecting the upper limits for intensity of land use).
   (b) 'Technical' restrictions, which result from the needs of the production process.
   (c) The usual restriction that negative values of variables are not permitted.
Environmental quality is an exogenous variable so far as the minimum requirements are concerned (restriction (a)). It is an endogenous variable so far as realisation above the minimum requirement is concerned (production function 1). In other words, environmental quality is

determined either by the minimum requirement formulated in restrictions or by economic reasons if it pays to raise environmental quality above the minimum level.

The character of models which corresponds to this structure should be dynamic because of the dynamic characters of the two major relations (1) and (2). The soil conservation models applying optimal control theory correspond to this requirement (see below).

The positive experience with these models, particularly in the USA, cannot be easily generalised,[27] for the following reasons.

Production and environmental quality with respect to soil losses are positively correlated, at least in the long run. Farmers are frequently aware of the positive correlation as Saliba, Esseks and Kraft have shown.[28] Hence one can use the one-dimensional objective function of profit maximisation with some justification, assuming the minimum quality by the restriction (a). This corresponds in principle to the familiar practices already used for some time in farm planning.

In other fields, like maintenance or restoration of the diversity of the landscape, there is a positive correlation between production and environmental quality e.g. with respect to plant production. However, negative effects resulting from input requirements of land and labour clearly exceed the positive effects. As a whole there is an inverse relation between environmental quality and productivity. Hence, the one-dimensional objective function does not make sense. Models must show the trade-off between production and environmental quality in order to show what incentives are necessary to implement a corresponding policy.

Economists will therefore have to look for a simplified view, which leaves dynamic relations in the black box. A more simplified version of the problem might be described as follows.

Given are:

1. The objectives for environmental quality.
2. The measures to achieve these objectives within an acceptable time horizon. They may include investments which require capital and land, annual inputs of labour and capital and restrictions imposed on producers which limit their freedom of decision.
3. The (static) production function, which relates agricultural production to 'traditional' inputs at given stages of environmental quality.
4. The quantity of 'fixed' factors.
5. The prices of products and inputs.

The task is to find a solution which maximises the annual profit from production subject to technical restrictions which result from the nature of the production process and the usual restriction that negative values of variables are not permitted.

The environmental quality to be realised is given by the objectives, which are exogenous variables or, more precisely, the measures to achieve these objectives are the true exogenous variables of the model since the relations between measures and environmental quality are not explicitly considered. This is certainly a fundamental weakness of the approach, but it corresponds to the present state of the arts which frequently permits the determination of only one point on the environmental function at best. We will have to live with this state for a while, especially since many ecologists do not understand the concept of an environmental function and are not prepared to intensify research in this field.

The present state of the arts justifies the static character of the model though it is applied in a dynamic world. It remains to be seen whether these disadvantages can be compensated for, at least partly, by comparative statics and simulation without entering the zone of measurement without data.

POLICY IMPLEMENTATION

Environmental problems are part of the category of externalities resulting from the conflict between individual and common interests. The major instruments to solve them are known:

research, in order to solve the problem by technical progress e.g. by biotechnology, thus making it non-existent as a problem,

education, in order to 'internalise' the problems and its social solution,

economic incentives,

regulations.

Research is the hope of policy makers. If biotechnology will do the job, public policy can avoid undertaking the unpopular task of promoting environmental quality by regulation or spending money that is not available. However, research might take too long and it seems questionable whether it can do the job alone unless fundamental changes in behaviour take place.

Education and extension, whose role has been emphasised by Saliba,[29] Esseks and Kraft,[30] are effective only if the measures recommended by policy correspond with the economic interests of individual farmers. Hence policy only has the choice between regulation and economic incentives, if the relations between environmental quality and productivity are inverse, as is mostly the case, except where strong soil erosion occurs.

Environmental policy-makers, usually short of financial means, tend to favour regulation. However, one has to consider that the farm sector is hard to control with its diversified structure of decision-making.

Farmers all over the world know their economic interests very well and they pursue them stubbornly. Especially in the market societies of the industrial countries they have been trained for generations to organise their farms according to the principle of maximum individual advantage. Environmental measures which are in conflict with the economic interest of individual farmers have therefore hardly a chance to be successfully implemented. One has to 'pay the farmers to love the land' as the *Economist* wrote recently. The institutional and the economic framework of the individual farms have to be shaped in such a way that the economic interests of the farmers coincide with the 'production of environmental quality' at the desired level. What is good for the country has to become good for the farmers not vice versa. Taxes and subsidies are the major instruments of such a policy. Economic research finds here a challenging field of activities. The task is not only to design the characteristics of an environmental policy but to co-ordinate these policies with other objectives of policy, like farm income, structural change, employment and, last and explicitly least, productivity. I believe the loss in productivity caused by the stronger consideration of environmental requirements has been frequently over-emphasised in this conference. Especially in the industrial countries with agricultural surplus production, greater environmental quality should be given priority over the increase in productivity.

NOTES

[1]Rawls, J., *A Theory of Justice*, Oxford University Press, 1971.
[2]Schweitzer, A., *Kultur und Ethik*, Sonderausgabe 1981, Kapitel XXI (translated by the author).
[3]Söderbaum, P., 'Economics in relation to ecology: a discussion of development concepts', (contributed paper).
[4]Jonas, H., *Das Prinzip der Verantwortung*, Frankfurt, 1979, S. 27 (translated by the author).
[5]Jonas, H., ibid., S. 390.
[6]Srivastava, U.K., 'Search for more fuel wood and better forest ecology in India' (Poster 147).
[7]Mill, J. S., *Principles of Political Economy*, Nottingham, 1897, pp. 497–8.
[8]Drake, L., 'Scenic values of agriculture' (Poster 145).
[9]Birowo, A. T. and Prabowo, D., 'The pressure on natural resources in Indonesian agriculture and forestry'. (See pp. 284).
[10]Farrell, K. R. and Capalbo, S. M., 'Natural resource and environmental dimensions of agricultural development: Coping with the tradeoffs'. (See pp. 273).
[11]Bromley, D. W., 'Natural resources and agricultural development in the tropics: is conflict inevitable?' (See pp. 319).
[12]Edwards, C., 'The role of natural resources in regional economic growth'. (See pp. 692).
[13]Farrell, K. R. and Capalbo, S. M., op. cit.
[14]Kramer, R., 'An international overview of soil conservation policy', (See pp. 307).
[15]Rask, N., 'Expanding agricultural markets through ethanol trade', (Poster 151).
[16]Da Rocha Ferreira, L. and Tourinho, O. A. F., 'An evaluation of the use of biomass as an energy source: The Brazilian Alcohol Programme' (contributed paper).
[17]Martin, G., 'Vegetable oils: Can they provide a solution to Third World agriculture energy problems?' (Poster 148).
[18]Mayeux, A. and Martin, G., 'Integration of a non-food oil plant into the agrarian system with a view to increase means of production without energy constraints' (Poster 149).
[19]Srivastava, U.K., op. cit.
[20]Ackello-Ogutu, A. C., 'The need for a new approach to fertilizer use and food production in the developing countries' (contributed paper).
[21]Saliba, B. C., 'Comparative measures of effectiveness in farm-level soil conservation' (Poster 154). Esseks, J. D. and Kraft, St E., 'Soil conservation: some behavioural insights' (Poster 158). Taylor, G. C., 'Soil erosion control. Observations from the US experience' (contributed paper). Kramer, R., op. cit.
[22]Eckholm, E. P.' *Losing Ground*, New York, 1978.

[23]Farrell, K. R. and Capalbo, S. M., op. cit.

[24]Wischmeir, W. H., 'Use and misuse of the universal soil loss equation', *Journal of Soil and Water Conservation*, vol. 31, 1976, pp. 5–9.

[25]Lanzer, E. A. and Mattuella, J. L., 'Farm economics of soil conservation in southern Brazil and its implications for agricultural policy decisions' (Poster 150).

[26]Farrell, K. R. and Capalbo, S. M., op. cit.

[27]Bhide, S., Pope, C. A. and Heady, E. O., *A dynamic analysis of economics of soil conservation: an application of optimal control theory*, Center for Agricultural and Rural Development, Report 110, 1982. Burt, O. F., 'Farm level economics of soil conservation in the Palouse area of the Northwest', *American Journal of Agricultural Economics*, vol. 63, pp. 83–92, 1981.

[28]Saliba, B. C., op. cit. Esseks, J. D. and Kraft, St E., op. cit.

[29]Saliba, B. C., op. cit.

[30]Esseks, J. D. and Kraft, St E., op. cit.

WALLACE E. HUFFMAN*

Changes in Human Capital, Technology, and Institutions: Implications for Policy and Research

The economic environment facing agriculture in much of the world during the past 15 years has been described as being turbulent (Schuh; Rausser *et al.*; Fishel and Kenney). The plenary, invited, contributed and poster papers and discussions at these meetings have focused upon many issues that relate to the theme, 'Changes in Human Capital, Technology, and Institutions', My purpose is (1) to highlight issues that were underemphasised under this theme and (2) to present implications for future research and policy. Part (1) is included because a number of important issues received very little attention in these meetings.

ISSUES THAT WERE UNDEREMPHASISED

In this section, issues that were underemphasised are discussed for each of the following areas (a) human capital for agriculture, (b) research and technology, and (c) institutions.

Human capital for agriculture
Investments in human capital (schooling, information, immigration and health) change the quality of human time and skills for decision-making. A large body of evidence shows that these investments have important effects in agriculture, households and labour markets, especially when the economic environment is dynamic (Schultz 1975; Welch 1978; Jamison and Lau 1982). This focus was missing from the contents of the conference.

In a technically and economically dynamic agriculture, farmers' schooling and agricultural extension have been shown to have relatively large marginal products in market economies. Productivity arises from farmers' enhanced allocative efficiency – ability to perceive, interpret and take appropriate action in response to new information. Allocative ability is important in market economies when farmers must make decisions on adopting new technologies and on the input and output mix when relative prices change (Huffman 1974, 1985). Related to this issue is

*Daniel Sumner and Gary Williams provided helpful suggestions, while Ulf Renborg encouraged a provocative format.

a possible threshold number of years of schooling that must be attained (e.g., 4–6 years or permanent literacy) before schooling has a significant effect on allocative ability. Also, does schooling enhance farmers' abilities to deal with greater uncertainty of a turbulent world? Finally, are farmers' schooling and agricultural extension substitutes for enhancing allocative efficiency of farmers? In centrally planned economies, and in China, very little is known about the effects of farmers' schooling on decisions and productivity of agriculture. With the exception of Chaudhri's paper, the importance of allocative ability of farmers in a dynamic environment received minimal attention in this conference.[1] I think this is a major oversight.

Schooling of adult farm household members (males and females) has been shown to affect their time allocation and household off-farm income. In an unstable agricultural environment, farm households can diversify their sources of income and reduce income uncertainty by having off-farm income, especially nonfarm wage and salary income, or by engaging in non-farm enterprises (Pollard and Meyer). The correlation of changes in non-farm wage rates and farm prices seems likely to be relatively low. Schooling has been shown to increase the probability of farmers' off-farm work (Huffman 1980; Huffman and Lange 1984; Rosenzweig 1980; Sumner 1982) and, in developed countries, to raise the wage rate received (Huffman and Lange 1984, Sumner 1982). Suh, Osburn, and Price (1982) also find that higher schooling levels of farmers increases their probability of off-farm work. Less evidence exists on the determinants of womens' participation in off-farm work. Other papers in these meetings that consider non-farm income of farm household members (e.g., Pollard and Meyer; Mukhopadyay) do not focus on the human capital component.

Schooling for rural people enhances occupational and geographical mobility. With sustained economic growth or a turbulent world, labour market conditions for particular types of labour or skills can be expected to change. Occupational mobility is required to prevent a serious poverty problem in rural areas. With occupational mobility, some able individuals may be gainfully employed locally, but others will need to move to a different location. Schooling for males and females is critical for making this transition. Furthermore, Psacharopoulous (1981, 1984) has summarised a large number of studies showing high social rates of return to investment in elementary schooling and contributions of education to economic growth.

Significant increases in expected length of life in many developing and developed countries have occurred over the past 15–30 years. This change has been labelled the life-span revolution by some (Ram and Schultz 1979). The production of good health is centred in the household, but we know very little about this production process. Infant mortality is negatively related to mother's schooling, and child health is positively related. Very little is known about the link between food or nutrient consumption and good health, including energy levels, number of days worked, and life expectancy.

Increased life expectancy of individuals also has implications for optimal schooling levels and other resource allocations of farm and non-farm households during their lifetimes. The 'new home economics' provides a useful framework for considering household production of health and other human capital components (Nerlove 1974; Michael and Becker 1973; Becker 1981). Cloud employs this framework for considering the productivity of human capital investments in women.

The potential for agricultural extension is enhanced in a dynamic agriculture. In almost all cases, when the economic and technical agricultural environment is changing, the demand for information increases. The econometric evidence for productivity of agricultural extension is strongest in the United States and weaker in developing countries (Huffman 1978). The organisation of extension, ties to productive indigenous agricultural research, and goodwill with farmers seem to be important factors for determining the productivity of agricultural extension. These are important human capital issues that deserve attention by agricultural economists.

Research and technology

Advances in knowledge are both the source of some of the changes in the technical environment facing agriculture and one source of solutions to problems encountered by agriculture in a turbulent world. Recent advances in biological sciences and computer technology provide potential for enhanced agricultural productivity and growth.

Little attention was given at these meetings to the issue of how to organise research so that agricultural sciences efficiently incorporate advances in basic knowledge. How do we quickly integrate advances in general sciences into applied agricultural sciences and agricultural technology? How do we set incentives for older scientists to stay up to date when rapid advances in knowledge occur? Longmire and Winkelman do raise the important issue of what should guide the allocation or reallocation of public agricultural research funds (e.g., comparative advantage, social rate of return). This is a very important issue for determining the social contribution of public agricultural research (Schultz 1983).

The efficient organisation of the international transfer of new biological technology is an important issue. The private sector seems to be more heavily involved in biotechnology than in the green revolution (Fishel and Kenney). This suggests that the mechanism for transfer may be different. Also, how should scientists be allocated internationally? Developing countries face strong competition for good agricultural scientists with developed countries and with international companies. Successful international borrowing of agricultural technology (by developing countries) requires an ongoing research enterprise and high-quality scientific talent (Evenson and Kislev 1973; Ruttan 1982, pp. 173–8). Very little agricultural technology is directly transferable internationally or between regions within a country.

The productivity of public agricultural research seems likely to be affected by the organisation and methods of financing public agricultural research. The establishment of successful agricultural research systems is a long-term process. The willingness of countries to fund public agricultural research differs considerably around the world (Judd, Boyce, and Evenson) and the reasons for these differences are largely unexplored. What is an efficient organisation of research for dealing with problems in a turbulent world? What role should farmers and other groups play in the decision-making process and in the funding process? Also, how can multiple disciplines be efficiently employed? Large problems need the expertise of several disciplines. However, multidisciplinary teams that look for problems to solve seem likely to be unsuccessful.

Institutions
In a turbulent and changing world, it is useful to consider institutions to be adaptable. Olson and Schmitt have presented papers at this conference dealing with new theories of public choice where public policy is endogenously determined.[2] (Also, see Becker 1983 and Peltzman 1976.) Theories of competitive pressure groups provide a framework for showing how minority groups in a population can have strong political influence. They must be relatively efficient at exerting political pressure. The new public choice provides a promising framework for explaining national agricultural trade and other policies. There is, however, relatively little econometric evidence to show the usefulness. Exceptions are von Witzke; Rausser and Freebairn; Guttman; Huffman and Miranowski; Huffman and McNulty. Can the models of the new public choices explain changes over time in the policies applied to agriculture in terms of changes in parameters that affect the distribution of benefits-costs of these policies among affected groups (see Gardner 1983)?

Alternative farm policies for dealing with a turbulent world economy have distributional implications. Some of these effects have been considered by Just and Zilberman (1984) but others include the distribution of benefits among farmers who have different managerial abilities, the incentive for managerial skill development in the future, and the long-term incentives for nonhuman capital investments.

IMPLICATIONS FOR RESEARCH

Based upon the state of knowledge in these broad areas of human capital, technology and institutions, I am suggesting a relatively small set of research implications. These are research issues that I think are relatively important across developing and developed countries. First, I am making an appeal for high-quality econometric research. I have detected a reluctance by authors of papers at this conference to put forward new theories of behaviour and econometric evidence to test their theories.

The only way that we can advance in our knowledge of the behaviour of agents and institutions is to provide sound econometric tests of competing theories. My specific suggestions for research are:

1. Identify the relative importance of farmers' schooling and experience, public extension and private information on farmers' abilities to adapt to a turbulent economic environment.

2. Identify the determinants of public funding for government farm programmes, agricultural research, agricultural extension and schooling for rural people.

3. Investigate effects of alternative farm programmes to deal with a turbulent world (a) on human capital attracted to agriculture and (b) on incentives for long-term capital investments in agriculture.

4. Investigate the determinants of part-time farming and implications for farm household welfare.

These ideas provide a starting point. The hard work of turning them into meaningful research projects and programmes is left to you.

IMPLICATIONS FOR POLICY

I am somewhat reluctant boldly to suggest policy implications for representatives from such a diverse set of countries. For a wide range of countries, the following policy implications do, however, seem to be relevant:

1. Permanent literacy should be established for rural populations in developing countries.
2. Average schooling completion levels of rural and urban populations should be equalised.
3. National agricultural research systems, especially in developing countries, should establish incentives to attract and keep at least a few high-quality agricultural scientists.
4. A country's trade, exchange rate and domestic food policies should not be permitted to preclude benefits from agricultural research.
5. Public agricultural extension should emphasise distribution of timely and new information and should not directly be associated with politics.

In conclusion, I think that human capital for farm people is a high priority when one considers the ability to adapt efficiently to changes in the economic environment associated with a turbulent world.

NOTES

[1] Although several papers in this Conference focused on farmers' adoption of new technology, none emphasised the role of farmers' schooling or agricultural extension.

[2] Berlan's concept of institutional transformation is descriptive. It does not contain a framework that yields testable propositions.

774   *Wallace E. Huffman*

REFERENCES

Becker, Gary S., *A Treatise on the Family*, Harvard University Press, 1981.
Becker, Gary S., 'A Theory of Competition Among Pressure Groups for Political Influence', *Quarterly Journal of Economics*, vol. 98, 1983, pp. 371–400.
Berlan, Jean-Pierre, 'From the United States to a World System: Technological Change, International Trade, and Agricultural Policy in the 20th Century', (this conference).
Chaudhri, D. P., 'Human Capital, Structures of Production and the Basic Needs', (this conference).
Cloud, Kathleen, 'Human Capital Development in Agricultural Households: Women, Equity and Efficiency', (this conference).
Evenson, Robert E. and Kislev, Y., 'Research and Productivity in Wheat and Maize', *Journal of Political Economy*, vol. 81, November-December 1973, pp. 1309–29.
Fishel, Walter L. and Kenney, M., 'Challenge to Studies of Biotechnology Impacts in the Social Sciences', (this conference).
Gardner, Bruce., 'Efficient Redistribution through Commodity Markets', *American Journal of Agricultural Economics*, vol. 65, 1983, pp. 225–34.
Guttman, Joel M., 'Interest Groups and the Demand for Agricultural Research', *Journal of Political Economics*, vol. 86, 1978, pp. 467–84.
Huffman, Wallace E., 'Decision Making: The Role of Education', *American Journal of Agricultural Economics*, vol. 56, 1974, pp. 85–97.
Huffman, W. E., 'Assessing Returns to Agricultural Extension', *American Journal of Agricultural Economics*, vol. 60, 1978, pp. 969–75.
Huffman, Wallace E., 'Farm and Off-Farm Work Decisions: The Role of Human Capital', *Review of Economic Statistics*, vol. 62, 1980, pp. 14–23.
Huffman, Wallace E. and Miranowski, J. A., 'An Economic Analysis of Expenditures on Agricultural Experiment Station Research', *American Journal of Agricultural Economics*, vol. 63, 1981, pp. 104–18.
Huffman, Wallace E. and McNulty, M., 'Endogenous Local Public Extension Policy', *American Journal of Agricultural Economics*, vol. 67 (1985).
Huffman, Wallace E. and Lange, M. D., 'Off-Farm Work Decisions of Husbands and Wives: Joint Decision Making', manuscript, Department of Economics, Iowa State University, April 1984.
.Huffman, Wallace E., 'Human Capital, Adaptive Ability, and the Distributional Implications of Agricultural Policy', *American Journal of Agricultural Economics*, vol. 67, 1985, pp. 429–34.
Jamison, Dean T. and Lau, L. J., *Farmer Education and Farm Efficiency*, Johns Hopkins University Press, Baltimore, 1982.
Judd, Ann, Boyce, R. and Evenson, R. E., 'Investments in Agricultural Supply: The Determinants of Agricultural Research and Extension Investments', *Journal of Economic Development and Cultural Change*, forthcoming.
Just, Richard and Zilberman, D., *Equity Implications of Agricultural Policy*, University of California, Agricultural Experiment Station Working Paper no. 303, July 1984.
Longmire, Jim and Winkleman, D., 'Research Resource Allocation and Comparative Advantage', (this conference).
Michael, Robert T. and Becker, G. S., 'On the New Theory of Consumer Behaviour', *Swedish Journal of Economics*, vol. 75, 1973, pp. 378–96.
Mukhopadyay, Sudhin K., 'Labour Use in Rice Cultivation: Male-Female Differential in Time Allocation', (this conference).
Nerlove, Marc, 'Household and Economy: Toward a New Theory of Population and Economic Growth', *Journal of Political Economics*, vol. 82, 1974, S200–S218.
Olson, Mancur, 'The Exploitation and Subsidization of Agriculture in Developing and Developed Countries', (this conference).
Peltzman, Sam, 'Toward a More General Theory of Regulation', *Journal of Law Economics*, 19, 1976, pp. 211–40.
Pollard, Stephen K. and Meyer, Richard L., 'Labour Allocation and Productivity of Men and Women on Thai Farms', (this conference).
Psacharopoulos, George, 'Returns to Education: An Updated International Comparison', *Comparative Education*, 17, 1981, pp. 321–41.

Psacharopoulos, George, 'The Contribution of Education to Economic Growth: International Comparisons' in Kendrick, J. W. (ed.), *International Comparisons of Productivity and Causes of the Slowdown*, American Enterprise Institute/Ballinger Publishing Co., Cambridge, 1984, pp. 335–60.

Ram, R. and Schultz, T. W., 'Life Span, Health, Saving and Productivity', *Economic Development Cultural Change*, vol. 27, 1979, pp. 399–422.

Rausser, Gordon C. and Freebairn, J. W., 'Estimation of Policy Preference Functions: An Application to U.S. Import Quotas', *Review of Economic Statistics*, vol. 56, 1974, pp. 437–49.

Rausser, Gordon C., Chalfant, J. A. and Stamoulis, K. G., 'Instability in Agricultural Markets: The U.S. Experience', (this conference).

Rosenzweig, M. R., 'Neoclassical Theory and the Optimizing Peasant: An Econometric Analysis of Market Family Labor Supply in a Developing Country', *Quarterly Journal of Economics*, vol. 94, 1980, pp. 31–56.

Ruttan, Vernon, *Agricultural Research Policy*, University of Minnesota Press, 1982.

Schmitt, Günther, 'The Role of Institutions in Formulation of Agricultural Policy: Their Repercussions on the Challenges of an Agriculture in a Turbulent World Economy', (this conference).

Schultz, Theodore W., 'The Value of the Ability to Deal with Disequilibria', *Journal of Economic Literature*, vol. 13, 1975, pp. 827–46.

Schultz, Theodore W., *An Economist's View of Agricultural Research*, University of Chicago, Agricultural Economics Paper no. 83:28, 1983.

Schuh, G. Edward., 'The International Capital Market as a Source of Instability in International Commodity Markets', (this conference).

Suh, Cong, H., Osburn, D. D. and Price, E. C., 'Farm Production and Off-Farm Employment in Areas of Rapid Rural Industrialization', (this conference).

Sumner, Daniel A., 'The Off-Farm Labor Supply of Farmers', *American Journal of Agricultural Economics*, vol. 64, 1982, pp. 499–509.

von Witzke, Harold, 'The Determinants of EC Agricultural Policies and Their Contribution to Turbulences in Agriculture', (this conference).

Welch, Finis, 'The Role of Investments in Human Capital in Agriculture' in Schultz, T. W. (ed.), *Distortions of Agricultural Incentives*, Indiana University Press, 1978, pp. 259–81.

EDWARD W. TYRCHNIEWICZ

The Food Chain, Markets, and Prices: Implications for Research and Policy

President Johnson's exhortation that agricultural economics should have a problem-solving focus and Vice President Renbourg's probing quest for policy and research implications provide a challenging assignment. Within the theme 'The Food Chain, Markets, and Prices', there have been many interesting papers presented at this conference, spanning from methodological and conceptual contributions to specific empirical analyses. Obviously, it is impossible to glean and identify every research contribution and policy implication from such a wide array in the short time available.

My observations reflect the personal biases of an academic agricultural economist who has been influenced by brief forays into several agricultural policy formulation processes in Canada, a number of short-term assignments in Third World countries, and almost a decade of academic administration! Clearly, others would bring different perspectives to this assignment.

The thrust of my paper is to identify continuing research needs in the area of food chain, markets, and prices that should be addressed by our profession. The remainder of my paper considers the following: (1) some general observations on why policy-makers do not always listen to agricultural economists, (2) the notion of growing interdependence, (3) market imperfections and distortions, and (4) continuing and emerging research needs in the food chain, markets, and prices.

WHY POLICY-MAKERS DO NOT ALWAYS LISTEN TO AGRICULTURAL ECONOMISTS

One of the recurring observations made in various papers and discussions at this conference was that policy-makers often ignored the well reasoned analysis and obvious policy advice offered by agricultural economists. There exists an apparent clash in the 'concepts of rationality' between agricultural economists and politicians. Perhaps we are overly critical of ourselves, given some of the following rather basic observations.

We must remember that more than just economic considerations enter into dealing with most policy problems. Politicans need to be re-elected on a fairly regular basis (at least in most countries). These politicians are prodded and influenced by various other 'stakeholders' (besides

776

agricultural economists). These include farmers, consumers, agribusinesses, other special interest groups and bureaucrats.

As potential contributors to the agricultural policy-making process, we need to recognise that the scenario faced by politicians gives rise to a *hierarchy* of often conflicting goals. At the top of the hierarchy we tend to find *political* goals. These may include survival as a nation, political stability and food security. Political goals would typically be followed by *general economic* goals such as price stability, reasonably full employment, and positive terms of international trade. Eventually, *agricultural* goals enter the picture with objectives of stability and adequacy of farm incomes, food self-sufficiency, farm price stability and orderly structural adjustments.

Clearly, this hierarchy and listing is incomplete and debatable. As agricultural economists we need to understand the existence of this hierarchy of conflicting goals (in some form) in every country, and the objective of policy-makers (politicians) to arrive at balances and compromises. Policy-making is the 'art of the possible'. 'Economic optimality of rationality' is only one dimension of this art.

THE NOTION OF GROWING INTERDEPENDENCE

Much has been said at this Conference about the growing interdependency within our turbulent world. McCalla and Josling in their paper entitled 'Agriculture in an Interdependent and Uncertain World: Implications for Markets and Prices' present a simple but useful framework for viewing and evaluating the degree to which a country's agriculture is integrated into the domestic and international economies. Domestically, the degree of integration can range from a traditional subsistence agriculture quite isolated from the rest of the economy, through a transitional agricultural sector, to a mature agricultural sector fully integrated into the domestic economy. Internationally, the agricultural sector can range from an autarchic (fixed relations) state quite independent of the rest of the world to an agricultural sector that is fully integrated into the world economy and completely exposed to the fluctuations and instability in the world economy.

This framework leads to some interesting policy implications for the food chain, markets, and prices. First, not all countries suffer the same fate from world economic instability. Clearly, a country whose agriculture is highly integrated into the domestic and international economies is affected more in economic instability than a country whose agriculture is isolated from domestic and international economic vagaries. Second, a country's range of options for the support of its agriculture is dependent upon the degree of integration both domestically and internationally. Third, the desirability of economic integration, trade liberalisation, and resulting stability in commodity markets is conceptually appealing. Yet, the reality is that there is a growing tendency towards protectionism, further destabilisation of world commodity markets, and even more uncertainty for exporters and importers.

These implications suggest a very crucial policy and research question for agricultural economists: what is the optimal degree of economic integration of a country's agriculture, both domestically and internationally? Is the ideal of a mature agriculture fully integrated into the domestic and international economies necessarily the most appropriate one?

MARKET IMPERFECTIONS AND DISTORTIONS

Underlying many of the papers and discussions at this conference is a lament that market imperfections and distortions are growing. Why is it that agricultural economists continue to be enamoured by the idealistic (and largely unattainable) concepts of purely competitive markets and free trade? The reality is that market imperfections and trade barriers are growing rather than decreasing. Perhaps we should devote more of our research efforts to understanding these imperfections better conceptually, and thus become more effective in conducting relevant policy analyses.

Increasing government intervention in domestic and international economies is happening in virtually every country. Administered pricing policies are more prevalent and government marketing institutions, including marketing boards, are often endowed with sweeping monopoly powers and mandates to restrict trade. These administered pricing policies and marketing institutions, coupled with a myriad of subsidy programmes have rendered the concept of 'natural comparative advantage' rather meaningless. The term 'competitive advantage' which encompasses these distortions seems to be more in vogue.

The role of multinational corporations is also significant. The paper by Dufour, Ghersi, and Saint-Louis entitled 'New Types of Multinational Firms in the Agribusiness Sector and the Implications of Their Emergence in the Least Industrialised World' presented the rather provocative hypothesis that changing structure and attitudes of multinational corporations may lead to their playing a greater future role in technology transfer and product marketing in Third World countries. This could include a greater willingness and flexibility to adapt to local conditions and to become partners in development with governments of Third World countries. The presence of some agribusiness economists, especially from multinational corporations, at this conference and on the programme, would have resulted in a more balanced perspective on the role of multinational corporations in the food chain.

Other marketing imperfections that are becoming increasingly obvious were mentioned in a number of papers. Inadequate marketing functions, especially in Third World countries, e.g., transport, storage and finance, have hindered market performance. Institutions and arrangements, such as GATT, World Bank and IMF, are not functioning as well as when they were established. The growth in counter trade, which is quite illogical when measured against standard economic norms, came up in a number of papers and discussions.

CONTINUING AND EMERGING RESEARCH NEEDS IN MARKETS, PRICES AND THE FOOD CHAIN

A number of fruitful research areas have already been identified. In this section I focus on some additional needs that are primarily empirical rather than methodological in scope. These needs are not listed in any particular order of importance.

Cost analysis for administered pricing policies
Several papers addressed this issue, but it requires further empirical analysis in both developed and less developed countries, especially as political pressures for deficit reduction continue to grow.

Market structure, conduct, and performance under various political and economic conditions
Although agricultural economists are doing some work in this area, the growing interventionist role of governments makes this a particularly critical research need.

Economic and social costs of 'induced' competitive advantage
Again, the tendency of government policies, programmes, and institutions to distance natural comparative advantages both domestically and internationally raises the need to identify the costs associated with these distortions, especially in Third World countries.

Improving market performance in Third World countries
Although somewhat mundane in comparison to previously identified research needs, improvements in transport, storage and grading are critical to the success of government policies relating to food security. The role of market information in improving market performance is also important.

Implications of multinational corporation and government co-operation in the pursuit of agricultural policy goals
Traditionally, multinational corporations have been viewed with suspicion (often justifiably) in their performance of technology transfer and product marketing. The emerging partnership with governments raises many questions and implications that need to be researched more fully.

The effect of the world financial and institutional framework (GATT, World Bank and IMF) on agricultural markets and prices
This framework successfully guided international economic relations

during the stable prosperity following the Second World War. The onset of instability, recession, and escalating foreign debts has raised questions about the effectiveness and relevance of GATT, the World Bank and the IMF as agents of stability and orderly economic growth. As policy analysts, we have a tendency to accept these international arrangements and institutions as 'given'. It is essential that research be done to evaluate the effect of these arrangements and institutions on agricultural markets, prices and the food chain, and recommend changes where appropriate.

CONCLUSION

These remarks are some random reflections from one perspective, and may appear to be an indictment of agricultural economists. I do not wish to leave the impression that the papers and discussion were inadequate. Rather, I have tried to identify some continuing and emerging research needs in markets, prices and the food chain that we must address if we are to function as problem solvers and be listened to by policy-makers.

PHILIPPE LACOMBE

Structure of Agriculture: Implications for Research and Policy

The object of this report is to pick out trends, new features and discernible gaps in work on agricultural structure as it has been presented at this conference, to show how the discipline is developing, and suggest new directions for research.

Taking into account the rich extent of the programme and the short time available, this report has to be only an outline, even a caricature, and provide a subjective view. However, Vice President Renborg has freed us from any doubts about this by inviting us to express our personal views; provocation can often be more useful than subtlety.

What do we mean by 'structure'? All the related elements making up forms of organisation and exchange, enjoying some level of stability and with some ability to recur. This definition obviously needs clarification but, keeping it as a provisional one, one can see emerging a common feature of the papers, i.e. a reading of the dynamics of agricultural structures on the basis of macroeconomic determinants. This common link undoubtedly arises from the pursuit of the well known process of integrating agriculture into trade, but today, as this conference has recognised, new factors are contributing to this integration. Let us first briefly recall them before discussing their consequences.

The coexistence of situations of surplus and shortage accentuates the competition between developed countries to secure LDC markets. This turns them into battle stakes, a factor which no doubt partly explains the importance attached to them by this conference. The trade brought about by this coexistence brings together agricultural structures of very different types.

Increasing unemployment slows down the process of structural change in agriculture.

Monetary factors play a very important role. The instability of exchange rates is a relatively new source of uncertainty. The increase in capital movements resulting from government debts, bank credits and budget deficits emerges on to an integrated (but uncontrolled) capital market which directs the volume and cost of credits. This creates a new form of dependence for agricultural production in relation to monetary mechanisms and policies, both domestic and foreign, particularly marked

781

for those countries involved in international trade and exposed to fluctuating exchange rates.

Agricultural production thus becomes a pawn in the exchange of goods, in movements of capital, and in relations between states.

The environment surrounding agriculture, the increasing decisiveness of whose role I have justifiably underlined, is becoming more complex, and more unstable. It results from a new situation which cuts through the relative stability of the 30 years since the Second World War. Even if the relations between agriculture and its environment have become more complex and diversified, possibilities emerge for adaptation under constraint, new determining factors enter into the picture, while the way in which traditional factors operate can change. This is the objective of the first part of my report, to evaluate the effects of these changes in the agricultural environment on analysis of agricultural structures. But this new situation gives rise to questions and debates not only about the way agricultural structures develop in different countries but also the status accorded to this view in our discussion. Part II will examine some of these arguments.

I   CONSEQUENCES OF THE NEW SITUATION

Changes in the environment of agricultural production give rise to new fields of interest and generate renewed interest in analysis of types of farm organisation and development policy instruments, with many writers emphasising the role of social groups.

1. New fields of interest

An immediate result of the recognition of new determinants is the appearance of hitherto little studied subject areas: in addition to agricultural trade between countries, which I shall review in Part II, monetary relations have come to be added to the factors usually brought into analysis of evolution of structures: factor endowment, productivity, demand elasticity.

To reach these new fields, we first have to reorientate our current view of agriculture: we often persist in analysing agriculture as a branch of activity which purchases inputs and satisfies a demand when agriculture becomes involved in the exchange of goods; it also becomes part of the monetary and financial markers, as well as of a network of diversified activities bringing about alternative uses for labour and capital.

In the monetary field, many papers give us information on the mechanisms of global quantities, econometric analyses which study their effect on the composition of production, conditions for trade, and change in terms of trade. A way towards some progress might lie in identifying the actors, analysing their interests and behaviour, and locating their areas of common interest or conflict. This kind of research into the logic involved seems necessary for understanding the management of money flows; it is also a precondition for any eventual organisation of capital markets, the desirability of which has sometimes been mentioned at this conference.

As far as individual agricultural producers are concerned, monetary variables – prices, interest rates, real and nominal exchange rates, monetary policy – have repercussions for production decisions which have still been little studied.

This often risky dependence on monetary factors added to the growth of farm capital and indebtedness underlines the interest in new sources of finance and problems of farm transfer. Several papers remind us of the difficulties experienced by family farms because of their lack of resources, and their dependence on the life cycle, and examines existing or easily complementable formulae to remedy their situation in forms of communal ownership, forms of land development, pluri-activity, legal title to the farm, to the land and to the workers, adjustment of inheritance arrangements etc; these are research suggestions with obvious institutional implications and from which emerge themes familiar to agricultural economists.

2. Types of farming and their development

The changes in macroeconomic conditions I have already indicated which make agricultural production more uncertain and more risky, give rise to various forms of adjustment. There seems to be unanimous agreement on the heterogeneity and diversity of types of farming, giving rise to such categorical statements as: 'there is no such thing as the average peasant farmer or typical farm'. In support of heterogeneity, the papers indicate the many forms of pluri-activity, the diversification of production systems, the setting up of new forms of organisation to make use of local resources, the existence of communal types of organisation etc, and the theme of the dual economy is often raised.

This result is not trivial. Analysis of farms through the model of the firm could lead one to believe in the progressive emergence of a dominant type of farm through elimination of the less well endowed units and accumulation of resources by the rest. In fact, for several years the thesis of promoting modernised family farms has probably been most prevalent and today's agricultural policies frequently refer to this mode. This recognition of diversity and heterogeneity thus opposes the linear, homogenising, reducing to a common denominator interpretation, to which we have so often been subjected in the past.

This movement in favour of heterogeneity is all the more remarkable in that it results from such varied intellectual starting points. Models drawn in the neoclassical mould illustrate the possibility of retaining heterogeneity and the conditions which explain it: the continued evolution of techniques while changes in price continuously alter the optimal combination of factors of production sought by producers.

Economists who are anxious to interpret types of farming in terms of macro-economic determinants underline the logic of diversity as emerging from the interplay of these determinants. Those who study changes in rural areas or rural societies always see more varied forms of production than those seen by administrators or agricultural policy makers. Statisticians confirm this general observation.

Finally, and surprisingly missing from the conference, Marxist thought, or at least some of its movements, accepts the idea that capital operating as a social link effects a permanent change in farm structure, giving way to new and varied types of organisation.

This finding of diversity often leads researchers to alter their way of approaching farms, which are no longer merely considered as farms (enterprises) but as households with consumption and investment needs which they must satisfy by mobilising resources with a wide range of uses in terms of systems of activity and capital investment. The basic identity frequently used for studying farms – 1 farm = 1 household = 1 exclusively agricultural activity = 1 farm income which has to finance consumption and investment – is today often called into question because of the diversification of activities and sources of income. Agricultural production thus becomes part of a family-based economy in which it is only one element. This shift in method of approach provides an opportunity for taking a closer interest in agricultural household consumption (level, composition, finance) and in localisation of activities.

This remarkable unanimity disappears when, seeking to complete the picture of agreement on heterogeneity, one asks a question about its constituent parts. This question has been very little tackled in either papers or discussions. For most papers, 'structures' are seen in terms of farm organisation. There is no attempt to combine these structures to understand their origins, their repetition, or to place them in a higher degree context which may be able to explain their dynamics. Perhaps even to propose such an idea would be considered futile by many speakers.

On the other hand, taking heterogeneity on board does not mean we can ignore two points concerning, first, taking account in economic policy of structures and their heterogeneous nature and, second, considering the social groups involved in these structures.

3. The instruments of development policy

The evolution of production conditions renews the debate on instruments of agricultural development policy. At the conference, this debate was limited to the case of developing countries.

Agreement was easily reached on underlining the importance of the role of prices and their inadequate levels. But the risk of contradictions in the resulting effects of changes in prices is also indicated: it is difficult to use price as a single policy instrument to simultaneously satisfy various objectives. I can understand the division of opinion between those wanting action on prices alone and those who think action on prices *and* on production structures is necessary to facilitate a response from the production system. However, the justification and forms of actions on structures have very often taken the form of appendices to papers and discussions. This seems to me regrettable, first because those in charge of development operations come face to face with them, and second, because action on prices is linked with action on structures: a price policy is also a structural policy (since it defines those farms able to continue and extend) while a structural policy is also a price policy (since it determines the performance of the production structure).

4. The role of social groups

Reference is certainly very frequently made to the importance of peasant participation, consulting their interests and getting them involved. In actual fact, much more frequently than an analysis, there is a simple, often conventional call for mobilisation of the actors involved.

Analyses on the constitution of an agrarian social movement, its role in managing a situation, or in sharing out the surplus are almost non-existent. Do we have to conclude, then, that for many speakers, these preoccupations are outside our scientific field? This is an extreme view, as Olson's paper shows, but for most of the papers and discussion, the question needs to be asked, and the answer would probably be affirmative.

The predominance of such an attitude is regrettable. The history of economic thought already shows the validity and the relevance of taking into account social categories more rigorously defined than by a simple reference to consulting those concerned. In considering the more limited field of agricultural economics, two arguments could be put forward in favour of more differentiated approaches.

In the first place, social groups are a determining factor in how structures evolve. Taking such a determinant seriously should lead to studying the social space occupied by the agricultural population in society. Through this space, peasant farmers can influence access to land, price relationships, the marketing system, allocation of public resources, and the role of the agricultural social movement. This social space is also the precondition for rural societies to become aware of their situation and contribute, under constraint, to the direction of their own development.

In the second place, collective action by farmers, or some groups among them, is the result of confrontation between economic interests dependent upon structures which agricultural economists quite rightly study with minute attention. In terms of this conference, a paradoxical view may be noted: the heterogeneity of structures is emphasised on the one hand, while at the same time talking of farmers as a homogeneous indistinguishable group whose role in collective and action and policy making is little studied. In this field Olson's communication provides particular relief. His proposals on group make-up and effectiveness seem applicable to analysis of the success, failures and operations of agricultural organisations. They also offer an invitation to pursue the study of the conditions required to change latent groups into working groups and, inversely, how economic and social structures favour, or do not favour, these transitions. Ignoring this question could lead to looking for explanations within groups without considering their mutual relationships.

5. A note on methodology

This review of work on structures and structural change, their original features, and their limitations can be concluded with a note on the methodological attitude of many authors of papers. These emphasise the multiplicity and complexity of the determining factors at work, whose result one cannot always predict. This is not a trivial observation; it indicates that the solution is not always strictly determined and the linear trends to which the preceding time period has made us accustomed are less frequently justified. In support of this, one could also note the attention given to the perverse effects indicated in relation to both interventionist and liberal policies.

A scientific caution emerges from these remarks which is favourable for identifying closed situations for which determinism is vital and open situations whose dynamic is uncertain. This is a not inconsiderable result if one admits that determinism is not indispensable in understanding social phenomena or in their interests. It is undoubtedly the crisis which, by weakening certainties, explains this methodological trend which leads agricultural economists to look again for contemporary questions on scientific determinism, as found in the works of Karl Popper.

This trend is opportune for identifying the themes of discussions and pinpointing unanswered questions which can be more deeply examined later.

II QUESTIONS AND DISCUSSIONS

Among the whole range of debates opened up by the papers given at the conference in the field of structures, two merit particular attention.

The first is the case of the relationship between the agriculture of developed and developing countries, for two reasons: (1) because of the scientific and political stakes involved, and (2) because our meeting, bringing economists from all over the world, is a particularly appropriate forum in which to tackle these questions.

In the second place, the remarks made below on the place and role of the notion of structure in our analyses invites us to consider the image agricultural economists have of this concept and the significance they allow it. With a view to clarification, I shall attempt to explain, in broad terms, the major well known differences between us in resorting to this notion of structure. This clarification seems to be a precondition for recognising the diversity of approaches, getting to the bottom of them, and questioning them together.

1. Relations between the agricultures of developed and developing countries

These relationships between countries at different stages of development seem to me to challenge agricultural economists in two particular areas: comparison of their structures, and analysis of the interrelationships between heterogenous agricultural structures.

(a) Comparison of structures It has been usual to insist on the specificity of production conditions in developed and developing countries. This might justify different methods, different forms or even separate sciences. In fact, during our conference, individual papers have been devoted to one or the other field. This very clear-cut distinction seems to me regrettable.

One gets a better understanding of the agricultural structures of developed countries from the research on agricultural structures carried out in developing countries. While the production condition may differ from one country to the next, the working methods and approaches seem comparable and likely to provide mutual benefit. Numerous examples can be cited from various fields: supply elasticities, migration, family organisation, relationship between the farm and the environment, etc. As the remarks of Polanyi remind us, observing modern societies in the light of developing societies stops us from separating economic phenomena from the rest of society as if they constituted an airtight and autonomous field.

It is true that there are risks of improper transfers of economic concepts or techniques, but this is due to the clumsiness of economists who tack a pre-established representation on to the real situation being studied, rather than seeking to understand how it works. This is also a risk in studying developed country agriculture.

This interest in comparing structures is further strengthened through the increasingly frequent communication between different agricultures because of trade.

(b) Interrelations between heterogeneous structures Relating the varied types of agriculture belonging to unequally developed countries gives rise to a double debate: scientific, about how to divide up agricultural activities, and political, on the direction of national food and agricultural strategies.

To simplify the usual concepts, location of production occurs according to comparative advantage, the market ensures communication between the various production regions, and international division of labour is thus found to be justified. In their most classical interpretation, these mechanisms offer such advantages that the economic policies to be implemented are self-evident. Given the questions at stake in this analysis, it seems to be important to carry to its limits the debate over the effects of competition between heterogeneous and unequal structures.

Consumption models for developing countries are similar to those for developed countries under the effect of imports made necessary through situations of extreme shortage, decided upon by governments, solicited by privileged social categories, or brought about by surplus situations in developed countries. This consumption model is thus not always oriented in favour of the operation and development of national agricultural structures. Developing countries' agriculture often finds itself both dependent on the export market, if it is an exporting country, but also on the import market, which provides products which are direct competitors with nationally produced or substitute products. And in this competition, the productivity gaps are such that LDC agriculture cannot rival that in developed countries.

Undoubtedly, the market offers advantages, frequently mentioned during the course of the conference, in terms of reducing surpluses and deficits but the characteristics of international agricultural trade provide contradictions to the thesis of international division of labour brought about by market mechanisms. Overproduction leads the developed countries to make price concessions or agree to export-linked advantages – credit, purchases, military protection, more or less overt political support. The market thus keeps an economic and political dependence; it may be a means of redistributing, but is also a way of dividing up the world. International trade cannot thus be analysed only in terms of supply and demand without explaining how they are directed and determined by the agricultural structures of the countries doing the trading.

2. On the use of the notion of structure

Although very little alluded to directly in our work, this question has always been implied, without there being any debate or argument about it. This can result in a poor appreciation of the dynamics of the discipline in this field. To begin to clarify the matter and encourage its study in greater depth, two concepts of the idea of structure can be set against one another. The way already prepared by earlier discussion, these concepts seems to be very clearly introduced by referring to the discussion between Berlan and Gonzalez-Vega on the problems of a particular agricultural change – setting up the maize-soya model.

In Berlan's exposé, this change results from the functioning of a structure characterised by a certain level of technical development and a given social organisation. It is the functioning of this structure which ensures change in the production model. In the comments by Gonzalez-Vega, the change in question is the result of adjustment of the price mechanism resulting from the encounter between, on the one hand, supply which works according to comparative advantage and, on the other, demand, dictated by changes in income.

From this example, one can distinguish a concept which sees in the idea of structure a means of clarifying, of precisely defining, the whole field of study, and a concept according to which the structure is a basic characterisation of the whole, giving it its operational logic.

According to a *first* concept, the notion of structure is a way of disaggregating global quantities while taking account of their organisations. The latter can make for efficient operations of economic mechanisms. In frequent cases the structure impedes economic operations; but adjustment of supply through price will end up doing it too. If one takes even a passing interest in the analysis of structures, it is simply to facilitate the movement towards rationality. One may also analyse structures to improve the representativeness of models; this process could then lead to research on constraints so as to take better account of the behaviour of the actors involved. Briefly, in this context, the economy is a process of adjustment through the price mechanism imposed on the social organisation which has then to adapt itself. Structures can thus have a second or secondary status.

Such a theoretical position often leads from description of a reality to confirmation of a norm. If economic science is a means not only of defining rationality but also of defining the conditions in which this rationality is beneficial to society, at least for a time, one can see that the researcher in economics can claim to define the norms of good operations.

According to a *second* concept, structure is a way of characterising the society being studied. Economic operation is not an adjustment procedure which is necessary at all times and in all places, independently of the social organisation, but the product of social links which make up a system. Rationality is not postulated, it is the result of research.

In this perspective, economic relationships are not a separate field, independent of social organisation, condemning other relationships to the role of exogenous variables or to an institutional role. The objective of the analysis is to find areas of connection, contradiction and complementarity between the various components of the society under study. These proposals reserve a privileged place for analyses of stratification which can pinpoint social relationships (who does what and how) and historical analyses to study how social groups develop, and their linkages.

Contrary to a widely held idea, this process excludes neither quantification nor model building but subjects them to preliminary knowledge, at least hypotheses, of the logic of operations of the whole being studied.

Surprisingly enough this view of the notion of structure has featured very little at the conference, although in the world at large it is often referred to by many agricultural economists; as evidenced by the frequency of systems analysis carried out by agricultural economists, the world of economic anthropologists and the various currents emanating from Marxism. As can be seen, there is a wide range of ideas on this theme, which cannot be reviewed here.

The concept is obviously full of risks and confronted with difficulties. On the one hand it faces the threat of monotony of hypotheses, verified by some researchers for all circumstances as if they offer the universal answer for all situations, the concessions having been predetermined before the research was even carried out! On the other hand, this approach generally covers broad fields, and has as a result to deal with delicate questions concerning the relationships between these fields;

technical progress and economic organisation, state and society, ecosystem and social dynamic. In Marxist analysis, there are innumerable debates on the identification and articulation of modes of production making up a social formation, and in the relationships between infrastructure and superstructure or between productive forces and social returns.

This attention given at the end of our conference to the concept of structure and its current status in our discipline, marks an opportune end to our discussions. To clarify and perhaps ultimately enrich these discussions on the status of structures in our analysis is undoubtedly a good way of finding out our differences when one is placed immediately on the methodological level. It is in any case a precondition for exchanges of views on the scientific nature of the view of structure we accept. For this, our Association should make room for the various currents of thought running through the agricultural economics profession. In this connection, it seems to me that the interpretation of structures as a foundation of the logic at work is over-represented in the world at large as much as in our organisation. If this organisation claims international status, it should be open to this wide range of currents and examine them in depth. This is also an excellent protection against the risk of creating an intellectual monolith. This wish, if it is shared, means that we are already involved in preparations for our next meeting.

Synoptic View

MICHEL PETIT
PRESIDENT-ELECT

The Status and the State of Agricultural Economics

At the end of this Nineteenth Conference of our International Association, opened by a Presidential Address reflecting on the scope of agricultural economics,[1] it is on the status and on the state of our discipline which I would like you to reflect. First of all, I must emphasise that the expression 'Agricultural Economics' is used here exactly with the same meaning as 'Economia Agraria' in Spanish, 'Economie Rurale' in French. This hesitation of the vocabulary reflects the nature of our discipline. Actually, none of these three expressions is strictly correct. This is precisely the problem which led Malassis, in another reflection on the object of our discipline presented to the European Association of Agricultural Economists to speak in terms of agricultural, agribusiness, and rural economics.[2] Let us stress that the difference of vocabulary does not correspond here to a difference of viewpoints on our discipline. It illustrates a problem of status: the field of agricultural economics is not defined only in terms of a scientific discipline. We shall come back later to this crucial question, but first I must specify what I mean by the state of agricultural economics. Our specialisation being defined by the use of concepts, hypotheses and methods of economics to the analysis of problems faced by agriculture in the broadest sense of this term, may one speak of the state of this utilisation in the world? Is this possible when account is taken of our extreme diversity?

It is obvious that the professional projects of our members, that is the objectives and the criteria used to judge the quality of our works, are extremely varied. Some mainly wish to make original contributions to the elaboration of economics as science; others want to find solutions to such major problems as hunger in the world or the conservation of natural resources; others still would like to participate in the solution of problems faced by the political authorities of their country or their region. Some of us, I am sure, believe that the ultimate test of the interest of our works is to know whether or not we bring something useful to farmers. The diversity of our professional projects also illustrates the diversity of the institutions we work in (universities, research organisations, government agencies, farm organisations, firms, etc.) and the diversity of the role given to scientists and technicians in the various societies, cultures and civilisations from which we come.

But beyond these diversities we have something in common; as illustrated for instance by the fact that we belong to the same international organisation. What we have in common, of course, is that we are agricultural economists. Thus, to discuss the state of our common project, i.e. the use of economics in agriculture, seems appropriate.

I have organised my presentation around three questions: where do we come from?, where are we now?; where do we go from here? The last question will permit us to reflect on our objectives and on our criteria of professional excellence. I shall use our work during this conference as illustrations. This seems justified on two accounts: first, it will facilitate communication by referring to something which we all know; second, such a conference constitutes an excellent opportunity to become more conscious of the diversity of approaches and of the main questions which preoccupy our colleagues throughout the world, even if all have not been equally well represented here.

WHERE DO WE COME FROM?

Our past, more precisely the intellectual traditions which influence us, must absolutely be taken into account if we want to be clearly conscious of what we are and to properly examine the relevance of our objectives and of our criteria of professional excellence; this justifies the question defining the object of this first part of my paper. The answer seems clear to me, even if its consequences raise fundamental ambiguities. We come from the 'agronomic' tradition and we claim to be fully fledged economists.

The 'agronomic' tradition
What is the exact meaning of this expression? For me, without ignoring the Roman agronomists or the concerns of Olivier de Serres, whose 'Mesnage des champs', written at the end of the sixteenth century, may be viewed as the forerunner of farm management, the real birth of 'agronomy' took place during the nineteenth century in western countries. From there it spread to most countries of the world as the scientific basis of modern agriculture. Agronomists behaved as the missionaries of scientific and technical progress in the countryside. This proselytism would be condemned by most of us today because it is much too closely linked with the scientism of that period. But it is from there that stems our concern for application.

The 'agronomy' of the nineteenth century must be understood in a broad sense. It is the use of all scientific disciplines which can clarify the problems of agriculture. In this sense, agricultural economics is clearly an 'agronomic' discipline; and this is widely reflected in most institutions of higher agricultural education and research in the world. Admittedly, like other social sciences, agricultural economics conquered its place late, and often with many difficulties.

Strikingly, it is roughly at the same time, in all western countries, that this 'agronomic' tradition was born. Even in new countries, as for instance were then the United States, the birth occurred at that time. Let us remember that the Morrill Act, creating the famous land-grant colleges in all the states of the Union, was passed in 1862; whereas in my own country, the Institut National Agronomique was only established definitively in 1879. This 'agronomic' origin has had lasting consequences until today:

1. an empirical and pragmatic attitude which favour eclecticism;
2. a good concrete knowledge of our object, which makes us sensitive to the interactions among the technical, economic, social and political dimensions of the problems under study;
3. as a result, a good disposition for multidisciplinary works.

The study of the problems of agriculture has thus been, since our origin, an essential characteristic of our discipline. But the reference to economic science is no less important.

Our claim to be fully fledged economists
One may say that ever since economists existed, they have not ignored agriculture. The Physiocrats viewed it as the only productive activity; and it is Ricardo who elaborated the concept of rent which, essentially, we still use today. Yet, it would not be perfectly legitimate to view ourselves as the direct intellectual heirs of these illustrious ancestors. They were fundamentally interested by the economy as a whole and not in solving the problems of agriculture.

The birth of agricultural economics was more the result of a meeting between the preoccupation of the agronomists and the contribution and rigour of the economic approach. This statement can be illustrated by an anecdote. In a paper published in 1965, Boussard[3] noted that Dumont, a famous agronomist, had rediscovered the marginal principle 70 years after the Austrian School. He was referring to a paper discussing priorities in the choice of agricultural investments, justly criticising the mistakes of a purely technical approach. What must be emphasised here is that the agronomist had been empirically led to a correct economic reasoning but he did not have a sufficient economic culture to place his analysis in a broader reference framework. In my little story, the agricultural economist is Boussard, a well-known member of our association. This story illustrates a general proposition. The study of problems faced by farmers, or by those who are concerned with agriculture for one reason or another, leads to an identification of economic questions. The scientific approach of the economist permits him then a greater degree of accuracy and rigour. This is particularly true in the realm of conceptualisation and in the articulation of hypotheses. We are all convinced of that, I am sure. And it is probably the attractiveness of this rigour which explains why some of us see disciplinary excellence as the ultimate criterion to judge the quality of an agricultural economist. With many others, I believe that such a point of view is too narrow. It ignores too much our agronomic origin. But if disciplinary competence is not sufficient to be a good agricultural economist, it is nevertheless indispensable. It is in that sense that we must be fully fledged economists. And if we believe Keynes, when he wrote that an economist who would only be an economist would not be a good one, our dual origin should not be an obstacle or an excuse for not being fully fledged economists.

WHERE ARE WE NOW?

If this dual origin, agronomic and economic, defines what agricultural economists are today, agricultural economics does not exist as a separate scientific discipline different from economics. On the other hand, it is clear that there are agricultural economists. Even in the most developed societies, agricultural activities are still specific enough to justify the specialisation of economists dealing with them. They must, however, remember that these activities are only a subset of the productive activities of that society. Experience shows that such a practical definition of the field of agricultural economics is sufficient. Finally, agricultural economists are economists who view themselves as such.

How, given these ambiguities of our professional objectives may we judge where we are? More precisely, what is the state of our discipline as it can be assessed at the end of this conference? To treat this question, I find it useful to decompose it in three sub-questions:

1. What are the topics preoccupying agricultural economists and are they relevant?
2. What are the economic foundations of our analysis?
3. What use do we make of analytical techniques? Are we threatened, as feared by Glenn Johnson by the danger of 'modernism', defined by McCloskey?[4]

Before tackling successively these three questions, two limits of the exercise undertaken here must first be emphasised. The nature of the papers presented at an international conference represents a very biased sample of our activities. Specific research projects and the very technical aspects of these research projects are necessarily under-represented, as are the studies designed to tackle the specific problems of a given decision-maker. Besides, presenting a paper in a conference session is a difficult task. The limits on the length of the papers prevent the authors from presenting all the aspects of their research. Very often the paper presents a synthesis of several years of research or the works of numerous authors. The author cannot justify the methods which were used. Thus it is difficult for the audience to assess critically the validity of the conclusions. In spite of these limitations, and particularly if one is conscious of them, examining the three questions listed above is worthwhile.

The topics
The first striking characteristic is their extreme diversity, going, for instance, from rather theoretical developments at the farm level to a criticism of the criteria of malnutrition, through the structure of agriculture, the handling of uncertainty, the international capital market or regional co-operation among developing countries. These examples only illustrate a diversity which is actually much greater, as revealed by a reading of the conference programme.

Of course such a diversity, which reflects the variety of agricultural economists' preoccupations is a great asset which must be maintained.

Another dimension of the diversity of papers presented during the conference relates to their nature: synthesis of an individual's works or the works of various authors, preliminary reflections prior to launching a research programme, synthesis of one author's reflections based on research but also on his long experience. My epistemological eclecticism leads me to believe that this again is a good thing. We can, and therefore we must, learn in different ways. The various sources of knowledge, the various approaches are, in my view, more of a complementary than of a competitive nature. I know that this point of view is not shared by everyone. But, at least, it leads us to raise important questions about how to judge the quality of our works. The double diversity just alluded to makes it difficult indeed to choose clear and simple criteria to judge professional excellence. One cannot rest satisfied with a judgement which would be expressed in too narrow 'scientific' terms.

What would be the criteria of disciplinary excellence? Very briefly research is deemed to be good if it contributes to the accumulation of economic knowledge, i.e. if it brings answers to a question which has been left open so far, or if it permits a fruitful reformulation of the question. For instance, the new household economics belongs to that category. Clearly, the main purpose of specialists in a discipline is to enrich or renew the existing theory.

In an applied discipline, such as agricultural economics, the starting point of the investigation and its objective are not expressed first in theoretical terms. One must refer to problems of agriculture. Of course such a contrast is over-simplified. The scientific approach in social sciences constantly goes back and forth between theory and practice: thus the opposition is not as clear-cut as suggested above. But even if the difference is only one of degree, the distinction is real.

To judge the quality of our works, one must therefore go back to the epistemological foundations of scientific criteria and keep, it seems to me, four 'classical' criteria:

1. the discourse must be clear and understandable by one's peers;
2. it must be free of internal contradictions;
3. it must be consistent with the observations of facts;
4. finally, it must be relevant.

The first two criteria imply expliciting one's hypotheses and being open to criticism, i.e. the two main characteristics of a scientific attitude according to Popper.[5] The last two criteria are less well recognised, thus they deserve to be further elaborated upon. Since there is no observation which can be independent of the observer's questions and assumptions, consistency with observation is, logically speaking, an extension of internal consistency. The point however is that this extension is often very convenient. And this justifies identifying it as a specific criterion of quality. Thus formulated, the three first criteria characterise objective knowledge. But perfection in this matter does not exist. Even if it is an ideal to pursue, objectivity can only be a relative quality; most often, it is possible to know in real life whether or not one is progressing in this respect. The fourth criterion, relevance, is of another nature. It relates to the interest of the new knowledge for the solution of more or less important practical problems. It is essential for an applied discipline, such as agricultural economics.

These criteria of quality are general and may be applied to any type of knowledge; but they will not be appreciated in the same fashion, depending on whether a research is more or less applied. Moreover, some works may deserve a good score on one criterion and much less on another. How can one class them in the same hierarchy? How can one choose between two works, one of which tests with great rigour an assumption having little interest, the other, dealing with a very important question, but providing a not very powerful test of the assumptions? Clearly, the evaluation will depend upon the point of view of the judge.

In order to make the evaluation easier, one could consider that relevance is a preliminary condition. Once having made sure that the research topic is relevant, one could worry about the first three criteria. Unfortunately, experience shows that such a solution is not satisfactory. The quest for relevance must be permanent, i.e. present at all steps of the research, influence all methodological choices and the interpretation of results.

Given this diversity in the application of quality criteria, a broad pluralism and much reciprocal tolerance among agricultural economists are called for. Examination of the economic foundations of our analysis will lead us to a similar conclusion.

The economic foundations of our works

Here again, diversity is very great, even in the papers that were presented at this conference. This diversity relates both to the place of explicit economic considerations and to the nature of the economic theory used as reference, even if most papers clearly used the neoclassical economic theory. This diversity is a good thing in the perspective of epistemological eclecticism presented above. The most encouraging development however is the extension of the theoretical field used as reference in our works. I have particularly in mind the interdependencies emphasised on several occasions, which led several authors to take explicit account of the international capital market or of the evolution of exchange rates. The attempts made to build general equilibrium models may be viewed in the same perspective.

By contrast, we are still too timid in our criticisms of the concepts and hypotheses of economic theory. Of course there are exceptions. After all, agricultural economists have made significant contributions to production theory, particularly regarding the fixity of factors of production, to the new household economics, to the theory of human capital, to intersectoral relationships, to the handling of the dynamics of numerous economic phenomena (recursive programming, adaptive process, dynamics of supply ...).

These contributions should encourage us not to rest satisfied with the theory of textbooks. It is true that in many of the above examples, contributions were made by economists who were at the margin between agricultural and general economics. Perhaps this shows that we are not yet completely fully fledged economists. Yet there is much to be done indeed. Analysis of practical problems of agriculture raises theoretical issues of a fundamental nature. To quote only a few examples: decision processes in family farms, consequences for the relationship between production, consumption, and savings decisions, nature of the dynamics of microeconomic adjustments to a constantly changing economic and social environment, nature and dynamics of economic and social relationships within rural communities at the local level, articulation among macro, meso, and microeconomic phenomena in every development process, consequences for the choice of a development strategy, determinants of agricultural policies. Perhaps we do not devote sufficient efforts to the identification and precise formulation of these theoretical questions and our conference may only have reflected this situation.

The techniques of analysis
This conference was not a very good place to judge the analytical techniques which we used. As indicated earlier, the limited length of the papers and their nature tend to eliminate discussions of this type. Thus, I cannot do justice to this question in spite of its importance. I would, however, like to call your attention to a striking contrast which I cannot explain. Having recently spent a year in the United States, I have become more conscious of the difference between research practices there and in France. In the US, emphasis is placed much more on the use of quantitative techniques for testing hypotheses without worrying enough, in my view, about the scope and significance of these hypotheses. In France, researchers are more worried about the global formulation of the problems they analyse without being much concerned with the rigorous test of the hypotheses. Clearly, the situation described here for the United States is very similar in Australia, Canada, Germany, and perhaps also the Netherlands. Does it reflect an excessive degree of modernism? The 'French' situation can probably be found elsewhere as

well. It does not suffer from that weakness, but should it be preferred? Restricting myself to the case of France, it is clear that the scientific debate was too much influenced there five or ten years ago by the participants' ideological positions. The growing use of descriptive statistics over the last few years is clearly a progress. But, the quantative estimation of the parameters of a model or the test of hypotheses through econometric methods remain very rare. Frankly speaking, my impression is that we have here two extreme situations, neither of which is satisfactory.

WHERE DO WE GO FROM HERE?

Raising questions about our future is useful mainly to know whether or not we should re-examine our objectives and our criteria of professional excellence. No one, of course, can pretend to bring definitive answers to these questions faced by all of us collectively and individually. I can only present here a few personal reflections with the purpose of nourishing the debate. For this, I suggest three questions:
1. Are we really conscious of the status of our discipline?
2. Which orientations should occupy our professional activities?
3. What consequences are there for our International Association?

Are we conscious enough of the status of agricultural economics?
In the old debate within economics between the desire to build a 'hard science', as rigorous as possible, at the cost of necessarily simplifying abstractions, and the wish to take into account the interactions with the social and political dimensions of the phenomena under study, I clearly lean towards the second attitude. This emphasis on the status of economics as a social science is, in my view, fully consistent with our 'agronomic' tradition and the applied character of agriculture economics. I know, however, that this choice is not shared by all. The dominant current in what we French would call Anglo-Saxon agricultural economics, very attached to the neoclassical theoretical reference, tends on the contrary to neglect the social dimension of the phenomena which we study. The point of view which I espouse here has important consequences for the definition of our professional objectives.

It suggests that our main role, as agricultural economists, is to explain and make explicit the mechanisms of the phenomena involved in any rural development process. Some social actors benefit, others suffer from it. To explain is to shed light on these conflicts which are sometimes hidden. In this sense, our role becomes one of social critique. And this immediately raises the question of our status, of our relationships with those who hold power and with the various categories of social actors. Answers to these questions cannot be given in general terms. They must be thought out case by case. But the questions are important and the fact that they have practically not been dealt with in this conference reflects, it seems to me, the domination of the neoclassical current which tends to ignore them.

Which orientations for our professional activities?
The diversity of topics in our conference was emphasised earlier. In this broad range, which must be made broader yet, I would like to call your attention to only a few points which are too often neglected or misunderstood.

The lack of data, or their inaccuracy, have been emphasised several times, in particular for many African countries. Did we draw all the consequences of this situation for us? In particular, do we exert sufficiently critical a judgement when interpreting the results of our research based on these uncertain data. In the case of agriculture, the lack of data often leads the agricultural economist to collect or to participate closely in the collection of data. Do we do it enough or with a sufficiently critical mind? Do we question enough the meaning of these data? Do we criticise the relevance of the concepts which the data are supposed to capture for rendering account of how micro-economic units function and evolve, be they production units, consumption units, accumulation and reproduction units? Personally, I feel that these elementary issues which often relate to the validity of fundamental economic concepts, are not raised often enough. Yet it is well known that the correspondence between such basic concepts as production, work, consumption, and reality is not immediate. The domain of agricultural economics is not only at the micro-economic level; I already indicated that it has been a progress for us to take into account many interactions among sectors within a national economy and among national economies. But the most serious theoretical difficulty which we face seems to me to be the articulation between the macro-economic level and the micro-economics of production units such as the peasant family. The fact that this difficulty was not explicitly enough recognised during this conference appears to me as the source of many frustrations, at least among some participants.

Finally, I would like to emphasise the interest for us of conducting the analysis of the determinants of agricultural policies. My own research has convinced me that, in the long run, the role of economic variables is essential. But, in the short run, this influence is exerted through the political process and, as a result, it does not obey a strictly economic rationality.

All of this does not mean that economic concepts are useless, nor that all efforts to quantify are doomed to failure. Experience shows, on the contrary, the outstanding generality of questions put in economic terms. Any society must give concrete answers to such questions as: how to feed itself?, through production or exchange?, with which resources in the first case? against what in the second? Besides, all economic reasoning implies some quantification. Even the analyses conducted in apparently qualitative terms imply orders of magnitude.

As a result, my general plea is that we must be rigorous, exert our critical minds, and be attentive to the relevance of the concepts which we use; in brief, we must take seriously the four criteria of professional excellence discussed above. The desire to rigorously analyse the problems of agriculture leads us to raise important theoretical questions. It also leads us to combine very diverse sources of information. As a result, collaborations are often necessary. The conditions of inter-disciplinary collaborations have been extensively discussed. Less well known are the conditions of a fruitful collaboration among agricultural economists working in institutions whose objectives are different – research, public administration, firms, consultants. Much could be gained, I am sure, from comparative studies of our practices in this matter. In the absence of such an analysis, one can at least say that the difficulties of this collaboration reflect the ambiguity of our discipline, constantly torn between the desire to accumulate knowledge and the need to solve problems. In this respect, the absence at our meetings of many specialised consultants is probably revealing. Whatever their reasons, their absence deprives us of an experience of analysing individual decision-makers' problems, (Glenn Johnson's third category). It is up to us to get organised so that we can mobilise their knowledge otherwise.

Consequences for our International Association
We must take our diversity and the inequalities among us more into account. Gathering only individual members, our Association is of course open to all agricultural economists of the world with the same rights and the same duties. But we do not have the power to suppress the inequalities. This situation justifies that we give particular support to our colleagues in countries where professional life is the least developed. It must also influence the policy of our new *Journal* and the conception of our conferences.

For the *Journal*, we are trying to constitute an editorial board which will be as representative as possible of the regions, of the main types of works done by agricultural economics, and of their main approaches. The editorial policy will aim at encouraging the publication of articles respecting the same plurality.

For our Conferences, it seems to me that we should revise their conception in order to satisfy better the diversity of interests among our members. All ideas and suggestions in this respect will be welcome. I promise you that the Executive Committee will study all of them carefully and our Vice President for Programmes will take them into account for the conception of our next conference.

CONCLUSION

Our diversity has been repeatedly stressed in this paper. The main lesson is that we must struggle to have the plurality of points of view respected. A real debate, without concessions made only for the sake of politeness, implies a great amount of courtesy. This implies much intellectual modesty and reciprocal tolerance, two virtues which are easier to preach than to practise. Still, I encourage you to try.

Regarding substance, if we want to remain faithful to our double tradition, agronomic and economic, we can, I believe, be inspired by A. K. Sen's presentation at the beginning of this conference. Let us ourselves avoid the ready-made answers of 'instant economics'. Let us show to our partners how economic analysis, i.e. first, the conceptualisation of problems in economic terms, permits one to pose them better and to contribute to their solution. It is in this manner, I believe, that we will be fully fledged economists and that we will fulfil our social role as agricultural specialists.

NOTES

[1]Johnson, Glenn L., 'Scope of Agricultural Economics', this volume.
[2]Malassis, Louis., 'Economie agricole, agroalimentaire et rurale', *Economie Rurale*, 1979, vol. 131, pp. 3–10.
[3]Boussard, J. M., 'Réflexions sur l'objet de l'économie rural', *Economie Rurale*, vol. 63, January–March 1965.
[4]McCloskey, Donald N., 'The Rhetoric of Economics', *Journal of Economic Literature*, vol. 21, no. 2, 1983, pp. 481–517.
[5]Popper, Karl, R., *The Logic of Scientific Discovery*, Harper and Row, New York, 1965.

INDEX* OF INSTITUTIONAL ATTACHMENT OF FIRST NAMED AUTHORS

Abbott, John C	FAO, Rome, Italy.
Anderson, Jock R.	University of New England, Armidale, Australia.
Anthonio, Q.B.O.	University of Ibadan, Nigeria.
Berlan, Jean-Pierre	INRA, Aix En Provence, France.
Binswanger, Hans P	World Bank, Washington, USA.
Birowo, A.T.	Ministry of Agriculture, Jakarta, Indonesia.
Boehlje, Michael	Iowa State University, Ames, USA.
Boussard, Jean-Marc	INRA, Paris, France.
Brinkman, George L.	University of Guelph, Ontario, Canada.
Bromley, Daniel W.	University of Wisconsin, Madison, USA.
Chataigner, Jean	INRA, Montpellier, France.
Chaudhri, D.P.	Australian National University, Canberra, Australia.
Csáski, Csaba	Karl Marx University of Economic Sciences, Budapest, Hungary.
Cuevas, Carlos E.	Ohio State University, USA.
Dufour, Jean-Claude	Laval University, Quebec, Canada.
Edwards, Clark	Economic Research Service, USDA, Washington, USA.
Eicher, Carl K.	Michigan State University, USA.
Farrell, K.R.	Food and Agriculture Program, Research for the Future, Washington, USA.
Fischel, Walter L.	Agricultural Research and Development Center, Ohio, USA.
Fischer, Günther	IIASA, Laxenburg, Austria.
Harsh, Stephen B.	University of Michigan, East Lansing, USA.

*The editors apologise for not including the names and institutions of joint authors and for any errors.

INDEX